AQA BUSINESS STUDIES for A2
Third Edition

Malcolm Surridge and Andrew Gillespie

DYNAMIC LEARNING

HODDER
EDUCATION
AN HACHETTE UK COMPANY

Every effort has been made to trace the copyright holders of material reproduced here. The authors and publishers would like to thank the following for permission to reproduce copyright illustrations:

P.6 © Envision/Corbis; p.11 © EVERETT KENNEDY BROWN/epa/Corbis; p.57 © Diana Bier Mexico Paseo Angel / Alamy; p.60 © David Pearson / Alamy; p.82 © UPPA/Photoshot; p.118 © AP/PA Photos; p.128 (top) © Justin Sullivan/Getty Images, (bottom) © Daniel Berehulak/Getty Images; p.132 © Miguel Villagran/Getty Images; p.136 © BERND OTTEN/AFP/Getty Images; p.140 © Hulton Archive/Getty Images; p.143 © Pixonnet.com / Alamy; p.144 © David Levenson / Getty Images; p.145 © Bill Pierce/Time & Life Pictures/Getty Images; p.158 © Getty Images/Atlantis, The Palm; p.161 NOAH SEELAM/AFP/Getty Images; p.210 with kind permission by Opodo; p.217 © Nicholas Bailey / Rex Features; p.229 © Matt Cardy/Getty Images; p.240 © Car Culture/Corbis; p.252 © Geoffrey Robinson / Rex Features; p.318 © Leslie Garland Picture Library / Alamy; p.344 © PA Wire/PA Photos; p.370 (left) © Nils Jorgensen / Rex Features, (right) ©2004 UPPA / TopFoto; p.371 © James Nielsen/Getty Images; p.380 © SAUL LOEB/AFP/Getty Images

Crown copyright material is reproduced with the permission of the Controller of HMSO and the Queen's Printer for Scotland.

Orders: please contact Bookpoint Ltd, 130 Milton Park, Abingdon, Oxon OX14 4SB. Telephone: (44) 01235 827720. Fax: (44) 01235 400454. Lines are open from 9.00 – 5.00, Monday to Saturday, with a 24 hour message answering service. You can also order through our website www.hoddereducation.co.uk

If you have any comments to make about this, or any of our other titles, please send them to educationenquiries@hodder.co.uk

British Library Cataloguing in Publication Data
A catalogue record for this title is available from the British Library

ISBN: 978 0 340 973 554

First Edition Published 2001
Second Edition Published 2005
This Edition Published 2009
Impression number 10 9 8 7 6 5 4 3 2 1
Year   2014 2013 2012 2011 2010 2009

Copyright © 2009 Malcolm Surridge and Andrew Gillespie

Hachette UK's policy is to use papers that are natural, renewable and recyclable products and made from wood grown in sustainable forests. The logging and manufacturing processes are expected to conform to the environmental regulations of the country of origin.

Cover photo from © Sophia Tsibikaki/iStockphoto.com
Typeset by Fakenham Photosetting Ltd, Fakenham, Norfolk
Printed in Italy for Hodder Education, an Hachette UK Company, 338 Euston Road, London NW1 3BH

Contents

How to use this book

This book gives you a comprehensive coverage of the AQA A2 specification. It builds on the AS specification that you have covered and cross-references the A2 materials with those that you studied at AS. This will help you to understand the relationships between the two specifications and to use AS material to underpin your study of the A2 subject matter when necessary.

This book is designed to help you to understand the key issues in each topic and the interrelationships between the various topics. Throughout the book we have introduced you to a range of theories and concepts which can be used to build arguments when responding to examination questions. These are not always mentioned directly in the specification but they will enable you to develop strong arguments and to make and support judgements. The book will also help you to learn how to use your knowledge effectively and to develop the right skills for success in the AQA A2 examinations.

Within each chapter there are also several features to help you understand the material. These are:

- Business in focus: this feature highlights the type of questions that might be asked in the exam and the issues you should think about when revising. What do you think? This feature should help to bring a topic to life by showing it in action in a real business. We hope to show you how the various theories and models can be applied to real business decisions.
- Examiner's advice: this feature is to help you reflect on what has just been covered in the book. How does it relate to other topics or your own experiences? What would you do in a given situation?
- Key terms: this feature will give you definitions for key terms.

At the end of each chapter we provide:

- A summary of the key points covered. If you want to get a quick idea of what a chapter is looking at then the summary is quite a good place to start.
- Quick questions. These are short questions to help you check whether you have understood the key points.
- Issues for analysis and evaluation. These sections highlight the possible connections between the theories covered in the chapter as well as issues that may involve judgements and are therefore evaluative issues. These features are there to help you pick out the key points in the chapter.
- Analysis and evaluation. These questions will help you to develop your examination skills. By practising these you can practise key skills such as applying your answers and evaluating the key points in your argument. Suggested answers are provided on *AQA Business Studies for A2 Dynamic Learning Network Edition CD-ROM* which accompanies this book.
- A case study. These are designed to help you to develop further the important skills of application, analysis and evaluation to prepare you for the types of questions that you will face in the A2 examinations. By answering these questions you will be able to develop vital examination skills. Suggested answers to these questions are provided on the CD-ROM noted above
- One step further. This provides extension material that is useful if you want to go beyond the specification or add further to your understanding of a topic.

Overall, we hope this book provides an interesting read and that you feel it provides a good coverage of the AQA specification and helps prepare you effectively for your exams. If you have any suggestions how we can improve the book in the future editions do not hesitate to contact us on wattgill@aol.com

Acknowledgements

For my parents, Alan and Bernice, with love.

Malcolm Surridge

With love and thanks to Ali, Clemmie, Roms and Seth.

Andrew Gillespie

We would also like to thank Colin Goodlad and Melissa Richards for their support and patience during the writing of this book.

Introduction to A2

Building on AS Business Studies

From studying AQA AS Business Studies last year you will know that there is a story that runs through AS Business Studies and on into the A2 specification. It is important that you understand this story because it sets out the philosophy of the specification and the extent of each part of the specification. It will help to guide you through your studies as well as helping you to prepare for the AS and A2 examinations.

AS Business Studies started with Unit 1, which considered the activities involved in starting a business. Therefore it considered small businesses and the process of planning. Unit 2 continued the story to include medium-sized businesses and to focus on how managers of small to medium-sized businesses can use tactical decisions (such as increasing capacity utilisation or recruiting new staff) to improve the performance of their businesses.

The A2 specification continues this story.

The A2 story

Unit 3 is based on large businesses, normally public limited companies that are trading nationally and internationally. The focus of this unit is on examining the functional strategies (human resources, operations, marketing and finance) that such businesses may adopt in order to achieve success. The story encompasses the ways in which businesses measure their performance and the strategies they may adopt (such as relocating overseas or adopting lean production techniques) to achieve the objectives they set themselves.

Unit 4 concludes the story. It continues to be based on large (possibly multinational) businesses, but it examines the internal and external causes of change that can affect a business. Therefore the initial focus of this unit is outside the business; all the previous units have looked at the internal operations of a business. This part of the story invites you to think carefully about the impact that internal and external causes of change can have on different businesses and to make some attempt to assess the likely impact of the various causes of change. The latter part of this unit is entitled 'Managing change' and considers the ways in which businesses manage change, as well as important factors in such management, including leadership and culture.

A2 assessment

The A2 assessment package comprises two compulsory papers. These papers can be taken each January and June.

Unit 3 – Buss3 (Strategies for Success)

This paper is worth 25 per cent of the total marks for the A level. The examination's duration is 1 hour 45 minutes. It comprises approximately five questions based on a decision-making case study including at least two numerical appendices. The paper carries 80 marks maximum. An example of this paper can be seen on page 230.

Unit 4 – Buss4 (The Business Environment and Change)

This paper is worth 25 per cent of the total marks for the A level. The examination's duration is 1 hour 45 minutes. It is presented in two sections.

▸ The first section is based on some research that you will have carried out prior to the examination.

This research will have been based on a research brief, which is available to you several months before the examination. The paper then offers you a choice of two questions, from which you have to choose one.

- The second section includes a choice of three essays from which you have to select one.

There are 80 marks in total for this paper – 40 for each section.

Unit 3

Introduction to Unit 3

Functional objectives and strategies

As we saw in Unit 2 of the AS specification, a business has a number of internal functions including marketing, finance, human resource management and operations. In a large business the managers or directors responsible for each of these functions will set functional objectives. This introduction looks at these functional objectives and considers how they can help the organisation to achieve its overall corporate objectives.

What you need to know by the end of this chapter:

• functional objectives and their relationship with corporate objectives
• the relationship between functional objectives and strategies.

Functional objectives and corporate objectives

Corporate objectives

Corporate objectives are the overall goals of the whole business. Corporate goals vary according to the size and history of the organisation, as well as the personal aims of the business's senior managers. The 'Business in focus' below states Sainsbury's corporate objectives and also a number of functional objectives that it will pursue and which will assist it in achieving its corporate objectives.

Corporate and functional objectives

Business in Focus

Sainsbury's corporate objectives

Two and a half years ago we outlined our plan to Make Sainsbury's Great Again ('MSGA'). Our vision is simple; we are here to serve customers well with a choice of great food at fair prices and, by so doing, to provide shareholders with strong, sustainable financial returns. This has driven everything we have done since we outlined our recovery plan in October 2004. The plan spans three years to March 2008 and as well as fixing a range of basics – such as product availability, supply chain, IT and price – we committed to make hundreds of small changes every day to improve our customers' shopping experience.

To enable us to measure our progress we set some key three-year targets:

1   To grow sales by £2.5 billion, with grocery contributing sales of £1.4 billion, non-food products sales of £700 million and convenience stores sales of £400 million.
2   To invest at least £400 million in improving product quality and our price position relative to competitors and to reduce buying costs to be passed on to customers through special offers.
3   To deliver operating cost efficiencies of at least £400 million.
4   To generate a positive cash flow from 2007–2008 onwards.

Source: Adapted from Sainsbury's Annual Report, 2007
http://www.j-sainsbury.co.uk

A business could pursue a number of corporate objectives, including the following:

- Growth, i.e. to increase the overall scale of the business.
- Diversification, i.e. looking to sell new products in new markets.
- To achieve the maximum possible profits in the long term.
- To develop innovative goods and services.

The setting and communication of clear corporate objectives allows senior managers to delegate authority to more junior employees while maintaining the organisation's overall sense of direction.

Web link

Find out more about J Sainsbury's corporate and functional objectives at http://www.j-sainsbury.co.uk.

Functional objectives

A functional objective is a goal that is pursued by particular functions within the business, such as human resources or marketing. A functional objective is likely to have a numerical element and a stated timescale. Thus, a business might set a financial objective which is a specific profit figure in relation to the capital available to the business. The objective will also set out the timescale within which this financial objective is to be attained.

Once clear corporate objectives have been set it is possible for the business to set targets at functional levels. The achievement of their objectives by the various functional areas of the business will contribute to the overall business achieving its corporate objectives. For example, a business that has a corporate objective of growth will require its HR function to set and achieve objectives to increase the size or productivity (or both) of its workforce to enable it to increase its supplies of goods or services. At the same time, the finance function may be setting itself goals of increasing the funds available to the business to allow the objective of growth to be financed properly.

The relationship between functional objectives and strategies

A functional objective is a goal that is pursued by a particular function of the business. A functional strategy is the medium- to long-term plan used to achieve the objective. Cadbury has set itself a number of functional objectives relating to the finance function, for the period up to 2011, including those set out below.

- Revenue growth of 4–6 per cent every year.
- Strong growth in shareholder dividends.
- A growth in the returns on the company's investments.

The company makes it clear that to achieve these financial objectives other functions within the busi-

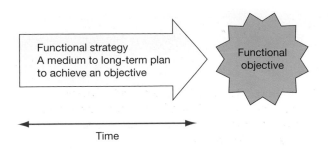

Functional strategies and functional objectives

A business such as Cadbury with a corporate strategy of growth, may set a functional objective within the HR department of developing a larger and more highly skilled workforce which will help the organisation to meet its corporate objectives. This will require the managers responsible for the human resource function to devise a strategy or plan to meet its functional objectives. The key elements of such a plan may include training employees, recruiting new staff and possibly relocating certain staff.

ness will have to take appropriate decisions. For example, the company's marketing department may have to develop new products or enter new markets to gain the 4–6 per cent growth in sales revenue each year. So, although functional objectives are set independently, they do require cooperation between the various functions that comprise a business.

Functional objectives should also contribute to the achievement of the business's corporate objectives. Cadbury may, for example, have a corporate objective of growth.

Functional objectives should be set first (and should contribute to the achievement of corporate objectives) and then the strategy should be devised to achieve the functional objective.

Summary

A business sets itself corporate objectives, which are targets or goals for the entire business, to be achieved over the medium to long term. In turn, the various functions (marketing, human resources etc.) of a business will set themselves functional objectives. The achievement of these functional objectives will assist the business in attaining its corporate objectives. To achieve their objectives the functions of the business will draw up functional strategies, which are medium- to long-term plans.

Business in Focus

Strange new beers

Barry Axcell, chief brewer at the world's third-largest brewer, SABMiller has come up with some outlandish concepts in beer; from blue beer and beer with the frothy 'head' in the middle of the glass, to beer which emits light.

But so far none of these innovations has yet made it behind the bar or onto the supermarket shelves. Mr Axcell says they have done lots of things which are technically possible, 'but if the market is not ready for it then it can just sit on hold for years and years or be shelved completely.'

As it is, he has overseen a number of marginally less unorthodox developments. SABMiller launched Miller Midnight, a black lager, into Russia, and suc-

cessfully produced a pineapple version of the Chinese beer brand Snow which the company part owns. Miller Chill brewed with lime and salt to tap into the Latinisation of American culture was launched in the US last year.

Even so, finding successful innovation in the mature UK beer market is difficult.

Source: Adapted from bbc.co.uk

Question:

1 How might the development of innovative products by the operations department of this multinational brewer affect the objectives and strategies of other functions within the business?

Green beer

Progress questions

1 Which of the following might **not** be a corporate objective of a large business?
   a diversification
   b growth
   c profit maximisation
   d relocation (1 mark)
2 Explain the difference between a functional objective and a functional strategy.
3 Explain, using examples, why the setting of a functional objective by the operations department of producing high-quality products will impact upon the objectives set elsewhere in the business. (8 marks)
4 Outline why the achievement of functional objectives should assist a business in attaining its corporate objectives. (6 marks)

Analysis and evaluation questions

D'Alcorn and Branson is a small company that manufactures organic chocolate. Its products are high quality and attract premium prices. Since its establishment seven years ago, the company has sold a limited range of products in the UK. Chief Executive Fran D'Alcorn believes that the company needs to set itself new goals if it is to develop further. Fran proposed to the Board that the company should seek to diversify and to make this its foremost corporate objective.

The company has introduced high-technology machinery onto its production line during the last two years, leading to major investment in training as well as a number of redundancies.

She proposed that the company should extend its product range to incorporate boxes of chocolates as well as drinking chocolate. In addition, she argued that the company should look to sell its products throughout the European Union as this represented a large and accessible market.

1 Analyse the implications for the company's marketing and operations functions of the decision to set a corporate objective of diversification. (10 marks)
2 To what extent is the corporate objective set by Fran D'Alcorn the only factor influencing the objectives set by the company's human resource function? (15 marks)

Section 1: Financial strategies and accounts

As with all topics in A2 Business Studies, you will have studied some elements of this subject during your AS level course. The major elements you will have studied are as follows:

- classifying costs (e.g. fixed and variable costs)
- the concept of contribution (selling price less variable costs)
- break-even analysis using calculations and charts
- the management of cash flow and the distinction between cash flow and profit
- sources of finance
- budgets and budgeting.

The A2 specification for business studies builds upon the subject knowledge and skills acquired during the AS programme. It is worthwhile looking back over your AS materials before starting to study A2 Financial Strategies and Accounts. More specific advice is given on any prior knowledge required at the outset of each chapter.

During your A2 programme you will study:

- financial objectives that are pursued by businesses and the factors that influence the choice of these
- company accounts in detail, considering their structure and interrelationships, and topics such as depreciation and working capital
- ratio analysis – a technique used to analyse company accounts
- investment decision-making – looking at financial and non-financial factors considered by businesses before taking a decision on whether to undertake major investments.

1 Understanding financial objectives

This chapter looks at the targets or goals that the financial department or section may set itself. The achievement of these targets or goals will assist the business in achieving its corporate goals or objectives. This chapter builds on some important topics from your study of AS Business Studies, not least costs, profit and cash flow. If you are unsure about the meaning of any of these terms and the distinction between cash flow and profit, you should look again at the relevant AS materials.

In this chapter we examine:

- the types of financial objectives that businesses pursue
- the external and internal influences on financial objectives.

The financial objectives of business

A financial objective is a goal or target pursued by the finance department (or function) within an organisation. It is likely that a financial objective will contain a specific numerical element and also a timescale within which it is to be achieved. The financial target will be set by the managers responsible for finance in the business, but will be consistent with other functional objectives and will also contribute to the achievement of the business's corporate objectives.

A business might pursue a number of financial objectives including those discussed below.

Return on capital employed (ROCE) targets

The return on capital employed (commonly referred to as ROCE) is calculated by expressing the net profits made by a business as a percentage of the value of the capital employed in the business. Stakeholders in a business can compare its current ROCE figure with those achieved by other businesses or by the same business in previous years.

A business might set itself a financial target of achieving a ROCE figure of 25 per cent. This means that its net profits for the financial year will be 25 per cent of the capital employed in the business. This financial objective is very precise and has the advantage of being relatively simple to measure and to compare with that achieved by other businesses and by the same business in previous years. To achieve such an objective (which is likely to be a higher figure than that achieved in previous years) can require actions to increase net profits as well as to minimise the value of assets used within the business. Anglo American, one of the world's largest mining groups with operations across the globe, set itself a ROCE target of between 37.47 per cent and 39.47 per cent for the financial year 2007–08.

As with the other financial objectives, this has considerable implications for other functions within the business. The marketing function may set objectives

Business in Focus

Toyota misses profits targets

The market for cars is in a trough, with sales at 1991 levels and car manufacturers in Detroit facing severe cash-flow problems. Even Japanese manufacturers are struggling, and perhaps the biggest sign that something is terribly wrong is that Toyota is even feeling the pain. The Japanese car manufacturer's sales dropped 32 per cent in September 2008 compared with September 2007, which was preceded by drops of 9.7, 18 and 11 per cent in prior months. Toyota has already lowered its global sales target for the year to 9.5 million units to reflect the trouble it has been experiencing in the American market, but recent news from Europe is that production is being cut there, as well.

The worst news for Toyota would likely be welcome news to the rest of the automotive universe: the Japanese giant only made $12 billion of profit this year – about 40 per cent below its profits target. Toyota's share price has also taken a hit during these challenging times, with its current value down about $23 per share from its recent peak of $58.76. The worst part about the car manufacturing market is that there appears to be no end in sight, which means there is more bad news to come; even from Toyota.

Source: Auto Blog http://www.autoblog.com

Questions:

1 What was Toyota's profit target?
2 What other financial targets might the company have set itself?

in terms of market share to improve profitability. At the same time the operations department may outsource some production to reduce the amount of capital that the business requires to conduct its trading activities.

Shareholders' returns

Shareholders' returns can be defined in more than one way. One approach is to take a short-term view and define it as the current share price and any associated dividends that are due in the near future. It is also possible to have a longer-term view of shareholders' returns and define it as a combination of short-term returns (both share prices and dividends) as well as future share prices and dividends. However it is defined, shareholders' returns focuses on generating profits and on increasing the value of the company as reflected in its share price.

Increasing shareholders' returns requires the support of the other functions within the business. Minimising costs can be an important element of any strategy implemented to achieve this financial objective, and this could have significant consequences for the operations and human relations functions within the business. Equally, the marketing function may aim to improve the business's product range and to increase added value in support of the achievement of this financial objective.

Shareholders can clearly benefit from a business pursuing a financial target of maximising its shareholders' returns. However, other stakeholder groups such as employees may be disadvantaged. This financial target is likely to result in a business seeking to cut its costs and this may result in a number of HR strategies that result in the loss of jobs; or certainly the loss of full-time permanent jobs in high-wage economies such as the UK. Equally, suppliers may suffer as businesses with this financial objective seek to drive down the cost of purchases of raw materials and fuel.

Cost minimisation

This financial objective has become better known over recent years due to the publicity given to low-cost airlines and easyGroup, and their strategies of cost and price minimisation. A financial strategy of cost minimisation entails seeking to reduce to the lowest possible level all the costs of production that a business incurs as part of its trading activities. In the case of the low-cost or budget airlines this has extended to minimising labour costs (some require employees to pay for their own uniforms), reducing administrative costs by, for example, using the internet for booking and using 'out of town and city' airports to reduce landing and take-off fees charged by airport authorities.

The financial objective of cost minimisation has clear implications for the objectives (and hence strategies) of other functional areas within the business. Clearly the managers responsible for the other functions should aim to operate with minimal expenditure in order to support the fulfilment of this financial objective. Such a financial objective is likely to support corporate objectives such as profit maximisation or growth.

Cash-flow targets

For many businesses cash flow is vital and an essential element of success. This is especially true of businesses that face long cash cycles. A cash cycle is the time that elapses between the outflow of cash to pay for labour and raw materials for a product or service and the receipt of cash from the sale of the product. House builders and pharmaceutical firms may face long cash cycles. The American house builder Hovnanian Enterprises Inc set itself a target of $100 million in cash flow from operations in 2008 and (surprisingly given the state of the American housing market at the time) announced towards the end of the year that it was confident of achieving this target.

Banks require a steady inflow of cash from depositors to enable them to engage in lending activities. The recent crises surrounding banks in the UK and other countries has, in part, been due to a lack of cash (or liquidity) being available to these organisations. Without cash banks do not have the necessary funds to avail themselves of possible profitable lending opportunities. Without cash a business is unable to meet its financial commitments as they fall due. If a business cannot meet its financial commitments it cannot continue trading.

Other businesses that may establish financial objectives in terms of cash flow may include businesses that are growing and need regular inflows of cash to finance the purchase of increasing quantities of inputs such as labour and raw materials. Failure to set such objectives may result in a business facing financial problems because it runs short of cash as its expenditure or outflow of cash 'runs ahead' of inflows of cash. Such a situation is described as over-trading.

The internal and external influences on financial objectives

A management team will be subject to a range of factors when setting its financial objectives. Some of these influences arise from within the business, while others are external. In 2008 many economies in the world were heading into recession. This made external influences particularly important on financial objectives at this time.

Internal factors

- **The corporate objectives of the business**. This might be the most important internal influence on a business's financial objectives. As we saw earlier, a financial objective must assist the business in achieving its overall corporate objectives. The corporate objectives are set first, followed by functional objectives, which are designed to complement them. Thus, a business that has profit maximisation as its overriding corporate objective may operate a financial objective of cost minimisation. Reducing costs as a financial objective should assist the business in maximising its profits.
- **The nature of the product that is sold**. The type of product can be a major influence on financial objectives. Businesses with long cash cycles (such as the American house builder Hovnanian Enterprises, mentioned earlier) are much more likely to set cash-flow targets as this should be a major focus of their management of finance. Alternatively, if a product's demand is sensitive to price (i.e. if its demand is price elastic), it may be more likely to persuade managers to implement and pursue a financial

objective of cost minimisation. This financial objective may allow price reduction with a positive impact on future sales and the business's sales revenue.

- **The objectives of the business's senior managers.** If the managers of the business hold large numbers of shares (perhaps as part of a share option scheme or as a result of founding the business), then increasing the shareholders' value might be an attractive proposition, especially if a long-term view is taken of this financial objective. On the other hand, managers may seek the recognition that accompanies the successful achievement of a corporate objective of growth. In such circumstances a financial objective of cost minimisation may be more appropriate.

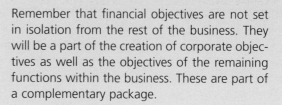

External factors

- **The actions of other businesses**. A business will be most unlikely to ignore the actions of its competitors when establishing its financial objectives. For example, a business operating in a highly price-competitive market might consider establishing an objective of cost minimisation to allow it more flexibility in pricing decisions. In contrast, a business that wants to achieve a higher ROCE target may seek to form alliances with its rivals or to develop a USP for its products to allow it to charge premium prices and to increase its profits margins.
- **The availability of external finance.** If a business is experiencing difficulty in raising capital then financial objectives are more likely to centre on profits and profitability. Achieving specific returns in terms of profit will assist in reassuring potential shareholders or investors as to the safety of their investments and the level of expected returns. It will also provide a source of capital for future investments.
- **The state of the market.** If the market for the

business's products is expanding it may lead a business's managers to set more expansive financial objectives, such as higher rates of shareholder returns or higher figures for ROCE. In contrast, in a market in which sales figures are stable or declining, financial objectives may be more cautious. Financial object... for cost minimisation or cash-flo... deemed more appropriate in these... The 'Business in Focus' feature ... below highlights the impact of a rec... business's financial objectives.

Business in Focus

Panasonic slashes profits forecast

Japanese consumer electronics firm Panasonic has cut its annual profit forecast by 90 per cent because of the global recession. The company now expects to report net profits of 30 billion yen ($315 million, £210 million) for the year ending in March 2009.

Panasonic made a net profit of 281.88 billion yen a year ago and had originally forecast a 310 billion yen profit this year. It said conditions were 'deteriorating sharply' because of falling consumer spending and tougher competition.

Source: Adapted from bbc.co.uk

Figure 1.1 Panasonic is one of Japan's leading electronics exporters

Progress questions

1 Define, with the use of examples, the term 'financial objective'. (3 marks)
2 Distinguish between cash flow and profit. (6 marks)
3 Explain **two** reasons why a public limited company might use ROCE as a basis for a financial objective. (8 marks)
4 What types of businesses might use cash-flow targets as a financial objective? Why? (5 marks)
5 Explain why a business entering an established market might choose to operate cost minimisation as a financial target. (6 marks)
6 What is meant by the term 'shareholders' returns'? (4 marks)
7 Explain why a business's finance department should not set its objectives without consulting the other functions of the business. (6 marks)
8 JHG plc builds oil rigs for use in locations across the globe. Explain how the nature of the company's product might influence its corporate objectives. (8 marks)
9 Why might the business's corporate objectives be considered the most important influence on its financial objectives? (6 marks)
10 Outline how the state of the market in which a business is selling might influence the financial objectives that it chooses. (6 marks)

Analysis and evaluation questions

1 Go Quick plc is a new entrant to the long-distance market for coach travel in the UK. The company has just started operating coach services between many of the UK's major towns and cities. The company operates with

a USP of low prices and is competing in a market with a number of larger established businesses such as National Express.

Go Quick plc has borrowed £62 million on a long-term basis to set up its business. The company's shareholders have been promised high returns and that the business will earn profits from its second year of trading. However, the investment in coaches and other equipment has led to a shortage of cash in the business during its first weeks of trading.

a Analyse the potential advantages to this company of pursuing a financial objective of cost minimisation. (10 marks)

b Discuss the likely consequences for the entire business of the adoption of the financial objective of cost minimisation. (15 marks)

2 Hagger Ltd is a chain of shops in London and southern England selling organic foods. The company has forecast a substantial fall in sales for a number of reasons. It expects consumers to spend less on relatively highly priced foods over the next three years. A new competitor has entered the market (a subsidiary of a large American organic food retailer) and is competing head-on with Hagger Ltd.

Hagger's Chief Executive has announced that she is to retire in 18 months and expects the company's financial performance to boost her retirement package.

a Analyse the likely impact on its choice of financial objectives of the changes in the market. (10 marks)

b Do you think that external influences are more important as an influence on its financial objectives than internal factors? Justify your answer. (15 marks)

Case study

Cadbury has announced a programme of job cuts as part of a major reorganisation of the company. In part these changes have been brought about by threat of a takeover by a private equity business, which would seek financial efficiencies and higher shareholders' returns.

The company is making itself more efficient through a 15 per cent reduction in the number of its employees and a similar reduction in the number of factories in which it makes confectionery.

That means around 7,500 jobs will go around the world over four years and ten confectionery sites will close – though Bourneville, as the company's home-sweet-home, is likely to be largely unaffected.

The reorganisation will cost it around £450m in a one-off charge. But Cadbury is hoping to reap a very substantial increase in its profit margins, perhaps as much as 40 per cent or 50 per cent.

However, Cadbury's story is about more than cost cutting. It is already the world's biggest confectionery company – and it believes it can become a lot bigger, by investing in developing markets and by manufacturing healthier and more glamorous products for richer consumers.

Cadbury, which is dropping the 'Schweppes' from its name, has also confirmed that a sale of its huge US drinks business – which makes Dr Pepper and Seven Up – is more likely than a stock market listing.

So what's the overall message from Cadbury today? It's 'do unto thyself before private equity does it to you.' And here's what should cheer up Cadbury's shareholders and the millions of people who have a stake in it through their pension funds: the profits from this sweeping reorganisation should go to them.

(40 marks, 60 minutes)

Questions

1 Explain what is meant by 'shareholders' returns'. (5 marks)

2 Analyse the possible financial objectives that Cadbury may pursue following this announcement. (8 marks)

3 Evaluate the likely influences on Cadbury's decision to establish a financial objective of reducing its costs. (12 marks)

4 To what extent is Cadbury's decision likely to please all of its stakeholders? (15 marks)

2

Using financial data to measure and assess performance

This chapter looks at the major documents that businesses in the UK use to report financial performance – the balance sheet and the income statement. These documents enable stakeholders to measure and analyse the performance of a business in financial terms. Stakeholders can use this information to assess an organisation's financial performance by making comparisons with the same business in earlier years or with similar businesses over the same financial year.

In this chapter we examine:
- how to analyse balance sheets
- how to analyse income statements
- how to use financial data for comparisons, trend analysis and decision-making
- the strengths and weaknesses of financial data in judging a business's performance.

Key terms

Assets are items owned by a business, such as cash in the bank, vehicles and property.

Capital is the money invested into a business and is used to purchase a range of assets including machinery and inventories.

Creditors are people or organisations to which a business owes money.

Liabilities represent money owed by a business to individuals, suppliers, financial institutions and shareholders.

Inventories are the raw materials and other items necessary for production to take place. They also include finished products that have not yet been sold.

Liquidity measures the ability of a business to meet its short-term debts.

Working capital is the cash a business has for its day-to-day spending.

How to analyse balance sheets

Since 2005 there have been significant changes to the way that public companies in the UK present their accounts. A European Union regulation required public companies to prepare financial statements complying with the International Financial Reporting Standards (IFRS) after 1 January 2005. This requirement has not yet been extended to private limited companies. As a consequence, different types of companies can present their balance sheets in different ways. This chapter will use the post-IFRS approach, but will use the old terminology alongside the new wherever possible. The key changes are set out in 'Business in Focus' below.

Examiner's advice

When considering financial statements such as balance sheets and income statements, do think about them from the perspective of a variety of stakeholders. It may be natural to consider them from the standpoint of shareholders and suppliers, but think of the conclusions that employees and customers may draw from the same financial information.

Business issues

IFRS changes to balance sheets

Since January 2005 the implementation of International Financial Reporting Standards (IFRS) throughout the EU has required that listed public companies present their balance sheets in a format slightly different from that used in the past. There are a number of differences in the terminology used on the IFRS balance sheet:

- Fixed assets are called non-current assets but continue to include tangible and non-tangible assets.
- There are two changes within the current assets section of the balance sheet: stocks are renamed as 'inventories' and debtors are now termed 'trade and other receivables'.
- Under current liabilities, creditors are referred to as 'trade and other payables'.
- Long-term liabilities are renamed 'non-current liabilities'.
- Reserves in the final section of the balance sheet are supplemented by 'retained earnings'. Retained earnings are profits that a company has generated which have not been paid out to shareholders.
- Shareholders' funds are termed 'total equity' or 'total shareholders' equity'.

There are some differences between the balance sheets of public and private limited companies as, at the time of writing, private limited companies have not had to implement the IFRS changes. In this chapter we will concentrate on the balance sheets of public companies, as it is reasonable to assume that in the future private limited companies will adopt a similar structure for presenting their balance sheets.

What is a balance sheet?

A balance sheet is a financial statement recording the assets (possessions) and liabilities (debts) of a business on a particular day at the end of an accounting period. The balance sheet only represents a picture of a business's assets and liabilities at a moment in time: it is commonly described as a 'snapshot' of the financial position of an organisation. Because of this, balance sheets always carry a date on which the valu-

ation of assets and assessment of liabilities took place.

Key balance sheet relationships

1. ASSETS = LIABILITIES
   This is the fundamental relationship that helps to explain why the balance sheet 'always balances'.
2. TOTAL ASSETS = CURRENT ASSETS + NON-CURRENT ASSETS
   Businesses need to invest in a range of assets if they are to operate efficiently.
3. LIABILITIES = SHARE CAPITAL + BORROWINGS + RESERVES

By recording assets and liabilities the balance sheet sets out the ways in which the business has raised its capital and the uses to which this capital has been put. The balance sheet provides a great deal of information for those with an interest in a business, and is the primary financial document published by businesses.

Balance sheets are an essential source of information for a variety of business decisions and for a number of stakeholders.

- **Shareholders** (and potential shareholders) may use balance sheets to assess a business's potential to generate profits in the future. Thus, they may examine the extent and type of assets available to a business. A high proportion of assets such as machinery and property may signify a potential for profit, depending upon the type of business.
- **Suppliers** are more likely to use a balance sheet to investigate the short-term position of the company. Thus, they may consider cash and other liquid assets a business holds and make a judgement about whether the business is likely to be able to pay its bills over the coming months. This may help a supplier reach a decision on whether to offer credit to the business in question.
- **Managers** will be interested in a balance sheet as an indication of the performance of the business. Thus, they may extract information to help them reach a decision on how to raise further capital for future investment. The amount of existing loans may be one factor influencing this decision.

The precise information drawn from the balance sheet will depend upon the stakeholder and the nature of their enquiry. However, it is important to appreciate that this particular financial statement contains a great deal of information.

Business in Focus

Carmakers have weak balance sheets

US carmaker General Motors was expected to run out of cash in the first half of 2009 after reporting third quarter operating loss of $4.2bn (£2.66bn) in 2008. Ford lost $2.98bn during the same period.

GM said it would cut jobs, laying off about 3,600 workers, as production is slowed at 10 plants. The company plans to cut $2.5bn in capital spending in 2009. It has also suspended merger talks with Chrysler to focus on current issues. Ford is to cut salary-related expenses in North America by another 10%.

The companies have spent $14.6bn in cash between them in the three months, weakening their balance sheets by reducing the amount of cash available.

GM posted a third-quarter net loss of $2.5bn, compared with a loss from continuing operations of $42.5bn a year ago. Revenue fell to $37.9bn from $43.7bn in the same period in 2007.

Meanwhile Ford's revenues fell to $32.1bn, down from $41.1bn in the third quarter of 2007. Vehicle sales in the US are at historic lows. Ford, which will accelerate plans to produce fuel-efficient cars, said it was looking at various solutions to support its balance sheet.

Source: Adapted from bbc.co.uk

Question:

1 What other actions might the two companies take to improve the cash position as shown on the balance sheet?

Assets

An asset is simply something that a business owns. Thus assets are what a business uses its capital to purchase. There are two main categories of assets that appear on the balance sheet. The distinction between the two categories is based upon the time the assets are held within the business.

1 **Non-current assets** (previously called fixed assets). These are assets owned by a business that it expects to retain for one year or more. Such assets are used regularly by a business and are not bought for the purpose of resale. Examples of non-current assets include land, property, production equipment and vehicles.

2 **Current assets.** This category of asset is likely to be converted into cash before the next balance sheet is drawn up. Therefore, cash and inventories (previously called stock) are examples of current assets as they are only retained by the business for a short period of time.

There is another classification of assets which, although it does not affect the balance sheet directly, is still important.

1 **Tangible assets.** These are assets that have a physical existence and have been traditionally included on a balance sheet. Tangible assets include:
   - land and property, which is frequently the most valuable asset owned by a business
   - machinery and equipment, a tangible asset that is likely to be of importance to manufacturing industries.

2 **Intangible assets.** These assets do not take a physical form. Examples include:
   - Patents and other rights – for example, the mobile telephone companies have paid the UK government substantial sums for licences to operate cell phones. These licences represent a valuable intangible asset for companies such as Vodafone.
   - Goodwill – this is the value of established custom and a good name to a business.
   - Brands – these can be included on a balance sheet if they were purchased or can be separately valued. However, many brands can fluctuate in value as they may have a relatively short life.

Since 1998 intangible assets have only been recorded on the balance sheet if they can be separately identified and money was spent upon their acquisition. This regulation brought UK accounting practice into line with international standards. It would be appropriate for mobile telephone companies to present their licences as intangible assets.

Liabilities

A liability is a debt owed by the business to organisations or individuals. Another way of thinking of a liability is that it shows the sources of the capital the business has raised in order to purchase its assets. As with assets there are a number of categories of liabilities.

1 **Current liabilities.** In many senses these are the equivalent of current assets. They represent debts owed by the business due for payment within one year or less. Examples of such short-term debt are overdrafts and tax due for payment. Trade and other payables (which were previously called creditors) are organisations such as suppliers to whom the business owes money. These are normally classified as a current liability because payment is normally due within a short period of time.

2 **Non-current liabilities** (previously called long-term liabilities). These are debts that a business does not expect to repay within the period of one year. Mortgages and bank loans repayable over several years are common examples of this type of liability.

3 **Total equity** (previously shareholders' funds). It may seem strange that the money invested into the business by its owners (shareholders in the case of a company) is a liability. However, if the company ceases trading, shareholders would hope for the repayment of their investment. Thus these funds (called total equity or total shareholders' equity) are liabilities.

Business in Focus

The BBC's balance sheet

The BBC published its accounts on 31 March, as it does each year. The net worth of the Corporation as measured by its net assets was virtually unchanged at £146.7 million compared with 146.6 million in March 2007. In both years the organisation's balance sheet recorded net current assets, although in 2008 this figure had fallen to 5.0 million from £6.1 million. At the same time the Corporation's long-term borrowing (non-current liabilities) remained constant and tiny at £0.3 million or just £300,000.

Source: BBC Annual Review 2007–8
http://www.bbc.co.uk/worldservice/us/annual_review/
2007/balance-sheet.shtml

Key term

A **consolidated balance sheet** is the total balance sheet for a business, including all its divisions.

Why does a balance sheet always balance?

The balance sheet is well named as at all times the assets held by a business must match its liabilities (including capital borrowed from its owners). Why is this the case?

First, there exists what accountants call the 'dual aspect' of constructing a balance sheet. Thus, any transaction that is recorded on the balance sheet has two effects that cancel out each other. The following examples highlight this point:

- If a business borrows £575,000 to purchase vehicles, the loan will appear as a liability as it is owed by the business to a bank or other financial institution. However, at the same time the business will have additional assets recorded on its balance sheet (in this case vehicles initially valued at £575,000). Thus this transaction will not cause the balance sheet to become unbalanced.
- Alternatively, the business might sell a non-current asset for cash. In this case the business will have non-current assets of a lower value, but its holdings of cash will rise by the same amount. In these circumstances the value of total assets is unchanged and the balance sheet still balances.

Another feature of the balance sheet that ensures that it continues to balance is reserves. Reserves are simply profit accumulated during previous years'

Figure 2.1 Assets, liabilities and reserves

trading and not paid out to the owners of the business. This accumulated profit is not held in the form of cash but is invested into a range of assets that are useful to the business and hopefully generate further profits. If a business is successful, purchases more assets and grows, then its value will increase and so will the value of the assets. It may borrow money to achieve this growth; if it does, liabilities will grow at the same rate. However, if it funds its growth out of profits, then the matching liability will be recorded as reserves indicating that the owners' stake in the business has risen in value. Remember that the owners' funds in the business are a liability as this represents money lent to the organisation.

The structure of a balance sheet

There are two possible formats in which the information on a balance sheet can be presented.

1 **The horizontal format.** This presents a business's assets and its liabilities alongside one another. This style of presentation is now relatively uncommon.
2 **The vertical format.** This is the most common format and all public companies are legally obliged to present their balance sheets in this way. In this chapter we will only consider the vertical format of the balance sheet.

The precise layout of balance sheets can vary a little according to the type of business, and this is more likely following the IFRS-led changes since 2005.

However, the structure is similar for all businesses. All balance sheets list assets – non-current first followed by current assets. Next, current liabilities are recorded, allowing a firm to calculate its working capital (simply current assets less current liabilities). Finally, the last section records the sources of finance both borrowed and provided by the owners.

Reading and interpreting balance sheets

Professional managers, potential investors and accountants can gain a great deal of information about a company from reading its balance sheet. In this section we will consider the balance sheet of one of the UK's best-known retailers, Marks & Spencer, to illustrate the uses of this financial statement.

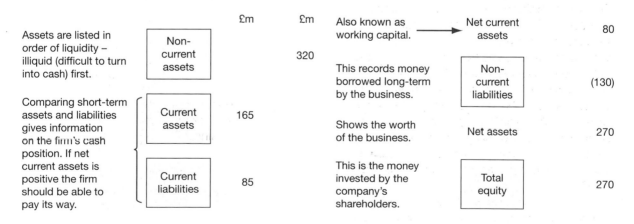

Figure 2.2 The basic structure of a public company's balance sheet in a vertical format

Marks & Spencer's consolidated balance sheet as at 31 March 2008		
	2008 £m	2007 £m
Intangible non-current assets	305.5	194.1
Tangible non-current assets	5673.8	4,340.5
Inventories	488.9	416.3
Receivables and cash	692.8	430.1
Total assets	7161.0	5,381.0
Current liabilities	1988.9	1,606.2
Net current liabilities	(807.2)	(759.8)
Non-current liabilities	3208.1	(2,126.6)
Total liabilities	(5197.0)	(3,732.8)
Net assets	**1964.0**	**1,648.2**
Share capital	628.0	629.2
Reserves & retained earnings	1336.0	1,019.0
Total equity	**1964.0**	**1,648.2**

Figure 2.3 Marks & Spencer's consolidated balance sheet

There are a number of features on the balance sheet that are worth examining when assessing the performance of the business in question. It is possible to make some assessment of the short-term financial position of the business as well as its longer-term strategy from reading the balance sheet.

The short term

Assessing a business's short-term situation entails examining its ability to pay its bills over the next 12 months. The balance sheet sets out a business's short-term debts (current liabilities) and also the current assets it has available to pay these creditors. The net position of these two factors is recorded as net current assets/liabilities. This is also known as working capital. If a business has more current assets than current liabilities it has a positive figure for working capital and should be able to pay its debts in the short term. However, if current liabilities exceed current assets, this may cause liquidity or cash problems, depending upon the type of business. Working capital is an issue we shall consider more fully in the next chapter.

The long term

This can be examined in a number of ways.

- Movement of non-current assets: a sudden increase in non-current (fixed) assets may indicate a rapidly growing company, which may mean that the company's financial performance might improve over the medium term.
- Considering how a business has raised its capital may also be valuable. As we shall see in a later unit, it is risky for a company to borrow too much. Thus a company raising more through borrowing (non-current liabilities) than through share capital and reserves might be vulnerable to rises in interest rates.

Business in Focus

Marks & Spencer plc

Figure 2.3 shows Marks & Spencer's balance sheet. The latest year (2008) is shown in the left-hand column. This method of presenting the latest data on the left is common in company's financial statements. Negative figures are shown in brackets.

We can see from the company's balance sheet that it operates with net current liabilities in both trading years. However, 2007 has a smaller negative figure than 2008. This shows us that Marks & Spencer's current liabilities exceeded its current assets by a smaller amount in 2007. Nevertheless, the company

did not have sufficient short-term assets to cover its short-term liabilities. This is not uncommon for retailers. They can rely on customers spending large amounts of cash daily in their shops, thus providing funds to settle short-term liabilities.

Marks & Spencer has increased the amount of capital that it has borrowed long term. This is shown by the increase in non-current liabilities. However, at the same time the company's value has increased substantially. Because its worth has increased significantly, a small increase in long-term debt would not be regarded as an important issue.

- Reserves provide an indication of the profits earned by the business. A rapid increase in reserves is likely to reflect a healthy position with regard to profits.

Working capital

Key terms

Current assets are items owned by a business that can be readily turned into cash. Examples include cash, money owed by customers (trade and other receivables) and inventories (stocks).
Current liabilities are short-term debts of a business, usually repaid within one year. An example is a business's overdraft.
Working capital is current assets minus current liabilities.

What is working capital?

Working capital measures the amount of money available to a business to pay its day-to-day expenses, such as bills for fuel and raw materials, wages and business rates. Much attention is given to the capital firms choose to invest in non-current assets, but of equal importance to the success of a business is the capital set aside to finance regular transactions.

Working capital is what remains of a business's liquid assets once it has settled all its immediate debts.

Examiner's advice

In some circumstances current liabilities might be greater than current assets. In this case, working capital will be negative (and called net current liabilities). As a negative figure it is likely to be in brackets.

It is possible to calculate the working capital of a business from its balance sheet by using the following formula:

working capital = current assets − current liabilities

On a balance sheet working capital may be labelled as net current assets. However, if current liabilities are greater than current assets, then it will be labelled as net current liabilities and the figure will be in brackets. This was the case with Marks & Spencer in Figure 2.3 above.

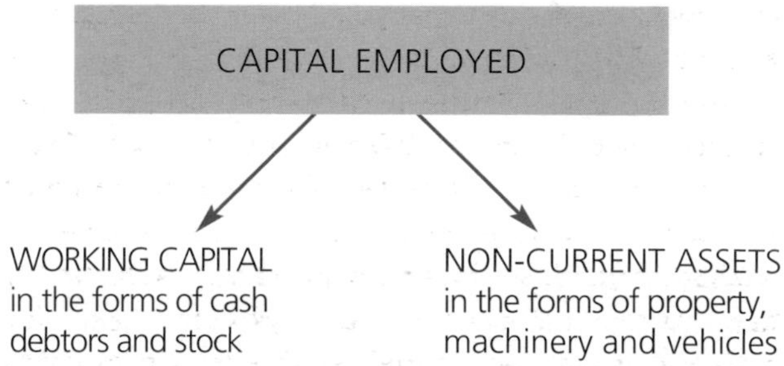

CAPITAL EMPLOYED

WORKING CAPITAL in the forms of cash debtors and stock

NON-CURRENT ASSETS in the forms of property, machinery and vehicles

Figure 2.4 A business's capital

Too much working capital?

It is too simple to argue that a business should hold large amounts of working capital to ensure it can always pay its debts in the short term and has spare assets in a liquid form (cash and debtors). Holding excessive amounts of working capital is not wise. The nature of liquid assets, such as cash and trade and other receivables, means that they earn little or no return for the business. Therefore a well-managed business will hold sufficient liquid assets to meet its need for working capital, but will avoid having too many assets in such an unprofitable form.

A number of factors influence the amount of working capital a firm needs to hold.

- The volume of sales – obviously a firm with a high level of sales will need to purchase more raw materials, pay a greater amount of wages and so on. Therefore, its need for working capital will be correspondingly higher.
- The amount of trade credit offered by the business. If a firm offers customers a lengthy period of time before they are required to pay, this increases the business's requirement for working capital. In effect, companies allowing trade credit offer their customers an interest-free loan.
- Whether or not the firm is expanding. In a period of expansion working capital requirements are likely to rise as the business purchases more fuel and raw materials. If a business expands without arranging the necessary working capital it is described as overtrading.
- The length of the operating cycle (i.e. the amount of time that elapses between the firm first paying for raw materials and receiving payment from customers). Some manufacturing industries (e.g.

shipbuilding) have long operating cycles and a correspondingly greater need for working capital.
- The rate of inflation. When prices rise rapidly, firms will require greater amounts of working capital to fund the increased costs of wages, components and raw materials.

As a rough guide, a firm holding current assets of twice the value of current liabilities would normally have sufficient working capital. It is also important for a business to have a significant proportion of its working capital in the form of cash. Cash, the most liquid of assets, is essential to pay the most immediate of bills.

The causes of working capital problems

Difficulties with working capital are a very common cause of business failure, even among firms that have the potential to generate a profit. The fundamental cause of problems in relation to working capital is poor financial management. Managers who plan ahead, forecasting their expected need for working capital against the likely inflow of cash, are less likely to encounter problems with working capital. If periods of potential difficulty can be identified, appropriate action can be taken.

A number of other causes of working capital problems can be identified.

- **External changes.** A number of changes in the economy can place pressure on a business's working capital. A sudden increase in interest rates will increase a firm's interest payments, and thereby drain cash from the business. The economy moving into a recession may restrict demand (especially for income-elastic goods such

WORKING CAPITAL
Essential, to pay for day-to-day expenses and keep the business operating

=

CURRENT ASSETS
- cash in the bank
- trade and other receivables due to settle their accounts soon
- inventories – raw materials and components

less

CURRENT LIABILITIES
(debts payable in the short term)
- debts repayable to the bank, e.g. overdraft
- trade and other payables who expect to be paid in the near future
- tax due to HM Revenue and Customs

NB An overdraft only represents a current liability if the bank calls for it to be repaid

Figure 2.5 Working capital

as foreign holidays and designer clothing), meaning a business's receipts from sales decline dramatically while expenditure is temporarily unchanged.

- **Poor credit control.** In a well-managed business emphasis is given to monitoring debtors to ensure that they settle their accounts and do so punctually. If a business fails to operate an effective system of credit control, then the incidence of bad debts may increase, resulting in a loss of revenue for the business. Furthermore, other customers may delay their payments, resulting in a lengthening of the working capital cycle.

- **Internal problems.** A business can suffer a variety of difficulties resulting in liquidity problems, as working capital proves insufficient to meet the needs of the business. Production problems can lead to a business incurring extra costs while suffering a decline in sales revenue. Similarly, misjudging likely sales can damage a business's working capital position. Production takes place and costs are incurred, including storage, while revenue is not received from sales.

- **Financial mismanagement.** Working capital or liquidity problems may arise simply because managers misread a situation by, for example, underestimating costs of production. Alternatively, they may invest too much in non-current assets as a consequence of overestimating the production capacity the firm requires. A business that borrows too much may not, in fact, improve its working capital position. The high and unavoidable costs of servicing the debts may place a strain on the liquidity position of the organisation.

> **Key terms**
>
> **Bad debts** refers to money owed to a business by its customers that is not expected to be recovered.
>
> **Overtrading** may occur if a business expands too rapidly without arranging funds to finance its growth.

How important is working capital?

Working capital is important to all businesses. It has been described as the 'lifeblood' of a successful enterprise. If any business is unable to pay its bills promptly, then it may be forced to close down as a

Technique	Advantages	Disadvantages	Suitable for . . .
reduce trade credit	• quick and simple to implement • under the control of the business	• may damage firm's image with customers • may result in loss of customers	small firms with few other options
negotiate extra credit with suppliers	• 'free' source of finance • may be able to implement quickly	• may lose out on price reductions available for prompt payment	larger businesses with secure financial reputation
negotiate additional short-term loans	• can provide immediate inflow of cash • minimal long-term impact	• can be very costly • may be difficult to arrange in times of financial crisis	firms experiencing short-term liquidity problems
cut production costs	• can improve profitability as well as liquidity • may enhance competitive position	• may lead to additional short-term costs, e.g. redundancy payments • may reduce quality if cheaper components used	businesses with potential to reduce expenditure without harming competitive position
careful financial planning	• minimal costs • improve business's competitive position	• may take time to have any impact • only eliminates problems relating to mismanagement	firms that do not normally experience liquidity problems
sale and leaseback	• can provide major injection of cash • all assets retained by business	• outflow of cash is necessary to retain use of asset • difficult to obtain the best price for an asset when selling under pressure	relatively large firms with valuable fixed assets, or those with surplus assets (in which case they may not be leased back)

Figure 2.6 Techniques for solving working capital problems

consequence of insolvency. However, working capital is of particular importance to certain types of businesses, requiring effective management of this important asset.

- **Small businesses.** This category of business can be especially vulnerable to problems with working capital for a number of reasons. Large firms often deliberately delay payments to small suppliers to improve their own liquidity position. They know that the smaller firm will not complain too much as it cannot afford to lose large orders. Secondly, small businesses often do not have access to sufficient funds to be able to improve their liquidity position easily. For example, banks may be unwilling to make loans to small businesses with few assets and experiencing liquidity problems.
- **Expanding businesses.** A growing business is likely to find its position with regard to working capital under pressure as it increases its expenditure on raw materials and components before it receives the revenue from selling its increased output. Even large firms can experience liquidity problems at this time.
- **Businesses with a long working capital cycle.** Many manufacturing businesses have substantial working capital requirements, simply because of the nature of their production. Firms engaged in shipbuilding may incur costs up to three years before they receive complete payment for their

Year	Value of asset on balance sheet at end of year	Amount depreciated annually
2008	60 000	20 000
2009	40 000	20 000
2010	20 000	20 000
2011	0	20 000

Figure 2.7 The Norfolk Ale Company

products. Clearly a firm that needs to generate large amounts of working capital as a part of its normal trading activity is especially vulnerable to changes such as slumps in demand.

Depreciation

> **Key term**
> **Depreciation** is the reduction of the value of an asset over a period of time.

What is depreciation?

Depreciation is the reduction of the value of an asset over a period of time. Thus, a brewery may purchase equipment for the brewing of beer at a cost of £80,000 and reduce its value as shown in Figure 2.7.

Figure 2.7 illustrates the effects of depreciation on the balance sheet and the income statement of the Norfolk Ale Company. The initial cost of the brewing equipment at the start of 2008 was £80,000. The company expects that this equipment will last for four years and have no resale value. The value of the asset falls by £20,000 each year, reflecting its decline in value. The amount of the decline in value (i.e. depreciation) is shown as an expense on the Norfolk Ale Company's income statement.

Why do firms depreciate assets?

Firms have to depreciate their non-current assets for a number of reasons. One of these is to spread the cost of an asset over its useful life. In the case of the Norfolk Ale Company it would have been incorrect to show the value of the brewing equipment as £80,000 throughout its life. Its resale value would decline for a number of reasons:

- the equipment would lose value as a result of wear and tear
- the availability of more modern equipment would

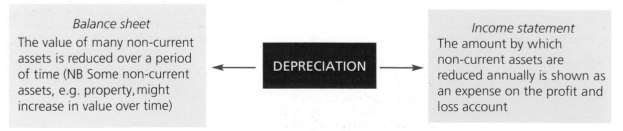

Balance sheet
The value of many non-current assets is reduced over a period of time (NB Some non-current assets, e.g. property, might increase in value over time)

DEPRECIATION

Income statement
The amount by which non-current assets are reduced annually is shown as an expense on the profit and loss account

Figure 2.8 Depreciation – a link between the balance sheet and the income statement

mean that the value of this 'older' style equipment would decline

- poor or inadequate maintenance of the equipment may mean expensive repairs are necessary, further reducing the brewing equipment's value.

Thus, reducing the value of an asset in line with these factors ensures that the value of the business recorded on the balance sheet is a relatively accurate indication of the true worth of the business.

Depreciation also allows firms to calculate the true cost of production during any financial year. The Norfolk Brewery would have overstated its costs in 2008 if it had allocated the entire cost of its new brewing equipment to that particular financial year. By depreciating the equipment by £20,000 each year for four years, one-quarter of the cost of the equipment is recorded each year on the Norfolk Ale Company's income statement. This helps to gain an accurate view of the profitability (or otherwise) of the business over the lifetime of the equipment.

Depreciation: a non-cash expense

Depreciation is an expense or a cost to a firm that is recorded on the income statement. However, depreciation is unusual in that it is a non-cash expense. Depreciation does not require a business to make any payment. It is recognition of the cost of providing a particular expense normally made at the time the asset was purchased. Depreciation is not a method of providing the cash necessary to replace the asset at the end of its useful life.

Why does depreciation matter?

Depreciation is an important matter to businesses for a number of reasons.

- Depreciation provides an accurate value of a business's assets throughout the life of those assets. This allows for a 'true and fair' assessment of the overall worth of the business at any time. Having an accurate figure for the overall value of the business is important for stakeholders such as investors.
- The amount of annual depreciation affects the overall value and profits of a business.

How to analyse income statements

> **Key terms**
>
> An **income statement** is an accounting statement showing a firm's sales revenue over a trading period and all the relevant costs generated to earn that revenue.
>
> A **loss** is a situation where a business's expenditure exceeds its revenue over a specific trading period.
>
> **Profit** can be defined in a number of ways, but is essentially the surplus of revenues over costs.

What is profit?

At its simplest, profit is what remains from revenue once costs have been deducted. However, in the construction of the income statement there are two main types of profit identified.

1 **Gross profit.** This form of profit is calculated by deducting direct costs (such as materials and shop-floor labour) from a business's sales revenue. This gives a broad indication of the financial performance of the business without taking into account other costs such as overheads.

2 **Net profit.** This is a further refinement of the concept of profit and is revenue less direct costs and indirect costs (or overheads) such as rent and

	Too much depreciation	Too little depreciation
Effects on balance sheet	fixed assets are valued at less than their true worth – value of business understated	fixed assets are overvalued giving a false impression of the company's worth
Effects on income statements	depreciation expenses are overestimated, reducing level of profits	low rates of depreciation will reduce the expenses incurred by a business. This will result in a business's profits being higher than they would otherwise be
Wider effects	business may look unattractive to prospective investors. Tax liability on profits may be reduced, but HM Revenue and Customs might investigate! Business may record surplus when asset finally sold	this may make the company more attractive to investors but will also increase its tax liability

Figure 2.9 The effects of depreciation

rates, as well as interest payments and depreciation. This gives a better indication of the performance of a business over a period of time as it takes into account all costs incurred by a firm over a trading period.

Net profit can take a number of forms.

- Trading or operating profit. This type of profit takes into account all earnings from regular trading activities and all the costs associated with those activities. However, this form of profit excludes any income received from, or costs incurred by, activities that are unlikely to be repeated in future financial years.
- Net profit before tax is a business's trading or operating profit plus any profits from one-off activities.
- Net profit after tax is the amount left to the business once corporation tax (or income tax in the case of a sole trader or partnership) has been deducted. This is an important form of profit. There are no more charges on this profit and the managers of the business can decide what to do with it.

Key Issues

Profit is one of the most commonly used words in business. Clearly it is important for a number of reasons. It acts as a signal to attract new businesses into a market and to encourage an existing business to grow. The pursuit of profit is an important business motive.

However, profit is not always the most important motive. Some businesses (e.g. charities and mutual organisations) do not aim to make profits. And profits that impose high social costs on others may not be highly valued. Businesses that generate high profits through polluting the environment or hiring sweatshop labour in less developed countries may attract criticism and lose sales in the long run.

Because of increased public awareness of ethical and environmental issues, many businesses are taking a long-term view of profit. They may be prepared to incur higher costs in the short term (through using more expensive materials from sustainable sources, for example) to maintain a positive corporate image and higher profits in the long term.

The quality of profit

It may seem strange, but some profits are better than others. Firms regard profit that is likely to continue into the future as high-quality profit. Thus, if a business introduces a new product onto the market and it immediately begins to generate a surplus and looks to have a promising future, then this will be high-quality profit. On the other hand, Merlin Entertainment, the company that owns Alton Towers, sold it for £622 million in 2007. If sold at a profit, this may have added to the company's overall net profit figure. This form of profit will not continue into the future and is therefore low-quality profit.

The amount of trading or operating profit earned by a firm is more likely to represent high-quality profit as it excludes any one-off items such as the sale of an asset at a profit. This level of profit might reasonably be expected to continue into the future, depending upon market conditions. Shareholders are interested in profit quality as it gives some indication of the company's potential to pay dividends in the future.

Examiner's advice

The quality of profit can be a powerful evaluative theme. It can be very helpful to remember that some types of profit are 'better' than others and to use this in your answers. Considering the quality of profit helps to bring a more strategic element into examination answers.

The structure of the income statement

Figure 2.10 provides an initial guide to the structure of the income statement as presented by most companies.

The income statement comprises four main stages:

1 First, 'gross profit' is calculated. This is the difference between the revenue figure (this can be called sales revenue or turnover) and the cost of the goods that have been sold. The latter is normally expressed simply as 'cost of goods'. This element of the income statement is sometimes called the trading account.

2 Second, 'operating profit' is calculated by deducting the main types of overheads such as distribution costs and administration costs.

3 Next, profit before taxation is calculated, which is arrived at by including interest received by the

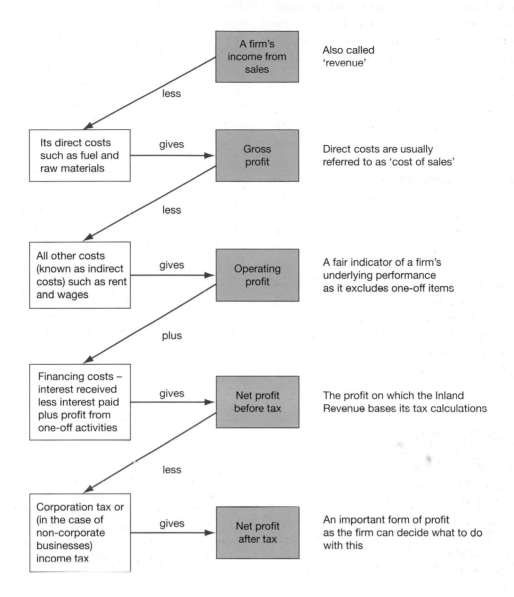

Figure 2.10 The basic structure of the income statement

business and interest paid by it. These are normally shown together as a net figure labelled 'financing costs'.

4 The final stage of the income statement is to calculate profit after taxation. This is arrived at by deducting the amount of tax payable for the year, and shows the net amount that has been earned for the shareholders. At this stage the company may indicate which profits are from continuing operations (those parts of the business that will be trading in the future) and which are from discontinuing operations. These can be seen in the case of Tesco plc in Figure 2.11.

Income statements and public limited companies

Public limited companies are required by law to publish their accounts. This means that they are available for scrutiny not only by the owners (shareholders), potential investors and bankers, but also by competitors.

When a company draws up its income statement for external publication it will include as little information as possible. Public limited companies usually supply no more detail than is required by law. This format is illustrated for Tesco in Figure 2.11.

Public limited companies also provide information on earnings per share on their income statements.

Earnings per share are simply the company's profits after tax divided by the number of shares the company has. Diluted earnings per share give a slightly lower figure as it takes into account all possible shares that could be issued by the company at that time, those issued plus those due to be issued as, for example, part of a share option scheme.

Group income statements

During the last 25 years many companies have been taken over by other companies to form groups. Each company within such a group retains its separate legal identity, but the group is also legally obliged to produce a group income statement (and balance sheet). A group income statement simply records the aggregated position of the group as a whole.

Examples of organisations producing consolidated accounts include The Body Shop International and Tesco (see Figure 2.11 for a summary of Tesco's group income statement). It is quite likely that the accounts of any large organisation you examine will be group accounts.

Income statements and the law

The legal requirements relating to income statements are set out in the Companies Act 2006. This legislation demands the production of financial statements including an income statement. It also

Summarised Group Income Statement for Tesco plc (Year ended 23 February 2008)		
	2008 (£m)	**2007 (£m)**
Revenue (sales excluding VAT)	47,298	42,641
Cost of sales	(43,668)	(39,143)
Impairment of the Gerrards Cross site		(35)
Gross profit	**3,630**	**3,463**
Administrative & other expenses	(839)	(815)
Operating profit	**2,791**	**2,648**
Finance income	262	221
Finance costs	(250)	(216)
Profit before tax	**2,803**	**2,653**
Taxation	(673)	(772)
Profit for the year from continuing operations	**2,130**	**1,881**
Profit/(loss) for the year from discontinued operation	–	18
Profit for the year	**2,130**	**1,899**
Earnings per share		
Basic	26.95p	23.84p
Diluted	26.61p	23.54

Figure 2.11 Tesco's summarised income statement
Source: Tesco plc http://www.tescoreports.com/downloads/tesco_report_final.pdf

specifies the information to be included in these accounts.

The income statement does not have to detail every expense incurred by the firm, but summarises the main items under standard headings. The Act sets out acceptable formats for presentation of the relevant data. A summarised form of one of these is shown for Tesco on page 26.

The notes to the income statements must disclose details of:

- auditor's fees
- depreciation amounts
- the total of directors' emoluments (earnings)
- the average number of employees, together with details of cost of wages and salaries, together with national insurance and pensions.

Companies must disclose the following:

- **Exceptional items** are large (usually one-off) financial transactions arising from ordinary trading activities. However, they are so large as to risk distorting the company's trading account. An example of an exceptional item was when the high street banks incurred unusually large bad debt charges.
- **Extraordinary items** are large transactions outside the normal trading activities of a company. As a result they are not expected to recur. A typical example is the closure of a factory or division of a business. These items have only been included in the income statement over recent years. In Tesco's case above, its store at Gerrards Cross in Buckinghamshire was damaged following the collapse of a tunnel over which the company was building a new store. Tesco has had to compensate Network Rail, the train operating companies and passengers. This cost is shown in the company's income statement.

There is no single format for a limited company's income statement. The Companies Act of 2006 sets out the minimum amount of information that must be included, though some modification can be made to ensure a 'true and fair view' of the business's performance.

The accounts of public limited companies also contain notes giving further details of the figures included in the income statement. Thus, in the case of Tesco, there was small number 6 next to the row in which the amount paid in taxation was entered. In a detailed explanation note 6 sets out the precise profit figure on which Tesco had to pay corporation tax and the rate at which it paid the tax (30 per cent). This depth of information is important to allow shareholders and other interested parties to make an accurate assessment of the financial performance of the business.

Interpreting income statements

A number of groups are likely to have an interest in a business's income statement. These stakeholders are illustrated in Figure 2.12.

- **Shareholders** are perhaps the most obvious group with an interest in the income statement. Shareholders will be interested in a business's sales revenue and operating or net profit. This will provide some guidance as to the performance of the enterprise, especially when compared with previous years. They will also be likely to examine the income statement closely to see how profits have been utilised. Some shareholders may seek the maximum dividend possible. Others may be interested in a longer-term return and welcome substantial reinvestment in the expectation of future profits.
- **Managers** use the income statement as an important source of information regarding the performance of the business. Managers are, of course, able to see the income statement in much more detail than that provided in the annual report and accounts. Published accounts contain the minimum amount of information required under law to avoid giving competitors any advantage. Managers will monitor sales performance through turnover figures and judge costs against sales

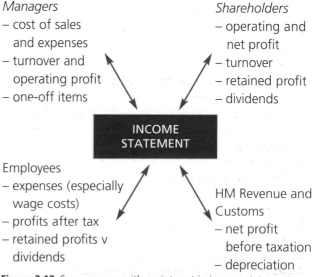

Managers
– cost of sales and expenses
– turnover and operating profit
– one-off items

Shareholders
– operating and net profit
– turnover
– retained profit
– dividends

INCOME STATEMENT

Employees
– expenses (especially wage costs)
– profits after tax
– retained profits v dividends

HM Revenue and Customs
– net profit before taxation
– depreciation

Figure 2.12 Some groups with an interest in income statements

revenue. If expenses and cost of sales rise by a greater amount than turnover, action may be necessary. Managers will also consider carefully the effects of one-off items on the account.

- **Employees** may be interested in profits after tax if their pay is related to company performance through a profit-related pay scheme. They may also be interested in the level of dividends if they are shareholders. The level of profits after taxation may also be an indication of the company's ability to fund a pay increase or, alternatively, of the security of their employment.
- **Revenue & Customs** is the organisation responsible for collecting corporation tax from companies on the government's behalf. HM Revenue and Customs will therefore scrutinise company accounts and use net profit before tax as the basis for their calculation of tax liability (the amount of tax to be paid). They may also check that the income statement meets all necessary standards (e.g. the basis upon which non-current assets have been depreciated).

Using financial data for comparisons, trend analysis and decision-making

Balance sheets

There are a number of features of a balance sheet that are valuable for comparisons, analysis and for assisting with decision-making.

The business's working capital position

A declining trend here would be shown by a smaller figure for current net assets or a larger negative figure for current net liabilities. A movement from a net assets figure to a negative net liabilities figure may be a cause for concern. It is easier to make a judgement if the trend of figures is compared with those for other businesses operating in similar markets. This can help to make a judgement as to the extent to which the change is due to a declining market situation. This could be due, for instance, to a significant fall in sales. Analysing this trend and conducting comparisons can help a business's managers to decide whether action (such as selling and leasing back non-current assets) is necessary to maintain the financial strength of the business.

The extent of the business's long-term debts

These are shown on the balance sheet under the heading non-current liabilities and represent debts which the business plans to repay in a period of over one year. If the figure for non-current liabilities is rising, especially if the value or worth of the business (as shown by net assets) is not increasing, may be a cause for concern. A business that borrows too much money may encounter problems in repaying it, especially if interest rates rise unexpectedly.

Examiner's advice

In the next chapter we consider a technique of financial analysis known as ratio analysis. This will help you to analyse trends in financial data and to make comparisons. You should return to this section when you have completed your study of the following chapter.

Income statements

Several key aspects of a business's income statement can be considered as part of the evaluation of a business's performance.

1 **Trends.** A better judgement can be made concerning a business if its performance in one year is measured against that of previous years. As in the case of Tesco, it is normal for businesses to present two years' figures alongside one another. Many companies also offer five-year summaries of financial performance. Using this sort of evidence it is possible to see what has happened to revenue, costs and expenses and profits over a period of time. It is important to look at the trends of sales revenue and profit for the year (i.e. after taxation). This gives you an insight into the company's success in selling products, in its markets and also its ability to control its costs and keep them below its revenues.

2 **The period to which the statement relates.** It is normal for an income statement to cover a period of one year. However, this statement can relate to a longer or shorter period. Such changes occur when, for example, the business changes the dates of its financial year. This either prolongs or shortens the year in which the change is made. A 20 per cent increase in profits may not appear so exceptional if the income statement covers a period of 15 months.

3 **Comparing gross and net profit.** The calculation of gross profit only includes direct costs (labelled as 'cost of sales'). Operating profit, on the other hand, takes into account all costs – direct and indirect. A rise in gross profit but a fall in operating profit may indicate that managers are not controlling indirect costs effectively.

4 **The business(es) to which the income statement relate(s).** Many companies trade as part of a group of businesses. In these circumstances the enterprise will produce an income statement (and a balance sheet) for the individual company and also one for the entire group. These latter accounts are referred to as consolidated accounts. These are an aggregation of the accounts of the individual companies that make up the group.

The strengths and weaknesses of financial data in judging performance

Window dressing balance sheets and income statements

Public limited companies are under considerable pressure to present their financial performance in the most favourable terms possible. There are a number of methods by which a company can improve the look of its balance sheet – these processes are called 'window dressing'.

- Some companies borrow money for a short period of time to improve their cash position just before the date on which the balance sheet is drawn up. This action may enhance the company's apparent ability to pay its short-term debts.
- An alternative method of improving a company's cash or liquidity position is through the use of sale and leaseback. This entails the sale of major non-current assets and then leasing them back. Many retailers have negotiated sale and leaseback deals on their high street properties.
- Businesses may maintain the value of intangible assets on the balance sheet at what might be excessive levels to increase the overall value of the organisation. This tactic is only possible when the assets in question (e.g. goodwill or brands) have been purchased.
- Capitalising expenditure, which means including as non-current assets items that might otherwise have simply been regarded as an expense and not included on the balance sheet. Thus a firm might spend heavily on computer software and include this as a fixed asset on the basis that it will have a useful life of several years. This action will increase the value of the business.
- On income statements businesses may bring forward sales to an earlier period and thereby boost revenue for a particular financial year. This

does result, however, in a lower figure in the next financial year.

There is a fine line between presenting accounts as favourably as possible and misrepresenting the performance of the firm, which is illegal. The authorities have made several adjustments to accounting procedures in order to restrict the extent of window dressing.

The importance of the balance sheet

The balance sheet is often referred to as the premier financial statement. It is important for a number of reasons.

- The fundamental use of the balance sheet is to provide a measure of the value or worth of a business. If a series of balance sheets over a number of years is examined, a clearer picture of a business's growth may emerge.
- A balance sheet paints a picture of the sources of capital used by a business. This allows stakeholders analysing the statement to assess whether the company has borrowed an excessive amount of capital, making itself vulnerable to rising interest rates.
- It is also possible to see if the business has used expensive sources of short-term finance (e.g. overdrafts) to purchase non-current assets. A well-managed business would normally use cheaper long-term sources (e.g. bank loans or mortgages) to finance the purchase of this type of asset.
- The balance sheet illustrates the cash (or liquidity) position of the firm and allows an assessment to be made of its ability to meet its debts or liabilities over the next few months.

However, the balance sheet is not a sound basis for analysing the performance of a business. Any effective analysis would require that other sources of information be used alongside the balance sheet.

- The **income statement** is another very important financial statement. An income statement records a firm's income, expenditure and ultimately profit or loss over some trading period. A much fuller analysis can be made of a business's financial performance by reading the income statement in conjunction with the relevant balance sheet.
- Any **financial statement** is a historical document recording what has happened in the past. This is

not necessarily a good indication of what may happen to the same business in the future.

- A balance sheet records financial information. It does not provide any real insight into the quality of the management team, the degree of competition provided by rival firms and any change that may be taking place in the external environment. For example, a sudden alteration in tastes and fashions would not be seen on the balance sheet until after the change has occurred.

The importance of the income statement

Unquestionably the income statement offers valuable information to a business's stakeholders. This financial statement gives details on a company's revenue, indicating whether or not it has grown. It also provides details about the costs incurred and how successful managers have been in controlling these. Finally, the level of net profit is of value to interested parties, as are the uses to which the profit has been put. This latter information might suggest how successful the venture may be in the future. If large amounts of profit are retained for reinvestment, the company may be expected to grow in the future and generate larger profits.

However, caution has to be exercised when interpreting an income statement. Inflation can distort accounts, exaggerating any increase in turnover that may have taken place. Firms attempt to window dress the income statement by bringing forward sales from the next trading period to increase turnover and profit. Profits can be altered by adjusting depreciation policies or by including one-off items as part of ordinary activities.

As with the balance sheet, an income statement alone is not a good indicator of a business's financial performance. It should be read in conjunction with the balance sheet. However, evaluating the performance of any business requires more than the current year's accounts. Analysts should consider the financial performance of a business over an extended period, perhaps five years. This allows trends in key variables such as revenue and profit to be identified. Furthermore, non-financial factors should be considered. The strength and actions of competitors, the growth (if any) in the market for the firm's products and the quality of a business's labour force are also factors that should be taken into account.

Business in Focus

Ryanair's profits slump

Irish low-cost airline Ryanair, which did much to pioneer the boom of cheap air travel, announced that net profits nosedived by 76 per cent in the first half when it was hammered by soaring jet fuel costs amid record high oil prices.

Net profits slumped to £76.85 million (95.3 million euros) in the six months to the end of September, compared with £326 million (407.5 million euros) in the equivalent part of 2007.

The Dublin-based airline, added that fuel costs more than doubled to 788.5 million euros in the first half, while revenues rose 16.5 per cent to 1.811 billion euros.

Oil prices had hit historic records above 147 dollars per barrel in July, but have since more than halved in value because of the prospect of a global recession and weaker energy demand.

Ryanair said it expected to break even this year because of lower oil prices, which traded at about 64 dollars per barrel on Monday. Jet fuel, or kerosene, is refined from crude oil.

Source: Adapted from Yahoo Finance
http://uk.biz.yahoo.com

Question:

1 Would this slump in profits have been predicted from looking at the company's most recent balance sheet and income statement?

The limitations of financial statements

By definition, financial statements such as the balance sheet and the income statement only include financial information. Inevitably they will not provide direct information on important factors such as the following:

- The quality of leadership of the business is not shown by financial data. Do senior managers have the necessary skills and experience to lead the business successfully and do they have the vision to inspire and direct the workforce?
- What is the position of the business in the market? It may have successful products that are selling well and generating acceptable levels of profit. However, the firm may be lagging behind in developing new products or in entering new markets and therefore likely to perform less well in the future. Financial analysis is unlikely to reveal this.
- What about the motivation and performance of the workforce? Balance sheets and income statements do not reveal productivity or levels of labour turnover, or even the rate of absenteeism, which can indicate the level of morale within the business.

Examiner's advice

Please remember that financial information is historical. It relates to previous years and, especially if the business environment is changeable, may not be a good indicator of the future.

One step further: cash-flow statements

A cash-flow statement is a document that is prepared to summarise the cash flows into and out of a business. It records the inflow and outflow of cash over an accounting period. The cash-flow statement is a required part of a public limited company's annual accounts.

The cash flow statement is different from a cash-flow forecast in that it states what actually happened with regard to cash flow rather than what was forecast. It differs from an income statement because it shows what has happened with regard to cash flow and not to profit. Profit is of little value to a business unless the cash that results from it has actually flowed into the business. The cash-flow statement tells interested stakeholders whether all the business's recorded profit has been realised in the form of cash.

The items in the cash-flow statement (for example the net cash inflow or outflow) can be significantly different from equivalent items on the income statement. This is what makes the cash flow so valuable: it gives an insight into the actual cash the business is receiving and not just the recorded level of sales. The income statement is vulnerable to window dressing in that sales can be brought forward to an earlier trading period to boost revenues. This is not possible with a cash-flow statement.

	Financial year ending 29 March 2008 (£m)	Financial year ending 31 March 2007 (£m)
Net operating cash flow from activities	1,069.8	1,292.5
Net cash outflow from investing and financing activities	(1,000.4)	(1,526.4)
Net cash inflow/(outflow) from activities	69.4	(233.9)
Effects of exchange rate changes	1.5	(1.5)
Opening net cash	47.0	282.4
Closing net cash	**117.9**	**47.0**

Table 2.1 Key information from Marks & Spencer's cash-flow statement, 2008
Source: Marks & Spencer Annual Report & Accounts 2008 http://corporate.marksandspencer.com/documents/publications/2008/annual_report_2008.pdf

Progress questions

1 Merrills Industries manufactures biscuits and other convenience foodstuffs. Identify three stakeholder groups who may have an interest in the company's balance sheet. Outline the likely nature of their interest. (9 marks)

2 Explain two factors that lead to a business's balance sheet always balancing. (6 marks)

3 Outline how the information recorded on a business's balance sheet can be used to assess the cash or liquidity position of the business. (7 marks)

4 Explain the difference between the net current assets and the net assets of a public limited company. (6 marks)

5 The net assets of Gujarati Products plc is £540 million. The company's non-current liabilities total £339 million. What are the possible implications of this position? (7 marks)

6 Smith and Whyte's reserves rose by £54 million last year. Outline the possible causes of this. (5 marks)

7 Explain two possible consequences of a retailer having too much working capital. (6 marks)

8 Explain why a manufacturing business that is expanding rapidly might face problems with its working capital. (8 marks)

9 Explain why a road haulage company will have to depreciate its non-current assets each year. (8 marks)

10 Outline why it is important to value non-current assets as accurately as possible. (6 marks)

11 Explain what is meant by high-quality profit. (4 marks)

12 Explain why an extraordinary item should be listed separately in a company's income statement. (5 marks)

13 Outline two aspects of a supermarket's income statement that might be of particular interest to a shareholder considering buying a large quantity of the company's shares. (8 marks)

14 Explain two reasons why a balance sheet can be considered a valuable document for stakeholders. (6 marks)

15 Outline three sources of information, other than its balance sheet and income statement, that might help an investor to assess the future prospects of a computer manufacturer. (8 marks)

Analysis and evaluation questions

1 A recent article described Benson plc (an oil company) as having a strong balance sheet. The company is investing its large profits (£6.6 billion in the last financial year) in extracting oil from difficult locations across the world. The company has recently appointed a new chief executive.

a Analyse what is meant by the phrase 'a strong balance sheet'. (10 marks)
b Discuss the value of Benson plc's balance sheets and income statements in assessing its future performance. (15 marks)

2 Marine Ltd is a rapidly growing company. Its range of flavoured waters has proved to be especially popular with children. The company has just persuaded Tesco to stock its products, although it has to grant the retailer 45 days trade credit.

a Analyse the possible reasons why Marine Ltd might experience problems in managing its working capital. (10 marks)
b Discuss the possible implications of the cash-flow problems for Marine Ltd. (15 marks)

Case study

Paul Ollington is one of Chester's best-known figures. He has been a local councillor for more than 20 years and has been a major contributor to local charities. However, he is perhaps most easily recognised as the owner of Ollington & Smart Photographers, with two shops in Chester and a further outlet in nearby Malpas.

Ollington's Photographers has been in business for over 30 years. Paul bought out his former partner several years earlier. However, Paul is now near retirement age and has to take a decision over the future of his business. In recent years Paul has been less motivated by his work as principal shareholder and managing director of the small business. Paul's accountant has urged him to sell the business given that the operator of a chain of photographic shops, Smith Photographic plc, has made an attractive offer. 'You may not receive an equal offer again, Paul, and if you are serious about selling you should not turn this down. You have said you are facing more competition and that people are producing more of their own photographs using computer

Ollington & Smart Photographers – Balance Sheet as at 31 March		
	2008 (£000)	2007 (£000)
Non-current Assets	180	192
Current Assets		
Inventories	48	60
Receivables	6	10
Cash	3	5
Less Current Liabilities	(62)	(72)
Non-current Liabilities	(95)	(95)
Assets Employed	80	100
Share Capital	25	25
Reserves	55	75
Total Equity	80	100

software. This is a moment for a positive decision: you need to change the direction in which the business is going.'

Paul was not decisive. 'I agree the position of the local economy has not been particularly strong over the last couple of years, but I have worked with several of my current employees for many years. I would hate to see them lose their jobs as a result of a takeover by Smith or another major firm. What's more, the sales figures have held up quite well in the circumstances. I need to think carefully about this.'

Questions

1 Identify **two** stakeholders who may have an interest in the balance sheet of Ollington. In each case explain the possible reasons for their interest. (6 marks)

2 Analyse the benefits that Ollington's Photographers may gain from taking action to window dress its balance sheet. (8 marks)

3 Smith Photographic plc is considering the purchase of Ollington & Smart. Consider the disadvantages of using a balance sheet as the basis of such a decision. (12 marks)

4 Paul's accountant has commented that there are strong reasons why he should sell the business at this time. Discuss the case for and against this view. (14 marks)

Case study

Rolls-Royce, is a world-leading provider of engines and services for use on land, at sea and in the air, and operates in four global markets – civil aerospace, defence aerospace, marine and energy. The company has invested heavily in technology and training its workforce, with the aim of improving its range of products and improving the environmental performance of its products.

Rolls-Royce has a broad customer base comprising 600 airlines, 4,000 corporate and utility aircraft and

Consolidated income statement (for the year ended 31 December 2007)		
	2007 (£m)	**2006 (£m)**
Revenue (sales excluding VAT)	7,435	7,156
Cost of sales	(6,003)	(5,566)
Gross profit	**1,432**	**1,590**
Administrative & other expenses	(918)	(898)
Operating profit	**512**	**693**
Finance income	718	1,196
Finance costs	(497)	(498)
Profit before tax	**733**	**1,391**
Taxation	(133)	(397)
Profit for the year	**600**	**994**

Consolidated balance sheet (as at 31 December 2007)		
	2007 (£m)	2006 (£m)
Non-current assets	4,206	3,620
Inventories	2,203	1,845
Trade & other receivables & cash	5,050	5,333
Total assets	11,459	10,798
Current liabilities	(4,754)	(4,462)
Net current liabilities	2,499	2,716
Non-current liabilities	(3,156)	(3,611)
Total liabilities	(7,910)	(8,073)
Net assets	**3,549**	**2,725**
Share capital	364	356
Reserves & retained earnings	3,185	2,369
Total equity	**3,549**	**2,725**

helicopter operators, 160 armed forces, more than 2,000 marine customers including 70 navies, and energy customers in 120 countries. Rolls-Royce is a technology leader, employing 38,000 people in offices, manufacturing and service facilities in 50 countries.

Annual sales total £7.4 billion, of which 53 per cent are services revenues. The firm's announced order book is £26.1 billion, of which aftermarket services represent 38 per cent, providing evidence of future levels of activity.

Questions

1 Explain what is meant by 'a consolidated balance sheet'. (4 marks)

2 Analyse the key trends in the company's income statements for 2006 and 2007. (9 marks)

3 Discuss the strengths and weakness of Rolls-Royce's balance sheet in 2007. (12 marks)

4 To what extent could an investor base a decision to purchase 1 million of the Rolls-Royce group's shares on the basis of this information? (15 marks)

3 Interpreting published accounts

This chapter builds on the material we studied in the previous chapter. It will introduce you to a range of simple mathematical techniques (collectively known as ratio analysis) which can be used to conduct a more in-depth analysis of a business's balance sheets and income statements. The chapter will also explain how to interpret the results of the ratio calculations and how to use these as the basis for decision-making.

In this chapter we examine:

- how to conduct ratio analysis, including the selection, calculation and interpretation of ratios
- the value and limitations of ratio analysis in measuring a business's performance.

Ratio analysis

There are a number of groups that are interested in the financial information provided by businesses and especially by public limited companies. Collectively these groups can be referred to as stakeholders and they may take an interest in the published accounts of a business for a variety of reasons. For example,

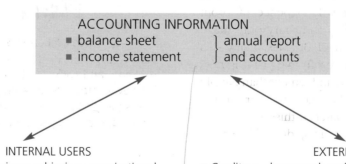

ACCOUNTING INFORMATION
- balance sheet   } annual report
- income statement   } and accounts

INTERNAL USERS
- Managers – is this business achieving organisational objectives? Is it using resources efficiently?
- Employees – is the business stable and jobs secure? – are they receiving fair pay in the light of the business's performance?
- Shareholders – what is the return on their investment? – how does this compare with alternative investments?

EXTERNAL USERS
- Creditors – how much cash does the business have? Will it be able to pay its bills?
- Government – what is the tax liability of the business?
- Competitors – how is the business performing in relation to other businesses?

Figure 3.1 Stakeholders and financial information

suppliers may want to judge the financial position of a business to evaluate whether they should offer the firm credit. Similarly, individuals contemplating buying shares in the business may try to assess the business's potential to make profits in the future. Figure 3.1 summarises stakeholder groups and their interest in a company's financial performance.

What is a ratio?

Ratio analysis allows stakeholders to evaluate a business's performance through the investigation of key financial statements such as the balance sheet and the profit and loss account. The key feature of ratio analysis is that it compares two pieces of financial information. By comparing two pieces of data in this way it is possible to make more informed judgements about a business's performance.

A comparison of the financial performance of two companies in 2008 can illustrate the advantages from comparing two pieces of data to make more informed judgements. J Sainsbury, one of the UK's largest retailers, announced a net profit of £479 million for the year. In comparison, J D Wetherspoon, a company that operates a nationwide chain of pubs, turned in a net profit of £54.2 million in 2008. A simple judgement would therefore suggest that J Sainsbury had performed more successfully. However, if we took into account the value of sales achieved by the two companies (its revenue), a more meaningful judgement could be made.

Table 3.1 shows that when we compare profit for the year with turnover, J D Wetherspoon's performance could be judged superior to that of J Sainsbury. J D Wetherspoon earned nearly 6 pence of profit from each £1 of sales, while J Sainsbury only made 2.69 pence of profit on each £1 of sales. Using this ratio (which is called the net profit margin) it is possible to make a more accurate judgement than simply comparing levels of profit. We shall consider the net profit margin in more detail later in this unit.

Ratio analysis allows managers, directors, share-holders and other interested parties to place key figures such as profits and turnover in context. Ratio analysis does not guarantee that a manager or share-holder will take a correct decision. The results of ratio analysis do, however, give decision-makers more information and make a good-quality decision more likely.

Types of ratio

There are a number of ways of classifying ratios. One approach is to identify five main categories of ratio.

1 **Liquidity ratios**, also known as solvency ratios, measure the ability of the business to settle its debts in the short term.
2 **Efficiency ratios** measure the effectiveness with which an enterprise uses the resources available to it. These are also termed internal control ratios.
3 **Profitability ratios** assess the amount of gross or net profit made by the business in relation to the business's turnover or the assets or capital available to it.
4 **Gearing** examines the relationship between internal sources and external sources of finance. It is therefore concerned with the long-term financial position of the company.
5 **Shareholders' ratios** measure the returns received by the owners of the company, allowing comparison with alternative investments. For obvious reasons they are also called investment ratios.

Examiner's advice

The AQA specification sets out ten ratios with which you should be familiar. These are the current and acid test ratios, ROCE, asset turnover, stock or inventory turnover, receivables (debtor) days and payables (creditor) days, gearing, dividend per share and dividend yield.

Company	Net profit (£m)	Revenue (£m)	Net profit as a percentage of revenue
J Sainsbury plc	479	17,837	2.69
J D Wetherspoon plc	54.2	907.5	5.97

Table 3.1 **Comparing the financial performance of two companies by using a simple ratio**

Typeof ratio	Liquidity ratios	Efficiency ratios	Profitability ratios	Gearing	Shareholders' ratios
Ratios used price–earnings	• current ratio • acid test (or quick) ratio	• asset turnover ratio • stock turnover ratio • debtor days	• net profit margin • gross profit margin • return on capital employed	• gearing – loans: capital	• dividend per share • dividend yield ratio
Purpose of ratios	to assess the ability of the business to pay its immediate debts	these provide evidence on how well the managers have controlled the business	provide a fundamental measure of the success of the business	assess the extent to which the business is based on borrowed money	give investors information on returns on their investment
Interested stakeholders	• creditors • suppliers • managers	• shareholders • managers • employees • competitors	• shareholders • creditors • managers • competitors • employees	• shareholders • managers • creditors	• shareholders • managers

Figure 3.2 Types of ratio

Sources of information for ratio analysis

The most obvious sources are the published accounts of the business or businesses concerned. In particular, ratio analysis requires access to a business's balance sheet and income statement. However, although this might be essential information, it is not all that is required to conduct an in-depth ratio analysis of a business. Other possible sources of information include the following:

- **The performance of the business over recent years**. Having an understanding of the trends of ratios over time can assist in making judgements. Thus a profitability ratio might appear fairly low, but if it represents a continuation of a steadily rising trend then the figure may be more acceptable to stakeholders.
- **Norms or benchmarks for the industry**. The results of ratio calculations should be judged against what is normal for the industry. Thus an investor might calculate that a company's debtor day ratio is 35 days (the number of days, on average, that customers take to settle their bills). This might be acceptable for a manufacturing business, but not for a fast-food business.
- **The economic environment**. A decline in profit ratios might appear to reflect an unsuccessful business. However, this might be more acceptable in the context of a severe economic recession in which sales and prices have declined.

Examiner's advice

It is easy to concentrate on how to calculate ratios and to underestimate the importance of interpreting the results. Some examination questions offer the results of ratios as part of the information given to candidates. This type of question places much emphasis on interpreting ratios and students should prepare themselves for this style of question.

Expressing ratios

Ratios are normally expressed in one of three forms:

1. as a proper ratio – for example, the current ratio is 1.6:1
2. as a percentage – ROCE expresses operating profit as a percentage of capital employed by the business
3. as a multiple – for example, inventories (stock) are turned over (or sold) five times a year.

Liquidity ratios

These ratios allow managers and other interested parties to monitor a business's cash position. Even profitable businesses can experience problems with liquidity and may be unable to pay their bills as they fall due. Liquidity ratios measure the liquid assets held by a firm (cash and other assets such as debtors that are easily convertible into cash). The value of these assets is then compared with the short-term debts or liabilities the business will incur. In this way stakeholders may evaluate whether the business's performance may be harmed as a result of liquidity problems.

Current ratio

This measures the ability of a business to meet its liabilities or debts over the next year or so. The formula to calculate this ratio is:

$$\text{Current ratio} = \frac{\text{current assets}}{\text{current liabilities}}$$

The current ratio is expressed in the form of a ratio, for example 2:1. This would mean that the firm in question possessed £2 of current assets (cash, debtors and stock) for each £1 of current liability (creditors, taxation and proposed dividends, for example). In these circumstances it is probable that the business would be able to meet its current liabilities without needing to sell non-current assets or raise long-term finance.

Examiner's advice

It is not necessary to learn the formulae for this and the other ratios that we shall consider in this chapter. These will be provided for you as part of the examination paper. You should concentrate on carrying out the calculations accurately, and on understanding what the results mean for businesses.

Using this ratio

- For years, holding current assets twice the value of current liabilities was recommended. This is no longer accepted, partly due to the use of computers in stock control and the widespread use of just-in-time systems of production. A more typical figure might now be 1.6:1.
- In spite of this, the 'normal' figure for this ratio varies according to the type of business and the state of the market. Fast-food outlets and banks typically operate with lower ratios, whereas some manufacturing firms may have higher ratios.

- Firms with high current ratio values (say, 3:1) are not necessarily managing their finances effectively. It may be that they are holding too much cash and not investing in fixed assets to generate income. Alternatively, they may have large holdings of stock, some of which might be obsolete.
- Firms can improve the current ratio by raising more cash through the sale of non-current assets or the negotiation of long-term loans. (NB: raising more cash through short-term borrowing will increase current liabilities, having little effect on the current ratio.)

Acid test (or quick) ratio

This ratio measures the very short-term liquidity of a business. The acid test ratio compares a business's current liabilities with its liquid assets (i.e. current assets less inventories (stock)). This can provide a more accurate indicator of liquidity than the current ratio, as inventories can take time to sell. The acid test ratio measures the ability of a firm to pay its bills over a period of two or three months without requiring the sale of inventories.

The formula for the acid test ratio is:

$$\text{Acid test ratio} = \frac{\text{liquid assets}}{\text{current liabilities}}$$

The acid test ratio is also expressed in the form of a ratio (e.g. 2:1).

Using this ratio

- Conventionally, a 'normal' figure for the acid test ratio was thought to be 1:1, giving a balance of liquid assets and current liabilities. However, by 2009, a number of businesses were operating successfully with acid test figures nearer to 0.7:1.
- The value of the acid test ratio considered acceptable will vary according to the type of business. Retailers might operate with a figure of 0.4:1, because they trade mainly in cash, and have close relationships with suppliers. A manufacturing business might operate with a ratio nearer to the standard 1:1.
- Firms should not operate over long periods with high acid test ratios, as holding assets in the form of cash is not profitable and does not represent an effective use of resources.
- As with the current ratio, the acid test ratio can be improved by selling non-current assets or agreeing long-term borrowing.

Liquidity ratios are based on figures drawn from the balance sheet relating to a particular moment in time. Because of this some caution should be exercised when drawing conclusions from this type of ratio. The actual figures on the balance sheet may be unrepresentative of the firm's normal position due to factors such as window dressing or a sudden change in trading conditions.

> **Key terms**
>
> **Debenture:** a long-term loan to a business carrying a fixed rate of interest and a specified repayment date.
>
> **Ordinary shares:** a financial security representing part ownership of a business that does not entitle the holder to a fixed payment from profits, but does confer voting rights.
>
> **Preference shares:** a financial security representing part ownership of a business that entitles the holder to a fixed payment from profits.
>
> **Inventories:** the amount of raw materials, components and finished goods held by a business at a given time.

Gearing

Gearing measures the long-term liquidity of a business. Under some classifications gearing is included as a liquidity ratio. There are a number of methods of measuring gearing; we shall consider the simplest form of the ratio. This ratio analyses how firms have raised their long-term capital. The result of this calculation is expressed as a percentage.

There are two main forms of long-term finance available to businesses.

1 **Non-current liabilities** – this includes preference shares and debentures (all have fixed interest payments). This is long-term borrowing and may be called loan capital.

2 **Total equity** – this arises from selling shares and increases in the value of the business.

The capital employed by a business is simply the total of these two. So this gearing ratio measures the percentage of a firm's capital that is borrowed.

$$\text{Gearing} = \frac{\text{non-current liabilities} \times 100}{\text{total equity} + \text{non-current liabilities}}$$

This measure of a business's performance is important because by raising too high a proportion of capital through fixed interest capital firms become vulnerable to increases in interest rates. Shareholders are also unlikely to be attracted to a business with a high gearing ratio as their returns might be lower because of the high level of interest payments to which the enterprise is already committed.

- A highly geared business has more than 50 per cent of its capital in the form of loans.
- A low-geared business has less long-term borrowing and a gearing figure below 50 per cent.

Much attention tends to be given to businesses that have high gearing and are vulnerable to increases in interest rates. However, this may be considered acceptable in a business that is growing quickly and generating high profits. Furthermore, a low-geared business may be considered too cautious and not expanding as quickly as possible.

Company	Date of balance sheet	Current assets £m	Inventories (stock)	Current liabilities £m	Current ratio	Acid test ratio
Next plc	26/01/2008	979.2	319.1	(1,042.5)	0.94:1	0.63:1
Rolls-Royce plc	31/12/2007	7,253	2,203	(4,754)	1.53:1	1.06:1
Cadbury plc	31/12/2007	2,600	821	(4,614)	0.56:1	0.39:1

Table 3.2 The liquidity ratios of three public limited companies
Notes: Next, a retailer, is able to operate successfully with lower levels of liquidity than Rolls-Royce, a manufacturer. In contrast, the results for Cadbury show the trend for even some manufacturers to operate with lower liquidity levels. In 2004 Cadbury's (or Cadbury Schweppes' as it was then) current ratio was 0.84:1 and its acid test ratio was 0.59:1.

Business in Focus

Companies face higher costs for borrowing

The 'credit crunch' has reached a new intensity, with the cost of borrowing money in London's money markets hitting a new high in relation to the Bank of England's base rate at nearly 7 per cent.

The London Interbank Offered Rate (Libor), the key measure of how much money costs on the City's open market, increased again, with the three-month rate, an important yardstick for business borrowing costs, particularly affected. It widened to almost 6.9 per cent meaning the three-month Libor is currently the highest it has been above the Bank of England's base rate for 20 years.

John Wraith of Royal Bank of Scotland warned of potential knock-on effects for the wider economy, as businesses and consumers start to face higher borrowing rates. 'It does starkly illustrate that a very material degree of monetary tightening has occurred through risk aversion in the money markets, without any direct change in the official monetary policy rate,' he said.

'A lot of borrowing in the corporate and individual sectors is linked to Libor and floating rates more generally, and the longer the escalated level of inter-bank rates continues, the greater the danger of spillover into the real economy.'

Source: Adapted from *The Daily Telegraph*
http://www.telegraph.co.uk/finance/markets/2815544/Credit-squeeze-grows-to-worst-for-20-years-as-cost-of-borrowing-hits-new-high.html

Question:

1 What are the implications of this news for companies with high rates of gearing (over 50 per cent)?
2 What actions might they take in response?

Using this ratio

- The key yardstick is whether a business's long-term borrowing is more than 50 per cent of capital employed.
- Companies with secure cash flows may raise more loan capital because they are confident of being able to meet interest payments. Equally, a business with well-known brands may be able to borrow heavily against these brands to increase long-term borrowing.
- Firms can improve their gearing by repaying long-term loans, issuing more ordinary shares or redeeming debentures.

Efficiency ratios

This group of ratios measures the effectiveness with which management controls the internal operation of the business. They consider the following aspects of the management of an enterprise:

- the extent to which assets are used to generate profits
- how well inventories are managed
- the efficiency of creditor control, i.e. how long before customers settle their accounts.

There are a large number of ratios that fall under this heading, but we shall concentrate on just four.

Company	Date of balance sheet	Non-current liabilities £m	Total equity + non-current liabilities (£m)	Gearing (%)
British Airways plc	31/03/2008	4,646	7,879	58.97
Rolls-Royce Group plc	31/12/2007	3,156	6,705	47.06
British Telecom plc	31/03/2008	14,216	33,864	41.98

Table 3.3 Gearing ratios of some leading companies
Notes: British Airways is heavily geared as it is significantly in excess of the 50 per cent standard maximum figure. The other two companies are less highly geared, although Rolls-Royce has little potential to borrow more without being regarded as highly geared.

Asset turnover ratio

This ratio measures a business's sales in relation to the assets used to generate these sales. The formula to calculate this ratio is:

$$\text{Asset turnover} = \frac{\text{revenue (turnover)}}{\text{net assets}}$$

Net assets are defined as total assets less current and non-current liabilities.

This formula measures the efficiency with which businesses use their assets. An increasing ratio over time generally indicates that the firm is operating with greater efficiency. Conversely, a fall in the ratio can be caused by a decline in sales or an increase in assets employed.

Using this ratio

- It is difficult to give a standard figure for this ratio as it varies significantly according to the type of business.
- A business with high sales and relatively few assets (a supermarket, for example) might have a high asset turnover ratio and earn low profits on each sale.
- Conversely, other businesses may have a high value of assets but achieve few sales, so having a

low asset turnover ratio. A high-class jeweller is an example of this category of business. The compensation for such a firm is that it normally earns a high level of profit on each sale.
- A business can improve its asset turnover ratio by improving its sales performance and/or disposing of any surplus or underutilised assets.

Inventory (stock) turnover ratio

This ratio measures a company's success in converting inventories into sales. Prior to the introduction of the IFRS rules in 2005, inventories were called stocks on financial statements. The ratio compares the value of inventories with sales achieved, valued at cost. This permits an effective comparison with inventories, which is always valued at cost. If the company makes a profit on each sale, then the faster it sells its inventories, the greater the profits it earns. This ratio is only of relevance to manufacturing businesses, as firms providing services do not hold significant quantities of inventories.

$$\text{Inventory or stock turnover ratio} = \frac{\text{cost of goods sold}}{\text{average inventories (or stock) held}}$$

	Data for the financial year ending 31/12/2008			Data for the financial year ending 31/12/2007		
	Revenue £m	Net assets £m	Result	Turnover £m	Net assets £m	Result
Rolls-Royce plc	9,082	2,531	3.59 times	7,435	3,549	2.63 times

	Data for the financial year ending 22/03/2008			Data for the financial year ending 24/03/2007		
	Revenue £m	Net assets £m	Result	Turnover £m	Net assets £m	Result
J Sainsbury plc	17,837	4,935	3.61 times	17,151	4,349	3.94 times

Table 3.4 Comparing asset turnover ratios

Notes: These results highlight the differences in assets turnover ratios between different types of businesses. Rolls-Royce achieves a clear improvement in sales in relation to the value of its assets. A significant increase in the company's revenue and a fall in net assets in 2008 resulted in the figure rising to a little over 3.5. In comparison, J Sainsbury is a very different company achieving much higher sales from an asset base which is larger. The slight decline from 2007 to 2008 may reflect the increasing competitiveness of the grocery market, or the company's investment in new assets which have not yet generated all the sales its management team expect.

In this form the results of calculating this ratio are expressed as a number of times a year. On 22 March 2008 Sainsbury held inventories valued at £681 million. During the company's financial year, which ended on that day, the company had achieved sales (at cost) of £16,835 million. The company's inventories turnover ratio was therefore 24.72 times.

The inventory turnover formula can be reorganised to express the number of days taken on average to sell the business's inventories.

$$\text{Inventory turnover ratio} = \frac{\text{inventories} \times 365}{\text{cost of sales}}$$

Our Sainsbury calculation would then become £681m × 365 ÷ £16,835m, giving an answer of 14.76 days. Thus, if Sainsbury sells its complete inventories every 15 days, it will sell its inventories approximately 24 times during a year.

Examiner's advice

Don't just think about finance in relation to ratios. Other aspects of a business's activities can have significant impacts on the results of ratio calculations. For example, if a business uses a JIT system of inventory control it is likely to have a much higher level of inventory or stock turnover.

Using this ratio

- The standard figure for this ratio varies hugely according to the type of business. A market trader selling fruit and vegetables might expect to sell his entire inventories every two or three days – about 100 times a year. At the other extreme, an antiques shop might only sell its stock every six months – or twice a year.
- A low figure for inventory turnover could be due to obsolete inventories. A high figure can indicate an efficient business, although selling out of inventories results in customer dissatisfaction.
- Improving the inventory or stock turnover ratio requires a business to hold lower levels of inventories or to achieve higher sales without increasing levels of inventories.

Receivables (debtors') days

This ratio (also referred to as receivables or debtors' collection period) calculates the time typically taken by a business to collect the money that it is owed. This is an important ratio, as granting customers lengthy periods of credit may result in a business experiencing liquidity problems. If a company has substantial cash sales these should be excluded from the calculation.

$$\text{Receivables (debtors') days} = \frac{\text{receivables (debtors)} \times 365}{\text{revenue}}$$

Using this ratio

- There is no standard figure for this ratio. In general a lower figure is preferred as the business in question receives the inflow of cash more quickly. However, it can be an important part of a business's marketing strategy to offer customers a period of trade credit of perhaps 30 or 60 days.
- A rise in this ratio may be due to a number of causes. A period of expansion may mean that a business has to offer improved credit terms to attract new customers, or a 'buy now pay later' offer may have been introduced.

This ratio may be improved by reducing the credit period on offer to customers or by insisting on cash payment. A more focused approach is to conduct an aged debtors' analysis. This technique ranks a business's debtors according to the period of credit taken. This allows managers to concentrate on persuading the slowest payers to settle their accounts.

Payables (creditors) days

This ratio (also referred to as payables or creditors' collection period) calculates the time typically taken by a business to pay the money it owes to its suppliers and other creditors. This is an important ratio, as delaying payment for as long as possible can help a business to avoid liquidity problems.

$$\text{Payables (creditors') days} = \frac{\text{payables (creditors)} \times 365}{\text{revenue}}$$

Using this ratio

- Businesses can improve their liquidity position by delaying payment, but this may result in poor relationships with suppliers who may suffer liquidity problems as a result of the delay in payment.

- Businesses may be charged interest on delayed payments, which can add to costs and weaken a business's liquidity position. The 'Business in focus' below outlines legislation in this area.
- By comparing payable days and receivable days a business can assess its liquidity position. If payable days is a lower figure then it is more likely that the business will experience liquidity problems as, on average, it is paying suppliers and other creditors more quickly than it is receiving payment from its customers.

Business in Focus

Late payment legislation

The Late Payment of Commercial Debts (Interest) Act 1998 and Late Payment of Commercial Debts Regulations 2002 gives businesses the statutory right to claim interest on late payments from other businesses. The law was originally introduced in November 1998 but was amended by European Union directive in 2002.

The law allows all businesses, including public sector organisations, to claim interest from any other business or organisation if payment is late. A late payment is defined as where the agreed credit period given by the supplier to the purchaser has expired. If no credit period has been specified by the supplier, the Act specifies a default period of 30 days, after which interest will accumulate.

Question:

1   Why might a small business be reluctant to claim interest from a large customer which buys a high proportion of its output and which regularly delays payment?

Profitability ratios

These ratios compare the profits earned by a business with other key variables, such as the level of sales achieved or the capital available to the managers of the business.

Gross profit margin

This ratio compares the gross profit achieved by a business with its revenue. Gross profit is earned before direct costs, such as administration expenses, are deducted. The ratio calculates the percentage of the selling price of a product that constitutes gross profit. The answer is expressed as a percentage.

$$\text{Gross profit margin} = \frac{\text{gross profit} \times 100}{\text{revenue}}$$

For example, in 2008 Sainsbury's gross profit was £1,002 million. This was achieved from a revenue amounting to £17,837 million. The company's gross profit margin is:

$$\frac{£1,002\text{m} \times 100}{£17,837} = 5.62\%$$

This gross profit margin may appear low, but a judgement should take into account the company's expectations, its performance in previous years and how other similar businesses, such as Asda, are performing. The 'Business in focus' below provides some of the answers to these questions.

Using this ratio

- The figure for gross profit margin varies depending upon the type of industry. Firms that turn over their stock rapidly and then can trade with relatively few assets may operate with low gross profit margins. Greengrocers and bakers may fall into this category. Firms with slower turnover of stock and requiring substantial fixed assets may have a higher figure. House builders may fall into this category.
- The sales mix can have a major influence on this ratio. A farmer selling eggs at a 10 per cent gross profit margin and renting out holiday cottages at a 40 per cent margin could improve the business's overall profit margin (but reduce its turnover) by discontinuing egg production.
- This ratio can be improved by increasing prices, although this may result in lower turnover. Alternatively, reducing direct costs (raw material costs and wages, for example) will also improve the figure.

Net profit margin

This ratio calculates the percentage of a product's selling price that is net profit (i.e. after all costs have been deducted). Because this ratio includes all of a business's operating expenses, it may be regarded as a better indication of performance than gross profit margin. Once again the answer to this ratio is written as a percentage.

$$\text{Net profit margin} = \frac{\text{net profit (profit before taxation)}}{\text{revenue}}$$

Continuing our example of J Sainsbury plc, the company's net profit for the trading year ending in March 2008 was £479 million. The company's net profit margin is shown as net profit margin is:

$$\frac{£479m \times 100}{£17,837m} = 2.69\%$$

Using this ratio

- Results of this ratio can vary according to the type of business, though a higher net profit margin is preferable.
- A comparison of gross and net profit margins can be informative. A business enjoying a stable gross profit margin and a declining net profit margin may be failing to control indirect costs effectively. This may be due to the purchase of new premises for example.
- Improvements in the net profit margin may be achieved through higher selling prices or tighter control of costs, particularly indirect costs.

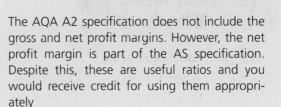

Examiner's advice

The AQA A2 specification does not include the gross and net profit margins. However, the net profit margin is part of the AS specification. Despite this, these are useful ratios and you would receive credit for using them appropriately

Return on capital employed

This is an important ratio comparing the operating profit earned with the amount of capital employed by the business. The capital employed by the business is measured by its total equity plus its non-current (long-term) liabilities.

The importance of this ratio is reflected in the fact that it is also termed 'the primary efficiency ratio'. The result of this ratio, which is expressed as a percentage, allows an assessment to be made of the overall financial performance of the business. A fundamental comparison can be made between the prevailing rate of interest and the ROCE generated by a business.

$$\text{Return on capital employed} = \frac{\text{operating profit} \times 100}{\text{total equity} + \text{non-current liabilities}}$$
$$\text{(capital employed)}$$

Using this ratio

- A typical ROCE may be expected to be in the range of 20–30 per cent. It is particularly important to compare the results from calculating this ratio with the business's ROCE in previous years and also those achieved by competitors.
- A business may improve its ROCE by increasing its operating profit without raising further capital or by reducing the amount of capital employed, perhaps by repaying some long-term debt.

Business in Focus

Sainsbury's profits rise 28 per cent

Sainsbury's crowned a three-year turnaround plan today by ringing up bumper annual profits of £488 million. The figure for profits before taxation, which was slightly ahead of forecasts, represents a rise of more than 28 per cent compared with the previous year. Sales for the year to 22 March 2008 rose by 5.3 per cent.

The retailer said it had exceeded a series of targets set down under the 'Making Sainsbury's Great Again' scheme, which was launched in 2005 by chief executive Justin King.

Chairman Philip Hampton said: 'This year has been particularly significant for Sainsbury's since it marked the completion of the Make Sainsbury's Great Again recovery plan announced in October 2004 and we moved from a period of recovery to growth.'

Sainsbury's has put on an extra £2.7 billion of sales during its turnaround plan, compared with a target of £2.5 billion. Customer numbers per week have also grown from 14 million to 16.5 million, it said.

Around 117,000 of the company's staff will also share a £47 million payout this year – an average of £401 each – as part of the success.

Source: *The Independent*, 14 May 2008
http://www.independent.co.uk

Question:

1 Why might a supermarket in a highly competitive industry be happy to achieve a net profit margin on sales of less than 3 per cent?

Company	Type of business	Date of accounts	Operating profit (loss)	Total equity + non-current liabilities	ROCE
Next plc *	Clothes retailer	01/07/2008	£197.9m	£742.6m	26.65%
Tesco plc	Retailer	23/02/2008	£2,791m	£19,901m	14.02%
Rolls-Royce plc	Engineering	31/12/2008	£562m	£6,656m	12.95%
Taylor Wimpey plc *	House builder	30/02/2008	(£1,474.9m)	£4,487.9m	−32.86%

Table 3.5 ROCE data for a selection of companies

Notes: The returns here vary enormously. The most eye-catching figure is that of Taylor Wimpey. The company's financial position has been severely affected by the onset of a recession in the UK in 2008 and a huge fall in house prices and the number of houses being purchased.

* These figures are based on six months' trading only.

Examiner's advice

ROCE is one of three key ratios used to assess the financial performance of businesses. The other two are the acid test ratio and gearing. Using these three ratios enables a company's short- and long-term liquidity positions to be examined, as well as being a fundamental measure of its profitability.

Do think about the ways in which a business may increase its ROCE figure if it is considered to be too low. This may have implications for all the functional areas of the business to increase profits and/or reduce the amount of capital employed in the business.

Shareholders' ratios

The results of this group of ratios are of particular interest to the shareholders of a company or to anyone considering purchasing shares in a particular company. They are also known as investment ratios. Shareholders can receive a return on their purchase of shares in two ways:

1 through dividends paid from the company's profits over the financial year
2 as a result of a rise in the price of the shares – called a capital gain.

Dividends offer a short-term return on an investment and may be of interest to shareholders seeking a quick return. However, other shareholders may seek a long-term return on their investment. They may be prepared to forego high levels of dividends in the short run to allow profits to be invested. They hope that the business will grow, increasing the price of shares and providing a capital gain for shareholders.

There are a number of ratios that may be used by shareholders. However, we shall concentrate on ratios that compare the dividends received against the capital investment made by shareholders when purchasing shares.

Dividend per share

This is an important shareholders' ratio. It is simply the total dividend declared by a company divided by the number of shares the business has issued.

$$\text{Dividend per share} = \frac{\text{total dividends}}{\text{number of issued shares}}$$

Results of this ratio are expressed as a number of pence per share.

In 2008 Marks & Spencer, one of the UK's best-known retailers, announced dividends totalling £343.6 million. The dividend per share for the company was calculated as follows:

$$\frac{£343.6m}{1,586.48m \text{ shares}} = 21.65 \text{ pence per share}$$

It is normal for dividends to be paid in two parts: an interim dividend halfway through the financial year and a final dividend at the end of the year.

Using this ratio

- A higher figure is generally preferable to a lower one as this provides the shareholder with a larger return on his or her investment. However, some shareholders are looking for long-term investments and may prefer to have a lower dividend per share now in the hope of greater returns in the future and a rising share price.
- It is wise to compare the dividend per share with that offered by alternative companies. However, it is also important to bear in mind how much has to be invested to buy each share. A low dividend per share may be perfectly acceptable if the company has a low share price.
- A business can improve this figure by announcing higher dividends (and therefore reducing the amount of profit retained within the business). This may prove attractive to some shareholders, but may not be in the long-term interests of the business, particularly if profits are not rising.

Dividend yield

This ratio is really a development of the previous ratio and provides shareholders with more information. The dividend yield compares the dividend received on a single share with the current market price of that share. This provides shareholders with a better guide to a business's performance, as it compares the return with the amount that would need to be invested to purchase a share. The result of calculating this ratio is given as a percentage.

$$\text{Dividend yield} = \frac{\text{dividend per share} \times 100}{\text{market price of share}}$$

Imagine a shareholder was considering investing in Marks & Spencer and noted that the share price on one particular day was 220 pence, and that the dividend per share for the company was 21.65 pence. He or she could calculate the dividend yield as follows:

$$\frac{21.65 \times 100}{220} = 9.84\%$$

Business in Focus

Debenhams cuts shareholder dividend

Debenhams has slashed its shareholder payout as it focuses its efforts on coping with a fall in sales and cutting its £1 billion of debts. Shareholders will receive 2.5 pence per share.

Reporting a 16 per cent drop in full-year profits to £110.1 million, Debenhams said it would manage the business 'tightly' after difficult and uncertain market conditions left like-for-like sales 4.2 per cent lower.

Despite the downturn in sales, Debenhams said it had grown market share in clothing and made further progress with its programme of store openings and refits. The company opened a total of 11 new outlets during the 2008 financial year, including department stores in Liverpool and Dunfermline.

Source: AOL News, 22 October 2008
http://news.aol.co.uk

Question:

1 Why might only some of Debenhams' shareholders be satisfied to see the company reduce its dividend per share?

Using this ratio

- A higher return will be regarded as preferable by shareholders seeking a quick return. Longer-term investors might settle for a lower figure, allowing the firm to reinvest profits and offering the possibility of higher profits and dividends in the future.
- Results for this ratio can vary dramatically according to fluctuations in the company's share price.
- This ratio can be improved by increasing the proportion of profits distributed to shareholders in the form of dividends.

The value and limitations of ratio analysis

Ratio analysis provides stakeholders with an insight into the performance of a business. However, to offer the maximum amount of information, the details gained from ratio analysis need to be compared with other data, such as that outlined below.

- **The results for the same business over previous years.** This allows stakeholders to appreciate the trend of the data. Thus, a low but steadily increasing figure for ROCE might be reassuring to investors.
- **The results of ratio analysis for other firms in the same industry.** We have seen that results expected from various ratios vary according to the type of firm under investigation. Thus, the inventory or stock turnover ratio will be much higher for a retailer selling perishable products than for a manufacturer. By comparing like-with-like a more informed judgement may be made.
- **The results of ratios from firms in other industries.** Stakeholders can compare the ratios of a particular business with those from a wide range of firms. This might allow, for example, a comparison between two firms experiencing rapid growth. The Centre for Inter-Firm Comparisons offers anonymous data on the financial ratios of many UK firms.

A significant weakness of ratio analysis is that it only considers the financial aspects of a business's performance. While this is undeniably important, other elements of a business should be taken into account when evaluating performance.

- **The market in which the business is trading.** A business that is operating in a highly competitive market might experience relatively low profits, reducing the results of ratios such as the return on capital employed (ROCE).
- **The position of the firm within the market.** A market leader might be expected to provide better returns than a small firm struggling to establish itself. However, the small struggling firm may be investing heavily in developing new products and establishing a brand identity. The struggling firm may generate large profits in the future.
- **The quality of the workforce and management team.** These are important factors in assessing a business, but not ones that will be revealed directly through ratio analysis. Indeed, a business that invests heavily in its human resources may appear to be performing relatively poorly through the use of ratio analysis.
- **The economic environment.** In general, businesses might be expected to perform better during periods of prosperity and to produce better results from ratio analysis. During the recession, which commenced in the UK in 2008, it is reasonable to expect the financial performance of many (but not all) businesses to decline.

One step further: the operating cash-flow ratio

The AQA specification sets out ten ratios with which you should be familiar. However, there are other ratios that can be of value, and the operating cash-flow ratio is one of these. It relies on the company's cash-flow statement as a principal source of information. We considered cash-flow statements in 'One step further' in the previous chapter (see pages 31–2).

The operating cash-flow ratio measures a company's ability to pay its short-term liabilities. It is measured by using the following formula:

$$\text{Operating cash-flow ratio} = \frac{\text{operating cash flow}}{\text{current liabilities}}$$

If the operating cash-flow ratio is less than 1, it means that the company has generated less cash over the year than it needs to pay off short-term liabilities as at the year end. This may signal a need to raise money to meet liabilities.

So, what is the advantage of using the operating cash-flow ratio, rather than the current or acid test ratios? The current asset ratio and others based on balance sheet numbers gauge liquidity as at the balance sheet date, whereas the operating cash-flow ratio uses the cash generated over an accounting period.

The operating cash-flow ratio can be used to compare companies across a sector, and to look at changes over time. A higher result from this ratio is preferable, but as with all liquidity ratios, it depends on the type of business and the industry in which it operates.

Progress questions

1 Explain, with the aid of an example, why a ratio might provide more detail on a firm's performance than a single piece of financial information. (7 marks)

2 Distinguish between efficiency ratios and profitability ratios. (6 marks)

3 Outline two sources of information that might be important when conducting ratio analysis. (6 marks)

4 Marsham Trading has current liabilities amounting to £2.8 million. Its current assets are: receivables £1.1 million, inventories £2.0 million and cash £0.9 million. Calculate the business's current and acid test ratios. (8 marks)

5 Explain two reasons why the results of liquidity ratios might be treated with caution. (6 marks)

6 Pelennor Products is a rapidly growing business providing IT services. The company's receivables (debtors') days ratio has increased from 33.2 days to 41.7 days over the past year. Outline the possible implications of this for the business. (10 marks)

7 Fangorn plc has seen an improvement in its gross profit margin over the financial year. At the same time its net profit margin has deteriorated. Explain the implications of this for the business and outline possible actions that the management team might take. (10 marks)

8 Explain why the return on capital employed (ROCE) is such an important ratio for stakeholders. (6 marks)

9 Why might the dividend yield ratio provide a better indication of a company's performance than the dividend per share ratio? (5 marks)

10 Outline two possible external factors that need to be taken into account when conducting ratio analysis. (6 marks)

Analysis and evaluation questions

1 The financial director of Steeple plc is concerned about the company's liquidity position. The house builder has experienced liquidity problems and the director is considering the results of some financial ratios that she has just calculated.

	This year	Last year
Acid test	1.01:1	1.19:1
Gearing	53%	46%
ROCE	8%	15%
Dividend per share	6.6 pence	6.4 pence

The company has just completed building a large housing estate in Dorset and the sale of the houses has just started. The company has also recently purchased land near to Birmingham on which it intends to build more houses.

a Analyse whether the company's director is right to be worried about the company's liquidity position. (10 marks)

b The company's chief executive believes that financial ratios are of little use to analyse Steeple plc's current position. Justify your decision. (15 marks)

2 Penhaligon plc manufactures components of computers and is UK market leader in its field. It is considering expanding into the US market, which is very competitive. The company is considering a major investment in extending its factory and introducing new equipment. This will enable it to reduce its workforce and become more cost effective in the long term.

The company has been highly profitable over recent years (its ROCE was 21.6 per cent in the last financial year), although its acid test figures are less impressive (latest figure: 0.91:1). However, the company will need to borrow an estimated £12 million to finance its plans. This will take its non-current liabilities to £304.6 million. The company's total equity is £300.8 million.

a Analyse how ratio analysis might help the company to make this decision. (10 marks)

b To what extent do you agree with the view that information on the market in which the company trades is the most important information needed to supplement the ratio analysis? (15 marks)

Case study

Retailing group Rohan is reported to have made a £229 million bid for the East-Anglia based supermarket chain Breckland Stores. A spokesperson for Rohan commented that Breckland represented a valuable addition and would enable the group to have a real presence throughout the UK. 'We have over 7 million customers in other parts of the UK, but East Anglia has been a black spot for us until now. This is the start of a period of rapid growth for us. We intend to increase our share of the European groceries market over the next year or two.'

City analysts were cautious about the takeover. One senior trader commented that Rohan had already expanded very rapidly and that the price paid for Breckland did not represent a bargain. 'The groceries market is increasingly global and the

Rohan group balance sheet as at 31 September		
	2008 (£m)	200 (£m)
Non-current assets	1182	842
Current assets		
Inventories	298	202
Receivables and cash	206	104
Less current liabilities	(662)	(577)
Non-current liabilities	(715)	(376)
Net assets	**309**	**195**
Share capital	225	105
Reserves	84	90
Total equity	**309**	**195**

Rohan's share price fell by 73 pence to 473 pence on the news of the takeover.

Rohan group – extracts from income statements		
	2008 (£m)	2007 (£m)
Revenue	6252	4944
Cost of sales	5413	4375
Gross profit	839	569
Expenses	527	399
Operating profit	312	170
Dividends	162	88

degree of competition is rising rapidly. Rohan is still relatively small in comparison with other supermarkets in the UK.'

Questions

1 Explain what is meant by 'net assets'. (4 marks)
2 Analyse the possible implications for Rohan's shareholders of the announcement of the proposed takeover of Breckland Stores. (8 marks)
3 Using ratios to support your arguments, assess the case for and against the Rohan Group spending £229 million on a takeover of Breckland Stores. (12 marks)
4 Discuss the value of ratio analysis is assessing the financial performance of the Rohan Group. (15 marks)

4 Selecting financial strategies

This chapter links very closely to Chapter 1. It sets out the ways in which a business might seek to achieve its financial objectives and the medium- to long-term plans it might put into place to achieve these targets. It will highlight the implications of using particular financial strategies for other functions within the business.

In this chapter we examine:

- the major financial strategies that may be adopted by large businesses
- how these financial strategies may relate to other functional areas within the business.

Key terms

A **financial strategy** is a medium- to long-term plan designed to achieve the objectives of the finance function or department of a business.

A **financial objective** is a goal or target pursued by the finance department (or function) within an organisation.

Retained profit is the profit that remains on the income statement once all additions to and deductions from revenue have been allowed for.

Investment has several meanings, but in the context of this chapter it refers to undertaking major programmes of expenditure, often over the long term, on which a return is expected.

Raising finance

A business may need to raise capital for a number of reasons:

- to purchase non-current assets such as production-line technology
- to pay for research and development
- to buy other companies
- to finance major advertising campaigns.

A business that is opting to raise finance as a financial strategy is likely to be a business that is expanding. Thus a business that has growth as a corporate objective may opt to raise finance as a key financial strategy. In recent years Vodafone has grown rapidly, mainly by purchasing (or taking over) mobile phone operators in other countries.

Much of this growth has been financed through borrowing.

However, a business has a number of options when considering the ways in which it may raise its finance for major investments such as those set out above. The method chosen will have significant implications for all areas within the business.

Using retained profits

Using profits retained from previous years' trading is an important internal and long-term source of finance for many businesses. There are distinct advantages for a business in using retained profits to finance its investment spending. First, the funding is available immediately without having to apply for and negotiate loans or organise the selling of shares in the company. Both of these methods of raising finance can take time and may require some considerable administration to complete. However, the major advantage of raising finance in this way is that it avoids interest charges that would be payable on a loan. It also helps to avoid increasing the business's gearing ratio, which is a likely consequence of taking out a large loan. This can be a major advantage for a business that is already heavily indebted. Using retained profits is also preferable in some ways to raising money through selling shares. Raising finance in this way means that a company will be expected to pay dividends to shareholders at some future time.

Examiner's advice

Opportunity cost is a very useful concept in business studies. It is useful for you to think in this way about many of the strategic decisions that a business takes. Thinking about the alternative that was foregone as the result of the decision may help you to assess the correctness of that action.

Of course this method of raising finance also has disadvantages. Using profits in this way has an opportunity cost. The money cannot be paid to shareholders as dividends if it is to be retained in the business. This may mean a reduction in the dividend per share and some shareholders may be dissatisfied, especially if they were seeking a short-term gain. One implication could be a fall in the company's share price if the decision is widely unpopular and significant numbers of shareholders sell their shares. It may also make it more difficult for the company to raise finance by selling shares in the near future.

However, there is another side to this argument. Not all shareholders will take a short-term view. Institutional investors such as insurance companies and pension funds buy large numbers of shares and many look for long-term returns on their investments. They may support the decision if they believe that the investment will increase the company's long-term profitability and ultimately dividends and the company's share price.

Key terms
Gearing examines the relationship between internal sources and external sources of finance.
Sale and leaseback is an agreement to raise finance by selling an asset, such as property, and immediately retaining its use on a long-term lease.

Business in Focus

Rangers increase retained profits

Rangers, the Scottish Premier League football club, has reported profits of over £3 million as a result of its involvement in the European Champions League this season.

The club narrowly failed to qualify for the last 16 of the tournament and is hoping for an extended run in the UEFA Cup by overcoming Panathinaikos in the round of 32 on Thursday night. But meetings with Barcelona, Lyon and Stuttgart in the group stages of Europe's elite club competition have already had a positive impact on the club's finances.

Financial results for the six months to 31 December 2007 show an increase of £3.8 million in profit before interest and tax to £3.1 million. Figures for 2006 showed a loss of £0.7 million.

The results also revealed a £10-million increase in revenue to £33.1 million, while retained profit increased by £3.8 million.

Source: Adapted from *Sporting Life*
http://www.sportinglife.com

Question:

1 Why might a professional football club welcome an increase in retained profit?

Borrowing

Businesses may choose to raise substantial sums through borrowing from banks or other financial institutions. This borrowing is likely to be long term and will appear on the company's balance sheet as a non-current liability. This type of long-term borrowing also has implications for a company's gearing as we saw in the previous chapter. If the borrowing is sufficient to take the gearing figure in excess of 50 per cent the company is said to be highly geared. This may result in the business having difficulty in repaying the debt and may lead to other functions within the business having less finance available due to the liquidity difficulties.

However, borrowing in this way has the advantage of being relatively quick to arrange, especially if the business has non-current assets (such as property, for example) that can be used as collateral against the loan. Collateral is security for the creditor – it can be sold to repay the loan if the business defaults on its payments. This is more likely to be an attractive option for raising finance if the market rates of interest are low and if finance is readily available.

Business in Focus

Italian Yellow Pages publisher struggles with debts

Italian yellow pages publisher Seat Pagine Gialle has started talks with Royal Bank of Scotland on 'enhancing its financial flexibility' under an existing loan agreement, the company has announced.

Seat expects to inform the Italian Stock Market of the outcome of the talks by the end of December, it said, adding that it will communicate the timing for the presentation of its new business plan at a later stage. Last week, Seat said it was taking no decisions on selling additional shares, after market speculation that it would raise share capital to ease its debt position.

At the end of September, Seat said its net financial debt had fallen to 3.105 billion euros, from 3.274 billion a year earlier. Seat shares have fallen in value as a result of the company's high debt level and concerns over its business model in the face of competition from Google in local advertising markets.

Source: Adapted from Interactive Investor
http://www.iii.co.uk

Question:

1   In what ways might Seat's ability to raise capital by selling shares be affected by its high debt levels?

Examiner's advice

Capital is a word with several meanings in business and you should use it precisely in examinations. In the way we are using it here it refers to the finance that is invested in the company, either as a result of selling shares, or by borrowing. It can also mean accumulated wealth that has built up in a business as a result of years of successful trading. Finally, it may refer to the machinery that is used within a business, such as production-line technology.

Selling shares

Another means of raising capital is to sell shares in the business. Clearly this is an option that is only available to companies, and only public limited companies can raise large sums in this way. This is because public limited companies can use the Stock Exchange or other similar markets to sell shares to the general public and to other organisations. The box below gives information about another market available to UK companies: the AIM.

Selling shares is a slower approach than borrowing and can be a relatively expensive one. It can also be a difficult proposition at certain times if the business's share price is declining. The sale of substantial quantities of shares may dilute the control that a particular group of shareholders holds in the organisation.

Business in Focus

The Alternative Investment Market (AIM)

The Alternative Investment Market (AIM) is a subsidiary market of the London Stock Exchange. It allows smaller companies to sell shares with a more flexible set of rules than is applicable to the London Stock Exchange's main market.

The AIM was launched in 1995 and has raised over £25 billion and more than 2,900 companies have chosen to join the market. In 2008, 1,586 companies were actively trading their shares on the AIM. The market is attractive to smaller companies as it has fewer rules and no requirements for the minimum value of the company or number of shares it issues.

Some companies that initially traded on the AIM have since moved on to join the main market, although in the last few years, significantly more companies transferred from the main market to the AIM. This is because the AIM has significant tax advantages for investors, as well as fewer rules for the companies themselves.

However, selling shares does offer significant potential advantages to a business. It does not commit it to regular interest payments, irrespective of the financial position of the business and in this way can help to protect a weak liquidity position. Instead the managers will be expected to pay a share of the company's profits to the shareholders (this payment is known as dividends). Clearly, if the company is experiencing a period of low profits it always has the option to reduce the amount it pays to shareholders in the form of dividends. In this way the sale of shares is a more flexible form of raising finance, which is adjustable (to some degree) to the circumstances facing the business.

Sale of assets

Some businesses may be in the fortunate position of holding surplus non-current assets or have investments in other companies that can be sold to raise finance. This is a good means of raising finance in that it avoids any sort of payments; however, it may result in the loss of assets which could increase in value in the future, or the loss of a source of income as in the case of shares held in other businesses.

A variant of selling assets has become popular in recent years. Businesses seeking to raise capital have sold assets that they require for future trading and have leased them back. This allows them to have a large amount of capital available and to retain use of the asset in question. The major disadvantage of this approach to raising capital is that it commits the business to permanent expenditure in the future to pay to lease the assets and retain their use.

The implications of a strategy of raising finance

A strategy of raising finance has profound implications for other areas of the business. This financial

Business in Focus

Sainsbury's latest sale and leaseback deal

J Sainsbury plc has struck a sale and leaseback deal on ten of its stores, raising £226 million to invest in other aspects of its supermarkets business. The deal with Morgan Stanley Dean Witter and Asset Trust follows an earlier £340 million sale and leaseback deal on 16 stores.

Ian Coull, property director, said the proceeds would 'deliver value for investment in our stores' improvement programme'. The deals are part of a wider move by Sainsbury's new chief executive, Sir Peter Davis, to make more use of the group's huge property portfolio. The company last week announced plans for an office and residential development above its Nine Elms store in south London. It is understood similar plans are in the pipeline for stores in Edinburgh and Peterborough.

Question:

1   Why do you think that J Sainsbury plc has chosen to raise £566 million to finance its investments by using this method of raising capital?

Business in Focus

Volkswagen's expansion plans

At Volkswagen's annual media conference in Wolfsburg, senior executives proudly announced that the company had sold a record number of vehicles in 2007 – 6.2 million. This helped to push up revenue almost 4 per cent to 108.9 billion euros (£85 billion).

The carmaker also has ambitious plans for the future. VW will raise capital to introduce 20 new models in the next three years, including vans and pick-ups, as part of a plan to sell a staggering 8 million cars by 2011. Volkswagen also announced that it was buying a controlling share in the Swedish truck-maker, Scania.

Volkswagen's chief financial officer, Hans Dieter Poetsch, said the firm was aiming to be the world's largest car manufacturer. 'We are currently looking at areas where we could build a new plant and we will also approach the market with products designed specifically for the US market. The only drawback is that we can only introduce the first product in early 2010.'

Volkswagen is expected to decide this summer whether it's going to open a new factory in the US. Once any decision is made, it would take around two to three years before production starts.

Source: Adapted from bbc.co.uk

Question:

1   How might Volkswagen intend to finance its expansion plans?
2   What would be the possible implications for other functions within the business of raising finance to build a factory in the US?

strategy is likely to accompany a programme of expansion which may mean that the business's human resource department needs to recruit more staff, retrain existing staff or relocate employees. The business's workforce plan will have to be written to support the financial strategy.

The implications of raising finance can be significant for the operations function of a business. It may entail research and development into new products or it could involve investment in new methods of production. In either event the managers responsible for these areas within the business are likely to have to manage programmes of change.

The marketing function of a business will be affected in a variety of ways. The marketing department may be required to research a changing market or to investigate new markets, possibly overseas. The development of new products may accompany a financial strategy of raising finance and the expansion of the business.

Key terms

A **profit centre** is an area, department, division or branch of an organisation that is allowed to control itself separately from the larger organisation.

A **cost centre** is an area, department, division or branch of an organisation for which it is possible to calculate costs (but not revenues). A marketing department might be an example of a cost centre.

Economies of scale are the factors that lead to unit or average costs *reducing* as an organisation increases its output.

Diseconomies of scale are the factors that lead to unit or average costs *increasing* as an organisation increases its output and becomes less efficient.

Implementing profit centres

What is a profit centre?

A profit centre is an area, department, division or branch of an organisation that is allowed to control itself separately from the larger organisation. It makes its own decisions, following corporate objectives, and may produce its own income statement for amalgamation with the rest of the business. So, a profit centre is some part of an organisation that is allowed to control itself as a separate element from the larger organisation.

- It can be **a factory or department** within a business. For example, BMW builds a new Rolls-Royce model at a factory in Goodwood in Sussex. This factory is a profit centre.

- It can be **a brand**. For example, Cadbury's Dairy Milk is a profit centre for the company.
- Some businesses use **geographical regions** as the basis for profit centres. Ford operates globally and Europe, for example, is a profit centre.
- **Groups of products** can be profit centres. Dairy Crest, the UK manufacturer of cheese and other dairy products, operates all its spreads (Utterly Butterly and Clover, for example) as a single profit centre.
- It is common for businesses, most obviously retailers, to manage each **branch** as a profit centre. French retailer Carrefour has hypermarkets throughout the world and each is a separate profit centre.

The managers of a profit centre can calculate costs and revenues and can make their own decisions in pursuit of corporate objectives. This financial strategy is more appropriate for larger businesses and especially those that sell diverse ranges of products or operate through a large number of outlets. The implementation of profit centres enables the businesses to manage the elements of its operations separately and to make at least some decisions in the context of a distinct part of the business.

This might be an attractive financial strategy for a business for a number of reasons (both financial and non-financial). There are a number of benefits from using profit centres as an integral part of managing a business.

The benefits of using profit centres

- Diseconomies of scale can be avoided. The trend towards globalisation has meant that some businesses have become too large to manage as a single entity. For example, HSBC trades in 83 countries and this is too large to operate as a single entity and to pursue corporate objectives such as expansion. It is important to divide the company in some way to ensure effective management and to prevent problems with coordination and communication. Decentralised decision-making allows areas to make decisions faster and be more responsive to changes in local conditions. In turn this assists the organisation in achieving its financial and corporate objectives.
- Delegating power and authority to centres improves motivation. HSBC is able to give senior managers in each country more authority to run their own affairs, boosting motivation. In turn the

Business in Focus

HSBC and profit centres

With its headquarters in London, HSBC is one of the largest banking and financial services organisations in the world. Its international network comprises some 10,000 properties in 83 countries and territories in Europe; Hong Kong; Rest of Asia-Pacific, including the Middle East and Africa; North America and Latin America.

Figure 4.1 HSBC is one of the world's largest financial institutions

HSBC provides a comprehensive range of financial services to 128 million customers through four customer groups and global businesses: Personal Financial Services (including consumer finance); Commercial Banking; Global Banking and Markets; and Private Banking.

In 2007 HSBC announced that the company's revenue for the financial year was US$8.601 billion (£58.40 billion) and that this had generated profits of US$24.21 billion (£16.14 million) for the financial year. The company confirmed its commitment to growth and stated that it would target emerging markets such as China and India as it believed rates of growth in these economies would be higher.

HSBC has divided itself into three 'core' profit centres: Europe, Hong Kong and North America. In 2007 HSBC saw Europe contribute £5.73 billion in profits and Hong Kong £4.89 billion, while the rest of the Asia Pacific region turned in a profit of £4.06 billion. Within these core profit centres other, smaller, profit centres operate. Thus senior managers at HSBC can analyse the performance of the UK market, as this is a separate profit centre within the European 'core' profit centre.

Source: Adapted from HSBC's Annual Report, 2007

http://www.hsbc.com

Question:

What disadvantages might HSBC experience as a result of operating profit centres?

---

bank is able to run branches as separate profit centres, allowing the potential to offer more motivating and challenging work to employees at a fairly junior level within the business. In a service industry such as HSBC it is of great value to be able to motivate staff by use of such techniques and thereby improve their performance. This will help the bank to achieve its growth objective, especially in emerging markets.

- Monitoring of performance is much easier. In 2007 HSBC made global profits amounting to over £16 billion, but this disguised a relatively poor performance by the North American division of the bank. The North American business only gener-

ated £60.7 million in profits (0.38 per cent of the company's profits), despite having 21.67 per cent of the company's assets available to it.

The drawbacks of using profit centres

- There is a danger that individual centres can become too narrowly focused. This means that the profit centres may lose sight of overall business objectives. Thus, the UK division of HSBC is focused on cost reduction, especially during the current recession, with the aim of protecting profit margins. However, this may not be entirely in tune with the bank's overall aim of growth.

- Performance of individual areas may be affected by local market conditions. The UK banking market is particularly competitive, especially as a result of mergers activity and the emergence of new financial services providers such as Tesco. It may not be realistic for HSBC to expect its UK division to match the profitability of some other regions of the world under these conditions.
- Some decisions may result from the use of profit centres. These may not be in the best interests of the entire business. Managers of profit centres may pursue their own agendas and not those of the business. This may mean that a financial strategy of implementing profit centres may not assist the business in achieving its corporate objectives.

Examiner's advice

Do consider the value of profit centres in relation to the type of business concerned. They may be attractive to a business that operates a large number of discrete sections or branches.

- Costs may rise. The use of a strategy based on profit centres means that a business is likely to have to invest heavily in training to provide staff with the necessary skills to manage more autonomously. In the short term this may damage the business's financial performance and make it more difficult to achieve certain financial objectives such as profit maximisation.

The implications of a strategy of implementing profit centres

There is a distinction between implementing and operating profit centres. Implementing profit centres means that the business will undergo a period of change as a more centralised system is replaced by a series of profit centres. This will have particularly significant implications for human resources and operations management.

The HR department of a business implementing profit centres is likely to have to take on a series of activities following the development of a new workforce plan. The plan may have to include the following to allow profit centres to be implemented successfully:

- a skills audit across the organisation to uncover

relevant skills among the existing workforce which had not been previously acknowledged
- the recruitment of new employees with the necessary skills to take greater control of managing financial and non-financial resources within separate branches or regions
- the redeployment of existing employees to new positions, often in different geographic locations
- the redundancies of some employees who may not have roles in the new organisation. These may include some relatively senior employees whose roles have in effect been delegated to more junior employees.

In addition, communication may become more important and possibly more difficult as more decisions are made at a lower level and greater amounts of information have to be disseminated throughout the organisation.

The operational implications of implementing profit centres are also significant. The operation of strategies of lean production may become more complex within an organisation that is likely to have become more decentralised. For example, the organisation of just-in-time production methods may be much more difficult. In addition, that business may not be able to benefit as fully from economies of scale if decision-making power is delegated to individual profit centres. For example, economies of scale which arise from purchasing in bulk may be dissipated if budgets are managed by different sections of the business and each makes individual purchasing decisions.

Cost minimisation

Key terms

Cost minimisation occurs when a business reduces its level of expenditure as far as is possible to allow it to provide goods or services of acceptable quality to its customers.

Offshoring describes the relocation by a company or a business process to another (lower cost) country. This may include manufacturing, or supporting processes such as customer service.

A business operates a strategy of cost minimisation where it reduces its level of expenditure as far as is possible to allow it to provide goods or services of acceptable quality to its customers. This strategy has received much publicity as a result of its use by budget airlines such as Ryanair and easyJet. Cost minimisation is likely to be an effective financial strategy in markets where demand for products is price elastic. That is, demand is sensitive to price reductions, and firms that can cut costs and pass on the benefits to customers can reap large increases in sales. Cost minimisation may also be an effective way of 'opening up' a market to consumers with lower incomes and thereby increasing sales.

Cost minimisation can be classified as a financial strategy as well as a financial objective. Businesses will seek to implement a cost minimisation strategy by implementing one or more of a number of policies.

Minimising labour costs

This may be important for firms supplying services, as many of them are likely to face wage and salary expenses which are a high proportion of total costs. Therefore cutting labour costs can have a substantial impact on overall costs of production. The implementation of this particular financial strategy may have a number of differing effects on the workforce as managers attempt to reduce expenditure.

- **Reductions in staffing levels**. This is the most obvious move and can have a significant impact on total costs, especially if the number of full-time employees is reduced significantly. However, it may lead to short-term increases in expenditure if redundancy payments have to be made. In addition, it may leave the organisation short of skilled and knowledgeable employees and therefore impair its performance.
- **Using more flexible workforces**. This type of workforce makes greater use of temporary and part-time staff, as well as zero-hours contracts, in order to match staffing levels more accurately to the needs of the organisation. The use of flexible workforces has the potential to cut labour costs by avoiding a situation where staff are paid when there is no work to be done.

- **Outsourcing**. This means that a business hires an outside organisation to carry out part of its work. It is common for businesses to use outside firms to maintain IT systems and to provide catering and cleaning services. Outsourcing cuts labour costs because the business only pays for such staff when they are required and is not responsible for certain fixed costs of employing people, such as paid holidays and pension contributions.

It is apparent that a financial strategy of cost minimisation that relies heavily on reducing labour costs will have huge implications for the business's human resource department. HR managers will be responsible for drawing up a new workforce plan to reduce costs and then implementing it.

Relocating

Many UK businesses have taken the decision to relocate to areas of the world where production costs are lower. Dyson, the innovative vacuum cleaner manufacturer, has moved its production facilities from Wiltshire to Malaysia, and Avon, the cosmetics company, has relocated its factories to Poland. The motive behind these decisions has been to lower the costs of production.

Producing in Eastern Europe or Asia will assist in reducing labour costs as wage rates are much lower. In Poland in 2007 unemployment was over 15 per cent and the average weekly wage was a little over £100. The equivalent figure for the UK at the time of writing is £461. Thus, for labour-intensive industries where employees require relatively few skills, relocating to a low-cost country can be an attractive proposition. Other cost savings may be achieved through cheaper land and property as well as fewer laws which can be expensive to adhere to.

Some businesses have partly relocated through a process known as offshoring. Using this approach businesses transfer part of their operations to a lower-cost location. The 'Business in Focus' below considers how expenditure on wages for IT staff in the UK has been affected by offshoring.

However, in the case of manufacturing the cost advantages may be offset to some extent by increased transport costs. There are other costs that businesses might incur as a consequence of relocating. There are the short-term costs of carrying out the relocation and ongoing costs associated with coordinating a business that may operate from different sites. Communication becomes more difficult as does the coordination of the business. Many of the costs may be hidden, for example lower productivity because of language barriers. Some financial services providers have reversed their policies of offshoring customer services operations to India as a consequence of increased levels of customer complaints about the quality of service received.

Examiner's advice

The value of relocation as a means of cost minimisation depends on the nature of the product and the market in which it is sold. The supply of some services, such as customer service for financial products, is not particularly dependent on location. Hence it can be relocated without creating too many difficulties or incurring large additional costs. Similarly, manufactures that sell their products globally may not be so dependent on a specific location as transport costs do not play such a large part in a move to Eastern Europe or Asia.

Relocating may have considerable implications for managers responsible for operations, as they are required to manage a production process spread across more than one country. There will be obvious transportation issues with the possibilities of delays in supplies of raw materials and final products. For managers of service operations there may be incompatibility of technical equipment, and production in different time zones may make the coordination of the production process even more complicated than normal.

Using technology

Technology can replace expensive staff for businesses located in high-labour-cost countries such as the UK. For example, low-cost airlines such as easyJet rely heavily on the internet to capture and process bookings by passengers for flights. It is also used to facilitate a speedy and inexpensive check-in procedure for passengers. This allows the company to employ fewer workers and to reduce its operating costs.

Technology may also be used on the production line to reduce production costs. This is a common practice in manufacturing. For example, most car

Business in Focus

Offshoring 'bad for IT pay in UK'

The pay and prospects of junior IT support staff in the UK have stagnated as services have been relocated to India, research has suggested.

Figure 4.2 More jobs in India, fewer in the UK

Annual salaries at the lowest end of the industry have not risen in five years, according to the Association of Technology Staffing Companies (ATSCO). The 'offshoring' of low-skilled jobs to cheaper locations in Asia has deterred people from entering the industry. This risked leaving a shortage of candidates for UK managerial positions.

According to ATSCO's and online CV provider iProfile's annual skills survey, which compares salaries across more than 75 per cent of the industry, average pay for low-skilled front-line staff has stalled at £18,000 for five years. In contrast, pay for managers has risen by more than 20 per cent over the period.

Source: Adapted from BBC News, 26 May 2008
http://news.bbc.co.uk/1/hi/business/7419916.stm

Question:

1 In what ways might the policy of offshoring IT jobs add to the costs of UK businesses in the long run?

manufacturers use robots to some extent on their production lines.

Key term

Capital expenditure is spending on new non-current assets such as property, machinery or vehicles.

Allocating capital expenditure

Capital expenditure is spending on new non-current assets such as property, machinery or vehicles. The way in which a business decides to spend its capital can have a significant effect on the operation of its finance department, and can also impact upon the other functions within the business. Businesses only have access to a limited amount of capital and any expenditure decisions normally have significant opportunity costs.

Investing in technology

Businesses may opt to do this to reduce the amount of labour deployed within the organisation and the associated costs. This approach will involve heavy initial expenditure on technology but may lead to a reduction in expenditure at a later stage. It also offers the potential advantage of increasing the productivity of the business. Nissan's car manufacturing plant in Sunderland has one the highest levels of labour productivity in Europe. In part this is due to the extensive use of technology on the production line. There are drawbacks, however. The initial costs are high and workers may need retraining in order to operate the technology efficiently.

Business in Focus

Abercrombie & Fitch to open flagship stores

Jeans and clothing brand Abercrombie & Fitch is still on track to open flagship stores around the world. Although the company has been hit hard by a 46 per cent drop in consumer spending in recent months, it has not postponed its plans. One of its new stores to be opened overseas will be in Paris.

The American-based retailer told investors it has recently received final approval to open an Abercrombie & Fitch flagship on the Champs Elysées in Paris in 2011. Abercrombie opened its first overseas store in London last year and opened its first European Hollister Co. mall-based store in a suburb of London last month.

The company said it is on track to open flagship locations around the world in 2009, including debuts of its namesake stores in Copenhagen and Tokyo along with Abercrombie & Fitch and Abercrombie stores in Milan. Also, Abercrombie continues to pursue lease arrangements for additional store locations in Europe and Asia.

The company began an international push about three years ago, hiring executives to oversee international business development. The first non-US stores opened that year were in Toronto and Edmonton, Canada, where the company now has several stores.

Source: *Fashion United*, 18 November 2008
http://www.fashionunited.co.uk

Question:

1   Why might a fashionable clothing brand decide to allocate its capital in this way?

Investing in other assets such as property

Some businesses invest heavily in property to enable them to trade effectively or possibly to support their corporate image. Thus supermarkets in the UK hold a portfolio of property in high street and out-of-town locations, which is essential to enable them to conduct their business effectively. Some also hold considerable amounts of land for possible development as sites, but also to prevent competitors from acquiring it. Hotels and restaurants may purchase desirable property in prosperous locations to support an upmarket corporate image. In both cases allocating capital expenditure in this way can help the business to achieve its overall corporate objectives.

Progress questions

1 Outline two reasons why a car manufacturer may need to raise large sums of finance. (6 marks)

2 Explain the benefits a business may receive from using retained profits to finance a major investment programme. (6 marks)

3 Explain why raising finance might be an appropriate financial strategy for a business aiming to sell in a global market. (8 marks)

4 Why might a business with a corporate objective of growth seek to raise finance through a mixture of selling shares and negotiating bank loans? (8 marks)

5 Why have many retailers with large numbers of stores chosen to raise finance through sale and leaseback? (8 marks)

6 Explain why implementing profit centres is a common financial strategy for large businesses with diverse product ranges. (8 marks)

7 Why might the implementation of profit centres as a financial strategy have significant implications for a business's HR department? (7 marks)

8 In what ways might a large business manufacturing non-branded T-shirts implement a financial strategy of cost minimisation? (8 marks)

9 Why might a UK manufacturer choose to allocate finance to investing in technology? (5 marks)

10 Which types of business might opt to allocate large sums of capital expenditure to the purchase of property? Explain your answer. (6 marks)

Analysis and evaluation questions

1 Prestige Hotels is aptly named. The company owns a number of luxurious properties in major cities in the UK and France. The company has been highly successful in recent years and its profits have grown steadily. Last year its ROCE exceeded 30 per cent.

The quality of the accommodation is not the only reason for its success. The staff are highly trained and loyal and the company's labour turnover is low. The hotel chain has a deserved reputation for providing excellent menus and the very best wines. It is highly successful in attracting wealthy people to become loyal customers. Prestige Hotels is considering targeting other cities in Europe in the future, but intends to plan its expansion carefully.

a Analyse the possible reasons why Prestige Hotels has selected a financial strategy of allocating capital expenditure. (10 marks)

b Discuss the likely consequences for the other functions within Prestige Hotels of the operation of this financial strategy. (15 marks)

2 Top Pizzas runs 59 fast-food restaurants across the UK. Chief Executive and major shareholder, Tony Curtis, thinks that the business could be managed more efficiently by implementing a strategy of profit centres. Over the last two or three years as the company has grown, its profit margins have declined. Tony has not been as hands on as he has wanted to be, although he still believes that he should make most of the decisions.

Top Pizzas supplies bargain-priced pizzas and offers cheap home delivery. It has expanded in part by undercutting its rivals in terms of price. Tony says that it is important to achieve high volumes of sales to help when negotiating with suppliers.

a Analyse two reasons why Top Pizzas may have decided upon a financial strategy of implementing profit centres. (10 marks)

b Tony is convinced that this is the right financial strategy for his business. Do you agree with him? Justify your decision. (15 marks)

Case study

EasyJet is well known for its strategy of cost minimisation. Although easyJet was virtually the only budget carrier when it launched in 1995, it now has several direct competitors including Ryanair, Virgin Express, Go and KLM/Buzz. EasyJet and the other budget carriers have reduced fares to levels lower than ten years ago.

EasyJet has won plaudits for operating one of the youngest fleets of aircraft in the airline industry, helping to reduce long-run operating costs. The company buys all its aircraft brand new from Boeing in Seattle.

Founder Stelios Haji-Ioannou has made easyJet a 'people's brand'. He has succeeded in showing that you do not need to offer tickets, free drinks and meals, use travel agents and have a complex system of connecting flights to survive. Business travellers will gladly forego these to save money, as long as standards of reliability and safety are up to scratch.

EasyJet has demonstrated the effectiveness of selling using the phone and the internet. One of the company's biggest cost savings is derived from the fact that it does not need to pay commission to travel agents, allowing it to sell seats at prices other airlines could not afford. EasyJet also became involved in the internet at the right point, and online seat sales now account for 90 per cent of all seats sold.

EasyJet's product relies on punctuality as well as cost effectiveness. Central to this is the ability to turn aircraft around quickly on the ground. Compared with the average hour and a half that it takes to turn a 737 around at Heathrow, easyJet's target time on the ground between flights is just 20 minutes – this takes a lot of organising by its staff.

As businesses seek to make cost savings in their travel budgets, easyJet is winning a bigger slice of the business traveller market. Its network of large city destinations and its flight timetables are designed to suit both business and leisure customers' needs. EasyJet calculates that companies could save up to 89 per cent on their travel budgets by using low-cost airlines.

Source: Adapted from *Event Magazine*
http://www.eventmagazine.co.uk
(40 marks, 60 minutes)

Questions

1 Explain what is meant by 'cost minimisation'. (3 marks)

2 Examine the ways in which easyJet has implemented its financial strategy of cost minimisation. (9 marks)

3 Discuss whether a financial strategy of implementing cost centres might become a necessity if easyJet continues to grow rapidly. (13 marks)

4 To what extent is the company's operations function most affected by its decision to minimise costs? (15 marks)

5 Making investment decisions

This chapter looks at the techniques that businesses can use to make major investment decisions. It considers the reasons why businesses undertake programmes of investment and will look at financial and non-financial methods of assessing the worth of alternative investment projects. This topic was not studied at AS level. However, obvious links exist with the financial strategies chosen by businesses – especially allocating capital expenditure, which we considered in the previous chapter.

In this chapter we examine:
- the financial techniques for making investment decisions
- the criteria against which businesses judge investment decisions
- the qualitative influences on investment decisions.

Key terms

Investment appraisal is a series of techniques designed to assist businesses in judging the desirability of investing in particular projects.

Profit is the surplus of revenues over total costs at the end of a trading period.

Cash flow is the movement of cash into and out of a business over a period of time.

Return on capital employed (ROCE) is the net profits of a business expressed as a percentage of the value of the capital employed in the business.

Introduction

Investment is an important term within business studies and often entails managers taking major decisions. Investment can mean a decision to purchase part or all of another business, perhaps as a result of a takeover bid. However, it is perhaps more common to use the term in relation to the purchase of a fixed asset or some other major expenditure. What is common is that all such actions involve a degree of risk. This must be judged against the likely return. The final decision will depend upon managers' assessment of these two factors.

Businesses take decisions regarding investment in a variety of circumstances.

- When contemplating introducing new products a business may assess the likely costs of and returns from investing in one or more new products.

- Expansion may entail evaluating whether or not to invest in new fixed assets as part of a planned programme of growth. Tottenham Hotspur Football club is set to invest an estimated £400 million in developing a new stadium, built in part on its existing ground, White Hart Lane. The club hopes to increase its sales revenue by attracting larger crowds into the new stadium, which will have a capacity of 60,000 spectators.

- Investing in new technology is often undertaken to reduce costs and improve productivity. For example, Luton Airport announced in 2008 that it had invested in a multilingual passenger communication system. The system, known as Aviavox, has the ability to communicate in nine different languages and is linked to the flight departure schedule, bringing benefits to passengers and improving the efficiency of the airport.

- Businesses may also use techniques of investment appraisal before spending heavily on promotional campaigns, developing new brands or products or retraining the workforce.

- In each circumstance, however, the business must adopt an appropriate appraisal technique to decide whether the returns received from an investment are sufficient to justify the initial capital expenditure.

Financial techniques for making investment decisions

A number of techniques are available to managers to assist them in taking decisions on whether to go ahead with investments, or to help in making a judgement between two or more possible investment opportunities. This section will look at three of the most important of these techniques: payback, the average rate of return and discounted cash flow.

These financial techniques are valuable but do depend upon a number of assumptions:

- that all costs and revenues can be forecast easily and accurately for some years into the future
- that key variables (e.g. interest rates) will not change
- that the business in question is seeking maximum profits.

There are two major considerations for managers when deciding whether or not to invest in a fixed asset or another business:

1 the total profits earned by the investment over the foreseeable future
2 how quickly the investment will recover its cost. This occurs when the earnings from the investment exceed the cost of the investment.

The process of assessing these factors is called investment appraisal and refers to the process of assessing one or more potential investments. Forecasting future costs and revenues can be a very difficult and at times expensive exercise to undertake. Forecasts about future revenues could prove to be inaccurate for a number of reasons.

- Competitors may introduce new products or reduce their prices, reducing forecast sales and revenues.
- Tastes and fashions may change, resulting in an unexpected slump in demand. The popularity of flying (as a result of low-cost airlines) has led to large falls in demand for cross-channel ferries and has led Eurotunnel to overestimate its sales.
- The economy may move into recession or slump (or, alternatively, into an upswing) resulting in sales figures radically different from those forecast.

Costs can be equally tricky to forecast. Unexpected periods of inflation, or rising import prices might result in inaccurate forecasts of expenditures. This can lead to a significant reduction in actual profits when compared with forecasts.

Companies that operate in a stable economic environment are much more easily able to forecast into the future as they have confidence that their predictions on the rate of inflation, likely rate of interest, level of unemployment and hence demand are as accurate as they can make them. A stable economic environment should lead to more accurate forecasts

Business in Focus

Nokia cuts its sales forecasts

Nokia, the world's biggest mobile phone manufacturer, has reduced its sales forecasts as it anticipates the economic downturn will hit sales of mobile phones harder than previously thought.

The company has already cut prices of its handsets by up to 10 per cent in the battle for market share. However, Nokia now thinks that sales across the industry will be lower than expected in 2008, with 1.24 billion handsets sold, instead of the earlier estimated 1.26 billion units.

Nokia also issued downbeat forecasts for 2009, and said sales of mobile phones will be down in 2009 compared with 2008, impacted by the continuing overall economic slowdown.

Nokia has been a poor predictor of its sales. In December 2000, Mr Ollila said, 'the best is yet to come' and predicted that globally 550 million handsets would be sold in 2001. The company was repeatedly forced to slash that prediction and in the end sales reached about 380 million handsets.

Sources: Adapted from the *Daily Telegraph* and *Times Online*
http://www.telegraph.co.uk
http://business.timesonline.co.uk

Question:

1 Why does Nokia, with the resources to carry out extensive market research, have such difficulty in forecasting its sales accurately?

of both costs and revenues associated with investment projects.

Investment appraisal and the other functions within a business

It is easy to regard investment appraisal as simply a technique to be used when a business is contemplating purchasing fixed assets. However, investment appraisal can be used in relation to a number of a business's activities across each of its functional areas, all of which involve significant investment expenditure. These might include:

- investing in a major new advertising campaign
- expanding into new markets, perhaps overseas
- attempting to adjust management styles and corporate cultures, possibly entailing reorganisation and retraining
- adopting new techniques of production, including JIT and kaizen
- researching and developing new products.

Investment appraisal is an important element of most aspects of business activity. It can help to quantify proposed actions by managers and provide important information, assisting managers to take good quality decisions.

Payback

Payback is a simple technique that measures the time period required for the earnings from an investment to recoup its original cost. Quite simply, it finds out the number of years it takes to recover the cost of an investment from its earnings. In spite of the obvious simplicity of the payback technique, it remains the most common method of investment appraisal in the UK.

Here is an example of payback:

Year	Cash outflow (£)	Cash inflow (£)
1	500,000	100,000
2		200,000
3		200,000
4		150,000

In this case the calculation is simple: payback is achieved at the end of year 3, when the initial investment of £500,000 is recovered from earnings – £100,000 in year 1 plus £200,000 in each of years 2 and 3.

Calculations can be a little more complex, however, as shown in the following example.

Year	Cash outflow (£)	Cash inflow (£)
1	500,000	100,000
2		100,000
3		200,000
4		300,000

In this case payback is achieved during the fourth year. The formula used to calculate the point during the year at which payback is achieved is as follows:

$$\text{number of full years} + \frac{\text{amount of investment not recovered}}{\text{revenue generated in next year}}$$

In the second example the investment has recovered £400,000 after three years. Therefore £100,000 remains to be recovered in year 4 before payback point is reached. During year 4 the investment will generate £300,000. Thus:

$$\text{payback} = 3 \text{ years} + \frac{100,000}{300,000} = 3\tfrac{1}{3} \text{ years, or three years and four months}$$

Figure 5.1 illustrates the concept of payback in the form of a graph.

Payback has the advantage of being quick and simple and this probably explains its popularity, especially with small businesses. However, it does have disadvantages. It ignores the level of profits that may be ultimately generated by the investment. For profit maximising businesses this may represent an important omission. Furthermore, payback ignores the timing of any receipts. The following example highlights this weakness.

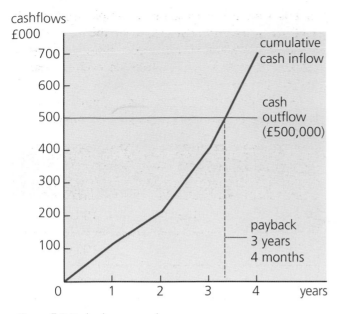

Figure 5.1 Payback on a graph

Average rate of return

The average rate of return (or ARR) is a more complex and meaningful method of investment appraisal. This technique calculates the percentage rate of return on each possible investment. The resulting percentage figure allows a simple comparison with other investment opportunities, including investing in banks and building societies. It is important to remember, however, that a commercial investment (such as purchasing CAD/CAM equipment for a production line) involves a degree of risk. The returns may not be as forecast. Therefore it is important that such an investment earns significantly more than the rate of interest available in the local building society. If the percentage return on purchasing the CAD/CAM equipment was identical to that on a high interest account in a building society, the latter would represent the better investment, as it carries little risk.

The formula for calculating ARR is:

$$\frac{\text{average profit}}{\text{asset's initial cost}} \times 100\%$$

$$\text{average profit} = \frac{\text{total net profit before tax over the asset's lifetime}}{\text{useful life of the asset}}$$

Two investment projects, A and B, each require an investment of £1 million. Their expected earnings are as follows.

Year	Project A cash Inflow (£)	Project B cash inflow (£)
1	500,000	100,000
2	300,000	200,000
3	200,000	300,000
4	100,000	500,000

Both investment projects achieve payback at the end of year 4. However, A is obviously more attractive because it yields greater returns in the early years. Payback does not take into account the timing of any income received.

Examiner's advice

Do not spend too long on investment appraisal calculations and do not carry out the same calculation repeatedly. If your answer is incorrect and you use it to support an argument in a later answer the examiner will credit it (in the later answer) as if it was accurate.

Business in Focus

Miller Reprographics
Purchasing new IT equipment for Miller Reprographics is estimated to cost £120,000 and a return of £220,000 over five years is anticipated.

The total profit from investing in IT over five years = £220,000 − £120,000 = £100,000

On an annual basis this is $\frac{£100,000}{5}$ − £20,000

Average rate of return = $\frac{£20,000}{£120,000} \times 100\%$

= 16.67%

Miller Reprographics may consider this to be an attractive investment as a rate of 16 per cent is considerably higher than that available on any interest-bearing account at a bank or building society, even allowing a premium for risk. However, the business may have an alternative investment offering a higher rate of return.

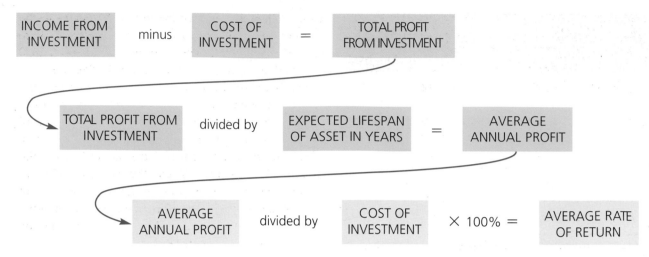

Figure 5.2 How to calculate average rate of return

The average rate of return is considered to be more useful than payback because it considers the level of profits earned from an investment rather than simply the time taken to recover costs. It also offers easier comparison with returns on other investments, notably financial investments in banks and building societies. However, this technique also fails to differentiate between investments that generate high returns in the early years and those that offer greater rewards later on.

Discounted cash flow

> **Key terms**
> **Discounting** is the reducing of the value of future earnings to reflect the opportunity cost of an investment.
> **Present value** is the value of a future stream of income from an investment, converted into its current worth.

The technique of discounted cash flow takes into account what is termed the 'time value' of money. The time value of money is based on the principle that money at the present time is worth more than money at some point in the future. Thus, according to this principle, £1,000 today is of greater value than £1,000 in one or two years' time. There are two major reasons why this time value principle exists.

1 **Risk** – having £1,000 now is a certainty; receiving the same amount at some point in the future may not occur. The full £1,000 payment may not be made; indeed no payment at all may be made. An investment project may fail to provide the expected returns because of a competitor's

actions, because of a change in tastes and fashions or as a consequence of technological change.

2 **Opportunity cost** is the foregone alternative. Even if no risk existed, the time value of money would still exist. This is because the money could be placed into an interest-bearing account generating a return. Thus, if we assume that a rate of 5 per cent is available on an interest-bearing account, £1,000 in one year's time is worth the same as £953 today. The reason for this is that by investing £953 at an interest rate of 5 per cent, we would have £1,000 after one year.

This time–value principle means that the longer the delay before money is received, the lower its value in present-day terms. This is called present value. Table 5.1 shows two investments requiring identical outlays. Both projects also receive the same cash inflow over a four-year period and would generate the same average rate of return (10 per cent). However, the majority of the cash inflow for project A occurs in year 1, while in project B this is delayed until year 3. The time–value principle would suggest that project A is preferable to project B. To show the effect of the time principle we need to calculate the present value of cash inflows and outflows through the use of discounting.

Discounting

Discounting is the process of adjusting the value of money received at some future date to its present value, i.e. its worth today. Discounting is, in effect, the reverse of adding interest. Discounting tables are

Year	Investment project A £000s	Investment project B £000s
0 (now)	(500)	(500)
1	400)	100
2	100	100
3	100	100
4	100	400

Table 5.1 **Two similar investment projects with different time patterns for cash inflows**

available to illustrate the effect of converting future streams of income to their present values. The rate of interest plays a central role in discounting – in the same way as it does in predicting the future value of savings. Table 5.2 shows the discounting figures and the value in present-day terms of £1,000 over a period of five years into the future. If the business anticipates relatively high interest rates over the period of the investment then future earnings are discounted heavily to provide present values for the investment. Lower rates result in discounting having a lesser effect in converting future earnings into present values.

The basic calculation is that the appropriate discounting factor is multiplied by the amount of money to be received in the future to convert it to its present value. Thus, at a rate of interest of 10 per cent, the present value of £1,000 in two years' time is £826 (£1,000 × 0.826). The present value of £1,000 received in four years' time is £683. This figure is lower because the time interval is greater and the effect of the time–value principle more pronounced.

From this example we can see that the rate of interest has a significant effect on the present value of future earnings. The higher the rate of interest, the greater the discount. Thus, the present value of £1,000 in three years' time is £751 if the rate of interest is assumed to be 10 per cent. However, if the rate of interest is estimated to be 5 per cent the present value is greater: £863.

The choice of interest rate to be used as the basis for discounting is an important decision by a business undertaking investment appraisal. The discounting rate selected normally reflects the interest rates that are expected for the duration of the project. However, as we shall see later, another approach is to choose the rate the firm would like to earn on the project and to use this as the basis of the calculation.

Net present value

Discounting expected future cash flows is the basis of calculating net present value. This method of investment appraisal forecasts expected outflows and inflows of cash and discounts the inflows and outflows. To calculate net present value we need to know:

Year	Discounting factor used to convert to present value assuming 10% rate of interest	Present value of £1,000 at a discount rate of 10% (£)	Discounting factor used to convert to present value assuming 5% rate of interest	Present value of £1,000 at a discount rate of 5% (£)
0 (now)	1	1,000	1	1,000
1	0.909	909	0.952	952
2	0.826	826	0.907	907
3	0.751	751	0.864	864
4	0.683	683	0.822	822

Table 5.2 **The process of discounting**

- the initial cost of the investment
- the chosen rate of discount
- any expected inflows and outflows of cash
- the duration of the investment project
- any remaining or residual value of the project at the end of the investment (if the investment is to purchase production equipment this may have scrap value once it is obsolete, for example).

The outflows of cash are subtracted from the discounted inflows to provide a net figure: the net present value. This figure is important for two reasons.

1 If the net present value figure is negative, the investment is not worth undertaking. This is because the present value of the stream of earnings is less than the cost of the investment. A more profitable approach would be to invest the capital in an interest-bearing account.
2 When an enterprise is considering a number of possible investment projects it can use the present value figure to rank them. The project generating the highest net present value figure is the most worthwhile in financial terms. In these circumstances a business may select the project – or projects – with the highest net present values.

Here is an example of calculating net present value. *Do it yourself* is one of the UK's most popular DIY magazines. The owners of the magazine, Bure Publishing, are investigating the production of an online edition and have conducted negotiations with two software houses regarding the development of a website for their new product, e-DIY. The two software houses offered very different ideas: one (proposal A) suggesting a basic product allowing Bure Publishing to offer access to the new website at a bargain price; the other (proposal B) proposing a more sophisticated product, to a higher technical standard, offering the opportunity for premium pricing.

The cash flows associated with these proposals over a five-year period are set out in Table 5.3. These show the cost of developing the website and the expected revenues, less operating costs for the site each year. Bure Publishing estimates that a 10 per cent discount rate would reflect likely market rates of interest.

Bure Publishing would opt for proposal A on the basis of this financial information, as the net present value for proposal A (the cheaper option) is higher than that for proposal B. The net cash flow for proposal A is also positive as cash inflows exceed outflows. Therefore the investment is viable. However, non-financial information may affect this investment decision.

A comparison of investment appraisal methods

The method of investment appraisal chosen will depend upon the type of firm, the market in which it

	Proposal A			Proposal B		
Year	Annual cash flows (£s)	Discounting factors at 10%	Present value (£s)	Cash flows (£s)	Discounting factors at 10%	Present value (£s)
0	(212,000)	1	(212,000)	(451,000)	1	(451,000)
1	46,000	0.909	41,814	89,400	0.909	81,265
2	57,500	0.826	47,495	115,000	0.826	94,990
3	63,250	0.751	47,501	122,500	0.751	91,998
4	69,000	0.683	47,127	144,275	0.683	98,540
5	71,000	0.621	44,091	140,000	0.621	86,940
	net present value		**£16,028**	net present value		**£2,733**

Table 5.3 Comparing Bure Publishing's investment projects using discounted cash flow

Method of investment appraisal	Advantages	Disadvantages
payback	• easy to calculate • simple to understand • relevant to firms with limited funds who want a quick return	• ignores timing of payments • excludes income received after payback • does not calculate profit
average rate of return	• measures the profit achieved on projects • allows easy comparison with returns on financial investments (bank accounts, for example)	• ignores the timing of the payments • calculates average profits – they may fluctuate wildly during the project
discounted cash flow	• makes an allowance for the opportunity cost of investing • takes into account cash inflows and outflows for the duration of the investment	• choosing the discount rate is difficult – especially for long-term projects • a complex method to calculate and easily misunderstood

Table 5.4 A comparison of techniques of investment appraisal

is trading and its corporate objectives. A small firm may be more likely to use payback because managers may be unfamiliar with more complex methods of investment appraisal. Small businesses also often focus on survival, and an important aspect of any investment will be how long it takes to cover the cost of the investment from additional revenues. Payback is therefore valuable for firms who wish to minimise risk.

Larger firms that have access to more sophisticated financial techniques may use the average rate of return or discounted cash flow methods. These methods highlight the overall profitability of investment projects and may be more appropriate for businesses where profit maximisation is important.

Investment criteria

Once the investment appraisal process has produced an answer, this needs to be compared with something in order to make a decision. There are a number of criteria that a business may use to make an investment decision.

The rate of interest

Average rate of return and net present value (NPV) methods produce figures that can be compared with the rate of interest. Any interest rate chosen for this

process will be based on the interest rate set by the Bank of England. In essence, the managers of the business will seek a return that will be greater than the current and forecast interest rates if the average rate of return is used or, if they are using NPV, the interest rate that is current should produce a positive net present value.

Using the interest rate as a criterion does involve a number of problems, however. First, many investment projects are long term and expenditure and returns may take place over many years. It is highly unlikely that interest rates will remain unchanged for this period of time. Therefore managers have to decide on a rate or range of rates to use in their calculations.

Second, investments involve risks – we consider this more fully in the section below. When choosing a minimum rate of return the management team has to build in an allowance for risk.

The level of profit

We saw in the chapter on interpreting company accounts that a series of ratios can be used to assess the profitability of a business. One of these (return on capital employed or ROCE) provides a figure which measures profits generated against the value of resources available to the business. It is not unusual for a business to set itself targets in terms of ROCE. Managers may insist that any new investment

Coca-Cola buys Abbey Well brand

Coca-Cola Great Britain has acquired Waters & Robson, the owner of the Abbey Well water brand. It will join premium water brand, Malvern, in the Coca-Cola portfolio. Abbey Well's water is drawn from a 117m-deep artesian well beneath the Northumberland countryside, before being bottled at the Morpeth plant, which generates annual sales revenues of approximately £11 million.

Abbey Well will be bottled and distributed by Coca-Cola Enterprises, which will take over its base in Morpeth, Northumberland on completion of the deal. The company's staff will also be employed by Coca-Cola Enterprises.

Sanjay Guha, President of Coca-Cola Great Britain, says: 'We have been looking for the right bottled water opportunity to expand the range of drinks we offer consumers for some time, and in Abbey Well we have acquired a natural, sustainable and high-quality British-sourced water.'

Source: Adapted from *Marketing Week*, 11 November 2008
http://www.marketingweek.co.uk

Question:

1 What criterion (or criteria) might Coca-Cola have used to judge the value of this investment?

project should generate returns which will at least match (and hopefully exceed) the business's overall target for ROCE.

Alternative investments

It would be unusual for a business to consider only a single investment project. Most managers contemplating a major investment will have other options. These could be very different investments or simple variants on the first proposal. The business may simply select the project or projects which perform the best subject to some minimum criteria in terms of profits or percentage returns. In such circumstances opportunity cost is an important concept for managers to bear in mind.

Investment criteria can be useful to you when responding to examination questions on investment appraisal. When judging whether or not a business should go ahead with a particular investment, it is important to think what criteria the business would expect the investment to meet. The case study may directly state these or they may be implied. In either case, by relating your answer to the criterion or criteria you have a basis for making a judgement that you are able to justify.

Assessing the risks and uncertainties of investment decisions

It is not a simple matter to assess the degree of risk involved in an investment decision. Risk is the chance of something adverse or bad happening. In the context of investment decisions there are two broad possibilities: costs may be higher than forecast or sales lower than expected.

Forecasting future sales can be a very difficult, and often expensive, exercise. Market research can be used, but it is costly and not always reliable. The difficulties in forecasting sales arise from a number of factors.

- **Timescales**. It is much harder to forecast sales accurately many years into the future. Over a longer timescale it is more likely that tastes and fashions may change or that new competitors or new products may enter the market.
- **New markets**. If an investment project is based on a business entering a new market (either in geographical or product terms) then the business has less experience and no financial records to use as a guide in forecasting sales. In 2007 Tesco entered the US market for groceries, setting up a series of small supermarkets throughout California. Early media reports suggest that these stores are not performing as well as expected. Apparently even one of Britain's largest companies does not find it easy to forecast its sales accurately.
- **Competitors' reactions**. Deciding on a particular

programme of investment may bring a business into competition with rivals in news ways. Entering a new market (as in the case of Tesco above), producing new products or developing new methods of production may all provoke a response from competitors. This may take the form of increased advertising, cutting prices or bringing out new products. Each of these actions will impact on the sales associated with the investment project. However, not knowing the type or extent of reaction in advance makes it very difficult to estimate its effect on future sales.

Equally, costs may rise above the forecast level, reducing the returns from the investment. In 2008 the price of oil and many other materials used in manufacturing rose unexpectedly. The price of oil rose to over $150 per barrel, leading to airlines such as British Airways saying that its profit margins had nearly disappeared as a consequence. Since this highpoint in spring 2008 the price of oil has dropped dramatically and unexpectedly. At the time of writing, in November 2008, its price is around $50 per barrel. The volatility of prices for such a fundamentally important product highlights the difficulties that firms face when attempting to forecast future costs of production.

Managers may seek to identify and manage the risk in an investment decisions by taking a range of actions, including the following.

- **Purchasing raw materials on forward markets.** This means that the firm concerned negotiates a price at the present time for a product to be delivered at some agreed date in the future. For example, many airlines have agreed future prices for the delivery of aviation fuel and therefore know for certain this element of their future costs. Although it removes the risk of a sudden increase in costs, it may be judged a mistake if prices fall between agreeing the deal and the delivery of the product.
- **Building in allowances for fluctuations in sales revenue and costs.** Prudent managers may opt to forecast a range of sales figures and costs of production which are based on their market research, but which allow for the market to change in some way that may be either adverse or favourable. Building in this flexibility in forecasting, and thinking about how wide the ranges for sales revenue and costs should be, will help managers to judge the degree of risk as well as the value of an investment project.
- **Ensuring the business has sufficient financial assets available.** If a business is trading in a volatile or rapidly changing market it would be

Business in Focus

Southwest Airlines' hedging strategy

Southwest Airlines is an American low-cost airline based in Dallas, Texas. It is the largest airline in the United States by number of passengers carried domestically per year (as of 31 December, 2007). In 2008 Southwest operated approximately 3,500 flights each day. The company buys enormous quantities of aviation fuel and has operated a very successful strategy of hedging against price rises.

What is hedging? Hedging is a financial strategy that lets airlines or other investors protect themselves against rising prices for commodities such as oil by locking in a price for fuel. It has been described as everything from gambling to buying insurance.

In the first three months of 2008, Southwest Airlines paid $1.98 per gallon for fuel. American Airlines paid $2.73 per gallon, and United paid $2.83 per gallon in the same period.

Since 1999, hedging its expenditure on fuel has saved Southwest $3.5 billion. It has sometimes meant the difference between profit and loss. In the first quarter, hedging savings of $291 million dwarfed Southwest's $34 million profit from its airline operations. Without buying its fuel in advance at a lower price, the company would have made a substantial loss.

Source: Adapted from Associated Press Report, 30 June 2008

http://www.msnbc.msn.com

Question:

1 What effect might the dramatic fall in oil prices have had on Southwest Airlines' hedging strategy in the second half of 2008?

sensible to make certain the business has sufficient resources to deal with any adverse circumstances. Tesco is likely to have sufficient finance to support its fledgling business in California even if sales do prove to be below forecasts for an extended period of time.

Is it worth using techniques of investment appraisal?

The results of investment appraisal calculations are only as good as the data on which they are based. Firms experience difficulty in accurately forecasting the cost of many major projects. It is even more difficult to estimate the likely revenues from investment projects, particularly long-term ones. It is perhaps possible to make an allowance to represent risk – for example, the possibility of a competitor taking actions that result in sales being lower than forecast. However, uncertainty – which cannot be measured – may make any investment appraisal worthless.

In assessing the value of numerical techniques of investment appraisal, some thought has to be given to the alternative. Without the use of payback and the like, managers would operate on the basis of hunches and guesswork. Some managers may have a good instinct for these matters, whereas others may not. As markets become more complex and global, the need for some technique to appraise investments becomes greater. It is more difficult for an individual or a group to have an accurate overview of a large international market comprising many competitors and millions of diverse individuals. Detailed market research to forecast possible revenues and the use of appropriate techniques of investment appraisal may become even more important in the future.

Qualitative influences on investment appraisal

The financial aspects of any proposed investment will clearly have an important influence upon whether a business goes ahead with the plan. However, a number of other issues may affect the decision.

- **Corporate image.** A firm may reject a potentially profitable investment project, or choose a less profitable alternative, because to do otherwise might reflect badly on the business. Having a positive corporate image is important in terms of long-term sales and profits and may be considered more important than gaining short-term advantage from profitable investments. In the UK the National Westminster Bank has invested heavily in internet banking and had planned to close many high street branches as part of this investment programme. However, the bad publicity given to branch closures by all banks led the National Westminster to reverse the closure decision. The firm's investment in internet banking may prove less profitable as a consequence.
- **Corporate objectives.** Most businesses will only undertake an investment if they consider that it will assist in the achievement of corporate objectives. For example, Rolls-Royce Engineering, a

Key Issues

Risk is an important factor within investment decision-making. Risk can be defined as uncertainty that is quantifiable or that can be measured. There are two major types of risk.

1 **Systematic risk** relates to the environment in which a project will operate. Thus, this type of risk could include a loss of sales and cash inflow due to, say, an adverse movement in the exchange rate.

2 **Specific risk** is associated with a particular project, such as launching a product which is entirely new and of which the firm has little experience.

Techniques of investment appraisal can incorporate an allowance for risk, perhaps by reducing cash inflows or increasing costs. More sophisticated techniques use the theory of probability to attempt to arrive at more accurate predictions.

Risk should be distinguished from uncertainty. Uncertainty is not measurable and cannot be included in numerical techniques of investment appraisal. An investment project which appears to have a high degree of uncertainty attached to it may not be undertaken because the firm in question may be unable to assess its likely costs and benefits.

company that publicly states its aim to produce high-quality products, may invest heavily in training for its staff and in research and development. This will assist in the manufacture of world-class aero engines and vehicles.

Business in Focus

Dell tries to save the planet?

Dell, one of the world's largest manufacturers of computers, has claimed it is now officially a carbon-neutral company – five months ahead of its own schedule.

The target was apparently met through improved energy efficiency at Dell's own facilities, combined with 'green' electricity purchases and investments in wind power in the US, China and India, totalling 645 million kilowatt-hours and creating savings of 400,000 metric tons of carbon dioxide.

Dell has invested $3 billion annually in green energy, and its consumption of green energy has increased almost tenfold to 116 million kWh in four years. Dane Parker, Dell's global environment, health and safety director, said the achievement reflects a long-established policy at Dell of saving energy, recycling, and other green practices.

Source: Adapted from Cnet News
http://news.cnet.com

Questions:

1 What financial methods of investment appraisal might Dell have used before deciding to invest funds in these ways?
2 What qualitative factors might have influenced its decision?

- **Environmental and ethical issues.** These can be important influences on investment decisions. Some firms have a genuine commitment to trading ethically and to inflicting minimal damage on the environment. This is a core part of the business philosophy of some firms. As a consequence they would not exploit cheap Third World labour or use non-sustainable resources. Other firms may have a less deep commitment to ethical and environmental trading but may avoid some investments for fear of damaging publicity.
- **Industrial relations.** Some potentially profitable investments may be turned down because they would result in a substantial loss of jobs. Taking

decisions that lead to large-scale redundancies can be costly in terms of decreased morale, redundancy payments and harm to the business's corporate image.

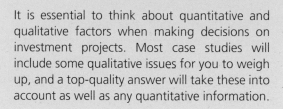

Examiner's advice

It is essential to think about quantitative and qualitative factors when making decisions on investment projects. Most case studies will include some qualitative issues for you to weigh up, and a top-quality answer will take these into account as well as any quantitative information.

Progress questions

1 Outline three business decisions that may require the application of investment appraisal techniques. (9 marks)
2 Explain why forecasts of sales revenues arising from an investment may prove to be inaccurate. (7 marks)
3 Why might investment appraisal be easier to conduct in a stable economic environment? (7 marks)
4 Thames Radio is contemplating investing in new broadcasting equipment. The cost of the investment is forecast to be £150,000. The expected additional revenue from being able to broadcast to a larger area is £40,000 per annum. What is the payback period of this investment? (5 marks)
5 Explain one disadvantage of using payback in the circumstances in question 4. (4 marks)
6 Outline the stages that have to be completed to carry out an average rate of return calculation. (6 marks)
7 Wessex Leisure is considering the purchase of a pleasure cruiser for use on the Solent. The *Meriden* is available at a cost of £900,000 and would cost £100,000 each year to operate. Over its ten-year life the cruiser would generate £280,000 in revenue each year. Calculate the average rate of return on this investment. (7 marks)
8 Explain what is meant by the 'present value' of a stream of earnings from an investment. (5 marks)

9 Chedgrave Printers Ltd is appraising the costs of and benefits from a new piece of machinery. The equipment costs £300,000 and has a working life of four years. The company expects to generate revenue of £120,000 each year if it purchases the machine. Calculate the net present value of this project assuming an interest rate of 10 per cent. (7 marks)

10 Outline two qualitative factors that an oil company may consider as part of the appraisal of a proposed investment to extract oil from the seabed under the English Channel. (6 marks)

Analysis and evaluation questions

1 Burrows Ltd owns a local newspaper in an area of high unemployment and intends to purchase new machinery for its printing room. The company intends to spend £1.5 million on the equipment and has priced it carefully. It has to make a choice from two brands of equipment, one of which has a very slightly higher net present value. The company relied on past records rather than market research to forecast sales.

The Chief Executive has decided that the company should raise the money it requires by a fixed interest bank loan. Some directors are concerned that installing the new high-technology equipment will lead to redundancies; others disagree. Last year Burrows Ltd's profits after taxation were £245,000.

a Analyse the benefits to the business of using net present value to compare the two pieces of machinery as investments. (10 marks)

b Discuss whether the business should give greater emphasis to quantitative or qualitative influences when taking this decision. (15 marks)

2 KJ plc is a mining company that has completed a survey of a region in a central African country which is rich in deposits of copper. Many of the company's directors are keen to invest in a partnership with the government of the country to mine the mineral. The company will have to invest £70 million before the project starts and its costs thereafter will be £12 million per year. The contract would last for five years and (at the current market price for copper) it could earn revenue of £40 million in the first year, and £50 million in each of the next four years. The central African country is very poor and the government came to power after an armed rising three years ago.

Some of KJ plc's directors would prefer the company to invest in expanding its opencast mining operations in the UK. The rising price of coal has made this more attractive. This project would cost £40 million and would generate annual profits averaging £10 million over the next five years.

a Explain why the finance director might think that investing in copper mining in Africa is a more attractive project in terms of profits. (10 marks)

b To what extent does the risk involved in this decision mean that the use of financial techniques of investment appraisal is of little value? (15 marks)

Case study

Transit plc is in the doldrums. The company is one of the UK's best-known train and coach operators. The company had enjoyed considerable success following the privatisation of rail services in the 1990s. Transit won the franchise to operate trains in the north of England and southern Scotland. Its trains won a reputation for arriving on time and for providing a comfortable and speedy service. At this stage in its life Transit was a rising star.

Chief Executive Craig Prescott had worked in transport companies in Singapore and the USA before coming back to the UK to head up the company bidding for the franchises to operate trains on a number of routes. Transit had run coach services for many years, but was looking to expand its business into related areas. Running trains on some lines in the UK meant that the company could use the skills already available.

By 2007 Craig Prescott and Transit were under pressure, and the threat of recession in 2008, along with a fall in the value of the pound, had made things worse. The company's sales had stagnated, profits were down significantly and the quality of service seemed to have declined. Passenger groups were complaining about high prices, late and outdated trains, poor catering facilities and dirty carriages. At a board meeting towards the end of 2008, Craig put forward two plans to his fellow directors.

Craig argued for growth as a way out of the company's troubles. 'I believe that we need to expand and to use our expertise in passenger transport. We have to generate increased profits and to capture the attention of investors in the City once again. There are two exciting possibilities open to us. The franchise for West Coast trains is up for grabs and I think we should bid for it. I have outlined likely expenditure and returns over the next five years for this investment (Appendix A). This would allow us to build upon the success we have achieved in running our existing franchises. The alternative is to invest in the rail network in Hong Kong. HK Transport operates the system out there and is looking for a partner to put in money and expertise. I have a number of contacts out there and the projections of income from an investment look good.'

Some directors were unhappy with Craig's proposals and said that the company should not invest in either of the proposals at a time when the whole world's economy was going through troubled times.

Questions

1 Explain what is meant by 'net cash flow'. (3 marks)
2 Calculate the average rate of return for the two investment projects and state which one the managers of Transit should select on the basis of your calculations. (9 marks)
3 Discuss whether the average rate of return was the best financial method of investment appraisal to use in these circumstances. (13 marks)
4 Some directors said that the company should not invest in either of the projects. Do you agree with them? Justify your view. (15 marks)

Year	West Coast trains net cash flows (£m)	HK Transport net cash flows (£m)
2009	(240)	(250)
2010	69	90
2011	101	95
2012	106	95
2013	108	150

Appendix A – forecast net cash flows for the two alternative investments

Section 2: Marketing strategies

At AS level the focus was on how medium-sized businesses changed their marketing activities to make the business more successful. For example, you may have considered changing the price to boost revenue or switching from one form of promotion to another. At A2 we are interested in 'the bigger picture'. We want to know more about why a business decides to compete in one market rather than another or why it chooses to offer one product line rather than another. We are also interested in the strategy businesses choose to use to compete against their rivals. For example, do they decide to compete with a low price strategy or by offering a premium product or service? How should managers position their business relative to the competition?

The study of marketing at A2 therefore includes:

- market analysis – understanding the scale of different markets, the particular features of a market including its growth and the trends of particular segments
- marketing strategy – how a business competes
- marketing plans – the detailed breakdown of how a strategy will be implemented.

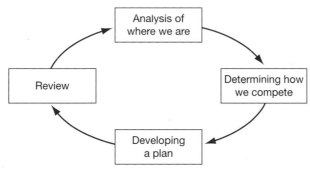

Analysis of where we are

6 Understanding marketing objectives

Marketing activities need a focus. To market anything effectively you need to know what it is you are trying to achieve, i.e. the marketing objective.

In this chapter we consider:
- the meaning of marketing
- the meaning and significance of marketing objectives
- the internal and external influences on marketing objectives.

What is marketing?

Marketing is the process by which a firm tries to identify, anticipate and satisfy customers' needs and wants and at the same time meet its own objectives. A firm will aim to provide goods and services that customers want and in return it will usually seek to generate a profit. Marketing therefore involves an exchange process in which both sides hope to benefit.

Effective marketing requires a good understanding of customers' requirements. This is usually achieved through primary or secondary market research, although in some cases managers may rely on their experience and intuition.

Marketing activities help organisations understand their customers. They also influence the customers' decisions to buy the product.

According to the American Marketing Association (2004), 'Marketing is an organizational function and set of processes for creating, communicating and delivering value to customers and for managing customer relationships in a way that benefits both the organization and the stakeholder.'

As you can see from this:

- Marketing is a function of the business, i.e. it is an element or part of the business. Other functions include finance, human resource management and operations. These functions must interact effectively for the overall corporate plan to be successful.
- Marketing is a process. This means that it is a series of stages rather than a one-off action. For example, managers will analyse the market to identify the market segments that exist. They will then target the segments of interest and decide how to position the business relative to the com-

petition. This is a process of segmentation, targeting and positioning (STP).

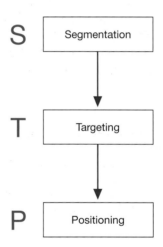

Figure 6.1 STP

- Marketing involves a relationship between the buyer and seller. In the past we have tended to see marketing as a transaction. For example, you sold someone a car. The aim was to find the right car for the buyer so the customer would feel he or she received value for money. However, businesses are increasingly realising the high level of costs and additional difficulties of finding new customers compared with keeping existing ones. For example, a car dealership would aim to provide customers with all the cars they wanted during their lives; the dealership would understand the needs of customer, provide a high-quality services and keep the customer informed of relevant new models and provide incentives to try and encourage them to come back. The idea would be to lock someone in to being a 'Lexus customer' or a 'Ford buyer'. It is much better to get your existing customers to keep coming back to you than to have to rely on constantly finding new ones. Marketing managers are increasingly trying to build relationships with customers: frequent flier plans, customer loyalty cards, newsletters and updates for customers are all ways of building a relationship. Once you have searched for books on Amazon you will find suggestions for similar books that you might like; the company is trying to provide you with additional services to build the relationship, so you trust its advice and want to come back and buy more from it.

- Marketing can refer to a business, a person, a place, an idea ... in fact anything at all! In politics these days great use is made of focus groups to understand what electors want, and this often influences the policy of a political party. Marketing was needed to secure London's bid for the 2012 Olympics. Manchester United is a global brand that needs to market itself. Anything and everything can be marketed, not just cans of cola or bars of chocolate.

Key terms
Segmentation is the process of identifying similar needs and wants within a market.
Targeting is the process of selecting which segments to compete in.
Positioning is the process of deciding how a product is perceived relative to the competition.

Examiner's advice

Remember that marketing is not just about 'making customers happy'– the business has to meet its objectives as well (e.g. to make a profit). There are likely to be trade-offs between what customers want and what the organisation can offer with the resources it has.

Also remember that decisions regarding the marketing mix can only be taken once you are clear what segment you are aiming for and how you intend to position your business.

Marketing responsibility and activities

Who is responsible for marketing and what does it involve? This depends. An entrepreneur who has just started up may have to do everything himself or

herself: marketing, finance and operations. In a bigger business there is likely to be a specialist department; there may even be several different sections to the marketing department. There may be people responsible for the various products the business offers, or different divisions or regions; there may be a sales team making contacts with potential clients, a research department gathering and analysing data and a brand manager controlling brand positioning and image. The precise jobs and priorities within the marketing function will depend on the nature of the business. In the soft drinks industry, for example, marketing may involve heavy expenditure on mainstream advertising to generate demand. In the industrial equipment market a sales team may be the central element of the marketing team; advertising may be less significant.

Key Issues

Advances in technology make it easier to find suppliers of products online. Advances in transportation make it easier to move products around the world. Trade agreements are making it easier to enter markets. These factors all combine to make markets more competitive. This makes it even more important for firms to understand their customers properly and meet their needs effectively if they want to survive and prosper.

What are marketing objectives?

A marketing objective is the target or targets set for the marketing function. As with all targets, these should not be imposed on individuals but discussed and negotiated with them so that they believe the objectives are feasible, understand the logic behind them and are committed to achieving them.

Typically, marketing objectives might include the following:

- **Sales targets** – for example, managers may have to boost overall sales by 15 per cent this year, or achieve specific sales targets for particular products or particular customer groups.
- **Market share** – sales targets will often be set in terms of market share. For example, when the iPhone was first launched it might have set a target of achieving a 10 per cent market share within two years.

Business in Focus

Market-oriented businesses

A market-oriented business is one where the customer is placed at the heart of everything the organisation does. Everyone in the business thinks about decisions from the perspective of the customer. This approach can be seen in the highly successful Zara fashion retailer.

Questions:

1 Discuss the possible reasons why some organisations are more market oriented than others.
2 How can a business try to ensure it is customer focused?

● **Brand awareness** – a company may feel that it is not recognised enough and not included on customers' 'shopping lists' when they are thinking of possible suppliers. They might therefore develop a promotional campaign to raise awareness (also called 'share of the mind'). This might be the first stage of a campaign to increase market share in the future.

Key terms

A **marketing objective** is a target set for the marketing function.
Market share measures the sales of one product as a percentage of the total market sales.
Sales growth occurs when the value (or volume) of sales increases.

An objective should be:

● specific, i.e. it should be clear exactly what the business is trying to achieve
● measurable, i.e. it should be clear how much the specific item is expected to change
● time specific, i.e. it should be clear by when a target should be achieved.

People in Business

Philip Kotler

Philip Kotler (born 1931) is Professor of Marketing at the Kellogg School of Management. His book *Marketing Management*, published in 1967, is a classic marketing textbook and bestseller; there are already 12 different editions.

Figure 6.3 Philip Kotler

In this book he developed a systematic approach to marketing in a way that had never been done before. According to Kotler: 'Marketing is not the art of finding clever ways to dispose of what you make. Marketing is the art of creating genuine customer value. It is the art of helping your customers become better off.'

Kotler has argued that the process of marketing develops over time, as does our understanding of what it does or should involve. At first Kotler focused on marketing as a transaction. Now he pays much more attention to relationship marketing, the idea that firms need to build customer loyalty and engage in a series of transactions with them during their relationship.

Source: *Marketing Management: Analysis, Planning, Implementation and Control*, Prentice Hall, 1967; 12th edn, 2006
Adapted from Economist.com, 12 September 2008

Influences on marketing objectives

The targets for marketing cannot be set in isolation from the other functions, or indeed from the objectives of the business as a whole. Imagine a restaurant booked up months in advance and without any space to fit in more customers. The marketing in this case might aim to sustain demand but not actually increase it because more capacity is not available. The operations constraints affect what marketing can achieve. If, on the other hand, the directors were pursuing a growth strategy and opening up several new restaurants a month, the marketing function would be working hard to generate new demand to fill them.

The influences on the marketing objective can be divided into internal and external factors.

Internal factors

The internal factors influencing the marketing objectives include the following:

- **Operations** – the capacity of the business will limit how much can be produced. The operations process will also affect the quality of the product and the flexibility that can be offered (e.g. the variety that can be provided). Particular strengths in operations (e.g. the speed of delivery or excellent design) is likely to feed in to the marketing strategy.
- **Human resources** – what a business is capable of producing will depend on the skills, attitudes and motivation of its staff. A business with a high level of diversity in its workforce, for example, may be in a relatively strong position to expand overseas because it may understand the cultures

Key term

A **marketing budget** involves forward financial targets set for revenue and the amount to be spent on marketing activities.

and needs of those markets better than its competitors.

- **Finance** – the finance function will determine what is affordable. A lack of finance may prevent the marketing manager from undertaking many of the activities he would like to. The finance function will influence the amount that can be spent on marketing, which is included in the marketing budget.

The marketing objective must be derived directly from the corporate objective. Does the business want to grow? How much? In what areas? In which markets? It must also be realistic.

A marketing objective of doubling sales may sound attractive, but if the firm does not have the capacity, the funds to invest in major promotions or the staff to implement such an increase then it is clearly not a good objective. Each function must act in harmony with the other functions.

The precise nature of a firm's marketing objectives will also depend on the culture of the business. Are managers ambitious and will they set high targets that stretch individuals? Or are they more conservative and likely to consolidate before expanding further? Are they innovative and constantly looking to launch new products and develop new markets, or do they prefer to focus on the core established business?

External factors

What is realistic as an objective will be affected by the external macro- and micro-environments. The macro-environment relates to factors well beyond the control of any one firm, such as political, economic, social, technological, environmental and legal factors (PESTEL). These changes may make sales more difficult to achieve. An ageing population might limit the sales of children's computer games. Technological advances might make certain types of televisions obsolete. Legal changes may limit sales opportunities; the banning of smoking hit cigarette sales, for example. Equally, PESTEL changes may create more sales possibilities. The expansion of the European Union (a political change) may make it easier to sell abroad. A booming economy may make sales easier.

The effect of any given change in the macro-environment on the likely sales of a business will depend on the nature of the change and the nature of the business. A fall in UK national income will hit demand for income-elastic products such as city centre apartments, health clubs and cruise holidays more than income-inelastic products such as shampoo, toothpaste and socks. Greater interest in environmental issues may have a greater impact on the demand for flights and cars than on the demand for ties and bread.

The micro-environment refers to factors in the immediate environment of a business, such as its suppliers, customers, substitutes and competitors. A substitute product is different from yours but performs the same function; a big promotional campaign by flower growers may hit sales of boxed chocolates, for example, as both are gift products.

Actions by competitors may also make sales more difficult. The lower prices approach of Aldi and Costco started to hit sales of higher priced supermarkets in the UK in 2008, for example, as the country moved into a recession. An objective may have to be adjusted as competitors change their approaches.

Key terms
The **income elasticity of demand** measures the percentage change in the quantity demanded given a percentage change in income.
Income elastic means that the percentage change in quantity demanded is greater than the percentage change in income.
Income inelastic means that the percentage change in quantity demanded is less than the percentage change in income.

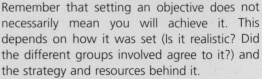

Examiner's advice

Remember that setting an objective does not necessarily mean you will achieve it. This depends on how it was set (Is it realistic? Did the different groups involved agree to it?) and the strategy and resources behind it.

However, if there is no objective it is difficult to know where you are headed, whether you are on track and whether or not you need to take action.

Key Issues

All planning should involve assessing the external environment and comparing this with internal resources in order to work out what to do next. The marketing objective will depend on the opportunities and threats of the external environment and the strength and weakness of the internal environment.

Summary

The marketing function is the interface between the business and its customers. Without customers there is no revenue. The marketing function will set objectives on what it is trying to achieve; for example, a certain level of sales or a given market share in a given time period. These objectives will be linked to the corporate objectives, i.e. the marketing function will aim to help the business fulfil its overall targets.

Business in Focus

The clothing market

The UK clothing retail market is heavily influenced by a number of external factors, which will influence the likely marketing objectives and strategies of any business in this sector.

These include:

- the ageing of the UK's population – this creates a challenge to some clothing retailers who need to adapt to the needs of older customers
- slower economic growth and non-food price inflation, which have reduced the funds consumers have available for clothing. This means growth in the sales of clothes may be slower.

Progress questions

1 Define marketing. (3 marks)

2 Explain what is meant by a marketing objective. (3 marks)

3 Give an example of a marketing objective. (3 marks)

4 Explain two benefits of setting a marketing objective. (5 marks)

5 What is meant by 'the external environment'? (3 marks)

6 State four functions within a business. (4 marks)

7 Explain two internal influences on a firm's marketing objectives. (6 marks)

8 Explain two external influences on a firm's marketing objectives. (6 marks)

9 Explain what is meant by market share. (3 marks)

10 Explain what is meant by sales growth. (3 marks)

Analysis and evaluation questions

1 Analyse the benefits to a soft drinks producer such as Coca-Cola of setting marketing objectives when entering a new region. (8 marks)

2 Discuss the factors likely to influence the marketing objectives for a business such as Unilever. (15 marks)

3 To what extent do you think marketing is the most important function of a car business such as Toyota? (15 marks)

Web link

For more information on Coca-Cola visit www.cocacola.com

For more information on Unilever visit www.unilever.com

For more information on Toyota visit www.toyota.com.jp

Case study

The furniture retailer MFI went into administration in November 2008. This means that it owed money to suppliers and these suppliers had asked administrators to recover their money. MFI said that sales for expensive items had fallen and this had caused cashflow problems; these had been made worse by difficulties borrowing money. Some stores continued to trade, but 26 closed immediately. When the announcement was made, MFI said that existing orders would either be met or refunded.

MFI facts

- Founded in 1964 as Mullard Furniture Industries.
- Mullard was the maiden name of the wife of one of the co-founders.
- Stores sold for just £1 in 2006 to private buyers.
- Employs more than 1,000 people.

The firm, which was bought out by managers in September 2008, had 110 stores and a workforce of more than 1,000 people. The downturn of the housing market due to the economic recession and

a lack of lending was a major contributor to MFI's decline. People stopped buying things such as new bathrooms and kitchens. The administrators were looking at selling some of the company's stores to raise funds.

MFI had also seen sales fall in recent years as it faced increased competition from newer rivals such as Ikea.

The GMB union said that MFI employees were saying the firm had been 'badly managed for some years'.

MFI said there were two potential buyers for the company.

(40 marks, 60 minutes)

Questions

1 Explain what happens when a business goes into administration. (6 marks)

2 Analyse the possible reasons why MFI sales have fallen in recent years. (10 marks)

3 If MFI was taken over, discuss the factors that might affect its marketing objectives. (12 marks)

4 To what extent do you think better marketing might have saved MFI? (12 marks)

One step further: relationship marketing

One of the main areas of interest in marketing in recent years is the growth of customer relationship management. Businesses are looking to build long-term relationships with their customers. For example, a bank wants you to bank with it and wants to understand the various stages of your life so it can offer you:

- money for university
- money to buy your first flat
- money for your first house
- money for your holidays

then to understand when to offer:

- pension advice
- investment advice
- insurance advice.

Amazon wants to understand what you like to read so it can offer you news of books you might like. So, marketing is no longer seen as a 'one-off' transaction – it is a series of ongoing experiences.

7 Analysing markets and marketing

In this chapter we examine:
- the reasons for and value of market analysis
- methods of analysing market trends
- the use of information technology in analysing markets
- difficulties in analysing data.

What is market analysis?

Market analysis occurs when a firm undertakes a detailed examination of the characteristics of a market. This is an essential part of marketing planning. Only by knowing the features of a market, and where it fits in that market, will a firm be able to plan effectively what to do next. A good understanding of markets should help the business to target the right segments and to market its products effectively in a focused way. A lack of analysis may mean the wrong markets are selected and/or the marketing is wasteful because it is not targeted.

Analysing a market involves gaining an understanding of the following.

- **The market size.** This may be measured in terms of the volume or value of sales. For example, in the soft drinks market a firm may measure the number of cans or bottles sold (volume) or the monetary value of the total sales (value). A firm must ensure that the market is big enough to generate sufficient returns to make it worth competing in. If a market is only worth £2 million a year in revenue but would cost, say, £10 million to enter then it is unlikely to be worthwhile.
- **The market share of firms within the market.** This measures the sales of a firm relative to the total market size. In some markets, such as banking, airlines, petrol stations, sugar refining and pharmaceuticals, a few firms dominate. These are called oligopoly markets. In other markets there are no dominant firms – there are many smaller firms competing; for example, the hairdressing, advertising and taxi markets tend to have a large number of relatively small firms.
- **The likely costs and difficulties involved in**

entering the market. What is the typical spending on marketing in the industry, for example? What are the main channels to market and how easy is it likely to be to access these? How brand loyal are customers?
- **The trends within the market.** For example, is the overall trend of sales upwards? At what rate is the market growing? For example, the growth of demand for takeaway foods has been rapid in recent years, whereas the growth in demand for high-fat foods has been slower. A firm will be reluctant to enter a declining market. When measuring the change in the size of the market, the firm will want to examine what is happening to the value of sales as well as the volume. If it finds the volume of sales has been going up but the value has been falling, for example, this means the average price has been falling. Will it be able to make a profit if this continues?
- **Patterns of sales.** Managers will also look for patterns within the overall trends. Are sales seasonal, for example? This could have implications for cash flow and production. Think of sun cream, fireworks, school clothes, textbooks, garden furniture and holidays. Are some segments growing faster than others (e.g. the demand for mints has grown faster than the demand for chocolate within the overall confectionery market)? This could have implications for new product development.

Key terms

The **value of sales** measures the amount of money spent on products in a market.
The **volume of sales** measures the number of units sold in a market.

When analysing markets, a business will want to analyse the position at a given moment in time and to monitor the trends over time.

Business in Focus

Business issues

Markets can differ considerably. The structure of a market can be measured by a concentration ratio. For example, a five-firm concentration ratio measures the market share of the largest five firms in a market.

Highly concentrated markets (i.e. dominated by a few firms) include tobacco, soft drinks, sugar, pharmaceuticals and banking. A market dominated by a few large firms is called an 'oligopoly'.

Markets with low levels of concentration (i.e. many small firms) include farming, hairdressing and advertising.

Why analyse markets?

It may be possible to set a marketing objective and develop a plan to achieve this target without gathering or analysing any data. You could simply rely on a hunch or your 'gut feeling'. Akio Morita, for example, is said to have launched the hugely successful Sony Walkman with very little reference to market research.

However, while this can obviously work it is likely to be a high-risk decision equivalent to trying to find your way around a house in the dark – you may get lucky but the chances are you will cause some damage. Gather valuable data and interpret it correctly and this is the equivalent of having the lights turned on – navigating your way around should be that much easier. You know where you are, you can see where you want to go and how to get there. The marketing spending by businesses can run into millions of pounds in some cases. Analysing markets should help to reduce risks and ensure marketing activities such as advertising are focused and relevant and do not involve waste.

Business in Focus

In the UK cosmetics market mainstream advertising is extremely important for the major brands. L'Oréal spends most on advertising across its L'Oréal Paris, Maybelline and Lancôme brands. Other high-spending brands include Max Factor, Rimmel and No.7. Two-thirds of make-up advertising is on press advertising, particularly in women's magazines. Beauty pages are very important to promote make-up brands. Advertising spending is between 4 and 5 per cent of turnover.

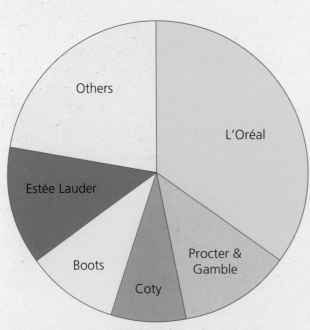

Figure 7.1 Advertising of make-up by media type, 2008

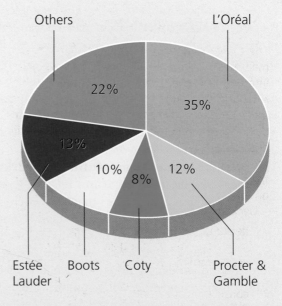

Figure 7.2 Spend on make-up, by advertiser, 2006–08*
*to May 2008 only
Source: Nielsen Media Research/Mintel

It is useful, therefore, to analyse the markets you are in or want to be in before you set an objective or develop a plan. Only when you know where you are and what is going on around you can you really set a target to say where you hope to end up in the future. Analysis is also important to determine where you are and what you might do next (i.e. it helps you assess the alternatives), and it helps you to assess the effectiveness of any action you take. If you are going to put resources into a particular marketing activity (advertising or promotion, for example) you need to know whether this will be a good use of funds.

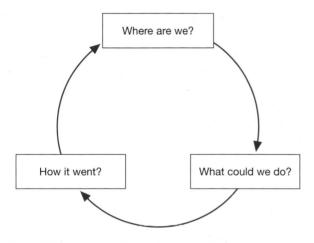

Figure 7.3 Market analysis and decision making

By undertaking a market analysis a firm should be able to identify existing market conditions. However, analysis will also be used to predict where the market is going in the future. Analysis should help identify possible opportunities and threats for the future. An opportunity is a future possible event that could benefit a business. A threat is a future possible event that could harm the business. Opportunities may include particular segments that are likely to grow fast; threats may be markets that are about to decline.

Methods of analysing trends

Managers are naturally interested in how markets will develop in the future as well as their present situation. It is important, therefore, for firms to look ahead when undertaking marketing. Marketing managers will be eager to forecast what sales in the market are going to be in the future. From this they can estimate the likely sales of their own products and produce their sales forecasts.

A firm's sales forecast sets out targets for overall sales and for particular products and services. It is a key element of a marketing plan.

To understand market trends managers might use one or more of the following methods of analysing trends.

Moving averages

If you look at the following sales data and plot the figures on a chart, you will see that the sales are quite erratic during the year. In June, for example, sales are relatively high, whereas in July they are lower.

However, although the sales clearly change from month to month, the overall trend is clearly upwards.

One way of plotting the underlying trend is to calculate the moving average. This looks at several periods at a time and averages out the data; by doing this, the effect of particularly high or low figures is reduced because an average has been taken.

For example, for a three-month moving average we average out the figures for January, February and March. Then we average out February, March and April; then March, April and May, and so on.

The three-month moving average highlights the underlying trend of the sales figures, as shown in Figure 7.5.

	sales £000		three-month moving average £000
January	9		
February	12	(9+12+15)/3	12
March	15	(12+15+15)/3	14
April	15	(15+15+18)/3	16
May	18	(15+18+21)/3	18
June	21	(18+21+19)/3	16
July	9	(21+9+18)/3	16
August	18	(9+18+21)/3	16
September	21	(18+21+24)/3	21
October	24	(21+24+12)/3	19
November	12	(24+12+24)/3	20
December	24		

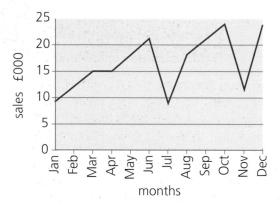

Figure 7.4 Sales

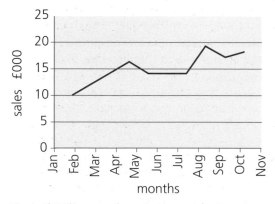

Figure 7.5 Three-month moving average

Extrapolation

To estimate the future sales in a market, managers may look back to identify trends that have occurred (using, for example, moving averages) and then, based on these, predict forwards. This is known as extrapolation. This technique is useful, provided the trends identified in the past continue into the future.

If, in fact, there has been a major shift in buying patterns (e.g. the timing of buying has changed or the economy has unexpectedly entered a recession) extrapolation could be misleading.

> **Key terms**
> **Extrapolation** involves identifying the underlying trend in past data and projecting this trend forwards. In Figure 7.7, for example, the underlying trend in sales figures is clearly upwards. If we assume this trend will continue we can project it forward and estimate future sales.
> **Correlation** occurs when there are apparent links between variables (e.g. promotional spending and sales).

sales

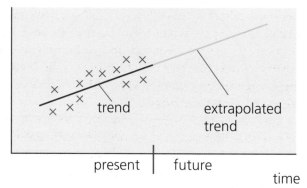

Figure 7.6 An extrapolated trend

Extrapolation is only likely to be effective if market conditions continue to develop in the future as they have in the past, i.e. extrapolation only works if past trends actually continue. The problem is that many markets are very dynamic and change rapidly. The market for cameras, for example, has seen rapid change in recent years with the arrival of digital cameras; in this situation extrapolation may be very misleading – examining the past may provide little indication of what is going to happen in the future. Sales can drop suddenly regardless of what has happened in the past, perhaps due to a recession, competitors launching a new product or a problem with production. In the 1990s farmers could hardly have predicted the collapse in the sales of beef due to the BSE crisis. In 2001 they could not have foreseen foot and mouth disease. Similarly, Coca-Cola could not have predicted the short-term drop in sales in 2000 when it had to take some of its products off the shelves temporarily due to a health scare. Few expected the UK recession of 2009.

Extrapolated figures must therefore be treated with caution – their reliability depends entirely on the extent to which the future will imitate the past.

Obviously firms can learn from past trends – retail sales are likely to increase in the run-up to Christmas, holidays in Spain are more likely to be popular in the summer, central heating is likely to be used more when the weather is colder and so on – but they must also look out for future changes in the market conditions. Rapid developments in technology, for example, can lead to major changes in terms of what we produce and how business is conducted, and this may make extrapolation more risky.

Correlation

Rather than using extrapolation, future market sales may be estimated using correlation. This process attempts to identify whether there is any correlation between different variables and the level of sales. Correlation occurs when there appears to be a link between two factors. For example, a firm might discover a correlation between its sales and the level of income in an economy – with higher income consumer sales might increase.

Correlation analysis examines data to see if any relationship appears to exist between different variables. This is important for marketing managers because, if they can identify the key factors which determine demand for their goods, and they can estimate what is happening to these factors (e.g. estimate income growth), they can estimate total market sales and then their likely sales.

In Figures 7.7 and 7.8 you can see examples of different types of correlation:

- 'Positive correlation' means that there is a direct link between the variables. An increase in advertising, for example, might lead to an increase in sales and vice versa. The sales of a product might be positively correlated with income levels and the number of customers in the market.

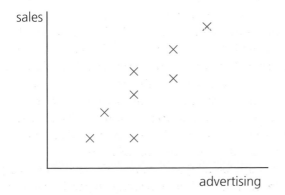

Figure 7.7 Positive correlation between advertising and sales

- A 'negative correlation' means that the two factors are inversely related; an increase in price, for example, is likely to lead to a fall in sales, so price and demand have a negative correlation.

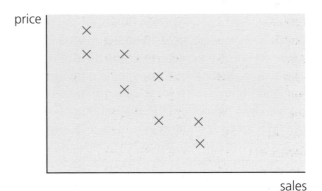

Figure 7.8 Negative correlation between price and sales

Business in Focus

Health service managers try to avoid bed crises by using weather reports to forecast when people will fall ill. The Meteorological Office has set up a unit using new technology to give doctors up to two weeks' notice of how many patients are likely to develop bronchitis, heart attacks and strokes. The service, which claimed to be the world's first, allows hospitals and surgeries to prepare for increases in demand using warnings generated by a supercomputer.

In the past the National Health Service has been caught out by sudden changes in the number of patients suffering respiratory and cardiovascular diseases. Meteorological Office experts say the timing was due almost entirely to changes in temperature and climatic conditions. According to a spokesperson, 'there is a very close link between weather conditions and illness. We can predict almost the day when large numbers of patients will seek treatment.'

More patients die in Britain from weather-related illnesses than almost any other country in western Europe. For every one degree fall in temperature, 1.37 per cent more people die; this is much higher than in other countries because the British are less well prepared; they do not dress warmly against the cold, their houses are less well heated or insulated and they take less exercise.

Source: *The Sunday Times*

Question:

1 Discuss other factors that are likely to influence demand for healthcare services.

It is important to note that correlation analysis simply identifies an apparent link between the two factors; it does not show cause and effect. For example, there is often a strong link between coffee drinkers and smokers; people who smoke often drink a lot of coffee as well. There is a link between the two but this does not mean that drinking coffee actually makes you smoke or vice versa. It may simply reflect a particular personality type. It is important to treat correlation figures with some caution, therefore. Just because sales figures and the amount of money spent on advertising expenditure are both increasing does not necessarily mean that the advertising is boosting sales. In many cases firms feel that if sales are higher they can afford to spend more on advertising, i.e. sales may determine advertising spending rather than vice versa. Alternatively, the increase in sales could be coincidental – it could be caused by factors other than advertising.

However, the more times the correlation appears to exist (e.g. if the firm has regularly advertised and at the same time sales have regularly increased), the more likely it is that managers will believe that a link does occur.

Other ways of estimating future sales

Using market research

Market research can be used to try to identify likely future trends rather than assuming they will be similar to the past. The value of this research depends on whether it is primary or secondary and the quality of the information. If a small sample is used, for example, the forecast is less likely to be accurate than if a larger sample had been used. Types of research might include test marketing (trying the product out in a given area) or surveys. A test market is a representative selection of consumers which the firm uses to try out a new product. Having seen the results in the test market the firm can estimate how the product might sell elsewhere and produce a sales forecast. By using a test market the firm can see customers' reactions before committing to a full-scale launch. If necessary, changes can still be made before the product is widely available. Many film companies, for example, show their films to a test audience before they go on general release, to assess the public's reaction.

Examiner's advice

In many of the case studies you are likely to face, a business will be making a major decision. In this type of situation large sums of money may be at stake and the future of the business may be at risk. It is possible but very unlikely that in this situation a decision will be made without some market analysis. You may question the way the analysis has been undertaken, but some information is likely to be better than none.

Key Issues

In marketing planning, as in all forms of planning, information is a vital resource. Getting good quality on time, at a reasonable cost and to the right people can make a difference to the competitiveness of a business. Amazon understands what its customers have looked at in the past, so it can recommend suitable books that might interest them in the future. Google can display adverts that link only to the search term you used, in the language you searched in. Banks can send you a cheque book before you run out of cheques. A hotel database can show that you prefer a ground floor room whenever you stay in their hotels. Tracking what customers do can help ensure marketing activities are tailor made to individual requirements. Looking for ways of gathering, maintaining and using good information is a key issue these days.

Key terms
Market research is the process of gathering, analysing and presenting data relevant to the marketing process.
Primary research uses data gathered for the first time.
Secondary research uses data that has been gathered previously (it uses the data for the second time).

The disadvantage of using test marketing is that competitors have an opportunity to see what you are planning to launch. This gives them time to develop a similar product and race you to launch first on a wide scale.

A test market may also give misleading results. This might be because the test market chosen is not representative or because competitors' actions lead to misleading results. For example, rivals might increase their promotional activities in the test market to reduce a firm's sales and lead it to believe that the new product will not do well.

Using your best guess

Managers could use their own experience or hire industry experts for their opinion of what is most likely to happen. This approach to forecasting is common if the rate of change in the market is great or if the firm is facing a new scenario and does not have past data to build on. In the Delphi technique, managers assemble a group of experts who are all asked individually for their views. These views are analysed and key areas extracted. These findings are circulated again to the experts for feedback.

The method of forecasting used by a firm will depend on the nature of the product and the market situation. When the National Lottery (now called Lotto) was launched in the UK, for example, Camelot (the organiser of the lottery) could have forecasted sales by looking at existing national lottery systems in other countries and tried to adjust this data to take account of the differences in culture and the precise nature of the system in the UK.

Camelot might also have used secondary research to identify gambling trends within the UK and primary research to identify customers' likely reaction to the lottery scheme. However, although the company probably used very sophisticated research techniques it is likely there was also an element of hunch in there too. After all, it was a completely new product within the UK and so there were no past data within this country to build on. Obviously once the lottery had been up and running for a few months the organisers were able to make better predictions of expected weekly sales because they were accumulating backdata and gaining a better insight into the market.

Forecasting

The benefits of forecasting

Inevitably a firm's external and internal conditions are likely to change and this can make it extremely difficult to estimate future sales. It depends in part how much good-quality data you have gathered and the rate of change in the environment. However, the fact that there are difficulties in forecasting does not necessarily make this a useless management tool. The simple process of forecasting makes managers think ahead and plan for different scenarios. This may help to ensure they are much better prepared for change than if they did not forecast at all.

Also, even though a forecast may not be exactly accurate it may give an indication of the direction in which sales are moving and some sense of the magnitude of future sales, which can help a firm's planning. Ultimately it may not matter much whether sales are 2,000,002 units or 2,000,020 units, but it makes a big difference whether they are 2 million or 4 million in terms of staffing, finance and production levels, i.e. provided the forecast is approximately right it can still be very useful even if it is not exactly correct.

Business in Focus

The flawed market research of new Coke

In 1985 the chairman of Coca-Cola announced, 'the best has been made even better'. After 99 years the Coca-Cola company decided to abandon its original formula and replace it with a sweeter version named 'New Coke'. Just three months later the company admitted it had made a mistake and brought back the old version under the name 'Coca-Cola Classic'!

Despite $4 million of research the company had clearly made a huge mistake. The background to Coca-Cola's decision to launch a new product was much slower growth in its sales in the 1970s, especially compared with Pepsi. Pepsi was also outperforming Coca-Cola in taste tests. The relatively poor performance was even more disappointing given that Coca-Cola was spending over $100 million more than Pepsi on advertising. The taste testing of the new recipe for Coca-Cola involved 191,000 people in more than 13 cities. Fifty-five per cent of people favoured New Coke over the old formula.

However, once the launch was announced the company was amazed by the negative response; at one point calls were coming in at a rate of 5,000 a day. People were most annoyed by the fact that Coca-Cola dared to change the formula of one of the USA's greatest assets.

What went wrong? Possibly one problem was that when undertaking the testing, customers did not know that choosing one cola would mean the other was removed, i.e. that if they chose a new flavour the old one would be withdrawn. Also, the symbolic value of Coca-Cola may have been overlooked.

Question:

1 Coca-Cola did extensive (and expensive) market research and yet still made a mistake. Does this mean that market research is a waste of time?

Business in Focus

The UK breakfast cereals market

- The market for breakfast cereals is well established in the UK. The vast majority of UK households buy cereals. This means the possibility for growth is limited.

- In recent years manufacturers have introduced premium products, which means the value of the market has grown faster than volume.

Table 7.1 UK retail sales of breakfast cereals, 2002–07

	000 tonnes	Index	£m	Index
2002	404	100	1,090	100
2003	409	101	1,117	102
2004	415	103	1,143	105
2005	419	104	1,169	107
2006	424	105	1,216	112
2007 (est)	432	107	1,280	117

Source: Mintel

It is also important to remember that sales forecasts can be updated. A firm does not have to make a forecast and leave it there. As conditions change and new information feeds in, the managers can update the forecast and adjust accordingly.

Gathering data

Many organisations are likely to have a great deal of data available to them. They may, for example, have details of customers' locations, their orders and the frequency of purchase. Part of developing a management information system is considering exactly what information needs gathering, how to collect it, how to analyse it and how to make the findings available to those who need it.

Gathering and analysing data has become a lot easier, faster and cheaper with developments in information technology. Store cards, such as Tesco Clubcard, enable the business to collect huge quantities of data on shoppers and their habits and to link this to the address of the card holder. Tesco can then build up a map of the UK and see how customers respond to different incentives and external changes such as more rain. This provides a detailed insight into UK shoppers which is invaluable to marketing decisions.

Managers can also use secondary sources of data, such as industry surveys produced by the media such as *The Financial Times* and the *Economist*. Secondary research is also available (for a fee!) from businesses such as Mintel (Market Intelligence – a market research company).

This does not mean that every business has all the information it needs at any moment, but there is a lot of data available at any time and managers need to be careful not to just gather more instead of thinking carefully about what they need. Think of applying to university – rushing to visit every university and get every prospectus is quite an inefficient and time-consuming way of going about things; much better to plan what you need and target key information.

Business in Focus

Mintel forecasts that sales of breakfast cereals between 2007 and 2012 will grow by 20 per cent by value. It arrives at this number by looking at underlying trends, such as:

- Eighty-seven per cent of households in the UK buy cold breakfast cereals. This means there are still 13 per cent of households that do not. Some of these are dieters who think that missing breakfast is a good way to lose weight. It may be possible to convince this group that eating breakfast is an important part of controlling your weight.
- The overall strategy should be to increase the frequency with which cereal is consumed and get consumers to buy premium brands. For example, they could increase the frequency by making it easier to eat on the move, and they could promote premium brands by stressing their organic nature or their healthy ingredients.
- The population is ageing; older consumers are more likely to have time to eat breakfast.
- The number of higher income earners is increasing and this should aid demand for premium products.

To produce its sales forecast, Mintel used correlations, market size data, and economic and demographic data. Using forward projections of these factors, a market size forecast is produced.

Key factors used were:

- the level of disposable income
- the changes in the number of high income earners
- the number of over 45s and families.

Table 7.2 Forecast UK retail sales of breakfast cereals, 2002–12

	000 tonnes	Index	£m	Index
2007 (est)	431	100	1,280	100
2008	430	100	1,322	103
2009	435	101	1,385	108
2010	437	101	1,430	112
2011	440	102	1,482	116
2012	442	103	1,536	120
% change 2002–07	7		17	
% change 2007–12	3		20	

The reliability of forecasts

Forecasts are most likely to be correct when:

- a trend has been extrapolated and the market conditions have continued as before
- a test market is used and is truly representative of the target population
- the forecast is made by experts (which may be the company's own sales forces) and they have good insight into the market and future trends
- the firm is forecasting for the near future – it is usually easier to estimate what sales will be next week rather than estimating sales in five years' time.

The importance of a sales forecast

A sales forecast acts as a goal against which a firm can measure its progress. It also drives many other decisions within the firm. For example:

- The production schedule will have to be closely linked to the sales forecasts to ensure the firm has the appropriate mix and number of products at the right time. Operations managers will need to know the likely pattern of demand to ensure there is sufficient capacity. As demand changes it may be that some products or services are withdrawn and resources can be switched into other areas of the business.
- The sales forecast will also influence the cash-flow forecast; only by knowing what sales are expected to be can the finance department estimate cash inflows. Having compared the expected inflows with expected cash outflows, the finance function can then decide if particular steps need to be taken, such as arranging an overdraft or loan facilities. The expected level of sales will also need to be know to estimate expected revenues and likely levels of profits. Break-even analysis highlights the likely profits at different levels of sales; the key

piece of information that is needed is what sales will actually be – this is what a sales forecast should tell you.

- Human resource decisions will also depend on the expected level of sales. Decisions about staffing levels and the allocation of staff to particular duties will inevitably be determined by the expected sales levels. Strong sales growth may require more recruitment, for example, whereas a drop in sales may require transfers or redundancies.

Key term
A **sales forecast** is an estimate of the volume or value of a firm's sales in the future.

The relationships between the sales forecast and the other functions are two way. A capacity constraint will limit total possible sales. A financial constraint may limit the amount of promotional activity that can be undertaken and limit potential sales.

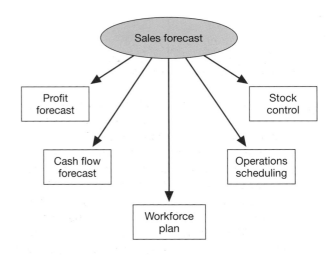

Figure 7.9 The relationship between sales forecasts and other functions

Why might forecasts be wrong?

Forecasts can only be predictions of the future. A variety of factors may make them wrong.

- **Customer buying behaviour changes suddenly.** For example customers may suddenly decide that a product is unsafe or unfashionable following a problem, such as a fault emerging with the product or ethical issues emerging regarding the way the product was produced. Changes in the weather might also change sales levels, along with other external factors such as economic change. Sales forecasts may therefore be wrong because of internal factors (e.g. poor quality control) or external factors (e.g. new entrants into the market).

- **The original market research was poor.** This may be because the sample was too small or was unrepresentative. Alternatively, it may be because the results were wrongly interpreted; this could be because the firm was in a rush to launch the product. In some cases the research may actually have been ignored – managers may have been certain that they knew best and gone ahead with the decision regardless of the findings of market research.

- **The experts were wrong.** Even the best-informed people can misread a situation and make mistakes – just look at the predictions of so-called experts before any horse race or football match, or the many different and often conflicting forecasts of growth in the economy that are often published in the papers.

Problems with analysing markets

There are always likely to be difficulties when analysing a market. For example:

- Data is likely to relate to the past; what you really want to know is what will happen next, but this is not as easy to do as analysing what has already happened.
- Data may not be in exactly the form you want; you want to know about the spending habits of 18 to 22 year olds but the secondary data focuses on 19 to 25 year olds, for example.
- It can take time to gather and analyse the data and then decide what action to take; by this time market conditions may have changed.

Information technology can enable data to be gathered, analysed and passed on more quickly, more cheaply and more effectively than in the past. This should enable better decision-making, better marketing decisions and less waste.

Business in Focus

In 2006 the marketing of TalkTalk's broadband services was so effective that demand created a 'customer service' nightmare. Charles Dunstone, the Chief Executive of the Carphone Warehouse which owns TalkTalk, admitted that the business was 'struggling to cope' with the more than 400,000 customers who signed up for high-speed internet access since the service launched in the first few months. Many could not get through to call-centre staff and had to wait weeks for their broadband connection.

Dunstone said resolving the customer service problems at TalkTalk was the group's 'number one issue'. Each day he held a daily 8.30 a.m. conference call of senior management in order to discuss 'What are we going to change and what happened with the changes we made yesterday?' The offer was so strong that the company simply did not anticipate the demand. He compared the broadband business to 'our own little sister, a little baby who's waking up every two hours and is disturbing the family and making our lives a nightmare. We must not lose sight of the fact that quite soon she will grow up into a beautiful young girl and we'll love her dearly.'

Dunstone said TalkTalk's biggest problem was a lack of call-centre capacity. The average caller had to wait three-and-a-half minutes for an answer, but many had to wait much longer. TalkTalk had 1,550 people working in its call centres at the time. It added another 400 when demand was higher than expected and aimed for 2,200 within six months. 'If it was a question of money, I'd spend it,' said Dunstone. 'You just can't do it overnight. There's no point putting people in until they're trained.'

Question:

1 To what extent were TalkTalk's problems due to poor sales forecasting?

Business in Focus

Marketing 'paralysed by facts'

Marketers used to struggle to get all the information they wanted about their customers. With the growth of the internet and other technological developments, the opposite is true: many marketing managers have so much data that 'analysis paralysis' has set in, according to Tim Calkins, a professor at the Kellogg School of Management in the US.

Calkins says that marketing managers need to become less preoccupied with gathering information and more focused on turning analysis into action. 'If all you do is know your customer really well, that doesn't help you.' For example, bad marketing plans can run for hundreds of pages without delivering a clear call to arms. They confuse strategy with tactics and overwhelm their audience with too much detailed information. Good plans realise they are tools for winning over colleagues to a desired course of action and have three or four memorable objectives linked closely to the company's profit goals.

Source: Adapted from A Jones in *The Financial Times*, 13 October 2008

Business in Focus

Customer relationships

Good customer relationships do not happen overnight; they rely on an effective communications strategy that is based on accurate data. Unfortunately, the data kept on customers is often out of date and can make a business appear out of date and out of touch with its customers, as well as being wasteful.

Organisations that invest in their data have a greater ability to send out targeted communications that are relevant, make customers feel valued, and encourage them to build a sense of loyalty to a brand.

Recent research conducted by Experian QAS revealed that 75 per cent of businesses across the globe thought they were losing business opportunities and revenue by not updating their databases. Despite recognising the value of their customer data, many organisations still do not have the structures in place to improve the quality of their data. Thirty-four per cent of organisations do not validate any of the information they collect on their customers and prospects, whether that be name and address, contact number, email address or bank account information.

The symptoms of a poor data strategy may not be immediately visible. It is only when other activities that rely on the data's accuracy, such as customer profiling, fail that a business starts to take note. Then it is often too late. Other less visible 'hidden costs' include wasted resources, lost productivity and ineffective marketing and communications spending, which can in turn hamper good customer relationships. Yet, damaged customer relationships are not the only symptom of poor contact data: businesses may also find themselves on the wrong side of the law.

Under new legislation, direct marketing companies that continue to 'make persistent and unwanted solicitations' will potentially face a maximum fine of £5,000 or, in some cases, up to two years in prison.

Direct marketing (i.e. direct contact with customers via mailings) to both existing customers and prospects has traditionally received bad press because of a perception that consumers are bombarded by 'junk mail' through untargeted and poorly managed marketing campaigns. While it would be unfair to judge everyone by this statement, marketers increasingly have to take the 'customer experience' and customer wishes into account. As people register with preference services and more information is available on individuals who pass away or move house, maintaining accurate data is no mean feat. This is supported by the Office of National Statistics, which claims that the average consumer database degrades by 14 per cent each year. With such a high level of database decay, it is crucial that marketers take more of a hands-on approach to their contact data. Contact data management needs to be part of a long-term data quality strategy with a defined timeline and targets for the capture, cleaning and suppression of data. It's not good enough to clean and suppress data once, occasionally or just before a specific marketing campaign. Data quality needs ongoing support and investment because we are not just talking about data, we are talking about customers.

Source: Adapted from Stuart Johnston in *The Financial Times*, 28 October 2008

Question:

1   Discuss the ways in which the use of information technology to manage customer relationships can benefit a business.

Use of information technology in analysing markets

Information technology refers to systems used to store, analyse, manipulate and exchange data. IT is increasingly becoming cheaper but more powerful, allowing organisations to analyse huge amounts of data relatively cheaply and relatively quickly. This should enable organisations to gain a better understanding of their customers. For example:

- They can analyse their till receipts to see the trends within their overall sales. How are sales of men's clothes at M&S doing compared with women's clothing compared with food?
- They can use their loyalty cards to link personal information on customers to their actual purchases; businesses can track exactly what different income groups, genders, postcodes and regions are buying.
- They can use software to help analyse data. For example, statistical packages can be used to identify correlations and then, based on future estimates of these factors, forecast sales. Databases can be used to store customer data, organise mailings and identify major clients more easily.

Summary

To make decisions about what marketing strategy to adopt, marketing managers should analyse their markets. This means identifying the state of the markets at the moment, changes that have happened and future possible changes. This is important in order to identify where and how to compete and to set targets. Target may be set in various ways, such as basing them on the past or using research. Market analysis is therefore an important aspect of developing a marketing strategy and plan.

Progress questions

1 What is meant by market analysis? (3 marks)
2 Explain two reasons why a business might want to analyse a market. (6 marks)
3 Explain two ways of measuring the size of a market. (4 marks)
4 Explain why producing a sales forecast is important to a business. (5 marks)
5 What is extrapolation? (3 marks)
6 Explain one way of producing a sales forecast, apart from extrapolation. (4 marks)
7 Explain how information technology can help a firm analyse a market (3 marks)
8 Explain two difficulties of forecasting sales. (6 marks)
9 What is a moving average? (2 marks)
10 Explain how developments in information technology have helped organisations undertake more effective marketing. (6 marks)

Analysis and evaluation questions

1 Analyse the possible benefits to a business such as Mars of undertaking market analysis. (8 marks)
2 Analyse the factors that might affect future sales of eggs in the UK. (8 marks)
3 Given that its markets are continually changing, to what extent is forecasting useful to a business such as Nestlé? (15 marks)

Web links

For information on Mars visit www.mars.com

For information on Nestle visit www.nestle.com

Case study

Key factors in the UK smoothies market:

- Sales of smoothies have increased by over 400 per cent between 2003 and 2007 and further fast growth is expected; having said this, growth is likely to be slower than in the past. Smoothies are relatively expensive and with the credit crunch demand may fall.
- With the growth in the market in recent years there have been many new entrants, including Tropicana.
- There has been increasingly heavy marketing expenditure to support the brands in the market. Television has started to play an increasingly important role in the promotion of smoothies, with Innocent, PJs, Ella's Kitchen and Tropicana all investing in TV campaigns.

Future trends in the market:

- The rate of future growth will, to a large extent, be dependent on economic conditions, although current levels of household penetration mean there is plenty of room for expansion.
- The challenge facing manufacturers is how to convince customers who are increasingly cost conscious that healthy eating should continue to be regarded as important and that smoothies can offer significant benefits, in terms of convenience and pleasure over alternatives such as fruit juices or fresh fruit, and are worth the price.
- Own-label products, fruit and fruit yogurt sales are likely to grow because they are relatively cheaper.
- In the US, made-to-order smoothies account for over 90 per cent of the market; this trend may develop in the UK.
- PJs is being repositioned as a low-price alternative, and discount own brands are likely to increase.

(40 marks, 60 minutes)

Questions

1 Explain why the growth of smoothies in the UK is likely to slow down. (5 marks)
2 Analyse the possible benefits to potential entrants to the UK smoothies market of undertaking a market analysis. (8 marks)

Table 7.3 **Forecast of volume and value of smoothies market, 2003–13**

	Million litres	**Index**	**Current prices £m**
2003	12	13	46
2004	13	14	53
2005	25	27	89
2006	57	62	178
2007	78	85	241
2008 (est)	92	100	282
2009 (fore)	104	113	317
2010 (proj)	107	116	328
2011 (proj)	114	124	351
2012 (proj)	124	135	384
2013 (proj)	136	147	422

3 Discuss the ways in which Innocent Drinks, a major UK smoothie manufacturer, might respond having analysed the data above. (12 marks)

4 To what extent are the sales of a business such as Innocent out of its control? (15 marks)

8 Selecting marketing strategies

A market analysis should enable a marketing manager to understand where the market is and where it is going. This should feed into developing a marketing plan.

In this chapter we examine:

- the meaning of marketing strategies
- the difference between low-cost and differentiation strategies
- the meaning and significance of market penetration strategies
- the meaning and significance of product development and market development strategies
- the meaning and significance of diversification.

Introduction to marketing strategies

Once a firm has undertaken market analysis it should have a good insight into the nature of its market and how it might develop in the future. Market analysis should provide information on the size of the market, the major firms competing within it and expected trends. Armed with this information, the firm can decide its objectives and determine the required strategy to achieve them.

Marketing objectives are quantifiable marketing targets; these may focus on the:

- level of sales
- composition of sales (e.g. the sales of one brand compared with another)
- timing of sales (e.g. in an attempt to smooth sales out over the year and remove seasonal patterns)
- brand image (e.g. positioning relative to competitors).

The marketing objective determines exactly what the firm is aiming to achieve in marketing terms. This will contribute to and be derived from the overall corporate objective. The marketing strategy is the plan a firm adopts to achieve its marketing objectives.

So, the marketing strategy is the long-term marketing plan aimed at achieving the marketing objectives. Imagine we want to increase sales by 50 per cent over the next five years. How can we do this?

1 We may decide to boost sales of our existing products. If we do this we could try to:
   - increase the amount existing customers buy when they purchase it (e.g. get them to spend more every time they visit our shops)
   - increase the number of customers (e.g. encourage people to switch to our shop)
   - increase the number of times they buy (e.g. more visits to the shop)
   - increase the amount they spend (e.g. get them to trade up to premium items).
2 Or we may decide to develop new products.

There are therefore many different ways of achieving an objective. Each strategy selected will have different implications in terms of the precise marketing activities being carried out.

Business in Focus

Barbie

Barbie has recently been experiencing increasing competition from Bratz dolls. To boost sales of Barbie, managers could target:

- those who buy Barbie already and try to get them to buy more
- those who used to buy Barbies but are older now, to try and get them to return to the dolls (e.g. adult collectors)
- those who do not buy Barbies but buy Bratz dolls; they could try to win over these customers
- those who do not buy dolls at all.

Each of these would be a different strategy to achieve the same objective of increasing sales.

Question:

1 Which of the above strategies would you recommend? Why?

Deciding on a marketing strategy

When deciding on a marketing strategy there are many issues to consider, such as:

- Where should the business compete and which segments should it target? For example, should the firm compete in a niche or try to compete head-on with the major players in a mass market? Should it compete in particular regions, in the UK as a whole or globally?
- What should it offer? For example, what product lines should it offer? How many different types of products should it offer? How similar should these be?
- How should it compete and position itself against competitors? For example, should the firm try to match competitors' offerings but sell them more cheaply (a low-cost strategy), or should it aim to differentiate itself and charge more (a differentiation strategy)?

Managers will make different decisions in answer to these questions.

- Lobbs, for example, is an exclusive shoemaker producing expensive made-to-measure shoes – this is a niche, differentiation strategy. Clarks competes much more in the mass market.
- Primark aims at the mass market via low prices; Karen Millen aims more for the expensive fashion market.
- The Ford Ka is for the younger driver (perhaps their first car); the Aston Martin DB7 is for the highly successful executive.
- Asda offers a range of foods aimed at the 'average' customer and seeks to maintain a lower price than competitors; this is a low-cost, mass-market strategy. Waitrose offers a more exclusive range of goods at a higher price, which is a differentiation strategy.
- The soft drink, Irn Bru, competes mainly in the UK; Coca-Cola is a global product. Sainsbury's focuses on the UK; Tesco is going global.

A firm's marketing strategy should aim to exploit its market opportunities and defend it against threats. It should naturally build on the firm's strengths and avoid entering market segments or offering products where its weaknesses will be exposed.

Figure 8.1 Forming a marketing strategy

Business in Focus

Unilever

Unilever is a large multinational business. Its mission is 'to add vitality to life. We meet everyday needs for nutrition, hygiene, and personal care with brands that help people feel good, look good and get more out of life.'

Its marketing strategy is now focused on what it calls 'power brands', i.e. key brands such as Dove and OMO that it wants to develop globally. These brand names will be extended to a wider range of products, but lesser-known brands have been or are being sold off. To achieve growth in the future Unilever is targeting emerging markets.

In these markets it has two strategies:

- to buy products for the first time
- to get customers to trade up.

What determines a firm's marketing strategy?

When considering a marketing strategy a firm's managers should consider the following:

- What is the firm trying to achieve, i.e. what are its marketing objectives? There is no point in cutting prices, for example, if the firm is trying to build an exclusive brand image. Similarly, there is little point diversifying if the firm's objective is to focus on its core products.
- What are the market opportunities? What market segments appear to be growing? Businesses will be unlikely to target declining markets or segments that are small relative to the investment needed to enter them and compete in them.
- What are the firm's strengths and key capabilities? What is it good at? Does it have any unique selling points (USPs)? Some businesses are good at innovating (e.g. W L Gore); others are good at extending the brand onto other products (e.g. Virgin); others are excellent at changing the price to match demand conditions (e.g. easyJet) – these key capabilities should influence the chosen strategy if a firm is to play to its strengths.
- What resources does the firm have? For example, what is its financial position? Will it be able to finance any plans for expansion, for example? Some firms have a good liquidity position and can finance growth internally. Others may be heavily in debt (highly geared) and therefore cannot easily borrow more, which might limit the marketing strategy.

The marketing strategy should therefore be firmly based on an effective SWOT analysis, which exam-

Figure 8.2 SWOT analysis as part of strategic planning

ines the **s**trengths, **w**eaknesses, **o**pportunities and **t**hreats facing a firm.

Analysing marketing strategies

There are several different ways of analysing the various marketing strategies. In this section we examine the Ansoff matrix, which examines strategies in terms of the products offered and the markets a business competes in, and Porter's model, which distinguishes between a low-cost and a differentiated strategy.

The Ansoff matrix and marketing strategies

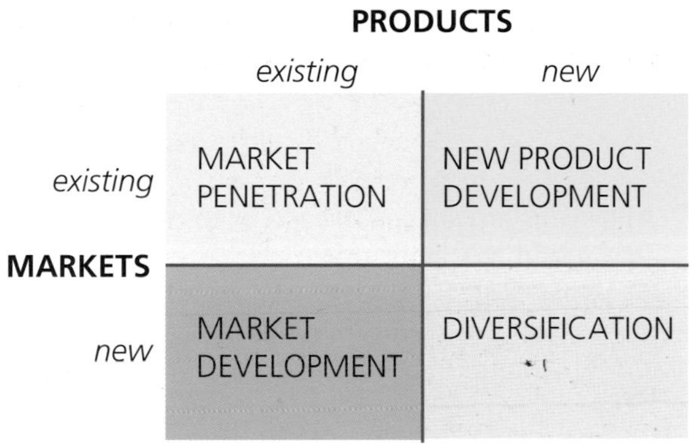

Figure 8.3 The Ansoff matrix

Market penetration

This strategy occurs when a firm tries to sell more of its existing products to its existing customers. To achieve more sales the firm may adjust elements of its marketing mix. For example, it may increase its spending on advertising or cut its price. This is a relatively low-risk strategy which can be implemented in the short term.

New product development

This strategy focuses on developing new products and offering these to existing clients. Firms operating in the soap, shampoo and laundry detergent markets, for example, are continually developing new brands for their customers. This strategy is risky in the sense that new products often fail. Only one in ten new products launched survives the first two years.

On the other hand, managers should have a relatively good understanding of the market and their customers' buying processes, and so they may feel confident that their offering will be successful despite the high failure rate of others.

Market development

This strategy occurs when a firm offers its existing products to a new market. For example, it may try and sell its products overseas or it may try and target new segments of its existing market. Many sportswear companies have successfully marketed their products as fashion items, for example. Chewing-gum companies have offered their product as an aid to giving up smoking, as something which helps prevent tooth decay and as a breath freshener; the product, therefore, has been offered to many new segments.

Diversification

This strategy involves offering new products to new markets. For example, a chocolate company may decide to diversify into the soft drinks market. This is a high-risk strategy because the firm may have only a very limited understanding of the production and marketing requirements of the new sector. If it is successful, however, it actually reduces the firm's risk because it is operating in two different markets. If sales decline in one market, demand may be sustained or even increase in another one.

Diversification is risky in the sense that managers are operating in an unfamiliar zone. Imagine that your senior managers at school decided to move the organisation into clothes retailing as well. Of course, it is possible they could run a business like this very well, but it would be completely different from running a school and they are likely to have real problems adjusting to the different circumstances. On the other hand, by operating in different markets managers are spreading the risks of demand falling; if demand falls in one market, sales in the other market may continue to sustain the business. Market penetration, by comparison, is safe in that managers are operating within their comfort zones; your school managers are still running the school but trying to make it bigger. The managers know the suppliers they want to work with, the competitors and market conditions. The danger is that the business is dependent on one market alone, which can make it vulnerable.

Key Issues

With growing international trade, looking for new markets overseas is becoming a key issue. Trade provides opportunities in terms of supply issues (e.g. where to produce products) and also demand (where to sell to). The emerging markets, such as China and India, are now the focus for many companies looking for fast growth. However, producers from these countries are also growing and are a threat to producers in more developed economies. Tata, the Indian conglomerate, has bought Corus, Jaguar and Landrover, and Lenovo, a Chinese company, has bought IBM's PC business.

Examiner's advice

Choosing where to compete (markets), what to compete with (products) and how to compete (positioning) are the key strategic decisions. Once these decisions are made the tactical decisions (i.e. the marketing mix) are more straightforward – if you know what to offer, whom to offer it to and what you are trying to achieve, the mix should follow logically. You start with the strategy and the mix follows from this.

Business in Focus

Mars 2008 corporate fact sheet

Mars, Incorporated is a family owned company, with six industry leading business units: Chocolate, Petcare, Food, Drinks, Symbioscience and, most recently, Wrigley Gum and Sugar (after it joined with Wrigley). Headquartered in McLean, Virginia, Mars, Incorporated operates in more than 79 countries. It is a recognised leader in confections with a wide range of product offerings including gum, mints, hard and chewy candies, lollipops and chocolate, Mars has approximately 65,000 associates worldwide and $28 billion in annual revenue.

The combination of Mars and Wrigley brings together two strong, international businesses and creates one of the world's leading confectionery companies. The portfolio spans a variety of categories such as confectionery items, main meals, side dishes, beverages, snack foods, frozen snacks, organic foods, pet foods, and now also includes Wrigley's vast portfolio of gum brands and sugar items.

Fast facts

- One of the world's largest family owned companies.
- Has over 317 sites world-wide, including 150 manufacturing facilities.
- Products are sold in more than 180 countries.
- Mars was founded in 1911, when Frank C. Mars started making and selling butter cream candies in Tacoma, Washington, U.S.A.
- Wrigley was founded in 1891, when William

Wrigley Jr. arrived in Chicago with $32 in his pocket and the ambition to start a business of his own.
- Mars' first blockbuster product was MILKY WAY®, invented by Frank and his son Forrest in 1923.
- In 1893, the Wrigley Company introduced Juicy Fruit® and Wrigley's Spearmint® gums, with Doublemint® making its debut in 1914.
- Mars established the Waltham Center for Pet Nutrition in 1965 in the U.K.

Mars brands

Chocolate M&M's® 3 Musketeers® Combos® Dove® Galaxy® Twix® Snickers® Mars® Milky Way® Kudos® Maltesers® Celebrations

Petcare
Pedigree® Whiskas® Cesar® My Dog® Sheba® Royal Canin® Kitekat® Frolic® Chappi® Winergy® Trill ® Waltham® Aquarian® Banfiels®

Food Uncle Ben's® Dolmio® Suzi-wan® Ebly® Masterfoods® Seeds of Change®

Drinks Flavia® Klix®

Mars Symbioscience focuses on innovative solutions that change the way we care for ourselves and the natural world, e.g. Mars Plantcare-Seramis®, Mars Sustainable Solutions

Wrigley gum and sugar
Starburst® Skittles® Lucas® Tunes® Lockets®
Kenman® Skwinkles® Rondo® Juicy Fruit® Orbit®
Altoids® Life Savers® Eclipse® Extra® Hubba
Bubba® Doublemint® Spearmint® Pim Pom® Sugus

Question:

1 Do you think the Mars strategy of operating in several different regional and product markets is a good one?

People in Business

Igor Ansoff

Igor Ansoff (1918–2002) is well known as a leading writer about business strategy. He lived in Russia until he was 18, then moved to America where he studied mechanical engineering and physics. He went on to work on strategic problem solving for NATO developing approaches. He later applied to business when he worked for Lockheed, an aerospace company. He went on to be the founding dean of the Graduate School of Management at Vanderbilt University in Nashville, Tennessee.

Ansoff is most famous for his 1965 book on strategy highlighting various processes and checklists he felt were required for managers to produce an effective strategy.

Low cost v differentiation

Another way of analysing marketing strategies was developed by Michael Porter in 1985. Porter distinguished between a low-cost and a differentiated strategy. A low-cost strategy focuses on providing similar benefits to competitors, but doing so at a lower price. This is the strategy adopted by companies such as Ryanair and Ikea. Managers of such organisations consistently look for ways of reducing costs to make their businesses leaner. They strip away costs to enable low prices. At Ikea, for example, you select your own furniture purchases, take them off the shelves on your own and take them to the tills. You then take them to your car – once again without help. You then assemble the furniture yourself at home. All of this means the labour costs of the business are reduced significantly. The stores themselves are out of town (reducing rents) and fairly basic in terms of design and layout (reducing decoration and maintenance costs).

To be successful with a low-cost strategy a firm must be able to deliver its products more cheaply than the competition. This may be achieved through economies of scale, special relations with suppliers or by removing some elements of the marketing mix. For example, a firm may try to make distribution more direct and so be able to avoid the middleman's profit margins; alternatively it may provide fewer additional services – some supermarkets, for example, compete on price by keeping overheads low and offering a more basic service and a more limited range of goods in the store itself.

The alternative approach is to differentiate your offering, i.e. to offer more benefits than your competitors. Provided the benefits are ones that customers want (e.g. better product range, a strong brand or high levels of customers service) this should enable you to charge a higher price. For example, Bang and Olufsen produces top of the range music systems for which it charges high prices because of the quality and design; Jo Malone produces expensive but distinctive fragrances. If a business is pursuing a differentiation strategy, the distribution of product or service is often exclusive; the firm is likely to want to keep a tight control over distribution to maintain an exclusive image. The products are often innovative and the firm may invest heavily in research and development. The promotional strategy is likely to emphasise the difference between this product and rivals' products.

Inevitably firms which do differentiate their offerings successfully may be imitated over time. Just look at the way in which Coca-Cola, Dyson and Pringles

Michael Porter

The concept of 'competitive advantage' was outlined by Michael Porter in 1985.

Porter argued that competitive advantage is a function of either providing comparable buyer value more efficiently than competitors (low cost), or performing activities at comparable cost but in unique ways that create more buyer value than competitors and, hence, command a premium price (differentiation).

You win either by being cheaper or by being different (which means being perceived by the customer as better or more relevant). There are no other ways. Behind Porter's idea was the value chain. This highlighted the different interrelated activities within a business and that lower costs or added value came from the activities within these elements and the way they link together.

In another book, called *Competitive Strategy*, Porter identified five factors that affect a company's profitability: buyer power, supplier power, rivalry, entry threat and substitute threat.

In a later book, *The Competitive Advantage of Nations*, Porter highlighted how the choice of location by an internationalising business might be a source of competitive advantage. He found that businesses from a particular industry often cluster together and this creates national advantages.

Further reading

Porter, M., 'How Competitive Forces Shape Strategy', *Harvard Business Review*, March–April 1979

Porter, M., *Competitive Strategy: Techniques for Analysing Industries and Competitors*, 2nd edn, Free Press, New York and London, 1998

Porter, M., *Competitive Advantage: Creating and Sustaining Superior Performance*, 2nd edn, Free Press, New York and London, 1998

Porter, M., *The Competitive Advantage of Nations*, 2nd edn, Macmillan Business, 1998

have been copied. At this point the firm will only be able to justify a higher price if it can continue to stress its role as the market leader or position itself effectively as the 'first of its kind' or the best. Dyson, for example, ran an advertising campaign emphasising that, 'if you want a Dyson you have to buy a Dyson', to highlight its uniqueness; Coca-Cola often stresses that it is the 'original'.

Remember that it is not just a question of choosing a marketing strategy – the business must be able to deliver it. If you choose a low-cost strategy, can the business actually get its costs down? Does it have a more efficient way of providing the service than others? Does it have better relations with suppliers? Is it avoiding some costs by missing out some stages (e.g. direct selling)? You cannot sustain low prices unless you somehow have lower costs so make sure this is feasible for the business. Similarly, if you offer a differentiated product, how is it differentiated? What value have you actually added? Is this sustainable or can it be imitated easily?

The worst of all worlds, according to Porter, is to get 'stuck in the middle', for example, offering a product with similar benefits to competitors at a higher price – this is a no win situation.

Why change a marketing strategy?

It may be necessary for a firm to change its marketing strategy for a number of reasons, such as:

- **It may have changed its marketing objectives** – rather than wanting more sales from a given product range managers may now seek to diversify (e.g. to spread risk).
- **Market conditions may have changed** – the slowing down of the rate of growth in the PC market has led firms like Microsoft to look for new markets to enter, such as computer games. The decline of the traditional film camera market has led Jessops to reconsider what it offers. Concerns over diet have made McDonald's think about how to make its offering seem healthier.
- **Competitors' actions** – a head-on attack from other firms may force an organisation to move into a new segment or to focus on particular areas of its business where it has a competitive advantage. The threat of supermarkets such as Wal-Mart attacking its core business led to Boots moving more into segments such as photography, optical and dental care.
- **The firm's own strengths** – as a firm develops its staff, technology and product range it may find that its strengths create new opportunities and this brings about a change in strategy.
- **Poor performance** – if your strategy is working well you are likely to keep on with it. If your strategy is failing you need to rethink. In 2008 Woolworth's went into administration. It had no

Business in Focus

Kellogg's

Kellogg's, the US breakfast cereal and snack maker, has said it will not change its marketing strategy to children despite concerns about obesity. Its managers said that the obesity issue was about calorie intake and exercise, not 'bad food'. Kellogg's plans to launch its Kashi brand of wholegrain cereals in the UK and will soon introduce a new version of All Bran to Japan.

The development illustrates how US food companies are responding to increased concern about the contribution of some processed foods to obesity, and marketing to children by highlighting efforts to develop healthier products.

The company's chief financial officer said: 'The whole issue with obesity is really calories in, calories out. There aren't any bad foods, it's all about balance.'

Concern about the role of food companies in contributing to obesity increased with a landmark lawsuit against McDonald's by New York teenagers who claimed the fast-food company played down the health effects of eating Chicken McNuggets. Kraft Foods has focused attention on the issue by voluntarily pledging to stop marketing in schools, advertising to children under 6 and shifting food promotions to the 6- to 11-year-old towards healthier items.

Asked whether Kellogg's would be changing its promotional strategy in the wake of Kraft's move, the company's chief executive said: 'We don't move based on what the competition does.'

Both Kellogg's and its main rival in the breakfast cereals, General Mills, have in the past year stepped up the introduction of cereals containing whole grains, including those aimed at children.

The chief executive said: 'Kids have been eating our products for decades. Offering options for what kids may want and what their mothers may want them to eat is certainly a thing we're interested in doing.' The vice-president in charge of marketing said: 'We think advertising cereal to kids is a very good thing to do and we'd like to do it more. Twenty-five per cent of kids walk out of the door in the morning having eaten nothing. We think that those kinds of problems are really much more significant and if we can put a dent in that, that would be very positive.'

Adapted from The Financial Times Limited 2008

Questions:

1 Should Kellogg's stop all advertising to children?
2 'We don't move based on the competition.' Is this a sensible strategy to pursue?

clear positioning in the market. Was it a sweets store? A music business? A children's clothes shop? It was not clear to a buyer why you would go there, and in each of its areas it faced attacks. In this situation (or hopefully before it happened) a business would reconsider its corporate and its marketing strategy.

A change in marketing strategy may be prompted by the possibility of exploiting an opportunity and/or to protect itself against threats or poor performance.

Business in Focus

Fads

In January 2008 the owner of home-decorating chain Fads warned of worsening conditions on the high street.

Strategic Retail, the owner of the home decorating chain, said trading conditions had 'deteriorated significantly' in the UK, with like-for-like sales dropping 6 per cent. The warning came after the collapse of rival MFI, which went into administration after it was unable to meet rent demands.

Strategic Retail has cancelled new stores and said it has changed its marketing strategy to reposition its stores and offer more discount products because demand for higher-end goods had dried up.

The company's losses widened to £855,000 from £26,000 in the same six months of last year. Revenues fell from £9.9 million to £8.9 million.

Strategic Retail said the impact of the dire economic climate was most acute at the group's larger, out-of-town Texstyle World stores in which trading is down by 11 per cent.

Questions:

1 Explain why Fads is considering changing its marketing strategy.
2 Discuss the factors that might determine the success of this change.

Overseas marketing strategy

One issue facing a firm when determining its marketing strategy is whether to focus purely on the domestic market or whether to expand overseas. Overseas expansion may be appealing for several reasons.

- **The domestic market is saturated.** Many markets in the UK are mature (e.g. the demand for microwaves, fridges and televisions). Companies can only generate replacement sales rather than many first-time buyers. In emerging economies such as Brazil, Russia, India and China the economies are growing much faster, creating opportunities for a rapid growth in sales.

- **The domestic market is subject to increasing competition or regulation.** Tesco cannot expand much more in the UK for fear of being blocked by the Competition Commission for having too big a market share. It has expanded overseas in countries such as South Korea, Thailand, the US and India to enable faster growth.

Business in Focus

Disneyland Paris

In 1992 Disney opened its holiday and recreation park 20 miles from the centre of Paris. It features two theme parks, an entertainment district and several Disney-owned hotels. By 2008 it had over 15 million visitors a year; however, at the start it encountered many problems.

These included:

- the very American menus on offer, which did not meet local tastes
- a ban on alcohol – not popular with the French who expected wine and beer on sale
- resistance from local politicians who felt that France was being invaded by American culture
- a policy by the American managers of demanding everyone spoke English at all meetings
- Disney's long list of regulations and limitations on the use of make-up, on whether facial hair, tattoos and jewellery were allowed; these policies were very unusual in France
- the name of the park; it began as Euro Disney Resort but is now Disneyland Paris.

Question:

1 Essentially, Disney encountered problems because it did not think enough about the local culture and customers. Why do you think these mistakes were made?

- **The benefits of particular market opportunities overseas**, for example a population of 1 billion in China that could be targeted.

Entering a foreign market does, of course, bring various problems. Perhaps most importantly the firm is unlikely to know the market as well as its domestic market. It will need to ensure it fully understands market conditions, including consumer buying behaviour, legal and economic factors and the possible response of the competition. Given that the market is not known as well, entering an overseas market can be seen as risky. This is why many firms entering overseas markets find a local partner to help them understand the market.

Business in Focus

Mothercare

Baby goods retailer Mothercare has experienced rapid growth in recent years, particularly in its overseas businesses. Although the UK outlook remained uncertain in 2008 and 2009 due to the recession, its sales overseas sustained the business. International sales grew 9 per cent in 2008. 'Only 0.5 per cent of the world's babies are born in the UK, that's 99.5 per cent outside the UK,' said the company's chief executive. The Middle East, Eastern Europe and Russia were among the company's best-performing markets. Mothercare currently has 24 stores in and around Moscow and plans to open another 40 stores in the next three years. It has outlined expansion plans for China and India too.

Question:

1 What problems do you think Mothercare might experience expanding outside of the UK?

Stages of entering an overseas market

Typically firms will begin to trade abroad by exporting. This means they will continue to focus on the domestic market but accept orders from abroad. This is a low-risk strategy – it simply involves a firm sending its products to other countries. It may at this stage do some marketing abroad, for example advertising its products or attending promotional events. If sales from abroad continue to grow the firm might

look for an agent or representative overseas. This means it has someone based abroad who knows its business well and understands local conditions. They will try and generate business for the firm and may be paid on commission. Again, the risk of this approach is relatively low.

A bigger commitment would be made when the firm finds a partner and form some type of joint venture or alliance. For example, it might collaborate on projects and share the profits. At this stage it is not just someone representing the firm, but someone who it is working with locally to generate more sales. For example, a drinks company might have an alliance with a local drinks company to share distribution costs or to gain access to some outlets. It might also franchise if that was appropriate. This would mean it was working with local partners who would better understand the political, legal, economic, social and technological issues in the overseas market.

If the market abroad looks as if it will prosper long term, a business might take over a foreign partner or invest itself to set up its own operations there. These two show real commitment and are major strategic decisions; this involves a high degree of risk and expenditure. Several UK businesses have found it difficult to succeed abroad because of the real differences in approach between regions.

Globalisation or localisation?

Once the decision has been made to enter an overseas market a firm must consider the extent to which it will adapt its offerings to local conditions. Is it possible to market the product in almost the same way in every country (as Gillette does with its razors), or will the marketing have to be adjusted for each market? If a firm pursues a global strategy this means it is adopting essentially the same marketing mix wherever it competes. A global marketing strategy has been adopted by firms in several markets such as jeans, soft drinks, cigarettes and luxury goods. A Rolex watch, for example, is positioned and marketed in a very similar way across the world.

One advantage of a global approach is that it offers marketing economies of scale, for example, the firm can develop one advertising campaign and one approach to packaging worldwide. However, this type of strategy does not respond to the requirements of different national markets and so the firm may lose sales to competitors who focus more on local needs. In markets such as food and drink and the media a firm may need to adapt significantly to local requirements. On the other hand, a more local approach may meet customer needs more precisely but may be more expensive and more complex to manage.

In reality, most companies will choose a balance between the global and local approach. Unilever, for example, has built several superbrands such as Dove. These are global brands selling in many different markets. They have the same name and logo everywhere. However, some adjustments are made in the way it is promoted to reflect local conditions. It calls itself a 'multi-local multinational'. This is reflected in its structure – it has brand managers who look after a brand globally and local country managers who look after all related issues in their areas. This approach is also called a 'think global, act local' strategy. Companies try to find economies of scale where they can by doing things the same but, where necessary, adjusting to the local market. McDonald's has the same basic brand image and approach everywhere but sells wine in France, does not sell pork in

Business in Focus

Diageo marketing overseas

Drinkers of whisky have tended to associate this drink with success. This is why the Johnnie Walker brand has used its image of a confident, successful striding man on its packaging for several years. However, people celebrate success in different ways and therefore Diageo, the group that owns the Johnnie Walker brand, has started to adjust its marketing. In China, for example, a recent advertising campaign has featured an extreme game of golf played by two young men culminating in shots taken from a golf cart, up a tree and even beneath the chin of a crocodile. Johnnie Walker has 34 per cent of the Chinese whisky market, making it the second most popular brand behind Pernod Ricard's Chivas Regal, which has a 50 per cent share. The market is certainly worth fighting for. According to the Scotch Whisky Association, whisky exports to China rose from £1.5 million in 2001 to £46 million last year. Not only are China's rapidly growing ranks of aspirational high earners eager to try upmarket international brands; the country's membership of the World Trade Organisation has also made scotch more widely available and affordable. Between 2001 and 2005, China cut import tariffs on spirits from 65 per cent to 10 per cent.

Diageo introduced its strategy for expanding in China two years ago, but understanding the complexities of a different regional market is not easy.

Chinese consumers drink whisky in a more diverse range of venues than western consumers, from traditional restaurants to trendy bars and nightclubs. Tastes and spending power vary greatly among Chinese consumers, depending on where they live. And Chinese drinkers have even found a new way to drink scotch – mixing it with iced green tea.

Diageo split the market into four consumer groups. 'The Chinese people are not monolithic,' said the managing director of Diageo China. 'The size of the market and the complex demographic composition leads to totally different consumption habits and patterns in different parts of China.'

The first, and most strategically important consumers for Diageo are 'guanxi men' – status-driven 35- to 45-year-olds for whom business entertaining plays a big role.

The second are 'strong independent women' aged 35 to 45.

The third group is 'upwardly mobiles' – 25- to 35-year-old men and women who want to be seen at the cutting edge.

The final group, the 'choice generation', are early twentysomethings who are eager to explore and experience something new.

Diageo has also constructed a framework of seasonal promotional activity built around important dates such as Chinese New Year and National Day.

A third strand to its strategy is event sponsorship. As a sponsor of the McLaren Formula 1 team, Diageo worked with different local authorities on initiatives to promote responsible drinking, culminating in last month's Chinese Grand Prix in Shanghai.

Diageo made the most of this by launching a digital marketing campaign that resulted in 11 million Chinese viewing its ad online in the week before the event.

Source: Adapted from Meg Carter, *Financial Times*, 14 November 2006

Question:

1 To what extent should companies like Diageo change their marketing strategies for different markets?

Muslim countries and adjusts the menu in different areas. Coca-Cola sells its main brands globally but has over 200 local brands that only sell in limited areas.

> **Key terms**
> **Globalisation** occurs when a business treats the world as one market and offers the same products to every country.
> **Localisation** occurs when a firm adapts what it offers to local market conditions.

Examiner's advice

When considering entering an overseas market, think about:

- the likely costs
- the likely risk
- the likely competition
- the understanding of the market
- the time frame
- the link with the firm's strengths and experience.

Assessing a marketing strategy

To assess a marketing strategy you should consider the following questions:

- Does it help the business to fulfil its marketing objectives (and therefore its corporate objectives) within the given time frame?
- Does it do this using the firm's resources and in a way which reflects the values of the brand and organisation?
- Is it sustainable, i.e. can you protect what you have achieved or is it easy for others to imitate, forcing you to move on before you can fully reap the gains of the strategy?

Summary

The marketing strategy is the long-term plan to fulfil the marketing objectives and ultimately the corporate objectives. This may be analysed using Ansoff's matrix, considering which products to offer and which markets to compete it. It may also be analysed using Porter's low-cost and differentiation strategies. The selection of the marketing strategy will depend on factors such as the external environment, the strengths of the business and competitors' actions.

Progress questions

1 What is a marketing strategy? (2 marks)

2 Outline the key features of the Ansoff matrix. (4 marks)

3 What is meant by market penetration? Give an example. (3 marks)

4 What is meant by market development? Give an example. (3 marks)

5 What is meant by market development? Give an example. (3 marks)

6 What is meant by new product development? Give an example. (3 marks)

7 What is meant by diversification? Give an example. (3 marks)

8 What is meant by a low-cost strategy (Porter)? Give an example. (3 marks)

9 What is meant by a differentiation strategy (Porter)? Give an example. (3 marks)

10 Explain two factors likely to influence a marketing strategy. (6 marks)

Analysis and evaluation questions

1 Analyse the factors likely to determine the marketing strategy of a new hotel business launched by Virgin. (8 marks)

2 To what extent is Mars' marketing strategy of diversifying into different product markets a good one? (15 marks)

3 Discuss the problems Primark might have moving from a low-cost strategy to a differentiation strategy. (15 marks)

Web link

For more information on Mars visit www.mars.com

Case study

Tesco, the UK's largest retailer, has chosen to open its first US store in the state of Arizona. The retailer, which is using Fresh & Easy as its brand name for its US venture, secured 20 sites in the Greater Phoenix area. Other outlets in Los Angeles and San Diego will open later this year. Tesco is targeting US grocers like 7-Eleven and locally run stores using a chain of convenience stores models. The Phoenix area was selected because of rapid growth in the region, Tesco said, predicting 2,500 jobs would be created by the first wave of openings.

'The Fresh & Easy Neighbourhood Market format is designed to draw customers back to their local neighbourhoods by offering high-quality, fresh and nutritious food at affordable prices,' said Tim Mason, head of Tesco in the US. 'Our company has enjoyed strong success in countries throughout Europe and Asia, and we are excited to bring that success to America.'

However, the US market is notoriously tough for UK businesses. Top retailers Sainsbury's and Marks & Spencer have failed to crack the tastes of the US consumer and both have withdrawn back across the Atlantic.

Tesco sees overseas investment as the key to corporate growth. It has 155 outlets in Thailand and has just opened its first store in Beijing. In the UK, further growth could well face investigation from the Competition Commission.

(40 marks, 60 minutes)

Questions

1 Explain why Tesco might want to expand overseas. (5 marks)
2 Analyse the factors Tesco might have taken into account when choosing Arizona as the location for its first store. (8 marks)
3 Discuss the factors likely to determine the success of Tesco's entry into the US market. (12 marks)
4 To what extent is entering overseas markets a better strategy for Tesco than market penetration in the UK? (15 marks)

9

Developing and implementing marketing plans

In this chapter we examine:
- the meaning of a marketing plan
- the components of a marketing plan
- the internal and external influences on a marketing plan
- issues in implementing a marketing plan.

Introduction to marketing plans

A marketing plan sets out in detail:

- the marketing objectives
- the marketing strategy
- the marketing budget
- the marketing activities.

A marketing plan should set out exactly what is going to be done when, who is responsible for each activity and what resources are needed for the activity. For example, imagine the strategy to launch a new product; the marketing plan would set out information such as:

- when the launch is
- what promotional activities will accompany the launch
- what activities need to be undertaken pre-launch
- how much can be spent on each activity
- who is responsible for the successful completion of each part of the plan.

So the plan is almost a checklist for managers to make sure they have thought through what needs to be done and to monitor the progress as activities are completed. The marketing plan also helps to integrate all the different elements of the business. It shows the human resources department when different staff will be needed. It shows finance what expenditure is going to happen when and when inflows might be expected. It shows operations when production is going to be required.

The benefits of a marketing plan

Marketing planning is useful for several reasons:

- By setting out in detail what it wants to achieve the firm should be in a better position to coordinate its activities.
- Managers can review the firm's progress by comparing the actual outcomes with the planned outcomes. If these are not the same it can analyse why these variances occurred and learn from this; this should then improve planning in the future.
- The process of planning is useful in itself because it forces managers to think ahead and consider what might happen and what they need to do to succeed. This should make success more likely.
- The plan should provide a sense of direction for all of those involved and help them to assess whether what they are doing is the right thing.

Many marketing decisions involve significant amounts of money and other resources. Managers will not want to commit such resources without a clear idea of how they are to be used and what is to be done at each stage. A plan of some form is therefore very desirable – without it there is likely to be a lack of coordination and direction.

However, getting the right plan means making sure that you have the right set of activities, that the strategy itself is right and that everyone delivers at each stage. The process of planning may itself have flaws and disadvantages.

The possible drawbacks of marketing planning include the following:

- It is possible for the plan to become out of date

because of changes in market conditions. In this case sticking to the plan can do more harm than good. Managers must be flexible and be prepared to review the plan regularly to check that it remains appropriate.

- It may take up valuable time and delay decision-making. The firm could spend so long planning that it actually misses out on opportunities.

To evaluate a marketing plan, managers, must consider several issues:

- Is it realistic? Can the firm actually achieve the goals that have been set?
- Does it help ensure that the strategy is achieved? To be successful a plan must obviously help the firm to achieve its overall goals.
- Is it affordable? Does the firm have the finance necessary for it to work?
- Does it fit with the firm's strengths?

The ultimate test of any plan is, of course, whether it actually works! To some extent this is in the hands of the firm, but it also depends on external factors. Even the most successful businessperson is usually willing to accept that luck played some part in his or her success. Succeeding when market conditions are against you is obviously more difficult than succeeding when the business climate is very favourable.

The marketing budget

A marketing budget is a quantifiable target which is set by a firm and which relates to its future marketing activities. It may involve a target level of sales for a particular product (a sales budget), or set out the amount a firm intends to spend to achieve its marketing objectives (an expenditure budget). The sales budgets may include targets for the absolute level of sales a firm would like to achieve, or for a desired level of market share; they may also include targets for particular regions or for particular types of customers or distribution channels. Marketing expenditure budgets, by comparison, set out the desired amount of spending on activities such as advertising, sales promotions, paying the salesforce, direct mailings and market research.

The size of the sales budgets is likely to depend on:

- **The level of sales a product has achieved in the past** – a firm may extrapolate a future sales target based on past trends.
- **The expenditure budget** – a firm may set a higher sales target if it is also intending to spend more on its marketing activities.
- **Market conditions** – actions by competitors and the state of the economy may affect the firm's expected level of sales.
- **Marketing objectives and strategy** – the target level of sales for a niche product is obviously likely to be lower than it is for a mass-market product.

The size of the marketing expenditure budget will depend on:

- **The firm's overall financial position** – the amount of money allocated to a particular function such as marketing will inevitably depend on what it has available to spend in total. In a successful year it may be easier to have a bigger budget than in an unsuccessful year. On this basis the marketing budget is likely to be lower when sales are lower and bigger when they are higher. This is often what actually happens within organisations, although in many ways this is not a particularly

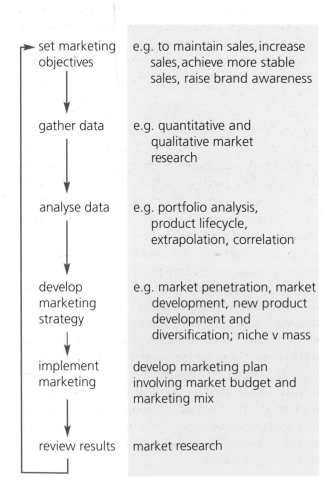

Figure 9.1 Scientific marketing model

sensible way to budget. In unsuccessful years the budget should arguably be higher (not lower) in order to improve the firm's sales, assuming of course that the firm can raise the funds needed to finance this. Unfortunately, though, the size of the budget does not just depend on what the firm would like it to be – it must depend on what the firm actually has available or what funds it can raise; as a result the budget may be lower at precisely the time when managers would like to increase it.

- **The firm's marketing objectives and strategy** – the amount of money allocated for marketing activities should clearly depend on what the firm is trying to achieve and the returns it expects to gain from its plans. When first launching a product, for example, the promotional budget is likely to be higher than it is for a more established product. Similarly, when first entering a new segment, spending on market research may be higher than in a 'normal' year.
- **The amount the firm expects to receive back** is also of critical importance: a firm is likely to be prepared to spend more on marketing a project with a high rate of return than on one which has a low expected rate of return.
- **Competitors** – a firm's budget is very likely to be affected by the amount its competitors are spending. If its competitors increase their spending on product development or promotion, for example, a firm may feel it necessary to increase its own expenditure to maintain its competitive position.

Of course, just because a firm has a large marketing budget does not mean that its marketing is necessarily more effective; the effectiveness of marketing activities will depend in part on the funds available, but it will also depend on whether the right activities have been chosen in the first place and how effectively they are being managed and implemented.

> **Key term**
> A **marketing budget** is a quantifiable target which is set by a firm and which relates to its future marketing activities.

How to set the marketing budget

The marketing budget should be set in consultation with those who will be responsible for undertaking the activities it involves. The amount of money to be spent on marketing overall, for example, should be agreed with the marketing manager. Given that the marketing manager is the person who will be held accountable if the budget is not hit, he or she should obviously be involved in deciding what the figure should be.

By involving the people who will actually have to achieve these financial targets the firm is more likely to gain their commitment. If, instead, people are simply told that they have to achieve certain targets without any prior discussion they are unlikely to feel much ownership of the budgets and as a result are unlikely to be committed to them. They may resent the fact they have not been involved in the process of setting the targets and consequently they may not be motivated to achieve them.

Furthermore, the process of discussing the targets may well highlight important issues which their superiors need to be aware of; the people who implement the policies are the ones who are most likely to know what is and what is not feasible and it therefore makes sense to make use of their expertise.

However, it is important not to get involved with prolonged negotiations over the size of a budget if this delays decision-making for too long. The process of budget setting can at times be quite slow and it is important to make sure it does not prevent managers from getting on with the job in hand, although targets do need to be set.

Also, superiors must be aware that subordinates may well try to set targets which suit themselves rather than the organisation. It is perfectly understandable, for example, if people exaggerate the likely costs of a project to make sure that they will be able to stay within their expenditure budgets. Similarly, employees may set relatively low sales targets to make sure they are easy to hit.

It is also important for managers to consider the size of the marketing budget in the context of the overall spending and income of the firm. Resources diverted towards marketing are clearly not available for use elsewhere and so there is an opportunity cost, which should be taken into account. As well as the overall size of the budget, managers must also consider the timing of the payments and earnings in relation to the firm's overall cash-flow position. A major marketing campaign, for example, may involve very heavy expenditure and managers must ensure this does not lead to liquidity problems.

Marketing planning and other functions

The marketing plan will have a direct effect on other functions within the firm. A reduction in price that increases sales, for example, may require investment in production equipment and greater recruitment or training. A decision to cease production of a particular brand may leave the firm with excess capacity, less revenue and the need to make redundancies.

At the same time, the marketing plan will also depend on these functions. For example, if a firm has a highly skilled workforce it may be able to build this into its promotional activities (think of football clubs and the way they promote their star players). The talents of the staff may also affect the design of the product – just think of the importance of designers in the software business. A firm's financial position is also important: a business with a strong financial position is more likely to be able to finance new product development than one with limited funds, for example. The production system can also make a difference: the capacity, the flexibility and the quality of the production will inevitably influence the nature of the marketing plan.

Implementing the marketing plan

Developing a marketing plan is one thing. Implementing it effectively is another. The implementation involves making sure you complete the activities as planned, on time, to budget and to the standards set. This means you must have set realistic targets and have had appropriate time set aside for activities. It also means you should regularly review progress at various stages throughout the

Business in Focus

Cains beer

Cains is using its Finest Lager to try to win over both real ale lovers and lager drinkers who are tired of the small number of heavily advertised lagers that dominate the UK. It is pitting its £500,000 marketing budget against the global drinks groups that regularly spend over £30 million on marketing their brand globally.

Figure 9.2 Cains beer

To build on the increasing interest in different drinks, Cains has a plan. This includes:

- **Marketing its local roots.** Cains is using its history in Liverpool to differentiate itself from rivals.
- **Quality.** Cains' Finest Lager uses superior ingredients: Maris Otter barley and top-quality Saaz hops. Cains' lager is cold matured for a full three months as opposed to the more typical 7 to 14 days of the mass-market brands.
- **Identity.** Unifying the portfolio through a single visual identity that echoes the architecture of Liverpool's Victorian heyday.
- **Innovation.** Using innovation and seasonal beers to create interest and encourage consumers to experiment. As well as the Finest Lager the company has launched a Fine Raisin Beer.

Source: Adapted from *The Financial Times*, 7 September 2005

Question:

1 Do you think that Cains is spending enough on marketing?

process. This means that at set times managers should consider whether they are on course relative to the plan. Have the right activities been completed on budget? If not, what is the impact of this on the remaining activities? If the plan has not been fulfilled managers must take corrective action to get it back on track.

Of course it may be that the environment has changed and that the plan itself is no longer viable. In this case it needs to be reviewed and adjusted. All decisions should be dynamic and should be constantly assessed. This is the feedback loop. The feedback enables managers to decide what to do next.

Problems of implementing a marketing plan therefore include:

- The external environment or marketing conditions may change, meaning the plan needs to be revised.
- Delays may occur, meaning some elements of the plan have to be reconsidered and amended or delayed as well. The launch of the website might be late due to technical problems or design conflicts, for example.

The fact that marketing plans do not always turn out as expected does not mean that planning itself is not useful. The fact you have a plan means you can see where you are relative to where you want to be and you can calculate how bad any unexpected changes are; without a plan you are operating in the dark.

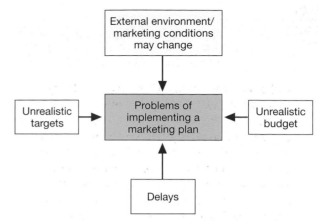

Figure 9.3 Problems of implementing a marketing plan

Marketing mix

The marketing mix is the combination of factors that influence a customer's decision about whether or not to buy a particular good or service. There are many different factors which make up the mix (think of all the things that influence your decision to buy the latest CD or computer game), but they are often categorised under the headings of:

- **price**, i.e. the amount the customer has to pay for the product, the payment terms and conditions (e.g. the length of time to pay)
- **promotion**, i.e. the way in which the firm communicates about the product (e.g. advertising, sales promotion, mailshots and via its salesforce)
- **place**, i.e. the way in which the product is distributed
- **product**, i.e. the actual good or service itself – its features, specifications, reliability and durability.

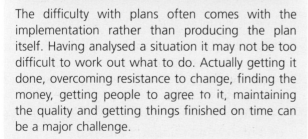

Key Issues

The difficulty with plans often comes with the implementation rather than producing the plan itself. Having analysed a situation it may not be too difficult to work out what to do. Actually getting it done, overcoming resistance to change, finding the money, getting people to agree to it, maintaining the quality and getting things finished on time can be a major challenge.

Examiner's advice

You will have studied the marketing mix at AS level. The focus there tended to be on individual elements of the mix and how these might be used to solve marketing problems. At A2 the focus is on the overall strategy; the strategy is supported by the marketing mix, i.e. a decision to enter an overseas market may need a different product, price and promotion. You need to think of the mix in the context of the overall strategy.

This approach to the marketing mix is known as the 4Ps model (Price, Promotion, Place and Product). Although quite a useful way of thinking of the mix, remember that there are in fact many different reasons why you might buy something which may not necessarily be under these headings. For example, you may be influenced by the people selling the product, past experiences at the store, whether you have to queue and the ease of payment. These different factors are all part of the marketing mix even though they do not fit under one of the 4Ps.

The role of the marketing mix is to implement the firm's marketing strategy. The strategy determines what goods and services are to be offered and in what markets. The mix determines how these products are presented to the customer.

The marketing mix should be linked directly to the strategy. If the strategy is to position the product at the upper end of the market this will influence the price charged, where the product is distributed, how the firm promotes the brand and the actual design of the product itself. A premium product, for example, is likely to have some form of USP, to be relatively highly priced and to be distributed through well-selected distribution channels. If, on the other hand, the firm repositions the product towards the lower end of the market the product is likely to be sold at a lower price, to have a more basic design and to be more widely distributed.

Figure 9.4 Relationship between company strategy and the marketing mix

The marketing mix will also be related to the particular stage a product is at in the product life cycle. In the introduction stage, for example, there is likely to be a great emphasis on promotion to launch the product; the promotion will tend to be informative at this stage to let customers know that the product exists.

Later on the promotional budget may be reduced and the emphasis is more likely to be persuasive.

> **Key terms**
> The **marketing mix** is the combination of factors that influence a customer's decision about whether or not to buy a particular good or service.

To be successful, all of the elements of the marketing mix must be well integrated. This means that the price, promotion, place and product should complement each other. Imagine that when you go shopping you find a well-known brand selling at a very low price in a cheap discount store – you may be suspicious that it is a fake because the price does not fit with the brand image. Similarly, a high-priced bottle of perfume will be unlikely to sell in a discount store because the elements do not fit together – the place is not complementing the price.

Summary

The marketing plan sets out in detail the marketing activities of the business. It will include the marketing objectives, strategy, tactics and budget. Producing a marketing plan is a useful exercise because it sets out in some detail what has to be done, when, by whom and involves a given budget. This should clarify for everyone within the marketing function and in other functions what they have to achieve at any moment and who is responsible for what.

Progress questions

1. What is a marketing plan? (2 marks)
2. State two items you might expect to be in a marketing plan. (2 marks)
3. What is meant by a marketing budget? (2 marks)
4. Explain two factors likely to influence the size of a marketing budget. (4 marks)
5. What is meant by the marketing mix? (3 marks)
6. Explain two factors that would influence a firm's marketing mix. (6 marks)
7. Explain two benefits to a business of producing a marketing plan. (6 marks)
8. Explain how the marketing plan is linked to the other functions of the business. (5 marks)

9 Explain two possible problems of implementing a marketing plan. (6 marks)

10 Explain two reasons why a business might change its marketing plan. (6 marks)

Analysis and evaluation questions

1 Analyse the possible links between the marketing plan for a new hotel chain launched by a major conglomerate and the other functions of the business. (8 marks)

2 Analyse the key elements of a marketing plan for a new headache cure launched by the pharmaceutical company GlaxoWellcome. (8 marks)

3 Discuss the factors likely to determine the size of the marketing budget of a business such as Marks & Spencer plc. (15 marks)

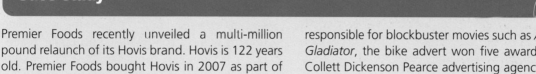

Case study

Premier Foods recently unveiled a multi-million pound relaunch of its Hovis brand. Hovis is 122 years old. Premier Foods bought Hovis in 2007 as part of its £1.34 billion purchase of RHM. It hopes this new campaign will revive sales and revive the fortunes of a group that has been under severe pressure with heavy debt after two major takeovers.

The relaunch attempts to restore an emotional connection between shoppers and Hovis by highlighting the company's long tradition and linking it to Britishness. The campaign will also highlight the 'healthy' properties of the bread that were a large part of its appeal when it was first made in 1886. The relaunch includes the return of the 'little brown loaf', a 400 gram unsliced loaf with the Hovis name baked into the side, familiar to generations of shoppers. In addition to its symbolic value, the loaf is ideal for smaller households, a growing market where Premier has lost sales to its rivals. Premier is also spending £10 million a year on cutting out additives and improving the quality of ingredients, while the bakeries have had a £5 million upgrade so that they can, for instance, lengthen the baking time to improve the flavour. This has already led to the success of a new 'softest ever' white loaf which has been gaining market share. New packaging also standardises the logo, and with a partially clear wrapper, shoppers can see the bread inside.

Hovis has a £13 million marketing budget. Millions have already been spent on making an advert which was first aired during Coronation Street and makes a deliberate reference to the 'Boy-on-the-Bike' Hovis commercial that was aired 35 years ago. In that advert, still remembered by many viewers, a lad pushes an old-fashioned baker's bike up a steep cobbled hill, to the strains of Dvorak's *New World* symphony. Directed by Ridley Scott, who was later responsible for blockbuster movies such as *Alien* and *Gladiator*, the bike advert won five awards for the Collett Dickenson Pearce advertising agency. At 122 seconds – one second for each year of the life of the brand – the new advert is an exceptionally long by TV standards. The narrative follows a boy from 1886 buying a Hovis loaf then running home through seven scenes from British history. The filming, in Liverpool, required 762 extras, including 15 Hovis employees, and shows World War I soldiers marching, suffragettes demanding the vote, bombsites, celebratory street parties and the miners' strike. *Coronation Street* regularly heads the lists of most-watched TV programmes, with audiences of around 10 million, so is an expensive programme during which to advertise. Premier has secured extra space on supermarket shelves in anticipation of strong demand. Also, although the group has closed and sold several factories in the past few months, it has kept one surplus bakery mothballed ready to meet demand.

Source: Adapted from *The Financial Times,* 7 September 2008

© The Financial Times Limited 2008

(40 marks, 60 minutes)

Questions

1 Explain two other forms of promotion Premier might use for Hovis, apart from advertising. (5 marks)

2 Analyse the factors Premier might have considered when deciding where and when to advertise Hovis. (8 marks)

3 Discuss the factors that might have determined the size of the marketing budget for Hovis. (12 marks)

4 To what extent will a large marketing budget guarantee the success of Hovis? (15 marks)

One step further: the seven Ps

All of us know the four Ps of the marketing mix very well, but you can always extend this to the seven Ps. The four Ps framework was developed by E Jerome McCarthy in 1965. He originally defined the marketing mix as 'a combination of all the factors at a marketing manager's command to satisfy the target market'. He later revised this to 'the controllable variables that an organisation can coordinate to satisfy the target market' (McCarthy and Perreault, 1987). McCarthy stressed the importance of analysing the mix in relation to the target market – something you should think about in exams. 'The marketing mix is not a standalone model … The focus has to be on the target market, otherwise the mix cannot succeed.' Since McCarthy there has been much debate about value of the 4Ps model. Some writers, like Booms and Bitner (1981), have sought to extend the list, in their case to seven Ps.

They add:

- **People** – this includes employees and suppliers. These communities are all involved in the marketing relationship and can affect the overall offering of the business. Well-trained, well-informed staff, for example, are likely to influence the customer experience.
- **Physical evidence** – these are the tangible aspects linked to the delivery of the product. For example, the store layout, the design and table layout of a restaurant or the fixtures and fittings of a pub; again, all of which contribute to the customer experience.
- **Process** – these are the elements of the customer buying process (e.g. the use of barcodes, scanning equipment and self-service tills, the queuing system and the payment methods) which can either make purchasing easy or unappealing. If you have ever had to wade through pages of documentation to organise insurance when you buy a PC you can appreciate how the process can lose customer goodwill.

So, when analysing the marketing mix do not feel you have to restrict yourself to the four Ps – there are many factors that influence your decision to buy!

Section 3: Operational strategies

At AS we focused on how managers solve operations problems or exploit operations opportunities. The emphasis was on short-term tactical decisions and involved topics such as:
- choosing suppliers
- managing quality.

At A2 the emphasis is more on long-term strategic issues such as:
- changing the scale of the business
- relocating the business
- introducing leaner operations methods.

We are particularly interested in how these operational decisions fit within the overall strategy of the business. While this is new material you will still be able to bring in your AS understanding. Successfully meeting quality targets, for example, is an important element of any operations strategy, and the effectiveness of an operation's plan will be measured in terms of unit costs, productivity and waste.

10 Understanding operational objectives

In this chapter we consider:
- the meaning of operations management
- operations objectives and their link with corporate objectives
- the internal and external influences on operations objectives.

Introduction to operations management

Operations management is the planning, organising, coordination and controlling of activities involved in the production of a firm's product or service. It is the management of the whole process that transforms inputs into outputs and adds value.

Operations management will include decisions regarding the following:

- **Where to produce.** What is the best location for the business? In the case of manufacturing this may be primarily driven by costs; in the case of retail it may be influenced more heavily by where customers are based.
- **What production facilities are needed.** What is the best scale of production? How many rooms should our hotel have? How many planes will our airline need? What capacity will our database need for our insurance business? How large should our production plant be?

- **What production methods should be adopted.** What is the best method of production? What is the best way of combining the firm's resources? How should the production be organised? How should the store or production plant be laid out? If we are a restaurant chain, will we have a standardised menu in every store or make each meal to customers' requirements? Will we have food pre-prepared?
- **Where to purchase supplies from.** Should we always try to have two suppliers for everything we buy, just in case one fails? How much stock do we need to hold to meet production and sales demands? Should we buy from local suppliers wherever we can? Should we take into account the way in which our suppliers produce (e.g. their environmental record)?

Examiner's advice

Operations is one function of a business. The operations activities will be determined by the overall strategy of the business and by the other functions. When considering what operations should or could do, do not forget the constraints of the other functions as well the corporate objectives.

Types of operations systems

There are, of course, many different types of production process – everything from an artist producing a few paintings a year to a bottling company turning out many thousands of bottles every day. These systems can be categorised in a number of ways, including:

- **Volume**: high-volume production includes bars of chocolate and soft drinks; low-volume production includes an architect and landscape gardener.
- **Variety**: high-variety operations include a tailor and a personal financial adviser who are capable of offering a wide range of products; low-variety operations include fast-food restaurants, which turn out a relatively limited variety of products.
- **Variation in demand**: products such as bakeries have relatively low fluctuations in demand; by comparison, the emergency services, such as the ambulance service, have a big variation in demand throughout the week.

- **Visibility**: this refers to the extent to which a business deals directly with its final customers. A manufacturing business has low visibility – it produces and sells to intermediaries who sell to the final customer; a hairdresser and an accountant have high visibility – they deal directly with their customers.

Types of operations processes

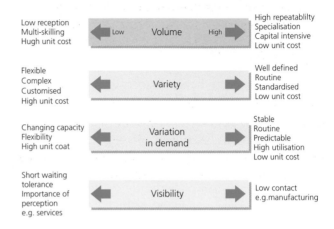

Figure 10.1 The 4 Vs of operations

Operational objectives

An objective is a target. A functional objective sets out what the business wants to achieve in a given functional area (e.g. marketing, operations, finance and human resource management).

Operations objectives might include:

- **Volume targets**, i.e. ensuring that the firm can produce the quantities demanded by customers at the time they want them without running out or having extensive queues.
- **Quality targets**, i.e. achieving an appropriate level of service and quality. For example, serving you within a given time in a restaurant, ensuring you are not waiting in a queue for longer than a certain time, ensuring that products are delivered to you in a certain time.
- **Efficiency targets**, for example producing products within a given time frame and ensuring the production is carried out as cost effectively as possible.
- **Environmental targets**, i.e. ensuring that operations are not excessively harmful to the environment. Targets might include reducing waste and pollution levels.
- **Innovation targets**, i.e. ensuring the products are

as up to date as they need to be, for example, perhaps they provide new benefits or are delivered in an innovative way (e.g. films online, making your own calendar online, online greetings cards).

- **Ensuring that your products are reliable and dependable**, so you do what you say and do not let customers down.
- **Ensuring the production system is as flexible as it needs to be**, for example in terms of the range of products that need to be provided.
- **Producing ethically**, for example ensuring that suppliers do not use child labour and that they are paid fairly.

Obviously achieving these different objectives simultaneously may be difficult (e.g. if you raise the quality criteria this may lead to an increase in costs). Adopting flow production techniques may lead to lower unit costs but reduces the amount of flexibility the firm has in terms of variety of products produced.

In an effort to boost productivity, the firm may demand much greater effort from workers, resulting in lower-quality products as work is rushed. The impact of any given operations target on other targets must be considered, therefore. An effort to reduce waiting times in doctors' surgeries may lead to patients being seen very quickly but the quality of advice may suffer.

Operations managers must also set targets in conjunction with other functions, such as marketing and finance (because these will affect what is desirable and attainable), they must determine the priorities and set appropriate operations targets.

> **Key terms**
> **Operations objectives** are targets set for the operations function, such as output levels or unit costs.
> **Flow production** occurs when items move continuously from one stage of the production process to another (e.g. a float glass process which operates continuously 24 hours a day).

Business in Focus

Starbucks

One hundred per cent of Starbucks espresso based coffee (including cappuccino and caffe latte) is going to be Fairtrade Certified; this will make Starbucks the largest purchaser of Fairtrade Certified coffee in the world. It will buy around 40 million pounds (volume) of fair trade coffee in 2009, leading to greater rewards for the community and small farmer organisations in countries such as Ethiopia and Rwanda.

The executive director of the Fairtrade Foundation UK said, 'The partnership between Fairtrade and Starbucks is good news for farmers, good news for coffee lovers and a wake up call to the wider coffee industry. The public has taken Fairtrade to its heart, and so we're delighted that they will soon be able to get 100 per cent Fairtrade Certified espresso drinks in Starbucks, from high streets to train stations and workplaces. Farmers need Fairtrade now more than ever, and even though these are difficult economic times, people across the country are staying loyal to their ethical values and to Fairtrade. We commend Starbucks for showing such visionary leadership in responding both to farmers' needs and consumers' interests.'

About the FAIRTRADE Mark and Fairtrade Foundation

The FAIRTRADE Mark is a certification mark and a registered trademark of Fairtrade Labelling Organisations International (FLO), of which the Fairtrade Foundation is the UK member. This independent consumer label appears on products as a guarantee that disadvantaged producers are getting a better deal. Today, more than 7 million people – farmers, workers and their families – across 59 developing countries benefit from the international Fairtrade system. By doubling its purchases of Fairtrade Certified coffee globally, Starbucks will help directly improve the lives of more than 100,000 farming families in developing countries across Latin America, Asia-Pacific and Africa and support programmes and projects like educational scholarships, medical clinics, basic infrastructure enhancements and quality improvement initiatives.

Question:

1 Discuss the possible benefits to Starbucks of buying only Fairtrade Certified coffee.

Figure 10.2 Typical operations objectives

The effectiveness of operations management may be measured using indicators such as:

- **Productivity**, for example the output per person, per factory or per machine. In a retail environment this may be measured by sales per employee or sales per square metre.
- **Unit costs**, i.e. the cost to produce one unit. The more efficient the process is the lower the unit cost will be.
- **The number of defects**, i.e. what percentage of the units produced or services completed is faulty. How many goods are returned? How many bills to clients are inaccurate? What is the level of customer satisfaction or dissatisfaction?
- **The speed of production**. Are items delivered on time? How fast is delivery relative to our rivals'?
- **The flexibility of production**, for example, how many different pack sizes of cereal can we produce? How many different A level subjects can our school offer?
- **The amount of waste generated**. Organisations will be trying to reduce the amount of products thrown away.
- **The amount of energy used**. To be more environmentally friendly and save costs, businesses will try to reduce energy usage.

Effective operations management should lead to better-quality products being produced more cheaply. Ineffective operations management, by comparison, is characterised by poor-quality products, delayed production and a failure to hit production targets.

Business in Focus

Shell

The multinational energy business, Shell, measures its performance using a number of different indicators. As well as measuring its financial position, such as its profits, it also considers its impact on stakeholders such as employees and society in general. Indicators of its operational performance include:

- CO_2 emissions
- sulphur dioxide, nitrogen oxide and methane emissions
- oil spills
- fresh water use
- waste
- fatal accidents
- occupational illness
- percentage of staff with access to staff forums (where their views can be represented)
- gender diversity.

Question:

1 Why do you think Shell is interested in measuring these indicators as well as profit?

The most appropriate measures of effectiveness depend on the nature of the business. An airline might measure the proportion of flights that take off and land on time. A call centre might measure how many calls are taken per day and how long it takes to answer them. A school might measure its absolute exam results or the value it has added to students' performance.

Key Issues

Many people like the idea of studying marketing because it sounds exciting and focuses on understanding the customers. However, operations lies at the heart of a business. Operations actually delivers the product, and most of us end up working in operations – we are the teachers, the accountants, the production line staff, the retail assistants, the doctors or the designers; we produce the products. The vast majority of the costs of a business are to do with the operations and that is why running our leisure centre, our hotel, our school or our cinema chain efficiently and effectively is so important.

Business in Focus

Marks & Spencer

In 2007 Marks & Spencer announced that it was to spend £200 million over five years on a wide-ranging 'eco-plan'. The plan aims to 'change beyond recognition' the way M&S operates. Initiatives within the 100-point plan include transforming the 460-strong chain into a carbon neutral operation; banning group waste from landfill dumps; using unsold out-of-date food as a source of recyclable energy and making polyester clothing from recycled plastic bottles.

'If you believe that all of us are going to have to espouse this green issue – whether it is climate, waste or whatever else – then there is no alternative,' said M&S chief executive Stuart Rose. 'And I also believe this is another way of differentiating ourselves – rather than just going down the normal bog-standard supermarket tactic of all pretending we're reducing prices by £70 million.'

Marks & Spencer calls its approach 'Plan A – because there is no Plan B'. It aims to reduce its environmental impact in all areas of the business, for example to:

- reduce the effect of its stores and delivery vehicles
- reduce the amount of packaging
- reduce the amount of energy, water and waste
- reduce ozone depleting HCFC gases with less harmful HFCs in their refrigerators
- source supplies from sustainable sources.

Question:

1 Should other retailers follow the Marks & Spencer approach?

Business in Focus

Ryanair

Operations decisions, like all business decisions, will need to be regularly reviewed as conditions change. This may lead to changes in targets and approach. In recent years, for example, many manufacturers have switched production to China because it is cheaper. However, as China's standard of living increases wages may rise and manufacturers may start to look elsewhere for production bases. Location decisions may change. Over time new production possibilities may also become possible. With ongoing improvements in technology, for example, much greater flexibility is now available even when mass-production techniques are being used; car factories can now produce in huge volumes but adapt each car for the requirements of the buyer.

Key terms

Productivity measures outputs in relation to inputs. Labour productivity, for example, measures the output per person.

Unit cost measures the cost of producing one unit; it is also called average cost.

Operations management and corporate objectives

The precise nature and priorities of operations management activities will depend on the overall corporate objectives and strategy. If the corporate objective is to double the size of the business then operations may have to increase capacity. If the corporate objective is to diversify then operations managers must be prepared to increase the flexibility of the business's production capabilities. If the focus is on profitability then operations may look to deliver efficiency gains; this may be through adopting different production methods or relocating production.

The operations objectives will therefore be directly related to and derived from the corporate objectives.

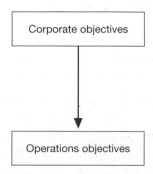

Figure 10.3 Corporate objectives leading to operations objectives

The corporate objective of Costco, for example, is to position itself as a low-cost retailer. To achieve this, the operations managers must:

- choose retail locations out of the city centre which are cheaper than central locations
- invest minimal amounts on display (large stacks of goods are displayed in huge quantities)
- buy in bulk to get better deals
- have a relatively low number of sales and administrative staff.

Figure 10.4 Costco

Figure 10.5 Pret A Manger

The food store, Pret A Manger, by comparison, stresses the freshness and quality of its foods and service. This requires:

- good-quality suppliers of fresh foods
- regular orders from suppliers so that the business is not left with high stocks at the end of each day (i.e. frequent small deliveries)
- well-trained staff who can produce good-quality sandwiches quickly.

Operations management and other functions

To achieve their goals, operations managers must work closely with the other functions of the business. For example, the marketing function must specify exactly what customers want and what they are willing to pay; marketing will also help determine what needs to be produced when. Meanwhile the finance function will specify what equipment and processes can be afforded and the level of costs that the operations function must achieve. The human resources function will also need to work with operations to know what numbers of employees are required, what skills they must have and what training requirements there are.

The relationships between operations and the other functions are two way. For example, the marketing department may set out what customers want but the production department must specify what it can actually produce. Similarly, the desired level of operations might determine human resource requirements but the numbers and skills of staff available also determine what it is feasible to produce.

Key Issues

A successful business is a combination on effective, efficient, interrelated activities. The operations function is crucial because it delivers the actual service or good. However, marketing has to assess and determine how to fulfil demand. Finance is needed to enable the business to undertake the activities, and human resource management is there to maximise the human input into the process. Corporate success comes through the combined actions of the different functions.

Influences on operational objectives

As we have seen the nature of the operational objectives that are set will depend on the corporate mission and the other functions of the business.

The corporate mission

This sets out the corporate values, objectives and strategy. Innocent Drinks will insist on production without preservatives. Lego prides itself on high quality, so Lego bricks must be made within 0.002 mm of each other in terms of their length, width or depth. Marks & Spencer has set several environmental targets and so operations must fulfil these by reducing waste and saving energy. Decisions by senior managers about the positioning of the product and how it will compete therefore have implications for operations managers and their objectives.

The other functions of the business

The targets for the volume, variety and quality of a product or service will depend on what marketing identifies as the key requirements to being competitive, and what marketing has promised customers. Finance may set required profit margins, which will influence the cost per unit operations must achieve.

The operations objectives will also be influenced by:

- **Demand** – the volume targets (i.e. how many to make) will obviously depend on the demand for the product. Demand will also influence the type of products produced in terms of their features, durability and reliability.
- **Past experience** – this may provide an indication of what is feasible and realistic given the resources of the business.
- **Competitors' actions** – if competitors are increasing the quality of their service you may have to do the same to match or surpass their offering. If your rivals can cut prices because of greater efficiencies you may have to look for ways of doing the same. Can you deliver as quickly and reliably as your competitors? Can you respond to individual customer requirements as easily?
- **Customer expectations** – customers are increasingly interested in where the materials used in the operations process are from. Are they sourced locally, supporting the local community? Are they ethically sourced (e.g. is it a Fairtrade product)? Is

the production process environmentally friendly? Organisations need to respond to such pressures, for example through using recycled paper, less packaging or more energy-efficient processes.

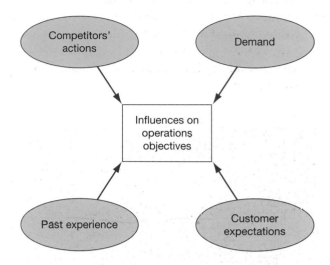

Figure 10.6 Influences on operations objectives

Toyota

In R&D (research and development), Toyota is continuing to focus its efforts in the three key areas of the environment, safety and energy. In particular, Toyota has positioned hybrid technologies as core technologies that can contribute to resolving environmental issues and it continues to undertake development with a commitment to leading the advancement of such technologies. Toyota is enhancing its hybrid vehicle line-up and also engaging in research and development for plug-in hybrids. Also, recently, as part of its response to energy diversification, Toyota launched in Brazil a flex fuel vehicle (a vehicle capable of running on fuel that consists of any percentage of ethanol mixed with gasoline, or on ethanol alone) that can run on 100 per cent bio-ethanol fuel.

Question:

1 Why do you think Toyota is focusing on the three key areas shown above?

easing efficiency

The efficiency of a firm is usually measured by the cost per unit. The more efficient a business is the lower the cost per unit; the less efficient it is the higher the cost per unit.

A key operations objective is to be more efficient. Productive efficiency will depend upon a number of factors, such as employees' productivity, the nature of the production process, the degree of innovation, the scale of production and the capacity utilisation.

Productive efficiency is a measure of the success with which a firm turns its inputs into outputs. The more efficient a firm is the more output it generates with its inputs, or the less inputs it uses to achieve a given level of output.

To become more efficient in production a firm will consider the following.

- **Labour productivity.** This measures the output per employee. Firms will usually try to increase the output per employee (provided that quality is maintained). An increase in productivity may be achieved through training, better capital equipment, better working practices (e.g. team working) or a change in management style.
- **The nature of the production process.** Firms must consider the nature of their market and their customer requirements and decide on the most efficient process available. For example, should the business tailor make each item to individual customers' requirements (this is called job production), or use flow production to continuously produce high volumes of similar products? Flow production, for example, is likely to require more investment in equipment than job production and is only likely to be efficient if there are high levels of demand for a relatively standardised product.
- **Capacity utilisation**, i.e. the extent to which a firm is making full use of its resources. A firm's capacity measures the maximum output it can produce given its existing resources. Capacity utilisation measures a firm's actual output in relation to its capacity. The lower the capacity utilisation the less resources are being utilised and the higher the unit cost is likely to be because resources are not being used efficiently.
- **The scale of production**. A firm must decide on the most appropriate scale of production. Up to some level of output a firm may experience economies of scale; by expanding, the unit costs may fall due to, for example, purchasing or tech-

nical economies. However, if a firm grows too big it may suffer from diseconomies of scale, i.e. unit costs may increase; this may be due to problems with communication, coordination and control as the firm gets too big. This is covered in more detail in Chapter 11.

- **Investment in innovation**. For example, increasing investment to develop new ways of providing a good or service can lead to cost savings. Online bookings rather than paper ones, car park payment via mobile phones rather than requiring machines to be maintained and emptied, and swipe cards to enter a building rather than a security firm can all save costs. More about innovation can be found in Chapter 12.

By improving its productive efficiency a firm can reduce its cost per unit.

- This means that it can then reduce the price per unit and still maintain the same amount of profit per unit. This should lead to an increase in sales. The extent to which sales increase depends on the price elasticity of demand. The more price elastic demand is the greater the increase in sales. By lowering its price the firm can offer better value for money and may achieve a competitive advantage over its competitors.
- Or it can maintain the same price and benefit from a higher profit per unit. This profit can be invested into the firm or paid out to the owners.

Greater efficiency is a key element of operations management. Organisations should constantly be trying to reduce inefficiency and reduce the cost per unit for any given level of service or quality.

Key Issues

Businesses will continually strive for greater efficiency. This is because they need to:
- reduce waste
- offset increasing costs elsewhere, such as wages
- compete against other organisations that are also constantly striving to be more efficient.

Examiner's advice

Remember that simply getting costs down is not necessarily an objective in itself. If you cut costs in the wrong way quality may suffer and the customer will no longer want your products. The objective would be to meet the desired quality criteria in the most efficient way possible, i.e. reduce costs while also achieving certain standards.

Progress questions

1 State two possible operational objectives, with examples. (2 marks)
2 What is meant by efficiency? (2 marks)
3 What is meant by productivity? (2 marks)
4 How can a business increase its efficiency? (3 marks)
5 How can an increase in efficiency help a business? (3 marks)
6 Explain the link between corporate objectives and operations objectives, with examples. (4 marks)
7 Explain how an operations decision can influence other functions. (5 marks)
8 Explain how other functions can influence operations objectives. (5 marks)
9 Explain what is meant by capacity utilisation. (3 marks)
10 Explain the disadvantages to a business of low capacity utilisation. (4 marks)

Analysis and evaluation questions

1 Analyse the ways in which a change in the corporate objectives and strategy might affect the operational objectives of an airline. (8 marks)
2 Analyse the possible benefits to an insurance company of increasing efficiency. (8 marks)
3 Discuss the factors likely to influence the operational objectives of a consumer electronics business. (15 marks)

Case study

Figure 10.7 The Nano

A team of 500 people worked on developing the Nano car. This car is 3 metres long, seats four people comfortably, can reach 65 mph and aims to revolutionise travel for millions. The 'People's Car' is the cheapest in the world at 100,000 rupees (£1,300); this is the same price as the DVD player in a Lexus! The Nano is produced by Tata, the Indian conglomerate. The company's chairman said at its launch, 'I hope this changes the way people travel in rural India. We are a country of a billion and most are denied connectivity,' he said. 'This is a car that is affordable and provides all-weather transport for the family.'

The aluminium shell contains a rear-mounted 33bhp two-cylinder petrol engine and weighs about half a tonne. The standard version comes with brakes, a four-gear manual transmission, seatbelts, windows and a steering wheel. It lacks a passenger-side mirror and has only one windscreen wiper. The deluxe version will have air-conditioning, while extras such as a radio and an airbag could be added.

The car is the culmination of five years' research and input from across the world, including Italy and Germany. But it was designed and made in India. Tata cut costs by minimising components, particularly steel, and taking advantage of India's low production costs. Because of its size, it uses less sheet metal, has a smaller and lighter engine than other cars, smaller tubeless tyres and a no-frills interior. The company has applied for 34 patents to cover its innovations. 'We shrunk it, made the engine smaller and used fewer materials but we haven't taken any shortcuts in terms of safety or emissions,' Mr Tata, the chairman, said.

The most basic Nano model is roughly half the price of the cheapest car available today. China's QQ3Y Chery and India's Maruti 800 are both about £2,550. The idea of millions of Nanos on the road alarms environmentalists. The chief UN climate scientist said that he was 'having nightmares' about it. Green campaigners point to India's terrible road system and rising pollution levels. 'Even if they claim it will be fuel efficient, the sheer numbers will undermine this.'

Source: Adapted from *The Times*, 11 January 2008

(40 marks, 60 minutes)

Questions

1 Explain the operational objectives that might be set for the operations function of the Nano division of Tata. (5 marks)
2 Analyse the factors likely to affect the demand for Tata's Nano car. (8 marks)
3 Discuss the ways in which Tata might be able to produce a car at this low cost. (12 marks)
4 To what extent does low-cost production guarantee that this new car from Tata will be a success? (15 marks)

11 Scale and resource mix

Choosing the right scale of production can have a big influence on the efficiency of a business and on how easy it is to manage. The efficiency, flexibility, quality and effectiveness of operations management will also be affected by the mix of resources used in a business.

In this chapter we examine:

- issues involved in choosing the right scale of production
- economies and diseconomies of scale
- capacity and capacity utilisation
- choosing the right combination of resources.

Introduction to scale

When we talk about the scale of production, we are referring to a firm's output level; this will depend on its capacity. The capacity is the maximum output that an organisation can produce at any moment, given its resources.

The capacity of a firm will depend on:

- its capital, such as office space, store space, level of machinery and equipment
- the existing level of technology
- the number and skills of its employees.

If a business increases its capacity it is increasing the scale of its production. Deciding on the correct scale for an organisation is a critical decision for its managers. If the capacity is too low compared with demand, they will have to turn away orders, possibly losing customers. If the level is too high compared with demand, they will have idle resources such as equipment and machinery.

The 'right' scale for a business will depend on:

- **The expected levels of sales**. The higher the level of demand, the greater the desired scale, assuming the demand can be sustained.
- **The costs involved in growing.** Can the business afford to expand? Expansion often involves investing in the short run and may take months or even years to gain a return. The organisation may not be able to produce on the scale it wants because it does not have the money to buy all the resources it needs.
- **The resources available.** For example, firms may

not be able to recruit sufficient numbers of staff if the skills they want are in short supply.

A firm can increase its scale by:

- investing in new capital such as IT systems, equipment and technology
- investing in labour, for example training the workforce to increase its productivity; hiring more employees to provide more 'people input'.

As a business grows and changes its scale it tends to experience efficiency gains (called economies of scale) up to a certain scale and then inefficiencies (called diseconomies of scale) after that.

Economies of scale

Economies of scale occur when the cost of producing a unit (the unit cost) falls as the firm changes its scale of production (its capacity level). There are several types of economy of scale.

Technical economies of scale

As a firm expands, it may be able to adopt different production techniques to reduce the unit cost of production. For example, a business may be able to introduce a production line. This is expensive in itself, but if it can be used to produce on a large scale the costs can be spread over many units, reducing the unit cost. At Mars' Slough factory, 3 million mars bars are produced each day.

Specialisation

As firms grow bigger, they are able to employ people to specialise in different areas of the organisation. Instead of having managers trying to do several jobs at once or having to pay specialist companies to do the work, they can employ their own staff to concentrate on particular areas of the business. For example, they might employ their own accountants or market researchers. By using specialists rather than buying in these services from outside firms, the business can make better decisions and save money. For example, a specialist finance director may be able to find ways of reducing the tax burden or organising cheaper sources of finance.

Purchasing economies

As firms get bigger, they need to buy more resources. As a result, they should be able to negotiate better deals with suppliers and reduce the price of their components and raw materials. Large firms are also more likely to get discounts when buying advertising space or dealing with distributors. If a firm can become a big customer of a supplier, the supplier will be eager to keep that deal and so is likely to offer better terms and conditions. The bargaining power of firms may mean lower unit costs and also better cash flow. In 2008, for example, Boots announced it would pay its suppliers 75 days after the end of the month in which an invoice is received. This means it can hold on to the money for a relatively long period and earn interest.

Businesses that grow also tend to benefit from 'learning by doing'. More experience of what to do, how to do it, what not to do and who to use to do it can make the whole process more efficient. This efficiency gain should not be underestimated. If you are trying to start a business, for example, there is a tremendous amount you simply do not know how to do; a more experienced business will have made the errors in the past and will now be getting it right and operating more efficiently.

Why do economies of scale matter?

Economies of scale can be important because the cost of producing a unit can have a significant impact on a firm's competitiveness. If an organisation can reduce its unit costs, it can either keep its price the same and benefit from higher profit margins, or it can pass the cost saving on to the customer by cutting the

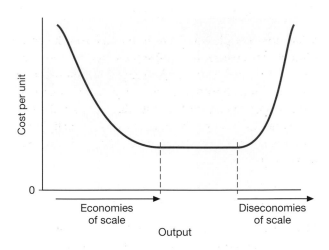

Figure 11.1 Economies and diseconomies of scale

price. If it chooses the first option, this may mean higher rewards for the owners or more funds for investment. If, on the other hand, it cuts the price, it may be able to offer better value for money than its competitors. The ability to lower price and still make a profit may be very important in a market with falling demand; this means such firms may be in a better position to survive a recession.

Firms with economies of scale may be able to price competitors out of the market if they wish; this can act as a threat to potential entrants who know they would be less efficient than the established business at first because they would be operating on a smaller scale and therefore may not want to take the risk of a price war. This means that economies of scale can act as a barrier to entry. For firms within a market economies of scale mean that business can respond to price cuts by others.

Diseconomies of scale

Diseconomies of scale occur when a firm expands its capacity and the cost per unit increases. Diseconomies of scale are often linked to the problems of managing more businesses. As organisations grow they have more products, operate in more regions, have more staff and simply keeping everyone focused and working together can be difficult. Diseconomies of scale can therefore occur for several reasons.

Communication problems

With more people involved in the business, it can be difficult to ensure that messages get to the right people at the right time. Although developments in information technology, such as emails and intranets, have helped, it can still be quite difficult to make sure everyone in a large business knows exactly what they are supposed to know when they are supposed to know it.

Coordination and control problems

Just as communicating properly gets more difficult in a large organisation, so does controlling all the different activities and making sure everyone is working towards the same overall goals. As the firm expands and sets up new parts of the business, it is easy for different people to be working in different ways and setting different objectives. It becomes increasingly difficult to monitor what is going on and to make sure everyone is working together. Culture differences are likely to emerge (for more on this see page 360) as differences in the values of parts of the business develop. The UK division will do things differently from the French division, the operations team see themselves as different from the marketing team. These differences in approach, management styles and values can lead to difficulties in terms of how they work together, causing inefficiency.

Motivation

As a firm gets bigger, it can become much harder to make sure everyone feels a part of the organisation. Senior managers are less likely to be able to stay in day-to-day contact with all the employees and so some people may feel less involved. In a small business there is often a good team environment; everyone tends to see everyone else every day and it is easier to feel they are working towards the same goal. Any problems can be sorted out quickly, face-to-face. As the organisation grows, its employees can feel isolated and have less sense of belonging. As a result, they can become demotivated.

Diseconomies of scale often occur when mergers and takeovers take place. Managers often anticipate economies of scale from sharing resources, synergy and the power of a large scale. In reality the difficulties of agreeing on standard policies, cultural clashes, different priorities and strategies can lead to significant diseconomies which lead to cost disadvantages

overall. In practice, most takeovers and mergers lead to worse financial performance for the combined companies than they achieved individually.

To avoid diseconomies of scale, managers use practices such as:

- having a mission statement to unify the business and outline the central purpose
- managing by objectives – an approach in which all employees are set targets tying them to the overall corporate objective
- using appraisals to review individuals' progress and ensure that they feel involved and as if they are acting in line with the overall aims of the business
- communicating regularly in a variety of ways to ensure people feel informed.

Examiner's advice

When considering expanding managers should:

- check if the demand is actually there to justify expansion – there is no point producing more if you cannot sell it.
- check if it is possible to staff the expansion
- check to see if the business has mechanisms in place (such as budgeting and appraisals) to try and ensure that diseconomies of scale do not occur if it grows.

Getting the 'right' size of firm is a crucial issue for managers. Firms want to be big enough to have market power and benefit from economies of scale, but not be so big that they suffer from diseconomies of scale. In industries such as brewing and telecommunications many firms have joined together to benefit from economies of scale. At the same time, other firms such as Cadbury, Hanson and ICI have split up into smaller units because of the problems of large size. There is, it seems, no ideal size. It depends on the particular nature of the business, its own culture and communication and the nature of the industry.

Capacity utilisation

The scale of an organisation is determined by the level of capacity it chooses. The bigger the scale, the greater the level of capacity. As mentioned earlier, not having enough capacity can mean the business cannot meet demand. Having too much capacity can mean resources are being wasted. The extent to which capacity is being used is measured by the capacity utilisation. The capacity utilisation of a firm measures the amount it is producing compared with the amount it could produce given its existing resources.

$$\text{Capacity utilisation} = \frac{\text{present output}}{\text{maximum output}} \times 100$$

To increase its capacity utilisation, a firm could increase the amount it is producing. However, there is no point producing more if it will not be able to sell the goods. A firm may need to boost demand, therefore, so that it can be sure to sell the extra output. It may try to do this in a number of ways, including:

- adjusting the marketing mix – changing elements of the marketing mix, such as promotion, the price or the distribution, can stimulate sales
- agreeing to produce products for other firms – sometimes producers of well-known brands also produce items for the supermarkets, which are sold with the supermarket's name on them (these are called own-label items). Although this may seem strange, because it is helping the competition, the manufacturers may actually benefit

because they are using their machinery at full capacity and this reduces the cost of each unit produced. When one firm gets another to produce for it, this is known as sub-contracting.

Figure 11.3 MV Emma Mærsk

International trade has benefited a great deal from the growth in containerisation. Using standard-sized containers has enabled much faster, much cheaper movement of goods and services. Container ships are designed so that no space is wasted. Capacity is measured in the twenty-foot equivalent unit (TEU), the number of standard 20-foot containers measuring 20 × 8.0 × 8.5 feet (6.1 × 2.4 × 2.6 metres) a vessel can carry (although in fact, most containers used today measure 40 feet (12 metres) in length). The loading and unloading is usually done by specialised cranes at the ports. Container ships now carry up to 15,000 TEUs on a voyage. The world's largest container ship, the MV Emma Mærsk has a capacity of 15,200 containers.

Emma Mærsk is a container ship owned by the A. P. Moller-Maersk Group. The number of crew on board is usually 13!

If a firm is operating below capacity and does not believe that demand will increase again, it may decide to close part of its production process and reduce its capacity. This is known as rationalisation. The banking industry has recently undergone massive changes as firms join together to rationalise their production.

Business in Focus

BMW suspend production

In 2008 Mini production had to be cut back and the factory closed for a month over Christmas, due to falling sales in the UK. The usual two-week shutdown for Christmas and the New Year was extended to four weeks. The decision affected around 4,700 workers across three shifts on the Oxford site.

Figures from the Society of Motor Manufacturers and Traders revealed that new car sales in the UK were down 23 per cent from a year ago. Mini sales in the UK were down 40 per cent compared with a year before. The national officer at Unite, a trade union, said: 'We understand the very difficult economic conditions car manufacturers are facing. We have robust agreements in place to protect our members as much as possible during these difficult times.'

Source: Adapted from bbc.co.uk

Questions:

1 Why did the factory have to be shut down for a month?
2 What does this tell us about the level of capacity compared with demand?

Key terms
Capacity measures the maximum a firm can produce given its existing resources at any given moment.
Capacity utilisation measures the amount a firm produces relative to its maximum output at any given moment.

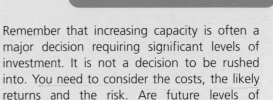

Examiner's advice

Remember that increasing capacity is often a major decision requiring significant levels of investment. It is not a decision to be rushed into. You need to consider the costs, the likely returns and the risk. Are future levels of demand likely to justify it?

Choosing the right resource mix

As we have seen, operations involves managing resources. It includes:

* deciding the best way of producing
* deciding the best resources to use and the combination of resources required (the resource mix)
* deciding where to get resources from (e.g. which suppliers)
* deciding how many resources to hold in stock.

When deciding how to produce a good or service, operations managers will consider the mix of

Business in Focus

Magners

In 2008 Maurice Pratt, the head of Irish drinks group C&C, maker of Magners cider, resigned after admitting his strategy had failed. For a while in 2006 the company experienced fast growth, but sales were hit after two successive wet summers and increased competition from larger alcohol makers, such as Scottish and Newcastle which produces Bulmers Original. The worsening economic situation in the UK did not help. 'The past two years have been very challenging for C&C Group and despite our best efforts we have not achieved our ambitions for the business,' said Pratt. The present chief executive said, 'As chief executive I have to be accountable and take responsibility for business performance. The company has to take important strategic choices and I have therefore decided it is time to stand aside and allow a new CEO to bring fresh thinking and impetus to the business.'

Back in 2006, when Britain enjoyed a heatwave, cider was advertised as a refreshing, cooling drink and quickly became popular. During the boom period the company expanded its capacity significantly, only to struggle when sales fell. It has now had to make redundancies and has relatively low capacity utilisation which has damaged profits.

resources to be used. Should more resources in schools be put into teachers, teaching assistants, learning support, computers, sports facilities or the canteen? The answer to this question is likely to depend on who you ask – a case could probably be made for all of these resources and many others. Some would argue that with more teachers the class sizes could be smaller and this would make a dramatic difference to the learning. Others might say that the money would be better used developing a virtual learning environment. Others might argue that diet has a big impact on how we learn. Given that finances are likely to be limited we cannot have all these different resources even though they might be useful; the question then is which are the best ones to focus on and which mix of resources would deliver the best outcomes? The same sorts of decisions face managers in all businesses. Would it be better to have more staff in our supermarkets or self-scanning equipment at the tills? Would it be better to spend more money to have stores in the centre of town or is out of town acceptable?

Businesses will, of course, have differing views on what is the best resource mix and this will affect the nature of the product provided. Dell put money into technology for many years and avoided much direct face-to-face contact with customers. Interestingly, in recent years Dell has felt that customers want advice and therefore more customer assistants and selling via retailers is desirable. In the whole area of customer enquiries many firms have switched towards computerised systems to direct the caller rather than having operators take the calls. This is reducing the human element of the process. However, some banks and insurance companies have started to reverse this trend and reintroduce 'people' on the end of the phone.

When analysing the resources mix, the combination of resources chosen will depend on factors such as:

- **The relative price of the resources.** In some developing economies where employees are relatively cheap many processes are very labour intensive. This means they use a high proportion of labour relative to capital (machines). The same processes in the UK may be more automated, using more machines because labour is relatively expensive.
- **The availability and value of different resources.** In some sectors there may be a shortage of land or land may be very expensive,

which might reduce the size of the offices or production facilities (or mean that the firm has to shift production elsewhere). Machinery or technology might not be available to do the job of a person – we have yet to come up with a computer program to design adverts or slogans, for example. However, in some cases we have tried to pool the knowledge of people into a program to reduce the number of people needed (e.g. NHS direct online is a series of yes/no questions which is linked to the knowledge gained from many doctors on illnesses to try and build a program to diagnose you automatically).

- **The nature of the product and process.** Cars can be produced by hand, for example, but for mass production the efficiency gains are so great that production lines are much more likely, i.e. mass-market products are likely to be produced by capital-intensive production methods.
- **The state of technology.** The flexibility of technology and the ability to use technology to complete tasks will affect the resource mix used. Cheaper, more effective technology has made farming far more capital intensive than it used to be, for example.

Becoming more capital intensive

A business may become more capital intensive by investing in more information technology, machinery, equipment or transport. This may involve:

- **Raising finance** – the business may try to finance this internally if it has the funds available. However, this can sometimes delay much-needed investment. Alternatively it may seek outside sources such as a loan (but this incurs interest charges) or investors (but this involves a loss of control).
- **Employee resistance** – some employees may resist the move towards greater capital intensity because they fear losing their jobs, they fear they will not have the necessary skills required to use it and/or they do not want to retrain.
- **Changeover** – introducing new equipment often involves disruption to the existing process. This can mean delays for customers if it is not planned properly and people are not kept well informed. There are often initial problems setting up processes, which can also cause delays. Effective project management is important (see page 391).

Business in Focus

Biofuels

As many countries demand more biofuels to replace oil as a source of energy, there is increasing pressure on Brazil's booming sugar cane industry to change the way it produces. Western firms now want more socially acceptable working practices.

Sugar cane cutters have been working Brazil's land since 1525, when Portuguese colonialists started growing the crop; they are now being replaced by machines because western firms have decided the way that employees are treated is unacceptable.

The Brazilian Sugar Cane Industry Association (UNICA) has said 80 per cent of the 500,000 jobs would be gone within three years and admitted that moving to a tractor-based system would adversely affect its migrant workforce.

The conditions of sugar workers was rarely noticed when the commodity was exported for sugar, but the position has changed now that Brazil is the world's second-largest exporter of sugar-based ethanol to use as a biofuel in petrol.

Behind the move to phase out sugar cane cutters are stories of exploitation that have damaged the image of Brazilian biofuels in big importing countries such as Sweden and potentially in Britain, where the government has stated that 2.5 per cent of all petrol must come from biofuels. Critics have accused Brazil's sugar cane industry of allowing child labour, high accident rates and workers earning as little as $1.35 (67p) an hour. Manual labour is also blamed for poor environmental practices such as crop wastage and the burning of stubble.

The importance of people

Although some processes, particularly in manufacturing, have become very capital intensive (just think of bottling plants, glass factories, car assembly plants and chemicals plants), the importance of people should not be underestimated. After all, it is people who think of the product idea, research the market, design the products, develop the operations process and manage the business.

Many businesses are focused on what we now call the knowledge economy: designers, consultants, advisers, trainers, architects, film producers, authors, investors, brokers, doctors and surgeons. These are all roles in labour-intensive organisations and the people play a vital part in adding value. Their knowledge is the key resource. This has major implications for human resource management in terms of:

- **Attracting the right people** to work for the business – think of how important people are to organisations such as Google, the Dreamworks film company, Goldman Sachs investment bank and Oxford University.
- **Keeping the right people** – if businesses want to keep good people they need to look at issues such as how they reward them, how they manage them and how their jobs are designed. In the case of highly able individuals who are employed for their knowledge, a more democratic style in which they are given freedom to develop their ideas may be important.
- **Managing people's knowledge** – having knowledge within an organisation is one thing, but making sure it is stored and shared effectively (see information management on page 382) is another. If a business can get people to compare and discuss ideas, brainstorm and problem solve together, it may well end up with better decisions.

Progress questions

1 What is meant by capacity? (2 marks)

2 State two factors that determine the capacity of a business. (2 marks)

3 What is meant by economies of scale? (2 marks)

4 Explain two economies of scale. (4 marks)

5 Explain two benefits to a business of achieving greater economies of scale. (4 marks)

6 What is meant by diseconomies of scale? (2 marks)

7 Explain two diseconomies of scale. (4 marks)

8 What is meant by 'a labour-intensive process'? Give an example. (3 marks)

9 Explain one advantage of adopting a more capital-intensive process. (4 marks)

10 What is meant by 'the knowledge economy'? (2 marks)

Analysis and evaluation questions

1 Analyse the factors likely to influence the resource mix adopted by a new restaurant. (8 marks)

2 To what extent is it advisable for a chain of health clubs to always try to get bigger? (15 marks)

3 Evaluate the importance of economies of scale in helping a soft drinks producer to be competitive. (15 marks)

Case study

Figure 11.4 Model T Ford

Ford Model T

The Ford Model T car was produced by the Ford Motor Company from 1908 to 1927. It was the first mass-market car produced at a price low enough for millions of people to be able to afford it. Ford was able to offer it at a relatively low price by developing assembly-line production. The first production Model T was built on 27 September 1908, at the Piquette plant in Detroit, Michigan.

Henry Ford said: 'I will build a car for the great multitude. It will be large enough for the family, but small enough for the individual to run and care for. It will be constructed of the best materials, by the best men to be hired, after the simplest designs that modern engineering can devise. But it will be low in price that no man making a good salary will be unable to own one – and enjoy with his family the blessing of hours of pleasure in God's great open spaces.' The Model T was the first car mass produced on assembly lines with completely interchangeable parts.

At the beginning the Model T was produced using assembly methods typical at the time; it was assembled by hand, and production was small. Ford's Piquette plant could not keep up with demand for the Model T, and only 11 cars were built there during the first full month of production. In 1910, after assembling nearly 12,000 Model Ts, Henry Ford moved the company to the new Highland Park complex. Ford developed the assembly line there and eventually cars were coming off the production line in three-minute intervals. By 1914, the assembly process for the Model T had been so streamlined it took only 93 minutes to assemble a car. That year Ford produced more cars than all other carmakers combined. The Model T was a huge commercial success, and by the time Henry made his 10 millionth car, 9 out of 10 of all cars in the entire world were Fords. In fact, it was so successful that Ford did not purchase any advertising between 1917 and 1923; in total, more than 15 million Model Ts were manufactured, more than any other model of its day. (Model T production was finally surpassed by the Volkswagen Beetle on 17 February, 1972.) However, for many years Ford refused to make any changes to the Model T. As other companies started to offer more comfort and better styling the Model T lost market share. Production ceased in 1927. The price of a Model T started at around $850 but by the 1920s had fallen to $300.

(40 marks, 60 minutes)

Questions

1 Explain two factors that might have influenced the demand for the Ford Model T. (5 marks)
2 Analyse the possible factors that influenced the design of the Model T. (8 marks)
3 Discuss the advantages and disadvantages of introducing capital-intensive production techniques in a business such as Ford. (12 marks)
4 Evaluate the reasons for the success of the Model T Ford. (15 marks)

One step further: productivity and operations management

A business's level of output is the total amount it produces. The success of operations management depends not just on the total output but also on the value and quantity of inputs used up in the production process. The aim of operations managers is to use as few resources as possible to produce a given output. At the same time, managers seek to maintain a given level of quality.

A business's productivity measures the output produced in relation to the inputs it has used. There are actually many different measures of productivity, such as:

- output per worker per hour or day or year (labour productivity)
- output per machine per time period (capital productivity).

The most commonly used measure is output per worker.

Labour productivity measures the output of the firm in relation to the number of employees. For example, if ten people produce 50 units in total each week, their productivity is 5 units each. The higher the productivity, the more is produced per person per time period.

Productivity is a crucial concept in operations management because it can have a significant effect on the costs of producing a unit. The higher the productivity, the more units each worker is making and, if wages are unchanged, the labour cost per unit should be cheaper. As a result, managers are constantly seeking ways to improve labour productivity because this means the firm will either make more profit per unit or can reduce the price to become more competitive.

Productivity may be increased by using a variety of techniques.

- **Increasing the number of hours worked** – If employees work more hours or more days each week, this could increase their output. However, this is not a long-term means of increasing employees' productivity because they are likely to get tired and stressed, and may therefore become less productive in the long term. Also, there is a limit to how many extra hours can be worked.
- **Training** – This is a very important way of increasing productivity. Training can increase employees' output by helping them to gain more skills and to learn new and better ways of doing things.
- **Investment in equipment and technology** – If employees have modern and more efficient machinery, they should be able to make more output. As a government business adviser said when commenting on UK productivity compared with that of other countries: 'A worker can be 100 per cent efficient with a shovel but it won't count if his international counterpart is equipped with a JCB!'
- **Changing the way the work is done** – If the way in which a product is made is changed this can affect the speed and the effectiveness of the

production process. Many firms have implemented teamworking in recent years, resulting in improved productivity levels.

- **Motivating employees** – If employees can be motivated (perhaps by offering more rewards or by giving people more responsibility) effort and productivity may increase.

While managers might be eager to increase productivity, employees may resist such efforts because:

- they do not want to work longer or harder
- they do not want to learn new skills
- they fear that higher productivity levels may lead to job losses
- they feel it is unfair that they are producing more unless they receive higher rewards.

12 Innovation

The business environment is constantly changing and firms need to adapt to these changes. This may require investment in innovation to develop new products and processes. Innovation can affect the costs and quality of a business's products.

In this chapter we consider:
- the meaning and significance of innovation and research and development
- the purpose and benefits of innovation
- the risks of innovation.

What is innovation?

The process of turning an idea into a saleable product or service is known as innovation. Innovation is defined as 'the successful exploitation of new ideas'.

Innovation allows businesses to develop new products and new processes. Apple may innovate by creating a new iPod (a product) and/or internally improving its communication systems (a process). Innovation can help you create new markets such as Nintendo shaping the family gaming market with its Wii games. It can help to create new ways of doing business, such as online booking of parking spaces.

However, innovation can also bring new competitors into your market. For example, Wrigley was threatened by Trident's entry into the chewing gum market, Kodak was attacked by Sony's entrance into the camera market, Gillette was challenged by King of Shaves' move into the razor market. It can also make markets obsolete (think of typewriters and VHS cassettes) if they do not keep up.

Given that customers are likely to be demanding more each year, innovation can be essential to help a business remain competitive by increasing the benefits it provides and/or reducing the costs of providing the product. Innovation may be essential just to keep pace with what competitors are doing (how many 'new improved washing powders' have you seen?). A failure to innovate may see a business lose market share.

The extent to which innovation occurs in some markets is clear. Just look at the razor market and you can see enormous innovations on a regular basis: more razorblades, better razorblades, faster, smaller electric shavers and shavers for women. The same is true in the toothbrush market: electric toothbrushes, tongue brushes, battery-operated toothbrushes. Other markets may seem to have less innovation (e.g. socks and pencils), but even here some progress is continually being made in terms of the way things are produced or the nature of the final product.

Figure 12.1 Types of toothbrushes

The aims of innovation may include:
- developing products which have a unique selling point, allowing a business to differentiate itself from the competition and earn higher profit margins
- developing better-quality products which meet customer needs more successfully
- developing more efficient ways of producing to reduce the cost per unit.

Business in Focus

Dyson

Figure 12.2 Dyson

James Dyson has always pulled things to pieces. He has always been interested in how they work asking, 'why does it do that?'. 'Just because it does' has never satisfied him as an answer. While he was at London's Royal College of Art, James Dyson developed the Sea Truck – a high-speed landing craft. Then came the Ballbarrow; its large red pneumatic ball stopped it sinking into soft ground. Then the Trolleyball boat launcher and the amphibious Wheelboat followed. Then one day he had an idea for a new type of vacuum cleaner. Five years and 5,127 prototypes later, he had developed a machine that had no bag and no loss of suction. Uninterested in new technology and wedded to vacuum bags (worth £250 million every year), major manufacturers turned James and his invention away.

James licensed his design in Japan. The Japanese loved the pink G-Force and, in 1993, the royalties allowed James to manufacture a machine under his own name, the DCO1. He patented his invention which meant he kept the rights to it. In 1999, after a lengthy court battle, Hoover was found guilty of infringing James' patent. Other manufacturers, unable or unwilling to develop their own vacuum cleaners, still try to copy Dyson technology and are taken to court. James and his engineers not only develop inventions, but also improve existing Dyson technology. For example:

- Dyson machines now have smaller multiple cyclones, which create greater centrifugal forces, capturing more microscopic dust.
- A Dyson Ball machine rides on a ball, pivoting on a single point, allowing it to go in any direction, unlike traditional vacuum cleaners that only move in straight lines.
- The company developed the Dyson digital motor, which is controlled by a microchip and spins at 98,000 rpm – five times faster than a Formula 1 car engine. Because of its speed, the digital motor is half the size and half the weight of conventional motors. With no brushes or fixed magnets, it doesn't emit carbon either.

One of the latest products was developed by a Dyson engineer who discovered that a high-speed sheet of air can act as an invisible wiper blade, literally scraping water from hands. With a 400 mph airflow, the Dyson Airblade hand dryer takes just ten seconds and uses less energy than warm air hand dryers. But it's only possible because of the Dyson digital motor.

Source: Dyson website

Questions:

1 Discuss the ways in which Dyson can try and ensure it comes up with new products.
2 Evaluate the factors likely to determine the long-term success of the Dyson Airblade.

- developing better ways of doing things (e.g. making it more original or more distinctive).

Successful innovation allows firms to keep ahead of their competitors and to keep finding better ways of doing things. This is often the key to long-term success in a market.

Innovation is often linked to research and development (R&D).

Business in Focus

Innovation in the shaving market

In the diagram below, from the *Economist*, it forecasts that given the rate of development in the number of razorblades being offered in recent years, if this rate continued a razor with 14 blades would be available by about 2020!

Blade running
Number of blades per razor system

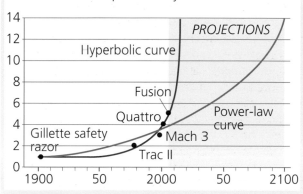

Figure 12.3

Research and development (R&D)

Research and development (R&D) is part of the innovation process. It refers to the generation and application of scientific knowledge to create a product or develop a new production process. For example, it may involve a team of employees at a confectionery company researching into a new flavour or a new variety of sweet and then trying out different versions until they have one they (and the customers) are happy with. Or it may involve another team in the business focusing on new ways of producing the confectionery.

In some sectors, such as the car industry, pharmaceuticals and energy, research and development can take many years and be very expensive. Glaxo calculates that on average a new pharmaceutical takes 10 to 15 years and costs £500 million on average to develop. However, research and development is often very risky. This is because you may never end up with an idea that is actually viable. Even if you do manage to launch a product, you may find that you do not have very long to recover the costs of development. In the software industry, for example, new products

are being developed very rapidly indeed; a successful film may only be showing for a few weeks.

Key term

Research and development (R&D) is the generation and application of scientific knowledge to create a product or develop a new production process which can increase the firm's productive efficiency.

People in Business

Akio Morita

Akio Morita was the founder of Sony. After serving in the Japanese navy he set up a small electronics company, Tokyo Telecommunications Engineering, with his friend Masaru Ibuka.

Figure 12.4 Akio Morita

Ibuka was an engineering genius who created many of the technical advances behind the brand Morita created.

The company became very successful in the 1950s when it produced a small transistor radio. The transistor was invented in America, but Morita bought a licence from Bell Laboratories to produce it in Japan. By the end of the decade Morita was exporting from Japan to the US and Europe. In 1958 he changed the company's name. After weeks of searching he found the name Sonus which is latin for 'sound'. He changed this to Sony because 'sony boys' is Japanese for whizz kids. In 1961 Sony became the first Japanese company to be listed on the New York Stock Exchange.

After further successes with televisions and videotape recorders Morita developed the Sony Walkman. This product (which changed the way we listened to music) was launched with almost no market research and against the views of many within the business.

'The public does not know what is possible. We do.' said Morita.

In 1998 the Sony Walkman was declared the number one consumer brand in America. Morita's famous view of globalisation was 'think globally, act locally'. In America Sony was seen as American; in Japan it was seen as Japanese.

Books: *Made in Japan*, Collins, 1987

Source: Adapted from Economist.com, 7 November 2008

Business in Focus

UK Research and Development Scoreboard

The government report on research and development in the UK highlights

- The top 850 UK companies in Research & Development (R&D) spent over £20 billion last year.
- Pharmaceuticals and biotechnology companies are now the biggest investors in R&D worldwide.
- Eighty-three per cent of UK R&D is conducted by the hundred most active companies.

- More than 81 per cent of global R&D occurs in five countries: USA, Japan, Germany, France and the UK.
- Global R&D intensity (R&D expenditure as a proportion of sales) has remained broadly constant at 3.5 per cent.

Source: Department for Innovation, Universities and Skills

Question:

1 To what extent do you think it matters whether UK firms invest in research and development?

Business in Focus

Innovation and swimming

Speedo's LZR swimsuit was introduced in February 2008. Thirty-eight of the 42 world swimming records that were broken in the following six months went to swimmers wearing LZRs.

To make the LZR, four innovations came together.

1 The fabric. The new suit is cut from a densely woven nylon-elastane material that compresses the wearer's body into a hydrodynamic shape but is extremely light. There are no sewn seams because the suit is bonded by ultrasonic welding. Ultrasonic welding removes 6 per cent of the drag that would otherwise occur. Compared with Speedo's previous suit, which was used by numerous gold medallists in the 2004 Olympic Games, the new material has half the weight yet triple the power to compress the body.

2 The suit has what Speedo calls an 'internal core stabiliser'– this is like a corset that holds the swimmer's form. As a swimmer tires, his hips hang lower in the water, creating drag. By compressing his torso, the LZR not only lets him go faster, because it maintains a tubular shape, but also allows him to swim longer with less effort.

In tests, swimmers wearing the LZR consumed 5 per cent less oxygen for a given level of performance than those wearing normal swimsuits did.

3 Polyurethane panels have been placed in spots on the suit. This reduces drag by another 24 per cent compared with the previous Speedo model.

4 The LZR was designed using a three-dimensional pattern rather than a two-dimensional one. It hugs a swimmer's body like a second skin; indeed, when it is not being worn, it does not lie flat but has a shape to it.

The results are a suit that costs $600 and takes 20 minutes to squeeze into! Some think the LZR improves performance by as much as 2 per cent – the difference between fourth and first place.

Source: Adapted from the *Economist*, 12 June 2008

Question:

1 Can you think of any other innovations in sport which have led to significant improvements in performance? Do you think they should be allowed?

Protecting successful innovation

If a firm manages to develop new products and new processes successfully it will naturally want to protect these from being copied or imitated by competitors. If an innovation is genuinely new a firm may protect it by taking out a patent. Under the 1988 Copyright, Designs and Patents Act the holder of a patent has the right to be the sole user of a process or manufacturer of a product for 20 years after it is registered.

The owner of a patent may sell the right to produce the product or use a process to others. This can be a valuable source of income to some organisations. If one firm suspects another of illegally producing a patented product or using its patented technology it can sue the offender. However, this can be costly and time consuming. To protect a product or process worldwide a firm must register the patent in different countries; this can also be an expensive and slow process.

By comparison, the work of artists, writers and musicians is automatically protected by copyright; copyrights do not have to be registered, although once again it is up to the copyright holder to sue offenders. Designs and logos can be protected by registering a trademark.

Sources of ideas

Firms may generate the ideas for innovation internally or externally. Internally ideas may simply come through discussion, employees' suggestion schemes, brainstorming activities or the firm's own research department, if it has one. However, to generate good ideas regularly requires a culture in which innovation is valued. This means people will be encouraged to question, to challenge and to improve the existing way of doing things (rather than adopting an attitude of 'it's always been done like that'). This means the business will want to build an innovative culture (see below).

Externally many new ideas are registered at the Patent Office; firms may search the patent office records and if they find a product or process they would like to use they can pay a fee to the owner of the patent for the right to use their technology. Alternatively, a firm might buy a franchise to produce under another firm's name; in return for this right a firm pays a fee and/or a percentage of its turnover.

A firm's customers can also be a valuable external source of new ideas. You will notice that many companies have a customer phone line or a comments book to gain feedback from their consumers on their service and to discover more about what customers really want. Innocent drinks, for example, has a 'banana phone' which customers can ring with their ideas.

> **Key terms**
> A **patent** provides legal protection for a new invention.
> A **franchise** occurs when one business (a franchisor) sells the right to use its name and processes to another (a franchisee).

Innovation, culture and structure

To encourage innovation internally a business will want a culture that encourages people to try out new ideas. If the standard way of doing things is to do as

Business in Focus

HP

HP provides technology solutions to consumers, businesses and institutions across the globe. Our offerings span IT infrastructure, personal computing and access devices, global services and imaging and printing for consumers, enterprises and small and medium-sized businesses. Our company employs over 140,000 people in 178 countries doing business in more than 40 currencies and more than 10 languages.

At HP, we believe that diversity and inclusion are key drivers of creativity, innovation and invention. Throughout the world, we are putting our differences to work to connect everyone to the power of technology in the marketplace, workplace and community. Creating a diverse, inclusive environment has been an ongoing journey of continuous action for many years. It has been a journey guided by deeply held values. Today, our diversity vision is one of global proportions. One that requires courageous, bold actions from many people throughout the world. We are proud to share what we have learned along the way and the aspirations we are actively working to achieve.

Question:

1 Discuss the ways in which having a diverse workforce might benefit a business.

you are told and if the people who keep their heads down and just follow instructions are the ones that get promoted then this will not encourage new ideas and new ways of doing things. Innovation therefore requires a culture that encourages people to try new ideas, that does not punish failure and that rewards those who do come up with new approaches. The commitment to innovation can be shown by the leaders of the business: what do they value, what do they recognise and praise? If you really want innovation to occur you need the senior managers to set an example. This will include making the funds available to those who need them to experiment and try ideas out. Apple, Hewlett-Packard, Intel and W L Gore, for example, are organisations that are said to have a particularly innovative culture.

The culture is important because it supports all other actions and highlights the priorities for the business. The culture is supported by and directly related to the structure of the organisation. Innovation requires the sharing of ideas and approaches. This is more likely in a structure that puts people together from different departments than one where individuals stay very much within their own area. By using cross-functional teams that cut across functional boundaries (e.g. bringing together

marketing, operations, finance and human resources), a project can be seen from different perspectives and this can help create new solutions to problems. Using Handy's models of culture, innovation is more likely to be a task culture than a role culture (see pages 365–6).

Key terms

The **culture** of a business refers to the values, attitudes and beliefs of employees; it reflects 'the way we do things around here'.

Key Issues

The extent to which a business is innovative will depend on the funding available for research and development. However, simply providing funds does not in itself generate creative ideas or bring about change. This will depend on other factors such as the culture of a business and its structure (do these help people share ideas?). This highlights how different aspects of businesses are all interrelated and how significant culture is in terms of everything a business does.

Business in Focus

W L Gore

'How we work at Gore sets us apart. We work hard at maximizing individual potential, maintaining an emphasis on product integrity, and cultivating an environment where creativity can flourish. A fundamental belief in our people and their abilities continues to be the key to our success. How does all this happen? Associates (not employees) are hired for general work areas. With the guidance of their sponsors (not bosses) and a growing understanding of opportunities and team objectives, associates commit to projects that match their skills. All of this takes place in an environment that combines freedom with cooperation and autonomy with synergy. Everyone can quickly earn the credibility to define and drive projects. Sponsors help associates chart a course in the organisation that will offer personal fulfillment while maximising their contribution to the enterprise. Leaders may be appointed, but are defined by 'followership'. More often, leaders

emerge naturally by demonstrating special knowledge, skill or experience that advances a business objective. Associates adhere to four basic guiding principles articulated by Bill Gore:

- Fairness to each other and everyone with whom we come in contact
- Freedom to encourage, help and allow other associates to grow in knowledge, skill and scope of responsibility
- The ability to make one's own commitments and keep them
- Consultation with other associates before undertaking actions that could impact the reputation of the company.'

Question:

1 Discuss the ways in which the approach at W L Gore affects how innovative the business is.

How much should a firm spend on innovation?

Innovation can be an important means of gaining a competitive advantage. Washing powder tablets, pyramid tea bags, combined shampoo and conditioners, razors with four blades are all examples of how firms have gained market share through innovative products. To compete and remain ahead of the market a firm may decide to invest relatively heavily in research and development. However, this does involve risk: simply putting more money into this area does not in itself ensure success and may be wasted funds which could have been used elsewhere. There is therefore an opportunity cost, which should be taken into account. To avoid the risk of investing in R&D a firm may pursue a 'me too strategy', whereby it imitates other firms rather than tries to break into new areas itself.

The amount a firm spends on research and development will therefore depend on its strategy. It will also depend on the nature of its market. In fast-changing markets such as consumer electronics the need to bring out new products is very strong – if you do not the chances are that your competitors will. Perhaps not surprisingly one of the biggest sectors for research and development spending is the pharmaceutical industry; to succeed in this market firms are continually striving to develop medicines which they can patent and which will bring them a stream of future income. The firm that develops a cure for the common cold, for AIDS or for Alzheimer's will make a fortune. There may be less pressure to invest in a more protected market – where the need to innovate is less intense or where the rate of change is slower.

Innovation as a strategy

While all businesses will be seeking to improve, some organisations put innovation at the heart of their strategy. These are companies in industries such as electronics, pharmaceuticals and computers (e.g. 3M, Intel, Google, Microsoft and Glaxo Wellcome). A failure to innovate in these industries mean you will fall behind. If innovation drives your strategy:

- You must be prepared to invest for the long term. There may be big projects that will only pay back over 15 years, if at all.
- You must be prepared for failure; not every new idea will work. The culture will have to encourage people to try. This means your Human Resource Management team must recruit people with ideas, people willing to challenge, and people looking to move things forward. You must provide a reward strategy and management style that fosters such creativity.
- Your marketing strategy may well be one of differentiation as you 'sell' the benefits of your new products and systems. The product may cost more money but the benefits are much greater for the customer. Alternatively, if the innovation is about finding cheaper ways of delivering the service then a low-cost strategy may be appropriate.

A strategy of innovation therefore has an impact on all the other functions of the business.

Business in Focus

Google

We're building a company around the idea that work should be challenging and the challenge should be fun. Having a few lava lamps, exercise balls, dogs and pool tables on hand doesn't hurt either

Additionally, we've become known for providing free, gourmet breakfasts and lunches, kitchens on every floor, a gym allowance (with on-site showers in our office building), lockers, bicycle racks and on-site massage. Recently, we've added a travel allowance to help you save transportation costs. We're green, too: recycling receptacles abound.

Google is dedicated to your career growth as well. We offer regular conferences, formal and informal training/learning opportunities, subsidised language classes and education-leave programmes.

Our culture allows you to invent technologies and solutions we haven't even imagined yet. After all, Googlers are our greatest asset!

Question:

1 How important do you think things like lava lamps, exercise balls and pool tables really are for Google?

Why might firms not invest in innovation?

There are many reasons why firms may fail to invest heavily enough in innovation:

- They may not be able raise the necessary funds. Innovation involves investment now in the hope of future returns. Firms that lack enough internal funds may struggle to borrow the money from banks. This may be because the banks are concerned that the research and development will not be successful and are not willing to take the risk.
- Alternatively, the bank may be willing to lend but the rates of interest charged may be perceived as too high. Even if a firm does have the necessary finance itself, some of the managers may be reluctant to use it in this area, preferring to use it elsewhere within the firm. For example, training or marketing may be seen as more of a priority than investing in research and development.
- The pressure from investors for short-term rewards may prevent managers from putting money into long-term projects. Investors may not be willing to wait for their rewards.
- The relatively low success rate may deter some firms from investing; even if firms manage to get a product to the launch stage, for example, it still has a very low chance of success. Firms are naturally reluctant to put money into projects which have a high failure rate, and may prefer to modify existing products instead.
- The business strategy may be to imitate what others do rather than take risks and try and be the pioneer.

Business in Focus

R&D and business performance

The Research and Development Scoreboard, a government report on R&D in the UK published in 2007, examined whether changes in business performance over the last five years – as measured by sales growth, profitability and stock market value – could be explained in terms of changes in investment in R&D over the same period.

Despite extensive analysis, no statistically significant relationships were found.

To some extent, this is not surprising because:

- there may be long lags between changes in investment in R&D and subsequent company performance
- the effects work at levels within companies that cannot be isolated at whole-firm level

- important variables are omitted from the data set available.

Our current conclusion here is that the relationship between R&D and business performance is complex rather than non-existent. Certainly, large firms with higher R&D as a proportion of sales have been judged by investors to be more successful over the recent past than their competitors.

Question:

1 Does the information above suggest firms should stop investing in research and development?

Progress questions

1 What is meant by innovation? (2 marks)

2 Why do many new ideas fail to be launched? (5 marks)

3 What is meant by research and development? (2 marks)

4 What is a patent? (2 marks)

5 Explain why the culture of a business can influence how innovative it is. (6 marks)

6 Identify two industries where research and development spending is likely to be high. Explain why. (6 marks)

7 Explain the factors that might determine how much a firm spends on research and development. (6 marks)

8 Explain two reasons why firms might be reluctant to invest in research and development. (6 marks)

9 How might greater innovation increase the sales of a consumer electronics business? (6 marks)

10 Explain two possible sources of ideas for innovation. (6 marks)

Analysis and evaluation questions

1 Analyse the possible benefits to Google of developing an innovative culture. (8 marks)

2 Evaluate the factors likely to influence how innovative an IT business is. (15 marks)

3 Discuss the factors likely to influence the research and development budget of a mobile phone producer. (15 marks)

Web link

For more on Google visit www.google.com

- may not have the funds
- may see short-term rewards
- Greater innovation can help electronic B as technology changes all the time
- Internally - through staff discussion etc
- Externally - looking at patents

Case study

GlaxoSmithKline

Headquartered in the UK and with operations based in the US, we are one of the industry leaders, with an estimated 7 per cent of the world's pharmaceutical market ... we care about the impact that we have on the people and places touched by our mission to improve health around the world ... we have a flair for research and a track record of turning that research into powerful, marketable drugs. Every hour we spend more than £300,000 (US$562,000) to find new medicines.

We produce medicines that treat six major disease areas – asthma, virus control, infections, mental health, diabetes and digestive conditions.

We also market other products, many of which are among the market leaders:

- over-the-counter (OTC) medicines including *Gaviscon* and *Panadol*

- dental products such as *Aquafresh* and *Macleans*
- smoking control products *Nicorette/Niquitin*
- nutritional healthcare drinks such as *Lucozade*, *Ribena* and *Horlicks*.

Our scientists are working hard to discover new ways of treating illness and disease. In addition to their wide-ranging talents, we use the resources of a company devoted to the application of science to improve the quality of life. It takes about 12–15 years and costs over £500 million to discover and develop a new medicine, so we need to be determined and innovative to develop our molecules into medicines as fast as possible . . .

We maintain a healthy product pipeline which ensures a flow of new products to people around the world.

Like all innovative pharmaceutical companies, we carry out a series of clinical trials to test each investigational drug for the potential to become a new medicine. The effect of the potential drug will often be compared to that of an inactive substance, a placebo, which is prepared to look like the drug so as to prevent bias during the trial. The investigational drug may also be compared against marketed medicines.

Phase I trials typically involve healthy volunteers. These trials study the safety of the drug and its interaction with the body, for example, its concentration and duration in the blood following various doses.

Phase II studies enrol patients with the illness an investigational drug is designed to treat. These trials evaluate whether the drug shows favourable effects in treating an illness and seek to determine the proper dose.

Phase III trials are designed to provide the substantial evidence of efficacy and safety required … before regulatory agencies will approve the investigational drug as a medicine and allow it to be marketed.

Therefore, a pharmaceutical company performs a comprehensive analysis of its studies for submission to regulatory agencies.

(40 marks, 60 minutes)

Questions

1 Explain the value of patents to GlaxoSmithKline. (5 marks)

2 Analyse why the launch of a new drug by GlaxoSmithKline can take several years. (8 marks)

3 Discuss the factors that might influence the research and development budget of Glaxo Wellcome. (12 marks)

4 To what extent does the success of a business such as Glaxo Wellcome depend on its research and development? (15 marks)

13 Location

The location of a business can affect its costs, its demand, its image and its ability to attract employees to work for it. The location decision is therefore a strategic decision that can affect the ability of the business to compete. The decision of where to locate can also reflect the values of the business, for example if it wants to help employment in a particular area. So, location choices should not be taken lightly and will involve decisions at the most senior level. In this chapter we examine:

- what influences a location decision
- how location decisions are made
- the benefits of an optimal location
- the advantages and disadvantages of optimal location
- the advantages and disadvantages of multi-site location
- issues relating to international locations.

Choosing a location

An important strategic operational issue facing businesses is where to locate their operations. A location decision can involve high levels of investment and have a major impact on competitiveness. The right location(s) may affect:

- the costs of production and of running the business
- the tax rates paid
- the availability of employees and the skills available
- demand for the products
- the ease of accessing markets.

Location decisions may involve several different elements: first which country, then which region and finally which specific plot of land.

The benefits of the optimal location

It may not always be possible to get the best (or optimal) location. You may find that a particular site is already taken or is too expensive. However, getting the best or nearly the best location can have several advantages:

- Lower costs may make the break-even output lower and reduce the risk of losses if sales are lower than expected.

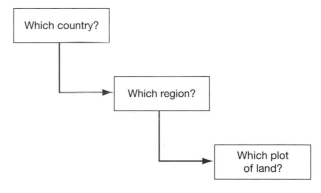

Figure 13.1 Levels of decision

- Being closer to the customer (and therefore possibly getting more customers as a result) may boost sales and profits.
- Overcoming barriers (e.g. it is difficult to export to some countries because of barriers to trade) may increase sales. By basing itself inside a customs union a firm may be able to sell in a particular country.
- It may add to the brand image. For example, having your flagship store on Fifth Avenue in New York or Convent Garden in London may be important for the status of your business.

Key terms

A **customs union** occurs when there are free trade agreements between member countries but these members have a common tax on products from non-member countries. The European Union is a customs union.

Business in Focus

Dov Charney

Dov Charney is the founder and chief executive of American Apparel, the largest T-shirt manufacturer in America. He is widely admired for almost single-handedly creating one of America's most successful fashion retailers, for devising his company's provocative approach to advertising and for treating employees better than his rivals.

Mr Charney opened his first shop in 2003. He now has over 140 stores in 11 countries selling casual clothes for men, women and children. Sales are over $300 million and the company has an 80 per cent gross profit margin, which is well above the industry average of 60 per cent. Its unbranded, brightly coloured and moderately priced T-shirts, sweatshirts, underwear and jeans have become extremely popular among the young, cosmopolitan group that Mr Charney says represents the 'world-metropolitan culture'.

From the beginning Mr Charney has put great emphasis on making his employees happy. Pay is performance-related, and amounts to $12 an hour on average, far above California's minimum wage of $6.75. American Apparel staff can buy subsidised health insurance for $8 a week. They are entitled to free English lessons, subsidised meals and free parking. Their workspace is properly lit and ventilated. When the company goes public employees will receive an average of 500 shares, expected to be worth about $4,500.

Anti-sweatshop activists praise Mr Charney as a pioneer of the fair treatment of garment workers. The benefits he provides are expensive: subsidising health insurance costs his firm $4–5 million a year;

subsidising meals costs another $500,000. He considers his contented workers the reason for his success. Treating them well means they are less likely to leave, which saves money. 'American Apparel is not an altruistic company,' says Mr Charney. 'I believe in capitalism and self-interest. Self-interest can involve being generous with others.'

Whereas Gap, another American fashion chain, outsources 83 per cent of its production to factories in Asia, all of the 4,000 or so workers involved in American Apparel's manufacturing process work in the same factory in downtown Los Angeles. But this is not because Mr Charney is opposed to outsourcing or globalisation. His motive, once again, is self-interest: it gives him control over every stage of production, and enables him to monitor the fashion market and respond quickly to new trends. In any case, he cannot outsource anything, he says, because he lacks the necessary infrastructure – and he has no plans to set it up.

Having become a public company, American Apparel now plans to open another 650 shops across the world. Retail analysts also doubt that American Apparel will be able to expand without resorting to outsourcing. Mr Charney insists that China is too far away for his T-shirt production, even though moving textiles by ship from Hong Kong to Los Angeles takes just 11 days.

Source: The *Economist*, 4 January 2007

Question:

1 Is American Apparel right to base its production in the US? Should other clothing companies follow this example?

Deciding where to locate

The decision on where to locate a business will be based on a combination of quantitative and qualitative factors. This means that it is a combination of factors that can be measured, such as the expected impact on costs and revenues (these are quantitative), as well as other factors that are less easy to quantify, such as the attraction of the surroundings and the quality of life in the area (these are qualitative).

Factors affecting a firm's location

- **The costs of a particular location relative to other options.** For example, the cost of land itself

will vary from area to area; so will the cost of labour and services such as electricity. Taxation rates can also vary significantly from country to country. The decision to locate can therefore have a significant impact on a firm's profits.

- **The availability of lower-cost locations abroad** has been a major factor for UK firms considering relocating to the Far East or Eastern Europe. Low-wage employees and a much lower cost of living often make it very financially attractive for UK firms to be based overseas.
- **The availability of government grants and incentives.** If, for example, a government offers low rents or lower taxes to attract firms, this can obviously act as an incentive to locate there. In the

last 20 years, for example, the development agencies in regions of the UK, such as Wales and Scotland, have been very effective at attracting overseas investment not just because of financial aid but also because of the general level of local and national government cooperation in areas such as planning permission. Governments often use a combination of push and pull techniques to encourage firms to locate in particular regions. Incentives such as grants help to pull firms to an area; refusing permission to build in other areas helps to push firms to locate where the government wants them to be.

- **The infrastructure of the region.** The availability of energy sources and transport facilities will affect the ease, speed and cost of production.

The importance of such factors will vary between industries, for example transport facilities are crucial to a wholesaler but less significant for an online insurance business.

- **The nature of the business itself.** The extent to which a firm has freedom over the location decision depends in part on what it actually does. A self-employed website designer, for example, may be able to work from home. A fast-food restaurant, by comparison, must be located somewhere near its customers, while a mining company must base its production facilities where the actual minerals are.

- **The location of the market.** In some cases, such as retailing, it will often be important to be close to the market. A central high street location is

Business in Focus

The risks of operating in different countries

'Risk Briefing' rates operational risk in 150 markets on a scale of 0 100. The overall scores are an aggregate of underlying scores for ten categories of risk: security; political stability; government effectiveness; legal and regulatory; macroeconomic; foreign trade and payments; financial; tax policy; labour market; and infrastructure.

Question:

1 To what extent do you think the table above should influence a firm's decision where to locate?

Table 13.1
Economist.com rankings
Operational risk
Countries, September 2008 (September 2007 score, if different)

Least risky				Most risky			
Rank		Score		Rank		Score	
1	Switzerland	8	(7)	**150**	Iraq	84	(88)
2	Denmark	10	(8)	**149**	Guinea	80	(79)
	Singapore	10		**148**	Myanmar	79	(78)
	Sweden	10		**147**	Zimbabwe	78	(77)
5	Finland	12	(10)	**146**	Turkmenistan	77	
6	Austria	14			Uzbekistan	77	
	Luxembourg	14		**144**	Venezuela	75	(74)
	Norway	14		**143**	Tajikistan	71	(70)
9	Netherlands	15	(13)	**142**	Eritrea	70	(69)
	Britain	15	(12)	**141**	Chad	68	
11	Canada	16	(15)		Ecuador	68	
	Hong Kong	16		**139**	Kenya	66	
13	France	17	(16)	**138**	Cote d'Ivoire	65	
	Germany	17	(16)		Nigeria	65	(67)
15	Australia	18	(16)		Sudan	65	
	Belgium	18					
	Malta	18	(19)				

*Out of 100, with higher numbers indicating more risk.
Source: Economist Intelligence Unit

more likely to attract business than a site located several miles away from the main shopping areas. In other industries, such as telephone banking, it is not so important to be close to the customer.

- **Market access.** The location of a firm may affect its ability to trade in particular markets. Firms based outside the European Union (EU), for example, must pay a tax (a tariff) to sell their goods within the EU. Firms located within the EU do not have to pay this tax. This is one reason why many Japanese firms set up in the UK in the last 20 years – if they have UK production facilities using a proportion of UK components they can export to other EU states and not pay a tariff; this obviously makes their goods more competitive compared with exporting from Japan.

- **Exchange rates.** If the pound is strong it is expensive for UK-based producers to export. On the other hand, it means UK firms have strong purchasing power overseas, which led some firms to relocate overseas at this time.

- **Political stability.** The political climate can have an impact on the appeal of a certain area. For example, terrorist threats in countries post 11 September 2001 have created instability in certain regions, and the UK's reluctance to commit to the single currency has meant some overseas investors have been wary of locating in the UK because they have been worried about the possible impact of being outside the 'euro zone'.

- **Resources.** A firm may locate in a particular area because of the resources it offers. Microsoft located near Cambridge in the UK because it wanted easy access to top graduates and research facilities.

- **Image.** A perfume company, for example, may benefit from being based in Paris or Milan but may not gain the same prestige from being located in Scunthorpe.

- **Quality of life**, for example, how attractive is the area in itself? What are the facilities like? What is the standard of living like?

- **Ethical issues.** Some firms have avoided locating in low-wage areas for fear of being criticised for 'exploiting' local staff or of taking jobs away from the UK. In many cases firms expand in areas where they already have established links (and therefore feel some responsibility to the community) rather than take jobs elsewhere. The Body Shop set up one of its manufacturing operations at Easterhouse in Scotland specifically to bring jobs to a deprived area.

Reasons for locating abroad	
Supply side issues	**Demand side issues**
• Overcome trade barriers e.g. locate within a customs union • Benefit from lower costs abroad e.g. in China	• Access global markets e.g. the fast growth BRIC economies of Brazil, Russia, India and China • Expand out of a mature market

Figure 13.2 Reasons for locating abroad

Business in Focus

Stakeholders Tata

In October 2008 India's Tata group abandoned plans to build the world's cheapest car in the eastern state of West Bengal. Tata group chief Ratan Tata said: 'We have little choice but to move out of Bengal. We cannot run a factory with police around all the time.' He was speaking after protests in a row over land acquired from local farmers.

The car, the Nano, is expected to cost about 100,000 rupees ($2,130). Tata had planned to make 250,000 cars a year at the Singur plant in West Bengal, rising to 350,000. The dispute in West Bengal highlights a wider problem between India's growing industry, which needs land, and its farmers, who are unwilling to give it up.

Mr Tata said the Nano will be built 'within this year but I can't tell you where. We have got offers from several Indian states but we have not yet finalised where to produce the Nano ... All these issues we will announce in the next few days when we have a clearer picture.'

Mr Tata said his group would still consider West Bengal as an investment destination in future. 'I value the considerable intellectual resources this state has, but something will have to change here,' he said.

He was speaking after meeting the West Bengal chief minister and his colleagues. 'This is a black day for Bengal. We will have so much more difficulty getting investments now,' said the state's industry minister.

The West Bengal government acquired 1,000 acres of land for the Nano project two years ago.

More than 10,000 farmers accepted compensation for their land, but just over 2,000 of them refused and demanded land be returned.

During the protests Tata's engineers and workers were attacked, prompting the group to stop work.

Question:

1 Discuss the factors that might determine where Tata now bases its factory.

Business in Focus

Disney

In the early 1980s the heads of Disney were looking for a location in Europe to open a new theme park. The first one outside the US was Japan and now Disney was looking for another base.

They initially came up with over 1,000 possible locations in Europe. By March 1985, the number of possible locations for the park had been reduced to four; two in France and two in Spain. Both of these countries saw the potential economic advantages of a Disney theme park and were offering financial deals to Disney. A strong possibility was a site near Toulon in southern France, not far from Marseille. The pleasing landscape of that region, as well as its climate, made the location a likely winner for the European Disney. However, thick layers of bedrock were discovered beneath the site, which meant construction would be too difficult. Finally, a site in the rural town of Marne-la-Vallée was chosen because it was close to Paris and its location was estimated to be no more than a four-hour drive for 68 million people and no more than a two-hour flight for a further 300 million. The agreement to build was signed in 1986.

Question:

1 How much do you think Disney should adapt what it offers at its theme parks in different countries?

Methods of making location decisions

A location decision is likely to be a combination of quantitative and qualitative analysis. This means that managers will consider what the numbers say (e.g. What is the likely rate of return in a particular location?) but also qualitative factors such as the effect on the quality of working life or the impact on the environment.

Quantitative analysis

The location decision can be absolutely critical to a firm because of its impact on costs and revenues and therefore profit. It can also be a difficult and expensive decision to change once it is made, which makes it even more important to get it right first time. To help ensure that the most financially attractive decision is made firms may use quantitative decision-making techniques. These are tools used to measure the value of a decision and may include the following.

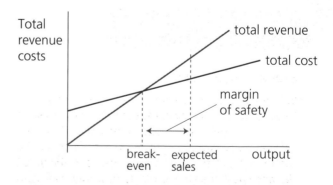

Figure 13.3 Margin of safety

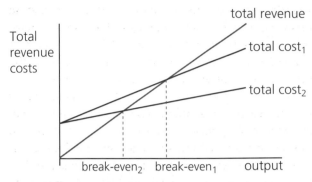

Figure 13.4 Lower variable costs reduce the number of units that need to be sold to break even

- **Break-even analysis.** A firm will want to know how many units must be sold in order to break even, i.e. for the revenue generated to cover the costs. It will also want to calculate the margin of safety, i.e. the extent to which sales could fall from the forecast figure before the firm starts to make a loss (see Figure 13.3). If the fixed costs of a particular location are lower than another (perhaps because of lower rents), this will reduce the break-even level of output – fewer units need to be sold to cover costs. Similarly, if the variable cost per unit is lower (e.g. due to lower wage rates) this will also reduce the break-even output (see Figure 13.4).

Business in Focus

Figure 13.5 The Atlantis

The Atlantis

Sol Kerzner is a London-based billionaire casino and hotel operator who recently opened a £1 billion resort called the Atlantis, in Dubai.

Aged over 70 this was one of the biggest risks of of Kerzner's career since he defied international opposition and opened the Sun City resort in Bophuthatswana, one of the independent tribal 'home-lands' of apartheid South Africa. He has invested £400 million into the 1,600-room Atlantis hotel and aquatic theme park in Dubai and spent hundreds of millions more expanding his existing One & Only hotel in the Arab emirate. He is also building a second One & Only on The World, a collection of man-made islands arranged in the shape of a map of the globe.

Atlantis is the biggest hotel in the Middle East. It sits on Palm Jumeirah, an artificial island in the shape of a date palm. The three-day grand opening party was attended by Sheikh Mohammed Bin Rashid Al-Maktoum, Dubai's ruler, and the most senior business executives in the region. Also attending were celebrities including Robert De Niro, Denzel Washington and Naomi Campbell. Kylie Minogue performed a concert and there was a fireworks display six times larger than the one at the opening of the Beijing Olympics. Locating the Atlantis in Dubai goes against so much that has made Kerzner one of the world's most successful hoteliers. He has created his privately held, £2 billion global hotel and casino brand by offering 'anything goes' hedonism. At his biggest flagship properties there has always been round-the-clock drinking and gambling. At the Atlantis there is no alcohol or gambling.

Kerzner says he is sticking to his formula of offering people something they have never experienced before. 'There's nothing like Atlantis for 1,000 miles in any direction, just like there was nothing like Sun City in Africa or Atlantis in the Caribbean when we opened there. We're offering the first $1 million-a-room resort; a water-based Disney-style theme park for all ages; restaurants by Nobu and Giorgio Locatelli for the adults. And we're doing it in an iconic building on the iconic development in the Gulf.' Kerzner points out that, with oil revenues coming in the local economy is still strong. 'There's no better example of growth than Dubai. Despite everything, most sectors are still expanding. The infrastructure is fantastic. Emirates [Dubai's airline] connects every big city on the planet.' Recent figures from accountants Deloitte Touche Tohmatsu confirm that the Middle East had the highest hotel occupancy rates in the world during the first half of the year, with Dubai leading the region at 85.3 per cent.

Question:

1 Discuss the factors that might determine the long-term success of the Atlantis.

- **Investment appraisal.** The decision to be based in a particular location is often a large-scale investment and as such firms are likely to undertake a detailed financial analysis of the expected payback period, the average rate of return and net present value. Given a choice a firm will usually choose the option with the quickest payback, the highest average rate of return and the highest net present value. In reality the decision may not be that straightforward, for example, one option may have a quicker payback but a lower average rate of return.

Qualitative factors

Although firms are likely to examine the potential impact on revenues and costs of selecting a particular site, the decision may also be affected by less measurable factors such as whether the location itself appeals to the managers, and the quality of life in the area. For example, many Japanese firms have been attracted to the UK because of the importance of the English language in business. It is also because English is learnt in Japanese schools – this makes it easier for these firms to set up here than in France, for example. The culture of the country and the extent to which you think you understand its traditions, its ways of working and its customers are all very important. According to Rugman (2000), the probability of an American multinational opening its first operations outside the US in Canada or the UK is 70 per cent; these are similar countries and therefore appear familiar territories. The probability of an American multinational opening its second operation in Germany or Japan is 2 per cent; these seem less appealing as the cultures are more different.

Once a few firms have set up in a location this can also act as an incentive for others to locate there, as they may think this proves it is safe and that networking (i.e. using the expertise and experience of others) will be easier. The growth of Hollywood as a film centre and Silicon Valley as a centre for computing are in part because the success of some firms has drawn in others.

Other possible qualitative factors which could attract managers to particular areas include the fact that they like the region or because they have particular attachments to the place. William Morris, for example, set up a car factory based in Oxford simply because he lived there. Managers might also choose a location because the name of the place enhances the product's image; a fashion house in New York

sounds more exclusive than a fashion house in Grimsby; an advertising agency in London may have more appeal than one in Dundee. The reasons a particular location is chosen are, of course, varied: in the case of call centres, some firms have located in the north east or north west of the UK because callers like the accent of people from these areas more than the accents of people from the south east. Although this factor may well impact on a firm's profits it is difficult to place an absolute value on an accent and so this also counts as a qualitative factor. Interestingly, other firms have located to India to cut costs.

Key Issues

With the growth of the knowledge economy in the UK the location of many businesses matters less than it did before and the qualitative factors become more significant. Web designers, computer programmers, artists and online businesses can be based almost anywhere – they are footloose; being near key supplies or key customers become less significant factors.

Types of location decision

There are in fact many types of location decision which managers may have to consider. There is the initial decision of where to set up the business. In many ways this is the easiest decision in that the managers have no commitments to existing facilities. On the other hand, it usually occurs at a time when money is tight and the firm will be heavily constrained by what it can afford. A key decision at this time is the desired capacity level – how big must the factory be? Or how much office space is needed? Managers may want to be optimistic about the possible growth of the business; at the same time they do not want to commit to large facilities and then find these are under utilised.

Once a firm is established it may have to consider relocating at some point in its development. This occurs when a firm wants to move its facilities. This may be necessary because the initial reasons for choosing a place have now gone (e.g. government grants have been withdrawn or tax rates have been increased), or perhaps because the firm has outgrown its premises.

When relocating, a firm may have more experience of the type of facilities it needs than it did when it first chose its location; it may also have greater financial resources than when it started up. However, relocation brings with it all sorts of new problems, including:

- staff who do not want to move (or the firm does not want to pay to relocate) – these people may need compensation
- there could be a period of lost production time during the move
- the costs of notifying customers and suppliers and administrative costs such as changing the firm's literature to include the new addresses.

A new location may also be part of an expansion process: a firm could be building new production facilities or opening up a new outlet, for example. The acquisition of new premises inevitably brings with it issues of management structure and control. A new facility will need controlling and the senior managers will need to decide on the best way of structuring the business, such as deciding what new jobs are created, what the reporting relationships will be and how to ensure effective communication.

Offshoring

Offshoring occurs when a business shifts production overseas ('off shore'). This has been common in recent years as many businesses have moved some of their operations to countries such as India, China, Turkey and Vietnam where production costs are so much lower. Printing, toy manufacturing, call centres, clothes production, shoe manufacturing and a great deal of manufacturing has moved abroad. Dyson, Burberry and MG are just a few examples of where production has gone offshore. Many support activities such as computing and accounting have also gone overseas.

The aim of offshoring is to reduce costs. In India, for example, there are many highly skilled computing and engineering graduates who are much cheaper and much easier to recruit than their UK counterparts. Moving to countries such as China may mean:

- lower wages
- less regulation
- less concern over methods of production and the impact on the environment
- lower or fewer taxes.

This all enables cheaper and more flexible production which may be difficult to match in more developed economies.

Business in Focus

Heathrow Terminal 5

Terminal 5 at Heathrow finally opened in 2008. This enabled the airport to serve another 30 million passengers a year. However, the decision to locate an additional terminal at Heathrow met huge resistance from various pressure groups. Environmentalists said it would mean more pollution. Defenders of the terminal said it was essential to improve the service for passengers and would create more jobs in the area. Work started in 2002 after a record public inquiry. The project cost £4.3 billion.

The main building is 400 m by 180 m and contains 105 lifts, 65 escalators and will consist of 80,000 tonnes of steel. You can fit 52 full-sized football pitches in its floor space and it is the largest free-standing building in the UK.

It has 30,000 square metres of reinforced glass and 5,500 glass panels have been used to glaze the terminal building and roof, giving the whole terminal a light and airy feel. The Terminal is located between Heathrow's two runways on land previously occupied by a sludge works. The project has successfully moved 9 million cubic metres of earth and two rivers have been diverted to create space for the new building.

Water from Terminal 5's rainwater harvesting and groundwater boreholes is being used for non-potable uses, reducing the demand on the mains water by 70 per cent. The harvesting scheme reuses up to 85 per cent of the rain that falls on Terminal 5's campus.

Question:

1 Discuss the factors that might have been considered before deciding to add an extra terminal at Heathrow rather than another airport.

The difficulty can be maintaining quality because you are not so close to the production. Several banks have moved their call centres back to the UK because customers felt the service was not good enough.

There may also be difficult ethical issues involved, for example, is it right to lose UK jobs by closing production here and moving it to another country? Is it right to pay much lower wages abroad than in the UK? Gap, Next, Primark and Nike have all faced criticism at some time over the way people working in their suppliers have been treated.

The choice of where to shift production to is affected by cultural issues as well as costs, i.e. moving to where you feel you know something about the culture. Japanese companies are starting to outsource to China, where large numbers of Japanese speakers can be found. German companies tend to outsource to Poland and Romania, where proficiency in German is common. French companies outsource to North Africa where France has many connections.

Although offshoring has increased in recent years as it has become easier for companies to base themselves in countries such as China, this does not mean that all production has gone. What tends to be left is higher value-added production activities such as design, research and development or the production of premium craft products.

> **Key terms**
> **Offshoring** refers to the relocation by a company of a business process from one country to another.
> **Business ethics** refer to what is regarded as right and wrong and what is acceptable behaviour.

Figure 13.6 A call centre abroad

Business in Focus

Offshoring

Many companies have moved their call centres abroad, particularly to India. However, some UK clients have complained that the people they are talking to do not know enough about Britain. In an effort to change this, some firms such as Infovision, which runs a call centre for the AA, has been training its Indian employees in the subtleties of British accents and culture. A month-long crash course in UK culture and pronunciation included television programmes such as *EastEnders* and *Coronation Street*, as well as information on festivals such as Christmas and Guy Fawkes' Night. Indian staff were introduced to British food, pubs, British education and shops, political parties and how to say the names of places and famous people. The thinking is that call-centre agents in India are more likely to be successful if they not only sound like the John Smiths and Karen Joneses they are helping, but also get to grips with the kind of lives the British lead.

Offshoring is on the rise. The technology research company Gartner recently predicted that up to 25 per cent of traditional IT jobs in the West today will have been outsourced to emerging markets such as India by 2010.

A report on the Indian economy from investment bank Goldman Sachs estimates that about 7 per cent of India's population speak English, making the sub-continent the second-largest pool of English speakers in the world.

The number of workers suitable for outsourcing in the service and IT industries has grown to 650,000 from 6,800 in 1986, the report says. HSBC pays Indian call-centre workers around £2,500 a year, compared with £18,750 in the UK. The average salary for highly qualified Indian business graduates is just £7,000, a fraction of the cost of MBA graduates in the West.

With the Indian call-centre agents' lucrative salaries come free meals and transport to and from work, as well as the public perception that being a call-centre worker is good work. The occupation carries kudos – a far cry from its image in the UK.

Accounting, financial services and the health and pharmaceutical sectors are increasingly using outsourcing. India, in particular, is well suited to carrying out research and development and to the manufacturing of drugs because of its highly trained workforce and good infrastructure.

The financial information and news group Reuters has already outsourced some of its IT operations to India and is also planning to recruit Indian journalists to report company results and other announcements.

Unions in Britain have lobbied against offshoring, and politicians have not been slow to address the issue. In the US, the issue is even more sensitive, as American companies are the largest users of offshore services in the world. The government has recently imposed restrictions on the outsourcing of US federal contracts.

Question:

1 Discuss the reasons why India may be such a popular location for offshore operations.

Business in Focus

Made in Britain

Many products are now produced abroad because it is cheaper. Even famous 'British brands' are often made overseas, such as most of Hackett's products or Burberry clothes.

A spokeswoman for Marks & Spencer said: 'You can still be a British brand but sell products that are sourced globally – like Marks & Spencer. The British manufacturing base has shrunk drastically over the years, but even if you don't manufacture here, it doesn't mean you are not a British brand.'

But if you do want to buy British, what is still made in the UK?

Clothes: the luxury brand Barbour, whose products are worn by the Queen, still has all its factories in the UK. All of its classic wax jackets are still made in South Shields, Tyne and Wear, where 180 skilled machinists are based.

Shoes: Charles Tyrwhitt makes its shoes here (but shorts abroad). Its website says: 'We still manufacture all our shoes in the UK and this is because the UK still makes the best shoes in the world. Unfortunately, investment in infrastructure and training has not been maintained sufficiently in other areas of UK manufacturing. We wish it had.' The town of Northampton has been manufacturing footwear since the 17th century. Even its football team rejoices in the nickname of 'the Cobblers'. There are still about eight factories there, including John Lobb, Tricker's, Crockett & Jones, Edward Green and Church's Footwear (owned by Prada). Church's employs more than 500 people in its manufacturing group in the area. Spokeswoman Jenny Mead says: 'Shoe-making has always traditionally been in Northampton, because of the oak woods for tanning material. We've build up a niche product here, and shoe-making skills have been passed down through generations of families. If we were to move elsewhere, we'd lose our tradition.'

Ceramics and homeware: Waterford Wedgwood (which owns the Royal Doulton, Waterford Crystal and Wedgwood brands) is based at plants in Stoke-on-Trent, along with Emma Bridgewater, Portmeirion Potteries, Royal Stafford and Moorland Pottery.

For furniture, DFS makes its sofas in Britain and has three factories in Yorkshire, Nottinghamshire and Derbyshire, while Marks & Spencer's made-to-order upholstered furniture is largely produced at its own 'eco-factory' in Wales.

While many electrical products are now made overseas, some are still produced here. Dualit has been making all its Vario toasters in Britain for 60 years and has its own factory in Crawley.

Bicycles: Brompton Bicycles, famous for its folding bikes, is one of the few companies to keep all its manufacturing in England – it has had a factory in Middlesex for the past 30 years. A spokesman for Brompton says: 'Most companies make their bikes in Asia, but we would never consider making them abroad because we want to stay British and we feel the quality is better here.'

Chocolate: Cadbury, one of the best-known British brands, has been making chocolate in Bournville, Birmingham, since 1879. But in 2007 it announced that it would close one of its factories, near Bristol, and shift some operations to Poland. A Cadbury spokesman said: 'It makes better business sense to transfer some production to Poland, but Bournville is Cadbury's spiritual home.' Most chocolates will still be made in Bournville but individual bars will be made in Poland.

Prestat has been making and selling chocolate since 1902, and the company still uses its original recipes at its North London factory, which employs 30 people. The company has just invested £250,000 on a bar-wrapping machine so that it could keep production in the UK.

Bill Keeling, managing director of Prestat, says: 'We consider ourselves to be a very English company and believe wholeheartedly in English production as being at the core of the company. Too many bars sold to UK consumers by iconic brands are being made abroad – it's utterly unnecessary. We aren't in the business of cutting costs to the bone at the expense of quality.'

Question:

1 What else can you think of that is made in Britain?

Multi-site locations

Many business will operate from many sites. In the case of retail operations this may be because there are different stores in different places. In the case of manufacturing it may involve different production bases in different locations.

By operating in different sites a business may benefit from:

- the gains of different resources in different locations (e.g. cheap labour in some countries, lower taxes in other regions)
- being closer to customers in different regions, enabling a better understanding of market needs and faster response times to local needs
- providing a safety net by splitting production to different sites so that if there are problems on one site production can continue elsewhere.

The disadvantages of multi-site location include:

- the problems of managing and coordinating operations that are geographically separate; simply from a management perspective this is difficult

- if some decisions are now taken separately rather than for the business as a whole there may be a loss of some economies of scale.

> **Key terms**
> **Localisation** refers to the extent to which a business adjusts to local market conditions.
> **Quality assurance** refers to a process by which organisations aim to prevent errors occurring.

Multinationals and overseas locations

A multinational business is one that has bases in more than one country. Examples of multinationals are Shell, Ford, Coca-Cola and Wal-Mart. Locating overseas naturally adds another dimension to any location decision. Many individuals in the UK, for example, have acquired properties in France or Italy, either as a second home or to go and live there, only to find it brings with it all sorts of problems they had not originally imagined. For example, acquiring properties abroad will involve an understanding of

Business in Focus

Toyota

During the almost 50 years since we first began exports, Toyota vehicles have found their way to over 170 countries and regions throughout the world. As our exports have continued to develop so has the localisation of our production bases, in line with our policy of 'producing vehicles where the demand exists'. Currently there are 52 bases in 27 different countries and regions. In addition, there are design and R&D bases in seven locations overseas, showing that from development and design to production, sales and service, Toyota has now achieved consistent globalisation as well as localisation.

There are a number of hurdles that this globalisation of production has to overcome. Among these the most important is 'quality assurance', which requires that 'no matter where Toyota vehicles are made, they have the same quality'. To put it another way, we don't put a label on our vehicles which says 'Made in such and such a country', we put the same label on all vehicles which reads 'Made by TOYOTA'. This means that we need to spread Toyota's manufacturing philosophy – the 'Toyota Way' – to all of our overseas bases. And on top of this it is important

that we minimise the necessary support that comes from Japan and let each of our overseas bases become self-reliant.

For example, the Toyota plant that recently commenced production in Texas made maximum use of the know-how which has been cultivated over the past 20 years by the Toyota plant in Kentucky. This is just the latest example of how the localised 'Toyota Way' is being passed on overseas.

Toyota believes that the way to achieve 'quality assurance' and to 'spread the Toyota Way' is by educating people: 'Making things is about developing people.' So, in 2003, we established the Global Production Center (GPC) within the Motomachi Plant in Toyota City. Furthermore, in 2006, we established regional GPCs in the United States, the United Kingdom and Thailand to carry out corresponding activities in the North American, European and Asia-Pacific regions respectively.

Question:

1 Discuss the advantages and disadvantages of Toyota's approach to locating its factories.

different legal requirements and processes. Overseas specialists will usually be necessary to make sense of the different requirements and to oversee the process of acquisition. Communicating and controlling facilities abroad may also prove more difficult simply due to the geographic distance between sites.

Why become multinational?

There are many reasons why firms might want to become multinational. These include:

- To benefit from lower costs overseas.
- To benefit from less regulation (e.g. fewer health and safety restrictions).
- To benefit from a greater pool of labour (e.g. locating overseas may enable the firm to recruit more cheaply or to benefit from particular skills). The labour market may also be more flexible, meaning that a firm can hire and fire staff more easily. The rights of employees in the UK, for example, have tended to be relatively low compared with those in other countries in the EU in terms of redundancy and dismissal rights and protection at work. This is one reason why the UK has been so attractive to overseas investors wanting to operate within the EU.
- To benefit from particular resources such as minerals.
- To benefit from market opportunities overseas. Firms may decide to expand overseas because the domestic market is saturated and there seems to be relatively slow growth compared with opportunities abroad, or simply because a firm identifies attractive possibilities in foreign markets. Opening up new stores or new factories abroad therefore provides an opportunity for growth. This then creates the possibility of economies of scale. By operating on a larger scale worldwide a firm may benefit from purchasing economies reducing the cost per unit.
- To be closer to their overseas customers; it may be easier to understand customer requirements and to provide a faster, more efficient service by being based in that country.
- To overcome protectionist trade barriers. Trading in China, for example, is very difficult unless a firm actually sets up there or at least has a form of partnership with a local firm. The Chinese government is eager to prevent what it regards as exploitation of the Chinese market unless western firms are actually investing into China at the same time.

Business in Focus

Entering India

In 2007 Wal-Mart entered the India market. It did this by signing an agreement to start a wholesale operation in equal partnership with Bharti Enterprises, an Indian conglomerate. Under the name Bharti Wal-Mart, the new company plans to open around 12 cash-and-carry stores by 2015.

Wal-Mart would like to grow at a faster rate than this in India. After all, it has huge potential. At current growth rates it will be the world's fifth-biggest consumer market by 2025, according to McKinsey, a management consultancy. However, around 97 per cent of Indian retailing is in the form of small, often family-run, stores rather than chains of supermarkets mostly of less than 500 square feet (46 square metres). This creates an opportunity for large retailers such as Wal-Mart, except for one thing: foreign firms are only permitted to own up to 51 per cent of shops selling single-brand products or to sell to others on a wholesale basis. They cannot open supermarkets directly. This limits what foreign retailers can achieve in the India market.

In 2008 Tesco also announced it would enter the India market by investing £60 million to open a wholesale cash-and-carry business based in Mumbai. The group has also signed a deal to help the retail arm of India's Tata group, Trent, develop its hypermarket business, for a fee. Chief executive Sir Terry Leahy added that the move would give the group 'access to another of the most important economies in the world'. At the time Tesco operated 3,729 stores employing more than 440,000 people in 13 countries across the globe, including Hungary, Slovakia, Malaysia and Thailand.

Question:

1 Discuss the factors Wal-Mart or Tesco should consider when choosing a new market to enter.

- To weaken trade union power. If a firm produces only in one country it is vulnerable to industrial action within that country. If, for example, there is a dispute with a trade union this could halt production completely; by having production facilities in several countries it is less likely production will ever be halted fully. Also it is more difficult for trade unions to organise themselves if they are in different countries so having, say, their factories in three different countries reduces the union power compared with having all three factories in one country.
- To overcome exchange rate problems; by producing in the market where it sells, a firm will not face the difficulty of fluctuating exchange rates which can suddenly make exports from its home country seem uncompetitive.

Is a low-cost location the best?

Although firms will often be seeking to increase efficiency and reduce their costs, this does not necessarily mean they will always seek the lowest-cost location. First, they may be influenced by qualitative factors – they may prefer to move to a location where they are familiar with the culture or language, for example. Second, they must consider the possible impact on quality. A cheaper location may not have the same access to high-quality resources. Third, a firm's location may impact on its revenue; a high street location may be an expensive option for a retailer but attract far more customers and so prove more profitable.

The location decision must therefore involve an overview of many different factors, including qualitative issues and overall profitability as well as costs.

Summary

Location can influence a firm's costs and revenues. It is a strategic decision in that once a decision is made it may be expensive and time consuming to move. Decisions may include which countries to operate in and whether to operate on several sites.

Progress questions

1 Explain how location decision can affect a firm's competitiveness. (5 marks)
2 What is the difference between quantitative and qualitative factors affecting a location decision? Give examples. (5 marks)
3 Outline two factors that might influence the location of a clothes retailer. (6 marks)
4 Outline two factors that might influence the location of a health club. (6 marks)
5 Outline two factors that might influence the location of a car production plant. (6 marks)
6 Outline two factors that might influence the location of a farm. (6 marks)
7 Explain how location can affect break-even output. (4 marks)
8 What is meant by a multinational business? (2 marks)
9 Explain one advantage of having multi-site locations. (3 marks)
10 Explain one disadvantage of a multi-site location. (3 marks)

Analysis and evaluation questions

1 Analyse the factors that might determine the location of a new theme park. (8 marks)
2 Discuss the importance of qualitative factors when locating the new head office of major global bank. (15 marks)
3 With reference to companies or industries you know, to what extent can the location of business influence its competitiveness? (15 marks)

Case study

Steiff

The world's most famous teddy bear is turning its back on China as Steiff moves to take production of its plush animals back to Germany.

Steiff is rejecting globalisation to keep the fur gleaming on the world's poshest bears. Fed up with poor workmanship, high staff turnover, delays and rising shipping costs, it is moving bear production back to its birthplace in Giengen an der Brenz.

Steiff's managing director said China was not capable of making a product to the level of sophistication it requires. It takes 18 months to train a worker to make a Steiff animal.

'If one of the glass eyes is a millimetre off, it means the adorable devoted look on the teddy bear's face ends up more like a stupid stare,' he said.

Steiff invented the teddy bear in 1902, branding its creations with a button in the bear's ear. In an effort to reduce the high cost of production, the company began outsourcing four years ago when it sent hundreds of staff to China to train the workforce.

Mr Frechen said: 'What we expect, they cannot produce.' The rapid turnover of the Chinese workforce has been a problem as staff chase higher wages.

'At one of our competitors, one morning a third of the employees didn't turn up to work.' Steiff makes an expensive product and the firm has no desire to compete with mass-market toymakers. However, the rising cost of manufacturing and shipping products from China is eroding the advantage of outsourcing a premium product. Delays have caused difficulties for a firm that has to respond quickly to fast-moving toy fashions.

The company suffered months of delays in the delivery of toys modelled on Knut, the famous polar bear cub in Berlin zoo. 'What we have learnt from the experience is that the things we do much better we do ourselves and that is how we keep our competitive advantage.'

Steiff was founded in 1880 by Margarete Steiff who, despite being disabled and wheelchair-bound from childhood, created a toy business sewing and stuffing felt animals. In 1903 the first Steiff bear was shown at a Leipzig trade fair where an American department store buyer ordered 3,000 and it became an immediate success.

(40 marks, 60 minutes)

Questions

1 Explain how Steiff's production methods may differ from those of a mass-market toymaker. (5 marks)
2 Analyse the possible reasons why Steiff originally chose to locate production in China. (8 marks)
3 Discuss the main factors that should determine the resource mix used when producing Steiff bears. (12 marks)
4 To what extent can the location of production influence the success of Steiff? (15 marks)

Lean production

Lean production aims to reduce wastage and thereby make a business more efficient. This may be crucial in an age of growing competition.

In this chapter we consider:
- the meaning and significance of lean production
- the effective management of time
- the meaning and value of critical path analysis.

Introduction to lean production

With greater globalisation and competition from all over the world the pressure is on organisations to become more efficient. They are often facing demands for increased pay and higher input costs, but cannot easily pass these on to their customers so, to maintain profits, there is a pressing need for greater efficiencies. Managers are constantly looking for ways of reducing the cost per unit. This does not necessarily mean producing cheaply – a Ferrari car, a Chanel dress and Jimmy Choo shoes are always likely to be expensive to make. However, many managers will want to find the cheapest way of producing at a given quality level. As we saw earlier, this may be achieved by innovation. It can also be helped by trying to become leaner in the way a product is produced.

Lean production aims to reduce all forms of waste in the production process. It is an approach that was developed most fully in Japan. Waste is called Muda in Japan and lean production aims to drive out all forms of Muda. This includes the waste of materials, of time, of energy and of human effort. Lean production streamlines operations so that costs are reduced and efficiency increased. To achieve this, a number of techniques have been developed (mainly in Japan) aimed at getting things right first time and reducing wastage levels.

According to Taichi Ohno (from Toyota) the seven types of waste include:

1 Defects; these only have to be put right later on and cost money or they have to be thrown away or reworked.

2 Overproduction of goods not demanded by actual customers; if they are not needed why produce them? They only have to be reworked or thrown away.

3 Inventories awaiting further processing or consumption; this represents idle money.

4 Unnecessary processing; why add features or extra work if it is not needed?

5 Unnecessary motion of employees; this wastes time and energy.

6 Unnecessary transport and handling of goods; again, a waste of resources.

7 Waiting for an earlier stage of the process to deliver; waiting time is idle time!

The techniques involved in lean production include:

- time-based management
- critical path analysis
- cell production (see page 173)
- benchmarking (see page 173)
- kaizen (see page 174)
- just-in-time (JIT) production (see page 174).

Time-based management

With the levels of competition in most markets increasing rapidly, businesses are always looking for new ways of out-competing their rivals. Many firms have tried to use time as a competitive weapon. If an organisation is able to produce an item in a shorter period of time than its competitors, or deliver it more rapidly to customers, more sales may result. Sony keeps producing new models of its products, for example, so that by the time the competition has copied the features of the last one, it has already moved on to a new version. Domino's Pizza has competed aggressively in the fast-food market by promising pizza delivery within 30 minutes. Similarly, Dell can produce a computer to a customer's specifications within weeks. Photo developers now promise a one-hour service. Opticians can produce glasses in hours. Amazon can deliver within 24 hours.

As customers become eager for 'instant' service, the ability to supply items as and when they are wanted may be crucial to a business's success. The growth of internet shopping, 24-hour telephone banking and home delivery by supermarkets all reflect a desire for quick, easy access to products. Firms must try to react by reducing the time it takes to develop products. Also, with new products being launched more frequently and with rapidly changing customer tastes, products do not tend to survive for as long as they used to in the past. Over 80 per cent of new products are likely to fail in the first few years. It may be important, therefore, to develop products very quickly to keep competitive in the market.

To speed up the development of products, businesses have adopted simultaneous engineering methods. These involve getting all the engineers and designers who are concerned with a project to work on it at the same time. Instead of having one person look at a product idea, develop it and then pass it on to the next person or department, time can be saved if everyone is looking at and discussing the work simultaneously. This process has become easier due to the increasing use of information technology. This enables employees to communicate and share information more easily.

> **Key term**
>
> **Simultaneous engineering** occurs when as many activities as possible involved in developing new products are undertaken at the same time, as opposed to in sequence, to save time.

Time-based management also involves building a flexible production system able to respond quickly and effectively to customer demand. This requires employees and equipment that can produce 'just in time' so that production reacts to orders. If production can be made to follow demand, firms should be able to gain a time advantage over their competitors.

An important element of time-based management is scheduling activities effectively so that they are undertaken as efficiently as possible. There are various ways to do this, including using critical path (or network) analysis.

Critical path or network analysis

To achieve productive efficiency managers will want to plan projects as effectively as possible to ensure that time and resources are not wasted. They do not want to have people and machines sitting idle unnecessarily or materials delivered well before they are required. To help them in the planning process managers may use network analysis, also called critical path analysis.

Network analysis is a method of organising the different activities involved in a particular process in order to find the most efficient means of completing the task. The aim is to complete the project in as short a time as possible. To do this a firm will determine the exact order in which activities have to be undertaken and identify which ones can be undertaken simultaneously to save time. Network analysis can be used in any type of project that involves several activities – anything from opening a new store to planning a new advertising campaign to organising the relocation of the firm. The technique was developed for DuPont in 1957 to speed up the building of a new plant.

To undertake network analysis managers must:

- identify all the different tasks involved in the process
- estimate the expected length of time each task will take
- determine the order in which tasks must be completed. For example, in some cases particular tasks cannot be completed until another one has taken place first (these are known as 'dependent' activities). In other cases activities can be undertaken simultaneously (these are known as 'parallel' activities because they can be undertaken at the same time as each other – 'in parallel').

The next step is to construct a network chart. This is a diagrammatic representation of all the activities involved in the project, the order in which they must be undertaken and the times each one will take.

When drawing a network diagram the following features are used:

- a circle (called a 'node') represents the start and end of an activity
- a straight line represents the activity itself.

A line showing an activity is labelled in the following way: above the line the name of the activity is given; below the line the length of time the activity is expected to take is shown – this is known as the expected duration of the activity. In Figure 14.1 activity B is expected to last ten days; activity A is expected to last four days; activity B can only be

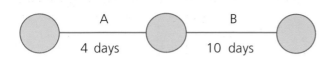

Figure 14.1

started when activity A is completed (that is why it only begins once A is complete).

In Figure 14.2 activities C and D can only be started after activity B has been completed. Activity E can only start when C and D are finished.

In Figure 14.3 we have added in some more activities. You can see that:

- activity F can start immediately
- G can start once F is completed
- H can start once E and G are completed.

All this information can be shown in Table 14.1.

We now have a whole network diagram. Remember the following rules when constructing a chart:

- The lines showing different activities must never cross.
- The lines showing activities should always begin and end at the mid-point of the nodes.
- The diagram must begin and end with one node.
- When drawing the activities and nodes, do not put the end node on any activity until you are sure

Activity	Preceded by	Duration (days)
A	—	4
B	A	10
C	B	3
D	B	1
E	C and D	5
F	—	6
G	F	9
H	E and G	3

Table 14.1

what comes next and whether anything else must also be completed before the following activity takes place.

Adding earliest start times and latest finish times

The next stage in producing a network chart is to show various information that can be calculated from the duration of each activity. This information is shown inside the node and to do this we now draw nodes in the following way:

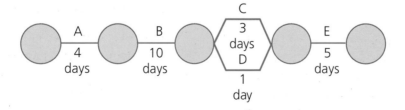

Figure 14.2

C.P.A = A,B,C
E & H

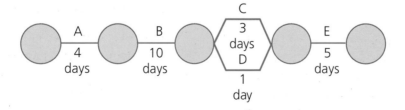

Figure 14.3

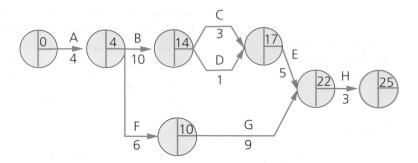

Figure 14.4

- The left-hand side shows the number of the node; this is used simply for reference and is done by numbering the nodes left to right.
- The right-hand side of the node is used to show two other pieces of information known as the 'earliest start time' (EST) of the next activity and the 'latest finish time' (LFT) of the activity before.

Earliest start times

The earliest start time (EST) is exactly what it says: it is the earliest time a particular activity can begin. This piece of information is shown in the top right of the node at the beginning of an activity.

As you can see in Figure 14.4, the earliest times have now been added. To calculate these figures you take the earliest start time of the activity before and add on the duration of that activity.

The earliest time A can start is day 0 (this is the first activity in the project); this activity takes four days so the earliest time that B can start is day 4. B takes ten days so the earliest C and D can start is 14 days.

E can only start when C and D are both finished. C takes longer than D so the project must wait for this activity to be completed before moving on; the earliest that E can start is therefore day 17.

If you have a choice of numbers to add on to calculate the earliest start time, choose the bigger number; the projects cannot continue until all previous dependent activities are finished, so you must wait for the longest one to be completed. Before H can start, for example, it must wait for both E and G to be completed, which means it cannot start until day 22.

By identifying the earliest start times a firm can see when materials are likely to be needed. This means that components and supplies can be ordered to arrive just in time to be used rather than arriving too early and sit around taking up space and costing money, or arriving late and delaying the whole

project. Materials and resources for activity E, for example, do not need to be ready until day 17.

Calculating the earliest start time is therefore an important part of developing a lean approach to a project and ensuring people and materials are coordinated and ready at exactly the right moment.

Latest finish time

The bottom-right space of a node is used to show the latest finish time (LFT) of an activity. Again this shows exactly what it says – the latest an activity can be finished without holding up the whole project.

Activity H must finish on day 25 – the day the whole project can be completed; since H takes three days it means the activities before must be finished by day 22 if the project is to be completed on time. Activity E must therefore be completed at the latest by day 22. Since E takes five days this means the activities before (C and D) must be finished by day 17. Given that C takes three days (which is the longer activity out of C and D), if this stage is to be completed by day 17 the stage before must be finished by day 14.

To work out the latest finish times, therefore, you work right to left deducting the duration of a particular activity from its latest finish time to get the latest finish time of the one before. If there are two or more activities involved (such as C and D), choose the longer duration.

Rules when calculating ESTs and LFTs

- To calculate the earliest start time of an activity, work left to right and add on the duration of the next activity to the previous earliest start time; if there is a choice, choose the biggest number to add on.
- To calculate the latest finish time of an activity, work right to left and deduct its duration from the previous latest finish time; if there is a choice of numbers, choose the largest number to deduct.

Total float time

Using the earliest start times and the latest finish times it is possible to calculate the total float time of an activity. The total float time shows how long an activity can overrun without holding up the whole project.

To calculate total float use the equation

Total float time = latest finish time − duration − earliest start time

For example, if activity D has to be finished by day 17, can start on day 14 and lasts one day then the total float is 2 days. This activity has two days' slack – it could overrun by two days and the project would still finish on time. By comparison, if activity B has to

> **Key terms**
> **Float time** is the length of time an activity can overrun without delaying the completion of the whole project. The **critical path** refers to activities that have no float time; if they overrun at all the whole project is delayed.

Activity	Preceded by	Duration (days)
A	—	4
B	A	10
C	B	3
D	B	1
E	C and D	5
F	—	6
G	F	9
H	E and G	3

Table 14.2

be finished by day 14, can start on day 4 and lasts ten days, its float is 0. There is no float – it must be completed on time or the whole project will be delayed. B is therefore known as a 'critical' activity because it has no total float. By identifying all of the critical

activities the firm can see which activities must be finished on time; this is known as the critical path.

The critical path for the project in Table 14.2 is ABCEH because these activities have no total float time. If they are delayed at all the whole project will be late and will not be finished in 25 days.

By identifying the activities on the critical path managers can see exactly which activities are the priority in terms of making sure they stay on time; the critical path also shows the shortest time in which a project can be completed.

Benefits of critical path analysis

When undertaking a critical path analysis:

- Managers must consider exactly what activities are involved in a project. This is a useful exercise in itself because it helps to make sure that nothing is forgotten. It also means that managers are likely to consult all the different departments and functions involved and this can help to improve everyone's understanding of the issues and challenges involved in getting the project completed.
- Managers can calculate the earliest time by which the project should be completed. This can be important information for customers (e.g. the firm can announce a release date) and is important to help plan the launch arrangements. It can also help the managers decide whether or not a deadline can be hit.
- Managers can identify the 'critical' activities that must be completed in time to get the whole project finished as quickly as possible. This means that they can focus on these specific activities and make sure they do not overrun. At the same time the amount of float time on non-critical activities can be calculated. While managers cannot ignore these activities entirely it may not matter so much if they overrun (provided they do not use up all their float time); it may even be possible to transfer labour and other resources from non-critical activities to critical ones to ensure the latter are completed promptly.
- Managers may be able to produce items or develop products more quickly than the competition, providing the business with a possible competitive advantage. By seeking to reduce the time taken for a project, network analysis is an important element of time-based management.
- Managers can implement just-in-time ordering. Network analysis shows the earliest start times for each activity. Using this the firm can order

materials and supplies to arrive exactly when they are needed and not before. This saves storage costs and also the opportunity cost of having money tied up in stocks. This can improve the firm's liquidity and free up cash which can be used elsewhere in the organisation.

- Managers can use network analysis as a control mechanism to review progress and assess whether the project is on target. If there have been delays the effects of the earliest start times and latest finish times can be reworked to see the effect on the completion of the project.

Although some of the estimates of the likely durations may prove to be wrong, and although external factors may cause delays, this does not mean that critical path analysis is unnecessary. On the contrary, by having a network diagram the effects of any delays can be relatively easily calculated in terms of the impact on the final completion date. Critical path analysis enables managers to understand the significance and likely dangers of any delay. Projects may still overrun, but managers should be able to predict if this is going to happen as soon as a problem emerges (rather than being taken by surprise) and if possible take action to get the project back on track.

Limitations of critical path analysis

Although critical path analysis can help business decision-making, it can have a number of drawbacks and limitations.

- It relies on the estimates for the expected duration. If these prove to be inaccurate the calculations for earliest start times and latest finish times, and so the critical path analysis, may be wrongly identified. The estimates may be incorrect because some managers may exaggerate how long an activity takes to make it easier for them to complete within the agreed time. On the other hand some managers may be too optimistic, particularly if these activities have not been carried out before. A more complex version of critical path analysis, called programme evaluation and review technique (PERT), includes a range of estimates for the durations of different activities; PERT produces a number of network diagrams based on optimistic, pessimistic and most likely durations of activities to take account of the fact that estimates cannot be completely relied on.
- If JIT is used for the delivery of materials, the ability to complete the project on time will depend

on the reliability of suppliers. If they are late this will prevent the next activity starting on time.

- Critical path analysis simply shows the quickest way to complete a project; it does not guarantee that this is the right project to be undertaking in the first place. It may be that the firm's resources could be used more effectively elsewhere.
- All projects must be managed properly if they are to be completed on time. Drawing up a network diagram is only the starting point. Managers must agree on who is responsible for each stage of the project. They must be given the resources and budget to complete in the time agreed. There must be an effective review system to make sure the project is on schedule and to agree what action to take if it is not. A network diagram can provide a valuable focal point for the management system, but it is up to the managers to make sure that everything is implemented correctly and that each activity is completed on schedule.

Other issues in critical path analysis

Before a project is started managers must agree on a definition of success. They must set out exactly what they want to achieve otherwise subordinates may cut corners to get the project done on time. The result may be that the project is completed quickly but that the quality is poor.

Managers must also agree on what resources and spending they are willing to commit to the project. Obviously the quickest way of completing a project will depend on what facilities and resources are available and how much the firm is willing to invest into getting it completed. With more people, more money and more machines the project could probably be speeded up. Whether particular activities can be conducted simultaneously will often depend on whether the firm has or is willing to invest in the necessary resources.

Managers will also be interested in the utilisation of resources throughout the project. It may be that certain activities could be undertaken simultaneously, but that as a result some weeks would require very high levels of personnel whereas in other weeks very few people would be needed. If it adopted such an approach a firm may have to bring in extra staff for the busy week and pay its existing staff to do little in the other weeks. Rather than have such fluctuations in staffing levels managers may want to shift activities around; this may mean that the project takes a bit longer but it may nevertheless be more desirable if it means that its full-time staff are fully employed each week.

Cell production

Cell production is a method of organising production around teams. It is another element of lean production. Instead of producing items on a production line, the process is divided into a series of different stages undertaken by teams or cells. Each team is given the responsibility for a stage in the process.

An advantage of this approach is that teams are responsible for a complete unit of work. Instead of each individual working on one simple task and having no real involvement with the final product, working in cells can give employees a sense of team spirit. It can also improve quality because teams have work for which they have overall responsibility and they can clearly see the results of their efforts.

Cell production can be very motivating for employees because they feel they have more control over their own work. The team members can organise among themselves when and how items are produced. They can also share their skills and expertise.

Team members are also likely to feel much greater responsibility for their work because the next cell has the right to refuse their work if it is poor quality. Cell production involves self-checking by team members.

Hackman and Oldham (1976) developed a model of job design which highlighted the key elements of a motivating job. This model stressed the importance of designing jobs in which individuals had:

- skill variety, i.e. they use a range of skills
- task significance, i.e. they are working on something that has some significance in terms of the overall business rather than just working on a small section and thereby not appreciating why what they do matters
- task identity, i.e. the work they do has a sense of competition (e.g. handing over a complete unit of work to the next stage of the process)
- autonomy, i.e. individuals have some independence to make decisions on how they do the work
- feedback, i.e. employees receive information on the quality of their work.

Cell production helps in most of the areas above and should therefore create more motivating work. Teams have control over what they do; together they produce a complete unit of work, they hand it over to the next cell, which will give feedback and each member of the cell may undertake a range of tasks. This should be more motivating than simply undertaking the same task again and again on a production line – in that system you probably have no idea why your part of the process matters, there is almost no skill variety or sense of task significance.

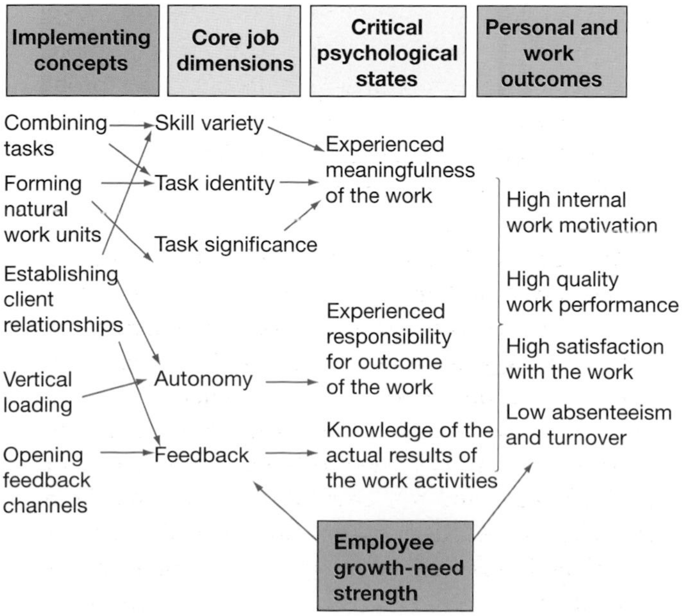

Figure 14.5

Benchmarking

Benchmarking occurs when one business measures its performance against other organisations. Firms benchmark against other organisations that are strong in particular areas. The aim of benchmarking is to learn from the best firms in the world and discover ways of improving operations. If you want to know how to manage large numbers of visitors, talk to Disney; if you want to know how to come up with great design, ask Apple; if you want to move things around reliably, talk to UPS.

Looking for the ways to improve corporate performance internally assumes that a business's staff know the best way of doing something, or how to improve it. Analysing the actions of other organis-

Key terms

Cell production occurs when the production process is divided into stages undertaken by teams.

Benchmarking occurs when one business decides to measure its performance against the leaders in the field.

ations, especially experts in the relevant business area, means a business is more likely to find the best solution. This is particularly true if firms benchmark against the best in the world. Benchmarking may be against other firms in the same industry or even against organisations in a completely different sector. It highlights the importance of being a learning organisation and not being complacent.

Firms may use benchmarking to help them improve in areas such as:

- the reliability of their products
- their ability to send out the correct bills (also called invoices)
- their ability to deliver items on time
- the time it takes to produce a product.

Organisations undertaking benchmarking are those most eager to learn and improve and those that are unafraid to seek outside help.

The benchmarking process

1 The firm must plan what it wants to benchmark, which firms it wants to benchmark with, how it is going to collect the data, what resources to allocate to the project and who is responsible for the project.
2 The firm must collect data from the other firm or firms. This may be through visits to their factories or offices.
3 The firm must analyse its findings to identify how it could improve its own process.
4 The firm must adapt its findings so it can implement the new methods in its own firm given its own circumstances.

The benefits of benchmarking

By undertaking benchmarking a firm should be able to:

- develop a better understanding of customers and competitors
- have fewer complaints and more satisfied customers
- reduce waste and improve quality.

Benchmarking can be difficult because some firms will naturally be unwilling to share their information. They may want to keep their methods and processes secret and might be reluctant to provide rival businesses with ideas on how to improve. One way of

avoiding this problem is to benchmark against firms in different industries.

Firms must also be careful about trying to copy another organisation's methods exactly. Every organisation has its own way of doing things, its own skills and its own circumstances. They may have to adapt the other firm's methods for their own use.

Key Issues

The pressure on businesses to be leaner is growing because their competitors are adopting these techniques and because there is greater competition. In markets such as clothes and computers customers are expecting more features at a lower price and firms have to find ways of becoming more efficient.

Kaizen

The belief that firms can always do better is known as 'kaizen'. Kaizen is a Japanese word meaning continuous improvement. The kaizen approach tries to get employees to improve what they do in some small way every day of every week of every year. If workers improve the quality of their work by 1 per cent every single day, the effect over just one year would be enormous. Too often, businesses seek dramatic changes instead of small, regular changes. If you want to improve your grades in your exams, it is unlikely that there is any one thing you can do which will lead to a sudden improvement in your marks. However, if you begin to change many things over time, your grade is likely to improve gradually.

Just-in-time production

Stocks are goods which have been produced or are in the process of being produced but which have not been sold yet.

All firms hold different types of stocks. Stocks can take a variety of forms:

- **Raw materials and components** are waiting to be used in the production process.
- **Works in progress or unfinished goods** are stocks of goods in the process of being manufactured.

• **Finished goods**, as the name suggests, are goods produced and ready to be sold. In the case of the manufacturer, these are goods waiting to be sold or delivered to the shops, or the final customer. Retailers hold finished goods on their shelves ready to be sold.

The way in which stocks are managed is an important element of operations management.

Holding stocks is important to firms because they are often needed to maintain production and to meet customers' demand. With stocks available, a business can produce at any time and has goods available for customers.

However, the problem is that holding stocks can be expensive and risky. For example, the more stocks a business has:

• the greater the warehousing space needed
• the more money there is tied up in stocks, which means the firm incurs a high opportunity cost because the money that is invested in stocks could be used in other ways
• the higher the security costs to protect the stocks
• the greater the risk; inevitably if a firm holds stocks there is the danger that they will perish or become obsolete.

The decision on how many stocks to hold is, therefore, a trade-off between the costs of holding the stocks and the problems which might occur if stocks are not held.

The minimum amount of stock that a firm wants to hold at any time is known as the buffer stock (or the safety stock). If the level of stocks falls below the buffer level, there may be a risk of running out; this could either halt production or mean that customers have to be turned away because no finished goods are available.

Several factors influence the level of buffer stocks a business holds:

• The rate at which stocks are generally used up – the faster stocks are used up, the more the firm will have to hold at any moment.
• The warehousing space available – the smaller the space the firm has for storage, the lower the level of stocks.
• The nature of the product – if the product is fragile or likely to depreciate, the firm will not want too much stock in case it breaks or loses value rapidly.
• The reliability of suppliers – the more reliable suppliers are, the fewer buffer stocks the firm needs to hold because it knows it can get more as and when required.
• The suppliers' lead time – the lead time is the time it takes for products to arrive from when they are ordered. If the lead time is two days, for example, this means that it takes two days for supplies to arrive once you have ordered them. The shorter the lead time, the smaller the amount of stocks a firm needs to hold. If, however, the lead time is long, the firm will need to hold more stocks to last while it waits for a delivery.

One particular approach to stock control is known as just-in-time (JIT) operations.

Just-in-time production occurs when firms produce products to order. Instead of producing as much as they can and building up stocks, firms only produce when they know they can actually sell the items. Similarly, components and supplies are only bought in by a firm as and when they are needed.

The aim of just-in-time production is to reduce a firm's stock levels by as much as possible; in an ideal world there would be no stocks at all. Supplies would arrive and be used to produce items that are sold immediately to the final customer. A just-in-time approach should provide a firm with tremendous flexibility, firms produce what is required, when it is required. In the past, firms have tended to try and estimate what demand would be and produce this amount in advance of actual sales. This system works provided demand has been estimated correctly.

JIT production should also reduce costs. With no stocks, the firm does not have to pay for warehousing or security. The firm also avoids the opportunity cost of having money tied up in stocks.

Just-in-time production should help minimise wastage. If goods are produced and left to accumulate as stocks, they are likely to get damaged, to depreciate, to go out of fashion or be stolen. JIT avoids these issues.

However, introducing a just-in-time system is complex and places many demands on a business, including:

Excellent relationships with suppliers

Businesses need to be able to rely on suppliers to deliver goods at precisely the right time. They cannot afford delays as this halts production. Also, the goods must be perfect quality; the manufacturer has no stocks to replace faulty supplies. A firm must be able to trust its suppliers completely.

Reliable employees

Because the business does not have many (if any) stocks at any stage of the process, the firm cannot cope with stoppages. If strikes occur, for example, the whole production process stops. A business cannot supply customers using stocks as none exist. JIT relies upon maintaining a good relationship between employers and employees.

A flexible workforce

To ensure that production can respond to demand, a firm needs a flexible labour force. This means that if someone is ill, another employee must be able to cover for them, or that if demand is high in one area of the business, people can be moved to that area to help out. Firms using JIT expect employees to be ready to work anywhere, anytime. People must change to meet the demand for different products because JIT is focused entirely on matching supply to customer orders.

Introducing just-in-time production involves:

- investment in machinery which is flexible and can be changed from producing one type of item to another without much delay
- training employees so that they have several skills and can do a variety of jobs (multi-skilling)
- negotiation with employees so that their contracts are flexible and allow them to move from one job to another
- building relationships with suppliers who can produce just-in-time as well.

Problems of JIT

Although the just-in-time process has many advantages, there are several potential problems or disadvantages as well.

First, the system relies on suppliers providing parts and components at exactly the time they are needed. If this type of flexible and reliable supplier cannot be found, the system breaks down. JIT can also cause problems if the suppliers fail to deliver on time. The manufacturer has no buffer stock and so cannot produce. The system also means that the firm is vul-nerable to action taken by employees. Any stoppage can be extremely expensive because production is halted completely.

Switching to JIT can also lead to an increase in costs because of the extra reordering. Because parts are ordered much more frequently, the firm may lose bulk discounts and will also have more administration costs.

Progress questions

1 What is meant by lean production? (2 marks)
2 What is time-based management? (2 marks)
3 What is critical path analysis? (2 marks)
4 What is float time? (2 marks)
5 What is just-in-time production? (2 marks)
6 Explain why firms hold stocks. (4 marks)
7 Explain two factors necessary for the successful introduction of just-in-time production. (6 marks)
8 What is meant by kaizen? (2 marks)
9 What is benchmarking? (2 marks)
10 Explain two possible benefits of cell production. (6 marks)

Analysis and evaluation questions

1 Analyse the potential benefits of just-in-time techniques to a supermarket. (8 marks)
2 Discuss the value of critical path analysis to a chain of coffee shops opening new stores in a new country. (15 marks)
3 Discuss the ways in which lean production can help a supermarket such as Asda to be more successful. (15 marks)

Case study

Zara, the clothes retailer, offers 'disposable fashion', with prices ranging from $33 for a red tank top to a black blazer for $145. Employing an army of 200-plus designers, Zara produces 12,000 different items a year. The fabric is cut in Zara's factory, then sub-contracted out to local workshops for stitching. The company offsets the higher costs of European labour by avoiding markdowns, keeping stocks to a minimum, and spending very little on marketing.

Tight control over design and production allows Zara to take a trend from catwalk to store shelf in as little as two weeks. Rival Gap Inc. takes about a year, albeit on a much larger scale, and the company is trying hard to get that process down to six months.

The chain's greatest advantage may be its sales-people, who act as grassroots market researchers. Each carries a wireless organiser that is used to punch in trends, customer comments and orders to headquarters. If an item does not sell, it can be off shelves in weeks. If it is successful, Zara designers know immediately and can churn out new versions in myriad colours. This year, Zara sold a pink men's dress shirt. Customers suggested they would prefer purple. Zara's in-house manufacturing sped into action and was able to get a new shirt into the store within days.

The company has a no-advertising policy. It depends mainly on its stores' elegant front windows to sell its merchandise. In New York, Zara has four outlets, including one on Fifth Avenue and one in SoHo. At the store on 34th Street, the company tore out the entire interior, added marble-like floors and high-tech lights to create a stunning 10,000-square-foot emporium. The crowd, mostly in their 20s, also includes more mature businesswomen.

Overseeing all these details is Zara's secretive founder, Armancio Ortega, who, with the rest of his family, owns 100 per cent of Inditex's shares.

Source: Adapted from Echison, W., 'The mark of Zara',
Business Week, Issue 3683 (2000)

(40 marks, 60 minutes)

Questions

1 Explain the meaning of just-in-time production. (5 marks)
2 Analyse the reasons why stock control is important to Zara. (8 marks)
3 Discuss the factors necessary for Zara's lean approach to be successful. (12 marks)
4 To what extent is Zara's success dependent on its just-in-time approach? (15 marks)

Section 4: Human resources strategies and accounts

The subject matter that makes up the management of human resources within A Level Business Studies is divided between the AS and A2 elements of the specification. The major parts of your AS programme will have included the following topics:

- introductory issues in employing people
- organisational structures
- measuring the effectiveness of the workforce
- motivation – in theory and practice
- recruitment, selection and training.

The A2 specification for business studies builds upon the subject knowledge and skills acquired during the AS programme. It is worthwhile looking back over your AS materials before starting to study this section. More specific advice is given on any prior knowledge required at the outset of each chapter.

As part of Unit Three of your A2 programme you will study the following:

- human resource objectives
- human resource strategies
- developing and implementing workforce plans
- developing competitive organisational structures
- managing employer–employee relationships effectively.

In addition, there are two topics within Unit Four of the A2 specification that are also closely linked to the management of human resources within an organisation. These are:

- leadership
- organisational culture.

Unit Four considers the importance of these topics in the context of managing change.

15

Understanding human resource objectives and strategies

A human resource (HR) function or department is responsible for the use of labour within the organisation. You will have already encountered some of these as part of your AS course: employing people; how organisations structure themselves; recruiting, selecting, training and motivating staff. In this section we will build on the AS materials and consider strategies that a business may adopt to achieve its human resource objectives.

In this chapter we examine:
- the HR objectives that businesses may pursue
- the internal and external influences on HR objectives
- the types of HR strategies that businesses may adopt.

Introduction to human resources

A business's human resource (HR) function or department is responsible for the use of labour within the organisation. Human resource management (HRM) views activities relating to the workforce as integrated and vital in helping the organisation to achieve its corporate objectives. People are viewed as an important resource to be developed through training. Thus, policies relating to recruitment, pay and appraisal, for example, should be formulated as part of a coordinated human resource strategy. HRM is an all-embracing integrated approach that aims to make the best use of human resources in relation to the business's overall goals. Human resource management involves the strategic planning of the management of employees.

In comparison, personnel management considers the elements that comprise managing people (recruitment, selection, wages and so on) as separate elements. It does not take into account how these parts combine to assist in the achievement of organisational objectives. At its simplest, personnel management within businesses carries out a series of unrelated tasks.

The most enthusiastic supporters of HRM are foreign-owned companies operating in the EU. However, in spite of the potential benefits, many firms do not engage in human resource planning and management.

> **Key term**
> **Human resource objectives** are the targets pursued by the HR function or department of the business.

The nature of human resource (HR) objectives

Human resource objectives are the targets pursued by the HR function or department of the business. The achievement of these goals should assist the business is attaining its overall corporate objectives. Tesco, the UK's largest retailer, has a number of corporate objectives, including: 'Developing the talents of its people through sound management and training practices, while rewarding them fairly with equal opportunities for all'. The company's human resource function will set itself a number of objectives to allow the business to achieve its objective. For example, it would set objectives relating to the provision of training to all of its 380,000 employees.

There are a number of HR objectives, the importance of which will vary according to the type of business, its products and the market in which it is trading.

Matching the workforce to the needs of the business

It is normal for the labour needs of a business to change over time. A business might grow, move overseas, replace employees with technology or take a decision to produce new products. Each of these actions will mean that the business will require a different workforce. Our earlier example of Tesco can apply here too. Tesco has grown rapidly, opened stores in central Europe, Asia and the United States. It has expanded its product range to incorporate financial services and personal services such as eyesight tests. This has required the company's HR department to recruit new employees, redeploy employees to a new location or to train employees to provide the necessary skills.

Meeting this objective is essential as it allows the firm to be as competitive as possible because the business needs to have sufficient employees to ensure that it can meet the needs of its customers and to provide the best-quality goods or services possible. Having a workforce of the correct size also assists the business in providing high-quality customer service. Ensuring that the business has the right number of employees to meet its customers' needs can be challenging for businesses that face seasonal demand, and is an important HR objective.

For example, the Royal Mail requires additional employees at certain times of the year, such as Christmas when demand for postal services is much higher. As a consequence the company's HR objectives will include the need to have a flexible workforce that can meet the varying demands of its customers. Fulfilling this objective requires ongoing action on the part of the HR function.

Remember that HR objectives that are decided by a business's HR managers have to support the business in the achievement of its corporate objectives. Thus, HR objectives can often be understood and maybe their relevance judged in the light of the business's corporate objectives.

Making full use of the workforce's potential

HR managers may select this as an objective if they feel that the business is not making the most effective use of its existing employees. Making more use of employees can result in an increase in output without necessarily incurring further costs. A workforce's potential can exist in a number of forms.

- **Skills**. It is possible that employees have some skills which they do not use as part of their working lives. This is entirely possible in a large business where managers may not be familiar with all of their employees. It is possible that employees have recognisable skills, such as speaking a second language or skills relating to information technology. Businesses can use a skills audit to identify such skills and then make use of them as and when appropriate.
- **Underutilised employees**. Some employees may find that their jobs are not really challenging. Their current roles may not stretch them or utilise their talents to anything like their full extent. This means that the employees are not contributing as fully to the business as is possible. On the other hand, some employees may not have sufficient work to occupy them fully; this would result in lower levels of productivity than might be expected. Identifying and responding effectively to this underutilisation of staff will improve the performance of the workforce.
- **Overworked or stressed employees**. The oppo-

Business in Focus

BT sheds 10,000 jobs in six months

In November 2008 British Telecommunications (BT) announced its intention to cut 10,000 jobs by the end of March 2009 to reduce costs. The cuts will mainly affect agency and contract staff, including offshore workers, the company said. BT said it had already cut 4,000 jobs, with a further 6,000 to go by March from its global workforce of 160,000.

News of the cost cuts sent BT shares 7.5 per cent higher. The company said the job losses were not a 'direct result' of the economic downturn. 'This is a reflection of the fact we have to become leaner,' BT chief executive Ian Livingston told the BBC. 'We need to do it in good times and bad.'

Questions:

1 Many of the job losses will be in the UK, with about 4,000 staff positions affected. Which HR objective might have prompted this decision?
2 Which corporate objective might this decision help BT to fulfil?

site circumstance to the above can occur, especially if a business is seeking to improve its profitability by reducing its operating costs. This can result in employees having excessive workloads or being asked to take positions within the organisation for which they are not properly trained or qualified.

> **Key term**
> A **skills audit** is a procedure used to identify the talents and abilities that employees have which may not be fully used by the business.

Maintaining good employer–employee relations

Maintaining good relations with employees is an important HR objective for all businesses. Good employer–employee relations give businesses a range of benefits.

- It makes strikes and other forms of labour disputes less likely. This avoids the business suffering from periods when it is unable to function normally due to a partial or complete loss of output. Such a scenario can reduce the business's revenue as well its profitability. It may also result in the long-term loss of customers who are dissatisfied with the lack of supplies.
- Research has shown that businesses with good industrial relations attract higher-calibre and better-qualified applicants for positions. This can assist a business in improving its performance. High-quality employees may be more creative, take better-quality decisions and provide a higher level of service for customers.
- Good employer–employee relations assist a business to maintain a positive corporate image which may have a positive effect on sales. A business that suffers from regular occurrences of industrial action may receive a lot of adverse publicity. This may result in a loss of customers who shun the business in the belief that employees are not treated well.
- With good relations, employer–employee communications may be highly effective, helping to resolve problems before they develop into a dispute. Efficient channels of communication between employer and employee may also improve the operation of the business in many ways by, for example, encouraging suggestions for improving production from employees.

The internal and external influences on HR objectives

Human resource managers are subject to influences from inside the business as well as external factors when deciding on the objectives for their department.

Internal influences on HR objectives

There are a number of internal factors that may influence a business's decision regarding which HR objectives to adopt and pursue.

- **Corporate objectives**. As with all functional objectives, those set by the HR department must assist the organisation in achieving its overall objectives. Thus, if the business has a corporate objective of maximising long-term profits, the HR objective might set itself objectives concerned with reducing labour costs or making the most effective use of the workforce. The low-cost airline easyJet has the corporate objective of operating at minimum cost and thereby remaining highly competitive in its particular market niche. In September 2008 the company cut 60 jobs at its headquarters in Luton to maintain its competitiveness.
- **The attitudes and beliefs of the senior managers.** The senior managers of a business can

> ### Business in Focus
>
> #### Tesco in the United States
>
> In 2007 Tesco started its expansion into the United States by opening 55 stores in southern California and Nevada. These stores have not been trading under the Tesco brand, but as 'Fresh & Easy' convenience stores. The company announced in 2008 that it intends to open a further 19 stores in northern California. The company has built one distribution centre to supply these stores and is in the process of building a second. Ultimately the company intends to build 1,000 stores along the entire western coast of the United States.
>
> #### Question:
>
> 1 In what ways might the development of the Fresh & Easy stores in the United Sates affect the objectives set by the company's HR department?

have an important influence on HR objectives. If they consider the workforce to be a valuable asset, they may want a long-term relationship with employees and may set objectives such as developing the skills of the workforce to their fullest extent. Alternatively, they may see employees as an expendable asset to be hired when necessary and paid the minimum rate possible. This can have considerable implications for the HR strategy operated by a business. We consider HR strategies more fully below.

- **The type of product.** If the product requires the commitment of a highly skilled labour force then objectives such as making full use of the workforce's potential may be most important. However, a key HR objective for a business selling products which are mainly produced by machinery and require little in the way of skilled labour may be to minimise labour costs through having the smallest possible number of employees at all times. Some retailers may focus on matching the workforce to the needs of the business as a prime objective because a number of their staff may be relatively low skilled and relatively easy to replace as necessary.

External influences on HR objectives

External factors will have a significant impact on the HR objectives that are set by businesses.

- **The state of the market**. A growing market will have a significant impact on the HR objectives pursued by a business. Sales of many products have fallen in the UK in recent times due to the onset of a recession. The media have carried a series of stories about how businesses are adjusting their workforces to reflect these changed times. The recession will have encouraged many businesses to think about matching the workforce to the needs of the business. The McDonald's story in the 'Business in focus' highlights that a rise in demand for the product requires increased staffing levels.

- **Price elasticity of demand for the product.** When demand for a product is strongly price elastic (i.e. demand is very sensitive to price changes) it is more likely that a business will opt for HR objectives that allow it to reduce labour costs. This can be seen in the case of budget airlines. If demand is price elastic, a reduction in price is likely to lead to a substantial increase in sales. Setting suitable HR objectives to match the

---

Business in Focus

McDonald's needs 4,000 new employees

While some service sector firms are cutting jobs, fast-food chain McDonald's aims to fill 4,000 new jobs in its UK restaurants.

Modernised branches and menu changes are said to be behind increasing demand for McDonald's meals, with the company reporting an increase of two million customers a month.

The company has refurbished half of its 1,200 branches and said it is on track to complete a £40m investment across 200 "Drive Thru" restaurants by the end of 2008.

It will also open up to 10 new restaurants in the UK this year.

Source: Adapted from bbc.co.uk

Question:

1 In what ways does this article indicate that the influences on a business's HR objectives can be a mix of internal and external factors?

---

need to minimise costs of production will be vital in these circumstances.

- **Corporate image.** Most businesses will set HR objectives that include maintaining good relations with employees. To become embroiled in an industrial dispute can be damaging to the image of a business and may lead to a loss in sales. This might be particularly important for large and potentially dominant businesses which may be vulnerable to accusations of abusing their power.

- **Employment legislation**. The UK government and EU authorities have passed a series of laws designed to protect labour in the workplace. The existence of such laws may encourage businesses to set HR objectives to develop the potential of their workforces as the law may make it difficult to hire and fire employees at will. In particular, a change in the law will have an impact on the objectives that a HR department pursues.

Human resource strategies

A human resource strategy is the medium- to long-term plan that is implemented to achieve the business's HR objectives. It is a central element of a business's approach to HRM. Why have firms adopted human resource strategies throughout the entire organisation rather than continued with the principles of personnel management?

A number of factors have persuaded UK businesses to implement human resource strategies.

- A principal argument is that the Japanese have had apparent success in managing people using this approach. The Japanese have been seen to gain significant competitive advantage from managing a human resource that produces high-quality products at minimum cost. It is human resource management that is credited with achieving this

match between employee behaviour and organisational objectives.

- Changes in organisational structure have led to many managers taking on responsibility for managing people within the organisation. Techniques such as delayering and the development of empowered teams have been an integral part of the implementation of human resource strategies. Acquiring, developing, motivating and rewarding employees are, it is argued, best done by managers and colleagues close to the employees in question. Under HRM, managers can carry out many of the more routine tasks of traditional personnel management.

- The increasing popularity of psychological approaches to motivation has encouraged the adoption of HR strategies. Human resource strategies demand styles of working that meet the

	'Hard' HRM	'Soft' HRM
Philosophy	See employees as a resource like any other available to the business.	Sees employees as different to, and more important than, any other resource available to managers.
Time scale	HRM seen as a short-term policy: employees hired and fired as necessary.	Takes a long-term view of using the workforce as efficiently as possible to achieve long-term corporate objectives.
Key features	<ul><li>Employees paid as little as possible.</li><li>Employees only have limited control over working lives.</li><li>Communication mainly downward in direction.</li><li>Leaders tend towards Theory X view of workforce.</li><li>Employees recruited externally to fulfil human needs – giving short-term solution.</li><li>Judgemental appraisal.</li></ul>	<ul><li>Managers consult with employees.</li><li>Managers give control over working lives to employees through delayering and empowerment.</li><li>Leaders tend towards Theory Y view of workforce.</li><li>Emphasis on training and developing employees.</li><li>Employees promoted from within, reflecting long-term desire to develop workforce.</li><li>Developmental appraisal.</li></ul>
Associated leadership style	Leaders operating this style of HRM are more likely to be at the autocratic end of the spectrum of leadership.	Leaders implementing 'soft' HRM are more likely to be democratic in nature.
Motivational techniques used	Probably mainly motivated by pay, with limited use of techniques such as delegation and teamworking.	Motivated through delegation and empowerment. Heavy use of techniques designed to give employees more authority.

Table 15.1 Approaches to human resource management

social and psychological needs of employees. The adoption of flatter organisational structures and psychological techniques of motivation are essential elements of HR strategies – organisations that adopt these techniques and structures would naturally move towards adopting some type of HR strategy.

However, the adoption of HR strategies by UK businesses is not as sweeping and as clear-cut as some might suggest. Surveys have indicated that many companies have opted to select only the elements of the human resource management package that fit in with their philosophies, management style and corporate objectives. For example, a firm might choose to implement rigorous selection and appraisal methods but ignore other aspects, particularly developing employees through training.

This means that there is not a single HR strategy or approach to HRM. Different firms have interpreted the HR philosophy in different ways.

- **'Hard' HR strategies**. Some firms operate 'hard' HR policies, treating employees as a resource to be used optimally. Such firms regard employees as yet another resource to be deployed as efficiently as possible in pursuit of strategic targets. Employees are obtained as cheaply as possible, controlled and disposed of when necessary.
- **'Soft' HR strategies**. Other firms use an HR system that can be regarded as 'soft'. This approach is based on the notion that employees are perhaps the most valuable asset a business has and they should be developed to maximise their value to the organisation. This makes a long-term approach essential. Employees are seen as a resource to be valued and developed over time and in response to changing market conditions.

Hard HR strategies

A hard HR strategy offers a number of advantages to a business.

- It makes it easier for businesses to adapt the size and composition of their workforces to match the needs of their customers. Thus, a business using this type of strategy will be prepared to hire and dismiss workers as necessary without the need to maintain the size of its workforce during a downturn in sales. This allows a business to cope more effectively when trading in markets that suffer from regular fluctuations in levels of demand.

- It can result in lower costs, especially in the short-term. Adopting a 'hard' approach to employees may mean that a business only uses employees with minimal skill levels and relies on the use of technology and a small number of highly skilled core employees to meet the needs of its customers. This means that the business may be able to reduce expenditure on its workforce by paying low wage rates (perhaps minimum wage) and to avoid heavy and regular expenditure on employee training. Such a strategy, if successful, may boost profits to the satisfaction of shareholders.
- A 'hard' approach to HR allows managers to retain control over the workforce and to direct operations as they wish. Under such an approach employees will be told what their duties are, with relatively little opportunity for discussion on how to complete a job and limited input in terms of suggestions on how to improve the production process. This approach can assist a business in maintaining its focus on its corporate objectives.

> **Key term**
> **Labour turnover** is the percentage of a business's employees who leave the business over some period of time (normally a year).

However, the 'hard' approach to HR can also bring about a number of disadvantages.

- The level of labour turnover might be very high. This can impose a number of costs on the business. Firstly, it has to recruit replacement employees. This can be costly in terms of advertising and using managers to select the new staff from the applicants. Secondly, even if the jobs are relatively unskilled some training is likely to be required which may involve further expenditure. Finally, new employees are likely to be less productive during the initial period of their employment, which will detract from the overall levels of productivity achieved within the business.
- Employees may be demotivated by this approach to employment. The failure of managers to develop a long-term relationship with employees will mean that it is unlikely that what Herzberg identified as motivators will be present in the job to any great extent. For example, the chance to

take responsibility for projects and opportunities for promotion will be limited. This approach relies heavily on pay as a motivator and ignores the potential of social and psychological factors to motivate employees and improve their performance at work.

Soft HR strategies

A soft HR strategy offers a number of advantages to a business, although in many cases these are the opposite of those discussed above.

* A soft HR strategy can help a business to build a reputation for being a 'good' employer. Good employers seek to offer their employees diverse and interesting jobs and the opportunity to develop their skills. The pay and conditions on offer are attractive and the employer ensures that employees receive regular training to improve their skills and enhance promotion prospects. Being regarded as a good employer allows businesses to attract higher-quality candidates, which in turn improve the quality of the workforce and the overall performance of the business. A recent survey showed that working for a respected employer was one of the most important factors to job seekers when applying for employment.

* A soft HR strategy can improve knowledge management within a business. This means that the business is more likely to possess a workforce with the knowledge and skills essential for the business to continue trading effectively. This comes about because this approach usually results in a lower level of labour turnover and therefore employees develop long-term working relationships with businesses, allowing them to bring experience to bear in decision-making.

* A soft HR strategy may also develop a more creative workforce. Employees will be given more opportunities to contribute to decision-making and to provide suggestions and ideas on improving the operation of the business. This can motivate the employees (by meeting what Maslow identified as an individual's higher needs) and also provide an organisation with some excellent ideas without incurring the costs of hiring consultants. Because these ideas are generated from people with a different perspective on the organisation they can be different and creative.

Of course, this type of human resource strategy does have its drawbacks.

* It can be very expensive, especially in the short term. The costs of training employees can be significant, particularly if they are given off-the-job training. These costs could be wasted to some degree if the employee leaves soon after completing the training, possibly as a consequence of being 'poached' by an unscrupulous rival. Higher rates of pay and good working conditions can also add to an employer's costs.

* It can be difficult and expensive to alter the workforce in response to a change in market conditions. The soft HR strategy is likely to rely heavily on full-time and permanent employees and thus the business might have surplus capacity if demand falls, and little potential to increase output if demand rises.

The approach to HR strategy used will obviously depend upon the type of business. It may be that businesses employing less-skilled employees may opt to use a harder approach as the costs of losing employees may be less and the potential from increasing responsibility within the organisation is less obvious. On the other hand, a more skilled workforce might be more suited to a softer approach to make the most effective use of their talents and to minimise the risk of highly trained, skilled and productive employees leaving the organisation.

Examiner's advice

It is essential, when dealing with questions on the advantages and disadvantages of the two types of HR strategy, to consider the nature of the business and its workforce. This may enable you to justify the use of a particular approach, either hard or soft.

HR strategies and competitive advantage

Adopting and implementing the right HR strategy has the potential to provide businesses with a significant competitive advantage over rivals. Using the right strategy should make the organisation more competitive, and to some extent this is borne out by the performance of Japanese companies.

Soft human resource management recognises the individual rather than producing personnel policies for the whole workforce. Reward systems, training and development, appraisal and communication are all geared to fulfilling the needs of the individual as well as those of the organisation. The key principle of HRM (or at least 'soft' HRM) is that each employee should be nurtured and developed in pursuit of the organisation's objectives. All aspects of the HRM 'package' should be coordinated to ensure coherence and to assist in the attainment of strategic targets.

If an organisation is successful in operating its HR strategy, the outcome should be motivated and creative employees who are committed to the firm and who do not seek to leave. Such employees should be aware of the goals of the organisation and understand how they can contribute towards the attainment of organisational targets.

Under this scenario a business should incur less recruitment costs, enjoy higher levels of productivity and a reduction in faulty products. It may attract top-class applicants to vacancies because of its reputation as a caring and enlightened employer. All of these factors should make the organisation more competitive and better able to cope with the rigours of operating in international markets.

However, in the real world there are differing views on the best HR strategy. Many businesses in the UK differ in their interpretation. Some take a 'hard' attitude, viewing employees as simply another resource to be used as effectively as possible. The latter approach has a much more short-term focus.

There are, however, theoretical arguments suggesting that whichever HR strategy is adopted, it may not enhance a business's competitiveness. Trade union recognition is a problem under the soft HR approach to managing employees. The strategy requires people to be treated as individuals and as such to contribute to the attainment of corporate objectives. Yet, in spite of a decline in their importance during the 1980s and 1990s, unions have a long-established role in businesses in the UK. But there is an obvious tension in an organisation that attempts to deal with its employees on an individual basis within a framework of collective bargaining. This tension may manifest itself in employee dissatisfaction or, in extreme cases, in industrial action. Both scenarios could prove extremely damaging to a business's competitive performance.

Further problems may exist if the culture of the organisation is not suited to a HR approach to managing people. Even a 'hard' HR strategy implies some degree of delegation and at least a limited commitment to training. This can involve a degree of expenditure and some managers may oppose the lessening of control that this entails. Furthermore, the adoption of any HR strategy may involve additional costs in the short term as managers and employees adjust to the new strategy and to revised roles within the organisation. The elevation of human resources to a strategic role may incite some opposition from those with responsibility for, say, marketing or finance. All of these factors can detract from the competitive performance of the organisation, especially in the short term.

One step further: Guest's model of human resource management

David Guest has developed a model of managing human resources within businesses that stresses the importance of integrating the various elements of the human resource strategy, which can result in better outcomes in terms of business performance. The integrated nature of this model supports the use of human resource strategies as part of human resource management rather than the use of personnel management.

Guest's model emphasises the close relationship between the business's corporate strategies and its HR strategies. However, the key point of this model is that HR strategy should lead to human resource outcomes that are strongly beneficial to the business. These are:

- commitment by employees to the business and its goals, involving higher levels of effort and cooperation
- the supply of quality goods and services (as a result of having a well-trained and motivated workforce)
- flexibility of employees in responding to innovation in the process of production and, more generally, to respond flexibly to changing circumstances.

Guest presented the HR outcomes as a package and argued that only if all three of the HRM outcomes were achieved could the organisation expect to see a change in the behaviour of its workforce and a consequent improvement in its workforce. This would result in improvement in the financial outcomes shown in the right-hand column.

HRM strategy	HRM practice	HRM outcomes	Behaviour outcomes	Performance outcomes	Financial outcomes
Differentiation (innovation) Focus (quality) Cost (cost-reduction)	Selection Training Appraisal Rewards Job design Involvement Status and security	Commitment Quality Flexibility	Effort/ motivation Cooperation Involvement Organisational citizenship	**High**: Productivity Quality Innovation **Low**: Absence Labour turnover Conflict Customer complaints	Profits Return on investment

Table 15.2
Source: Guest (1997)

Progress questions

1 Of what is the following a definition: '… considers the elements that comprise managing people (recruitment, selection, wages and so on) as separate elements'? (1 mark)
2 Which *two* of the following are HR objectives?
   a increasing market share
   b maintaining good employer–employee relations
   c matching the workforce to the needs of the organisation
   d maximising capacity utilisation. (2 marks)
3 Distinguish between personnel management and human resource management. (5 marks)
4 Outline two external factors that might influence a large retailer's HR objectives. (6 marks)
5 Which of the following is *not* an external influence on HR objectives?
   a the state of the market
   b price elasticity of demand
   c corporate objectives
   d corporate image. (1 mark)
6 Explain why the type of product that the business produces might affect its HR objectives. (5 marks)
7 Explain the difference between 'hard' and "soft' HR strategies. (5 marks)
8 What is likely to be the major motivational technique used within a 'hard' HR strategy? Why? (6 marks)
9 Outline two possible disadvantages of using a 'soft' HR strategy. (6 marks)
10 Explain why a university might opt to use a 'soft' HR strategy. (5 marks)

Analysis and evaluation questions

1 The chief executive of one of the UK's largest multinational companies commented recently: 'My firm trades in a highly challenging market in which it is vital to produce new products on a regular basis and to be price competitive. The company's hard HR strategy is the best option in the circumstances.' He continued to say that the company had been successful in controlling its costs and that this had been very popular with the shareholders.

   a Analyse the major features of the company's hard HR strategy. (8 marks)
   b To what extent do you agree with the chief executive's view? (15 marks)
2 Carbone and Caccachio Ltd manufactures a range of processed foods, including a popular range of low-calorie ready meals. The business is well known for the quality of its products and uses this as a USP. The business has been successful in recent years and its sales have grown steadily, though they are

strongly seasonal. The company has suffered from some criticisms from its workforce for not consulting over major decisions.

The company faces strong and growing competition from European rivals. As a result it is seeking to sell its products in new markets, including Russia.

a Explain and justify two human resource objectives that the company should set itself. (8 marks)

b Discuss whether external or internal influences are likely to have a greater impact on the company's human resource objectives. (15 marks)

Case study

John Lewis is one of the UK's best-known and popular retailers. The company operates:

- 27 John Lewis department stores
- 194 Waitrose supermarkets (www.waitrose.com)
- an online and catalogue business, johnlewis.com (www.johnlewis.com)
- a direct services company, Greenbee (www.greenbee.com)
- a production unit and a farm.

The company employs 69,000 permanent staff and in 2008 had a turnover of nearly £6,800 million. The company faces tough competition from rivals such as Debenhams and Tesco.

All the permanent staff are called 'partners' and share in the benefits and profits of the business. The extract below, from the company's website, sets out the philosophy behind the company's human resource strategy.

Ensuring the happiness of Partners is at the centre of everything we do. Our founder, John Spedan Lewis, had a vision that placed the happiness of the members above all else and made everyone a co-owner of the Partnership.

1 **Owners of the business working together, self-responsibility, collective responsibility**
   We're owners, but with ownership comes responsibility; we take responsibility for our own success and failures. By working together, the Partners each contribute to our collective success and we always acknowledge the role of others in our achievements.

2 **Job satisfaction, enjoyment and fun**
   We're excited by what we do and believe that happy Partners need job satisfaction and fun, both at work and at play. Part of the job satisfaction for Partners comes with the training, development and career opportunities open to them and the knowledge that Partners can grow with the business for many years. One per cent of total pay and bonuses is spent by Partners as they see fit. The money goes on the care, well-being and leisure activities of working and retired Partners.

3 **Open information and dialogue**
   We are a unique and vibrant democracy. We share knowledge and information about the business between Partners, giving everyone the opportunity to contribute to decision-making as well as to challenge and question. We recognise every Partner's right to be listened to and heard regardless of their point of view.

4 **Shared profits**
   Profits are shared fairly among Partners, and everyone receives an equal percentage of their salary as an annual bonus; 20 per cent in 2007–08. This gives everyone in the business a shared purpose and a really tangible reason to serve customers to the absolute best of their ability.

5 **Care of Partners when working and in retirement**
   We believe that Partners need to be supported in difficult personal times. We have dedicated Partners and a number of ways that we ensure the confidential care of working Partners. We are committed to keeping our non-contributory pension scheme open at a cost of £85 million, in 2005–06.

   Source: John Lewis website
   http://www.johnlewispartnership.co.uk
   (40 marks, 60 minutes)

Questions

1 Explain one possible reason why the John Lewis Partnership offers so much detail about its human resource strategy on its website. (5 marks)

2 Analyse the type of human resource strategy that is used by the John Lewis Partnership. (8 marks)

3 Discuss the major influences on the company's human resource objectives. (12 marks)

4 To what extent do you think that the company's human resource strategy is the correct one? (15 marks)

16 Developing and implementing workforce plans

A workforce (or human resource) plan assesses the current and future capacity of a business's workforce, and sets out actions necessary to meet the business's future workforce needs. You will have already encountered some of the actions necessary to carry out workforce planning as part of your AS course. In order to turn a plan into reality the business may need to recruit employees and provide training. In this chapter we will develop these aspects of your AS studies and see how they fit into the strategic process of planning an organisation's future labour needs and changing the workforce to meet its requirements.

In this chapter we examine:
- the components of workforce plans
- the internal and external influences on workforce plans and how to judge their importance
- issues that may be encountered by managers when implementing workforce plans
- the value to businesses of using workforce plans.

> **Key terms**
> **Human resource management** (HRM) is the process of making the most efficient use of an organisation's employees.
> **A workforce (or human resource) plan** assesses the current and future capacity of a business's workforce, and sets out actions necessary to meet the business's future workforce needs.

The components of workforce plans

Workforce planning is one of the core activities of human resource management, whatever style is operated. Workforce planning entails a number of stages.

1 The starting point of workforce planning is to consider the overall or corporate objectives of the business. The workforce plan must contribute to the achievement of the business's overall or corporate objectives.

2 The next stage is to take a strategic view of employees, and to consider how human resources can be managed to assist in achieving the business's corporate objectives. This may entail considering factors such as the use of technology and how this might complement or replace some human input into the production process.

3 At this stage, those responsible for workforce planning will have to make a judgement about the size and type of workforce the organisation will require over future years.

4 This desired future workforce is compared with that available to the business at the time of planning.

5 Once this comparison is complete the firm can decide upon policies (e.g. recruitment, training, redeployment and redundancy) necessary to convert the existing workforce into the desired one. This process is shown in Figure 16.1 below.

The workforce plan will specify the business's desired workforce and how the business will implement its human resource policies. An important element of the plan is a skills audit to identify the abilities and qualities of the existing workforce. This

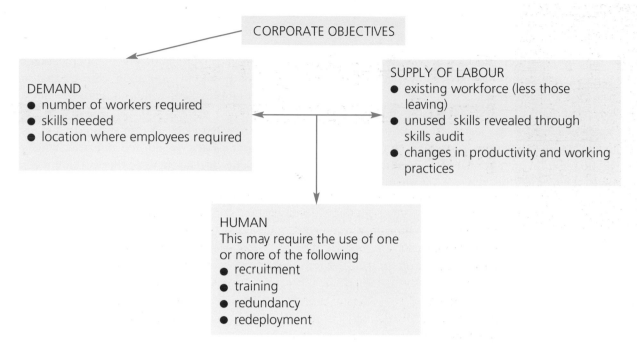

Figure 16.1 Workforce planning

may highlight skills and experience of which managers were unaware. For example, some employees could possess language skills which could prove invaluable to a business that trades overseas.

> **Key term**
> **Labour turnover** is the proportion of a business's staff that leave their employment over some period of time, normally one year.

A business's workforce plan will contain at least the following information.

- Information on the business's current workforce. This will set out:
  - the number of employees the business currently has
  - the skills and qualifications possessed by its current employees
  - where its employees are currently employed (for multinational companies this could be in many different countries)
  - the age profile of its employees, which will help to forecast likely future changes due to retirement etc.
- **An analysis of likely changes in the demand for the business's products**. In turn this will affect the business's need for labour in the forthcoming period. Clearly changes in demand will have a significant effect on the number of employees that are needed, especially if the business is heavily dependent upon employees as a central part of the production process. This is the case for many businesses providing services, such as banks and hospitals.
- **An analysis of the likely factors affecting the supply of labour**. This could include a wide range of factors, including forecast rates of labour turnover for the business; factors affecting the local labour markets, such as the entry of a new business in the local area, which may recruit heavily; or the arrival of large numbers of migrants from Eastern Europe into the local labour market.
- **Recommendations on actions needed to acquire the desired workforce.** These actions are likely to set out changes in recruitment, training, redeployment and redundancy. The workforce plan will set these out in detail and will also explain the impact on each element of the business and also the timescale over which the changes will be implemented.

A workforce plan assists a business in using its human resources effectively and at minimum cost in pursuit of its corporate objectives.

Human resource managers require specific information when developing workforce plans.

- They need to carry out research to provide sales forecasts for the next year or two. This will help identify the quantity and type of labour required.

Clearly, rising levels of sales will have an impact on the number of employees required. Such a situation may mean that more employees are required to directly provide the goods or services for customers, but also more employees in roles such as managers and administrators.

- Data will be needed to show the number of employees likely to be leaving the labour force in general (and the firm in particular). Information will be required on potential entrants to the labour force. Sources of this type of information could include the government or local authorities.
- Information regarding future wage rates for the types of employees that it hires. If wages are expected to rise, businesses may reduce their demand for labour and seek to make greater use of technology. Alternatively, a multinational business may transfer production to areas or countries where wage rates are lower.
- Information on the numbers of people entering specific training or education courses that may result in employment within the industry in question.
- The plan will reflect any anticipated changes in the output of the workforce due to changes in productivity or the length of the working week.
- Technological developments will impact on planning the workforce. Developments in this field may reduce the need for unskilled employees while creating employment for those with technical skills.

Business in Focus

UK employees' working hours

New research shows that UK workers are among the hardest working people in Europe, with those in full-time jobs putting in an average of 41.4 hours per week - one and a half hours more than the average for the 27 members of the EU.

Only Romanians and Bulgarians are putting in longer hours, according to research compiled by the European Foundation for the Improvement of Living and Working Conditions (Eurofound).

The French and Italians worked the fewest hours - with an average of 37.7 and 38.4 hours per week.

UK workers also get less annual leave than the average EU worker, getting an average of 24.6 fully paid days, compared to an EU average of 25.2.

Weekly hours worked by male full-time employees exceeded those of their female counterparts, with men working 2.3 hours more than women in the 27 EU member states.

The group found a substantial gap between the length of the working week in Eastern and Western Europe. Those in the 12 countries that have joined the EU since enlargement began in 2004, work an average of 40.6 hours a week compared with 39.5 hours per week for workers in those 15 countries that were the original members.

Slovakia was the only new EU member to have recorded a considerable reduction in working hours over the past few years, Eurofound said.

Source: Adapted from bbc.co.uk

Question:

1 How might human resource managers for a multinational company such as Nestlé make use of this information as part of their planning?
2 How useful do you think this information would be for these managers?

Bulgaria – 41.7
Romania – 41.7
UK – 41.4
Czech Republic – 41.2
Austria – 41.1

Table 16.1 **Longest weekly hours**
Source: Eurofound

France 37.7
Italy 38.4
Denmark – 38.6
Portugal – 38.8
Belgium – 38.8

Table 16.2 **Shortest weekly hours**

The process of HR planning can be assisted by a business creating a HR planning group which brings together senior human resource managers and also key managers from the other functions (marketing, operations and finance, for example) within the business. This can speed up the process of HR planning and help to ensure that it truly meets the needs of all parts of the business. The process is also dependent upon the availability of accurate and up-to-date records on all employees. These can assist managers in analysing likely future trends of labour turnover and also identifying employees with particular skills. This analysis is easier if the records are available in electronic format.

Internal and external influences on workforce plans

HR managers have to take a number of factors into account when drawing up workforce plans. Some of these factors are external to the business and others are internal.

External factors

Sales forecasts

Estimating sales for the next year or two can be a prime influence on workforce plans. This helps the business to identify the quantity and type of labour the firm will require to meet the expected demand for its products. Businesses experiencing rising sales will expect to recruit more employees. At the time of writing the UK is entering a recession in which demand for goods and services will fall. As a consequence businesses from many sectors of the economy are announcing redundancies. Examples of such businesses include BAE Systems (aerospace manufacturer), AstraZeneca (pharmaceuticals), British Telecommunications (BT) and Yell (the company responsible for Yellow Pages).

In some circumstances businesses may not immediately adjust their workforce plans in the light of changes in sales forecasts. If a downturn in sales in expected to be short term it may be worth maintaining employment levels, especially if the workers concerned are highly skilled. In November 2008 employees at car manufacturers Land Rover and Jaguar were offered three months' leave if they agreed to a 20 per cent pay cut. A spokesperson for Tata, the parent company, said that this was an innovative and voluntary solution to 'current trading conditions'.

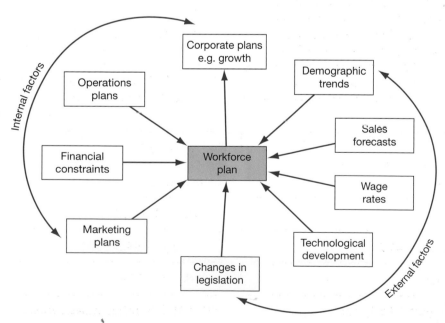

Figure 16.2 Factors influencing workforce plans

Demographic trends

Workforce planners need information on potential entrants to the labour force, which depends on demographic factors such as migration and birth rates. This can be a major influence on their decision-making.

Key Issues: migration

Figures released by Office for National Statistics (ONS) show that a long-term trend of more people coming to live in the UK than leaving to live elsewhere has continued. Figure 16.3 below shows the trend since 1998. Although people have left the UK to live overseas there have consistently been larger numbers opting to move from overseas to live in the UK. What this means is that the UK population rose by almost a quarter of a million in 2007 – the second-highest recorded annual increase since 2004.

The impact of such migration on the labour supply varies according to the skills of those leaving and entering the UK. Some of those entering the UK may not be of working age and others may have relatively low skills. However, from November 2008 the UK government has implemented a new points system to restrict some categories of migrants to those with skills that are in short supply in the UK. The UK's membership of the European Union means, however, that citizens of most of the 27 member states are free to enter the UK and to live and work here.

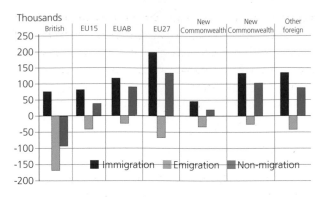

Figure 16.4 Total international migration estimates by citizenship

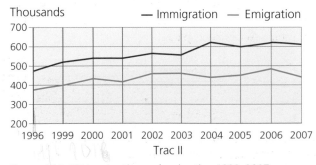

Figure 16.3 UK immigration and emigration 1998–2007

Wage rates

If wages are expected to rise, then businesses may reduce their demand for labour and seek to make greater use of technology. This may entail a large investment by businesses in technology and also in training the remaining employees to operate the technology efficiently. The inward migration into the UK has helped to keep wage rates down. A greater supply of labour tends to depress wage rates and many immigrants (especially those from Eastern Europe) have been prepared to work for relatively low wages by UK standards.

Technological developments

Changes in technology will impact on planning the workforce, as they may reduce the need for unskilled or even skilled employees, while creating employment for those with technical skills. Workforce planners liaise with operations managers to investigate the impact of introducing technology into the production process. For example, potteries have introduced technology onto their production lines for cups, saucers and other types of crockery and this has led to a reduced need for employees.

Changes in legislation

Employment laws may limit the number of hours employees can work each week or may require businesses to offer employees benefits such as paternity leave. Such changes may mean that a business requires greater amounts of labour or persuade it to replace labour with capital equipment. In 2008 the UK government announced its intention to introduce an Equalities Act which would impact on businesses' recruitment policies. The Act of Parliament would also allow businesses to discriminate in favour of female and ethnic minority candidates of equal ability, though companies would not be forced to use positive discrimination.

Internal factors
Corporate plans

These set out the goals of the entire organisation. Corporate plans relate to the business's mission statement. The goals included in corporate plans may include:

- growth
- increased market share
- competing in new markets (perhaps overseas)
- earning the highest possible profits.

A corporate plan suggesting expanding into a new market could, for example, have significant implications for employees. More employees might be required, possibly with different skills. If the expansion involves entering a market overseas, some employees may be redeployed, or some may be made redundant. Finally, in some circumstances jobs may be lost as part of expansion if this involves joint ventures allowing some rationalisation and staffing reduction.

Marketing plans

Marketing plans detail a firm's marketing objectives and how they intend to achieve these objectives (marketing strategy). The achievement of marketing objectives assists a firm in attaining its corporate objectives. If a firm plans to increase market share it may introduce new products. This might require the workforce plan to create a labour force with different skills through recruitment, training and redeployment.

Operations plans

This type of plan details a business's objectives in relation to operations management. As with marketing plans, the objectives in operations plans are a central part of a firm's corporate strategy. Plans for production inform a business's workforce plan. Operations may become capital intensive, requiring fewer employees with greater skills. Alternatively, a business might wish to give employees more responsibility for operations as it adopts total quality management. This may require the workforce plan to prepare for delayering and empowerment.

Financial constraints

Workforce planning operates within tight financial guidelines. Training, recruitment, redeployment and even redundancy are expensive. Firms operating a 'soft' approach to HRM may be prepared to grant a larger budget for workforce planning as they seek to develop their employees. On the other hand, advocates of 'hard' HRM would wish to effect workforce planning with minimal costs.

The type of business

The type of workforce required by a business is highly likely to be influenced by the type of business and its circumstances. In turn this will impact on the process of workforce planning. For example, a business committed to global growth may have to have redeployment of experienced employees as a central feature of its workforce plan. In contrast, innovative businesses may require diverse workforces (different ages, educational backgrounds and cultures) to generate and assess unique and creative ideas as a basis for new products.

Issues in implementing workforce plans

Once a workforce plan is complete and approved by the senior managers or directors of a business, it has to be implemented. This process is likely to involve recruiting, training, redeploying and making employees redundant, depending on the circumstances facing the business. There is a range of factors or issues that can affect the process of implementing a workforce plan.

Examiner's advice

When responding to questions on issues relating to the implementation of workforce plans, it is important to appreciate that the impact of these factors can be both positive and negative. It is also important to recognise that workforce plans do not always reduce the size of a business's workforce; they are also used to expand it.

Key Issues: methods of reducing the size of a workforce

Research conducted by the Cranfield School of Management shows that compulsory redundancies is the most common method used by UK businesses to reduce the size of their workforces. A compulsory redundancy takes place when a business takes a decision that a job no longer exists and the post holder loses his or her job against their will. In contrast, voluntary redundancies take place when employees volunteer to leave the workforce in return for compensation. Outsourcing or outplacement occurs when jobs that were previously carried out by the business's employees become the responsibility of the employees of another business.

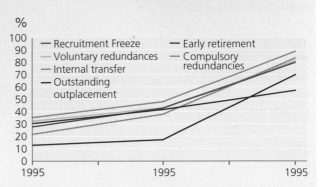

Figure 16.5 Methods for reducing employment levels
Source: Personnel Today http://www.personneltoday.com

Employer–employee relations

If a workforce plan entails a significant reduction in a business's workforce through redundancies or the redeployment of employees to other areas of the UK or to other countries, its implementation may damage the working relationship between the business and its employees. If the changes to the size and location of the workforce are implemented compulsorily, the workforce may resist its implementation and may take industrial action such as strikes in an attempt to prevent its implementation. Such a series of events may damage the business's financial position due to a loss of sales and revenue.

> **Key terms**
> **A trade union** is an organisation formed with the objective of protecting and enhancing the working conditions and economic positions of its members.

Conversely, good employer–employee relations can assist the process of implementing workforce plans. One major advantage can arise from the involvement of trade unions or other employee representatives in the planning process. The involvement of such groups can bring greater knowledge and different perspectives to the process. For example, a trade union might have conducted research into labour market issues, such as migration, and be able to advise human

Business in Focus

Trade union negotiates with firm over job losses

In 2008 Paramount Foods announced it was planning to cut 144 posts from its workforce of 488 in Salford, where it manufactures bases for pizzas. Among the company's customers is the supermarket chain Asda. Paramount Foods plans further job losses at its factory on Deeside, where the pizza toppings are made. Here, more than half of the 241-strong workforce could go.

The GMB union will begin consultation with employers on Tuesday. It also wants talks with Asda, which has cut its orders with Paramount. A 90-day consultation period over the proposed job losses will end in September.

The firm's managing director Phil Ryle has said the firm will 'do everything in our power' between now and September to minimise the number of job losses. The union's North-West regional officer Mark Jones said: 'The GMB will do everything we can to see what alternatives there are to these redundancies.'

Question:

1   To what extent might the GMB trade union assist and hinder Paramount Foods in the implementation of its workforce plan?

resource managers of likely trends in specific sectors of particular labour markets. Good relations between employers and employees can also be useful in providing an effective channel of communication with employees, reducing the chances of rumours and misunderstanding causing problems at any stage of the implementation of the plan. If new employees are required or if redundancies are necessary, a trade union or other group representative of employees may assist in the relevant selection procedures and reduce the possibility of conflict or disputes.

The cost of implementing workforce plans

All workforce plans are subject to some financial constraints. The implementation of the workforce plan will have to be carried out within a certain budget. This limits the extent of the spending of the human resource managers in putting their plans into action. Implementing workforce plans can entail a number of different forms of expenditure.

- **The cost of recruiting and selecting new employees**. To increase a labour force in this way can entail advertising (sometimes nationally or even internationally), screening applications and operating a selection procedure using interviews and/or other methods such as psychometric testing. These activities are expensive in terms of direct costs as well as the cost of using human resource employees in these ways. The Chartered Institute of Personnel and Development estimates that the average cost of recruiting a single new employee is £4,333.
- **Training costs** can be substantial. Most new employees will require some training, if only induction training. However, other forms of training may be required to improve the skills and performance of employees to match those set out in the workforce plan.
- **Making redundancy payments to staff**. This can be expensive, with the law requiring that a payment of up to £495 for each year of employment is made. The cost of making a single person redundant can run to many thousands of pounds.
- **Redeployment** can also be a costly exercise. This may involve paying the costs that the employee incurs in moving to another part of the UK, or even overseas. These may include the legal and professional costs of selling and buying houses, other costs such as fitting out new houses and transport costs.

However, operating within a financial constraint does also offer some benefits. Human resource managers may look carefully, for example, at the skills that are available to the business internally before opting for an expensive external recruitment programme. Equally, it can provide a line of argument to use when negotiating with trade unions or other employee representatives and a reason for not paying higher sums of redundancy pay, for example.

> **Key term**
> **Induction training** is the provision of job-related skills and knowledge given to a new employee within a business.

Corporate image

A corporate image is the public's perception of a business. Increasingly businesses wish to present themselves in the most favourable light possible. They recognise that they might gain a competitive advantage from being held in high esteem by their stakeholders, and especially their customers. Being seen to offer high quality training schemes can assist in this regard. On the other hand, making large numbers of employees redundant can damage a business's reputation and may harm its commercial performance. In 2008 British Telecommunications (BT) revealed that it planned to make 10,000 employees redundant and stressed that there would be no compulsory redundancies in an attempt to minimise the harm to its corporate image.

Implementing workforce plans can also have a positive impact on a firm's corporate image. The creation of new jobs or the implementation of a major scheme of training can help to improve the image of a wide range of business. Many businesses issue press releases to announce positive HR actions that may have been taken as part of the implementation of their workforce plans. You will commonly see companies such as Tesco announce the creation of new jobs as part of an expansion plan. The creation of the new jobs will have been built into the business's workforce plan. Coordination with the company's marketing department will ensure that a positive news story is reported.

The value of using workforce plans

The process of planning can be highly beneficial to businesses. Workforce planning is no exception. It offers management the opportunity to coordinate and integrate the business's entire human resource management activities and hence to avoid any inconsistencies or waste of resources through duplication of activities.

Workforce planning offers businesses other benefits as well.

* The in-depth investigation of likely future events will encourage HR managers to think of the most effective (and cost efficient) ways of responding to these events. Managers have time to reflect on and discuss their responses and to consider the full implications of proposed actions. In this way all the data relating to any HR decisions can be collected and considered at length. This avoids crisis decision-making and reduces the likelihood of errors.
* HR managers are afforded the opportunity to consult with other managers with responsibility for other functions within the business, such as marketing or finance. This allows HR decisions to be taken in an integrated fashion and to have the greatest possibility of assisting the business in achieving its corporate objectives.
* Workforce planning gives HR managers the opportunity to assess whether the business's human resource objectives are feasible given the constraints (for example, finance) under which the function operates. It should also afford the opportunity to change the HR objectives.

However, workforce planning can go wrong and be of limited value to a business. The value of workforce plans depends, to a great extent, on the accuracy of the company's forecasting of its future labour needs. In particular it will depend upon the company's ability to forecast the level of demand for its goods and services with some degree of accuracy. If the company underestimates demand it may have insufficient labour available and the result may be dissatisfied customers. On the other hand, employing too many staff leads to unnecessary costs and reduced profit margins. There are many reasons why forecasts of future sales (and therefore the required labour force) may be inaccurate. There may be a sudden and unexpected change in customer tastes. In 2008 firms selling vegetable seeds experienced a surprising increase in demand (up to 40 per cent) for their products due to the increasing popularity of growing vegetables. The economy may perform differently from what was expected. In 2006 few economists were forecasting that many countries would go into recession in 2008. Finally, competitors may alter their behaviour by bringing out new products, or new competitors may emerge. So, forecasting

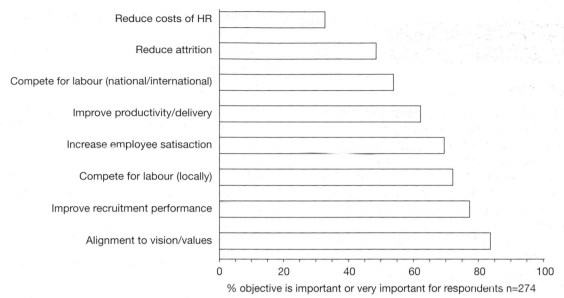

Figure 16.6 Employer branding objectives (in order of importance)
Source: CIPD http://www.cipd.co.uk

labour demand can be a tricky business, especially if the forecast extends several years into the future.

The exact value of workforce planning will depend on the circumstances in which it is being conducted. The experience of the managers engaged in the process will play a part, as will the volatility of demand for the products that the business sells. The time and resources devoted to the planning process will also affect the quality and accuracy of the outcomes and therefore its value. Finally, the timescale to which the plan relates is also important: the further into the future the plan extends, the less value it is likely to provide to the organisation.

One step further: employer branding

Brett Minchington is sometimes credited with 'discovering' the concept of employer branding. Employer branding is defined as creating the image of the organisation as a 'great place to work' in the minds of current employees and other key stakeholders such as potential employees, customers and suppliers.

A company brand is used to gain customer loyalty and therefore increased profits through differentiation. An employer brand can be used to similar effect by HR and organisations, to compete effectively in the labour market and drive employee loyalty through effective recruitment, engagement and retention policies. A business's employer brand will inevitably be linked to the way in which the organisation is perceived by the general public and key stakeholder groups.

Employer branding is how an organisation presents and sells what it has to offer to both potential and existing employees. A strong employer brand should connect an organisation's values, HR strategy and HR policies and be inseparable from the business's corporate brand. It will make the business an attractive employer in terms of pay and conditions but also job satisfaction, training and the possibilities of promotion. The successful development of an employer brand should lead to a business being regarded as 'a good employer'.

There are a number of reasons why a business would want to engage in employer branding. Figure 16.6 illustrates the most important ones.

Progress questions

1 Define the term 'workforce plan'. (2 marks)

2 State four items that would be likely to be included in a workforce plan. (4 marks)

3 Describe three possible sources of information for a workforce plan drawn up by a food manufacturer based in Devon. (6 marks)

4 Explain why sales forecasts are such an important influence on workforce plans for all businesses, but especially those supplying services. (6 marks)

5 Outline two other external factors that might influence the workforce plan drawn up by a large supermarket such as J Sainsbury. (6 marks)

6 Explain two internal factors that might influence the workforce plan of the low-cost airline easyJet. (6 marks)

7 A manufacturing business has taken a decision to switch to capital-intensive production. How might the business's workforce plan assist in effecting this change successfully? (8 marks)

8 How might a trade union assist HR managers in implementing a workforce plan? (6 marks)

9 Explain why a pharmaceutical company implementing a workforce plan during a period of rapid growth might allocate a large budget to its HR department. (8 marks)

10 Explain two possible benefits that workforce planning might provide to a UK restaurant chain considering its first overseas expansion into Europe. (8 marks)

Analysis and evaluation questions

1 Easysleep plc is one of the largest hotel chains in the UK, providing budget-priced accommodation for travellers in locations throughout the UK. The company has just bought a small restaurant chain specialising in pasta and pizzas and intends to develop it to provide restaurants alongside its most popular hotels. Some employees are unhappy at this move, believing that the hotels need investment to improve the standard of accommodation. Customer numbers have been falling and employees are worried that their jobs are not safe.

a Analyse why this business should draw up a workforce plan. (10 marks)

b To what extent do you agree with the view that the company's sales forecasts will be the most important influence on its future workforce planning? (15 marks)

2 Liddell Ltd manufactures wooden furniture and is based in a high-unemployment area of south London. The company is facing a difficult period of trading and its order books are nearly empty. However, one of its rivals has closed and is selling some of its production-line machinery cheaply, which could help Liddell Ltd to cut its production costs. The company's managers believe that if they can be more price competitive sales could increase.

Many of the company's employees are members of APTU – a trade union. Relations with the trade union have been good and the union representative is urging the company to construct a new workforce plan for the next three years.

a Analyse the possible sources of information that Liddell Ltd could use to construct its workforce plan. (10 marks)

b Will the trade union make it more difficult for the company to implement its workforce plan? Justify your view. (15 marks)

Case study

Rolls-Royce announced today that it is consulting employee representatives about a proposed reduction of 140 jobs at its Assembly and Test facility in Derby, UK, which forms part of the Group's Civil Aerospace business.

Today's announcement represents the first stage in a more general programme aimed at matching the Group's capacity more closely with the expected levels of demand. The Group currently employs around 39,000 people globally, of whom around 60 per cent work in the UK.

Rolls-Royce has been reviewing the possible impact of current economic uncertainties, delays on individual programmes, such as the Airbus A380 and the Boeing 787, and the benefits of the Group's continuing focus on efficiency. While it is too early to be specific about the precise implications for the number and location of job reductions, the Group's current assessment is that in 2009 it will be necessary to implement job reductions across the various sectors and functions of around 1,500 to 2,000 on a worldwide basis, including the reduction announced today.

The costs of the changes in the workforce in 2009 are expected to be balanced by the savings achieved in the course of the year, as is the case in 2008. These reductions account for around 4 per cent of the total workforce and will have an effect globally.

To put these proposed reductions into context, Rolls-Royce announced in January that it would continue its focus on efficiency by reducing by 2,300 during 2008 the number of staff working in overhead functions, a programme that is now largely complete. To minimise compulsory redundancies, the Group reduced its temporary workforce and, where possible, relied on voluntary severance, natural attrition and avoided recruitment. It has continued to recruit to support growth in key areas of the business and, importantly, maintained its commitment to apprentice and graduate recruitment. Rolls-Royce will adopt a similar approach in 2009 so as to reduce, as far as possible, the impact of the proposed reductions.

Sir John Rose, Chief Executive, said: 'We are determined to maintain our focus on cost reduction and competitiveness as the world economy enters a challenging period. It is too early to determine the precise effects of the global economic downturn and programme delays. However, we wanted to give all our employees an early indication of the likely scale of the job reductions we expect in 2009.'

Source: Adapted from http://www.rolls-royce.com/media

(40 marks, 60 minutes)

Questions

1 What are the key elements of Rolls-Royce's workforce plan for 2009? (5 marks)
2 Analyse the possible benefits that Rolls-Royce receives from workforce planning. (8 marks)
3 Discuss the major influences on the company's workforce planning for 2009. (12 marks)
4 Do you think that corporate image will be the most important issue for the company when implementing its workforce plan? Justify your view. (15 marks)

Competitive organisational structures

An organisational structure is the way in which a business is arranged to carry out its activities. In this chapter we will build on the material you covered in Unit Two of your AS Business Studies course and especially issues such as levels of hierarchy, spans of control, delegation and workforce roles. This chapter will consider the particular issues facing larger businesses when deciding on the organisational structure to adopt and how they organise their employees to give themselves the greatest possible competitive advantage.

In this chapter we consider:
- the types of organisational structure that firms might use
- the factors that influence a business in its choice of organisational structure
- how organisations adapt their structures to improve their competitiveness.

> **Key terms**
> An **organisational structure** is the way in which a business is arranged to carry out its activities.
> **Levels of hierarchy** refer to the number of layers of authority that exist within an organisation.
> A **span of control** is the number of subordinates directly responsible to a manager.

Introduction to organisational structure

An organisational structure, which may be shown in an organisation chart, sets out:

- the routes by which communication passes through the business
- who has authority (and power) and responsibility within the organisation
- the roles and titles of individuals within the organisation
- the people to whom individual employees are accountable and those for whom they are responsible.

Businesses change the structure of their organisation rapidly and regularly; some managers believe that they should be continually reorganising their firms to meet the demands of a dynamic marketplace. By improving the organisational structure on a regular basis a business is better able to meet the needs of its customers.

Types of organisational structure

Businesses can adopt a number of organisational structures according to a number of factors, such as the size of the organisation, the environment in which it operates and the personal preferences of the owners and senior managers. We will discuss the factors influencing the choice of organisational structure in detail in the next section of this chapter.

Formal or traditional hierarchies

This structure shares decision-making throughout the business and gives all employees a clearly defined role, as well as establishing their relationship with other employees in the business. It is common for this type of organisational structure to be based upon departments and, because of the dependence upon agreed procedures, it can be bureaucratic.

Figure 17.1 A traditional hierarchy

Business in Focus

The organisational structure of Cadbury Schweppes plc

Source: Cadbury World Study Tour Booklet, page 13
http://www.cadburyworld.co.uk

Question:

1 This shows the organisational structure of the multinational confectionery and soft drinks company before it separated (or de-merged) from its soft drinks division in May 2008. Looking at this chart, can you think of reasons why Cadbury Schweppes might have split itself into two?

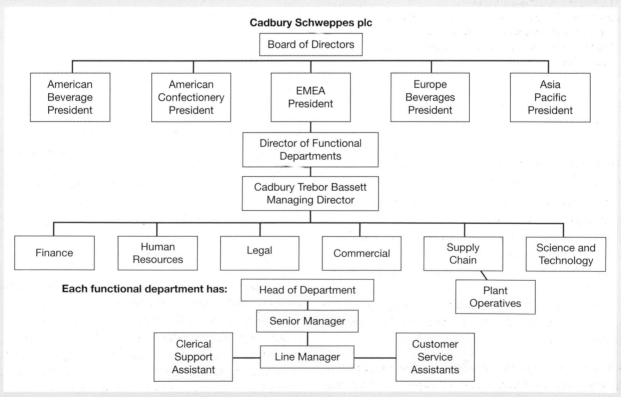

Figure 17.2 The organisational structure of Cadbury Schweppes plc

This type of structure normally has a number of other features.

- It is a relatively 'tall' hierarchy with the associated narrow spans of control.
- The organisation will be centralised, with the most important decisions taken by senior managers.
- Hierarchy is important and senior managers expect to be treated with respect.
- Tradition is important and change is often implemented slowly.

Communication in formal organisations is principally downwards and uses established routes moving down from senior to junior employees. This structure allows specialists to operate (for example in marketing and finance) within their area of expertise. They can generate new and very innovative ideas, but other areas of the business may be unaware of such developments. Employees are aware of lines of command and communication and the position of their department or unit within the organisation. All employees appreciate the possibilities for promotion that exist in the business.

The disadvantages of this structure can become more apparent as the organisation grows in size. Departments may bid for resources in an attempt to increase their size and prestige within the business, rather than because this will benefit the organisation. Furthermore, as the business becomes larger, decision-making can become slower as communication has to pass through many layers within the organisation. Simultaneously, coordinating the business's attempts to achieve its objectives becomes difficult. Senior managers become more remote and may take decisions that are not appropriate to local situations or to the needs of particular groups of customers.

Traditional organisational structures can be found in the following types of businesses:

- long-established businesses such as merchant banks in the City of London
- family businesses operating on a relatively small scale.

Matrix structures

This type of organisational structure is task orientated and is intended to overcome many of the problems associated with the traditional or hierarchical structure. It is a combination of a vertical chain of command operated through departments or units and horizontal projects of product teams. A typical matrix structure is illustrated in Figure 17.3.

Businesses using matrix structures put together teams of individuals with the specialist skills necessary to complete a particular project. Each individual within the project team brings a particular skill and carries appropriate responsibilities. The aim is to allow all individuals to use their talents effectively irrespective of their position within the organisation. So a project manager looking to develop a new product may be able to call on IT and design skills from relatively junior employees elsewhere in the organisation.

Matrix structures focus on the task in hand – launching a new product, opening new retail outlets, closing down factories or entering overseas markets for the first time. Project groups often have strong senses of identity in spite of being drawn from various areas in the business. This is because they are pursuing a clearly defined objective providing team members with a sense of purpose and responsibility.

Matrix structures bring problems with them. Employees can find it difficult having two managers (project managers and departmental managers) because of divided loyalties. They can be uncertain about which parts of their work to prioritise and conflict can result. Matrix structures have a reputation for being expensive to operate: administrative and sec-

Advantages	Disadvantages
• Authority and responsibility are clearly established. • Specialist managers can be used effectively. • Promotion path is clearly signposted. • Employees are often very loyal to their department within the business.	• The organisation can be slow to respond to customer needs. • Communication, and especially horizontal communication, can be poor. • Inter-department rivalry may occur at the expense of the performance of business as a whole.

Table 17.1 **The advantages and disadvantages of traditional hierarchies**

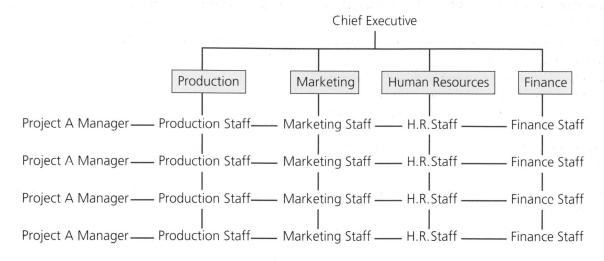

Figure 17.3 A typical matrix structure

Advantages	Disadvantages
• Focuses on tasks necessary for business success. • Encourages organisations to be flexible and responsive to customers' needs. • Motivates and develops employees by providing varied and challenging tasks.	• Employees can have divided responsibilities. • Conflict can occur between project and departmental managers, reducing performance of organisation. • Heavy expenditure on support staff may be required.

Table 17.2 **The advantages and disadvantages of matrix structures**

retarial staff can be costly when used in support of a number of projects.

Entrepreneurial structures

These are frequently found in businesses operating in competitive markets and particularly in those where rapid decisions are essential. Television and radio news organisations, for example Sky News, often operate with an entrepreneurial structure. A few key workers at the core of the organisation – frequently the owners in the case of small businesses – make all the major decisions. The business is heavily dependent upon the knowledge and skills of these key workers. Power radiates from the centre under this structure, as illustrated in Figure 17.4.

Entrepreneurial structures are suited to markets where rapid decisions are essential and where organisations are small enough to be controlled effectively by a few trusted employees. It is a structure frequently used by charismatic and dynamic leaders: Alan Sugar used this approach in managing his elec-

tronics company Amstrad during the early years of the business. Because all-important decisions are taken at the centre, little use is made of hierarchies and the organisation is relatively 'flat'.

However, there are distinct drawbacks to the

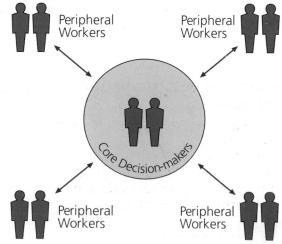

Figure 17.4 The entrepreneurial structure

entrepreneurial structure. Its effectiveness depends upon two factors:

1 The quality of management and decision-making by the 'core' employees. If decisions are delayed or if the workers lose touch with the market the business is unlikely to perform effectively.
2 As the business grows, the 'core' employees experience increasing difficulty in managing the business. The volume of work may overwhelm them and the quality (and speed) of decisions may suffer. At this point the business may adopt another structure.

Informal structures

This type of structure exists where the organisation does not have an obvious structure. This is common is the case of professionals (doctors and lawyers, for example) where they operate as a team. The professionals normally receive administrative support from others within the organisation.

This form of organisational structure allows highly trained and motivated employees to organise their working lives and to take decisions with a high degree of independence. However, it is less appropriate for many businesses as it lacks coordination and control by senior managers.

Examiner's advice

The A2 specification looks at large businesses and so the size of the business is an important influence. This makes entrepreneurial structures and informal structures less relevant to the types of businesses on which examination questions may be asked. However, these two structures should not be ignored.

The choice of organisational structure

When deciding upon an organisational structure a business will take into account a number of factors. These can be separated into internal and external influences.

The size of the business

This is arguably the key factor. As the scale of the

business increases an entrepreneurial structure, for example, becomes unsuitable. As the business grows further the chain of command is likely to be lengthened, encouraging the removal of some layers of hierarchy and broader spans of control as a consequence.

On page 203 we saw the organisational chart for Cadbury Schweppes plc. Prior to its de-merger this was a large company, earning a revenue of nearly £8,000 million in 2007 from selling confectionery and soft drinks in markets across the world. The company employed over 55,000 people globally in the same year. The size of this business makes it necessary to break it into smaller units in order to manage it. You will see that Cadbury Schweppes organised itself regionally into American, European and Asia Pacific divisions. It also split itself into beverages and confectionery divisions. The sheer size of the organisation made (a complex) hierarchical structure inevitable.

The nature of the product supplied by the firm

If the firm supplies a diverse range of products it may organise itself traditionally – perhaps in the form of divisions reporting to the board of directors. Hard Rock Café operates in this way. It was originally started as a restaurant business, by Peter Morton and Isaac Tigrett, but later expanded into hotels and casinos. Key areas of the business, such as casinos, have some degree of independence, but operating within the overall structure of the organisation. Such circumstances may allow a more entrepreneurial structure, at least to some extent, if a large business is subdivided into a number of much smaller entities.

The skills of the workforce

The higher the level of skill the typical employee has, the more likely it is that businesses will organise along matrix or informal lines. Groups of professionals, such as management consultants or surgeons, may simply carry out their professional duties with administrative support from the organisation. This may mean that the business is more likely to operate with an informal structure or a matrix structure, depending on the type of business and the products it supplies.

However, in the case of less-skilled employees a hierarchical structure may be preferred. It could be argued that a large organisation employing relatively

Business in Focus

BAE Systems (Australia)

BAE Systems (Australia) is a leading manufacturer of communications, electronic warfare systems, military air support, air defence, mission support segments and intelligence, surveillance and reconnaissance.

The company has 2,700 employees, and is part of the larger British-based BAE Systems. The company is designed to meet the evolving requirements of operating in the defence industry. The company prides itself on delivering the most efficient, value for money products and solutions for its customers. We draw on the strengths of our global company to develop capabilities which ensure the protection of Australia and its assets.

The company operates in a complex market. It is no longer one of single suppliers. The supply chain for defence equipment is a matrix of interconnecting companies working to the same end, drawing on each other's skills and abilities to deliver to customers the most integrated and sophisticated systems available.

Our culture is one of partnerships and long-term working relationships with suppliers, customers and partners alike. We pride ourselves on creating flexible, entrepreneurial teams with an emphasis on strong teamwork and seamless performance.

Source: http://production.investis.com/tenix/aboutus/aboutbaeaus/

Question:

1   Why does BAE Systems (Australia) operate a matrix structure?

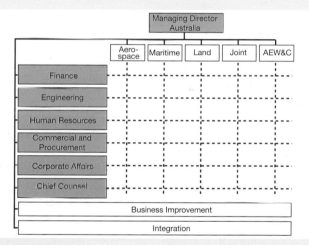

Figure 17.5 BAE Systems' organisation chart

unskilled workers will perform better with a more formal structure and more authority retained further up the hierarchy.

Key term
The **culture** of a business refers to the attitudes, ideas and beliefs that are shared by the employees in a particular business.

The culture of the organisation

This can be a major influence on the structure it adopts. If a business has a highly innovative culture whereby it wishes to be a market leader selling advanced products, then it may adopt a matrix structure to minimise bureaucracy and to allow teams to carry out the necessary research and development and market research. On the other hand, an organisation which places importance on tradition (and derives its commercial success from appearing conventional) may be best suited to a formal hierarchical structure. This structure places emphasis on positions rather than people and this factor encourages the continuance of existing policies and practices. Some high-class hotels may fall into this category.

The business's strategic objectives

An innovative and highly competitive organisation may opt for a matrix structure in order to complete tasks effectively. The matrix structure is task orientated and set goals and can permit employees to be rewarded for achieving such goals. This can increase the performance of the business's workforce and the competitiveness of the whole organisation. On the other hand, a business focusing on quality of design and production (as opposed to growth) may suit an entrepreneurial structure. This could operate with the intention of encouraging creativity and innovation.

> **Key term**
> **Delayering** is the reduction of the number of layers of hierarchy within an organisation's structure.

The environment in which the business is operating

Fierce competitive pressures may encourage delayering in an effort to reduce costs. The process of delayering, if successful, will allow reductions in costs and increased price competitiveness. This can be an attractive strategy for a business supplying services where labour costs are frequently a high proportion of total costs. Firms that operate in markets subject to rapid change (such as technology) may opt for a matrix structure (in at least a division of the business) to ensure that the organisation can complete the necessary tasks to ensure it remains competitive in terms of product development. The matrix structure would also help to eliminate the possibility of inflexible hierarchies getting in the way of rapid decision-making.

Adapting structure to improve competitiveness

Organisational structures are subject to constant change. Changes in technology, changes in competitors' behaviour, changes in government policies and changes in tastes and fashions can all act as a catalyst for a change in an organisation's structure. For example, a new competitor entering a market might result in an increase in price competitiveness, necessitating existing firms to cut costs. Reducing the size of the workforce and adapting its structure may be one way to achieve this.

There is a range of methods a business may use to alter its organisational structure as it attempts to achieve its corporate objectives.

Delayering

As already mentioned, delayering is the reduction of the number of layers of hierarchy within an organisation's structure. A number of businesses have implemented large-scale delayering programmes over recent years. Many such businesses have opted to remove middle managers from their organisational structures.

The increasing level of competition in international markets, and particularly from businesses in the Far East, has forced UK firms to reduce their costs. This trend to cost reduction has been given further impetus by the onset of a recession in many countries, starting in 2008, creating a greater need to reduce costs to survive a period in which sales are likely to decline.

The need to delayer has not been limited to organisations in the private sector. In 2008, as a consequence of cuts in its funding, Transport for London (TfL) announced plans to delayer to reduce its operating costs. Transport for London is the local government body responsible for most aspects of the transport system in Greater London in England. Its role is to implement the transport strategy and to manage transport services across London.

Delayering has been encouraged further by the widespread acceptance of management theories emphasising the benefits that may result from fewer layers of hierarchy. Modern writers on business have identified significant competitive benefits to be gained from giving relatively junior employees greater authority and control over their working lives. This combination of the need to reduce costs and the move to enhance the role of shop-floor employees has put the jobs of middle managers at risk.

Advantages	Disadvantages
• It reduces costs by removing a number of expensive middle managers. • It can improve responsiveness by bringing senior managers and customers closer together, speeding up decision-making. • It can motivate employees lower down in the organisation by giving them greater authority and control over their working lives. • Communication may improve as there are fewer levels of hierarchy for a message to pass through. • It can produce good ideas from a new perspective as shop-floor employees take some decisions.	• It can lessen organisational performance as valuable knowledge and experience may be lost. • Morale and motivation may suffer because employees feel insecure. • Some businesses may merely use the excuse of delayering for making a large number of employees redundant. • Because delayering means employees have to take on new roles within the organisation, extensive (and expensive) retraining may be required. • It can lead to intolerable workloads and high levels of stress among employees.

Table 17.3 **The advantages and disadvantages of delayering**

Delayering is credited with creating 'flatter' organisations, which some describe as 'leaner and more responsive'.

Delayering on its own is unlikely to achieve very much. Components of HRM strategy that typically accompany the process of delayering include:

- a greater emphasis upon teamworking
- cross-functional working, possibly through the use of a matrix structure
- increased employee involvement in decision-making through a process of empowerment.

It is essential that managers implementing a policy of delayering incorporate one or more of the above factors to achieve an effective outcome. These factors will function as replacements for the coordination and controlling role of the organisation's missing levels of hierarchy.

Examiner's advice

Delayering is a 'live' topic at the moment. Many firms are using this approach as a means of improving their performance. Delayering has important links with motivation through providing junior employees with enhanced roles. However, an important evaluative line is to consider why firms delayer: is it simply to cut labour costs or because of a genuine belief in the benefits of employees having greater control over their working lives?

Key terms
Delegation is the passing of authority (but not responsibility) down the organisation structure.
Centralisation exists when the majority of decisions are taken by senior managers at the top (or centre) of the business.
Decentralisation is the passing of authority from those working at the centre of the organisation to those working elsewhere in it.

Centralisation and decentralisation

Centralisation and decentralisation are opposites. A centralised organisation is one in which the majority of decisions are taken by senior managers at the top (or centre) of the business. Centralisation can provide rapid decision-making as few people are likely to be consulted. It should also ensure that the business pursues the objectives set by senior managers.

Decentralisation gives greater authority to employees lower down the organisational structure. In recent years many businesses decentralised for a number of reasons.

- Decentralisation provides subordinates with the opportunity to fulfil needs such as achievement and recognition through working. This should improve motivation and reduce the business's costs by, for example, reducing the rate of labour turnover.
- Decentralisation is doubly beneficial to management. It reduces the workload on senior managers, allowing them to focus on strategic (rather than operational) issues. At the same time

it offers junior managers an opportunity to develop their skills in preparation for a more senior position.

- Many junior employees in the organisation may have better understanding of operational matters and delegation may allow them to use their skills and understanding to good effect.

However, some businesses remain centralised. This might be because the senior managers like to remain in control of the business and to take the major decisions. The decision to centralise may reflect the preferred style of management of the business's senior managers and their desire to retain authority. This may occur when employees are relatively low skilled and the organisation is likely to perform more effectively if power remains at the centre of the organisation.

Flexible workforces

> **Key terms**
>
> **Flexible workforces** exist when businesses place less reliance upon permanent full-time employees and make greater use of part-time and temporary workers.
>
> **Temporary workers** have contracts of employment that only exist for a specific period of time – perhaps six months.
>
> **Annualised hours** operate when an employer states the number of hours employees must work over a year. Weekly working hours can be varied to suit their circumstances.

In recent years a number of trends have emerged in the UK's workforce.

- **Rising numbers of temporary workers.** The number (and proportion) of workers on temporary contracts (for a fixed time period) within the UK rose steadily from the early 1980s until 2000, since when it does appear to have levelled out. In 2008, 1.37 million UK workers were recorded as being on temporary contracts.

Business in Focus

Opodo decentralises

Opodo is a European company owned by nine of Europe's leading airlines, including British Airways and Air France. Opodo offers a 'competitively priced' online global travel service with access to flights from over 500 airlines, over 65,000 hotel properties and over 7,000 car hire locations worldwide, as well as travel insurance. Opodo launched its first website in Germany in 2001, its UK site in 2002 and currently operates in nine countries.

In 2007 the company achieved net profits of €6.6 million on sales of €1,300 million. Ignacio Martos, chief executive of Opodo, said that one major reason the company had achieved its financial and other objectives was because the business had concentrated on its core business and had simplified its

●●●●● opodo.co.uk
let the journey begin

Figure 17.6

organisational structure through decentralisation. The company's decision to decentralise enabled it to concentrate on developing its operations and to invest heavily in IT for the next few years. Opodo states that it intends to maintain 'state of the art' technology and to develop a comprehensive and reliable booking engine giving customers first class customer service.

Sources: Adapted from Opodo website http://opodo.com

	Total employment (millions)	Full-time employees (% of total)	Part-time employees (% of total)	Temporary employees (% of total)	Self-employed (% of total)
1992	25.17	65.37	21.94	5.6	10.26
1995	26.25	64.56	24.43	7.1	10.38
2000	27.98	65.75	25.05	7.0	8.8
2004	28.38	63.91	26.00	5.25	9.8
2008	29.41	64.47	24.99	5.4	12.90

Table 17.4 Trends in employment in the UK 1992–2008
Source: Office for National Statistics, www.statistics.gov.uk

- **Part-time working**. The number of employees within the UK who work part time has also increased year on year. The latest survey in 2004 indicated that 25 per cent of all employees worked part-time – about 7.5 million people.
- **Self-employment**. This form of employment has generally been increasing over recent years, and particularly since 2004. The Labour Force Survey in 2008 showed that approximately 3.8 million people in the UK can be classified as self-employed.
- **Contractors and consultants.** Many businesses have replaced full-time employees with consultants or have contracted out duties to other organisations. For example, it is common for firms to employ contract staff to design and manage IT systems rather than use permanent full-time employees in these roles.
- **Full-time permanent employees**. Firms use fewer full-time employees than was the case in the 1990s. Such employees are relatively expensive as the firm incurs all the costs of employment, such as making pension contributions and providing training. Using consultants and contractors avoids these costs and ensures employees are only hired when needed. Full-time employees tend to be highly skilled and perform central roles within an organisation.

UK businesses have opted for workforces containing increasing numbers of part-time and temporary employees. Labour forces with high proportions of these types of employees are called flexible workforces.

Core and peripheral workers

One way in which a flexible workforce could be organised was part of a 'flexible firm'. This idea was developed by John Atkinson and The Institute of Manpower Studies. They contended that flexible firms comprise a core workforce and a peripheral workforce, as illustrated in Figure 17.7 below.

Figure 17.7 The organisation of a firm with a flexible workforce

The business's core workers would be highly qualified and trained and would be motivated and would be in permanent full-time employment with security of employment. In contrast the peripheral workers would only be hired when necessary. They may be low skilled or have highly specialised skills that are not required all the time. An example of the latter category could be experts on environmental pollution. This would allow the business to respond to fluctuations in demand without incurring the ongoing costs of employing all its workers on a permanent basis. The peripheral workers could be employed part time or by using temporary contracts.

Other methods of flexible working

Businesses can also employ people flexibly using:

* **annualised hours contracts** – employees working in this way are expected to work, say, an average of 38 hours each week, but can be employed to work longer hours during busy weeks, with an equivalent reduction in working hours during quieter periods

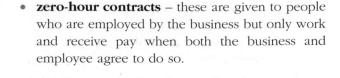

Business in Focus

Zero-hour contracts in the retail industry

Employers' bodies have slammed trade union plans to lobby government for a ban on the use of 'zero-hour' contracts. Delegates at the Public and Commercial Services Union (PCS) annual conference in Brighton earlier this month voted for a campaign to ban contracts that don't guarantee work.

The PCS claimed that the contracts allowed employers to abuse employees by keeping them waiting around for work, and not offering proper training or job security. Delegates called for a campaign, in conjunction with the TUC if possible, aimed at curtailing or banning the use of zero-hour contracts.

But the British Retail Consortium insisted that many employees enjoyed having flexible terms. 'It is wrong to characterise zero-hour contracts as exploitative,' said a spokesman. 'They offer flexible working opportunities that many people appreciate. Often employees want to stay at a firm, but can't commit to permanent hours for family or other reasons, and it is in both their interests and the employer's to keep them on a zero-hour contract.'

Source: Personnel Today
http://www.personneltoday.com

Question:

1   Are zero-hour contracts of equal value to all types of retailers?

* **zero-hour contracts** – these are given to people who are employed by the business but only work and receive pay when both the business and employee agree to do so.

Key terms
Homeworking refers to anyone who works from home for a significant part of their working week.
Teleworking has a similar meaning to homeworking, but implies that this style of employment is dependent upon technological forms of communication.
Outsourcing means finding a people or business outside the organisation to complete part of the production process.

Homeworking

Homeworking refers to anyone who works from home for a significant part of their working week. Homeworking is also sometimes referred to as teleworking. Homeworking is an increasingly important feature of the operation of many businesses in the UK and throughout the world. Over 25 per cent of the UK workforce 'sometimes' works at home. But the number of people working 'mainly' at home is over 2 per cent of the workforce at 681,000, and this is almost a doubling of the number who did so in 1981 (346,000).

The Labour Force Survey now also identifies people who work 'partially' from home (i.e. more than one day per week), and people working 'sometimes' (less than one day a week) from home. The 'partially' category accounts for 3.5 per cent of the workforce, 932,000 people. Thus the trend towards homeworking is accelerating.

Home workers are on average better qualified than the employed workforce as a whole.

In the case of people working partially from home the difference is marked – 41 per cent have degrees as opposed 16 per cent in the workforce as a whole. Only 24 per cent of this group have either no or only secondary-level qualifications.

Non-manual work accounts for about 80 per cent of the work done at home, and the majority of this involves the use of ICT: 61.2 per cent of those working at home at least one day per week use a telephone and computer to do so.

British Telecom is one of many British firms encouraging and supporting employees in homeworking. Why have businesses advocated homeworking?

* Many managers have argued that homeworking

has a positive effect on the motivation of employees. Homeworking naturally allows employees greater responsibility for their own work. Interestingly, some studies suggest that homeworking can reduce stress levels, especially those associated with commuting.

- Employment costs incurred by businesses can be substantially reduced as a consequence of homeworking. Firms can reduce their capacity, avoiding the need to pay expensive office rents in city centres. Other savings to businesses can take the form of reducing travelling expenses and the need for social facilities at work. A survey by the Henley Centre has suggested that for each employee converted to homeworking a business saves £6,000.
- Employees can actually spend more time working as travelling time is eliminated and time spent gossiping with colleagues is reduced. Thus, there is the potential for increasing productivity and employee performance.

The UK government has expressed support for homeworking on environmental grounds, as any significant reduction in commuting offers society substantial benefits in terms of reduced pollution. In view of the apparent benefits of homeworking and governmental approval, it seems surprising that homeworking has not been adopted on a larger scale. However, a number of factors have influenced firms, as well as individual employees, in their decisions not to adopt teleworking.

At times during the 1990s office rents were relatively low and this eliminated a major incentive for businesses to encourage homeworking. The same is true now as the economy moves through a recession. At the same time many companies have 'downsized', creating vacant space within their offices which is almost impossible to sell or lease. Once the main financial inducements have been removed the attractiveness of homeworking to businesses is sharply diminished.

Many companies have operated trials into the costs and benefits of homeworking. Inevitably these have attracted much media attention. However, the outcomes of such experiments have often been to retain the status quo and keep the majority of employees at the office. Many businesses, especially those in the financial sector, have drawn back from the move to have significant numbers of employees working at home.

As long ago as the 1930s, Elton Mayo wrote that the social dimension was an important aspect of employment. Homeworking eliminates much contact with fellow workers and certainly removes the opportunity to indulge in workplace gossip and banter. Failing to fulfil the social needs of employees at work could damage motivation and performance. Furthermore, there is some evidence that it is the social isolation inherent in homeworking that has resulted in numerous employees opting to return to more traditional patterns of employment.

Some employers are reluctant to encourage homeworking as they feel that employees may not work as hard if they were not closely supervised. It may be that a more democratic style of leadership is likely to promote and encourage homeworking among employees.

Many forms of employment are not suited to homeworking. If a job involves significant communication with colleagues on a regular basis, or if it requires the skills of a number of people simultaneously, homeworking is unlikely to be an effective method of organising the workforce.

Outsourcing

Outsourcing means finding a person or business outside the organisation to complete part of the production process. Businesses may decide to outsource to reduce their labour costs and this can be an attractive option if the type of employee required is highly skilled and/or the business does not require their services all of the time. Sometimes work may be outsourced because the business does not have employees with the skills necessary to complete the work. Examples of the type of work that is outsourced can include cleaning, the provision of IT services and management consultancy services.

Outsourcing brings obvious advantages in terms of reducing labour costs. The business does not have to contribute to pension funds or the government's national insurance scheme on behalf of the employee, provide training or paid holidays. However, communication between outsourced workers and permanent employees can be more difficult and the level of motivation of such workers can be low.

Conclusion

The balance between advantages and disadvantages of employing flexible workforces depends upon the circumstances. Flexible workforces arguably offer the greatest potential to businesses when the employees

The case for . .	. . . and the case against
• Flexible employees are cheaper because firms avoid many of the costs of full-time employment (such as pension contributions). Wages are also generally lower. This makes the firm more price competitive, which may be important in an increasingly global market. • Flexible workforces assist businesses in dealing with fluctuations in demand. Being able to call on part-time or self-employed workers at a busy time avoids the problems associated with unfulfilled orders. At quiet times firms do not have expensive workers with little to do, and do not have to pay to make employees redundant. • Firms can reduce training costs by subcontracting work to other organisations or by hiring self-employed workers. Businesses acquire staff with up-to-date skills without having to pay for their training. This is particularly useful in industries subject to rapid change, such as the microelectronics industry. • Flexible patterns of employment allow businesses to have access to highly specialised skills without bearing the costs of permanently employing what can be hugely expensive workers. Thus, even relatively small businesses may hire self-employed systems analysts to carry out highly technical work with their computer systems.	• Communication is tricky with flexible workforces. More employees, unfamiliar with one another and with different patterns of attendance, make it difficult to pass on information. Formal and informal communication is poorer, causing lower-quality customer service and damaging the firm's image. • The turnover of staff is higher with flexible workforces. Lack of job security leads people to move to permanent employment when possible. High rates of labour turnover mean workers are unfamiliar with their duties and firms incur greater recruitment costs. • Morale can be lower with flexible workforces. Security needs may not be met through these forms of employment and employee performance may be hampered by this factor. The failure to form groups at work – or the regular breaking up of these groups – may mean that social needs also remain unfulfilled, leading to lower levels of motivation.

Table 17.5 The case for and against flexible workforces

in question are either highly skilled or have few skills. Highly skilled employees are expensive to hire and may require constant retraining to ensure their skills remain up to date. Employing such people through temporary contracts, or as self-employed workers, may provide benefits without incurring heavy long-term expenditure.

Equally, employees with few skills may be hired on a part-time, flexible-hours or temporary basis. This allows firms to have the appropriate amount of labour available to meet varying levels of demand. High levels of turnover of staff may not be a problem in such circumstances, as training is likely to be minimal.

One step further: global delayering

The Boston Consulting Group (perhaps best known for developing the Boston Matrix) has spent some time researching delayering and has produced a

Examiner's advice

You must think about the advantages and disadvantages of flexible workforces in relation to the type of business under consideration. Factors such as the stability of patterns of demand and the degree of price elasticity may shape your opinion on its value.

number of articles on this topic. Its most recent article (2006) considers a more complex type of delayering: global delayering.

The Group argues that advantages of delayering (lower costs, quicker decision-making and improved communication) can be achieved in a global context. The Group argues that the benefits of global delayering may be greater than can be achieved through the domestic variety. The authors of the article argue that it is easier to ignore inefficiency at a global level and therefore easier to do nothing about it. The implementation of a strategy of global delayering will have to stretch across several, and perhaps many, countries. However, the Group believes that delayering forces senior managers to look closely at and address many other issues in an organisation that may reduce its international competitiveness.

For example, the concept of global delayering may be very necessary in global businesses that have grown through takeovers. Takeovers can result in the bringing together of businesses with different organisational structures and may result in too many layers of hierarchy. The buying business may be more interested in thinking about the new customers and products this purchase may give. Thoughts as to rationalising functions such as finance may not be at the front of executives' minds, although it offers potential for significant cost savings. You can find out more about global delayering by reading the Boston Consulting Group's article at the web address given below.

Source: Boston Consulting Group

Adapted from http://www.bcg.com

Progress questions

1 Explain the key distinctions between a hierarchical organisational structure and a matrix structure. (6 marks)
2 Outline two factors that may determine the effectiveness of an entrepreneurial organisational structure. (6 marks)
3 Explain why a large, multinational business might be expected to choose a hierarchical organisational structure. (8 marks)
4 Outline the ways in which the skills levels of its workforce might affect the choice of organisational structure chosen by a design company. (6 marks)
5 Explain why the drawbacks of delayering might be felt in the short term, whereas the benefits might only arise in the long run. (8 marks)
6 Explain possible reasons why a policy of delayering on its own may be unlikely to achieve much in terms of improving the performance of the workforce. (6 marks)

7 Explain, with the aid of examples, the term 'flexible workforce'. (3 marks)
8 Outline two ways in which a major ice cream manufacturer might increase the flexibility of its workforce. (8 marks)
9 Outline two reasons why some firms make little attempt to make more use of home-working to increase the flexibility of their workforces. (6 marks)
10 Explain the possible ways in which a UK high street bank might make use of outsourcing. (8 marks)

Analysis and evaluation questions

1 GKX plc is a well-established operator of hotels throughout Europe, though its profits have declined over recent years. The company employs 5,350 people, and 90 per cent of its staff work full time on permanent contracts. The business's hotels are sited in locations popular with tourists seeking the sun and also skiing in the winter months. Approximately 50 per cent of the hotels are used for beach and skiing holidays.
The company has a hierarchical structure based on a head office in London and a series of regional managers across Europe, and each hotel has a manager and deputy as well as staff responsible for functions within the hotel, such as catering. The company's head office in Mayfair has a staff of over 350 including a number of specialists in areas such as IT, public relations and interior design.
   a Analyse the possible disadvantages to GKX plc of operating a hierarchical structure. (10 marks)
   b Discuss the actions GKX plc could take to make its workforce more flexible. (15 marks)
2 Charles Fik plc has lost market share over the last four years. It now holds 34 per cent of the UK market for the manufacture of glass products. The company has used a hierarchical structure with nine levels of hierarchy and employs 12,000 people in six locations across the UK. The retiring chief executive wished to avoid managers operating with wide spans of

control. The company comprises four divisions which deal with different parts of its product range.

Demand for glass is very sensitive to the state of the economy and is also higher in summer when more construction work takes place. The company has been active in research and has a research department which, although creative in the past, has been less successful in recent years.

a Analyse possible reasons why the company opted to use a hierarchical organisational structure. (10 marks)

b Discuss the ways in which the company might adjust its organisational structure to improve its competitiveness. (15 marks)

Case study

Thomson Reuters, the international news agency, reported a slight slowdown in growth in sales revenue during the second quarter (April to June) of 2008, but said it was well placed to withstand the worst of the economic recession. The company's sales revenues in the second quarter increased by 7 per cent year on year, down from the 8 per cent increase recorded in the first three months of the year. Growth in the company's markets division (which provides the latest financial data to investment banks and other institutions, and includes the Reuters and Thomson news businesses) slipped from 9 per cent in the first quarter to 7 per cent in the second. The company, formed in April from the merger of Canadian group Thomson and the 157-year-old Reuters business, confirmed guidance that full-year revenues would rise 6 per cent to 8 per cent.

A company spokesman said it was difficult to predict trading conditions going into 2009, but detected recent signs of increasing confidence. 'People are feeling a little better than they did a few weeks ago, but that's fragile and that could change.'

He said the company was insulated by its global sales, with revenues in Asia up 15 per cent, offsetting weaknesses in New York and London. Areas such as healthcare and scientific data were 'not recession related' and the tax and accounting arm was likely to benefit from probable legislative changes after the US presidential election.

The spokesman said the merger would result in more than 1,000 jobs being shorn from the 52,000-strong workforce over the next three years. About 140 editorial jobs are going (though about 70 posts are being created) and redundancies this year will total in the 'high hundreds'. Thompson Reuters is seeking to establish a competitive organisational structure.

'There will be some follow-on reductions over the next year. But the lion's share is being done this year,' he said. 'I hesitate to give a number, but my best estimate is over 1,000.'

The cuts were relatively modest when set against the 5,000 job losses at Reuters in the seven years before the merger, he added. 'I view this as just a sensible delayering as a result of bringing two companies together.'

Source: Adapted from the *Guardian*, 13 August 2008
http://www.guardian.co.uk
(40 marks, 60 minutes)

Questions

1 Explain what is meant by a 'competitive organisational structure'. (5 marks)
2 Analyse the possible ways in which Thompson Reuters might make its workforce more flexible. (8 marks)
3 Assess the difficulties the newly merged company might face in implementing a new organisational structure. (12 marks)
4 Will the benefits of Thomson Reuters' delayering exceed its costs? Justify your decision. (15 marks)

Effective employer– employee relations

This chapter looks at the relationship between employers (usually represented by managers) and employees in the workplace. A good relationship can be of great value in improving the competitive performance of the business. Although this chapter builds on your general understanding of the management of people within businesses, it does not build on any specific aspect of your study of AS Business Studies.

In this chapter we examine:
- the nature and importance of communication
- how employers manage communications with employees
- the methods of employee representation
- the methods of avoiding and resolving industrial disputes.

The nature and importance of communication

> **Key term**
> **Communication** is the transfer of information between people.

The theory of communication

Communication is the transfer of information between people. A transmission mechanism is simply the means by which one person communicates with another (e.g. by letter or email).

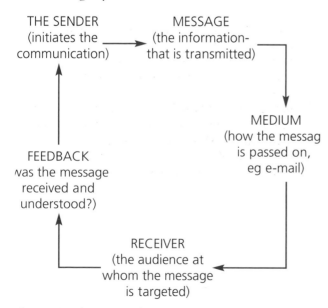

Figure 18.1 The process of communication

Communication involves a number of elements as shown in figure 18.1.

Figure 18.2 An advert by Marks & Spencer plc

Advertising is an example of business communication, as shown by this example from Mark & Spencer's website. The company is linking together its different methods of advertising communication.

- The **sender** is the company who commences the process of communication.
- The **message** is the information that the business

wishes to send to its audience. In the case of Marks & Spencer it wishes to convey information concerning clothes for sale.

- The **medium** is the way in which the message is communicated. Marks & Spencer chose to use the internet to transmit their message – but also made reference to television as a medium.

The **audience** is the target group at whom Marks & Spencer aimed this message – adult men and women, but those who are still relatively young. **Feedback** in this case could take the form of the company analysing the number of people who respond to their website and place online orders while the television advert is running alongside the internet version.

Businesses engage in communication for a variety of purposes, as illustrated in Figure 18.3. This communication can be **internal**, i.e. with other individuals or groups within the business. Thus, a memo sent from the director of human resources to team leaders concerning overtime rates would be an example of internal communication. **External** communication takes place between a business and other organisations or individuals. For example, a business providing details of job vacancies as part of the process of external recruitment would be communicating externally.

Communication can also be classified in other ways.

- **Formal communication** is the exchange of information and ideas within and outside a business using official channels. Examples of formal communication include board meetings or team briefings, and communication through email, memos and letters.
- **Informal communication** takes place outside the official channels of an organisation – gossip is an obvious example.

Effective communication

Effective communication is an essential element of business success. A survey by the Institute of Management and UMIST stressed the importance of good-quality communications within businesses. The survey reported that good communication could assist employees of all types within a business.

- Good communication makes it easier to implement change – an important issue in a business environment subject to rapid and continual change.
- Good communication encourages and develops commitment to the business from employees at all levels within the organisation.
- Effective communication helps to ensure that the

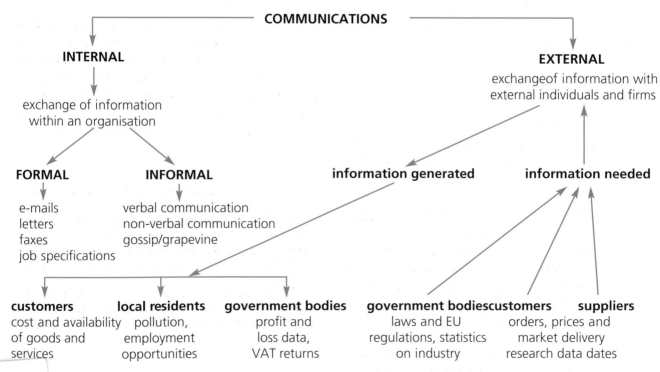

18.3 Internal and external communication

business is coordinated and that all employees pursue the same corporate objectives.

The role of a manager in a modern organisation is to communicate with everyone – shareholders, the media, superiors, customers and suppliers. The measure of today's managers is more about how well they communicate than what they communicate. Good-quality communication by managers with the business's stakeholders offers many benefits.

Successful decision-making requires that managers have access to as much relevant information as possible. The key management roles of planning, prioritising, coordinating and controlling depend upon access to information. This emphasises the importance of good communication to businesses.

A business that has not set up good systems of communication with other stakeholders such as customers and suppliers is unlikely to have effective systems in place with which to communicate with employees. It is to this aspect of communication that we now turn our attention.

Managing communication with employees

Communication is the cornerstone of the coordination of employees. In large businesses it is easy for different departments or parts of the organisation to pursue different objectives. Regular and effective communication can help to ensure that all employees remain closely focused on agreed corporate objectives.

The communication medium

There are a number of techniques or mediums through which managers at all levels in the organisation might choose to communicate with their subordinates; equally, these techniques may be used for upwards communication.

- Meetings can occur in a variety of forms, including formal meetings between trade unions or other groups representing employees, or less formal discussions between individual representatives of the two sides. Social events may also provide a forum for the exchange of information.
- Presentations are frequently used in businesses to explain policies and procedures to large groups of employees. Many presentations use Microsoft PowerPoint. Detailed information (especially

relating to employment and working practices) can be exchanged using this software.

Technology can be used by larger businesses to communicate with their employees, and this can be of particular value to businesses that operate in several locations, especially if these locations are in different countries.

- **Electronic mail (email)** allows people throughout the world to communicate with each other via their computers for the cost of a local telephone call. Messages are stored on servers and can be accessed by the recipient through the use of a password. This is particularly useful for quick international communication between employers and employees groups across different time zones, as messages can be stored until the recipient is available.
- **Intranets** are electronic, computer-based communication networks, similar in nature to the internet but used internally by individual businesses. They are ideally suited to large companies, especially those with a number of locations. They provide an email service as well as access to information of interest to large numbers of employees.
- **Video conferencing** allows people to communicate face-to-face while in different locations, nationally or internationally. It saves time and avoids the need for employers and employees to travel to meetings.

The precise method or methods that a business elects to use to communicate with its employees will vary according to the circumstances and the nature of the business. A business that is large, with employees in a number of locations, possibly in different countries, may rely more on electronic communication, though other means of communication will also be used.

> **Key terms**
> **Delegation** is the passing of authority down the organisational structure.
> **Empowerment** is giving employees greater control over their working lives.
> **Trade unions** are organisations of workers established to protect and improve the economic position and working conditions of their members.
> A **works council** is a forum within a business where workers and management meet to discuss issues such as working conditions, pay and training.

Issues in communicating with employees

The effective management of communication with employees is not simply about choosing the right medium through which to exchange information. Other factors make up an effective employer–employee communication package.

Appreciating the nature of effective communication

Good-quality communication is normally two-way communication. This means that information will flow in both directions between employers and employees or their representatives. Two-way communication allows for feedback to establish that the message has been received and understood. However, it has much more potential than this. It affords the opportunity for employees to offer ideas and suggestions which may result in some excellent ideas for improving the way in which the business operates. The opportunity alone to offer suggestions may improve employees' motivation, and thereby their performance, by providing a sense of recognition and an opportunity for achievement if ideas and suggestions are effective. Finally, two-way communication can alert managers to potential problems which may result in confrontation and conflict if not resolved at the earliest opportunity.

Using the appropriate style of management

The writings of Elton Mayo, and especially the Hawthorne experiment, offer evidence that employees respond positively to receiving attention from managers. Later research has strengthened this link. Abraham Maslow developed his hierarchy of needs, and argued that good communication underpins some of the higher-level needs identified in his theory. The need for recognition, for example, relies heavily upon managers communicating with subordinates. Similarly, Frederick Herzberg wrote that direct communication (rather than through unnecessary layers of hierarchy) was an important means of improving employee motivation. Electing to manage in a style that offers employees the chance to participate in decision-making does more than provide a forum for communication – it encourages it as well.

Adapting the organisational structure to encourage effective communication

We saw in the previous chapter that businesses can organise themselves in different ways. By opting for a structure which allows employees to have greater authority and control over their working lives, employers can encourage communication at all levels within the organisation. Using techniques such as delegation and empowerment has costs in terms of loss of power for managers and in terms of training relatively junior employees to take on more demanding roles. However, alongside the benefit of improved communication, the performance of employees should also improve as levels of motivation increase.

Good communication can have a positive impact upon employee motivation and performance. Praise and recognition are widely seen as motivators, but rely upon communication. Effective communication

Business in Focus

The world's largest brewery

Belgium-based brewer InBev announced it has agreed its £35 billion purchase of the US's Anheuser-Busch to create the world's largest brewer. The new company will be one of the leading consumer product firms in the world.

Anheuser makes Budweiser – the most popular beer in the US – while InBev produces Stella Artois and Beck's.

The brands of the combined company include Stella, Budweiser, Beck's, Hoegaarden, Leffe, Brahma, Staropramen, Michelob and Rolling Rock.

InBev, itself formed by a giant merger of Brazil's AmBev and Belgium's Interbrew several years ago, has promised that Budweiser's headquarters will remain in St Louis, Missouri while none of Anheuser-Busch's US breweries will be closed.

The combined business will have annual sales of $36.4 billion, equivalent to 46 billion litres of beer a year.

Source: Adapted from bbc.co.uk

Questions:

1 Why might the managers of the new company face possible problems in managing communications with its employees?

2 What actions might they take to reduce these problems?

can also give employees important feedback about their performance and help to improve it in the future.

It has become more difficult in some ways to manage communication effectively between employers and employees over recent years. Mergers and takeovers continue to create larger and more complex business. It is not uncommon for businesses in different countries to merge, or for one to buy another in a takeover deal. As a consequence, the need for effective communication between employers and employees can increase. At such a time job losses may be expected and effective communication will be essential to quell rumours and to negotiate mutually acceptable deals. However, the scale of the new business and the possible absence of effective mechanisms for communicating can make this process very difficult.

Collective and individual bargaining

When communicating with employees about issues such as pay and conditions, there are two broad approaches that managers can take in negotiations.

Collective bargaining

Collective bargaining is a tradition for which businesses in the UK are noted. Collective bargaining entails negotiations between management and employees' representatives, usually trade unions, over pay and other conditions of employment. Collective bargaining can only occur if the employer recognises the right of a trade union or other representative group to act on behalf of the workforce. Under a collective agreement the terms negotiated by the employees' representatives are binding upon the entire workforce – this is the 'collective' aspect of this form of negotiation.

In spite of the tradition of collective bargaining in the UK, for many years it became less common. Simultaneously, the proportion of firms recognising trade unions for the purposes of collective bargaining declined. However, the situation was reversed to some degree by the passing of the Employment Relations Act, which came into force in 2000. Under this Act a trade union with a membership exceeding 50 per cent of the employees in any particular business (or part of a business where negotiations take place) can demand union recognition and thereby the right to reintroduce collective bargaining. If a union has more than 10 per cent of the workforce as members it can call for a ballot and needs the support of 40 per cent of the employees to be successful. The newly formed Central Arbitration Committee may settle disputes about union recognition.

The European Union may help the reintroduction of collective bargaining into the workplace. In 2000 the EU announced that it was planning to make consultation with employees on a range of items compulsory for companies with over 50 employees.

The use of collective bargaining as a means of communication between employers and employees in the UK declined for a number of reasons.

- Since the early 1980s trade union membership in the UK has declined. As a consequence the influence of unions waned, allowing businesses to move away from collective bargaining more easily.
- Governments have passed legislation designed to restrict the power of trade unions and to allow labour markets to operate more freely, thereby discouraging collective agreements.
- Employers have introduced strategies that emphasise and reward individuals and teams. This represents a change of approach from collective employer–employee relationships conducted through trade union officials.

Individual bargaining

The move away from collective bargaining has been driven by a change in philosophy within many modern businesses. The adoption of the principles of human resource management has resulted in many enterprises seeking to make the most effective use of each and every member of the workforce. This has had two main consequences.

1 Instead of paying a standard wage or salary to every worker carrying out a particular role (as would have been likely under collective bargaining), individual bargaining means that workers may be paid according to their contribution. This may reduce the labour costs of a business and has the potential to provide financial motivation for employees.
2 The other side to individual bargaining is that some businesses seek to develop their employees to encourage them to make the maximum possible contribution to the performance of the business.

Other firms have simply chosen not to recognise trade unions in the hope of being able to keep wage increases and costs to a minimum without the upward pressure of collective bargaining.

In spite of the move away from collective bargaining in the early years of the new millennium, individual bargaining is most commonly used when employees have substantial skill levels and the ability to negotiate their own packages of pay and conditions. Nevertheless, it has led to a different pattern of communication between employers and employees.

Many employees in the UK have their pay determined by one of two systems, as follows.

1 Pay reviews are frequently used in the public sector to settle the pay levels for groups such as teachers and nurses. A committee of 'experts' considers all the relevant information before arriving at a decision.

2 Management determines pay unilaterally. It is used in some workplaces, often as part of a decentralised arrangement. Management decisions commonly reflect the current rate of inflation.

These methods of settling pay and working conditions may involve minimal communication between employers and employees.

Methods of employee presentation

Employees are not only represented by trade unions in their negotiations with employers. In fact, in the UK only a minority of workers are members of a trade union. In this section we will consider the various ways in which employees can be represented in negotiations with employers.

Trade unions

A trade union is an organisation of workers established to protect and improve the economic position and working conditions of its members. A number of different types of trade union exist, although a series of amalgamations over recent years has resulted in the distinctions between them becoming less clear.

Trade unions are normally organised on a regional basis. For example, Unite operates in regions throughout the UK and Eire. Each region has a regional office staffed by full-time union employees (called organisers or officers). The region is made up of a number of branches (more than 6,000 in total in the case of Unite) and each branch has an elected shop steward. The shop steward communicates with employers on behalf of the union's members and reports back to members regarding management

Business in Focus

Unite

Created through the merger in 2007 of Amicus and the Transport and General Workers Union (T&G), Unite has 2 million members. The new union represents workers in the public and private sectors and in almost every industry and profession; it is the dominant union in manufacturing, energy, transport, finance, food and agriculture. It also represents members working in the National Health Service, education, local authorities, government departments and the voluntary sector.

With a network of more than 500 salaried officers and thousands of trained workplace representatives, Unite is instrumental in improving working practices and training and development initiatives for thousands of UK workers.

decisions. The head office has an administrative, statistical and legal staff and the senior officials of the union. Other trade unions operate similar structures.

Most trade unions in the UK have similar objectives. These focus on improving the economic position of their members by fulfilling the following objectives:

- **Maximising pay** – unions engage in collective bargaining to provide their members with the highest possible rates of pay.
- **Achieving safe and secure working conditions.**
- **Maintaining job security** – arguably this is the most important objective of a modern trade union and one that is difficult to fulfil in the light of pressures resulting from globalisation, the recession that started in 2008, and the increasing use of technology in the workplace.
- **Participating in and influencing decisions in the workplace** – trade unions may achieve this through collective bargaining or through having representatives on works councils and other employer–employee committees.

Business in Focus

The declining power of trade unions in the UK

Union membership rose from the 1950s until the mid-1970s. Since then it has fallen steadily, and despite a slight increase in 2000 membership had declined to an estimated 6.6 million by 2006.

This decline has occurred for a number of reasons:

- **Legislation to control the activities of unions.** The Conservative governments of the 1980s and early 1990s passed a series of Acts to limit the impact of unions on business activities. In particular, this legislation made secret ballots on disputes mandatory and restricted the number of pickets.
- **The decline of traditional industries.** The coal mining, shipbuilding and steel industries were strongly unionised. The fact that these industries have declined in importance and employ far fewer people means that the unions associated with them have also become less important.
- **The increasing number of small businesses.** There has been a rise in the number of small businesses in the UK since the 1980s. These firms are not strongly unionised because they employ few people (and many are part time) and relationships are such that a union is often considered unnecessary.
- There have been **significant changes in the composition of the UK's workforce** in recent years. More employees are now female and part time and less likely to be members of unions. Simultaneously, fewer young employees have entered the workforce because of falling birth rates and thus unions have had fewer potential recruits. The public sector has retained a high proportion of employees who are members of a trade union; numbers in the private sector have declined sharply.

At the same time the number of trade unions has declined due to a series of mergers.

In addition, many unions have social objectives, such as lobbying for higher social security benefits, improved employment legislation and improved quality of provision by the National Health Service.

Trade unions achieve their objectives by carrying out a range of functions to the benefit of their members.

- Their most important and time-consuming function is protecting members' interests over issues such as discrimination, unfair dismissal and health and safety matters.
- They negotiate pay and conditions for their members through collective bargaining.
- Trade unions provide their members with a range of personal services, including legal advice, insurance, education, training and financial advice.

Employers can also benefit from the existence of trade unions for the following reasons:

- They act as a communications link between management and employees.
- Professional negotiation on behalf of a large number of employees can save time and lessen the likelihood of disputes occurring.

Examiner's advice

Do not just think about trade unions in a negative sense. They offer many benefits to employers such as acting as a channel of communication, offering advice on issues such as health and safety and may be proactive in preventing disputes.

Trade unions are responsible for collective bargaining in the workplace. They negotiate with employers on behalf of their members on matters such as pay, conditions and fringe benefits. Unions are in a better position to negotiate than individuals in that they have more negotiating skills and power.

Works councils

A works council is a forum within a business where workers and management meet to discuss issues such as working conditions, pay and training. Employee representatives on a works council are normally elected. It is common for works councils to be used in workplaces where no trade union representation exists. However, in businesses where works councils and trade unions co-exist, the former is normally excluded from discussing pay and working conditions.

Employees like to know what their employers are planning, and since 6 April 2008 all UK employers with 50 or more staff are obliged to keep employees regularly informed. Under the new European Union regulations, companies will be required to establish formal works councils on demand.

Before 6 April 2008, the obligation only applied to organisations with 100 or more employees. But this has now been extended, and a significant number of UK employers will have to get acquainted with the new legal regulations. The EU takes works councils seriously: non-compliant employers may face fines of up to £75,000 and could have a works council imposed on them that is ill-suited to their business.

Business in Focus

Works council consulted

2,700 jobs are to be cut at Peugeot Citroen, the French car company, because of falling demand in Europe. The job cuts will affect assembly-line workers, managers and office staff.

The company, which experienced a 17% drop in sales in the last quarter of 2008, expects sales volumes to fall by at least 10% in 2009.

In October, Peugeot Citroen started "massive" production cuts in the wake of a global downturn, and cut its profit forecast for 2008.

Peugeot Citroen human resources director Jean-Luc Vergne said urgent action was needed in order to protect the future of 200,000 employees.

The carmaker also plans to move 900 workers from its French factory in Rennes to other sites, under a plan which is to be presented to its works council on 2 December.

Source: Adapted from bbc.co.uk

Question:

1   In what ways might the Works Council assist Peugeot Citroen in taking major decisions such as this one?

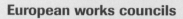

Business in Focus

European works councils

European works councils bring together employee representatives in a multinational company from across Europe, to inform and consult them on the group's performance and prospects. European works councils can help trade unionists and employee representatives to respond to the decisions that employers increasingly take on a European and global basis. European works councils affect any business with at least 1,000 employees and at least 150 employees located in two or more Member States of the European Union.

A European works council is made up of at least one elected employee from each country in which the multinational is based and representatives from senior management. They normally meet annually and discuss issues affecting employees throughout the organisation. These include health and safety, merger proposals, the closure of plants and the implementation of new working practices such as teamworking.

Although European works councils have been operating for several years, it is only since January 2000, when new regulations came into force, that multinational firms in the UK have been obliged legally to have this type of works council. These regulations mean that more UK companies have to implement European works councils and UK employees have gained new rights.

At the time of writing, in November 2008, the directive relating to European Works Councils was being amended, though the details of any changes are not available currently.

Other types of employee representation

Employee representation can take other forms. Employers may allow the development of any arrangement which allows communication to take place. For example, a factory or office committee may be established. These committees can have members/employees elected by the workforce as well as the employer's representatives. They discuss such matters as working conditions, employment and production changes, safety and welfare matters. To be effective committees should meet regularly. If disillusionment is to be avoided, such committees should be seen to have a real effect on how matters are determined. This requires that the workforce be regularly informed about the committee's work.

Alternatively, a staff association may be formed to provide employee representation. Staff associations usually operate on behalf of a single company or even a part of a larger business. Staff associations are often independent from external influences and this can be a reason for them to be popular with both employees and employers. However, it can also limit their effectiveness in the long term, which often depends on the input and commitment of a small number of individuals. As a result it is not uncommon for staff associations to eventually merge with a larger trade union. This is especially likely when employees seek to negotiate collectively their terms and conditions.

Methods of avoiding and resolving industrial disputes

Key terms

An **industrial dispute** is a disagreement between an employer and its employees, usually represented by a trade union, over some aspect of the terms or conditions of employment.

Industrial action refers to any measure taken by trade unions or other employee groups meant to reduce productivity in a workplace.

Business in Focus

Days lost in disputes

Source: Office for National Statistics (www.statistics.gov.uk)

Question:

1   Why might there be more days work lost due to industrial disputes in the public sector?

Year	Days lost in disputes in the private sector (000s)	Days lost in disputes in the public sector (000s)
1996	299	856
1997	163	71
1998	165	117
1999	172	70
2000	136	363
2001	128	397
2002	200	1,123
2003	130	369
2004	163	742
2005	59	99
2006	98	656

Industrial disputes and industrial action

An industrial dispute is a disagreement between an employer and its employees, usually represented by a trade union, over some aspect of the terms or conditions of employment. Trade unions or other employee groups can take a number of actions as part of an industrial dispute. Such actions are called industrial action. Industrial action refers to any measure taken by trade unions or other employee groups meant to reduce productivity in a workplace.

Trade unions or other employee groups can take a number of different types of industrial action.

- **Strikes.** Workers can withdraw their labour so long as this course of action is agreed through a secret ballot. Strikes may be continuous or a succession of one-day actions.
- **Picketing.** This occurs when strikers stand at entrances to a place with an industrial dispute, to attempt to persuade others not to cross the picket line and go into work, thereby breaking the strike action. Legislation restricts the number of people able to picket at any one time.
- **Work to rule.** Under this action unions dictate procedures to be followed by members in the course of working. This leads to employees being less productive and output declining.
- **Sit in.** A sit in takes place when employees occupy a workplace for a specific period of time, thus causing production to be stopped.
- **Go slow.** Similar to a work to rule, this is a measure designed to slow production and reduce workers' productivity with adverse effects on the firm's profits.
- **Overtime bans.** Under this sanction employees are not prepared to work beyond their normal hours, reducing the flexibility of the labour force. Overtime bans may mean employers have to recruit more employees, incurring additional costs.

Examiner's advice

Do not think that industrial action just refers to strikes. This is normally the final resort. Do also remember that the threat of industrial action may be used by trade unions or employee groups to persuade employers to negotiate or to give ground in negotiations.

Methods of avoiding industrial disputes
No-strike and single-union agreements

The field of industrial relations has seen a number of developments that have limited the power and influence of trade unions within the workplace.

A 'no-strike deal' is an agreement between employers and unions whereby in return for a pay and conditions package a union agrees to refrain from strike action for an agreed period. Often such agreements are accompanied by a commitment by both parties to go to binding arbitration in the event of a dispute. This reassures the union that it is not making itself too vulnerable by agreeing not to take industrial action. A no-strike agreement can benefit a trade union in a number of ways.

- By presenting itself as non-confrontational the union may attract a greater number of members from within the workforce, increasing its income and strength.
- A less confrontational stance might allow the union to appoint worker directors, increasing the union's influence and role in decision-making.
- Such agreements can improve the public perception of trade unions. This will assist the union in its activities in other businesses and industries and may persuade employers to recognise it.

A further advantage of no-strike deals is that they may lead to a single-union agreement, strengthening the position of the union within the business.

Single-union agreements have become more common over the last 20 years. Under this type of deal employees agree to be represented by one union. This makes negotiation simpler for the employers (as there are only two parties to the discussions) while reducing the possibility of disputes between rival unions. Single-union deals also assist in maintaining good communications between employers and employees, lessening the possibility of industrial action.

Advisory, Conciliation and Arbitration Service (ACAS)

ACAS is an independent and impartial organisation established to prevent and resolve industrial disputes. ACAS's mission is to improve the performance and effectiveness of organisations by providing an independent and impartial service to prevent and resolve disputes and to build harmonious relationships at work. ACAS offers a number of services to employers and employees:

- preventing and resolving industrial disputes, particularly through the use of arbitration and conciliation
- resolving individual disputes over employment rights, including individual cases of discrimination and unfair dismissal
- providing impartial information and advice on employment matters such as reducing absenteeism, employee sickness and payment systems
- improving the understanding of industrial relations.

ACAS was established in 1975 by the government, during a period of industrial conflict, to provide advice on industrial relations matters. Initially ACAS's role was mainly the resolution of industrial disputes. More recently the organisation has focused on improving business practices to reduce the possibility of industrial disputes. In the new millennium, demand for ACAS's services is greater than ever: the number of cases in which it is involved has almost tripled since 1979. Much of ACAS's work nowadays is conciliating in disputes between an individual employee and his or her employer. This trend reflects the decreased influence of trade unions in modern businesses.

Methods of resolving industrial disputes

> **Key terms**
> **Arbitration** is a procedure for the settlement of disputes, under which the parties agree to be bound by the decision of a third party.
> **Conciliation** is a method of resolving individual or collective disputes in which a neutral third party encourages the continuation of negotiations and the postponement of industrial action.

It is normal for industrial disputes to be resolved without unions taking any form of industrial action. The decline in industrial disputes in the UK over recent years has, in part, been a consequence of the effective use of the measures outlined below.

Arbitration

Arbitration is a procedure for the settlement of disputes, under which the parties agree to be bound by the decision of an arbitrator whose decision is in some circumstances legally binding on both parties.

The process of arbitration is governed by Arbitration Acts 1950–1996. There are three main types of arbitration.

1 **Non-binding arbitration** involves a neutral third party making an award to settle a dispute that the parties concerned can accept or not.
2 **Binding arbitration** means that the parties to the dispute have to take the award of the arbitrator.
3 **Pendulum arbitration** is a binding form of arbitration in which the arbitrator has to decide entirely for one side or the other. It is not an option to reach a compromise and select some middle ground. This system avoids excessive claims by unions or miserly offers by employers.

Business in Focus

Jersey's ambulance crews threaten industrial action

Ambulance crews threatening to withdraw overtime after finding out they earned less than civil servants answering 999 calls have been urged to take their pay dispute to arbitration. If no agreement is reached between Ambulance Service Organisation members and their employers, the withdrawal will come into force on Saturday.

Mick Pinel, the head of employee relations at Jersey's Human Resources department, said that he believed the paramedics and ambulance technicians were breaking a no industrial action or impairment of service agreement signed in 1999 when the Association broke away from the Manual Workers Joint Council.

Charlie Gouyet, the president of the Ambulance Service Association, said that his staff had intimated that they were not against going to arbitration, but would do so when they were ready and had prepared a case.

Source: Adapted from *The Jersey Evening Post*,
November 2007
http://www.thisisjersey.com

Conciliation

This is a method of resolving individual or collective disputes in which a neutral third party encourages the continuation of negotiations and the postponement (at least) of any form of industrial action. Conciliation is sometimes called mediation. The conciliator's role does not involve making any judgement on the validity of the position of either party. The conciliator encourages the continued discussions in the hope that a compromise can be reached.

Industrial tribunals

Industrial tribunals are an informal courtroom where legal disputes over unfair dismissal or discrimination can be settled. Industrial tribunals were established in 1964 and are to be found in most major towns and cities in the UK. Each tribunal comprises three members: a legally trained chairperson, one employer representative and an employee representative. Most employee complaints are still settled by industrial tribunals.

One step further: Does conciliation work?

New research, led by Dr Paola Manzini of the Department of Economics at Queen Mary College, University of London is critical of the contributions made by mediators (or conciliators) in helping to resolve industrial disputes. The potential ability of third parties (such as the government in tackling the firefighters' industrial action) to make contributions to settle strikes may lead to severe inefficiency.

The research, funded by the Economic and Social Research Council (ESRC), examined the effect on negotiations of the presence of third parties not directly involved in industrial action but able to provide additional resources to help reach agreement. Collaborating with Clara Ponsati of Universitat Autonoma de Barcelona, the researchers observed that since the third party, or 'active mediator', had no direct claim to the dispute, the only threat against the other parties was to withhold the additional resources, thus stalling any agreement.

Dr Manzini said: 'We found that the mere possibility that the mediator may intervene in negotiations creates the potential for delays, in the hope of pressurising them into conceding extra resources. On the other hand, so long as the amount of resources that the mediator can make available is sufficiently small, the bargainers' incentive for stalemate is reduced.'

The study highlights the motivation for governments to decentralise negotiations and to avoid becoming directly involved in negotiations. The report says its findings suggest that the Government should use legislation to limit its involvement as far as possible by introducing tougher requirements for firms to consult their workforce before taking decisions which may gave a great impact on jobs.

Source: Queen Mary College, University of London http://www.qmul.ac.uk/news/newsrelease.php?news_id=55

Progress questions

1 Describe the process of communication. (4 marks)
2 Explain the benefits a rapidly expanding business might receive from having effective communication links with its employees. (8 marks)
3 Explain two ways in which a major UK retailer with 80 stores might improve communication with its employees. (8 marks)
4 Outline the difference between collective and individual bargaining. (4 marks)
5 Explain the benefits a large multi-site business may receive from having a highly unionised workforce. (8 marks)
6 Outline the benefits an employer might receive from negotiating a single-union agreement. (6 marks)
7 Outline two benefits a trade union might receive from negotiating a 'no-strike' agreement. (6 marks)
8 Outline why staff associations might not be particularly effective in the longer term. (4 marks)
9 Explain the difference between conciliation and arbitration. (4 marks)
10 Explain the benefits that might result from the use of binding arbitration to resolve an industrial dispute. (6 marks)

Analysis and evaluation questions

1 Venables Ltd is a traditional manufacturer of biscuits and cakes. The company has over 2,000 employees, low labour turnover and five locations in the north of England. Over 60 per cent of the company's workforce are members of six different trade unions.
   a Analyse the reasons why this company might have problems communicating effectively with its workforce. (10 marks)

b Discuss the advantages and disadvantages to Venables Ltd of having over half its workforce represented by trade unions. (15 marks)

2 Harper plc is a large insurance company based in the City of London. The company's 2,500-strong workforce is represented by a trade union. The company's managers are unhappy at having to recognise the union and do not communicate regularly with the union. The company has experienced a rising number of disputes with its employees.

a Analyse the benefits and drawbacks to the company of its workers being represented by a trade union. (10 marks)

b Discuss the actions this company could take to reduce the chance of industrial disputes in the future. (15 marks)

Case study

Figure 18.4 The Public and Commercial Services Union

Hundreds of thousands of civil servants are to be balloted on taking industrial action for three months in a pay dispute, it has been announced.

The Public and Commercial Services Union said around 270,000 members will vote on a rolling programme of industrial action which will extend into the New Year. The PCS will also try to coordinate any strikes with other unions, which could cause huge problems for the Government. Every single department will be affected, including the Home Office, Education and Transport departments as well as the Work and Pensions department.

PCS General secretary Mark Serwotka said the ballot followed growing anger over the Government's policy of trying to limit pay rises in the public sector to 2 per cent this year.

He complained this was disproportionately hitting some of the lowest-paid workers in the country.

Mr Serwotka told a press conference in Brighton, where the TUC Congress opens on Monday, that the Government did not have the 'faintest idea' of how workers were struggling to pay rising fuel and food bills when their pay was falling below the rise in inflation. Civil servants were facing 'desperate' decisions on whether to have a holiday or even buy presents for their children, he claimed.

A series of strikes have already been held this year by coastguards, immigration officers, driving test examiners, passport and jobcentre staff. But if members approve the new wave of industrial action it would be the biggest bout of strikes by civil servants for years.

The PCS will hold a ballot of all the union's members, running from 24 September to mid-October, asking them to back a national, civil service-wide strike followed by a rolling programme of targeted industrial action against Government departments.

Sky's political correspondent Jon Craig said: 'Unions are making the point that while public sector workers are being asked to accept pay rises around 2 per cent, inflation is on the increase. Union bosses claim the rate is much higher than the Government's own figures.'

Source: Adapted from Sky News
http://news.sky.com

Questions

1 Explain what is meant by 'industrial action'. (5 marks)
2 Analyse the possible problems the government may face in communicating effectively with members of the PCS. (8 marks)
3 Discuss the actions the government may take to prevent future disputes of this type. (12 marks)
4 To what extent do you agree with the view that conciliation is the only way to resolve this dispute? (15 marks)

Unit 3 Assessment

Waters Engineering plc

Waters Engineering continues the tradition of engineering for which Birmingham was world famous in the past. However, despite its reputation for quality products, it is experiencing increasing difficulty in competing with other firms (mainly located elsewhere in the European Union), partly due to a lack of scale and because labour and capital productivity remain substantially below levels achieved by competitors. The company's profits have steadily declined, falling to £1.7 million two years ago and to £1.35 million in the last financial year.

The European market is very important to the company, although it has struggled to be price competitive with major European producers. The marketing department of the company has been involved in negotiations with other functional managers prior to drawing up new marketing objectives to guide the organisation as it attempts to increase its sales within the markets of other members of the European Union. It is almost certain that one marketing objective will be to increase European market share for a range of products by 2.5 per cent annually for the next four years. Several marketing managers believe that internal factors should be the main influence on the company's new marketing objectives.

The company has an overriding corporate objective of growth. To achieve this it has introduced a financial strategy of cost minimisation. However, it is experiencing difficulties in cutting labour and production costs, in part due to opposition from the workforce (as well as some managers), and partly because it has had to spend heavily on marketing.

As part of its strategy of cost minimisation the company has sought to reduce wage costs. The directors of Waters Engineering are involved in a dispute with the union that represents many of its employees over last year's pay rise. The Amalgamated Union of Engineering Workers (AUEW) made a claim for an average wage rise of 5.7 per cent backdated three months, and the company offered an increase of 1.9 per cent with no backdating. The negotiations dragged on and last week the AUEW members in Waters Engineering voted in favour of taking industrial action. A strike is planned for next week.

The company is contemplating two alternative investments as part of a process to improve its competitiveness. Some directors favour investment in computer-aided manufacturing equipment to improve the performance of the company's production line. Although opposed by the AUEW, the managing director supports this move, arguing that it will 'bring the company into the twenty-first century'.

An alternative view is that the company should invest heavily in staff training, allowing the adoption of new methods of production including just-in-time production and a widespread adoption of teamworking. It is expected that this approach would allow empowerment of the workforce with the intention of improving labour productivity levels.

The director of finance has estimated the expected costs and returns associated with the two approaches and these are shown in Appendix A.

Appendix A Financial information

	Cam equipment Net cash flows (£m)	Retraining and empowerment Net cash flows (£m)
Initial investment	(25.5)	(18.7)
Year One	7.2	1.9
Year Two	7.4	5.1
Year Three	7.7	8.5
Year Four	7.9	11.4
Year Five	8.3	13.6

10% discount factors	Year One	Year Two	Year Three	Year Four
	0.91	0.83	0.75	0.68

Appendix B HR data

Number of employees	1,989
Number of employees who are members of AUEW	762
Labour turnover rate (average of last three years)	14.7%
Index of labour productivity (industry average = 100)	86
Index of wages paid (industry average = 100)	99

Appendix C Other data

Number of suggestions for improving production from employees last year	11
Percentage increase in number of breakdowns of production line equipment last year	66
Average number of errors per batch of 100 items produced	7.1
Average increase in customer complaints per year over last three years	18.4

Questions

1 Using either payback and average rate of return or net present value (using 10 per cent discounting factors), calculate the expected returns from the two alternative investment projects. (10 marks)

2 Some marketing managers believe that 'internal factors should be the main influence on the company's new marketing objectives'. To what extent do you agree with them? (18 marks)

3 Discuss the ways in which Waters Engineering might resolve its industrial dispute with the Amalgamated Union of Engineering Workers (AUEW). (18 marks)

4 Using all the information available to you, complete the following tasks:

a Analyse the case for Waters Engineering investing in computer-aided manufacturing equipment.

b Analyse the case for Waters Engineering investing in staff training to improve productivity.

c Make a justified recommendation on which option the company should choose. (34 marks)

Unit 4

Introduction to Unit 4

Corporate aims and objectives

This chapter is an introduction to Unit 4. It examines what a business is trying to achieve, which is set out in its mission statement, which in turn helps to share a business's aims and objectives. These are probably the most important influence on the corporate strategies that it adopts. We have considered the concepts of functional objectives and functional strategies in Unit 3, but in Unit 4 we consider these topics at a whole business or corporate level. This chapter also considers the different views that stakeholders may have on strategic decisions and the extent to which such differences may have the potential to cause conflict.

In this chapter we examine:
- the nature and purpose of mission statements
- the corporate aims and objectives that a business may pursue
- the corporate strategies a business may adopt to achieve its aims and objectives
- the different perspectives of different stakeholders on business decisions.

Mission statements

A mission statement sets out what a firm is trying to achieve, i.e. the reason it exists. For example, a firm may set out to be 'the lowest-cost producer in the industry' or to 'maximise the returns for our shareholders'. The mission may include a statement of what the firm believes it is, what it values, which markets it wants to compete in and how it intends to compete. Mission statements commonly focus on:

- corporate values
- non-financial objectives
- benefits of the business to the community
- how consumers are to be satisfied.

By setting out a mission everyone within the firm knows what they should ultimately be trying to do. All of their actions should be directed towards the same thing. This should make decision-making easier: when faced with a series of options managers can compare them in relation to the overall objective of the business. Mission statements can also motivate

Sun Healthcare Group's new mission and logo

The Sun Healthcare Group is a leading American healthcare provider, delivering healthcare products and services to thousands of people every day. The company and its subsidiaries employ over 30,000 people in the United States. The company has announced that it will be introducing a new visual identity, replacing its nearly 15-year-old look. This re-branding will be implemented during the first part of 2009.

The new logo, a sun resting in the palm of a hand, reflects the company's new mission statement: Caring is the Key in Life. 'While we are not changing the essence of our mission, which is to provide ethical, quality care for our patients and residents, we are changing how we talk about it. Our old statement was too long and, as often happens with mission statements, no one could remember it,' said Rick Matros, Sun's chairman and Chief Executive.

'We felt we needed a logo that better represented, both in its colour and symbolism, our new mission statement,' said Matros. 'Our new colours and our new logo, a hand holding the sun, represent the act of caring by providing support to all whom we serve with a sense of warmth. Furthermore, by bringing that caring attitude to everything we do, we live out our mission.'

Source: Adapted from Yahoo! Finance, 6 October 2008

Question:

1 Does Sun Healthcare Group really need a new mission statement and logo?

people – they know exactly why they are there and what the business is trying to achieve, and this can give them a sense of belonging and direction.

However, some mission statements are so unrealistic, or clearly just public relations exercises, that employees pay little attention to them. In other organisations managers clearly ignore the mission statement and so other employees lose faith in it as well. Imagine that the mission of your organisation was supposed to be 'to delight all of our customers', but every time you had an idea to improve customer service it was ruled out on the grounds of cost; you would soon realise that what the managers *said* they wanted to do was not the same as what they *actually* wanted to do. A mission statement will only have value, therefore, if the behaviour of everyone within the firm supports it. In these circumstances it can be a powerful way of uniting people and developing a corporate spirit.

A further criticism of some mission statements is that they are overloaded with jargon. However, this is not always the case. Some are clear and concise and can impart a sense of purpose and direction.

'To create value for customers to earn their lifetime loyalty ...' (Tesco)

'To enable people and businesses throughout the world to realize their full potential.' (Microsoft)

'To enrich people's lives with programmes and services that inform, educate and entertain.' (The BBC)

Corporate aims and objectives

Corporate aims

Aims are long-term plans from which company objectives are derived. Businesses do not normally state aims as numerical targets, but rather in qualitative terms. For example, the Dutch airline KLM states that its corporate aim is 'to achieve profitable and sustainable growth'. In contrast, Tesco's aims are growth and diversification.

Corporate aims (and mission statements) are set by the directors of the business and are intended to provide guidance for setting corporate and functional objectives and also to guide and assist more junior managers in their decision-making. Thus, for example, managers throughout Tesco will take decisions intended to achieve the corporate aims of growth and diversification. In this context opting to open supermarkets in China and to sell electrical products and clothing are all strategic decisions which the company has taken with the intention of meeting its corporate aims.

From its corporate aims (and from its mission statement) a company can set quantifiable objectives, such as gaining a 35 per cent share of a particular market in Europe within three years.

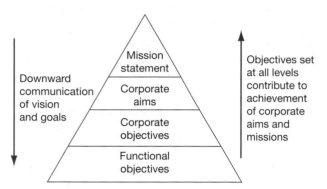

The hierarchy of objectives

Corporate objectives

Once a firm has established its mission it can set its objectives. The objectives turn the mission statement into something which is more quantifiable. Rather than simply being a statement of intent, an objective sets out clearly what has to be achieved.

Corporate objectives are medium- to long-term goals established to coordinate the business. Objectives should be quantified and have a stated timescale, such as to earn a 20 per cent return on capital next year.

To be effective objectives should be SMART. SMART objectives must be:

Specific – they must define exactly what the firm is measuring, such as sales or profits.

Measurable – they must include a quantifiable target, for example a 10 per cent increase.

Agreed – if targets are simply imposed on people they are likely to resent them; if, however, the targets are discussed and mutually agreed, people are more likely to be committed to them.

Realistic – if the objectives are unrealistic (for example, they are too ambitious) people may not even bother to try and achieve them. To motivate people the targets must be seen as attainable.

Time specific – Employees need to know how long they have to achieve the target – is it two or three years?

An example of a good objective might be: 'to increase profits by 25 per cent over the next four years'. By comparison, a bad objective would be 'to do much better' – it is not clear what 'doing better' actually means, how it will be measured or how long you have to achieve it.

Businesses may have a number of objectives, and these are considered below.

Survival

This objective is for the company to continue to trade over a defined period of time, rather than to submit to some form of commercial pressure and be forced to cease trading. This is an important objective, even for the largest of businesses at certain times. Times when survival becomes a key objective include:

- periods of recession or intense competition
- times of crisis, such as during a hostile takeover bid.

Profit maximisation

Profits are maximised when the difference between sales revenue and total costs is at its greatest. Some firms seek to earn the greatest possible profits to satisfy their shareholders' desire for high dividends. This might be a shorter-term objective. Others may pursue the longer-term objective of providing acceptable levels of dividends, but also growth in the value of the company and therefore in the share price. This can provide shareholders with long-term financial benefits.

Growth

Many businesses pursue growth because their managers believe that the organisation will not survive otherwise. If a firm grows, it should be able to exploit its market position and earn higher profits. This benefits shareholders (in the long term) by providing greater dividends as well as offering better salaries and more job security to the employees and managers of the business. We saw earlier that Tesco

Business in Focus

Ford and General Motors (GM) face tough times

General Motors delivered the starkest warning from the car industry yet when it said yesterday it would run out of cash in the first half of next year. The world's biggest car manufacturer said that this year's cash levels would approach the bare minimum required and that next year the company would be in a worse position unless it gets government help, or sells assets, or the economy improves.

The grave warning came as GM and Ford turned in terrible financial results and Ford announced thousands of job cuts.

GM, which lost $4.2 billion (£2.7 billion) at its operating level in the third quarter, said 'estimated liquidity during the remainder of 2008 will approach the minimum amount necessary to operate its business' and said cash levels next year would be even weaker. Pre-tax losses were $2.5 billion, exceeding the worst expectations.

GM also revealed that it had abandoned merger talks with Chrysler. GM and Chrysler have been exploring a merger to try to pool their cash and cut costs, but that too would depend on an injection from the American government of about $10 billion. The abandonment of the merger leaves both GM and Chrysler with few hopes to strengthen their business without outside intervention.

Ford and GM will cut thousands of managerial and administrative jobs. GM is pushing through cuts that have already been announced, while Ford yesterday detailed new job losses after clocking up operating losses of $2.98 billion in the third quarter.

Ford's losses amount to more than $3,000 for every car produced in the three months to 30 September.

Source: Adapted from *Times Online*, 8 November 2008

Question:

1 What effect might the the banking crisis and the recession have had on the corporate objectives pursued by GM and Ford?

---

has set itself the aim of growth and this will have been transferred into quantified objectives, possibly relating to sales figures or grocery market share in other countries.

Diversification

Adopting this objective allows a business to spread its risk by selling a range of products (rather than one) or through trading in different markets. Thus, if one product becomes obsolete or a market becomes significantly more competitive, then the alternative products or markets may provide a secure source of revenue for the business while it seeks new projects. Diversification avoids a business having 'all its eggs in one basket' and has been the principle behind the creation of conglomerate businesses.

Improving corporate image

This has become a more important objective for many companies recently. Companies fear that consumers who have a negative view of them will not purchase their products. This applies to any action that damages the company image. Some airlines have pursued this corporate objective for fear of losing customers who believe that they are damaging the environment through their commercial activities.

The objectives pursued by a business vary according to its size, ownership and legal structure. Thus, for example, survival might be important to a newly established firm, profits to a large public limited company and satisficing to a family-owned private limited company.

Corporate strategies

A corporate strategy is a long-term plan to achieve the business's corporate objectives. For example, if a firm's target was to increase profits, it might try and do this by reducing costs or by increasing revenue; these would be two strategies to achieve the same goal. Similarly, if a firm was trying to boost overall sales the managers might take a strategic decision to do this by trying to sell more of its existing products or by increasing sales of new products; again these would be two different ways of achieving the same end goal.

Strategies tend to involve a major commitment of

resources and are difficult to reverse. For example, the decision to invest in new product development is likely to involve a high level of finance and take several years. Strategic decisions also tend to involve a high level of uncertainty. Over time market conditions often change significantly and so firms must change their strategies to cope with unfamiliar conditions.

The value of producing a clear strategy is that it sets out the firm's overall plan; this helps employees develop their own plans to implement the strategy. If employees know that the firm wants to diversify, for example, they know that it is realistic to consider market opportunities in new segments of the market. In contrast, if they are aware that the strategy is to boost the firm's market presence in a particular region, they are likely to focus on putting more resources into this area.

The decisions made about how to implement the strategy are called 'tactical decisions'. Tactical decisions tend to:

- be short term
- involve fewer resources
- be made more regularly and involve less uncertainty.

International corporate strategies

A global strategy

A global market is one that is worldwide in scope. There is an increasing number of examples of products which are sold in global markets. Soft drinks such as those produced by Coca-Cola and Pepsi Cola, and sports clothing supplied by Nike or Adidas, are both examples of products sold in global markets. A global market requires firms to compete in all its component markets to be competitive.

To succeed in global markets businesses need to adapt strategies that reflect the particular needs and demands of these markets. Key elements of a global strategy may include the following.

- Being competitive in all markets across the world.
- Producing a standardised product for all markets to benefit from economies of scale.
- Organising and controlling the business from the centre.
- Coordinating activities in different countries and markets to maximise efficiency.
- Seeking to minimise costs in all possible ways, including locating production capacity in low-cost countries.

- Bringing new products to the market ahead of competitors.

A global strategy is most appropriate when global patterns of demand are not dissimilar and a single product (possibly with slight variants) is likely to meet the needs of the global consumer.

A well-designed global strategy can help a business to gain a competitive advantage in some potentially very large markets. The competitive advantage can arise from a number of sources.

- **Efficiency**. This can arise from economies of scale as the business operates in more markets and sells to greater numbers of customers. A global strategy may also derive its efficiency from using cheap resources, such as raw materials or labour, from other nations.
- **Risk**. A global strategy may allow the business to spread operational risks by producing in several locations, reducing the chance of adverse weather or political unrest disrupting production. The global strategy can also permit a business to operate in numerous economies meaning the chance of an economic downturn in all its markets simultaneously is most unlikely.
- **Reputation**. Businesses operating global strategies may be able to develop a strong brand identity in global markets, encouraging global brand loyalty.

This type of strategy does have drawbacks. It can arouse opposition in some local markets due to a perceived imposition of foreign cultures and loss of differentiated products. The fast-food retailer McDonald's has been criticised on these grounds in a number of countries, notably India and France. Many people would regret the development of global and standardised products.

Multi-domestic strategy

Businesses operating a multi-domestic strategy produce different products for different countries and markets. Decisions are taken at a local level wherever possible to allow the business to meet the needs of different customers. This strategy can encourage an entrepreneurial spirit at relatively junior levels in the organisation and high levels of innovation. Activities such as research and development may be conducted in local markets and supplies may be sourced locally.

Japanese car manufacturers have operated highly effective multi-domestic strategies, especially in the

Business in Focus

VW CEO claims no market for 'world cars'

As car buyers around the world become savvier, car manufacturers can no longer afford to build a single car for the entire global market. At the two extremes, a customer in a western country wouldn't seek the same specifications and features that someone in an emerging market would, even though they could be buying the same car. A number of carmakers have realised this and have set about creating new global design centres whose job it is to customise and tailor a single model for different markets.

Volkswagen is wary of the developing trend. Speaking with the *Financial Times*, VW CEO Martin Winterkorn told reporters that the days of building one car for the whole world were 'dead and buried'. To help boost sales, VW is developing unique models for major centres like North America, China and India and is expected to launch 20 new models within the next three years.

'In the coming years, we will make the VW group the world's most international carmaker. The days of a "world car" are dead and buried. Our customers in China or India expect us, as a global player, to offer entirely different solutions than we do in the US or western Europe,' Winterkorn explained.

Pictured above is a model of VW's Up! concept,

Voltswagen's Up!

whose production version will eventually replace the Lupo as VW's new entry-level model. Officials presented a number of different versions of the car at recent motor shows, reflecting the trend to develop unique versions of a single model instead of a single world car.

Source: Motor Authority, 14 March 2008
http://www.motorauthority.com

Question:

1 What are the costs and benefits of VW's new global strategy?

lucrative American market. They have customised car designs to meet the tastes of American consumers. For example, Toyota released the Tundra with V8 engines, which look like a heavy-duty pickup truck with a powerful engine. Nissan gave its American employees responsibility for the design and development of most of its vehicles sold in North America.

This strategy is attractive in many ways, in particular as it allows for differentiated products in global markets. However, the most obvious and fundamental drawback is that it increases costs in comparison with a global strategy, as economies of scale are lost.

Examiner's advice

You should look to master a number of theories and models relating to all aspects of Unit 4. The style of question here will not be to ask you to write about a specific theory or model, so having a range of theories and models at your fingertips will be a distinct advantage in developing arguments and making judgements.

Models of business strategy

There are many models and theories of business strategy. We will consider two in the following section and a further one in 'One step further' on page 242.

Ansoff's matrix

Igor Ansoff developed his matrix in 1957. His matrix measures the degree of risk associated with various growth strategies. The model highlights that risk is reduced by strategies that mean the firm remains in familiar markets and sells familiar products. The model gives an organisation four strategic options for growth.

1 **Market penetration**: This involves increasing sales of an existing product and thereby penetrating the market further by either promoting the product heavily or reducing prices to increase sales. This may mean increasing revenue by, for example, selling to existing customers.
2 **Product development**: The organisation develops new products to aim within their existing market, in the hope that they will gain more custom and market share. In order to be successful the company will develop and innovate new products in place of existing ones. The new products are sold to existing customers in existing markets. Companies such as Microsoft have adopted this strategy, developing products such as X-box.
3 **Market development**: The organisation here adopts a strategy of selling existing products to new markets. Basically the product remains the same, but it is marketed to a new group or potential buyers. Kellogg's did this when it placed its breakfast cereals into the 'eat healthily anytime' market.

4 **Diversification**: This is the most risky strategy for growth. By diversifying, businesses seek to sell new products to new customers or markets. As the business is unfamiliar with both the products and its customers, the chance of failure is increased. Some organisations diversify quite successfully; Virgin is a well-known example of a business that uses this strategy.

Porter's generic strategies

Michael Porter first wrote about his generic strategies in 1985 in *Competitive Advantage: Creating and Sustaining Superior Performance*. Porter's generic strategies are ways of gaining competitive advantage by giving a firm, brand or product an 'edge' that rival products do not have. Porter's generic strategies are shown in the figure below.

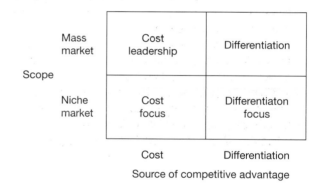

Porter's generic strategies

Porter set out three generic strategies.

1 **Cost leadership** through providing basic products at minimum cost. A cost leadership strategy means that a business seeks to produce its products at the *lowest* possible cost. This gives it flexibility in pricing: it can increase market share by selling at prices below those of its rivals and still generate profits; alternatively it can set its prices at the general industry level and reap higher profit margins on each sale. A business adopting this strategy needs to be confident that it can achieve the lowest costs in the industry, perhaps through its scale or by efficient techniques of production or by use of kaizen groups. It is important that competitors will not have access to these

Ansoff's matrix

same sources of low-cost production or the competitive 'edge' will be lost.

2 **Differentiation** by creating products that are unique. This means that the products might have different features, designs, functions, after-sales support or durability from those offered by rivals. For example, Apple stresses the fact that its latest iPod Nano is thinner than any rival MP3 player. Depending on the type of industry it is in, a business may only be able to sustain a differentiation strategy if it has one or more of the following: an effective research and development department, a highly skilled and efficient workforce able to supply top-quality goods or services, and a good marketing department able to bring the unique features of the product to the attention of the right group of consumers.

3 **Focus** on offering a specialised service in a niche market. Within this strategy Porter identified two elements: focus on cost or focus on differentiation. Businesses using focus strategies target niche markets. SAGA targets its products at consumers who are aged over 50. These products include holidays, insurance and other financial services. This strategy is more likely to succeed when the businesses concerned have a good and clear understanding of the particular consumers they are targeting. A focus strategy has to be in terms of either cost leadership or differentiation. In addition, the focus has to offer something extra that competitors do not provide. SAGA's products are tailored to meet the specific needs of the over 50s, and the company promotes its many years of experience in the market.

Michael Porter was adamant that companies have to choose a particular strategy and not attempt to follow some 'middle course' with elements of more than one strategy. He pointed out that a cost leadership strategy requires a business to look inwards and to examine its internal functions to minimise costs. In contrast, a differentiation strategy calls for a business to look outwards at its customers to meet particular aspects of their needs.

Business in Focus

Ryanair's business strategy

It was a stunt only Michael O'Leary, the outspoken chief executive of low-cost airline Ryanair, could pull off. The airline's fuel bill has almost doubled in the past year and the looming recession means fewer people are flying abroad. So what did O'Leary do last week? He announced that the airline would slash fares. He admitted that this, together with the sky-high oil price, could push the airline into its first ever loss for the year.

Shares plummeted by almost a fifth on the news, coming just weeks after O'Leary had indicated that Ryanair's fares would have to rise to meet its higher costs. Howard Wheeldon, an analyst at BGC Partners, called the announcement that fares could fall 5 per cent this year, and accompanying results, an 'unmitigated disaster'. But is O'Leary as crazy as he would like us to think?

Neil Glynn, from NCB Stockbrokers, thinks he isn't. 'I wouldn't describe that announcement on cutting fares as a gamble,' he says. 'It's very much in line with Ryanair's business model.'

The strategy goes something like this: by heavily discounting fares, Ryanair will sacrifice some revenue in the short term in the hope of winning more business from more expensive rivals. Once uncompetitive rival routes are axed, Ryanair will be able to raise its fares again. On cue, Ryanair's website has started advertising a sale, offering a million seats for £1 each including taxes.

All the media reports of Ryanair slashing fares are great free advertising. Not advertised of course are ways Ryanair is boosting its income, for example by raising its credit card handling charge to £4, and charging passengers £6.10 for a large gin and tonic, a 25 per cent hike compared with 2006.

Source: *The Observer*, 3 August 2008

Question:

1 In what ways might this strategic decision represent a risk for Ryanair?

Different stakeholder perspectives

> **Key terms**
> A **stakeholder** is any group or individual with an interest in a business and its activities.
> **Social responsibility** is managing a business so as to take into account the interests of society in general and especially of those groups and individuals with a direct interest in the business.

Any business has a number of stakeholder groups with interest in its affairs. The table below identifies some of the major groups and some of the interests that they might be expected to have.

Over recent years businesses have become much more aware of the differing expectations of their stakeholder groups. Previously managers operated businesses largely in the interests of the shareholders. A growing awareness of business activities among the general public has complicated the task of the management team of a business. Today's managers have to attempt to meet the conflicting demands of a number of stakeholder groups. The table below highlights the different demands stakeholders might place on a business.

The terms 'stakeholders' and 'social responsibility' are interrelated and thus difficult to distinguish. Social responsibility is a business philosophy proposing that firms should behave as good citizens. Socially responsible businesses should not only

> ## Examiner's advice
>
> The table below contains the primary stakeholders for most businesses, but a number of others exist. When writing on stakeholders it is important to develop answers fully. This is impossible if you attempt to cover too many stakeholder groups – just concentrate on a small number of the ones that are most relevant to the circumstances.

Stakeholder group	Possible nature of stakeholders' interest
1. Shareholders	• Expectation of regular dividends • Rising share prices • Preferential treatment as customers – for example through lower prices
2. Employees	• Steady and regular income • Healthy and safe working conditions • Job security • Promotion and higher incomes
3. Customers	• Certain and reliable supply of goods • Stable prices • Safe products • After-sales service and technical support
4. Suppliers	• Frequent and regular orders • A sole-supplier agreement • Fair prices
5. Creditors	• Repayment of money owed at agreed date • High returns on investments • Minimal risk of failure to repay money owed
6. The local community	• Steady employment • Minimal pollution and noise • Provision of facilities (e.g. scholarships, arts centres or reclaimed areas) for local community

Stakeholders and their interests

operate within the law, but should avoid pollution, the reckless use of limited resources or the mistreatment of employees or consumers. Some businesses willingly accept these responsibilities partly because their managers want to do so, partly because they fear a negative public image.

There are many ways in which the strategies adopted by businesses may cause conflict between stakeholder groups. For example, a business pursuing what Porter would identify as cost leadership would aim to generate high returns for its shareholders through increasing profitability. However, this may entail paying minimal wages to employees and also seeking to minimise other costs related to employment, such as expenditure on training and pensions.

Business in Focus

More on Ryanair

Four hundred Ryanair pilots and cabin crew will be forced to take one week of unpaid leave this year as the budget airline cuts back flights from Dublin and Stansted.

Michael O'Leary, the chief executive of Ryanair, said the airline's executives would also receive a pay cut of at least 10 per cent because of the financial difficulties facing the sector. The unpaid holiday will be imposed on staff at Dublin and Stansted and, based on an average Ryanair salary of €60,000 (£47,000), will cost them about €1,150 each in lost earnings.

Source: *The Times*, 8 October 2008
http://business.timesonline.co.uk/tol/business/industry_sectors/transport/article4901947.ece

Equally, a strategy of differentiation may entail a business investing heavily in research and development to create innovative goods or in training staff to provide the highest-quality services. In either case such strategies may result in reductions in short-term profitability. Thus, employees may be satisfied with such a strategy but shareholders seeking a quick return on their investment may be dissatisfied.

One step further: the balanced scorecard

The balanced scorecard was developed by RS Kaplan and DP Norton and first published in the *Harvard Business Review* in 1992.

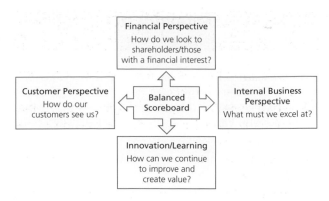

The balanced scorecard
Source: http://www.supershareware.com

A balanced scorecard can be defined as 'a strategic planning and management system used to align business activities to the mission statement of an organisation'. A balanced scorecard attempts to help to manage the business better at all levels in pursuit of the company's mission statement.

The scorecard looks at the financial and non-financial elements of a business's operations from a variety of perspectives. To use the balanced scorecard path a management team first must know (and understand) the company's mission statement, i.e. its purpose or vision.

The four perspectives that the balanced scorecard considers are:

- the financial perspective
- the internal business perspective: how its internal processes are operating
- the employee perspective
- the customer perspective.

Taking this approach allows managers to look at the business from four important perspectives and gives a 'balanced' picture of its overall performance. This highlights the aspects of the business's activities that need to be improved. The balanced scorecard includes both quantitative and qualitative measures and links the assessment of the business's performance to the strategy that it has adopted.

The scorecard produces a balance between the four key business perspectives and how the organisation views itself and how others see it. In some senses it brings together the notion of strategy and the different perspectives of stakeholders.

Progress questions

1 Distinguish between a mission statement and a corporate aim. (5 marks)
2 What benefits might a large multinational company gain from having a mission statement? (7 marks)
3 Explain two criticisms of mission statements. (6 marks)
4 Explain the relationship between corporate aims and corporate strategies. (6 marks)
5 Why might oil companies such as BP pursue a corporate objective of improving their corporate images? (8 marks)
6 How might Ansoff's matrix assist managers in assessing the risk of a particular strategy? (7 marks)
7 Outline Michael Porter's generic strategy of cost leadership. (6 marks)
8 Why did Porter argue that a business should not try to mix strategies of cost leadership and differentiation? (6 marks)
9 In what ways might the objectives of Marks & Spencer plc's shareholders and employees differ? (6 marks)
10 How might a strategy of cost leadership lead to conflict between stakeholders? (8 marks)

Analysis and evaluation questions

1 Harmer plc offers holidays in Spain to tourists aged 18–25. The company uses cheap hotels in popular resorts on the coast with reputations for a lively nightlife. The company has to compete with other companies that target their products at a wider age range. Apart from its much larger rival, Club 18–30, Harmer plc is the only specialist operator aiming holidays at this age group.
Harmer plc uses charter flights that operate late at night to keep costs to a minimum, and this has proved effective.
  a Analyse the potential advantages to this company of adopting a strategy of cost leadership. (10 marks)
  b Discuss whether a strategy of cost leadership will automatically be in the interest of the company's consumers. (15 marks)
2 Logger plc has recently adopted a mission statement. This was decided upon by a new chief executive, following its merger with its largest rival. The company is the dominant firm in the global market for kitchen appliances.
The new chief executive has persuaded the board of directors to operate a global strategy rather than a multi-domestic strategy, which several of its closest competitors have decided upon.
  a Analyse the case for having a mission statement. (10 marks)
  b Do you agree with the decision to adopt a global strategy? Justify your decision. (15 marks)

Case study

Anyone who has followed Apple since its inception knows that the very idea that Apple could actually compete on the same level as its competitors on price is a shocker. Steve Jobs went out of his way to create good-looking devices with a unique experience so he wouldn't have to charge less for his computers and it worked like a charm. Mac sales have never been higher, and it's quickly becoming apparent that people are more than willing to spend the additional cash to own a Mac. And yet, the rumours that Apple will sell an $800 Mac simply won't go away.

Now, I'm a firm believer that Apple *should* start lowering its prices to appeal to more consumers and take the fight to Hewlett-Packard and Dell, but if Apple's plan next week is to offer cheaper Macs, I can't help but wonder if this is Apple's new strategy going forward.

I think it is.

Remember when we all made a fuss over how high the price of the original iPhone was? Do you remember when we all rejoiced as Apple announced that the lower-end iPhone would retail for $199?

And if you look at the iPod, now you can spend as little as $49 for the iPod Shuffle, $149 for an iPod Nano, and $229 for the iPod Touch. And just in case you want an Apple TV, the entry-level price of $229 isn't too bad for a set-top box with that kind of functionality.

Do you see what I'm getting at here? Apple is quickly becoming a company that offers high-quality products at a relatively affordable price. And if it decides to sell a Mac for $800, I don't think there's any debating the fact that Jobs has decided to change his company's business model.

And what a change that would be. As I mentioned, Apple is a boutique vendor on a number of levels and has decided that it would rather offer products for a higher price than play the pricing game. But as economic conditions change and people need to think more about their wallets than they may have over the past few years, Apple feels it needs to change its course and compete more effectively against HP and Dell.

Will it work? I can guarantee that it will. But what will it do to Apple's image? As long as the company continues providing high-quality products that easily eclipse the competition, I don't think it will have anything to worry about on that front either.

Questions

1. Explain what is meant by 'an innovative company'. (4 marks)
2. Use Ansoff's matrix to analyse Apple's strategy up to the launch of the i-phone. (8 marks)
3. To what extent is Apple's apparent decision in the interest of all the company's stakeholders? (12 marks)
4. Is the author of this article correct to 'guarantee' that Apple's change of strategy will work? Justify your view. (15 marks)

Section 5: Assessing changes in the business environment

19

Businesses and the economic environment

This chapter introduces you to a range of economic factors and considers the possible effects of changes in these factors on different types of large businesses. The chapter encourages you to think about the positive as well as the negative consequences of changes in these external factors and to reflect on the ways in which different businesses will be affected. Throughout this chapter we will consider the strategies that large businesses may deploy in response to changes in the economic environment.

In this chapter we examine:
- recent trends in key economic variables
- the impact of economic variables on different types of businesses
- the effects of globalisation and developments in emerging markets
- the strategic responses of businesses to changes in the economic environment.

Key terms

Economic activity relates to the level of spending, production and employment in the economy at any given time.

Gross domestic product (GDP) measures the value of a country's total output of goods and services over a period of time, normally one year.

Economic growth is the rate of increase in the size of an economy over time.

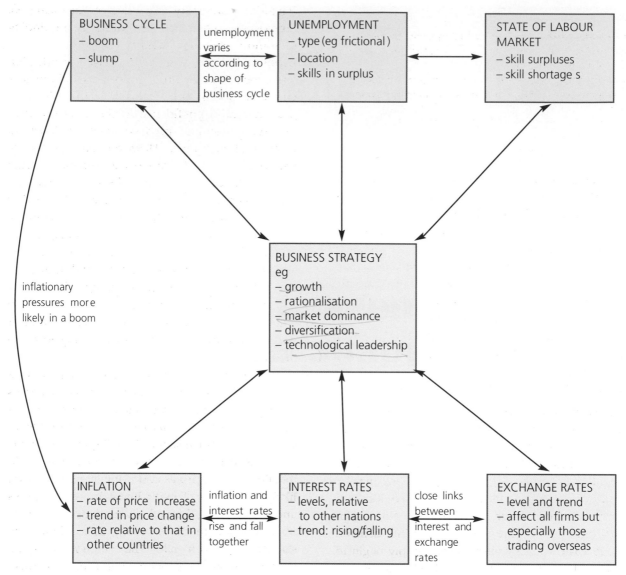

Figure 19.1 Business strategy in an integrated business environment

The economic environment and business strategy

A business's strategy is simply the long-term plans through which it seeks to attain its corporate objectives, i.e. the objectives of the whole business. For example, a business may have growth as a major corporate objective and will develop plans to achieve the desired rate of growth. These plans may include increasing innovation as part of the development of new products, entering new markets or pursuing a policy of takeovers and mergers. Figure 19.1 summarises the major economic variables that might impact upon strategic planning and decision-making. The diagram also emphasises the interrelationships that exist between the elements that make up the economic environment for businesses.

Factors such as interest and exchange rates, the business cycle, inflation and unemployment combine to shape one aspect of the environment within which businesses operate. Thus, as the economy moves through the various stages of the trade cycle, rates of inflation and unemployment may change. Equally, interest rates may be adjusted to dampen the effects of the business cycle, creating further implications for firms. Finally, the strategic decisions taken by businesses in response to opportunities and constraints that appear in the economic environment also determine that environment. Thus a decision to rationalise because the economy is moving into recession may contribute to the economic downturn.

The business cycle

All countries suffer fluctuations in the level of activity within their economies. At times spending, output and employment all rise; during other periods the opposite is true. The value of a country's output over a period of time is measured by its gross domestic product (GDP) – this figure is dependent upon the level of economic activity. A rising level of economic activity will be reflected in a higher level of GDP.

The business cycle describes the regular fluctuations in economic activity (and GDP) occurring over time in economies. Figure 19.2 illustrates a typical business cycle.

Trade cycles generally have four stages:

1 **Recovery or upswing** – as the economy recovers from a slump, production and employment both begin to increase. Consumers will generally spend more in these circumstances as they are more confident in the security of their employment. Initially businesses may respond cautiously to signs of increasing consumer confidence. No major decisions are required to meet rising demand while spare capacity exists: firms simply begin to utilise idle factories, offices and other assets. As business confidence increases firms may take the decision to invest in further non-current assets (factories, machinery and vehicles, for example). Employees experience less difficulty in finding jobs and wages may begin to rise.

2 A **boom** follows, with high levels of production and expenditure by firms, consumers and the government. Booms are normally characterised by prosperity and confidence in the business community. Investment in fixed assets is likely to increase at such times. However, many sectors of the economy will experience pressure during booms. Skilled workers may become scarce and firms competing for workers may offer higher wages. Simultaneously, as the economy approaches maximum production, shortages and bottlenecks will occur as insufficient raw materials and components exist to meet demand. Inevitably this will result in their prices rising. The combination of rising wages and rising prices of raw materials and components will create inflation. It is the existence of inflation that usually leads to the end of a boom.

3 A **recession** occurs when incomes and output start to fall. Rising prices of labour and materials mean that businesses face increased costs of production. This will begin to eat into their profits. In circumstances such as this the UK government has tended to raise interest rates in an attempt to avoid inflation. Falling profits and rising interest rates are likely to lead to plans to invest in new factories and offices being delayed or abandoned. The level of production in the economy as a whole may stagnate or even fall. The amount of spare capacity within the economy will rise. Some businesses will fail and the level of bankruptcies is likely to rise.

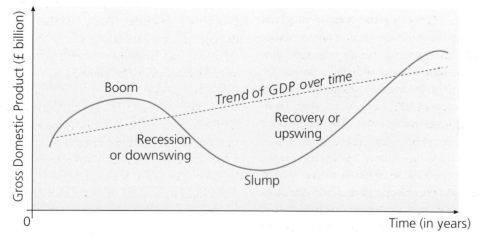

Figure 19.2 The stages of the business cycle

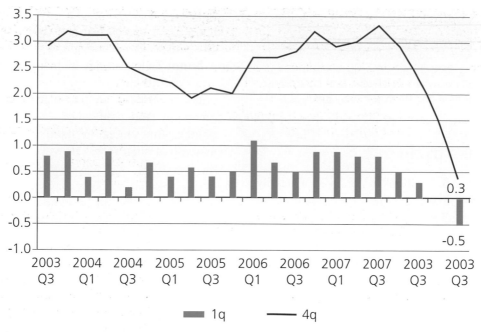

Figure 19.3 Real GDP growth in the UK 2003–08
Source: National Statistics Online
http://www.statistics.gov.uk

4 A **slump** often, but not always, follows a recession. In some circumstances an economy may enter the upswing stage of the business cycle without moving through a slump period. Governments may take action to encourage this by, for example, increasing their own spending or lowering interest rates. A slump sees production at its lowest, unemployment is high and increasing numbers of firms will suffer insolvency. (Note: limited companies become 'insolvent', while the term 'bankruptcy' applies to individuals, sole traders and partnerships.)

Figure 19.2 illustrates a smooth and regular trade cycle in operation. In reality the change in gross domestic product is likely to be irregular as economic cycles of different duration and intensity operate simultaneously. The business cycle is a major influence on the performance of businesses. As the economy moves from one stage of the cycle to another, businesses can expect to see substantial changes in their trading conditions.

The quarterly data in Figure 19.3 has been adjusted to remove the effects of rising prices so that the underlying trend is revealed. This is why the data is described as 'real'. Gross domestic product (GDP) fell by 0.5 per cent in the third quarter of 2008, compared with zero growth in the previous quarter.

The effects of the business cycle

Table 19.1 identifies some actions that different large businesses might take in response to the business cycle. However, not all businesses are equally affected by the changing trading conditions.

A number of businesses may find that demand for their products is relatively unaffected as the business cycle moves through its stages. Producers and retailers of basic foodstuffs, public transport and water services may notice little change in demand for their products. This is because these are essential items consumers continue to purchase even when their incomes are falling – demand for them is not sensitive to changes in income.

Demand for other categories of products is more sensitive to changes in income levels and therefore the stages of the business cycle. Examples include foreign holidays, electrical products such as televisions and CD players, and construction materials such as bricks and windows.

Thus, firms selling basic foodstuffs might have to take little or no action to survive a recession; in fact, demand for their products might increase as consumers switch from more expensive alternatives. At the other extreme, businesses supplying materials to the construction industry could be hard hit as firms delay or abandon plans to extend factories and build

Stage of business cycle	Key features	Likely reactions by businesses
Recovery or upswing	• Increasing consumer expenditure. • Existing spare capacity used. • Production rises. • Business confidence strengthens. • Investment increases.	• Opportunity to charge higher prices. • Rising numbers of business start-ups. • Businesses take decisions to invest in fixed assets. • Business operate nearer to (or at) full capacity.
Boom	• Rate of inflation increases. • Bottlenecks in supply of materials and components. • Some firms unable to satisfy demand. • Profits probably high – but hit by rising costs.	• Firms face increasing pressure to increase prices. • Businesses seek alternative methods to increase output. • Wage rises offered to retain or attract skilled labour. • Managers plan for falling levels of demand.
Recession	• Government increases interest rates. • Firms reduce production as demand falls. • Spare capacity rises. • Business confidence declines and investment is cut. • Profits fall.	• Firms seek new markets for products – possibly overseas. • Some products may be stockpiled. • Workers laid off – or asked to work short-time. • Financially insecure firms may become bankrupt.
Slump	• Increasing number of bankruptcies and insolvencies. • Government lowers interest rates. • High levels of unemployment. • Low levels of business confidence and consumer spending.	• Firms offer basic products at low prices. • Businesses may close factories to reduce capacity. • Large-scale redundancies may occur. • Marketing concentrates on low prices and easy payment deals.

Table 19.1 The trade cycle and business actions

new offices. Their position might be made worse by a fall in demand for new houses as hard-up consumers abandon schemes to move home.

Firms supplying these products may be significantly affected by the business cycle:

- leisure air travel
- sports and leisure goods
- jewellery
- household furniture
- cars.

Firms supplying these products are unlikely to be affected to a great extent by the business cycle – in fact demand may rise for some of these products in a recession/slump:

- fuel, including gas and electricity
- cigarettes and tobacco
- petrol
- water and sewage services.

Figure 19.4 The UK construction industry is particularly sensitive to the effects of the business cycle.

Government policy and the business cycle

Governments attempt to offset the most extreme effects of the business cycle. The UK government is no exception in this respect and it has taken a number of high-profile actions in an attempt to lessen the effects of the recession that started in 2008. The government implements counter-cyclical policies to limit the fluctuations in gross domestic product and hence the consequences of these fluctuations for businesses. These counter-cyclical policies have implications for businesses in the same way that the business cycle does.

In a slump the government seeks to lessen the impact of falling confidence among businesses and declining expenditure by individuals and businesses. By reducing interest rates and possibly cutting the level of taxes paid by individuals and businesses the level of economic activity may remain relatively stable. Recent governments have favoured reducing interest rates in the expectation that they will encourage firms to undertake investment programmes as borrowing money becomes cheaper. Similarly, consumers may spend more if credit is less expensive. In March 2009 the Bank of England reduced its base rate (which influences most other interest rates in the economy) to 0.5 per cent. This was its lowest rate ever.

At the other extreme, a boom may result in governments raising interest rates in an attempt to lower the level of economic activity. Higher interest rates are likely to discourage investment by businesses and spending by consumers. Reducing expenditure in this way can assist in avoiding resources becoming too scarce as firms attempt to produce more than available resources will allow.

Businesses need to take into account the likely effects of counter-cyclical policies when considering their responses to changing trading conditions brought about by the business cycle. Such counter cyclical policies can be beneficial as they avoid the need for firms to prepare for the worst excesses of boom and slump.

Business strategy and the business cycle

The business cycle is a permanent feature of the economic environment for firms, and one that is receiving a great deal of publicity at the time of writing. All that changes is the stage of the cycle through which the economy is passing. The effects of changes in the business cycle vary from industry to industry. Firms selling goods whose demand is

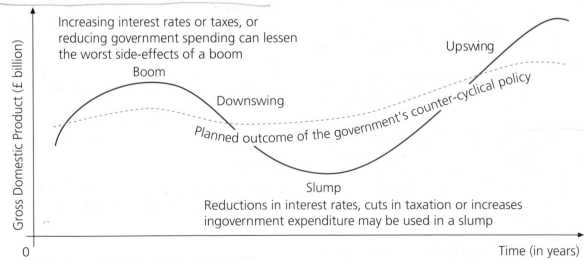

Figure 19.5 Counter-cyclical policies and the business cycle

sensitive to changes in income (known as income elastic goods), such as designer clothes and foreign holidays, may find that sales rise in a boom and fall during recession. Conversely, businesses selling staple products such as foodstuffs, where demand is not income elastic, may be relatively unaffected by the business cycle.

It is possible to argue that the business cycle will only provoke short-term responses in many firms, because its effects are relatively short-lived. Booms and slumps do not last for ever and businesses can take actions to see them through difficult trading periods. During boom periods managers may increase prices to restrict demand and increase profitability; they may subcontract work to other firms or seek supplies from overseas. Equally, in conditions of recession or slump, lay-offs may occur or short-time working may take place, while overseas markets are targeted to increase sales. Well-managed firms will predict the onset of a boom or slump and take appropriate action in advance. Short-term responses may be all that are required if governments are successful in eradicating the more extreme effects of the business cycle.

Decisions of a more strategic nature may be more likely if the effects of the business cycle are expected to be prolonged. Many businesses fear that the recession, which began in 2008, will be a deep and lasting one. The prospect of such a recession may persuade firms to close factories or to permanently reduce capacity. In contrast, a lengthy period of prosperity may encourage the expansion of productive capacity and the innovation of new products as consumers' income rises.

Business in Focus

Businesses respond to recession

1 Vauxhall offers sabbaticals

Car manufacturer Vauxhall has offered its workforce at one factory the chance to take a sabbatical on 30 per cent pay. General Motors approached unions at the plant in Ellesmere Port, Cheshire, with the plan last Thursday. Under the scheme, staff would stay away from work for up to nine months between January and September 2009 on less than a third of their basic salaries.

A spokesman said the company wanted to avoid making any compulsory redundancies. He said it was 'working with unions to cut structural costs and get us through 2009 without losing staff'. He added: 'We want to avoid any forced redundancies.'

If successful, the sabbatical plan could be rolled out at Saab, Opel in Europe and other Vauxhall plants in the UK. But the company said it did not expect there to be a 'huge take-up' on the sabbatical offer. Vauxhall employs more than 5,000 people in Luton and Ellesmere Port. In October, the Ellesmere Port plant stopped production for 14 days because of falling sales in Europe.

Source: Adapted from BBC News, 13 December 2008
http://news.bbc.co.uk/1/hi/england/merseyside/7781345.stm

2 Banks cut jobs permanently

Many IT jobs are under threat in the financial services sector as two leading banks, HSBC and Credit Suisse, announced plans to slash their workforce. The recession has started to impact the workface as more than 1,150 job cuts were announced yesterday across the UK financial sector. HSBC will cut another 500 jobs following a review of the business and 'current economic conditions'.

'We deeply regret taking this step, but we consider it essential to ensure our business is operating as efficiently as possible and that we are best placed to deal with the economic downturn and maintain our levels of customer service,' HSBC, UK managing director, Paul Thurston said.

Swiss banking firm Credit Suisse said it is cutting around 650 UK jobs, representing about 10 per cent of the company's UK workforce. A spokesperson for the Swiss bank blamed 'market conditions and projected staffing levels required to meet client needs'.

Source: Adapted from CIO, 3 December 2008
http://www.cio.co.uk

Question:

1 Why might these large multinational businesses have responded in different ways to the recession?

Interest rates

> **Key term**
> Interest rates are the price paid for borrowed money.

The rate of interest can best be described as the price of borrowed money. Most textbooks and newspapers refer to the interest rate as if there is only a single rate. In fact there are a range of interest rates operating in the UK economy at any time. However, the base rate of interest is set officially and all other interest rates relate to this.

For many years the government (or the Chancellor of the Exchequer) took responsibility for setting the base rate of interest. However, in May 1997 the government gave the Bank of England responsibility for setting interest rates. The Bank of England's Monetary Policy Committee (MPC) meets each month and takes decisions on whether to alter the base rate of interest.

Rates of interest normally vary according to the period of time over which the money is borrowed and the degree of risk attached to the loan. Changes in interest rates have significant effects on businesses and the environment in which they operate. Recent UK governments have relied heavily upon interest rates to control the level of economic activity in the economy and to avoid the worst effects of the business cycle.

BANK OF ENGLAND'S BASE RATE

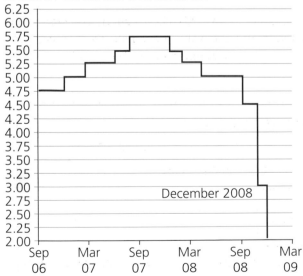

Figure 19.6 The base rate in the UK, September 2006 to December 2008

Interest rates and consumer spending

Interest rates affect the level of spending by UK citizens. The level of their spending is dependent upon interest rates for a number of reasons.

- Consumers are more likely to take a decision to save during a period in which interest rates are rising. The return on their saving is greater and will persuade some consumers to postpone spending decisions. Conversely, when rates are falling consumers might save less and spend more.
- Changes in interest rates alter the cost of borrowing. Many goods are purchased on credit – electrical goods, cars and caravans and satellite TV systems. If rates fall then the cost of purchasing these goods on credit will decline, persuading more people to buy them. Demand for consumer durables is sensitive to interest rate rises and sales of these products decline significantly following an upward movement in the base rate.
- An increasing number of UK consumers have mortgages. A rise in interest rates will increase the amount paid each month by householders. This reduces the income available for expenditure on other products. Demand for a range of products will fall in these circumstances. A fall in rates will have the opposite effect.
- Britain's population is steadily ageing, meaning that more people are dependent upon pensions and savings. This means that their income is highly dependent upon the rate of interest and this makes consumer expenditure highly sensitive to rate changes.

Business and changes in interest rates

Interest rates affect businesses in a number of ways. It is not simply a case of whether they rise or fall: businesses also take into account the overall level of rates. Thus a small increase in interest rates may have little impact if rates are low. This is unlikely to be the case when rates are high before the change is introduced.

- A change in interest rates will affect a firm's decisions on investment and expansion. Thus, rising rates may cause the postponement or cancellation of investment plans. Businesses may decide to invest in other countries if they feel that interest rates may be volatile or high relative to other countries.
- Changing interest rates affect consumers' spending decisions. As a result of increasing interest rates

consumers may decide to save more (attracted by high rates) or to delay spending decisions requiring borrowing. Purchases of products such as cars, white goods (e.g. fridges and cookers) and televisions are sensitive to changes in interest rates. Consumers may demand more of these products when interest rates fall.

- Interest rates also affect the value of the pound in terms of other currencies. Increases in interest rates tend to exert upward pressure on exchange rates; similarly, falling rates encourage the value of the pound to decline. Thus rising interest rates may make it more difficult for exporters to sell their products overseas. We will consider the effects of exchange rates on business strategy more fully later in this unit. Figure 19.7 illustrates the relationship between interest rates and exchange rates.

Businesses tend to take a long-term view of interest rates. Rates can be altered each month, and strategic decisions are rarely taken on the basis of factors that may alter again within a month or two. However, a country with a reputation for having persistently high rates, or for interest rate volatility, may be unattractive to businesses. Volatile rates make long-term planning more difficult. Unpredictable changes in interest rates may have significant effects on domestic demand and the exchange rate (in turn affecting overseas consumers). In these circumstances firms may seek to relocate overseas and diversify into products for which demand is less dependent upon interest rates.

But are all businesses equally affected? The answer to this is no. A number of types of businesses are particularly susceptible to changes in interest rates. These include the following.

- Businesses supplying luxury products such as sports cars, jewellery and expensive hotel accommodation. These sorts of products will be among the first to be cut from consumers' budgets following a rise in interest rates and become attractive to consumers following a fall in rates.
- Businesses that are heavily involved in overseas trade. Interest rate changes influence exchange rates and this, as we shall see later, directly determines the prices of exports and imports.
- Businesses whose products are frequently purchased on credit. Prices of goods purchased in this way fluctuate directly with the rate of interest. Thus a rise in rates may lead to a significant fall in sales of fitted kitchens as the increased interest charges mean consumers have to pay more.

Clearly any business's response to rising rates will depend to some degree on the extent to which its sales are sensitive to changes in interest rates. Suppliers of fuels and basic foodstuffs may take little or no action to maintain sales revenue. Those offering products on credit or luxuries are more likely to respond by use of tactics such as interest-free periods of credit or 'buy now, pay later' deals. These techniques are used extensively by businesses manufacturing and supplying personal computers and domestic furniture. Alternatively, businesses might accept lower prices and reduced profits – if they can afford to do so.

Interest rates and exchange rates

An important link exists between the domestic rate of interest and the value of a nation's currency. This relationship is summarised in Figure 19.7.

3. Demand for pounds increases raising the price (exchange rates) of pounds.

2. Foreign investors purchase pounds to invest in UK banks and other financial institutions.

1. UK becomes a more attractive location for foreign investors seeking high returns.

Rise
Interest Rates
Fall

1 UK becomes less attractive to foreign investors as UK banks and other financial institutions cut rates.

2. Foreign investors sell pounds to purchase other currencies to enable them to invest overseas.

3. Supply of pounds increases depressing the price (exchange rate).

Figure 19.7 The relationship between interest rates and the exchange value of the pound

Changes in the UK's rate of interest will lead to an alteration in the exchange value of the pound sterling. Thus, following a 1 per cent rise in UK interest rates the following changes could occur:

- the value of one pound rises from $1.45 to $1.60 and
- the pound is worth €1.25, rising from €1.15.

When interest rates rise the pound will increase in value against most foreign currencies. Similarly, a reduction in interest rates causes a fall in the exchange value of the pound.

As interest rates fall in relation to the rates available in other countries, the UK will become a less attractive target for international investment. Foreigners with money to invest will be tempted by the high returns available from banks in other countries. To take advantage of the relatively higher rates overseas, investors will withdraw funds from UK banks to invest abroad. To do this they will have to exchange their sterling for the currency of the country in which they wish to invest. This will mean that an increased supply of sterling will be put onto the world's currency markets. As with most products, an increase in the supply of pounds will tend to lower its price – in this case the exchange rate.

Exchange rates

Key terms

A currency **appreciates** when its value rises against another currency or currencies.
An **exchange rate** is the price of one currency expressed in terms of another. For example, £1 might be worth €1.1.
Depreciation occurs when the value of a currency declines against another currencies or currencies.

An exchange rate is simply the price of one currency expressed in terms of another. Thus, at a particular time, the pound may be worth US$1.45 or 2,900 Japanese yen.

London is one of the premier international centres for buying and selling foreign currencies: each day transactions total billions of pounds. Exchange rates between most currencies vary regularly according to the balance of supply and demand for each individual currency.

Why do firms buy foreign currencies?

The main reason businesses purchase foreign currencies is to pay for goods and services bought from overseas. Firms purchasing products from abroad are normally expected to pay using the currency of the exporting country. For example, Sainsbury's purchases wine from Chile. Chilean wine producers would expect to be paid in their local currency –

Business in Focus

The effects of interest rate cuts

Retailers and companies with high levels of gearing were pleased by the Bank of England's shock decision to cut the base rate by 1.5 per cent. The share prices of many retailers rose following the news. Marks & Spencer rose by 14.5 pence to 259.25 pence, while the Kingfisher Group was 2.7 pence better at 129.9 pence. Debenhams – which is both a retailer and has large debts – has also seen a significant rise in its share price.

Not everyone is convinced by the Bank's move. Mic Mills, senior trader at ETX Capital, said: 'This is a much bigger cut than expected, and in fact, it's being seen as a bit of a panic move. Long-term, it's the right decision and we need monetary loosening

to give the economy a boost. But traders are thinking, if we've really got to cut rates to 3 per cent, then how bad is it out there? Recessionary fears were bad before; they just got a whole lot worse.'

Source: *Guardian*
http://www.guardian.co.uk

Questions:

1 Why might Debenhams have been pleased by the cut in interest rates?
2 Do you think that big cuts in interest rates might lead to some companies cutting back on production and investment? Explain your view.

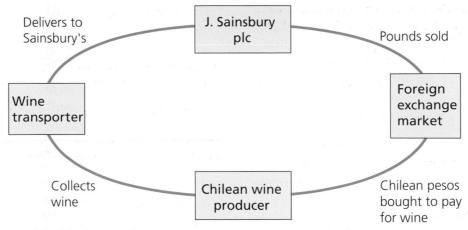

Figure 19.8 The operation of the foreign exchange market

The exchange rate of pounds	Prices of UK exports overseas (in foreign currencies)	Prices of imported goods in the UK (in pounds)
Appreciates (rises)	Increase	Fall
Depreciates (falls)	Fall	Increase

Table 19.2 **The effects of changes in the value of sterling**

Chilean pesos (Ch$). Thus traders acting on behalf of Sainsbury's would sell pounds sterling in order to buy pesos on the foreign exchange market. This process is illustrated in Figure 19.8.

Demand for foreign currencies may also arise because individuals and businesses wish to invest in enterprises overseas. Thus a UK citizen wishing to invest in a South African business will require South African rands to complete the transaction.

The effects of exchange rate changes

Exchange rates can change significantly over time. A rise in the value of a currency is termed appreciation; a decline in its value is called depreciation.

In July 2008 £1 exchanged for US$2.02. Just under six months later, in December 2008, the exchange rate was £1 = $1.48. This meant that the value of the pound had depreciated by just over 25 per cent over the period. Alternatively, the value of the American dollar had increased (or appreciated) by the same amount.

Changes in the value of currencies affect the prices of exports and imports as shown in Table 19.2.

Using the information in Table 19.2 we can see that the fall in the value of the pound against the American dollar during 2008 would have had the following effects:

- Prices of UK exports to America (for example Scotch whisky) would have fallen by approximately 25 per cent.
- American imports to the UK would have been up to 25 per cent more expensive. However, the price the Americans received in dollars would not have changed. It is likely, however, that because prices were higher in the UK they would sell smaller quantities of their products.

Small changes in the UK's exchange rate occur all the time as demand for the currency and supplies of it alter. A series of slight rises and falls over a period of time is not necessarily a major problem for industry. Of more concern is a sustained rise or fall in the exchange rate – or a sudden and substantial change in the exchange rate. In the latter stages of December 2008, the pound fell heavily in value against major currencies such as the dollar and the euro. This offered UK exporters significant advantages in terms of price competitiveness in American and European markets, though it resulted in rising import costs.

Exchange rate changes can create uncertainty for a number of reasons.

- If firms agree deals priced in foreign currencies, they may receive more or less revenue from a particular transaction than expected if the exchange rate alters in the intervening period. Thus, a deal to sell whisky to America may give Scottish distillers less revenue than anticipated if the contract is agreed in terms of dollars and the pound then rises in value against the American dollar. In these circumstances the amount of dollars stated in the contract will convert into a smaller number of pounds, causing a shortfall for the exporter.

- Changing exchange rates can affect prices and sales in overseas markets, even if the exporter avoids direct exchange risk by insisting on payment in domestic currency. For example, a London-based clothes designer may sell clothes overseas, but stipulate that they are paid in pounds sterling. A rise in the value of the pound may mean that foreign retailers are forced to increase the prices of the clothes to maintain profit margins. As a consequence sales may be lower than expected, giving the London-based design company less revenue than forecast.
- Competitors may respond in unexpected ways to exchange rate changes. Foreign firms may reduce prices to offset the effects of an exchange rate change, putting rivals under pressure to do the same or lose market share.

Price elasticity can be an important part of a discussion on the possible effects of exchange rate changes. If overseas demand for a product is price inelastic, then an increase in the exchange rate may not be too harmful. It might be that Americans will continue to buy Scotch whisky when the price rises.

Examiner's advice

Remember that products are not sold on the basis of price alone. When considering the likely consequences of a change in exchange rates it is important to note that factors such as quality, reputation, after-sales service and meeting delivery dates are important influences on buyers' decisions.

Business in Focus

The euro

On 1 January 1999 a single European currency – the euro – was introduced into 11 European Union countries. Austria, Belgium, Finland, France, Germany, Ireland, Italy, Luxembourg, the Netherlands, Portugal and Spain all adopted the new currency. Euro notes and coins were not be available until 1 January 2002 and until then participating states used their domestic currency (Italian lira, Dutch Guilders etc...). By 30 June 2002 old banknotes and coins had been withdrawn from circulation. The 11 countries locked the foreign exchange values of their national currencies to the euro and shared the new currency.

Convergence between the economies of participating countries is viewed as an absolutely necessary condition for a single currency. The economic criteria to be met by the participating countries (as agreed in 2006) are:

- annual inflation of less than 2.6 per cent
- government deficits (government income less than spending) of below 3 per cent of gross domestic product
- national debt to be less than 60 per cent of gross domestic product

- long-term interest rates below 5.9 per cent.

There are a number of sound arguments for the UK joining the euro. The biggest potential beneficiaries could be UK businesses.

- Cheaper transaction costs would result for UK companies if the euro replaced sterling. No longer would it be necessary to exchange currencies when trading with other countries using the euro, meaning the commission charges would be avoided.
- Being within the euro zone would assist the UK in attracting inward investment, which is vital for jobs and prosperity.
- A major benefit would arise from the stable exchange rates that would operate throughout Europe. Trading in euros would remove the risk of adverse exchange rate movements and potential loss of earnings from international trade.
- Prices would become transparent. As all goods and services would henceforth be priced in the same currency through much of Europe, comparing the prices of suppliers would become a simple process.

In this case demand may alter little. If demand is price elastic, exporters might be badly affected by a rise in the exchange rate, but benefit greatly from a fall.

Business strategy and exchange rates

Fluctuations in exchange rates create a great deal of uncertainty for businesses trading internationally. When exchange rates are volatile, businesses become uncertain about earnings from overseas trade. This adds to the risk businesses incur as part of their trading activities.

Firms like to operate in a relatively risk-free environment and to reduce uncertainty. The undesirable consequences of exchange rate changes can be reduced through the use of techniques such as forward foreign currency markets. This sets a guaranteed exchange rate at some future date (when transactions are completed), meaning that the amount received from overseas trading is more certain. However, fixing an exchange rate in this way does not guarantee a particular level of sales. Furthermore, the bank arranging this service may require a fee.

Exchange rate changes are more of a problem in markets where fierce price competition occurs. In these circumstances demand is more likely to be price elastic and businesses are under pressure to respond quickly to any change in exchange rates.

Businesses may respond to the pressures of exchange rate changes by seeking to create productive capacity in overseas markets to avoid the effects of changing currency values. A number of foreign motor manufacturers located in the UK have revealed that they are considering relocating in the euro zone in Europe to avoid the difficulties imposed by fluctuations in the value of the pound against the euro. In particular Toyota has argued strongly for the UK to adopt the euro to eliminate exchange rate risk.

An alternative approach, currently used by Toyota, is to require suppliers to price their products in a different currency. The company, which sells cars throughout Europe, has announced that it intends to pay UK suppliers in euros. As a result, fluctuations in the exchange rate will have less impact on the company as it pays suppliers in the same currency that it receives from European customers.

How might UK firms respond to a rising value of the pound?	How might UK firms respond to a falling value of the pound?
EXPORTERS	**EXPORTERS**
• allow prices to rise in foreign markets reducing probable sales. Remember exporters receive the same price in pounds for each overseas sale, but will sell less in this situation • leave prices unchanged in overseas markets in terms of foreign currency. Sales should be unchanged but the exporter will receive fewer pounds from each sale Neither of these options is attractive to exporters – rising exchange rates are bad news.	• could allow prices to fall in overseas markets as a result of the exchange rate change. They will receive the same amount in pounds from each sale but should achieve higher sales • increase their prices to maintain price levels in terms of the foreign currency. Sales should remain constant (depending on competitors' actions) and revenue should rise in pounds as a result
DOMESTIC PRODUCERS	**DOMESTIC PRODUCERS**
• reduce prices to compete with cheaper imports • enjoy the benefits of cheaper imports of materials and components • emphasise other elements in the marketing mix, e.g. the quality of the product	• enjoy increased sales as a result of rising prices of competitors' imported products, assuming foreign businesses do not hold prices down • increase prices (to some extent) to enjoy increased revenues from each sale • must beware the increased cost of imported raw materials and components

Table 19.3 Changes in exchange rates

Business in Focus

UK's manufacturers remain gloomy

The CBI has found that, despite a fall in the value of the pound, orders placed with UK manufacturers have continued to fall sharply. A monthly survey by the employers' organisation the Confederation of British Industry, also found that a balance of 42% of firms say they expect output to fall over the next three months.

Expectations for production in the coming months remain at their lowest since the recession of 1980. CBI economist Ian McCafferty said the figures made "depressing reading".

Manufacturers have also reported the biggest fall in export orders since October 2003, according to the CBI's monthly industrial trends survey. It showed a balance of 33% of firms reporting export orders lower than normal, as the downturn deepened among the world's developed economies.

"It is worrying that, despite the 20% depreciation in sterling over the past year, export orders remain so weak," McCafferty said. "Our export competitiveness is increasing but many of our key export markets are contracting rapidly."

Source: Adapted from bbc.co.uk

Question:

1 What actions might exporters take when, despite a fall in the exchange rate of the pound, sales continue to fall?

Inflation

Key terms

Cost-push inflation happens when firms face increasing costs due to rising wages or increasing costs of raw materials and components.

Demand-pull inflation occurs when the demand for the country's goods and services exceeds its ability to supply these products.

Inflation is a persistent rise in the general price level and an associated fall in the value of money.

The Retail Prices Index (RPI) measures the rate of inflation based on the changes in prices of a basket of goods and services.

What is inflation?

Inflation can be defined as a persistent rise in the price level and the associated fall in the value of money. For many businesses a low rate of inflation is not a problem. So long as wages are rising at about the same rate or higher, a low constant rate of price increase simply serves to help maintain demand. Inflation only becomes a major problem for businesses when it is high, rising rapidly or (worst of all) is doing both together.

Inflation in the UK, and in many industrialised nations throughout the world, has been at historically low rates over the last 15 years or so. Despite a rise in UK inflation rates to over 5 per cent (as measured by the Consumer Price Index) in late 2008, inflation

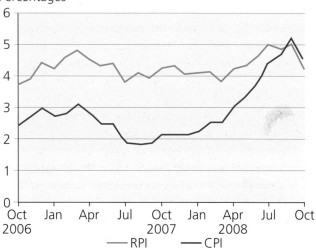

Percentages

Figure 19.9 Inflation in the UK 2006–08
Source: www.statistics.gov.uk

in the UK is forecast to fall back to around 2–2.5 per cent during 2009.

How is inflation measured?

The UK government measures the rate of inflation by use of the Retail Price Index (RPI) as well as the Consumer Price Index (CPI). The CPI was introduced in December 2003 and operates alongside the RPI. The CPI measures the average monthly change in the prices of goods and services purchased by households in the UK, and the government will use this to set targets for inflation in the future. The RPI and the

CPI are both calculated using more than 650 separate goods and services for which price changes are measured throughout the country.

The main difference between the CPI and the RPI is that the CPI excludes housing and Council Tax costs. The use of the CPI as the official measure of inflation brings the UK into line with most other European countries. The CPI gives a lower rate of inflation than the RPI. Figure 19.9 illustrates that this is normally the case.

The causes of inflation

There are a number of factors that may cause inflation. Economists tend to classify inflation as caused by demand-pull or cost-push factors. The cause of inflation can be an important factor for businesses as it provides some indication of likely future government policies to control inflation.

Demand-pull inflation

Demand-pull inflation occurs when the demand for the country's goods and services exceeds its ability to supply these products. Thus prices rise generally as a means of restricting demand to the available supply. The underlying cause of this might be the government allowing firms and businesses to have too much money to spend, perhaps as a consequence of cutting taxes or lowering interest rates.

Demand-pull inflation normally occurs at the boom stage of the trade cycle, when the economy is at full stretch with most of its resources in use. At this high level of production, shortages and bottlenecks occur in supply. Because resources and labour become relatively scarce, firms offer higher prices and wages and inflation is the result. Governments are alert for the first signs of demand-pull inflation and prepared to raise interest rates to prevent the economy overheating and prices rising.

Cost-push inflation

Cost-push inflation occurs when firms face increasing costs due to factors such as rising wages or increasing costs of raw materials and components. This type of inflation can arise from a number of sources.

- **Wage rises**. If trade unions and employees are successful in negotiating pay increases significantly above the rate of inflation then further price rises might be the result. This becomes more likely

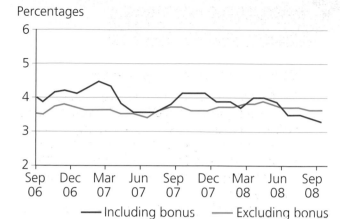

Figure 19.10 Growth in average earnings 2006–08
Source: www.statistics.gov.uk

if productivity is not increasing, allowing businesses to offset some of the increased wage costs against additional production. Some business analysts became concerned in 2006 that pay rises were running at a level that might prove inflationary. However, this pressure had evaporated by autumn 2008, as shown in Figure 19.10.

- **Imported inflation**. One of the hidden causes of inflation is rising import prices. The UK is susceptible to this type of inflation as it is an 'open' economy importing large quantities of raw materials, components and finished goods. Import prices rise when the exchange rate is falling and more pounds are required to purchase a given amount of a foreign currency. Although exporters might complain about rising exchange rates, they do help to control inflation.

Expectations and inflation

Expectations are an important part of the process of creating inflation. If managers and businesses anticipate rising inflation they might take actions which, in fact, further fuel the inflationary process. If firms expect their suppliers to increase the prices of raw materials and components they may raise their selling prices in anticipation of this. This avoids any possibilities of lower profits if costs rise before prices can be increased. The action also provides a windfall profit in that for a while firms sell at higher prices while their costs have not risen.

Trade unions build their expectations of inflation into their wage demands for the coming year. If, as in 2009, inflation is forecast to be around 2.5 per cent, this is likely to be the base figure for a wage rise. In such circumstances, unions will demand a 4 or 5 per cent increase in wages to give their members an increase in their standard of living. Unless productivity rises, paying workers wage rises in excess of the rate of inflation may result in businesses having to increase their prices.

Consumers, by their actions, can also add to inflation. If they expect prices to rise in the near future they may make major purchases immediately to avoid the price increases. If the economy is near to full capacity (i.e. it is in a boom) this can add to demand-pull inflation. A large number of consumers deciding to purchase consumer durables may result in price rises as producers are unable to respond to the orders and shortages occur.

Thus, the expectation of inflation can sometimes contribute to its existence. Governments wishing to control inflation have to be seen to be acting against it in order to reduce the expectations of future price rises.

The impact of inflation on business

Inflation can have a number of effects on businesses.

- Many businesses may suffer falling sales in a period of inflation. Consumers might be expected to spend more during inflationary periods as they would not wish to hold an asset that is falling in value. However, research shows that people save more (perhaps due to uncertainty) and sales fall for many businesses.
- It can be difficult to maintain competitiveness (and especially international competitiveness) during bouts of inflation. Rising wages and raw material costs may force firms to raise prices or accept lower profit margins. Firms operating in countries with lower rates of inflation may gain the edge in terms of price competitiveness under such circumstances.

The impact of government on anti-inflationary policies

The UK is experiencing a period of low inflation, as illustrated in Figure 19.9. In part this is due to the government's effective control of inflationary pressures. This has meant that businesses are frequently affected more by anti-inflationary policies than by inflation itself. Over recent years the UK government has controlled the worst effects of inflation in a number of ways.

- Rises in interest rates have been the government's main weapon. Increasing the base rate reduces the possibility of demand-pull inflation occurring. Consumers are discouraged from spending their money by higher rates on savings accounts and they are less likely to buy on credit as it is more expensive. Businesses reduce investment as borrowing becomes more expensive. Output and sales decline and the inflationary pressure reduces. We saw in an earlier chapter that changes in interest rates can have significant implications for businesses.
- Successive governments have introduced legislation designed to restrict the power of trade

Business in Focus

Dramatic changes in inflationary expectations

Inflation rate expectations among the public plunged by a record amount in November from a record high three months earlier, a Bank of England survey showed yesterday. The average expectation for inflation over the coming year stood at 2.8 per cent, compared with a record high of 4.4 per cent in August, the BoE/GfK NOP Inflation Attitudes poll showed. It was the biggest drop since the survey was launched in November 1999.

The reversal partly reflects the sharp drop in energy prices, which had pushed inflation to above 5 per cent this year – more than twice the Bank's 2 per cent target. When asked to state the current rate of inflation, respondents to the survey gave a median answer of 4.9 per cent, compared with 5.4 per cent in August.

While policymakers were concerned earlier this year that expectations of high inflation were at risk of becoming entrenched, those worries have now been overtaken by fears that Britain's economy is heading into a long and painful recession.

Source: *The Independent*, 12 December 2008
http://www.independent.co.uk

Question:

1 What effects might this dramatic change in inflationary expectations have on the decisions of major supermarkets such as Tesco?

unions. Acts controlling picketing and making ballots compulsory before unions can take industrial action have served to reduce trade union power. This legislation has lessened the chance of cost-push inflation while reducing the number days lost to strikes and other industrial action.

- Over time the government has reduced the expectation of inflation. Recently inflation in the UK reached its lowest rate for over 30 years. This has helped businesses to be confident in setting prices and avoided unions putting in excessive (and inflationary) pay claims. The low rate of inflation enjoyed by the UK has also been one of a number of factors persuading foreign firms to move to Britain. The effect of the recession has led to retailers reducing prices in an attempt to persuade consumers to spend more. Such decisions are likely to reduce consumer expectations regarding inflation.

We will consider government policies to control the economy in more detail in the next chapter.

Inflation can offer some benefits to businesses, however. Some analysts suggest that low and stable rates of inflation may be beneficial. A steady rise in profits can create favourable expectations and encourage investment by businesses. Inflation can also encourage long-term borrowing and investment by businesses as the value of their repayments (in real terms) declines over time.

Inflation in the UK has been at low levels over recent years. This has offered UK businesses a number of advantages.

- Costs are much easier to control in periods when prices are rising slowly.
- Pricing strategies are easier to establish (and simpler for consumers to understand) when inflation is low.
- If UK inflation is lower than that experienced by other nations, businesses based in the UK may receive a competitive advantage. Rival firms located in other countries may face increased costs and face pressure to increase their prices in an attempt to maintain profit margins.
- Sales forecasts are more likely to prove accurate during periods of relatively low inflation. During bouts of severe inflation consumers may switch to cheaper overseas products or decide to save against an uncertain future.
- Government policies to reduce inflation may have adverse effects on businesses, reducing the levels of expenditure on the business's products.

In an environment of relatively stable prices, as experienced by the UK over recent years, businesses may be willing to expand capacity through investment and to develop new products. Price stability removes an element of risk from business planning, engenders confidence among senior managers and may result in more positive business strategies. Arguably, the low rate of inflation enjoyed by the UK over recent years has been one factor encouraging foreign firms to locate in this country.

However, businesses' responses to a period of inflation will depend upon the perceived cause of inflation, the level of inflation and the confidence they have in the government's ability to control price rises. Inflation caused by high levels of demand (so-called demand-pull inflation) may encourage firms to expand to meet the high and potentially profitable levels of demand. Even cost-push inflation (fuelled, for example, by high wage claims) may not be regarded as too damaging if the resulting inflation is at a low level and the government appears capable of preventing price increases from accelerating.

Unemployment

Unemployment remains an important issue in most countries. It is important because it represents a waste of resources if labour is unused – if all available workers were used the country concerned would be able to produce more and its citizens would enjoy a higher standard of living. The social effects of high and prolonged rates of unemployment can be devastating: poor health and crime are just two factors associated with unemployment and poverty.

Key terms

Unemployment exists when people who are seeking work are unable to find any employment.

Counter-cyclical policy is operated by the government with the intention of reducing the worst effects of booms and slumps.

Cyclical unemployment is caused by the operation of the business cycle rising in slumps and falling in booms.

Frictional unemployment exists because people may be temporarily out of work between leaving one job and starting another.

Structural unemployment occurs due to fundamental changes in the economy whereby some industries reach the end of their lives.

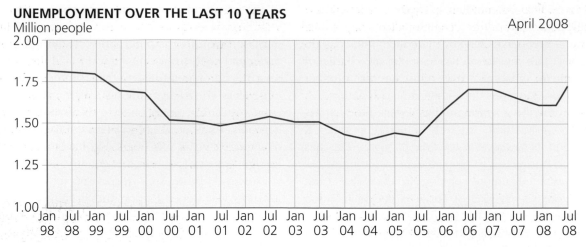

Figure 19.11 UK unemployment
Source: Adapted from from BBC News, 17 September 2008

Types of unemployment

People can be unemployed for a number of reasons. Governments find it useful to distinguish between the various types of unemployment, as each type requires a different remedy. Although many different types of unemployment exist, we shall focus on three main types.

Structural unemployment

Economies continually change: some industries die and others emerge to replace them. Structural unemployment occurs due to fundamental changes in the economy whereby some industries reach the end of their lives. Structural unemployment occurs for a number of reasons:

• the adoption of new methods of production
• significant and permanent changes in demand
• increasing competition from overseas
• rising income levels meaning demand for some products declines.

But structural change in the economy also offers opportunities to businesses. Rising incomes and technological developments have led to the development of the mobile phone industry. This industry employs a large number of people in manufacturing the product, supplying networks and in retail outlets.

Structural unemployment is a difficult problem for governments to solve. Because large numbers of employees may no longer have the skills that employers require, training is an important part of any solution. Other approaches include encouraging foreign producers to establish themselves in the UK to provide employment for those with skills not

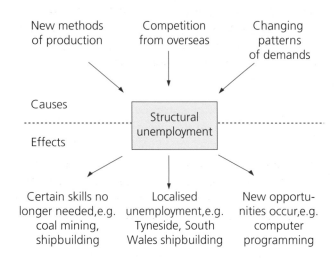

Figure 19.12 Causes and effects of structural unemployment

needed by domestic businesses. The UK has been particularly successful in attracting motor vehicle producers from throughout the world.

Cyclical unemployment

This type of unemployment arises from the operation of the business or trade cycle – a topic we considered in detail earlier in this chapter. The boom stage of a business cycle will see this type of unemployment minimised as firms increase their production levels. At this stage of the business cycle those who have been unemployed for some time (and with relatively few skills) may find work.

At the other extreme, much of the unemployment experienced during a slump will be cyclical. Figure 19.11 highlights the effect of cyclical unemployment as unemployment can be seen to reduce as the business cycle moved into a boom between 2002 and 2005. Some firms have moved to protect themselves against cyclical unemployment by the introduction of profit-related pay. Such schemes allow pay to fall during a recession along with profits, reducing the need to make workers redundant. We saw earlier in this chapter that the car manufacturer Vauxhall offered its employees a nine-month sabbatical on 30 per cent pay as a response to the economic downturn.

Frictional unemployment

People moving between jobs cause frictional unemployment. If a person leaves one job they may not be able to move into a new position immediately. While they are searching for new employment they are classified as frictionally unemployed. The government providing improved information on job vacancies available may reduce the level of frictional unemployment. A healthy economy will have some amount of frictional unemployment as people move between jobs.

Business and changing unemployment levels

Rises in unemployment can have serious implications for businesses, though the precise impact and likely responses of firms will depend upon their circumstances and the type of unemployment.

Examiner's advice

It is important to relate the impact of unemployment – or changes in other economic factors – to the precise type of business under consideration. Some businesses rely heavily on labour as a key element of production – this is more likely to be true of businesses that supply services. Hence a change in the level of unemployment will have a greater impact on this type of business.

Cyclical unemployment might result in businesses suffering from falling sales. In the short term firms may be able to add any surplus production to stocks. Alternatively businesses may seek new markets, perhaps by selling overseas. Not all businesses will be equally affected by changes in unemployment levels. Businesses selling essential products may be relatively unaffected by cyclical unemployment, while suppliers of luxury products could suffer substantial reductions in sales.

Structural unemployment can have a significant effect on businesses because it is frequently highly localised and often very persistent. Thus high levels of unemployment suffered by former coal mining communities had considerable implications for most businesses in the locality. Unemployment brought about by the decline of an industry also has an impact upon associated industries. For example, falling production in the UK's shipbuilding industry contributed to the decline in the country's steel industry.

Business in Focus

Santander cuts 1,900 UK bank jobs

Santander, the Spanish owner of Abbey, Alliance & Leicester and Bradford & Bingley, is to cut 1,900 jobs at the three British banks next year. A mixture of compulsory and voluntary redundancies is expected, though talks with the four unions representing staff have only begun today. The bank has 23,000 staff after the acquisitions of the Alliance & Leicester and Bradford & Bingley, 15,000 of which are at Abbey, 7,000 at A&L and 1,000 at B&B.

The bank stressed that the job losses were not in reaction to the financial crisis but part of the planned £180 million of annual cost savings identified at the time of the A&L acquisition earlier this year. Santander stressed that 'there will be minimal impact in branches and call centres' as the focus of the programme would be on back office and support roles.

Santander has been the principal beneficiary of the financial crisis in the UK, picking up rival businesses on the cheap. After the merged Lloyds TSB and HBOS, Santander will be the second-largest provider of mortgages in the UK and the third-largest savings institution.

The Spanish bank has been ruthlessly successful in cutting costs in the past, axing 7,000 jobs in three years after buying Abbey in 2004 – against earlier targets of just 3,000 – as technology replaced a range of jobs. The job cuts add to the thousands already made across the financial services industry.

Source: The *Daily Telegraph*, 12 December 2008
http://www.telegraph.co.uk

Question:

1 Santander is one of a number of businesses cutting jobs in the UK at the time of writing. What are the disadvantages to businesses such as Santander of taking such decisions?

Business in Focus

Migration

Migration is the movement of people between different countries. Over the last 20 years the UK has experienced relatively large numbers of people leaving (emigrants) and entering (immigrants) the country. The number entering the UK has accelerated since the expansion of the European Union in 2004, which entitled the citizens of many east European countries (most notably Poland) to live and work in the UK.

The graph opposite shows net migration into the UK, which is the balance between inflows (immigrants) and outflows (emigrants). The UK has seen more people enter than leave in each of the ten years illustrated.

Below are the top 20 occupations in which registered workers from EU accession countries were employed between May 2004 and December 2006:

1 Factory worker: 270,180 registered workers
2 Warehouse operative: 39,545
3 Packer: 32,210
4 Kitchen and catering assistants: 31,305
5 Cleaner, domestic staff: 27,630
6 Farm worker/farm hand: 22,345
7 Waiter, waitress: 20,050
8 Maid/room attendant (hotel): 18,125
9 Care assistants and home carers: 15,745
10 Labourer, building: 14, 245
11 Sales and retail assistants: 14,260
12 Crop harvester: 9,655
13 Food processing operative (fruit/veg): 7,885
14 Bar staff: 7,420
15 Food processing operative (meat): 6,645
16 Chef, other: 6,130
17 Driver, HGV (Heavy Goods Vehicle): 4,540
18 Administrator, general: 4,690
19 Fruit picker (farming): 4,390
20 Carpenter/joiner: 3,460
TOTAL TOP 20: 425,360

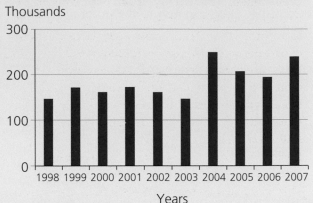

NET MIGRATION TO/FROM THE UK - 1998-2007

Figure 19.13 Net migration to/from the UK, 1998–2007

The impact of migration depends upon a number of factors and not just the size of the net migration flow. If migrants possess suitable skills and are primarily of working age they offer substantial benefits to UK businesses. They can assist in overcoming skill shortages and reduce the expenditure that firms must make on training. In addition, the increased supply of people onto the labour market may help to prevent wages from rising. This is especially likely if migrants are willing to work for lower wage rates.

The impact of migration varies between different regions of the UK and also between different industries. The list on the right shows the main industries that attracted migrants between 2004 and 2006.

Source: Adapted from BBC News, 22 May 2007 and 19 November 2008 http://news.bbc.co.uk

Question:

1   In 2008 the UK economy moved into recession. How might a net inflow of migrants affect the competitiveness of business in such an economic situation?

If there is a need to reduce output then rationalisation and redundancy might follow and factories and offices may be closed. Research and development plans may be abandoned or postponed as firms seek to reduce their costs to match their (reduced) revenues. The predicted fall in the level of demand may encourage the firm to diversify, possibly into foreign markets. Businesses may consider mergers with other

firms to help reduce costs or to broaden product ranges.

Periods of low unemployment cause different problems for businesses and provoke different responses. Falling unemployment and accompanying skill shortages create problems that take time to solve. Businesses look to the government to assist through the provision of state training schemes and the development of relevant vocational courses in schools and colleges. Recent UK governments have attempted to support industry in these ways.

However, businesses can take action.

- Skill shortages encourage the development of capital-intensive methods of production in manufacturing and service industries. Using technology to replace labour can boost productivity thereby enhancing international competitiveness.
- Businesses may relocate to take advantage of more plentiful and cheaper sources of skilled labour. However, this may require location outside Europe as most of the EU is experiencing similar skill shortages.
- Businesses may invest in training schemes to develop the required skills in their employees.
- This may entail giving relatively junior or unskilled employees additional skills to enable them to carry out a wider range of activities. This can be a risky approach, however, as unscrupulous competitors may entice away skilled employees once training is completed.

The skills shortage creates difficulties for many businesses, but opportunities for others. Recruitment agencies and firms providing training for other businesses may enjoy increasing demands for their services during a period of skill shortages.

Economic growth

Economic growth is an increase in the value of goods and services produced by a nation's economy. This links closely with the business cycle, which we considered in an earlier chapter. If the rate of economic growth is negative (i.e. if the economy is getting smaller) for a successive six months, then it is said to be in recession.

Economic growth is normally measured by an increase in gross domestic product (GDP). In 2007 the GDP of the UK was £1,266,000 million. The population of the UK is approximately 60 million, giving a GDP per head (or per capita) of £21,100. Governments seek to increase this figure over time as it represents a rise in the country's standard of living.

Most countries' economies experience economic growth over a period of time, though in the short term economies may stagnate or even decline in size. Figure 19.14 illustrates the economic growth rates for the UK from 1978 until 2011, with the final four years being forecasts.

Governments aim to maintain steady and sustained economic growth over a period of time. However, this is a difficult target to achieve, as the operation of the business cycle tends to create the fluctuations apparent in Figure 19.14. Governments use counter-cyclical policies (including control via interest rates and taxation levels) to attempt to eliminate the more extreme fluctuations. High rates of

The benefits	The drawbacks
• high rates of economic growth provide the government with increased tax revenues permitting greater expenditure on health, education and transport benefiting all businesses and citizens in the UK and encouraging further growth • growth provides opportunities to all in society. Individuals benefit from greater chances of promotion; high levels of consumer spending encourage enterprise. Businesses small and large may thrive in a growing environment • businesses generally enjoy higher sales and increased profits. Expansion is likely for firms selling income elastic products such as cars and foreign holidays. Growth creates new markets for products	• not all regions within an economy benefit equally during periods of economic growth. Firms selling in the south of England are likely to enjoy increases in sales while those in less prosperous regions such as Wales and the north of England may only see a marginal increase in revenues • growth may result in shortages of labour and other resources. This may result in higher wages, costs and prices fuelling inflation and creating uncertainty among the business community • growth places individuals and businesses under pressure. Workloads increase and decisions may be rushed. In these circumstances it may prove impossible to maintain the quality of management and businesses may lose coordination and a clear sense of direction

Table 19.4 The benefits and drawbacks of economic growth for businesses

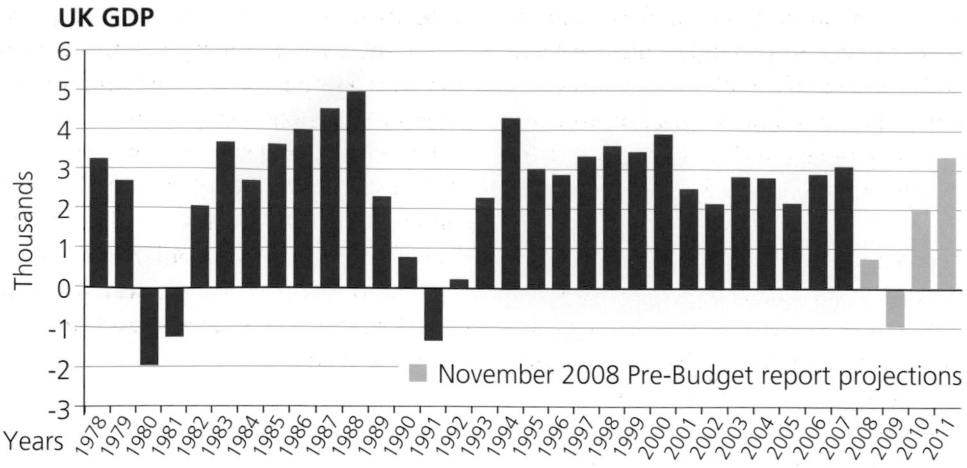

UK GDP

Figure 19.14 UK GDP

economic growth are not desirable, as they tend to result in slumps whereby economic growth may become negative. This can be seen in the period 1988–1991 in Figure 19.14.

Governments can stimulate growth as a consequence of their economic policies. Short-term growth can be encouraged by cuts in interest rates and taxation which fuel borrowing and spending, prompting greater output and hence economic growth. The danger is, however, that firms and individuals purchase products from overseas, promoting growth in foreign economies. Supply-side policies may be implemented to achieve sustained economic growth. This type of policy entails increasing the productive capability of the economy by improving the skills of the workforce, encouraging more people into employment and promoting competition within markets to increase output and GDP.

The case for economic growth is not clear-cut. Growth brings disadvantages as well as advantages. These arguments are summarised in Table 19.4.

Globalisation and growth

The fact that economic growth is not always an advantage has been highlighted in the well-publicised opposition to further economic development and especially to globalisation. Opponents of uncontrolled economic growth argue that other factors such as a clean environment, the protection of plants and wildlife and adequate leisure time contribute to the standard of living as much (and maybe more than) consumer products. As societies become richer this argument may become even more persuasive. We will consider the effects of globalisation fully on pages 267–271.

The economic environment as a single entity

In this chapter we have looked at the major economic factors individually and considered how they might affect the decisions taken by businesses. However, in reality managers and directors do not consider a single economic factor when assessing the behaviour of an economy and constructing their responses to changes in the economic environment. Instead, they assess the state of the economy by taking into account all the factors that can be used to judge its performance. It is important to judge the state of the economy by considering all the relevant key variables such as unemployment, and bearing in mind their interrelationships.

In 2008 the UK economy is moving into recession and is experiencing the start of what could be a quite severe downturn in the business cycle. This will attract the headlines, but any detailed analysis of the economy will also consider the effects of changes in other economic variables.

First, the exchange rate of the pound has fallen significantly against the currencies of some of the UK's major trading partners such as the USA and the European Union countries that use the euro. This has the potential to offer increased export sales to businesses that sell in the USA and Europe. The increase in sales will be more likely if the product that is sold is price elastic and foreign consumers respond positively to price reductions in their own currencies. However, the decline in the international value of the pound could increase costs for businesses that import large amounts of raw materials and components from overseas.

The economy moving into recession is also likely

to reduce the rate of inflation. Some analysts expect it to fall to very low rates. Surprisingly, this can lead to firms facing falling sales. If inflation is very low, or even non-existent, it may result in wages not rising to compensate for rising prices and this may result in falling levels of demand, especially for consumer goods, as consumers feel less well off.

Finally, rising unemployment can have a number of effects. It can result in falling levels of sales as consumers have less money to spend as a result of an increasing number becoming jobless. However, rising unemployment tends to depress wage levels and this may help a business to maintain its price competitiveness. This may be a particularly important factor for businesses that employ large numbers of people and where labour costs represent a high proportion of total costs.

Examiner's advice

The effects of changes in the economic environment and the consequent change in business strategy will depend upon the type of business, the markets in which it operates and the extent of the changes. This chapter provides you with general guidance, but you must think about the precise effects and consequences in the light of the situation you are faced with.

• Globalisation

Key terms
Globalisation is the trend for many markets to become worldwide in scope.
A **global strategy** exists when a business produces a single product (possibly with slight variants) to meet the needs of consumers across the global market.

What is globalisation?

The world's economies have developed ever-closer links since 1950 in trade, investment and production. This process has resulted in globalisation, and is not new. However, its pace and scope have accelerated in recent years, to include more industries and more countries.

At its simplest, globalisation refers to the trend for many markets to become worldwide in scope. Because of globalisation many businesses trade throughout the world, whereas in the past they may

have focused on one country, or possibly a single continent such as Europe. Improvements in global transport systems and communications, notably the internet, have encouraged this trend.

However, there are many people who do not view globalisation as a beneficial trend. The term globalisation brings to mind visions of large numbers of protesters confronting police forces in towns and cities across the world. We will consider the aspects of globalisation that have caused such responses later in this section.

Why is there a trend towards globalisation?

Many governments and businesses believe that increased and freer trade between nations will offer prosperity and growth for all countries and businesses. Globalisation, they argue, has already brought many benefits: global food production has risen steadily over the last 20 years and malnutrition rates have fallen accordingly. Citizens in less-developed countries have access to healthcare, often supplied by foreign businesses.

For its supporters globalisation offers an opportunity rather than posing a threat. The leaders of the world's major economies and big businesses are committed to protecting and promoting global commerce and trade and emphasise the benefits it can bring. Research in 2006 estimated that the typical UK family has benefited from globalisation in terms of cheaper products and a wider product range as a result of globalisation. The research suggested that the benefits of globalisation are worth £7,000 a year to the typical family.

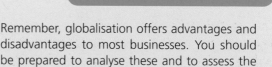

Examiner's advice

Remember, globalisation offers advantages and disadvantages to most businesses. You should be prepared to analyse these and to assess the overall impact on the business in question.

FALLING TRANSPORT AND COMMUNICATIONS COSTS

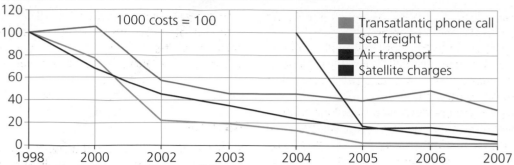

· **Cost of three minute telephone call from New York to London**
· **Average ocean freight and port charges per short ton of import and export cargo**
· **Average air transport revenue per passenger mile**

Source: HM Treasury, used on bbc.co.uk

GROWTH OF MULTINATIONAL FOREIGN OPERATIONS

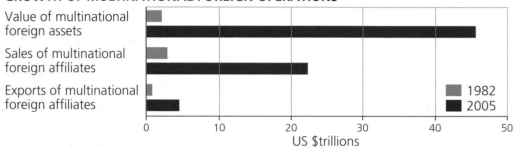

Figure 19.15 Falling transport and communication costs and the growth of multinational operations
Source: UNCTAD, used on bbc.co.uk

Business in Focus

Globalising the car manufacturing industry

For many years, the major market for the car industry was the United States – the single largest car market in the world – and US producers were the major players in the world market. But now the US represents less than one-quarter of the world industry, and its market share will decline further.

Stephen D'Arcy of PricewaterhouseCoopers believes all the growth in the global auto industry in the next decade will come from emerging market countries such as India, China and eastern Europe.

And that means the fastest-growing segment in the car industry will be the small car, the only size that will be affordable to the growing middle classes in these countries.

Consultancy firm Ronald Berger estimates that global demand for small cars, those costing less than $10,000 or 10,000 euros, will grow by 30 per cent in the next five years to 18 million, including 6 million in the BRIC countries (Brazil, Russia, India and China).

Major companies developing low-cost cars include Renault, Fiat, Peugeot, Daewoo (GM), Hyundai and

GLOBAL CAR OWNERSHIP
forecast for car ownership millions

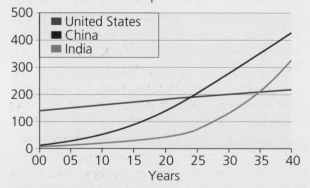

Figure 19.16 Global car ownership

Daihatsu (Toyota), as well as Chinese firms Geely and Chery and Indian companies Tata and Maruti. These companies are aiming to sell their products in markets throughout the world. The demand for similar types of vehicles in many markets enables major car manufacturers to put into place a global strategy.

The car industry is also going through a profound revolution in its method of production.

Lean production techniques are lowering the cost of making small cars and making it more efficient for car companies to change models quickly, in response to changing consumer taste.

The big car groups are moving to a global production system, in which their factories anywhere in the world are identical, based on global design and manufacturing best practice. 'The reality is that in today's economy you've got to be able to compete across borders in virtually every market,' says Toyota's North American president Jim Press.

That ability puts pressure on smaller companies who cannot match their productivity. However, it does allow the car companies, if they wish, to localise their product mix to suit each region.

Source: Adapted from BBC News
http://news.bbc.co.uk

Question:

1   What are the benefit and drawbacks of globalisation to smaller car manufacturers such as Tata?

Globalisation and business

Globalisation offers a number of opportunities to businesses from any country and not just the UK.

- **Increased sales, revenues and profits.** Being able to trade freely in international markets offers the chance to increase sales substantially and to enjoy higher revenues and profits – if the business is sufficiently competitive. It has become possible to sell similar products to billions of global consumers and this has offered unrivalled opportunities for growth. Companies such as McDonald's and Cadbury have derived enormous benefits from this increased access in terms of rising revenues.

- **Cheaper resources.** Increased volumes of trade also make more resources available to businesses and allow them to source raw materials and, of course, labour significantly more cheaply than in the past. For example, many UK manufacturers, including the train-maker Hornby and cosmetic manufacturer Avon, have moved production facilities to China and Poland respectively to take advantage of cheaper labour. This has only been possible as a result of reduced costs of transportation and political and economic changes that have made it possible for UK businesses to locate in these countries.

- **Economies of scale.** The increased scale of production gives greater potential to benefit from economies of scale. This is especially true if it is possible to implement a global strategy whereby a similar product can be sold to consumers across the world. This means that fixed costs, such as research and development, can be spread across larger volumes of production, lowering unit costs.

At the same time the company is likely to benefit from marketing and purchasing economies.

- **Developing different products for different markets**. The increased scale of production and access to large overseas markets such as China and India means that foreign companies can produce cars that meet the needs of local consumers. Thus, for example, increasing awareness of environmental issues and limited incomes mean that most Asian car consumers will wish to purchase small cars. The products that will be required will be different from those purchased in North America.

But globalisation brings drawbacks for all businesses too.

- **Downward pressure on prices.** All businesses have access to cheaper sources of raw materials and labour, enabling them to reduce costs and selling prices. This has led to a sharpening of price competition. Prices of clothing, footwear and electronic products have fallen in the UK over recent years, once inflation is taken into account. This means that for businesses to remain competitive in markets such as these it is imperative that they are able to reduce prices to match the general market trend. Some businesses have, however, recognised that they cannot compete in terms of price with producers based in countries with lower costs. As a result they have adopted strategies to differentiate their products by, for example, developing a USP based on quality or advanced technology.

- **New producers.** Established businesses in markets in Europe and North America have found themselves facing new competition from businesses in developing countries. For example,

Petro China is China's largest company and was only founded in 1999. However, by 2007 it had generated annual revenues of more than £75 billion and profits of £14 billion. Clearly this company has become a fierce global competitor drilling and refining oil. Established producers have found that many markets have been subject to increased levels of imports from producers in countries such as Russia and India.

- **Increased need for investment**. Globalisation, by sharpening competitive pressures, has increased the pressure for businesses to invest to compete with firms from around the globe. Investment is required to produce new products which are differentiated from those currently available, or to increase the skills and productivity of the businesses' workforces. These competitive strategies require investment in research and development (R&D) or in training employees.

- **The threat of takeover**. Globalisation has seen the development of larger businesses more able to face the full force of global competition. Many businesses have taken over smaller competitors to give them greater economies of scale and, in some cases, a brand name that is familiar in other parts of the world. Smaller successful businesses might be particularly vulnerable to takeover because of the globalisation of markets.

Business in Focus

Ittiam Systems

Ittiam Systems was created by Srini Rajam in 2001. The company supplies IT services to other businesses and is skilled in developing Digital Signal Processing (DSP) Systems. The company's headquarters are in Bangalore, India and it has marketing offices in the US, UK, France and Taiwan. Ittiam Systems is also represented in Israel, Japan, Taiwan, South Korea and Singapore.

Ittiam Systems earns its living from devising products; both off-the-shelf components compatible with its customers' systems and also custom-made products. Revenue is mainly generated through licensing of its ideas and its designs. The company is recognised as a world leader in its field and has received global awards to this effect.

The company currently employs over 200 people.

Why is globalisation controversial?

One of the reasons that globalisation is so controversial is that different groups can interpret it in many different ways. For some groups globalisation is a uniquely threatening word. It prompts visions of large multinationals dominating the world, selling Coca-Cola and Big Macs to consumers in pursuit of ever-higher profits. Many pressure groups fear that globalisation threatens the environment as well as national cultures, and predict that it will make the rich nations richer while impoverishing developing countries.

Citizens in rich and poor countries alike see the threat posed by globalisation to their local cultures and have acted to protect them. In India consumers wrecked McDonald's restaurants for violating Hindu dietary laws. At the same time Canadian communities are fighting to keep out the giant Wal-Mart chain for fear it will destroy neighbourhood shopping centres. Some people fear that the development of larger and more powerful global businesses offer threats to their jobs (lost to countries where wages are lower) and their way of life – being sold products that are unfamiliar to their cultures.

Business in Focus

The World Trade Organisation (WTO)

The WTO was created in January 1995 as a forum for trade negotiations and with the brief to resolve trade disputes. It cooperates with other international organisations in pursuing its aim of ensuring that trade flows as freely and smoothly as possible. It administers and polices existing and new free-trade agreements, settles trade disputes between governments and organises trade negotiations. In October 2003 the WTO had a membership of 144 countries. China joined in 2001 while Russia is seeking entry. The WTO's role in promoting world trade has attracted ferocious opposition from anti-globalisation protesters, resulting in violent scenes at WTO meetings, most notably in Seattle in 2000.

Strategies in response to globalisation

Globalisation is likely to remain a hot potato for governments and big businesses alike for the foreseeable future. Some consumers from developed and developing countries can be expected to continue to voice their opposition to the actions of businesses that damage their local cultures and their local environments. Multinationals need to achieve a tricky balance in their strategic planning between achieving their ambitions to operate in a global market while ensuring they do not alienate large numbers of the consumers who make up that market.

Unfortunately for big businesses they operate in an environment in which information on their activities is increasingly available and consumers are better informed than ever before. Some companies have already recognised that there are significant commercial advantages in being seen to react to at least some of the demands of the anti-globalisation campaigners. International furniture retailer IKEA has announced that it will protect the world's ancient forests by only using timber from sustainable sources. Other multinationals may be more reluctant to respond until and unless the protesters' actions begin to have substantial financial consequences.

Some multinationals may opt for strategic alliances with businesses from other parts of the world to respond the changes in the world economy that have been created by globalisation. This has been apparent in the car manufacturing and supermarket industries. For example, Tesco has sought a deal with a Chinese supermarket group (Ting Hsin) as a first step to operating in what is a very different market for a food retailer.

Others will seek to establish production capacity throughout the world and to sell differentiated products targeted to meet the needs of consumers in local markets. Toyota has adopted this strategy, producing different cars for the American and Asian markets. We considered such multi-domestic strategies more fully in the previous chapter.

Developments in emerging markets

Key terms

An **emerging market (or economy)** describes a country with low incomes per head, but one which is enjoying high rates of economic growth.

The **BRIC countries** are Brazil, Russia, India and China and are often referred to as prime examples of emerging markets.

Economic growth is the rate of increase in the size of an economy over time.

A **multinational business** is one that has production capacity in more than one country.

The rise of emerging markets is inextricably tied up with globalisation. Globalisation is the result of the freeing up of trade by reducing political and legal barriers to it and improving international communications and transport links. These developments have allowed economies such as China and India to thrive. Freer trade and political systems have allowed businesses to thrive in emerging markets and have encouraged established producers to locate in these countries. At the same time domestic businesses have grown rapidly. These changes, in total, have helped the emerging economies to achieve very high rates of economic growth.

Emerging economies: key players of the future?

China has received much attention in the media as a rapidly growing economy and an economic powerhouse of the future. The economy has achieved rapid rates of growth (around 10 per cent per annum over the last seven years) and has produced enormous quantities of manufactured goods. In 1980 the Chinese economy was about 25 per cent of the size of the UK's; by 2005 it was larger. However, it is a mistake to think of China as the only emerging economy. There are a number of other economies with enormous potential. India's population is nearly as large as China's and the country has specialised in providing services. We saw earlier that Ittiam Systems is an example of an Indian company that is able to compete successfully in global markets, illustrating India's growing economic power. Other key emerging market countries are Brazil and Russia. These countries benefit from sizeable populations as well as other resources such as oil and gas. Together

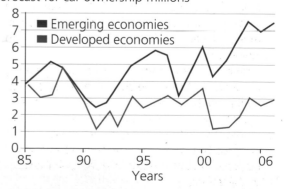

GLOBAL CAR OWNERSHIP
forecast for car ownership millions

Figure 19.17 GDP growth rates in developed and emerging economies

these four emerging markets are referred to as the BRIC countries. Other emerging economies include South Korea, South Africa, Mexico, Bulgaria, Hungary and Romania.

The growth rates achieved by the emerging economies is much higher than that achieved by developed economies such as France and the UK, as is shown in Figure 19.17.

Business in Focus

Emerging markets fizzing for coke

Coca-Cola has seen third-quarter pre-tax profits rise 16% to $2.1bn (£1.03bn) fuelled by strong sales growth in China and Russia, and growing demand for water and juice drinks

Revenues at the US company rose 19% to $7.7bn. Sales rose more than 10% in China, Russia, India and Brazil, while sales in established markets were boosted by a growing preference for non-fizzy drinks such as Powerade and Minute Maid. This was in spite of a sales fall of 2% in Europe attributed to poor weather.

Demand for Coke and its other drinks in emerging economies is counteracting sluggish growth in North America, where sales grew by just 1% over the period. Concerns about obesity levels and the amount of sugar in soft drinks popular with children have had a negative impact on sales in the US and Europe.

Growth in sales of non-carbonated drinks outstripped those of their fizzy counterparts, rising 14% year-on-year compared with 6% sales growth in fizzy drinks, reflecting this trend.

Foreign sales, in general, were also boosted by the weak US dollar.

Coca-Cola acknowledged that its growth was being driven by international markets but added that it had seen some "signs of progress" in its North American business.

"We are demonstrating our ability to create shareowner value from the combined strengths of our brands and our global reach," said chief executive Neville Isdell.

Source: Adapted from bbc.co.uk

Question:

1   What other benefits might emerging economies offer to Coca-Cola, apart from rising sales?

The strengths of emerging economies

Emerging economies have numerous strengths and this allows them to offer real benefits to businesses.

- **Enormous labour resources**. China and India are the world's two most populous nations, with 1.3 billion and 1.1 billion inhabitants respectively. As a consequence the two economies have workforces each in excess of 500 million people. In China this allows wages to be very low and has permitted the production of manufactured goods at very low costs. India's workforce is nearly as large as China's and many Indians speak fluent English. An increasing proportion is highly educated, allowing the country to provide large numbers of employees for the global IT industry.

- **Large markets**. The large number of citizens in emerging economies also means that Russia, Mexico, China and India are important markets for many companies because of the number of consumers and the fact that their incomes are rising rapidly. Companies such as McDonald's and Coca-Cola have targeted increasing sales in these countries as their incomes rise. For some companies, such as those supplying tobacco, these markets can be exceptionally attractive as levels of health education are lower than in developed economies.

- **Rapid growth rates**. Many of the emerging markets are achieving rapid rates of growth. The Chinese economy is growing at around 10 per cent each year and India is achieving growth rates in excess of 6 per cent. In 2008 Russia's economy grew by 8 per cent and South Korea's by 4.5 per cent. This growth means that many consumers have increasing disposable incomes to spend on consumer goods such as cars, clothes and electrical goods. Emerging economies are increasingly attractive markets for many multinational businesses because of the number of consumers and their rising incomes.

- **Natural resources**. Some of the emerging economies, notably Brazil, benefit from extensive natural resources. Brazil has huge amounts of timber, agricultural land and mineral resources. This has been reflected in the value of its exports, as shown in Figure 19.18.

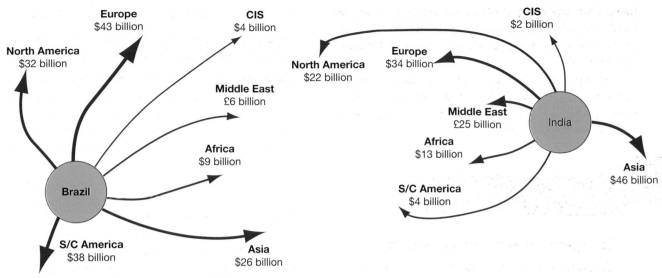

Figure 19.18 Exports from Brazil and India, 2007
Source: World Trade Organisation
http://www.wto.org

Weaknesses of emerging economies

- **Poor transport infrastructures**. India has a congested and fragmented road structure and this limits the locations that are feasible and cost-effective for multinational companies; the government has agreed to prioritise improving this. China has invested heavily in developing its transport and communications, yet problems remain, especially in areas away from its east coast.
- **Inflation**. This is a pressing problem for several of the emerging economies, despite the economic downturn since 2008. China's rate of inflation was 6.2 per cent in 2008, India's 6.1 per cent, Mexico's 5.3 per cent, Brazil's 5.8 per cent and Russia's 14.1 per cent. This poses a number of problems for businesses that opt to locate in these countries. Interest rates may increase as governments attempt to reduce rates of inflation, and the companies might find the cost differentials that attracted them to locate there in the first place are slowly eroded.
- **Import restrictions**. It can be difficult to export to countries such as India, China and Russia. The governments may impose taxes or other restrictions on imports or limit the ability of foreign businesses to operate there. Foreign supermarket chains have experienced problems in breaking into the Indian market because of the reluctance of the Indian government to admit them. The Indian government also imposes high import taxes on some products. Until 2007, for example, the

Indian government imposed high taxes on imported motorcycles.
- **Lack of appropriate skills**. Some decisions to locate production capacity in emerging economies have not been successful as employees have not had the necessary skills. For example, Lloyds TSB removed its call centres from India following complaints from customers who said staff did not have the necessary local knowledge to carry out their duties effectively.
- **Vulnerability to recession**. Although they have achieved spectacular rates of economic growth in recent years, countries such as India and China are poor in international terms. For example, India is home to 40 per cent of the world's malnourished children. Because of this vulnerability a downturn in spending across the world can lead to companies closing production facilities in the emerging economies, resulting in large increases in unemployment. This was observed in India and China during the latter part of 2008 when falling exports led to the closure of factories and offices. Multinationals may also find it more acceptable to close down some of their overseas facilities first when sales fall. Some observers fear social unrest, especially in China if rates of growth slow significantly and large numbers of people become unemployed suddenly. Equally, continued and dramatic falls in the prices of resources such as oil can have severe adverse effects on economies such as Russia and Brazil.

Strategic responses to changes in the economic environment

The economic environment is an important factor for many businesses and changes are likely to provoke a range of responses, as outlined below.

- **Relocation**. If the economic position in a particular economy deteriorates then it may be that a business will relocate to a different country where the economic conditions are more favourable. This may be an appropriate response to an economic downturn if an economy is moving towards recession or suffering higher rates of inflation than other countries, damaging price competitiveness. This strategy has been made easier by the relaxing of barriers to trade and improving global transport links. However, the global economy is increasingly integrated and an economic downturn in one economy is likely to be experienced by others, though not necessarily to the same degree.
- **Selling new products or entering new markets**. These are strategies that Ansoff would recognise and are included in his matrix. Businesses may opt to enter markets in countries whose economies are buoyant or to sell products that are 'recession proof'. Globalisation and the emergence of economies such as India and China may encourage such strategic responses among firms whose products are in demand across the globe.
- **Retrenchment or cost cutting**. Retrenchment essentially means that a business downsizes and operates with a smaller productive capacity. Managers will identify less profitable (or major loss-making) areas of the business and eliminate these in the expectation of making the entire enterprise more efficient. Cost cutting may be a less dramatic strategy, but can help a business to maintain an acceptable level of profitability during a period of adverse economic conditions.
- **Mergers and takeovers**. By increasing its scale a business may be better equipped to deal with the rigours of global markets. It may enable a business to benefit from economies of scale and to control costs more effectively and be price competitive. Mergers and takeovers may enable a business to extend its product range and to compete in other markets. In this way the strategy may help to protect the business against an adverse economic environment by providing new products whose sales are not as vulnerable to falling incomes or rising costs.
- **Joint ventures and alliances**. This strategy falls short of a full merger or takeover but offers similar benefits. It can be an effective way of gaining access to a new market or a means or reducing costs, not least through the achievement of substantial economies of scale.

The precise strategic response taken by any business will depend upon a range of factors including the nature of the product that the business sells, the financial position of the business and the extent of the change in the economic environment. However, a key influence on any decision about strategic responses to changes in the economic environment will be the extent of any change and the period over which it is expected to last. Thus the emergence of economies such as India, Brazil and China or the globalisation of markets may provoke a range of responses, many of which are outlined above. In contrast, an economic downturn or a period of inflation that are expected to be of limited duration may only lead to tactical responses such as changing prices or other elements of the marketing mix.

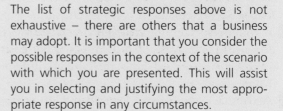

Business in Focus

House builders decide to merge

Taylor Woodrow and George Wimpey are to merge, creating a £5 billion house construction business with operations in Britain and the US. The companies are understood to be in the final stage of negotiations; an announcement to the London Stock Exchange is expected soon.

The deal is the latest in a series of mergers and acquisitions in the sector, which included Barratt's purchase of Wilson Bowden for £2.2 billion, agreed earlier this year, the sale of Crest Nicholson to a consortium of HBOS and Sir Tom Hunter for over £700 million and the purchase of McCarthy & Stone by HBOS for £1.1 billion.

The proposed all-share deal between Taylor Woodrow and George Wimpey will be structured as a nil-premium merger. Peter Redfern, Wimpey's chief executive, is expected to step into the same role at the merged entity, with Norman Askew, the current chairman of Taylow Woodrow, expected to chair the new company. Taylor Woodrow's chief executive, Ian Smith, has been tipped to leave the combined group.

A source close to the deal said: 'Both companies have strong complementary businesses and, while there is concern about the US market, if we put the two together it should add strength.' By merging the third- and fourth-biggest house builders in the country, the deal will catapult the new group into the FTSE100 index and create huge cost savings, in part through redundancies. It is expected that around 10 per cent of the 14,000-strong combined workforce could lose their jobs. The combined operation will have an output of 30,000 homes a year.

Both companies have been affected by the slowdown in the American property market. More than 50 per cent of Taylor Woodrow's business is in America, while Wimpey also has a significant presence in the country. However, it will be in Britain that the combined operation will look to grow business through cost savings and the merger of their land banks.

Source: The *Daily Telegraph*, 26 March 2007
http://www.telegraph.co.uk

Question:

1 What are the strengths and weaknesses of this response by the house builders to a looming world recession?

Progress questions

1 An economy is in the upswing stage of the business cycle. What are the most common features of this stage of the cycle? (4 marks)

2 Outline two ways in which a company manufacturing digital televisions might be affected by a recession. (6 marks)

3 Examine two factors that might determine a business's response to a rise in interest rates. (6 marks)

4 Explain two ways in which a UK-based manufacturing business, trading across the EU, might be affected by a fall in UK interest rates. (7 marks)

5 Archer & Sons, based in Norwich, purchases raw materials from overseas and sell half its output in foreign markets. Consider the probable effects on the company of a rise in the exchange value of the pound. (8 marks)

6 Explain why price elasticity of demand may partly determine the responses of a business to a substantial change in exchange rates. (7 marks)

7 Consider the responses of a large insurance company to a steady fall in the rate of unemployment. (8 marks)

8 Examine the ways in which an international airline might respond to a large and unexpected rise in the rate of inflation in its home market. (8 marks)

9 Outline why a business would be more likely to monitor long-term interest rates. (6 marks)

10 In what ways might a hotel chain in the UK respond to a high rate of UK economic growth? (8 marks)

11 Explain two advantages of globalisation for a major UK supermarket such as Tesco. (6 marks)

12 What disadvantages might McDonald's face as a result of globalisation? (6 marks)

13 Why might a car manufacturer opt for a multi-domestic strategy in the face of globalisation? (8 marks)

14 Why might emerging economies such as India and China offer opportunities to multinational businesses such as Vodafone? (7 marks)

15 Explain two risks for a clothes manufacturer of locating in an emerging economy. (7 marks)

Analysis and evaluation questions

1 Patten plc is a manufacturer of tyres for cars, lorries and buses and sells its products across the world, though its main markets are the UK and the rest of the EU. It imports large quantities of rubber from Malaysia to make its products. Patten plc's products are recognised as top quality and it is able to charge a price premium because of this. The company's Chief Executive has recently stated that the recent rise in the value of the pound against the euro and the US dollar has weakened its financial position.

At the same time the rate of inflation in the UK has risen significantly above the expected rate, though it remains below that experienced in the EU. This change has been accompanied by a small increase in the rate of economic growth from 2.7 per cent to 3.0 per cent. This has been a surprising figure given that growth rates in the USA have slowed from 2.5 per cent to 1.9 per cent.

a Analyse the effects of a rise in the exchange value of the pound for this company. (10 marks)

b To what extent do you think the economic environment in which Patten plc trades has become less attractive for the company? (15 marks)

2 The managing director of Spangles Ltd was looking at some UK economic forecasts which had been given to him.

His company organises luxury holidays in Europe, the United States and Asia. In recent years the company has struggled in the face of an adverse economic environment.

However, the managing director believes that a dramatic improvement in the economic environment in which Spangles Ltd trades will occur over the next two to three years. He thinks that the company's strategies should reflect this forecast improvement.

a Analyse the possible ways that the company may respond to a 'dramatic improvement' in the economic environment in which it trades. (10 marks)

b To what extent do you agree with the managing director's assessment that the economic environment in which the company trades will improve dramatically? (15 marks)

3 Damly plc is a successful manufacturer of vacuum cleaners. Its products are based on sophisticated technology which means that it operates more efficiently than those of rivals such as Hoover and Dyson. The company was located in Edinburgh, but three years ago its management team took the decision to relo-

Economic factor	Next year	The following year	The year after
Value of £ against the US$	1.55	1.67	1.88
Value of £ against the EU€	1.07	1.09	1.01
Growth in GDP	1.5	1.9	2.9
Inflation	2.2	2.2	2.3
Unemployment rate (%)	5.6	5.3	4.9
Interest rates	2.75	3.00	3.25

cate the company's factories to a huge factory near Shanghai.

The company has kept its head office and much of its research and development in Scotland and is continuing to invest heavily in producing the more advanced products. The managing director has commented that she intends to spend an increasing amount on R&D in future years.

a Analyse the benefits to the company that may arise from globalisation. (10 marks)

b Do you think that the risks of locating its factory in China will outweigh the benefits? Justify your view. (15 marks)

Case study

The number of people out of work in the UK rose by 137,000 to 1.86 million in the three months to October 2008 – the highest level since 1997. This took the unemployment rate up to 6 per cent from 5.8 per cent previously, the Office for National Statistics said. At the same time the exchange value of the pound fell to a record low against the euro as the unemployment figures revealed the weakness of the UK economy.

Several companies have announced big job cuts as the economic downturn begins to hit hard. Economists said that to see so many job losses at this stage of a recession is very worrying as increases in unemployment usually lag behind the operation of the trade cycle.

The number of people claiming unemployment benefit rose for a tenth consecutive month and climbed above the 1 million mark for the first time in eight years. HSBC, lorry manufacturer Leyland and Spanish bank Santander, which runs Abbey, Alliance & Leicester and parts of Bradford & Bingley, are among the many firms to have announced job cuts in recent months.

On Wednesday, rail and bus firm National Express said it would cut up to 750 jobs as it acted to save costs. The trade union umbrella body the TUC has predicted that 2 million people will be out of work by Christmas, and says half a million people will be facing their second Christmas out of work. People at all levels within a business are expected to be vulnerable to the rising level of unemployment. Managers are expected to be hit hard by job cuts, with the Management Consultancies Association forecasting up to 360,000 will lose their jobs by 2010.

Source: Adapted from bbc.co.uk

(40 marks, 60 minutes)

Questions

1 Explain one possible effect on UK exporters of the pound reaching a record low against the euro. (5 marks)

2 Analyse the possible reasons why National Express has decided to cut its costs given the changes in the economic environment described in the passage. (8 marks)

3 Discuss the ways in which the lorry manufacturer Leyland might be affected by the recession in the UK. (12 marks)

4 Do you think that all businesses should respond in the same way to the onset of a recession? Justify your view. (15 marks)

Case study

Tesco has announced its first foray into China with the purchase of a 50 per cent stake in a 25-strong hypermarket chain for £140 million ($260 million). The joint venture with the Ting Hsin chain ends a three-year search by Tesco for a foothold in the Chinese market. Tesco currently has a presence in 12 countries, including Hungary, Poland, South Korea, Taiwan and Japan.

'China is one of the largest economies in the world with tremendous forecast growth,' said Tesco's Sir Terry Leahy.

Ting Hsin is the largest food supplier in China and owns the Hymall chain of stores, of which Tesco will have a 50 per cent stake. Hymall opened its first outlet in September 1998 and is now one of the leading hypermarket operators in the country, with French chain Carrefour and US-owned Wal-Mart among its rivals. The business serves around 2 million customers a week and is valued at £280 million, with sales of £330 million. Most of its stores are located in 'high quality' shopping mall developments in the east, north and northeast of China, Tesco said.

Combining their talents, Ting Hsin will offer its local knowledge and operating expertise, while Tesco will add its supply chain, product development and store operation prowess to 'improve the shopping experience'. 'Hymall is already a leading retailer in Shanghai, China's largest retail market and the chain of 25 hypermarkets provides an excellent base of stores from which we can grow together,' said Sir Terry Leahy.

Ting Hsin chairman Wei Ying-Chiao said: 'This new strategic partnership with Tesco will bring new management expertise and technology know-how to help grow the business even further.'

Source: Adapted from bbc.co.uk
(40 marks, 60 minutes)

Questions

1 Explain one possible effect on Tesco of the globalisation of world markets. (5 marks)
2 Analyse the possible disadvantages to Tesco of the globalisation of the groceries market. (8 marks)
3 Discuss the possible reasons why Ting Hsin might have agreed to the deal with Tesco. (12 marks)
4 To what extent does Tesco's decision to move to China represent a sensible strategy for the company? (15 marks)

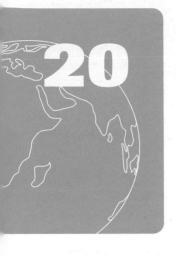

20

Businesses and the political and legal environment

This chapter builds on the previous one and does not relate directly to any materials you covered as part of your AS course. It considers the actions that the government takes in an attempt to provide a more supportive economic environment for businesses and the effects of these actions on businesses – they are not always as intended. It also examines the legal framework that the UK and EU authorities have created for businesses. As we cover these topics we will consider how a variety of businesses have reacted to changes in their political and legal environments.

In this chapter we examine:

- the government's economic policies
- the effects of the government's intervention in the economy
- political decisions affecting trade and access to markets
- the impact of legislation relating to businesses
- the different responses of businesses to changes in the political and legal environment.

Key terms

Economic policy: a series of actions (such as changing interest rates and altering rates of taxation) through which the authorities attempt to create the best possible economic environment for businesses and individuals.

The economy: the complex interaction of millions of consumers, thousands of businesses, and governments in supplying a wide range of goods and services.

Economic activity: the level of production, spending and employment occurring in an economy at a given point in time.

Balance of payments: a record of a country's trade and financial transactions with the rest of the world over a specified period of time, normally a year.

Balance of payments (current account): a financial record of a nation's trade in goods and services with the rest of the world over a specified period of time, normally a year.

Introduction

The operation of the UK's economy affects everyone and every business in the country. Changes in the level of production, employment or prices can have significant consequences for managers, for employees and for consumers. However, we cannot consider the UK economy in isolation. The UK is a part of the wider EU economy and is an important component of the global economy that is assuming ever-greater importance. Not surprisingly, the government has a number of objectives for the economy and all of its policies are intended to fulfil these objectives.

As early as 1945 the government had established economic objectives that still broadly apply today. These objectives are as follows.

- **Price stability**, i.e. controlling the rate of inflation as measured by the consumer price index. In the 1980s the UK suffered high rates of inflation, but they have declined steadily since that time. Since 2004 inflation has been around 2.5–3.4 per cent. Having an inflation rate below that of other nations offers firms a potential price advantage.
- **Steady and sustained growth in the economy**, allowing greater levels of production. Economic growth offers firms and individuals the potential for increased incomes and greater prosperity. Most western economies (including the UK) aim for a growth rate of 3–4 per cent, although some devel-

oping economies such as China have achieved annual rates in excess of 10 per cent.

- **A low rate of unemployment** – it is impossible to have everyone in the economy employed. Unemployment in 2009 is hovering around the 2 million mark, still a relatively low figure when compared with over 3 million unemployed in the 1980s. Unemployment represents a major waste of resources by an economy.
- **A balanced balance of payments**, avoiding long-term deficits and surpluses. Governments usually aim to avoid deficits on the current account of the balance of payments. This means the value of goods and services sold overseas should at least be equal to the value of imports of goods and services. On occasions governments seek to avoid the exchange rate rising, which can contribute to a balance of payments deficit on the current account.

The Bank of England has responsibility for operating some of the government's economic policies, which we shall consider in more detail later in this chapter. The Bank recently restated the government's economic objectives.

The Government's central economic policy objective is to achieve high and stable levels of growth and employment. Price stability is a precondition for these high and stable levels of employment and growth. In the past inflation has contributed to the UK's poor economic performance, not least by holding back the long-term investment that is the foundation for a successful economy.

Most governments would be satisfied if they could manage the economy to achieve the following targets in relation to the economy:

- the rate of inflation below the government's 2004 target of 2 per cent annually
- less than 5 per cent of the workforce unemployed
- steady economic growth at rates of 2–3 per cent each year
- avoiding large deficits on the current account of the balance of payments as a result of the value of imports of goods and services exceeding exports of the same.

However, managing the economy to achieve these objectives simultaneously is not an easy task. Many governments over recent years have failed to achieve these objectives. In part this is because in introducing policies to attain one objective, others become less achievable. There is a trade-off, as illustrated in Figure 20.1. Government economic policies designed to achieve objectives such as higher rates of economic growth and reductions in unemployment can have undesirable consequences. A consequence of higher growth and lower unemployment might be increasing inflation as shortages of raw materials, factories and offices, as well as skilled labour, force up prices. Another result might be increasing imports as individuals and consumers spend increasing sums of money on imports, causing a balance of payments problem.

The government's economic policies

> ## Key terms
> **Supply-side policies** are designed to improve the free operation of markets and therefore the total amount that is produced (or supplied) by the economy.
> **Direct taxes:** taxes on income and wealth, e.g. income tax, corporation tax and inheritance tax.
> **Indirect taxes:** taxes on spending, e.g. value added tax.
> **Interest rates:** the price of borrowed money.
> **Fiscal policy:** the use of taxation and public expenditure to manage the level of economic activity.
> **Monetary policy:** controlling the amount of money and/or interest rates within the economy in order to achieve the desired level of economic activity.
> **Privatisation:** the process of transferring organisations from the state to the ownership and control of individuals and other businesses.

Possible		possible
low unemployment	TYPE OF GOVERNMENT POLICY	price stability

expansionary government ← → contractionary government

| high rates of economic growth | policies increasing level of economic activity | policie reducing level of economic activity | 'balanced' balance of payments (current account) |

Figure 20.1 Government policies and economic objectives

The government operates a number of different policies with the aim of providing the best possible economic environment for UK businesses. This entails adjusting the level of activity in the economy to avoid the excesses of booms and slumps. The government's economic policies can be divided into three categories.

1 **Monetary policy**. Using this policy the government (or the Bank of England acting on its behalf) manipulates the amount of money and/or interest rates within the economy in order to achieve the desired level of economic activity.

2 **Fiscal policy**. This refers to the government's use of taxation and public expenditure to manage the economy. By adjusting the levels of taxation and government expenditure, the government can alter the level of activity within the economy.

3 **Supply-side policies**. These are designed to improve the free operation of markets and therefore the total amount that is produced (or supplied) by the economy. Privatisation is one type of supply-side policy, along with limiting trade union power and providing training for unemployed workers.

Monetary policy

This type of economic policy involves adjusting the amount of money in circulation and hence the level of spending and economic activity. Monetary policy can make use of one or more of the following:

- altering interest rates
- controlling the money supply
- manipulating the exchange rate.

Although at times all three techniques have been used, more recently governments have tended to rely upon altering interest rates to manage the economy. Since May 1997 the Monetary Policy Committee of the Bank of England has had responsibility for setting interest rates. The Monetary Policy Committee sets interest rates monthly with the aim of achieving the government's target for inflation while attaining long-term growth in the economy. Table 20.1 highlights the aims that may lie behind the authorities altering interest rates and, importantly, the implications for individuals and businesses.

Broadly speaking, rises in interest rates depress the level of economic activity and reductions promote an expansion of economic activity.

Rising interest rates	Falling interest rates
The likely **objectives** of increasing interest rates include the following: • reducing the level of consumer spending • limiting inflationary pressure in the economy • slowing the level of economic growth (as measured by GDP) • avoiding increasing imports creating a deficit on the balance of payments In general higher interest rates will assist in dampening down an economic boom.	Reductions in interest rates may be introduced with the following **objectives** in mind: • reducing levels of unemployment • stimulating the level of production in the economy • promoting exports sales by reducing the exchange value of the pound • increasing rates of economic growth in the economy Reducing interest rates can assist an economy in recovering from a slump.
The likely **consequences** of increasing interest rates include the following: • many businesses may experience falling sales as consumers increase savings • demand for products purchased on credit may decline significantly • businesses cancelling or deferring investment plans • firms reduce borrowing by, for example, cutting levels of stocks • increased value of sterling increasing the prices of exports while reducing import prices In general higher interest rates will assist in dampening down an economic boom.	The **consequences** for businesses and individuals of falling interest rates include the following: • demand and sales are likely to increase • production is likely to be stimulated by increasing employment • export sales of price sensitive products may increase while imports become less competitive • businesses may undertake increased investment promoting growth in industries such as construction

Table 20.1 Changes in interest rates – objectives and implications

Interest rates are the price of borrowed money. Although the Bank of England sets the base rate, many other interest rates operate in the UK. The precise rate of interest charged on a loan depends on several factors, including the time period of the loan and the degree of risk attached to it.

In the UK, expenditure is sensitive to changes in interest rates. One prime reason for this is mortgage interest payments. Millions of UK consumers have mortgages. A rise in interest rates increases the payments made on mortgages, leaving less money available for other types of expenditure. Similarly, a cut in rates reduces mortgage payments, freeing money for other forms of expenditure.

Effects of changes in interest rates

The impact of rising interest rates will depend upon the size of the change as well as the initial rate. A small increase at a relatively high level of rates will have little impact, while a larger increase from a low base rate will have a significant impact.

Not all businesses are affected equally. We can identify several categories of businesses that are particularly susceptible to changes in interest rates.

- Small firms are often affected greatly by changes in interest rates as they have smaller financial reserves and a relatively greater need for borrowing. The Bank of England estimates that every 1 per cent rise in interest rates costs the UK's 1.5 million small firms an extra £200 million in interest rate payments. Significant rises in interest rates can lead to substantial increases in bankruptcies among small firms.
- Even larger firms with high levels of borrowing (and therefore high levels of gearing) can be affected by alterations in interest rates. For example, a rise in rates can lead to a hefty increase in interest payments, forcing firms to reduce costs elsewhere or to pass on the extra expenses in the form of higher prices – if this is possible. Alternatively, a cut in interest rates offers a substantial reduction in expenses to such firms, improving their competitiveness.
- Firms trading overseas are affected by alterations in interest rates. Rising interest rates tend to lead to an increase in the exchange rates as individuals and businesses overseas purchase sterling to invest in UK financial institutions to benefit from higher rates. A fall in interest rates would have the opposite effect.

However, it is not only the direct effects of altering interest rates that affect businesses. The use of interest rate policy by the authorities can have a profound impact upon the general economic environment in which businesses operate. The Bank of England's Monetary Policy Committee changes

Other economic variables	Rising interest rates	Falling interest rates
unemployment	unemployment increases as levels of production decline	unemployment declines as the level of economic activity rises
inflation	falling demand and output reduces inflationary pressure	increasing output and spending causes prices to rise fuelling inflation
economic growth	will slow as businesses cut output and investment and spending declines	is stimulated by cheaper loans and rising business investment and increasing consumer expenditure
exchange rates	value of the pound is likely to rise	exchange value of the pound generally falls
balance of payments (current account)	fewer imports purchased improving the current account balance	increased spending will 'suck in' imports worsening current account balance

Table 20.2 Interest rates and other economic variables

interest rates to assist the government in achieving its economic objectives. This means that altering rates affects the level of unemployment, inflation and growth existing in the economy. They also change managers' expectations of these key economic variables affecting their day-to-day and strategic decisions.

Table 20.2 illustrates the relationship that exists between the level of interest rates and key economic variables such as economic growth and unemployment.

Fiscal policy

Fiscal policy is the use of government expenditure and taxation as a means of controlling the level of activity within the economy. In particular a government's fiscal policy is the relationship between the level of government expenditure and the amount raised in taxation in any given year. The fiscal year runs from 6 April to 5 April the following year.

The balance between taxation and government expenditure is determined annually when the Chancellor of the Exchequer announces the annual budget. The government can operate two broad types of fiscal policy.

1 **Expansionary fiscal policy** entails cutting taxation and/or increasing government expenditure on items such as health, education, social services, defence and transport. The effect will be to increase the amount the government borrows to fund its expenditure (known as the public sector borrowing requirement or PSBR) or to reduce the surplus held in the government's coffers at the end of the fiscal year.

2 **Contractionary fiscal policy** is brought about by reducing government expenditure or increasing taxation, or by both policies simultaneously. The effect is to increase the government's PSBR or to reduce its surplus on its budget for the fiscal year.

Figure 20.2 summarises the operation of fiscal policy. Fiscal policy can help to stabilise the economy (avoiding the worst effects of the business cycle) through the operation of the 'automatic stabilisers'. For example, lower unemployment when the level of economic activity is high means temporarily lower social security spending, higher income tax receipts and higher National Insurance contributions. Higher company profits generate higher corporation tax receipts, and higher spending by consumers yields higher VAT receipts and excise duties. These factors together will have a contractionary effect, dampening an economic boom.

Tax and expenditure policies can have immediate effects on the level of economic activity, although the precise effects will depend upon the types of tax altered and the nature of government expenditure.

Direct taxes

These are taxes on income and profits and include income tax and corporation tax (levied on company profits). Direct taxes take a larger amount from individuals earning high salaries and companies announcing handsome profits. The government can forecast with some accuracy the effects arising from an increase (or reduction) in income tax. Although the overall effect may be predicted, the implications for individual businesses will vary according to the type of product supplied. Firms supplying luxury goods (long-haul foreign holidays, for example)

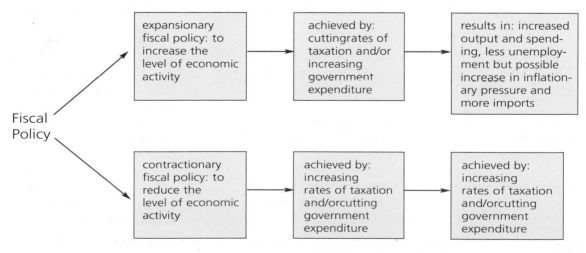

Figure 20.2 The operation of fiscal policy

might be significantly affected by a change in income tax rates, especially for those earning higher incomes, while those selling basic foodstuffs may be relatively unaffected.

Indirect taxes

VAT (value added tax) and other taxes on spending are classified as indirect. Changes in this type of taxation can have a rapid effect on the level of economic activity, although its effects are difficult to predict. An increase in VAT will cut consumer spending, reducing demand for goods and services and eventually lowering the level of economic activity. However, the extent of the fall in demand will depend upon the price elasticity of demand for the goods in question. Consumers will continue to purchase essentials such as fuel and food, although demand for products associated with DIY, for example, may decline. An important side effect of increasing indirect taxes is that it is inflationary.

Government expenditure is the other half of fiscal policy. Governments may spend more in two broad categories.

1 **Transfer payments** are expenditure on unemployment benefits, pensions and other social security payments. Changes in expenditure on these items will have a rapid impact as they are received by relatively poor members of society who will most likely spend the increase or cut back if necessary almost immediately. An increase in transfer payments often results in substantial increases in demand for basic goods such as food, public transport and gas.

2 **The infrastructure**, which governments improve through their spending on housing, roads and flood protection. Investment in these areas can increase the level of economic activity by boosting demand for the services of construction firms while reducing costs for other firms. A new road, for example, might cut a business's transport costs.

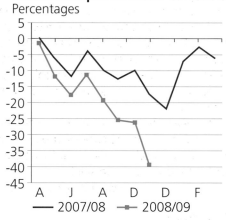

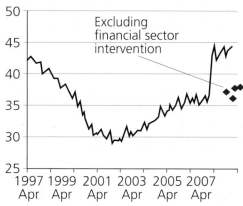

Figure 20.3 Public sector borrowing and public sector debt as a percentage of GDP

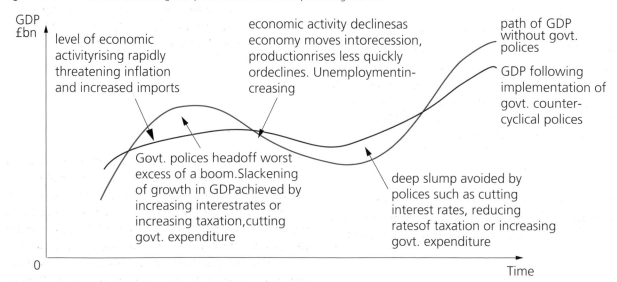

Figure 20.4 Government economic policies at work

This, however, is a much slower method of altering the level of economic activity.

Fiscal policy has not been an important part of the economic armoury of recent governments, although the UK government cut VAT from 17.5 per cent to 15 per cent as part of its attempts to lessen the effect of the recession that began in 2008. Government expenditure fluctuates with the business cycle because of the automatic stabilisers discussed earlier, but generally the trend has been to have a relatively neutral fiscal policy (neither expansionary nor contractionary) and to rely upon the use of interest rates to control the economy. Figure 20.3 shows that there has been a decreasing trend in public expenditure over recent years, reflecting a change in philosophy about government intervention in the economy and the lessening importance of fiscal policy.

The two graphs in Figure 20.3 show the increasing indebtedness of the UK government as it increased expenditure to try to reduce the effects of the recession that started in 2008. It is apparent that government spending has risen substantially since 2002 and this data excludes the cost of the financial intervention to support banks such as HBOS in 2008.

EU and government policies

At the time of writing the UK has not reached a decision on when to join the European single currency – the euro. The government states that it will adopt the euro 'when the conditions are right'. Operating the single currency in 14 member states (and possibly more than 25 in the future) requires the economies to be at similar stages in the business cycle and to pursue common economic policies to avoid their economies becoming unsynchronised. When (and if) the UK does adopt the euro the government at Westminster will lose a substantial degree of control over economic policies. The European Central Bank (the EU's equivalent of the Bank of England) sets interest rates for all member states. Fiscal policy may be decided domestically, but is subject to the overall control of the EU.

Supply-side policies

These are a range of measures intended to improve the operation of free markets and the amount that is produced by the economy. They can take a number of forms.

Business in Focus

Interest rates at 57-year low

The Bank of England's rate-setting body voted unanimously to cut rates to 2% this month. The Monetary Policy Committee (MPC) agreed that a cut in the Bank rate from 3% to 2% was the minimum needed.

Minutes from the meeting show a bigger move was considered, but was rejected over concerns that it could hit the pound and undermine confidence in the economy.

However, expectations of further hefty cuts have caused the pound to fall to another record low against the euro, with one pound worth 1.0867 euros. Analysts have said the minutes indicated that UK interest rates would fall further in the months ahead.

MPC minutes showed that the committee considered that a cut in the Bank rate to below 2% might be justified given the problems facing the economy. However, it noted that financial markets were expecting a one percentage point cut, and "there was a risk that going further could cause an excessive fall in the exchange rate". It felt that, "an unexpectedly large cut could undermine confidence in the economy more widely."

The weak state of the UK economy was also emphasised by the release of new unemployment data, which showed the highest jobless total for more than a decade.

Source: Adapted from bbc.co.uk

Question:

1   In what ways might a major UK supermarket, such as J Sainsbury, be affected by the reduction in interest rates mentioned in the article?

Labour market measures

In recent years UK governments took a range of measures intended to allow labour markets to operate more effectively. In the 1980s and early 1990s successive Conservative governments reduced the power of trade unions to permit labour markets to operate more freely. By reducing the power of trade unions businesses were enabled to implement policies to allow them to use labour more flexibly and efficiently. For example, employees were able to carry out a range of duties, rather than a limited role to avoid demarcation disputes. Disputes and confrontations became less common as a consequence of a series of laws.

Other policies have been implemented to encourage the effective operation of the UK's labour markets. The unemployed have been encouraged back into the labour force through the provision of training programmes designed to equip them with employable skills, by limiting the availability of unemployment benefit to those in genuine need and the cutting of income tax rates on low earners to encourage people into the labour force.

Privatisation

This is the process of transferring organisations from the state to the ownership and control of individuals and other businesses. In the 1980s and 1990s many major state enterprises were sold into the private sector, a selection of which are shown below.

1981 Cable & Wireless
1984 Enterprise Oil, Jaguar, British Telecom
1986 British Gas
1987 British Airways, Rolls-Royce, British Airports Authority
1988 British Steel
1989 Water companies

The policy has continued in recent years, although it has slowed as the state owns relatively few enterprises. Since 2000 the London Underground system has been partly privatised as has air traffic control and the port of Dover. The UK began a worldwide fashion for privatising former state-owned businesses; since 1990 the policy that has been copied by governments across the globe.

The arguments in favour of privatisation are formidable.

- By removing potentially inefficient monopolies privatisation offers consumers the possibilities of lower prices and better-quality products. Businesses in competitive markets cannot afford to be inefficient. The policy is based on the unshakeable belief in the superiority of private enterprise.
- Private businesses are more likely to pursue long-term policies to increase the prosperity of the businesses, to the benefit of all in society. In contrast, the objectives of the former nationalised industries were unclear and inconsistent – often little more than breaking even.

- The process of privatisation has provided huge sums of revenue for the government. By 2008 the figure exceeded £42 billion. This has enabled the government to reduce its borrowing and to cut taxes. The proceeds from privatisation played an important part in creating a society in which enterprise was valued and rewarded.

In recent years governments have tended to move away from the policy of full privatisation, preferring to see the public and private sectors cooperate on a range of projects. Two systems have been used:

- Public–Private Partnerships (PPP) are collaborations on relatively small-scale projects using private and public sector money.
- In contrast, a Private Finance Initiative (PFI) relies entirely on funding from the private sector. This approach is used for major capital projects, such as building schools and hospitals. The building of the Norfolk and Norwich hospital is a well-known example of the operation of PFI in the UK.

However, the drawbacks of privatisation have become increasingly apparent.

- Critics have argued that privatisation has not, in fact, resulted in more efficient industries. The establishment of watchdogs such as OFGAS and OFTEL have highlighted that left to their own devices the newly privatised companies might exploit consumers through excessive prices and poor-quality products. Furthermore, the well-publicised problems facing the UK's railways have provided further ammunition for those opposed to privatisation.
- Some economists have argued that having thousands of UK citizens as shareholders in privatised businesses has not encouraged long-term strategies to be implemented by the businesses. Shareholders, having limited understanding of business, have looked for a quick return. This has encouraged managers to maximise short-term profits – a policy not necessarily in the long-term interests of the company or the economy.

The perceived shortcomings of privatisation have led to a mild backlash against the policy. Countries such as New Zealand have created new nationalised industries, and even California has taken steps in this direction. Government proposals to privatise the UK's air traffic control encountered much opposition and resulted in only partial privatisation. It may be that nationalisation is no longer a dirty word.

Other supply-side measures

Governments have tried to make other resources more freely available by removing controls on the operation of markets that provide capital and land. The negotiating of the free movement of capital throughout the EU has been a major factor in increasing the funds available to UK enterprises. Similarly, the removal of rent controls has made the property market operate more effectively.

Government intervention

The issue of privatisation is at the forefront of the debate about the extent to which the government should intervene in the economy. The Conservative governments of the 1980s and 1990s argued that the state's role in the economy should be minimised to allow markets and businesses to operate with the maximum degree of freedom. In part this was achieved through the policy of privatisation, but also by the reduction in government subsidies and grants to industry and by legislation limiting the state's role in business matters. For instance, wages councils (responsible for setting the wages of many low-paid workers) were abolished and regulations governing markets such as telecommunications and financial services were relaxed, allowing new suppliers and greater competition. This approach to managing the business environment is described as laissez-faire and puts faith in a greater degree of self-regulation by businesses.

There are, not surprisingly, advantages and disadvantages to businesses arising from trading under a government that takes a laissez-faire approach to economic management.

Businesses benefit through less interference in their activities. Government intervention tends to raise costs (insisting on the employment of safety officers, for example) reducing the competitiveness of UK businesses. This can be a major handicap for firms operating in highly price-competitive markets where small cost differentials can lead to substantial loss of sales. By removing the requirement to pay national rates of pay, wages may fall in poor regions such as the north of England and Wales, attracting new businesses and making existing businesses more competitive. Supporters of the laissez-faire approach argue that the UK has been extremely successful in attracting overseas producers because of the lack of regulation of businesses. They contend that govern-

ments cannot prevent the operation of global market forces, and that it is a waste of money to try. Finally, the laissez-faire approach helps to promote an entrepreneurial society in which individuals take responsibility for their own economic welfare and are

Business in Focus

The minimum wage

The national minimum wage will rise to £5.73 an hour in October, Prime Minister Gordon Brown has announced. It will rise by 3.8 per cent from £5.52. For 18- to 21-year-olds the rate will be £4.77, up from £4.60, while 16- to 17-year-olds will get £3.53, up from £3.40.

The government said that 1 million people would benefit from the increase, two-thirds of whom would be women. Mr Brown said that the minimum wage had gone up by 60 per cent since the policy was introduced by the government in 1999. The original level when the minimum wage was launched was £3.60 an hour. It was last increased in October 2007.

Business Secretary John Hutton said: 'The national minimum wage remains one of the most important rights introduced by the Government in the last decade. Before it was introduced, some workers could expect to be paid as little as 35 pence an hour. Our legislation has ensured that can no longer happen. I am proud of the minimum wage. It makes a real difference to the lives of many of our lowest-paid workers and protects them from exploitation. It also creates a level playing field for business and boosts the economy.'

Sceptics who predicted that job losses would be the result of implementing the national minimum wage have been proved wrong according to the Income Data Services (IDS). More than 2 million workers benefited from the new pay floor, especially women and part-time workers.

Source: Adapted from bbc.co.uk

Question:

1 Discuss whether the apparent success of the minimum wage suggests that the government should play a larger role in determining pay rates for other groups, such as directors.

more creative and hard working as a result, to the benefit of all in society.

However, many individuals and groups oppose the laissez-faire style of economic management. They argue that it is vital that governments support struggling industries in poor regions to prevent heavy unemployment and poverty. The government intervened in 2008 to support the UK's banks during a time of a shortage of credit and, at the time of writing, is rumoured to be planning to offer state aid to Jaguar and Land Rover. Governments should recognise that economic change is inevitable, and attempt to soften the blow of economic restructuring of this type. Allowing businesses to regulate their own activities with minimal interference from the authorities is likely to result in unscrupulous businesses exploiting workers (through low wages and poor conditions) and consumers (by charging excessive prices). Some controls, it is argued, are essential to prevent this happening, particularly where a business faces little competition and exploits its monopoly power.

Political decisions affecting trade and access to markets

The trend towards the globalisation of markets has been encouraged by a series of decisions by governments. In this chapter we shall consider two key decisions.

Greater freedom of trade

The World Trade Organisation (WTO), which we profiled in the previous chapter, has played a prominent role in developing increased freedom to trade. The economic case for an open trading system based on multilaterally agreed rules is simple enough and rests largely on commercial common sense. But it is also supported by evidence: the experience of world trade and economic growth since the Second World War. Tariffs on industrial products have fallen steeply and now average less than 5 per cent in industrial countries. During the first 25 years after the war, world economic growth averaged about 5 per cent per year, a high rate that was partly the result of lower trade barriers. World trade grew even faster, averaging about 8 per cent during this period.

Lowering trade barriers is one of the most obvious means the WTO uses to encourage trade. The barriers concerned include customs duties (or tariffs)

and measures such as import bans or quotas that restrict quantities selectively. From time to time other issues such as red tape and exchange rate policies have also been discussed at WTO meetings.

The General Agreement on Trade and Tariffs (GATT) was the WTO's predecessor and existed until the end of 1994. Since GATT's creation in 1947–48 there have been eight rounds of trade negotiations. A ninth round, under the Doha Development Agenda, is now underway – and has been for seven years! At first these focused on lowering tariffs (customs duties) on imported goods. As a result of the negotiations, by the mid-1990s industrial countries' tariff rates on industrial goods had fallen steadily to less than 4 per cent.

Although the actions of the WTO have attracted much opposition from pressure groups, it has encouraged nations to take political decisions aimed at freeing trade and promoting economic growth. The current round of talks at Doha has stalled, but this should not detract from the WTO's achievements and those of its predecessor GATT.

Extending the European Union

The European Union currently has 27 member states constituting a market of over 475 million people – larger than the markets of Japan and the USA added together! In 2004, the EU expanded to 25 states with the entry of Cyprus, the Czech Republic, Estonia, Hungary, Latvia, Lithuania, Malta, Poland, the Slovak Republic and Slovenia. In 2007 Bulgaria and Romania joined, taking the total to 27. Turkey has made an application to join the EU, while others that were part of the former Soviet Union (Ukraine, for example) are expected to do so in the near future.

The enlargement of the EU offers businesses considerable opportunities. Since 2004 there have been 100 million extra consumers freely available to businesses in the UK and other established EU member states. Firms expect to achieve increased sales and perhaps to benefit from economies of scale in supplying this enlarged market. High-technology and service industries (e.g. telecommunications and banking) are likely to face relatively little direct competition from these countries.

Furthermore, firms have chosen to locate in countries such as Poland and Hungary to benefit from lower costs and, initially at least, fewer controls on business activity. The states of Eastern Europe have proved particularly attractive to manufacturers seeking to expand or transfer their European productive capacity.

There is, of course, a downside to the expansions of the EU. Greater competition is likely to appear in some industries where the relatively undeveloped economies of eastern and southern Europe have an advantage. Analysts fear that western Europe's agricultural industry may be threatened by a surge of cheap imports from the new member states. The productive potential of Poland's agricultural industry alone is awesome. Jobs may also be lost in economies where labour is relatively expensive as the competition from the east increases.

Pan-European strategy

The increasing size of the EU market will place firms under greater pressure to develop strategies to sell their products successfully in 27 diverse countries. A single strategy is unlikely to suffice.

Managers responsible for developing strategies to sell products throughout Europe will need to consider a number of issues.

- The acceptance that Europe is not a single market, not even 27 countries, but a series of localities all of which are different in some way and need different products and different approaches to marketing. This means that differences in products and marketing campaigns are essential, making it more difficult to achieve economies of scale.
- Increasing Europe's borders has made it bigger, more varied and more difficult to sell to successfully as languages and cultures become more diverse.

Examiner's advice

These are only two examples of political decisions that have contributed to the shaping of the environment in which businesses operate. Many others have taken place and you should be prepared to use them to support your arguments as necessary.

- Market intelligence becomes less available as one moves east and south. This makes it more difficult for managers to assess market and production potential within the proposed new member states of the EU. For example, pricing can be a difficult issue: firms wish to generate the highest sales possible, but to avoid allegations of dumping cheap goods.

The legal environment

The law is a framework of rules governing the way in which our society operates. These rules apply to businesses as well as individuals. The legal framework affects businesses in a number of ways, affecting almost all areas of business activity. Marketing, production, employment, relationships with customers and competitors and even the establishment of the business itself are examples of business operations influenced by the law.

Employment legislations

Employment Protection

Individual Labour Law

This legislation relates to the rights andobligations of individual employees

Examples include:
- Sex Discrimination Act, 1975
- Race Relations Act, 1976 Disability
- Discrimination Act, 1995
- National Minimum Wage Act, 1998

Collective Labour Law

This body of law covers the activities oftrade unions and the conduct ofindustrial relations.

Examples:
- Employment Acts, 1980 and 1982
- Trade Union Act, 1984
- Trade Union Reform and Employment Rights Act, 1993
- The Employment Relations Act, 1999

Figure 20.5 Employment legislation

Individual labour law

This aspect of employment legislation refers to the rights and obligations of individual employees. The amount and scope of individual labour law has increased in recent years, in part encouraged by the growing influence of the European Union on business matters in the UK.

A number of the most important Acts relating to individuals in employment are explained as follows.

- The Equal Pay Act 1970 rules that both sexes should be treated equally in all matters relating to employment. Equality in the workplace has been strengthened by European Union legislation, e.g. the 1975 Equal Pay Directive.
- The Sex Discrimination Act 1974 made discrimination on the grounds of sex or marital status illegal in recruitment, promotion, training and dismissal. The Act created the Equal Opportunities Commission to monitor the effectiveness of the Equal Pay and Sex Discrimination Acts. The commission was given the tasks of encouraging the elimination of sexual discrimination in the workplace and promoting equal opportunities.
- The Race Relations Act 1976 made it illegal to discriminate, in relation to employment, against men or women on the grounds of colour, race, nationality or ethnic or national origin. As in the case of sex discrimination, individuals have the right to take a claim for discrimination to an industrial tribunal. This Act also established the Commission for Racial Equality.
- The Disability Discrimination Act 1994 deems that employers who treat a disabled person less favourably than others without proper reason are behaving illegally. Employers are also required to make reasonable alterations to the working environment to assist those with disabilities in remaining employed.
- The Working Time Regulations 1998 is European Union legislation (hence the term 'regulation') which set a limit of 48 hours on the time that employees could be required to work each week. Employees can opt to work longer hours if they wish, but employers cannot insist that they do so without inserting an appropriate clause in their contract of employment. The regulations also gave employees an entitlement to four weeks' paid annual leave.
- The highly publicised National Minimum Wage Act 1998 came into force on 1 April 1999. The key features of this legislation are:

- a general hourly minimum wage rate – £5.73 an hour from October 2008
- a minimum rate of £4.77 an hour for 18–21 year olds
- all part-time and temporary workers must be paid the minimum wage.
- Employment Equality (Age) Regulations 2006 has several features.
- The main theme of this EU-inspired law is that it is unlawful to discriminate against workers under the age of 65 on the grounds of age.
- Making someone redundant or barring workers from training or promotion because they are too old – or too young – is illegal.
- As they approach 65, workers have to be given six months' notice that their employer wants them to give up their job and retire.

Business in Focus

Worker loses discrimination case

British Airways has successfully defended itself against accusations that it religiously discriminated against a worker by banning her from wearing her Christian cross.

Nadia Eweida, 56, who said her BA bosses banned her from wearing a small cross around her neck, lost her case before an employment tribunal which said she had breached the firm's regulations without good cause.

In a statement the airline said it was "pleased" at the decision.

Miss Eweida said she was very disappointed. 'I'm speechless really because I went to the tribunal to seek justice, but the judge has given way for BA to have a victory on imposing their will on all their staff."

She has vowed to proceed with her case if her solicitor agreed.

"It's not over until God says it's over," she said.

Source: Adapted from bbc.co.uk

Question:

1 British Airways won this case, but in what ways might the company have suffered as a result of it?

In addition, from December 2003, employers became liable for tackling discrimination against employees, agency and other workers on grounds of sexual orientation (whether heterosexual, gay or lesbian or bisexual). At the same time it became unlawful to discriminate on the grounds of religion or religious belief. These changes followed earlier developments which widened the scope of sex and race discrimination law by making it unlawful for employers to discriminate against individuals even after they have left their job, for example in providing references to future employers.

Key Issues

Unfair dismissal is the termination of a worker's contract of employment without a legal reason. Legislation relating to unfair dismissal only relates to workers once they have been in a particular job for one year or more. There are a limited number of reasons why an employee might be dismissed:

- where a job no longer exists – this is redundancy
- gross misconduct – reasons for this include, for example, theft from the employer or behaving violently at work
- failing to carry out duties in 'a satisfactory manner'
- another substantial reason, e.g. the ending of a temporary contract.

All other reasons for dismissal are considered unfair. Employees who think they have been unfairly dismissed can claim compensation by taking their case to an industrial tribunal.

Collective labour law

This group of laws applies to the operation of industrial relations and collective bargaining as well as the activities of trade unions. For many years the law did not play a significant role in employer–employee relationships. However, this philosophy was changed when the Conservative governments of the 1980s and early 1990s passed a series of Acts intended to restrict the power of trade unions.

- The Employment Act 1980 states that employers are no longer obliged to negotiate with unions – many unions were derecognised as a consequence. It also restricted picketing to employees' own place of work, thereby outlawing 'secondary picketing'. Closed shops were only permitted if supported by at least 80 per cent of the workforce in a secret ballot.
- The Employment Act 1982 increased the support required for closed shops to 85 per cent to make their continuation legal. It also made trade unions liable for damages if the union supported illegal industrial action.
- The Trade Union Act 1984 made a secret ballot of employees a legal requirement before industrial action is lawful.
- The Employment Act 1988 protects union members from disciplinary action by their union for refusing to take part in strike action or picketing, despite a ballot in favour of industrial action.
- The Employment Act 1990 finally outlawed closed shops. Employees taking part in unofficial strike action could be dismissed without being able to make a claim of unfair dismissal.
- The Trade Union Reform and Employment Rights Act 1993 made it compulsory for unions to give employers a minimum of seven days' notice before taking official industrial action. It also abolished wages councils and minimum pay rates.
- The Employment Relations Act 2000 states that a trade union with a membership exceeding 50 per cent of the employees in any particular business can demand union recognition and the right to introduce collective bargaining.

Health and safety legislation

Health and safety legislation has been enacted to discourage dangerous practices by businesses and to protect the workforce. The legislation is designed to prevent accidents in the workplace, and has developed steadily over the last 30 years.

The main Act in the UK is the Health and Safety Act of 1974. This is an example of delegated legislation whereby Parliament gives responsibility to government departments to update the scope of the legislation as necessary. This process avoids any particular aspect of legislation taking up too much of Parliament's time.

The Health and Safety at Work Act gives employers a legal obligation 'to ensure that they safeguard all their employees' health, safety and welfare at work'. The Act covers a range of business activities including:

- the installation and maintenance of safety equipment and clothing
- the maintenance of workplace temperatures

- giving employees sufficient breaks during the working day
- providing protection against dangerous substances.

Businesses are required to protect the health and safety of their employees 'as far as it is reasonably practicable'. This means that the business concerned must have provided protection appropriate to the risks. Thus, a chemical manufacturer would be expected to provide considerable protection for its employees.

The Act also requires employees to follow all health and safety procedures and to take care of their own and others' safety. The Health and Safety Executive (HSE) oversees the operation of the Act and carries out inspections of businesses' premises. The HSE also carries out investigations following any serious workplace accident.

The impact of employment and health and safety legislation on businesses

It is easy to assume that employment legislation simply constrains business activities and therefore has a purely negative effect on businesses. However, this is not the case. Employment legislation can have positive and negative effects on businesses and their activities.

Employment legislation can help to motivate the workforce. Employees who work in a safe and secure physical environment will be more contented and probably more productive. Employers will also avoid the costs, delays and bad publicity caused by accidents at work or employee complaints about poor conditions. Furthermore, freedom from arbitrary dismissal may encourage a more cooperative, flexible and productive workforce, enhancing the performance of the business.

Employment legislation restricting the powers of trade unions has encouraged the development of more flexible workforces. The ending of closed shops and the requirement for union recognition in many circumstances made it easier for businesses to implement changes in working practices, improving the productivity and competitiveness of UK businesses. Firms were able to adopt single-union deals, making collective bargaining simpler and ending damaging and costly demarcation disputes (disputes between unions concerning the respective roles of their members in the organisation).

Following the legislation of the 1980s and 1990s, the UK has some of the most employer-friendly employment legislation in the western world. This has helped the country to attract the lion's share of foreign investment entering Europe. The UK is an attractive site for overseas businesses because its favourable employment legislation helps to minimise labour costs. The UK is the major recipient of inward investment into the European Union.

However, in spite of the employer-friendly approach in the UK, employment legislation does increase costs above the level that would exist if no legislation were in place. To take an example, the national minimum wage, introduced in 1999, raised the wages of an estimated 3 million employees. It is estimated to have added approximately 1 per cent to the nation's wage bill. Similarly, the requirement (under the Disability Discrimination Act) to make 'reasonable' alterations to the working environment to enable the employment of disabled employees adds to costs of production.

Employment legislation also requires firms to employ greater numbers of non-productive workers such as human resource managers and safety officers. These employees add to the costs of production without making any direct contribution to the output of the business. Inevitably, costs increase as a consequence.

The effects of legislation may be greater on small firms who have fewer resources and are less able to keep up with changes in employment laws and may not be able to afford to respond in the appropriate manner. Larger firms have expert human resource specialists and are more likely to be geared up for change. They may also be able to afford specialist employment lawyers to advise them on avoiding some of the effects of a new piece of employment legislation.

Consumer protection legislation

Key terms
Consumerism is an approach that places the interests of the consumer at the heart of discussions about business decisions or activities. This could be contrasted with trade unionism, which places the interests of workers first.
Consumer protection is a term used to describe a series of acts designed to safeguard consumers against:
- businesses charging excessively high prices or rates of interest
- unfair trading practices, for example selling quantities less than those advertised
- unsafe products such as children's toys with sharp objects or toxic paint
- having insufficient information on which to take purchasing decisions.

Since 1973 the Office of Fair Trading has overseen consumer protection in the UK. The OFT's Consumer Affairs Division seeks to improve the position of consumers by giving consumers information to allow them to make better choices when purchasing goods and services. It also protects consumers by prosecuting offenders against consumer legislation and negotiating voluntary codes of practice with producers.

Consumers in the UK have become more informed and less accepting of poor products or unscrupulous trading practices by businesses. Consumers often conduct research (aided by organisations such as *Which?*) before making major purchases. This trend is known as consumerism and is considered in detail below.

Key Issues

Consumerism is an organised movement that has developed steadily in the UK since the 1970s. Its objective is to persuade businesses to behave in more socially responsible ways and to consider the interests of consumers.

The consumer movement developed in response to a number of factors:

- the increasing technical complexity of products
- a better educated and informed general public
- the increasing market power of large businesses
- publicity given to unethical and socially irresponsible behaviour by companies, for example causing pollution.

The champion of the consumer movement is the Consumers' Association. This organisation publishes *Which?* magazine, giving reports of product testing and comparisons between brands. However, pressure groups such as Greenpeace and Friends of the Earth have encouraged the introduction of environmentally friendly products.

In recent years the pressures of consumerism have resulted in firms supplying lead-free petrol, aerosols without CFCs and foodstuffs free from genetically modified products. In more general terms, consumerism has forced firms to adopt safer and non-polluting methods of production and waste disposal.

There is a considerable quantity of consumer protection legislation in the UK. The acts listed below represent some of the highlights.

- Sale of Goods Act 1979 – the basic requirement of this act is that the goods sold should be:
  - of merchantable quality – must be undamaged and unbroken and must work properly
  - fit for the particular purpose
  - as described by the manufacturer.
- Consumer Protection Act 1987 – under this Act producers are liable for any harm to consumers caused by their products.
- Weights and Measures Act 1986 – this Act states the weights and measures to be used in trading. Weights and measures must be guaranteed in terms of accuracy.
- The Consumer Credit Act 1974 lays down that consumer credit can only be given by licensed organisations. It also sets out the terms under which credit may be given.
- Control of Advertising is necessary to protect the public from improper use of the power of advertising. It involves a combination of legal controls and self-regulation:
- The Trade Descriptions Act 1968 makes misleading descriptions of goods and services an offence.
- The Advertising Standards Authority supervises the operation of this code of practice. It is an independent body; its members are not in the advertising industry. The ASA protects the public interest and deals with complaints from the public.
- The Consumer Protection from Unfair Trading Regulations 2007, introduced from May 2008, specifically bans a number of practices which have been deemed to be unfair to the consumer. An example of a practice that is banned is aggressive selling by businesses. The Regulations have also amalgamated a lot of the consumer harms under previous legislation, such as Trade Descriptions Act 1968, as well as keeping pace with new scams which are continuously being evolved and developed by scammers and rogue sellers.

The impact of consumer protection legislation on businesses

Increases in the scope of consumer protection have had a number of implications for businesses. Meeting the requirements of consumer credit regulations, for example, entails additional processes and personnel, thereby increasing costs. Under this legislation, consumers expect firms to supply products that are safe and of consistently high quality. They expect the processes used in production to avoid any pollution, and raw materials to be from sustainable sources. All of these expectations mean that production costs are greater, partly owing to additional costs of materials and employing extra workers to carry out the necessary checks.

Consumerism has resulted in higher expectations on the part of consumers, in areas not necessarily covered by legislation. Consumers require firms to provide advice and technical support and effective after-sales service and to behave in a socially responsible manner.

Examiner's advice

It is easy to just think of laws as constraining business activity. Of course this is true, but legislation also offers opportunities to many businesses. For example, health and safety laws requiring firms to provide safety clothing and equipment provides sales for businesses supplying such equipment. Legislation requiring food products to have 'use by' dates created a small industry supplying specialised inkjet printers for use on production lines.

Environmental protection

The government has passed a series of Acts of Parliament designed to protect the environment. Two acts are of particular importance.

1 The Environmental Protection Act 1991 introduced the notion of integrated pollution control, recognising that to control only a single source of pollution is worthless as damage to one part of the environment means damage to it all. This Act requires businesses to minimise pollution as a whole.

2 The Environment Act 1995 established the Environment Agency with a brief of coordinating and overseeing environmental protection. The Act also covered the control of pollution, the conservation of the environment and made provision for restoring contaminated land and abandoned mines.

The government imposes fines on firms that breach

legislation relating to the protection of the environment. These are intended to force firms to bear the full costs of their production (including external costs), although environmental pressure groups and other critics believe that the sums are not sufficient to deter major businesses with budgets of billions of pounds annually. The government also attempts to encourage 'greener' methods of production through the provision of grants. The government has created

Business in Focus

Water company fined for pollution

At Ipswich Crown Court, Anglian Water was fined a total of £150,000 for allowing a sewage treatment plant to pollute drains on four occasions, and told to pay the Environment Agency's costs of £28,973.

The water company admitted offences relating to discharges of ammonia and improperly treated sewage from its works in Newmarket, Suffolk.

Four offences were considered by the court:

- In January 2006, the level of ammonia discharged from Newmarket Sewage Treatment Works was more than twice the level allowed.
- In July 2006, large amounts of improperly treated sewage were discharged into the Soham Lode waterway over a fifteen-hour period after a pump failed. Over the next 48 hours, 1,200 dead fish were removed from the river by Environment Agency officers and the public, according to the Agency.
- On 4 September 2006, waste water containing excessive amounts of ammonia was discharged into the public drain after a mechanism failed.
- In April 2008, sewage was discharged into the public drain.

Anglian Water was given fines of £40,000, £80,000 and £30,000 for the first three of these offences, and asked for the fourth to be taken into consideration in sentencing.

Source: Adapted from bbc.co.uk

Question:

1 Is a fine the most effective way of controlling pollution by large businesses such as Anglian Water plc?

the Carbon Trust which, since April 2001, has given capital grants to firms that invest in energy-saving technologies. The intention is to slow the onset of global warming by reducing emissions of carbon dioxide. In a similar vein, government funding is also supporting the development of environmentally friendly offshore wind farms to generate 'clean' electricity.

The EU has also passed hundreds of directives relating to environmental protection. The UK is also a signatory to a number of international agreements intended to provide environmental protection on a global scale. For example, the UK government has attended a number of Earth Summits at which targets for reducing the production of carbon dioxide have been agreed.

Strategic responses to changes in the political and legal environments

The political and legal environment can have a major impact on the way in which businesses operate and also their costs of production. Because of this, businesses may adopt a variety of strategies in response to changes in this aspect of their external environment.

- **Relocation**. If a government implements new legislation which increases costs or raises taxes, perhaps on company profits, businesses may respond by relocating to another country with more favourable corporate tax regimes and business laws.

- **Changing production methods.** This might be an appropriate response to changes in laws on environmental protection or to new employment laws. In the latter case a business might seek to reduce the number of employees in its workforce. However, such changes can be costly, especially in the short term. However, changing production methods to a more environmentally friendly approach may offer the business additional benefits in terms of improving corporate image.

- **Producing new products.** A new product range may be necessary to meet environmental laws. For example, furniture manufacturers may only use wood from sustainable sources and need to change the products they manufacture to meet this requirement. This strategy may also be necessary due to changes in the law. For example, many pubs have created outdoor smoking areas following a ban on smoking in public places in England from July 2007.

The precise strategic response taken by any business will depend upon a range of factors including the nature of the product that the business sells, the financial position of the business and the extent of the change in the political or legal environment. Changes in health and safety legislation, for example, are likely to have significant effects on businesses

Business in Focus

UK business taxes are unpopular

Over a quarter of businesses in the UK could be relocated due to unpopular tax policy, according to new reports. A study by Tenon Group found that 26 per cent of business owners are thinking about relocation due to the UK's high tax levels. The figure rose to 30 per cent for business owners who had previously experienced a recession.

Some 37 per cent of respondents admitted that high corporation tax (on company profits) was the primary reason for possible relocation, with 16 per cent citing capital gains tax as a cause.

Andrew Jupp, head of tax at Tenon, said:

'Entrepreneurs are genuinely struggling in the current legislative and economic environment and the government must heed this call for help in order to avoid losing some of the country's most talented business people.'

Source: GAAP web
http://www.gaapweb.com

Question:

1 What problems might a business experience when relocating to another country during a period of recession in the UK?

involved in construction, agriculture or manufacturing, but may be less significant for some businesses in the service sector.

Examiner's advice

The list of strategic responses above is not exhaustive – there are others that a business may adopt. It is important that you consider the possible responses in the context of the scenario with which you are presented. This will assist you in selecting and justifying the most appropriate response in any circumstances.

Progress questions

1 Outline the difficulties a government may encounter when attempting to achieve its economic objectives simultaneously. (7 marks)

2 Distinguish between monetary and fiscal policy. (4 marks)

3 Outline the possible effects of a fall in interest rates on a multinational business manufacturing consumer durables such as televisions and freezers. (8 marks)

4 Explain how a government might use fiscal policy to increase the level of economic activity. (7 marks)

5 Outline two supply-side policies that a government may use. (6 marks)

6 Explain two possible employment laws that might increase the costs of UK businesses. (4 marks)

7 How might UK health and safety legislation help to make a workforce more productive? (6 marks)

8 Outline two ways in which business activities might be constrained by consumer protection legislation. (6 marks)

9 Explain two ways in which employment legislation might make the UK a less attractive location for footloose multinationals. (6 marks)

10 Explain two implications for UK businesses of the implementation of the National Minimum Wage Act. (6 marks)

Analysis and evaluation questions

2 In 2004 the EU expanded significantly with the addition of ten new member states, mainly former communist countries from eastern Europe. In 2007 two further new members were admitted: Romania and Bulgaria. These states are diverse, with income levels far below those of western European states such as France, Germany and the UK. Production costs in the new member states are low: the average Polish hourly wage rate in 2006 was little more than 15 per cent of that in the UK.

a Analyse the effects of the expansion of the EU on a UK low-cost airline such as Ryanair. (10 marks)

b To what extent do you think that UK businesses in general will benefit from the expansion of the EU eastwards? (15 marks)

2 Cooper plc builds and maintains oil and gas rigs which are used by oil companies in the North Sea and other locations across the world. The company has an enviable safety record and puts great emphasis on the health and safety of all its employees. The company's financial director is critical of the legal environment in which UK companies operate. He believes that there are far too many laws which normally only add to costs of production. He argues that such legislation only disadvantages UK companies such as Coopers plc.

a Examine the ways in which health and safety legislation might affect Cooper plc. (10 marks)

b To what extent do you agree with view that UK and EU legislation always disadvantages businesses such as Coopers plc? (15 marks)

Case study

High street stores are hoping for a big cut in interest rates next week after figures showed that retail sales plunged this month with further falls forecast for the run-up to Christmas.

A survey released yesterday by the CBI showed that 62 per cent of firms reported lower sales in the first half of November compared with a year ago.

The CBI's survey balance slid to –46 this month, from –27 in October. The more negative the figure, the worse the picture. Analysts had predicted a deterioration to –35. The figure matched the reading in August, the lowest since records began in 1983.

Several retailers have released dire sales figures in the last week, with Woolworths and MFI entering administration and DSG, which owns Dixons and PC World, reporting its biggest ever loss. Sales at John Lewis were down 13 per cent.

Andy Clarke, chairman of the CBI's distributive trades panel and retail director of Asda, said: 'Christmas is going to be extremely tough this year, with retailers having to work harder than ever to keep the tills ringing. The added pressure of changing millions of prices, to reflect the cut in VAT, will be an unwelcome and costly burden.' He added that items such as consumer durables, furniture, carpets and DIY goods were being hit the hardest.

Most sectors linked with the housing market suffered a decline in sales and only footwear and leather goods showed any sales growth. There was also a big decline in sales volumes in the grocery sector, bringing two years of continuous growth to an abrupt end. Retailers' confidence in their sector remained especially weak, and 37 per cent expect the retail business situation to deteriorate over the next three months.

The CBI figures will put more pressure on the Bank of England's monetary policy committee to cut interest rates when it meets next week. It slashed 1.5 percentage points off rates earlier this month to leave them at 3 per cent. Economists have predicted that the MPC would now cut rates by at least another half point.

Source: The *Guardian*, 29 November 2008
http://www.guardian.co.uk
(40 marks, 60 minutes)

Questions

1 Explain, with the aid of examples, what is meant by the term 'monetary policy'. (4 marks)
2 Analyse how the government expected its cut in VAT (from 17.5 per cent to 15 per cent) to improve the economic environment for high street retailers. (8 marks)
3 Evaluate the other economic policy decisions the UK government could take to try to improve the economic position of high street retailers. (12 marks)
4 Discuss the actions that major high street retailers might take in response to this economic environment and the government's policy decisions. (15 marks)

21 Businesses and the social environment

Businesses are a part of society and are affected to varying extents by social change. The factors arising from changes in society vary and, at the time of writing, factors such as migration and the increasing need to protect employment may be argued to be important social factors affecting the activities of businesses. The chapter also considers the ethical behaviour of businesses. This has become a more important influence on the activities of businesses over time, and represents a distinctive USP for a number of organisations.

In this chapter we examine:

- social responsibility and changes in the social environment
- the ethical environment and developments that have taken place
- how businesses respond to changes in the social environment.

Introduction

Stakeholders are individuals or groups within society that have an interest in an organisation's operation and performance. Stakeholders include shareholders, employees, customers, suppliers, creditors and the local community. The interest that stakeholders have in a business will vary according to the nature of the group.

Over recent years businesses have become much more aware of the expectations of stakeholder groups. In the past managers were expected to operate businesses largely in the interest of the shareholders. A growing awareness of business activities and the rise of consumerism has complicated the task of the management team. Today's managers have to attempt to meet the conflicting demands of a number of stakeholder groups.

Social responsibility

Social responsibility is a business philosophy that emphasises that firms should behave as good citizens. They should not merely operate within the law, but should consider the effects of their activities on society as a whole. Thus, a socially responsible business attempts to fulfil the duties that it has towards its employees, customers and other interested parties.

Collectively these individuals and groups are termed a business's stakeholders.

It is difficult to meet the demands of all these stakeholders simultaneously. For example, paying employees higher wages may reduce the dividend paid to shareholders.

Meeting social responsibilities has many implications for businesses, including:

- taking into account the impact of their activities on the local community – protecting employment and avoiding noise pollution, for instance
- producing in a way that avoids pollution or the reckless use of finite resources
- treating employees fairly and not simply meeting the demands of employment legislation
- considering the likely sources of supplies (and

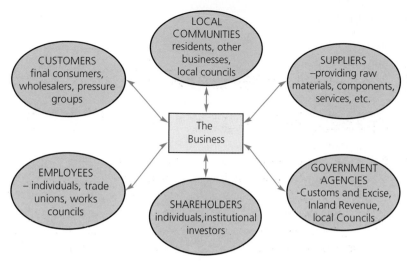

Figure 21.1 Examples of a business's stakeholders

whether they are sustainable) and the ways in which suppliers meet their social responsibilities.

Some businesses willingly accept these responsibilities, partly because their managers want to do so, partly because they fear a negative public image. It can be argued that socially responsible behaviour can pay off for businesses in the long term, but may entail additional short-term expenditure.

Examiner's advice

Figure 21.1 shows the primary stakeholders for businesses, although others exist. When writing about stakeholders it is important to develop answers fully. This is impossible if you attempt to cover too many stakeholder groups – just concentrate on a few.

Stakeholder group	Possible nature of stakeholder's interest
Shareholders	• Expectation of regular dividends • Rising share prices • Preferential treatment as customers – for example lower prices
Employees	• Steady and regular income • Healthy and safe working conditions • Job security • Promotion and higher incomes
Customers	• Certain and reliable supply of goods • Stable prices • Safe products • After-sales service and technical support
Suppliers	• Frequent and regular orders • A sole supplier agreement • Fair prices
Creditors	• Repayment of money owed at agreed date • High returns on investments • Minimal risk of failure to repay money owed
The local community	• Steady employment • Minimal pollution and noise • Provision of facilities (e.g. scholarships, arts centres or reclaimed areas) for local community

Table 21.1 Stakeholders' interests

Areas of social responsibility

The nature of a business's social responsibility will vary according to the nature of the business. A petro-chemicals company is more likely to be concerned with polluting the environment than a bank. On the other hand, in an age of rapid developments in information technology, banks may see their social responsibility to be the maintenance of employment. We can identify a number of key elements of social responsibility beyond the responsibilities a business has to its shareholders.

1 **Responsibilities to consumers**. The consumer has become a force to be reckoned with over recent decades and this has been reflected in the development of consumerism. Increasingly consumers have been better informed about products and services and prepared to complain when businesses let them down. The rise of consumerism has meant that businesses have been required to behave more responsibly by looking after the interests of the consumer.

2 **Responsibilities to employees**. Businesses have a variety of responsibilities to their employees that are not a legal requirement. For example, firms should provide their employees with training to develop their skills as fully as possible and make sure that the rights of employees in developing countries (where employment legislation may not exist) are protected fully. This may mean paying higher wages and incurring additional employment costs.

3 **Responsibilities to the local community**. Firms can benefit from the goodwill of the local community. They can encourage this by meeting their responsibilities to this particular stakeholder group. This may entail providing secure employment, using local suppliers whenever possible and ensuring that the business's operation and possible expansion does not damage the local environment.

4 **Responsibilities to customers**. Customers are critical to businesses. Offering high-quality customer service, supplying high-quality products that are well designed and durable and at fair and reasonable prices should create satisfied customers and quite possibly generate repeat business.

5 **Responsibilities to suppliers**. Businesses can promote good relations with suppliers by paying promptly, placing regular orders and offering long-term contracts for supply. These are not legal requirements, and might result in higher prices for materials and components, but may also assist suppliers to meet their own responsibilities, for example in the maintenance of employment.

Business and social responsibilities

Stakeholder and shareholder concepts

The importance of social responsibility to businesses is a matter of considerable debate. Businesses accept the need to make a profit for their owners and the need to operate within the law. More contentious is the expectation that a competitive business will take into account the obligations it may have to society in general. This is known as the stakeholder concept whereby a business considers the needs of its stakeholders – and not just its shareholders.

In spite of the growing popularity of the stakeholder concept, there are opponents to the philosophy. A school of thought exists that supports what is known as the shareholder concept. This view advocates the management of businesses to meet their responsibilities to shareholders by maximising profits. This should result in increasing share prices and higher dividend payments. The needs of other stakeholders are regarded as of secondary importance.

In what ways can businesses accept their social responsibilities?

Businesses can take a variety of decisions and actions allowing them to meet their responsibilities to their stakeholders in general.

- For manufacturing businesses the impact of their sources of supply can be considerable. Using sustainable sources for resources means that future generations will have access to the same materials. Body Shop International's refusal to use any materials that are unsustainable or any components that have been tested on animals reflects a sense of responsibility to many relatively poor communities in developing countries and to animals.

- Many manufacturers have considerable potential to pollute the environment. Altering production processes (sometimes at considerable cost) can reduce or eliminate many forms of pollution. A report by the Environment Agency stated that Southern Water was one of the worst polluters in the UK and that its poor record had resulted in

Business in Focus

Shell fined over pollution

Shell UK Oil Products Ltd has been fined £18,000 by Grimsby Magistrates' Court for polluting the groundwaters close to its Toothill Petrol Filling Station at Yarborough Road, Grimsby.

The cost of cleaning up the underground contamination, which has been paid by Shell to Anglian Water, is estimated to be about £5 million, the court was told on Wednesday (25 June 2008). The company was also ordered to pay £53,198 Environment Agency costs.

Magistrates were told that the pollution happened between January and May 2000 when unleaded petrol was lost from an underground petrol storage tank into a major aquifer, known as the Flamborough Chalk, underlying the Grimsby area.

Source: The Environment Agency
http://www.environment-agency.gov.uk

Question:

1   Is it the fine or the fear of adverse publicity that is more likely to influence Shell's actions?

fines of £73,000. In response Southern Water announced a £540 million investment programme to improve its environmental performance.

- Socially responsible firms put employees before profits. Maintaining employment, even when the level of sales is not sufficient to justify this, is an important means of fulfilling social responsibilities, as is the continuation of unprofitable factories to avoid creating unemployment blackspots. These types of policies are only really sustainable in the short term, unless the business in question is earning handsome profits elsewhere.
- Choosing suppliers is an increasingly important issue for firms that are keen to confirm that their raw materials and components come from socially responsible firms. Many firms operate a code of conduct for suppliers, including restaurant chain McDonald's. The fast-food company operates a code of conduct prohibiting suppliers from using

child labour and insisting upon basic health and safety standards. The company has a contractual right to inspect suppliers' premises to ensure the code of conduct is implemented.

- Supporting the local community is an important way of fulfilling social responsibilities. It can provide the public with a clear perception of the 'caring' side of modern businesses. BT, one of the largest telecommunications companies in the world, received an award for its support of the children's charity, Childline. BT donated £1 for every customer who signed up to the company's 1571 call minder service. This action improved the company's reputation and increased sales of the 1571 service by 25 per cent.
- Over 70 per cent of the UK's best-known companies (those making up the FTSE 100) are members of Business in the Community. This organisation exists to assist member companies in 'continually improving, measuring and reporting the impact that their business has on their environment, workplace, marketplace and community'. However, the state of the economy can influence the level of charitable donations given by businesses. In 2008 charities reported that corporate donation had declined by 20 per cent.

Environmental threats and opportunities

The media take a great interest in business activities in relation to the environment. When firms are found to be guilty of some act of pollution adverse publicity is likely to follow. Society expects higher standards of environmental performance than in the past.

There are many potential causes of damage to the environment. The major environmental concern identified by the government is global warming. This is caused by the release of a concoction of industrial gases (principally carbon dioxide) that has formed a layer around the earth. This layer allows the sun's rays in but prevents heat escaping, causing the so-called 'greenhouse effect'. Other problems include the pollution of rivers and land and the dumping of waste, some of which is toxic and harmful to wildlife and humans alike.

Businesses contribute in many ways to the creation of environmental damage.

- The emission of gas through production processes pollutes the atmosphere.
- Pollution is caused by transporting raw materials and products, particularly using road vehicles which emit noxious gases and create congestion

and noise. A report by the EU suggested that pollution from vehicles in the UK could be responsible for up to 40,000 deaths among elderly people each year.

- The sea is polluted by businesses using it as a 'free' dumping ground. The North Sea is one of the most polluted stretches of water in the world.
- Natural environments are destroyed as a result of activities such as logging (cutting down trees for commercial purposes, as in the Amazon rainforest) and building homes on greenfield sites.

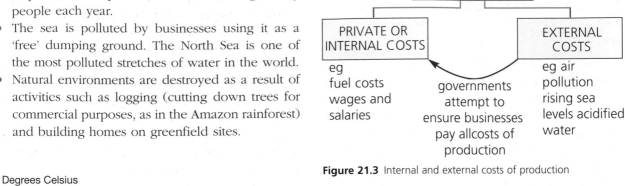

Figure 21.3 Internal and external costs of production

Costs of polluting the environment

Businesses are acutely aware of their private costs, i.e. the costs of production they have to pay themselves, such as expenses for raw materials and wages. These are easy to calculate and form part of the assessment of profitability. However, environmental pressure groups and others have pressed for businesses to acknowledge the costs they create for other groups in society – the external costs of production.

Noise, congestion, air and water pollution all impose costs on other individuals and groups in society. A firm extracting gravel from a quarry may create a number of external costs. These could include congestion on local roads caused by their lorries. This would impose costs in terms of delay and noise pollution on local residents. The destruction of land caused by the quarrying could create an eyesore for people living nearby and may reduce the value of their properties. Dust may be discharged into the atmosphere. The quarrying firm will not automatically pay for these costs. It requires government action to ensure that they pay these external costs as well as their internal ones.

Thus, the total costs of production equal internal or private costs plus external costs borne by third parties. By ensuring that firms pay all the costs associated with the production of a product, governments can avoid what is termed market failure. Market failure could occur as a result of pollution because suppliers may not be charged the full costs of production and oversupply might result, as profits are high.

Degrees Celsius

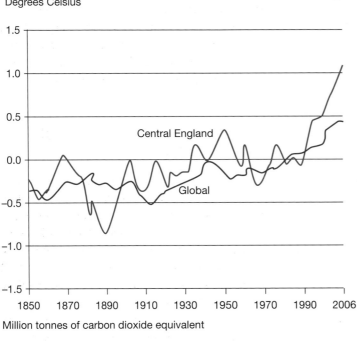

Million tonnes of carbon dioxide equivalent

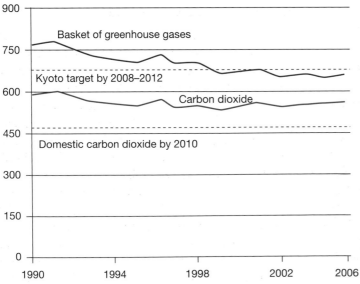

Figure 21.2 Global warming and gas emissions
Source: Social Trends, 2008
http://www.statistics.gov.uk

Implications of environmental control for businesses

The need to alter business practice to take account of environmental protection has implications for most aspects of business activity.

- **Production**. Firms face pressure to redesign products to use less materials and packaging and to make these materials biodegradable or recyclable. These requirements affect all types of businesses. For example, house builders are under great pressure to build on brownfield sites (land previously used for building, often in cities and towns) and to protect the countryside by minimising the use of greenfield sites. Strict controls on production techniques are intended to minimise pollution.
- **Purchasing**. Businesses are encouraged to seek sources of supply that are sustainable and do not damage the environment and to use recycled materials. For example, the paper industry makes a great deal of use of recycled materials and uses this as part of its promotion.
- **Marketing**. Businesses use their 'green credentials' as an important component of their marketing strategy. Adverts will make reference to environmental protection and even projects to improve the environment. Packaging will confirm the company's concern to avoid pollution. This is particularly important to firms that are seen to have great potential to pollute (BP and Shell, for example) or for those who use this aspect of their operations as a USP – Body Shop International is an example of the latter.
- **Human resources**. New processes and procedures in manufacturing make some jobs and skills obsolete, creating a need for redundancies or retraining. Environmental management has resulted in many businesses needing employees with new skills requiring a retraining programme or recruitment. Environmental managers seek to minimise the effects of the business's activities on the environment and to ensure that the firm meets new legislative requirements as they emerge. Businesses may also seek to hire employees skilled in resource management and having the ability to influence corporate decisions to ensure the development of management strategies designed for the most efficient use of scarce natural resources.

The implications of environmental protection are profound, especially for the so-called polluting sector (e.g. chemicals and oil extraction and refining). They require a corporate response from senior managers within a business. But as with many external influences the environment provides opportunities for businesses as well as constraints.

New markets have been created for businesses supplying training in environmental management. Firms also offer to supply environmental control equipment to adapt production processes to minimise the possibility of environmental harm. Equally, a market exists for testing equipment to monitor emissions or the toxicity of waste products. Finally, businesses can use environmental policies as a means of obtaining a competitive advantage. BMW, for example, promotes itself as a manufacturer of cars that are almost entirely recyclable. This could prove attractive to environmentally aware consumers.

Why should businesses accept social responsibilities?

It is easy to argue that by meeting their social responsibilities businesses are likely to reduce profitability. Providing workers with ongoing training, investing in facilities for the local community, trading with suppliers who do not use cheap child labour and only engaging in non-polluting production techniques will all increase costs, reducing a business's profitability and limiting its international competitiveness.

However, this is a relatively simple view and there are more subtle arguments in favour of businesses fulfilling their obligations to society.

- Some businesses have a high profile with regard to issues of social responsibility. Thus, the public sees Shell and BP as having enormous potential to pollute. The directors of these companies have recognised this and regard socially responsible behaviour as an important competitive weapon. As an example, Shell supports education and produces much valuable material for use in schools and colleges. In particular the company gives information on environmental matters. Clearly both Shell and BP hope that being seen to be socially responsible will improve their sales.
- Sometimes behaving in a socially responsible manner may reduce costs. Treating employees with respect and paying slightly above the going rate may improve motivation and performance and reduce labour turnover. For businesses where labour represents a high proportion of total costs

(banking and insurance, for example) this could represent an important saving.

- In markets where little product differentiation occurs, adopting a socially responsible stance may improve sales and profits. The Co-operative Bank is alone in the banking sector in promoting its ethical and socially responsible views. In recent years its profits have risen significantly.

It may be that social responsibility might reduce profits in the short term, but over a longer timescale the marketing advantages may dominate and profits could increase.

Corporate social reports

Key term

Corporate Social Reports (CSRs) are documents setting out a business's targets for meeting its social obligations and the extent to which previous social targets have been achieved.

Increasingly analysts are not assessing businesses solely in terms of profits. It can be argued that businesses should also be judged in terms of their records on pollution, consideration of their employees and support for the community. A proportion of businesses are engaging in social responsibility reporting. This form of reporting includes the costs to the business of acting in a socially responsible manner (charitable donations, for example) and the benefits received, which are usually difficult to quantify in monetary terms. A few businesses include their social reports within their annual reports. A 'successful' business might not be the most profitable, but the one of most value to all sections of the community in which it operates.

The trend to social and environmental reports continues with most of the UK's largest firms producing some form of social and environmental report. However, the quality of the reports is improving, though some do not cover all the relevant issues. Many companies do not have their Corporate Social Reports (CSRs) independently audited to confirm their accuracy. A further criticism is that some firms do not analyse their supply chains. This means that suppliers could engage in practices such as employing children without it being revealed in the CSR. It is possible that the impact of the recession from 2008 might reduce the number of businesses prepared to devote resources to producing a CSR, or to improving its quality and extent.

Business in Focus

Diageo is the UK's most admired company

Drinks company Diageo has made it to the top of the 'Most Admired Companies' list – just as the Government launches a new assault on the binge drinking culture. The company, which makes Christmas favourites Bailey's and Archers, has been pushed to the top of a table published by *Management Today*, knocking troubled retailer Marks & Spencer off the top spot and out of the top ten altogether.

Matthew Gwyther, editor of *Management Today*, described this year's list as 'a particularly brutal game of snakes and ladders', with many traditional entrants falling out of favour due to difficult economic conditions.

Last year's list contained three leading retailers, Sainsbury, Tesco and M&S. This year, only Tesco remains in the top ten, and it has been pushed from second place to number five. Britain's biggest retailer has topped the list a record six times in the past.

'There have been catastrophic reversals of fortune for companies such as M&S and surprise appearances for corporate tortoises-turned-hares, Diageo and Unilever,' Mr Gwyther said.

The list is decided by peer reviews within company sectors and investment analysts, which were completed this summer. Experts were asked to score the company's quality of marketing, ability to attract, retain and develop talent and quality of goods and services. Awards were given for each of these criteria, with the company with the highest overall score topping the list.

Source: The *Daily Telegraph*, 1 December 2008
http://www.telegraph.co.uk

Question:

1 Should the management teams at Sainsbury, Tesco and Marks & Spencer pay any attention to the results of this survey?

Business in Focus

Extracts from Morrisons corporate social report

Morrisons is the UK's fourth-largest food retailer and publicises that it takes its responsibilities to the environment and society in which it operates very seriously. The company is large and has:

- 375 stores throughout the UK
- 10 million customers visiting its shops each week
- 117,000 staff.

Below are the social targets that Morrisons achieved as part of its corporate social responsibility programme.

CSR Programme 2007
Key highlights

- We have cut our emissions by saving 115,718 tonnes of carbon.
- We include our own supply chain – produce packing, food production, bakeries and meat processing – in our Carbon Footprint, to benefit from our carbon emissions reduction strategy.
- 5% reduction in Group energy use, with over 110,000 colleagues trained in energy awareness.
- Reduced the amount of packaging we use for own-brand products by 7 per cent.
- Cut carrier bag use by over 110 million.
- New 'Recyclopedia' packaging labelling campaign.
- All fresh fish counters certified under the Marine Stewardship Council (MSC) Chain of Custody traceability programme.
- 100% British fresh beef, pork, lamb and chicken
- 100% of own-brand tissue paper products certified by the Forest Stewardship Council (FSC).
- Values workshops for over 1,000 colleagues.
- £1.23 million raised for our Charity of the Year, Asthma UK.

Source: Morrisons Corporate Social Report, 2008
http://www.morrisons.co.uk

Question:

1 What competitive benefits might Morrisons receive from publishing a CSR each year?

The changing social environment

At any time there are a number of factors of work that promote change in the social environment in which businesses work and require socially responsible businesses to respond in certain ways. Current issues may include the following.

The increasing threat of unemployment

The onset of the recession in the UK in 2008 was accompanied by a significant rise in the level of unemployment. By December 2008 the number of people unemployed in the UK had risen to over 1.8 million, the highest level for more than ten years. This posed a challenge for businesses seeking to act in a socially responsible manner and to protect employment. At a time when sales were falling along with profit margins, it would have been a brave decision to maintain employment levels within a business when an improvement in the economic situation appeared to be some way off.

The increasing importance of the environment

Many UK consumers are increasingly aware of, and concerned by, the threat that the activities of businesses pose to the environment. This concern has manifested itself in two main ways. Some people have protested against the activities of businesses such as airlines, which are deemed to be responsible for substantial amounts of pollution. For example, in 2008 protesters blockaded Stansted Airport as a protest against the negative environmental impact of aviation. Their actions received much publicity. This can result in affected businesses receiving adverse publicity and may have negative effects on sales. Other businesses whose activities are considered to be damaging to the environment may experience falling sales and revenues.

Business in Focus

Renault is going for gold ready for 2012

An electric commuter car is on the way from Renault, and the company is working flat-out to have it ready for the London 2012 Olympics. The eco-vehicle will rely on battery power and be charged up overnight. And it will be a bespoke machine, designed and engineered from the ground up to run solely on electricity.

Patrick Pelata, Renault's director of product planning, said: 'If we are ready, the new all-electric car could be launched in time for the London Olympics. We are maximising things to aim for then, and the car would be sold from that point onwards. Because of the high tax rates in the UK, this would be a valuable market for us.' Pelata hinted the car – likely to be similar in size to the Twingo – could come with two different sizes of battery. Owners could use a smaller, lighter unit for weekday journeys, then easily swap to long-range cells for weekends.

'We are considering renting out the battery with a monthly payment scheme. There would be a higher payment to charge it in the middle of the day, a lower one at night,' he added.

Renault's strategy on all-electric transport currently involves two other vehicles. A version of the next Mégane, set to debut at October's Paris Motor Show, is being developed for the Israeli market. Due to be launched in 2011, it will be powered by solar panels fitted to the roof of the owner's house. And the firm is also working on an electric Kangoo for use by commercial fleets in mainland Europe.

Source: *Auto Express News*, 23 April 2008
http://www.autoexpress.co.uk

Question:

1 What risks might Renault be taking in responding to a change in the social environment in such a positive manner?

Changes in the composition of the UK population

The UK is subject to large migrationary flows. There have been substantial inflows of migrants from parts of Asia and also eastern Europe leading to the UK's population size passing 60 million, and the rate of increase is the highest since the 1960s. This has led to a demand for different types of products (as well as offering new sources of labour supply). It is estimated that more than 1 million people from Poland alone have come to live in the UK since that country became a member of the EU in 2004. This development has led to a new market niche and suppliers of Polish products such as foods and books have appeared. It is not just small businesses that have responded to the creation of this niche market. In May 2008 Tesco launched a Polish language website to enable it to supply homesick Polish migrants in the UK with products from 'home'.

The UK's ageing population

The population of the UK is steadily ageing, with larger numbers of people in the older age groups. In 2005, 34 per cent of the UK's population (20 million people) was over 50. In 2025 it will be 40 per cent (about 25.5 million people). In 2005 16 per cent of UK citizens were over 65 – that is expected to rise to 21 per cent in 2025, as many as 13.5 million people. There are expected to be 4.5 million people in the UK aged over 85 in 2025. Figure 21.4 illustrates the main trends in the age structure of the UK's population until 2041.

The older age groups represent substantial segments of markets for many products, and businesses have responded to the increased spending power of older groups. Firms supplying products including holidays, clothes, insurance and housing have designed products for the older age group.

UK's ageing population
Projected population by age (millions)

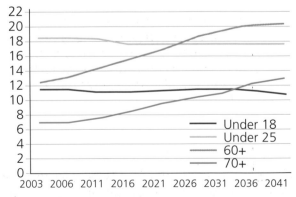

Figure 21.4 The age structure of the UK's population 2003–2041
Source: Government Actuary's Department, from bbc.co.uk

	2003	2026	Average annual increase
Under 25	226,000	254,000	1,000
25–34	797,000	1,048,000	11,000
35–44	923,000	1,460,000	23,000
45–54	834,000	1,415,000	25,000
55–64	947,000	1,792,000	37,000
65–74	1,061,000	1,559,000	22,000
75 and over	1,659,000	2,359,000	30,000
Total	**6,447,000**	**9,886,000**	**150,000**

Table 21.2 **One-person households by age in the UK, 2003–2026**
Source: News Distribution Service
http://nds.coi.gov.uk

The rise in the number of single-person households

People in the UK are increasingly living alone, meaning that the country is comprised of more, smaller households. This has significant implications for businesses of all types. Table 21.2 illustrates how the number of single-person households in the UK is expected to rise until 2026. This trend has implications for businesses supplying houses, consumer durables and even food where smaller packet sizes may be more commonly purchased.

Examiner's advice

The above is only a small selection of ways in which society is changing. It may be that new factors will emerge during your course of study and you should consider the implications that these have for businesses and how they may respond.

Business ethics

Business ethics can provide moral guidelines for decision-making by organisations. An ethical decision means doing what is morally right; it is not a matter of merely calculating the costs and benefits associated with a decision. Individuals' ethical values vary. Ethical values are shaped by a number of factors, including the values and norms of parents or guardians, those of religion, and the values of the society in which a person lives and works. Most actions and activities in the business world have an ethical dimension.

What are ethical decisions?

Ethical behaviour requires businesses to operate within certain moral guidelines and to do 'the right thing' when taking decisions. What exactly is ethical behaviour? This is a tricky question. An ethical decision would take into account the moral dimension, but not everyone would agree what is ethical. Some may argue that it is not ethically wrong for supermarkets to charge high prices for basic foodstuffs; others would disagree. Different moral values make a decision as to whether a business is behaving ethically a tricky one to reach.

The following scenarios arguably illustrate examples of diverse businesses taking moral decisions.

- Starbucks, the world's largest coffee retailer, has donated £100,000 to a development programme run by the UK charity Oxfam in the East Hararge region of Ethiopia. In this region farmers struggle to produce high-quality Arabica coffee because of

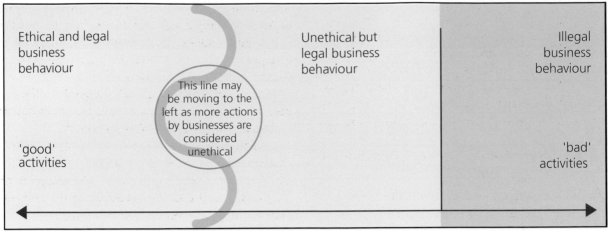

Ethical and legal business behaviour	Unethical but legal business behaviour	Illegal business behaviour

This line may be moving to the left as more actions by businesses are considered unethical

'good' activities

'bad' activities

Business activities

Figure 21.5 Legal and ethical behaviour

poverty and a hostile climate. The money will be spent on improving irrigation as well as providing seeds and tools. Starbucks experts will also offer advice on improving coffee yields and quality, and on strengthening the growers' marketing cooperative. Starbucks and Oxfam also plan to pool ideas on alleviating rural poverty in Ethiopia.

- Primark, the high street discount retailer, sources much of its clothing in Bangladesh. The company regularly conducts unannounced inspections of its suppliers' factories. Primark pays for these audits and provides training for its suppliers' employees.
- A Work Study Foundation report complimented McDonald's, the fast food chain, for creating jobs in deprived areas within the UK. The report also noted that many of McDonald's managers worked their way up within the company and, when initially recruited, had few qualifications.

Each of these decisions could be judged to be financially disadvantageous to the business in question. It is therefore possible to argue that they have been taken because the businesses believe that it is the morally correct course of action. However, some may contend that there are 'hidden' commercial benefits from each of the decisions.

Business in Focus

Google – an ethical customer

Google hasn't even celebrated its 10th birthday yet, and it's already one of the most influential companies in the technology industry. From the beginning, however, Google has been dedicated to conducting business responsibly and reducing its impact on the environment. The most prominent example is Google.org, the company's philanthropic arm, which is committed to using the power of information and technology to address some of the world's most challenging problems: Climate change, poverty, disasters and disease. As of January 2008, the organisation had already committed over $75 million in investments and grants around the world. Google encourages its staff to become involved in these efforts at all levels and routinely communicates the importance of ethics and compliance to its employees. Additionally, Google is working with a group of other companies, NGOs and academics to help develop a global code of conduct for how to deal with governments that suppress free expression and privacy. As Andy Hinton, Google's global ethics and compliance officer, puts it, 'World-class technology is only the tip of the iceberg at Google. Google wants to change the world for the better in very fundamental ways. That's part of what makes us a "different" kind of company.'

Source: Ethisphere website
http://ethisphere.com

Question:

1 Why might it have been easier for a relatively new business, such as Google, to operate ethically throughout the organisation?

Ethical codes of practice

As a response to consumer expectations and, in many cases, competitive pressures businesses have introduced ethical codes of practice. By 2008 over 85 per cent of the UK's major businesses (the FTSE 100) operated an ethical code of practice. They are intended to improve the behaviour and image of a business.

Common themes in ethical codes of practice may include:

- promoting products with integrity and honesty
- minimising possible damage to the environment by, for example, using sustainable sources of raw materials
- competing fairly and avoiding collusion or other anti-competitive practices
- taking into account the needs of the business's stakeholders.

An ethical code of practice states how a business believes its employees should respond to situations that might challenge the values of the business. The first part of an ethical code of practice sets out the values in which the business believes.

The nature of the code will depend on the business concerned. Banks may concentrate on honesty, and chemical firms on pollution control.

Companies normally publicise ethical codes of practice, as in the case of the pharmaceutical company AstraZeneca plc below. The company produces its ethical code of behaviour in 47 languages. Many companies believe that being seen to behave ethically is an important element of the marketing strategy of many businesses.

Ethics and profits

A conventional view is that if a business behaves ethically, its profits are bound to suffer. Any of the following ethical actions is likely to increase costs of production and possibly reduce profits:

- using more expensive resources (perhaps recycled or from sustainable sources)
- training employees to behave in an ethical manner
- treating animals with respect
- implementing safety systems beyond the legal requirements

However, the argument is not as simple as it might appear at first.

The Co-operative Bank is an example of a business that has its ethical stance as a central part of its marketing strategy. The Bank's ethical position is unique within the UK's financial sector and has resulted in an improved performance by the business. In 2008, despite the problems facing the UK and international banking industry, the Co-operative Bank posted pre-tax profit of £46.2 million for the 28 weeks to 26 July, up from £45.5 million in the same period of 2007. A large proportion of the bank's customers came from the prosperous A and B social classes who hold substantial (and profitable) balances with it. A survey showed that 89 per cent of the Co-operative Bank's staff are proud to work for the organisation.

This example highlights that there are marketing advantages from being seen to behave ethically. Businesses may attract new customers and (as in the case of the Co-operative Bank) customers with more money to spend. A reputation for ethical behaviour can provide a business with a USP (unique selling

Business in Focus

AstraZeneca plc

We continue to widely communicate our policies and standards to employees worldwide to ensure awareness and understanding of our commitments.

Listed here are our Group codes, policies and principles that are relevant to our corporate responsibility.

These are supported by internal standards and guidelines that help our people to understand the detail of what our high-level commitments mean in practice.

Everyone at AstraZeneca is required to be aware of, and conduct their activities in accordance with our Code of Conduct and all supporting policies and applicable codes, and the laws and regulations of the countries in which we work and do business. Our commitment includes operating to the highest of the standards required by these various authorities. Managers are responsible for promoting awareness and supervising compliance by their teams, and for providing assurance on these matters to the AstraZeneca Board.

Source: AstraZeneca website
http://www.astrazeneca.com

point). This can be particularly valuable when products provided by rivals are similar, and may explain some of the success of the Co-operative Bank's approach. A positive corporate image may also assist businesses by allowing them to charge higher prices and enjoy increased profits on each sale.

Benefits also exist in terms of recruiting the best employees. A business that is successful and has a good reputation is attractive to potential employees. High-calibre employees may be recruited in these circumstances and valuable employees will be less likely to leave. Ethical behaviour can help to develop a talented workforce.

However, a high-profile ethical stance is not a guarantee of profits. For example, Body Shop, despite its strong ethical stance characterised by its opposition to testing products on animals, experienced several years of financial problems before it was purchased by L'Oréal in 2006.

Businesses introducing ethical practices for the first time may face other costs leading to reduced profits. Training is an obvious cost – for a company to be ethical all employees must carry out their everyday activities in the right ways. Firms may also need to spend heavily on adapting production processes to reduce the possibility of pollution. These factors make it probable that profits will be lower, at least in the short run.

Changing views towards ethical behaviour

A series of accidents and incidents during the 1980s and 1990s fuelled a call for businesses to behave in more ethical ways and to introduce morality into decision-making. Serious accidents such as the leaking of toxic gas from Union Carbide's plant in Bhopal, India in 1984 (an estimated 7,000 died and 500,000 were injured) and the sinking in 1987 of P&O's *Herald of Free Enterprise* outside Zeebrugge harbour leading to the loss of 194 lives, led to criticisms of business practice. Firms were viewed as more interested in profits than in behaving in a responsible manner. The air of mistrust deepened with a series of business scandals, including the fraudulent use of the Mirror Group's Pension Fund by Robert Maxwell.

The call for a more moral approach to business was reinforced by the report of the Cadbury Committee in 1992. A key recommendation of the committee was to strengthen the role of non-executive directors in the hope that they would ensure greater morality in corporate decision-making. Non-executive directors do not take an active role in the management of the company and are well placed to control unethical and undesirable practices.

Since that time many businesses have recognised that standards expected of businesses have risen and that a clear competitive advantage can be gained from adopting an ethical stance. In 2008, 85 of the FTSE 100 companies operated an ethical code. And the ethical approach was not limited to large firms. A Mori survey showed that in 2003 less than half the population (48 per cent) believed that British business behaved very or fairly ethically; by 2006, that figure had risen to 58 per cent. Those who believed British business behaved not very or at all ethically fell from 41 per cent in 2003 to less than a third (32 per cent) in 2006.

Some businesses have adopted highly ethical stances and have publicised their change of strategy. For other companies, developing an ethical approach has required the creation of a unique selling point in markets containing many similar businesses selling undifferentiated products.

Creating an ethical business culture

An ethical business culture exists when all employees in a business behave in a moral manner as a normal part of their working lives. This offers businesses a number of advantages in terms of marketing, particularly in relation to corporate image. Furthermore, businesses with a reputation for ethical behaviour may be more successful in attracting high-quality employees.

However, although senior managers may appreciate the benefits of changing the corporate culture to enable the adoption of an ethical stance, it may be less apparent to employees further down the organisational hierarchy.

The first issue to be resolved is the introduction of an ethical policy into the organisation. The Institute of Business Ethics offers advice to managers seeking to make this change. This information is highlighted as follows.

Six key stages in implementing an ethical culture within a business:

1 Find a champion – make sure that the change has the public support of the Chief Executive.
2 Discover the issues – discover the ethical issues employees are likely to encounter.
3 Benchmarking – look at the policies introduced by other firms and copy good practice.

4 Test the idea – try out the new approach on a small part of the business first. This will help to iron out teething problems.

5 Code of conduct – issue this to everyone to make sure that all employees, suppliers and interested parties are aware of what is expected of them when taking decisions.

6 Make it work – ethical elements should be introduced into training programmes and especially into induction programmes.

Some businesses have enjoyed great success in developing ethical values within their organisations. Texas Instruments (better known as TI) took the approach of ensuring the organisation behaved ethically by encouraging each individual employee to be ethical in all aspects of their work. This extended to issuing individual employees with cards offering advice on what to do when faced with ethical dilemmas and identifying more senior staff able to offer support.

Introducing ethical approaches and codes of conduct can conflict with existing policies. In some senses a democratically led organisation with high-quality, two-way communication lends itself to implementing change. Such an organisation might be more responsive to a new culture, although there is potential for conflict in a business managed in this way. First, in a democratically managed business employees are unlikely to respond well to a new culture imposed upon them without consultation. Indeed, they may wish to play a substantial role in shaping the new culture, which might conflict with the objectives of the senior managers.

Second, in an organisation with a high degree of delegation employees take responsibility for some decisions and may, if empowered, have considerable responsibility for controlling their daily work. Imposing a new and uniform culture in such an environment may prove difficult. Employees may resent any loss of independence in how they conduct their working lives. This can be a tricky dilemma for even the most highly skilled managers.

Is ethical behaviour simply another form of PR?

Certainly businesses would like to be perceived as more ethical. There is little doubt that some businesses have adopted a more ethical stance that is genuine. Companies such as Body Shop and the Co-operative Bank have based much of their marketing on their strong moral principles. This can prove to be a profitable decision as well as a moral one. Ethics is seen as good business by many firms at a time when a more informed public demands moral behaviour from firms.

The danger for businesses adopting token ethical stances is that the attentions of the media and pressure groups might reveal the superficial nature of their principles. This could be a public relations nightmare causing substantial damage to the business's public image and profits. However, for firms in the tertiary sector, the temptation to pay lip service to ethical behaviour may prove irresistible.

For many firms however, the decision regarding their ethical position will depend upon an assessment of the potential costs and benefits. If the costs of ethical behaviour exceed the benefits, a superficial adoption of moral principles is the most likely outcome. However, if a commercial advantage can be gained without incurring too many additional costs, then a complete change of corporate philosophy might result.

Responses to changing social and ethical environments

We have already identified a number of strategies that businesses might adopt in response to changes in the social and ethical environments, notably developing an ethical culture to persuade consumers of the strong moral principles underlying the business. There are other actions that businesses can adopt in response to changes in the social and ethical environment.

- **Adopting new techniques of production**. This may entail using sustainable resources, or reducing carbon emissions that are the by-product of the production process. In contrast, it could mean using different resources in production, perhaps, for example, relying heavily on migrant labour. As we saw earlier, such decisions are likely to increase production costs but can form the basis of a distinctive marketing campaign.

- **Developing a new corporate image**. This may involve publicising genuine actions that the business has taken to meet the needs of its stakeholders more fully or to operate throughout the organisation in the most ethical fashion. In part this may require the business to implement an ethical code of conduct and to train its employees. Alternatively, it may be based on a marketing campaign to change stakeholders' perceptions of the business. As we saw above it may depend upon the extent to which the ethical stance is genuine.

- **Developing a new product range or entering new markets**. The ageing of the UK's population, for example, may mean that house builders adjust their product ranges to build more bungalows and developments including sheltered housing. The growing size of the market may persuade holiday companies to provide products aimed at the 50+ age group. Other businesses may decide to target all their products at this age group.

The precise strategic response taken by any business will depend upon a range of factors, including the strength of the competition that the business faces, the financial position of the business and the type and extent of the change in the social or ethical environment. Businesses may be most likely to react strategically to changes that they believe to be long term. Thus the fashion among many consumers towards thrift in 2008 may prove to be short term and not worthy of developing new product ranges.

Examiner's advice

The list of strategic responses above is not exhaustive – there are others that a business may adopt. It is important that you consider the possible responses in the context of the scenario with which you are presented. This will assist you in selecting and justifying the most appropriate response in any circumstances.

Progress questions

1 What is meant by the term 'social responsibility'? (3 marks)
2 Identify the interests that consumers and employees may have in a business. Why might these interests clash? (7 marks)
3 Outline the responsibilities that a retailer such as Tesco might have to its suppliers. (7 marks)
4 Explain two advantages that a business may receive from operating in a socially responsible manner. (6 marks)
5 Explain the possible ways in which a multina-

tional manufacturing business might fulfil its social responsibilities. (7 marks)
6 Outline the possible reasons why the business in question 5 might want to fulfil its social responsibilities. (7 marks)
7 Explain the differences between a business that operates legally and one that operates ethically. (6 marks)
8 What difficulties might a large multinational business face when trying to implement an ethical code of conduct? (8 marks)
9 Explain why ethical behaviour by businesses is increasingly important as a competitive weapon. (8 marks)
10 What factors might prevent an ethical business from being highly profitable? (6 marks)

Analysis and evaluation questions

1 BudgetFly has enjoyed a remarkable ten-year trading period. The company has seen its passenger numbers rise from 20,000 in 1998 to nearly 30 million by 2008. The company flies numerous routes within the UK and throughout Europe. It has plans to introduce low-cost flights to the United States and Canada.

The company's profits have dipped in recent months, partly due to falling sales as consumers have cut spending in the face of the recession and the falling value of the pound. The company is operating with very tight profit margins as it competes with easyJet and Ryanair. It has also received criticism for its contribution to damaging the environment.

a Analyse social factors that may affect a low-cost airline based in the UK, such as BudgetFly, over the next few years. (10 marks)
b To what extent do you think it is essential for BudgetFly to be seen to be a socially responsible business? (15 marks)
2 Rickshaw Graves is an investment company that promotes itself as being strongly ethical. The company employs 50 analysts and administrators in its offices in London, and is small in comparison with many of its rivals. It refuses to invest any funds in businesses that

damage the environment, produce weapons or military equipment, or exploit less developed countries. It charges higher than average commission and fees for its services. An article in a financial journal was highly critical of the company's ethical stance. It concluded that Rickshaw Graves was certain to be less successful than its competitors as it could not invest in all businesses.

a Examine the reason why Rickshaw Graves might have decided on a policy of ethical investment. (10 marks)

b To what extent do you agree with view that Rickshaw Graves is certain to be less successful than its competitors? (15 marks)

Case study

Wal-Mart Stores Inc's chief executive said he sees changes in the habits of the chain's customers as they contend with the recession, and also said Wal-Mart had offered to help the government with health care and environmental issues. Wal-Mart is the world's largest retailer with operations throughout the world. Wal-Mart achieved sales of just over £260,000 million in 2007 and in 2008 has 1.2 million employees worldwide. It owns Asda in the UK.

The company has been criticised in the past for paying more attention to profits than to its social responsibilities. Despite having a highly publicised code of ethical conduct, the company has been subject to much criticism for the allegedly unethical actions of some of its senior employees.

'The number one issue today is (consumers') concern about their job,' Lee Scott said on NBC's 'Meet the Press'. 'In our pharmacy group, we have increases in prescription drugs, but not at the same rate it was,' he said. 'What we're seeing is an increase in self-treatment.'

Strained consumers are also changing the food they buy at Wal-Mart, Scott said. 'We're seeing an increase in food storage as people are cooking more at home,' he said. They are 'using leftovers more extensively' and buying more frozen food.

Small businesses are also changing how they buy goods, he said. Cash-strapped restaurant owners are visiting the stores more frequently to buy supplies as one day's cash flow allows them to buy supplies for the following day.

Scott, who will retire in early 2009, also said he sees a role for Wal-Mart in the debate around issues such as the environment and health care, which he has previously said 'profoundly' affect the chain's shoppers and business.

Wal-Mart has 'reached out' to President-elect Obama's team to work on the US health care and energy issues, he said, adding that people critical of Wal-Mart's involvement in political debates were 'on the wrong track'.

'These are not times to be self-serving,' he said. 'We have a responsibility to participate.'

Source: Adapted from STV.TV
http://news.stv.tv
(40 marks, 60 minutes)

Questions

1 Explain, with the aid of examples, what is meant by 'unethical actions'. (6 marks)

2 Analyse the social responsibilities that Wal-Mart might have during a period of recession. (8 marks)

3 To what extent is it impossible for a business the size of Wal-Mart to implement an ethical code of conduct successfully. (11 marks)

4 Discuss the case for and against Wal-Mart's apparent decision to become more socially responsible. (15 marks)

22 Businesses and the technological and competitive environment

The chapter commences by considering changes in the technological environment and the ways in which this can affect the products that businesses and consumers require and the production process itself. This chapter also considers the factors that cause change in the competitive environment in which businesses trade. This is strongly influenced by topics we have already considered, such as globalisation and the emergence of economies such as China. As with all the chapters looking at external causes of change, they should be seen as creating opportunities as well as posing threats.

In this chapter we examine:

- the factors that cause technological change
- the competitive environment and developments that have taken place
- how businesses respond to changes in the technological and competitive environment.

Technological change

In the eighteenth century, news of technological developments spread at the rate of one mile per year. In the first few years of the twenty-first century people and businesses throughout the world learn quickly of technological changes, and the rate of technological progress is increasingly rapidly. The last few years have seen a number of technological advances having significant implications for businesses. The internet has probably been the biggest single technological factor leading to change in business behaviour, but other sources of technological change such as bio-technology are also having and will continue to have substantial effects on business behaviour.

Technology and marketing opportunities

Technological advances have created new markets for new products and new ways to sell them.

Technology and new products

New technology can open up new markets for businesses. In 1990 mobile telephones were unheard of by most people. By November 2007 there were an estimated 3,300 million in use across the world. Companies such as Nokia and Vodafone have grown as a consequence of the developments in this field of communications technology. Markets for MP3 players, satellite navigation systems and laptop computers have been created as a consequence of technological advances. Today they are multi-billion pound markets selling products to millions of consumers. Smaller, niche businesses have also developed, based on technological products, and we consider two very different examples below.

- Tesco takes on X factor – Tesco is investing in a new product called 1Click2Fame. Recording booths will be set up in Tesco stores to allow aspiring celebrities to perform song and dance numbers. The results will be shown on the internet and the winner will win £100,000. Tesco and its backers believe that this product will attract 10,000 entrants and the mobile booths will move from store to store to make it as widely available as possible.

- Glasses to help correct the vision of the world's poorest people – Professor Josh Silver of Oxford University has used simple technology involving fluids, syringes and special hollow lenses to create glasses that wearers can adjust themselves to correct their own vision. This removes the need for specialist advice from an optometrist. Over 30,000 pairs of the spectacles have already been distributed to people in low-income countries, enabling wearers to continue working and to lead normal lives. However, Silver is ambitious for his project and not to make money, but to help the needy. He wants to distribute 100 million pairs of spectacles annually. He is negotiating with various interested parties to make his vision a reality.

Using technology in the products themselves, rather than in the production process, also offers great advantages to businesses. Firms possessing a technological lead over rival producers are frequently able to charge a high price for their products – at least until the competition catches up. This technique of price skimming is likely to boost profits. Possessing a technological edge may attract new customers to a business. Toyota's Prius hybrid car offered environmentally aware consumers the chance to buy a vehicle that switched off its petrol engine at low speeds and used a self-charging electric motor in its place. Toyota's hybrid car was the first on the market and recognised to be of high quality. The company had a waiting list for this product despite its premium price.

Technology and promoting and selling products

One of the world's largest businesses – the Microsoft Corporation – has developed alongside the technological revolution in software and computing. Microsoft has benefited from technology in terms of being able to develop new products but also from using technology to promote and market its products. Technological advances have allowed the company to produce new products such as its software and gaming equipment (e.g. the X-box) as well as providing a means to promote and sell its products online as consumers can download the company's software at any time.

It also has used technology as a basis for product development and to encourage consumer loyalty. Microsoft's Office product (Word, Excel etc.) is designed to be used with its Windows operating system but is also highly compatible with the company's internet browser (Explorer). Thus technology has offered the company the opportunity to develop and sell a suite of products, rather than a single one.

Business in Focus

Amazon

Amazon was started by Jeff Bezos in a garage in California in 1994 and started selling on the internet in 1995. The company, which is now the world's largest online retailer, is based in Seattle in America and is nearly three times larger than its nearest online retail competitor. In 2007 Amazon made a profit of £435 million on sales of £9,800 million. It employs 17,000 people worldwide.

Amazon started as an online bookstore, but soon diversified to product lines of VHS videos, DVDs, music CDs, MP3 format music, computer software, video games, electronics, furniture, food, toys etc. The company has negotiated deals with companies such as 'Toys 'R Us' to enable it to supply more bulky items.

Amazon has established separate websites in Canada, the United Kingdom, Germany, France, China and Japan. The company was unprofitable for many years as Jeff Bezos continually cut the company's prices to increase market share. The increasing scale of the business enabled it to negotiate better prices with suppliers and to pass these on to customers in the form of lower prices. In this way the business expanded rapidly.

The company relies heavily on technology to operate its business. It uses the latest technology in its huge warehouses and its website incorporates technology which allows potential customers to browse selected pages of books. Finally the company uses technology to keep records of individual consumers' purchases, allowing it to target its marketing of new products and also to offer a service of acting as a market should its customers wish to sell their books once they have read them.

Other businesses rely entirely on technology to distribute their products. Apple is famous for producing innovative technological products, but the company also uses technology to distribute its products. Its iTunes store allows purchasers to download music, music videos, television shows, applications, iPod games, audio books, various podcasts, feature length films and movie rentals. It is also used to download applications for the iPhone and iPod touch.

Using technology in this way offers substantial cost advantages. Apple does not have to pay to distribute its products nor does it have to pay retailers commission on each sale. This increases the company's profit margin and increases its flexibility in pricing decisions. The company also receives marketing benefits in that it can easily collect large amounts of data about its customers and their preferences, enabling it to target its future marketing effectively.

Technology and production processes

Technology and communications

Technological advances also affect the ways in which businesses operate. Communications within businesses have been transformed by technology. Businesses can communicate simply, cheaply and (most importantly) quickly across the globe. Developments such as video conferencing have allowed employees in a business to see and talk with one another while at different locations.

This offers considerable benefits in terms of use of time and reduction of costs to multinational businesses, or even those operating more than a single site in the UK. Similarly, email allows employees and organisations to communicate immediately and messages can be sent to many recipients at the same time.

The development of extranets has created closer links between businesses, helping to improve efficiency. Companies like the giant American retailer Wal-Mart share sales data through an extranet with suppliers such as Proctor & Gamble, to enable production and deliveries to match demand in the stores. Wal-Mart estimates that this improved its stock control enormously when introduced and saves it $2 billion in costs each year.

Technology and production

New technology offers a range of benefits to businesses and consumers. Perhaps the major advantage of technology to businesses is that it allows the development of new methods of production resulting in lower costs. This permits the firm to enjoy higher profits on each sale. However, in an increasingly competitive global market firms seek to improve their market position by offering high-quality and sophisticated products at low prices. Using ever-more sophisticated technology in planning and producing products is one way of achieving lower costs.

Figure 22.1 Computer-aided manufacture at Vauxhall's factory at Ellesmere Port

The process of manufacturing in many industries has been transformed by automation, whereby machines do jobs previously carried out by people. The most dramatic aspect of this has been use of computer-controlled technology on the production line. The use of computer-controlled technology is an integral part of lean production. Its use allows businesses to control the production line to supply variants on a standard product to meet the precise demands of consumers. Thus Vauxhall's car factory at Ellesmere Port uses computer-aided manufacturing systems to produce different colours and styles of cars in succession in response to customers' orders. This is part of the company's JIT (or 'pull') manufacturing system.

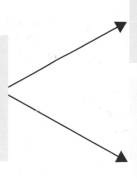

CAD
Computer-aided design – this allowsdesigners to produce new products and components using 3-D models displayed on computer screens. CAD makes it easy to develop and redraw designs.

CAPP
Computer-aided process planning –identifies the most efficient ways inwhich to manufacture products.

CAM
Computer-aided manufacture –computers are used to operate robotsand other machines on the productionline. Linking CAD and CAM allows newdesigns to be accommodated quicklyinto the production process. CAM canalso be used to order raw materialsand

Figure 22.2 Computer-aided design, computer-aided manufacture and computer-aided process planning

Business in Focus

Virtual design at Boeing

Before the first 787 Dreamliner rolled out of the Boeing factory in 2008, designers at the American aeroplane manufacturer, Boeing, created a virtual aeroplane to test and check their ideas before production of the aeroplane started.

Using a French software system, the American designers assembled an entire virtual Boeing 787 Dreamliner to check that the several hundred thousand parts that make up the airliner fitted together. Every component will have been modelled in 3D geometry, milled and shaped on digital machine tools, assembled several times in virtual factories, and maintained by people who have 'crawled' into digital equipment bays. Any parts that did not meet tough standards were redesigned to overcome problems.

The benefits of this approach were seen when the first Dreamliner was built: the model was assembled with few difficulties occurring. The costs of this process were also much cheaper than the traditional technique of actually constructing a prototype airliner to discover the potential problems.

The use of CAD and CAM has assisted in improving productivity levels in many manufacturing industries, helping to keep costs down and enhance productivity. Because of this its use has spread to many industries including food processing and the manufacture of pottery.

Technology in not only used in production processes in the manufacturing sector. It is also widely used by businesses that supply services. For example, companies such as Aviva (formerly Norwich Union) supply insurance policies using the internet. Policyholders enter their requirements onto the company's website and complete their personal details. Aviva's technology computes the price and deducts the appropriate sum from the customer's credit card before downloading the policy to the customer's computer. The whole production process is based on technology.

Technology and human relations

Humans within businesses are always affected by technological change. This is particularly true when new technology is introduced onto the production line. Such changes may simply lead to some minor changes in the duties of employees, or they can result in enormous changes for a business's workforce. For some it may be redundancy: replaced by technology as part of the process of automation. Many high street banks have made workers redundant owing to advances in technology. Other employees may be required to undertake duties dramatically different from those with which they are familiar as a result of the increasing use of technology, for example in the banking sector.

Employees' reactions to technological change can be equally diverse. For some employees it may represent an opportunity. They may have a chance to acquire new skills, to make their jobs more secure and enjoy higher incomes. The new working prac-

Business in Focus

The internet

The internet links computers across the world, allowing communication and increasing commercial activities to be conducted electronically between users worldwide. It originated on 30 October 1969 when a small team of researchers headed by computer scientist Leonard Kleinrock at the University of California transmitted the first message between networked computers. In 2008 it was estimated that nearly 22 per cent of the world's population were using the internet – approximately 1.46 billion people.

The original uses of the internet were for electronic mail (email) and for transferring files of data between computers. The development of the World Wide Web, enabling navigation of internet sites, expanded dramatically during the 1990s to become the most important component of the internet. By 2008, 65 per cent of UK households had access to the internet at home.

The commercial possibilities of the internet have been exploited by many businesses. E-tailing (selling products on the internet) has become increasingly important to a range of retailers. In 2008 John Lewis announced that sales on its website exceeded those achieved by its flagship store on Oxford Street in London. By 2010 it is forecast that annual online spending in the UK will amount to £39,000 million.

tices may offer great benefits. Technology can allow employees greater control over their working lives, leading to increased responsibility and the possibility of achievement. This can result in greater motivation.

Others may fear technological change as it increases job insecurity. This is likely to be true of those with few skills carrying out tasks that may be easily automated. Fear of unemployment may lead to industrial action as workers seek to protect their jobs. In such circumstances the introduction of new technology may be awkward and expensive. Redundancy payments may be expensive and corporate images may suffer.

New technology-based products create jobs and

Business in Focus

Google's culture

Though growing rapidly, Google still maintains a small-company feel. At the Googleplex headquarters almost everyone eats in the Google café (known as 'Charlie's Place'), sitting at whatever table has an opening and enjoying conversations with Googlers from all different departments. Topics range from the trivial to the technical, and whether the discussion is about computer games or encryption or ad serving software, it's not surprising to hear someone say, 'That's a product I helped develop before I came to Google.'

Google's emphasis on innovation and commitment to cost containment means each employee is a hands-on contributor. There's little in the way of corporate hierarchy and everyone wears several hats. The international webmaster who creates Google's holiday logos spent a week translating the entire site into Korean. The chief operations engineer is also a licensed neurosurgeon. Because everyone realises they are an equally important part of Google's success, no one hesitates to skate over a corporate officer during roller hockey.

Google's hiring policy is aggressively non-discriminatory and favours ability over experience. The result is a staff that reflects the global audience the search engine serves. Google has offices around the globe and Google engineering centres are recruiting local talent in locations from Zurich to Bangalore. Dozens of languages are spoken by Google staffers, from Turkish to Telugu. When not at work, Googlers pursue interests from cross-country cycling to wine tasting, from flying to frisbee. As Google expands its development team, it continues to look for those who share an obsessive commitment to creating search perfection and having a great time doing it.

Source: Google's corporate website
http://www.google.com/corporate/culture.html

Question:

1 In what ways does Google's culture assist the business in embracing technological change?

unemployment at the same time. For example, automated telephone switchboards have resulted in a loss of jobs for telephonists. Direct dial numbers and electronic answering systems have made telephonists obsolete in many firms. Simultaneously, employment has been created in industries manufacturing and maintaining the automatic telephone systems.

The reaction of employees to technological change may depend upon the culture of the business. Businesses operating with a traditional culture that places great emphasis on bureaucracy and convention may experience difficulties in adapting to technological change. The existence of a task culture may make the process less difficult. It may be most appropriate if the managers of businesses that are affected by technological change develop a culture that is responsive to change and one where employees' attitudes are to embrace change rather than to resist it.

Threats and technological change

However, technological change can be threatening as well as providing opportunities for businesses. The impact of technological change has been profound on one of the UK's most familiar organisations: the Royal Mail. In the first half of the 2008–09 financial year the company saw its volume of business fall by 4 per cent as its average daily postbag declined by 5 million letters each day. The major reason for this change is increasing competition from email and digital delivery of information. Royal Mail expects the volume of letters it handles to decline at 7 per cent per annum over the next few years. The company has estimated that the decline in its volume of business has reduced its operating profit by $500 million annually.

The threats of rapid changes in technology are considerable. Firms in high-technology markets will face demands to research new products and to implement more efficient methods of production. Thus, commercial pressures may exist to improve technology used in products and processes. New technology, in whatever form, can be a major drain on an organisation's financial resources. Installing new technology on the production line will involve a heavy capital outlay and disruption to production while the work is completed. Thus, a business may lose sales revenue at the time its expenditure rises significantly. Some firms may experience difficulty in raising the funds necessary to purchase new tech-

nology. Costs of research and development can be huge and many years may pass before any return is received on them.

Businesses operating in markets experiencing rapidly changing technology can be left behind – or find it too expensive to keep up with other producers. Small firms can be particularly vulnerable even if they are well managed. This is one factor leading to mergers and takeovers in markets supplying high-technology products. The series of mergers and takeovers in the world car manufacturing market has been brought about, in part, by the

Business in Focus

Shopping firm jobs under threat

Up to 280 jobs with a shopping company are under threat at seven locations. Shop Direct Group Ltd said it was moving from mail order towards online and the way it dealt with customers had changed.

It said about 278 staff were being offered other shifts or the chance to 'up-skill', but if this was rejected, they would face compulsory redundancy. Jobs are at risk at Worcester, Bolton, Preston, Burnley, Sunderland, Crosby in Merseyside and Newtown, Powys. Up to 65 jobs are under threat at Worcester, but the firm had not said how many jobs were at risk at the other six sites. The firm has had nine shopping brands, including Littlewoods and Littlewoods Direct.

Since 2005 online sales had increased from 18 per cent of products sold online to more than 50 per cent now, the company said. This figure was expected to rise to at least 70 per cent of total sales by 2011, it added.

The company said it would soon start a formal consultation with workers and was working with trade unions and the management team. Group chief executive Mark Newton-Jones said: 'We have seen a progressive change in the way customers engage with our contact centres. As a result, we need to re-align our resources to meet changing customer demand.'

Source: Adapted from bbc.co.uk

Question:

1 How might Shop Direct Group Ltd have lessened the impact of this change on the business through planning?

high costs of developing new products and especially environmentally friendly ones. Sir Alex Trotman, the former chief executive of Ford, has forecast that the global market for car manufacture will eventually comprise three large companies, and the extent of investment in technology is one factor driving this change.

New production methods do not always work effectively from the start. Some teething problems are inevitable following the introduction of state of the art technology onto production lines. Workers will take time to adapt to what is required of them and the technology may not behave as expected. This may result in lower levels of productivity and higher production costs.

Changes in the competitive environment

> **Key terms**
>
> The function of the **Competition Commission** is to monitor proposed mergers and to prevent monopolies operating against the public interest.
>
> In theory, a **monopoly** is the only supplier of a particular product. The law considers a firm with 25 per cent or more of a market to be a monopoly.
>
> **The Office of Fair Trading** is a government organisation established to ensure that firms are complying with relevant legislation.
>
> **Restrictive practices** are actions by producers preventing the free-working of markets.

A business's competitive environment is made up of a number of factors. It includes the power of rivals and the potential rivals that the business faces in a battle to win customers and market share, but it also includes its customers and its suppliers and the influence they wield. The competitive environment faced by a business can change in a number of ways.

New competitors

The arrival of a new business into a market poses an obvious threat to existing firms. A new business is likely to take at least some customers from the firms already trading on the market and this becomes more likely if the market is not growing. In this case the only way a new business can gain sales is at the expense of businesses that are already trading. Such a situation is a 'zero-sum' game in that the total number of customers lost and gained must total zero.

Business in Focus

Watch out Nike!

College student Li Aihua wears his tattered, grungy Li Ning basketball sneakers with pride.

'Li Ning is our Olympic gymnast and his brand is China's most famous so I like to support them,' the student at the South China Agricultural University said, sitting in Guangzhou's chic Shangxiajiu shopping area.

Li Ning, the company founded by the Chinese gymnast who won three gold medals at the 1984 Los Angeles Games, and other sportswear makers such as Anta, China Hongxing and Kangwei still lag global giants Nike and Adidas. But they are catching up fast.

'They understand the Chinese market better than international players, and their prices are lower,' said Rui Wu, an analyst at JP Morgan. 'Li Ning is definitely the market leader because it started earlier than the others.'

In 2006, Nike controlled roughly 16.7 per cent of China's sportswear market, compared with Adidas's 15.6 per cent, ZOU Marketing says. Li Ning claimed third place with a 10.5 per cent slice, and Anta fourth with 4 per cent, but those figures are climbing as aggressive marketing lifts their brand recognition.

Some foreign investors have seen the writing on the wall. Houston Rockets owner Les Alexander, who provided a home for basketball superstar Yao Ming (China's top sports celebrity) invested $30 million for a stake in Anta, which raised $406 million in its Hong Kong IPO last year.

In 2006 Li Ning struck a five-year $1.25 million deal with US basketball celebrity Shaquille O'Neal. It also has sponsorship deals with US National Basketball Association (NBA) stars Damon Jones and Chuck Hayes.

Source: Reuters website, 21 February 2008
http://www.reuters.com

Question:

1 Why does the emergence of Li Ning represent a significant change in the competitive environment of companies such as Nike and Adidas?

The extent of the change in the competitive environment will depend upon the scale of the new competitor, and whether its products will be appealing to customers in the market. A large business that is diversifying into a new market may pose a major threat to established producers, especially if its product is differentiated. In contrast, a small business seeking to gain a foothold in a small segment or niche of the market may hardly represent a change in the competitive environment. In November 2008 the global mobile phone manufacturer announced over 600 job losses as it cut back its production. One reason for this, the company admitted, was competition from Apple and its successful iPhone.

Dominant businesses

A dominant business is able to have a substantial influence over market prices and in some cases may determine them with other, less powerful firms, following its lead. A dominant firm is likely to be the largest in an industry and to hold the greatest market share. As a consequence it will probably be highly profitable, though it may not be highly efficient and innovative, especially if its supremacy is not immediately challenged.

Dominant businesses may emerge through internal or organic growth as in the case of Microsoft. Other firms may achieve dominant positions in their markets as a result of a strategy of takeovers and mergers. It is this approach that Vodafone has used to create its market power.

A famous example of a dominant business is Microsoft. Microsoft was established by Bill Gates in 1975 and operates in a number of markets, including computer hardware (the Microsoft mouse), home entertainment (X-box) and cable television (it has its own American channel). However, it is in the global computer software market that the company is dominant. Its Windows operating systems and Microsoft Office suite of products are sold in every country in the world. The company has been estimated to have over 90 per cent of the world's computer software market.

Business in Focus

Competition policy

Competition policy is intended to create free and fair competition within markets in the UK and throughout the European Union. The aim is to provide consumers with quality products at a fair price, allowing producers the opportunity to earn reasonable profits. Unfair competition can arise in a number of ways.

- Monopolies can abuse their power and exploit consumers by charging high prices and supplying outdated products. In 2006 Tesco was investigated by the Competition Commission over alleged abuses of its monopoly position in the UK grocery market.
- Mergers and takeovers can create monopolies with the power to exploit consumers. In 2000, in a famous ruling, the Competition Commission rejected the proposed takeover of Manchester United Football Club by BSkyB. The main reason given was that this takeover would prevent television rights to football being sold in a free and fair market.

- Restrictive practices exist when businesses interfere with the free operation of markets. Restrictive practices may take the form of producers making agreements to share out a particular market between them or forcing retailers to stock all of a firm's products by threatening to withdraw all supplies. Such practices make markets less competitive.

The UK's approach to competition policy is described as 'pragmatic'. This means that the authorities do not believe automatically that monopolies or mergers are damaging and anti-competitive. Each case is investigated and a decision is taken on whether the monopoly or mergers is 'against the public interest'. Only if it is judged to be so will any action be taken. Restrictive practices are viewed differently: they are considered to be against the public interest unless the firms concerned can prove otherwise.

Coca-Cola too dominant in China?

The Chinese authorities have announced that they are reviewing Coca Cola's bid to buy Chinese juice company Huiyan.

US drinks giant Coca Cola is attempting to take over the Chinese firm in a $2.5 billion (£1.4 billion) bid.

The bid by Coca-Cola has caused public anger in China over the possible move of a well-known national business into foreign ownership.

Coca Cola is a globally recognised brand and the company is keen to increase its presence in the country's fast-growing drinks market.

It agreed to pay 12.20 Hong Kong dollars per share - about three times the firm's closing price last Friday - for Huiyan, because of the firm's market share.

Huiyan had a 44% share by sales value of the Chinese market for pure juice, and 42% for nectar in the first half of 2008 (data from AC Nielsen).

A spokesperson for Huiyan said that Coca Cola was preparing the documents to send to Beijing competition authorities.

'We are prepared to accept the decision of the Ministry of Commerce one way or the other,' said Matthew Mouw, vice president for strategic development at Huiyan.

Source: Adapted from bbc.co.uk

Question:

1 Why might the Chinese authorities oppose this takeover bid?

If a business is becoming more dominant in a market this represents a threat for its competitors. The growing power of a single business may lead to its rivals losing sales and market share and a decline in profitability. The dominant business's competitors may have to invest in new products, new marketing campaigns and cut prices to protect their market positions. This may become increasingly difficult to do if the dominant business uses its market power ruthlessly to increase its power within the market.

Changes in buying power of customers

The major feature of the competitive environment for some businesses is the scale and power of their customers. An increase in the power of a single large buyer can pose difficulties for a business, particularly if it is relatively small and the dominant customer purchases a large proportion of its output.

In such circumstances the change in the competi-

Supermarkets and suppliers

At last, it is said, competition watchdogs have found the 'smoking gun' they have spent years hunting for: hard evidence that the big supermarkets use their muscle to bully suppliers and extract unreasonable price cuts.

The Competition Commission, which is nearing the end of its third full-scale inquiry into the grocery business in seven years, last week ordered Asda and Tesco to hand over millions of emails sent and received over a five-week period in June and July. They leapt into action after unearthing email evidence that the big two supermarkets had been threatening suppliers and demanding cash payments to finance this summer's round of supermarket price wars. The emails, it is understood, employed 'threatening language'.

The grocers, naturally, are denying any such wrongdoing. Tesco responded in typically robust fashion, denying the claims and accusing the competition authorities of making 'prejudicial' allegations. Asda insists there has been some horrible mistake and is certain that it will be exonerated.

Suppliers' lobby groups claim the big chains can squeeze suppliers until their financial viability is in doubt. But they have provided no hard evidence to show how this is done. The supermarkets say this proves there is no problem, but the suppliers' lobby groups say simply that they are so frightened of being delisted – having their goods taken from the grocers' shelves and contracts not renewed – that they dare not complain.

Source: The *Guardian*, 25 August 2007
http://www.guardian.co.uk

Question:

1 What benefits might small suppliers receive from dealing with large supermarket chains?

tive environment could have a range of adverse consequences for the business.

- The customer will have increased bargaining power and may be able to negotiate substantial reductions in the price at which products are supplied. The customer may use the threat of transferring to another supplier to achieve its ambitions. Being forced to sell at lower prices could reduce, or in extreme cases eliminate, the supplier's profit margins.
- Customers may request changes in the specifications of products to be supplied or may impose tough conditions in terms of delivery dates or the quality or appearance of products. Such outcomes are likely to put the supplier under pressure and to increase costs of production. Once again the ultimate effect could be to reduce profits.
- A dominant customer may ask for generous trade credit terms. Thus the customer may request a 60-day trade credit period. This can cause liquidity problems for suppliers, not least because the size of the order will mean that the sums involved are substantial. In such circumstances the supplier may have to negotiate expensive overdrafts with its bank.

Most of the UK's large supermarkets have come under a great deal of criticism for the way they deal with their suppliers. The 'Business in Focus' on page 324 considers this is more detail.

Changes in selling power of suppliers

In contrast to dominant customers, some businesses find that a major influence on the competitive environment in which they trade is the power of their suppliers. Powerful suppliers who hold a dominant position in a market have control over prices and this power is increased if the product they sell has few or no substitutes.

The implications for businesses can be severe, especially if the supplier provides a large percentage of the resources used by the business. In this event, a policy of increasing prices as the supplier's market power increases can squeeze the business's profit margins.

In 2007 and 2008 many small businesses in the UK complained about the actions of their energy suppliers. The UK's largest gas supplier, British Gas, received the largest number of complaints about poor customer service and its pricing policies, according to a survey by Energywatch.

Responding to changes in the technological and competitive environments

Changes in the technical and competitive environments provide opportunities as well as posing threats. A business may respond to a change in the technical environment by embracing the change. If it is a technical change in relation to the products the industry supplies a business may attempt to be a market leader and to supply the most technologically advanced products possible. This offers benefits in terms of developing a valued brand image and making demand for products less price elastic, or less sensitive to price changes as the products become more desirable. Such an approach may boost profits.

Equally, a business may adopt the most up-to-date technology in its production processes. This can permit a highly efficient service and can reduce costs. In either case the performance of the business may be enhanced. Budget airlines such as easyJet use technology which allows them to adjust their online prices if a surge in demand occurs. Thus, if a particular flight is proving popular the company's website technology responds to this by raising prices to improve profit margins in the face of increasing demand.

An alternative approach may be to emphasise the traditional element of a business's products. This involves operating in a niche market to attract consumers who wish to avoid some aspects of the technological age in which we live. So some pubs present themselves as refuges from the latest technology and ban mobile phones and do not have electronic gaming machines or piped music.

The ways in which businesses may respond to changes in their competitive environment may be equally diverse and will clearly depend upon the nature of the change. The entry of a new competitor into a market, or the emergence of a dominant business, may provoke a number of strategic reactions. Affected businesses may seek new markets or develop new product ranges. Alternatively, they may seek alliances or mergers with other businesses in the same industry to increase their own market power in response to these changes in the competitive environment.

Changes in the competitive environment that manifest themselves as increasing the power of suppliers can create major difficulties for businesses, especially if no alternative suppliers exist. In this situation managers may consider the production process and ways in which the business may adapt to reduce its reliance on the products sold by the supplier in question. Other strategies in this situation could include taking over the supplier (in what may be a hostile action) or negotiating favourable deals with smaller rival suppliers in the hope of fostering greater competition.

Examiner's advice

The list of strategic responses above is not exhaustive – there are others that a business may adopt. It is important that you consider the possible responses in the context of the scenario with which you are presented. This will assist you in selecting and justifying the most appropriate response in any circumstances.

One step further: Porter's five forces model

Michael Porter's famous 'five forces of competitive position' model provides a simple framework for assessing and analysing the competitive strength and position of a corporation or business. Porter's five forces model can be used to good analytical effect alongside other models such as the SWOT and PEST analysis tools.

Porter's five forces model suggests points under each main heading, by which you can develop a broad and sophisticated analysis of competitive position, as might be used when creating strategy, plans, or making investment decisions about a business or organisation.

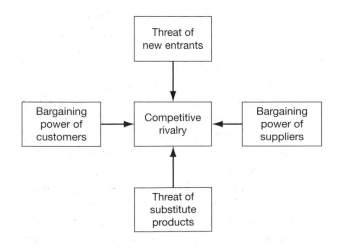

Figure 22.3 Porter's five forces

Five forces analysis looks at five key areas, namely competitive rivalry, the power of suppliers, the power of buyers, the threat of substitutes and the threat of entry.

1. Competitive rivalry

Competitive rivalry is a major force. If entry to an industry is straightforward then competitive rivalry is likely to be high. If it is easy for customers to move to substitute products, for example from oil to gas as a fuel, then again rivalry will be high. Generally competitive rivalry will be greater if:

- there is little differentiation between the products sold between customers
- competitors are approximately the same size as each other
- the competitors all have similar corporate strategies
- it is costly to leave the industry and so businesses do not do so.

2. Power of suppliers

Suppliers are a vital element of an effective organisation. Raw materials are needed to complete the finished product of the organisation. Suppliers can be highly powerful. This power arises from:

- the number of suppliers that are operating – fewer suppliers means more powerful suppliers
- the cost involved in changing suppliers – if it is difficult suppliers have greater power
- the lack of a substitute for the supplier's product.

3. Power of buyers

Buyers or customers can exert influence and control over an industry in certain circumstances. This happens when:

- the products are similar and it is easy to find substitutes
- products have a high price elasticity of demand, i.e. customers are sensitive to price
- switching to another supplier's product is cheap and straightforward.

4. Threat of substitutes

A substitute is an alternative product that offers purchasers similar or the same features and benefits. The threat of substitute is high when:

- price of that substitute product falls
- it is easy for consumers to switch from one substitute product to another
- buyers are willing to substitute.

5. Threat of new entrant

The threat of a new organisation entering the industry is high if entry barriers are low, i.e. when it is easy for an organisation to enter the industry. An organisation will look at how loyal customers are to existing products, how quickly they can achieve economies of scale, whether they would have access to suppliers, whether government legislation would prevent them or encourage them to enter the industry.

Progress questions

1 Outline two major technological changes that have affected UK businesses since 2000. (4 marks)

2 Technological change can affect products and processes. Carefully distinguish between these two types of technological change. (4 marks)

3 Examine the ways in which technological change can result in opportunities for businesses offering services. (6 marks)

4 Explain the difficulties a business might face if trading in a market subject to rapid changes in technology. (6 marks)

5 Explain what is meant by a business's 'competitive environment'. (4 marks)

6 Why might the entry of a new firm into a market change the competitive environment for established producers? (6 marks)

7 How does the existence of a small number of large supermarkets in the UK affect the competitive environment of small suppliers to the UK grocery market? (8 marks)

8 In what ways might the UK government influence the competitive environment in which businesses operate? (6 marks)

9 What possible effects might a dominant and large supplier have on a small manufacturing business? (8 marks)

10 What factors make the UK airline market highly competitive? (8 marks)

Analysis and evaluation questions

1 Below is an extract from the MyTravel website.

MyTravel.com is one of the biggest names in UK travel and part of the Thomas Cook Group of Companies. Every year MyTravel.com provides thousands of happy customers with holidays, city breaks, flights and cruises ... all easy to find, fully bookable online, and updated every minute of every day.

We understand that our customers need so much more than a great choice of travel options, resorts and accommodation. That's why the MyTravel.com website also provides you with extra services such as free resort guides, plus upgrades, pre-bookable holiday car hire, travel insurance, foreign currency, theme park tickets, and even airport car parking and pre-departure airport hotel stays!

And when you consider that we have hundreds and hundreds of worldwide destinations to choose from (with departures from over 20 UK airports), and exclusive online prices, discounts, offers and savings, then you'll know why we're confident that you'll find something to exactly match your travel needs on MyTravel.com.

a Analyse the benefits that MyTravel might receive from being one of the biggest businesses in the UK travel agency market. (10 marks)

b To what extent do you think MyTravel has benefited from recent changes in the technological environment. (15 marks)

2 Danton Ltd is a small-scale manufacturer of shampoos and soaps. The company is a relatively small supplier in a market dominated by larger businesses. It supplies to one of the UK's largest hotel chains and also to Tesco and Asda. The company's management team is considering entering the EU market.

The company has been through tough negotiations with its customers in recent months and has had to accept reduced profit margins. It is also aware that an American manufacturer is poised to enter the UK market. The company's costs have risen and its labour productivity figures have declined, placing it below all of its major rivals in this regard.

a Examine the ways in which technological change may provide an opportunity to Danton Ltd. (10 marks)

b Discuss the actions that Danton Ltd might take in response to its changing competitive environment. (15 marks)

Case study

Asda has overtaken its rival Sainsbury's for the first time to become the UK's second-biggest online grocer. The Wal-Mart-owned supermarket chain grew its home shopping grocery sales by 71.8 per cent for the 12 weeks to June, compared with the same period last year, according to TNS Worldpanel figures.

The revelation will increase the pressure on Sainsbury's in the growing home shopping market, although both supermarkets' online grocery sales are dwarfed by market leader Tesco. It is understood that Sainsbury's grew online sales by just 17.3 per cent over the same 12-week period to 15 June.

Asda declined to comment on any comparison with Sainsbury's but confirmed its online grocery sales had grown by more than 70 per cent for the 12 weeks to 15 June. Asda's chief executive, Andy Bond, admitted last year that it had been slow to exploit the full potential of grocery home shopping, but since then it has been rapidly expanding its coverage in the UK. For the seven days to 15 June, Asda grew home shopping sales by 56 per cent, while Sainsbury's was thought to have increased sales by 8.3 per cent in comparison to the same period in the previous year.

Sainsbury's declined to comment on the figures but said that its total online grocery sales over the past year – as opposed to a 7-day or 12-week period – were ahead of Asda's. Sainsbury's has suffered intermittent technical problems since mid-June with its online grocery site, which have now been fixed.

The online shopping battle is set to intensify in the autumn, when Asda relaunches its website. A key goal is to increase online sales of non-food products, but ultimately Asda wants to offer customers a fully integrated grocery and non-food shopping experience. Sainsbury's is also gearing up for a major online non-food push, including clothing.

In the wider grocery sector, Tesco had a 31.3 per cent share of the market, Asda was 16.9 per cent and Sainsbury's had 15.9 per cent for the 12 weeks to 13 July 2008.

Source: Adapted from *The Independent*, 28 July 2008
http://www.independent.co.uk
(40 marks, 60 minutes)

Questions

1 Explain how the changing technological environment in which UK supermarkets operate might influence their marketing activities. (7 marks)
2 Analyse how Tesco, as the dominant business in the grocery market influences its competitive environment. (8 marks)
3 Discuss the major factors that make up Asda's competitive environment. (11 marks)
4 Do you think that the technological environment poses a threat or an opportunity for Sainsbury's? Justify your view. (14 marks)

Section 6: Managing change

23 Introduction to change

Starting points

Change is the one predictable element of business. You may not know what is going to change, but you know something is! These changes may be due to internal or external causes.

In this chapter we consider:
- the causes of internal change
- the causes of external change.

Introduction

The one constant in business is change. All businesses are constantly undergoing change. Just think of your school and the changes it will have experienced in recent years: new qualifications, new style exam questions, some staff leaving and some joining, new investment in facilities, new students, changes to the structure of the staffing and changes to what competitors are providing and how well they are doing. Standing still is not an option – change happens whether you like it or not. The ability to survive and prosper depends on your ability to respond to and adapt to change. As Charles Darwin wrote: 'In the struggle for survival, the fittest win out at the expense of their rivals because they succeed in adapting themselves best to their environment.'

External change

Some change will be external. It happens *to* you. For example, change may come from any of the PEST (political, economic, social, technological) factors you studied earlier in this book. Change is happening all the time in the external environment (e.g. new taxes, new laws, new technologies) and your job as a manager is to anticipate such change and prepare for it; hopefully preparing to exploit the opportunities it creates and/or minimise the threats it generates. Of course, the nature of the change and the significance of any particular change will depend on the industry we are examining. Technological change is clearly vitally important in the computer games console market; economic change may be more significant in the construction industry; political regulations may be critical in the banking sector following massive government intervention in the banking crisis of 2008.

The significance of change for any business will depend on the particular circumstances of the business: an economic recession may hit health clubs and leisure centres but benefit takeaway pizza companies and tent manufacturers. A global business may be less sensitive to changes in the UK than one that operates solely within this country.

The rate of change may also vary over time. The UK economy underwent a period of relative stability in the late 1990s and early 2000s; inflation stayed relatively constant around 2 per cent, the economy grew around 2 to 3 per cent each year and unemployment was relatively low. Then in 2007 and 2008 came the global credit crisis. Suddenly businesses could not borrow, the UK economy went into a recession, the government had to step in to save several banks and share prices fell dramatically. This

became a time of very radical change and unpredictability, making planning incredibly difficult. Who would have predicted in early 2007 that the UK government would have to nationalise banks, that the UK would enter a recession, that interest rates would be slashed, VAT cut and the government would pump billions of pounds into the economy to try and preserve growth? The whole business environment, not only in the UK but globally, was shaken up and managers were operating in a whole new world.

> **Key terms**
>
> **PEST analysis** is a way of analysing the external macro-environment of business. It examines political, economic, social and technological factors. It can also be known as PESTEL analysis, referring to political, economic, social, technological, environmental and legal factors.

Business in Focus

Marks and Spencer plc

In November 2008 Marks and Spencer (M&S) plc reported a fall in profits of over 30 per cent for the first half of the financial year. Managers reassured investors it would maintain the dividend for its investors. M&S executive chairman, Sir Stuart Rose, blamed the wider economy for the profit slump: 'The UK economy is having a very difficult time and we can't defy gravity. If I believed we had a bad business plan I would change it.'

According to Rose, the economic environment had changed dramatically in the past year and the company was encountering the 'most difficult retail conditions since the early 1990s. M&S is a very strong business in a very weak economy.' He said that recently trade had been 'volatile' because consumer confidence had been shaken by the financial crisis that had led to real problems for the high street banks. Rose added that 'Interest rates should come down so hopefully we will see some blue sky towards the end of 2009'. In fact, interest rates were cut a few days later by 1.5 per cent – a very significant cut.

M&S's response to the fall in profits included an

advertising campaign featuring boyband Take That and TV actor Robson Green, as well as regular M&S faces Twiggy and Erin O'Connor. It also offered promotions such as 'Dine in for £10' to increase the value of its food and compete against discount retailers such as Aldi.

M&S also dramatically scaled back its spending plans for this year and delayed a costly store refurbishment programme and UK expansion plans. However, it continued to expand overseas planning to open 15 stores in India and recently opening its first store in China.

Questions:

1 Explain why Marks and Spencer's managers maintained the dividend even though profits had fallen.
2 Examine the changes in the external environment identified in the passage above which seem likely to affect the success of Marks and Spencer.
3 Analyse the likely impact of these changes on Marks and Spencer.
4 Discuss whether Marks and Spencer plc is right to continue its expansion plans in China.

The effects of change can be seen in many different industries. The travel industry, for example, has undergone major reorganisation in recent years due to the growth of the internet. Customers are searching around more and often going direct to the hotels and resorts, bypassing travel agents. The music and television industries have been transformed by online media. The photography industry has been revolutionised by the digital revolution. By comparison, industries such as trouser presses, art galleries and garden seeds may have experienced less change.

Key terms

The **macro-environment** refers to external factors, generally beyond the control of a business, which will affect its success such as the economy, the level of technology and social factors.

Other sources of external change come from the competitive environment. This includes the organisations that a business is dealing with on a regular basis, such as:

- **Their competitors** – new competitors into the market can pose a new threat to the existing providers of a product. Just think of Branston launching its beans to attack Heinz, or Cadbury launching Trident gum to attack Wrigley.

- **Suppliers** – all business have to buy in some supplies. Suppliers may try to increase prices, may have quality problems or may change their terms and conditions, all of which will force a business to reconsider its own decisions.
- **Buyers** may also try to negotiate new terms.
- **Providers of substitute products** and their marketing actions may affect your own business. Better marketing of laser eye treatments will affect sales of spectacles, for example.

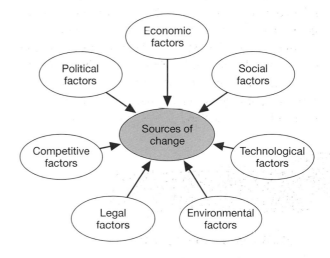

Figure 23.1 External PESTEL and competitive forces as sources of changes

Business in Focus

Panasonic

In 2008 the Japanese consumer electronics firm Panasonic cut its annual profit forecast by 90 per cent because of the global economic downturn.

The company said it now expected to report net profits of 30 billion yen ($315 million, £210 million) for the year ending in March 2009. It said conditions were 'deteriorating sharply' because of falling consumer spending and tougher competition.

Panasonic cited the rise in the value of the yen as another reason for weaker profits. A stronger yen cuts the exporter's overseas earnings.

Source: Adapted from bbc.co.uk

Question:

1 How might the managers of Panasonic now react to the global economic downturn and the strong yen?

Internal change

Change can be internal as well as external. Staff may want higher rewards or to be treated differently, for example. Over time, staff may feel they should be consulted to a greater extent or that greater efforts should be made to ensure they have a good quality of life at work. Over the years employees in the UK have gained greater rights when it comes to health and safety and consultation, for example. These developments require changes within the business such as the way that staff are managed.

The changes that affect a business can therefore come from within (internal change) or from outside (external change). In many cases external change will bring about internal change as the firm has to respond and react given the altered environment.

Analysing change

Of course, when analysing any change we should take account of the nature and the rate of the change. The UK's population is ageing, for example, but this has not happened suddenly; managers could have and should have expected this and planned accordingly. Other changes are more rapid and less predictable. Gradual change is called 'incremental change'; dramatic change is called 'transformational change'.

Change can create threats for business or opportunities. In fact, the same change will be a threat to some and an opportunity for others. In part the effect depends on what the change is, but also it depends on the internal position of each business, the quality of the management and the extent to which the

Business in Focus

Boeing

Boeing had to delay the first flight of its 787 Dreamliner aircraft until 2009, having previously aimed to get it off the ground before the end of 2008. There had already been a quality problem with the fasteners holding the planes together which had delayed progress by a year. About 3 per cent of the fasteners on the four test jets had been incorrectly installed by suppliers, being either too far apart or too close together.

Production was then held up due to a 58-day strike by machinists. The labour dispute was finally ended when trade union members voted by 74 per cent in favour of a four-year deal. The dispute had centred on pay and job cuts. The eight-week strike cost Boeing an estimated $100 million (£61.8 million) a day in lost income. The striking machinists lost about $7,000 each in wages during the dispute.

The union – the International Association of Machinists and Aerospace Workers – said the new contract that had been negotiated would protect over 5,000 factory jobs, and would prevent some jobs from being out-sourced. Change in this case was brought about by union action.

Source: Adapted from bbc.co.uk

Questions:

1 Discuss the possible effects on Boeing of a 58-day strike.
2 Should Boeing managers have agreed to the employee demands at the start of the dispute?
3 How might the dispute affect the relations between managers and employees in the future?

Key Issues

You cannot avoid change; the key issues are whether you can foresee it and whether you can adapt to it. MG Rover, KwikSave, Woolworths and MFI are all business that could not cope. Tesco, Ryanair, General Electric, Coca-Cola, McDonald's and Sony are companies that (so far) have managed to gain from change. They are proactive and are able to embrace change.

change has been expected and prepared for. For example, the recession in 2008 depressed the share price of many companies. This may have been a threat to some businesses because there was a danger of takeover, but an opportunity for other companies to buy rivals for a lower price. It depends on the funds each business has, their strategies for the future and their ability to combine with rivals.

Proactive v reactive approaches to change

Proactive managers look ahead and anticipate change wherever they can. A reactive approach waits for change to happen and then responds. Obviously a proactive approach is better in terms of planning ahead and having the resources to identify and exploit opportunities. However, in some cases the change may be unexpected either because it could not be easily anticipated and/or because the managers were not looking properly. Kodak was slow to respond to the rise of digital cameras because it did not see companies such as Sony and Fujitsu as real competitors; instead it was still watching traditional producers of cameras such as Nikon and did not see the long-term threat of digital. Even Microsoft has been guilty of not anticipating change – it took several years of the growth of the internet for the company to realise its potential and divert resources to online-focused products.

> **Key terms**
> **Marketing myopia** is a term that was introduced by Theodore Levitt and describes organisations that are short sighted and miss the trends developing within their markets, such as Kodak and digital cameras.

Summary

Change cannot be avoided in business and in many cases you will not want to avoid it because it can bring opportunities – just ask investors in eBay, iTunes, X factor, Ryanair, Blackberry, Sky and Nintendo. However, it can bring threats as well and

People in Business

Alvin Toffler

Alvin Toffler is a business writer who coined the phrase 'future shock' in an article that was first published in 1965. The term is now quite commonly used. It refers to what happens to society when too much change happens in a very short time, causing confusion and chaos. His first book was also called *Future Shock*, and was followed by *The Third Wave* and *Powershift*. All of these books are about change: the first focuses on how it affects organisations; the second about where it is taking them; and the third is about who can control change. Toffler was the first to point to the acceleration of change in business. He also highlights the significance of the information revolution we have experienced. 'The advanced economy,' wrote Toffler, 'could not run for 30 seconds without computers.' His book *Revolutionary Wealth*, written with his wife, discusses the growth of the 'prosumer' – a consumer who is also part-producer of what he or she consumes, e.g. the person who designs their own kitchen or bathroom using a store's software, buys from the store and then assembles it themselves.

Books:
1 *Future Shock*, Bantam Books, 1970; Pan Books, 1979
2 *The Third Wave*, Morrow, 1980
3 *Powershift: Knowledge, Wealth, and Violence at the Edge of the 21st Century*, Bantam Books, 1990
4 *Revolutionary Wealth*, with Toffler, H., Alfred A. Knopf, 2006

Key Issues

Change is getting faster in many industries because businesses are operating in global markets with more competition.

Technological change is getting faster, reducing the costs of producing some products, of communicating and creating new markets.

challenge or cause dramatic upheavals in an industry (think of music, broadcasting and education). Of course the shape and nature of change can differ significantly; it may be internal or external, slow or rapid, predicted or unexpected.

Progress questions

1 Outline two changes that have occurred at your school or college in the last few years. (6 marks)

2 Outline one way in which *you* have personally changed in the last year. What caused the change? (5 marks)

3 Outline a change in the UK economy in the last year. Explain, with examples, how this is an opportunity for business. Explain how it may be a threat. (8 marks)

4 Outline a change in the UK social environment in the last decade. Explain, with examples, how this is an opportunity for business. Explain how it may also be a threat. (8 marks)

5 Explain two possible causes of internal change within a business. (6 marks)

6 Explain two ways in which a significant fall in income in the economy might affect a business. (6 marks)

7 Explain two ways in which a fall in the exchange rate might affect a business. (6 marks)

8 Explain two ways in which an ageing population might affect a business. (6 marks)

9 Explain two ways in which the launch of a new product by a competitor might affect a business. (6 marks)

10 Explain two ways in which the law can affect a business. (6 marks)

Analysis and evaluation questions

1 Analyse the effect of one recent change in the external environment on UK retailers. (8 marks)

2 Discuss the factors likely to determine whether a recession in the UK is an opportunity or threat for a UK hotel chain. (15 marks)

3 Using examples of businesses and industries you know, to what extent do you think external change is more dangerous than internal change? (15 marks)

Case study

Wal-Mart sees opportunities amid the crisis

In 2008 there was huge concern about the state of the global economy. The UK, for example, went into recession. Many businesses were laying off staff and there were several business closures. For many firms this was a gloomy time but Wal-Mart, the largest US retailer, said it could see 'extraordinary opportunities' in the global retail landscape created. The company's chief executive said that 'there are probably things that the government might allow you to do that they would not have allowed you to do in the past', while saying that Wal-Mart would take a 'thoughtfully aggressive' approach to any opportunities. For example, it might be possible to look to acquire sites from retailers that were going out of business; in the past permission to expand in these areas might not have been allowed for fear of Wal-Mart dominating in a particular region. There was

also the possibility 'to negotiate very good rents' because of less demand in a recession. 'If you are a local politician, do you want those stores to go dark? Or do you want to have Wal-Mart taking them over and creating local jobs?' said Wal-Mart's chief executive.

These remarks came as Wal-Mart, whose US sales exceed $300 billion, continued to slow the expansion of its network of more than 2,500 supercentres. It plans to open between 142 and 157 of the stores next year, down from an expected 191 this year.

The retailer is also looking at new smaller store formats and an enhanced focus on online sales to drive growth. The new store formats will include a smaller 'high-efficiency' version of its supercentre that will be the retailer's 'second growth platform' and could help drive significant expansion. The new stores, he said, would support a parallel expansion of Wal-Mart's online presence, where 'site-to-store' pick-up orders now account for about half its online sales. 'Online is, without doubt, a very significant opportunity for us, and one that you will see us invest in much more in the future.' There are also plans to move even further away from pure retail operations, such as a long-term agreement with the largest US online contact lens provider, 1-800-contact, that includes an in-store presence. The company said it was unlikely to try and move into banking after it withdrew its attempt to secure an industrial bank licence two years ago in the face of major opposition from banks and from labour groups.

Source: Adapted from Jonathan Birchall, 2 November 2008,
The Financial Times Limited 2008
40 marks; 60 minutes

Questions

1   Explain two factors in the external environment (apart from the economy) that might affect Wal-Mart. (5 marks)

2   Specify two changes in the economic environment of the UK and analyse how they might affect a retailer such as Wal-Mart. (8 marks)

3   Discuss the factors likely to determine the success of Wal-Mart's smaller store formats. (12 marks)

4   To what extent is a recession really likely to be an opportunity for Wal-Mart? (15 marks)

24 Internal causes of change

In this chapter we examine in detail possible internal causes of change. We will consider:
- changes in organisational size
- the impact of new owners/leaders
- poor business performance.

Changes in organisational size

Internal change can occur as a result of the challenges and opportunities of growth. Many owners and managers will want their firms to grow. There are several reasons for this:

- Larger firms may benefit from economies of scale. This may mean lower unit costs and can result in higher profit margins or lower prices.
- Larger firms have more power over their markets, for example, they may be able to negotiate better deals with their suppliers and distributors; they may also be able to bargain for better positioning for their advertisements in the media.
- Larger firms tend to be safer from takeover simply because they are more expensive to buy. Managers who are interested in their own job security will therefore have an incentive to make their firms bigger and as a result protect their own jobs.
- Larger firms have more status. Managers will often want the praise and recognition that comes with building up a business.

The growth of a business may happen internally or externally. Internal growth occurs when the firm sells more of its products. External growth occurs when a firm acquires or joins up with another.

Internal growth is often slower – it may take some time to penetrate a market and increase sales. External growth is naturally faster and more sudden because a firm acquires another organisation's sales in one go.

However, all forms of growth bring about changes because there are more people to organise, more products to provide, more markets to operate in and more decisions to be made. This can lead to changes in the structure of the business and its culture.

> **Key terms**
> **Economies of scale** occur when a change in the capacity of a business results in lower unit costs.

Adjustment during growth

As an organisation grows, its managers must examine the firm's structure and the roles of people within the business. Many firms start off as sole traders. The founder is the boss and he or she makes all the major decisions. This type of enterprise is able to respond quickly to market conditions and the founder has complete control. He or she can make decisions without having to consult others and has a clear overview of the business situation.

The next stage, as a firm grows, usually involves more people being hired to deal with the additional business. At this stage there may well be a good team spirit. Individuals share out tasks among themselves and can communicate easily with each other to sort out any problems. Employees feel they are all working towards the same goals. Individuals share jobs, help each other out and generally deal with things as and when they come up; there may not be formal job descriptions at this stage.

If, however, growth continues it may be necessary to develop a more formal structure within the organisation. To avoid too many people doing the same thing, or to avoid things not getting done at all, it usually becomes necessary to clearly define what each job involves. More rigid job descriptions become the norm and a more formal structure evolves with defined lines of accountability.

At this point the people at the top of the organisation are less directly involved with the day-to-day work. Their approach must be less hands-on simply because they cannot do it all themselves; this means that the senior managers must learn how to delegate and let others do the frontline work for them. In larger organisations managers must focus on the overall planning, coordinating and controlling rather than the actual doing.

For some managers the transition from the 'boss' (the person who does things himself or herself) to 'manager' or 'leader' – the person who focuses on the overall direction of the business and delegates day-to-day tasks to others – can be a very difficult one; they can find it hard to remove themselves from direct contact with the job and their customers. In many firms the senior managers continue to intervene too much, even though the business has grown, because they cannot 'let go'; the danger of being too interventionist is that this undermines subordinates. Furthermore, managers who cannot relinquish control inevitably place a block on the size of the firm – if they always want to know exactly what is going on, the business as a whole cannot grow very big.

Keeping control of a growing business

As an organisation grows it naturally becomes more difficult for managers to keep control of all of its activities. There are more people to manage, more products to oversee and more things to do. The internal and external environments become more complex. Managers must therefore develop ways of keeping everyone informed and focused, and ensuring that employees know exactly what is happening and how their actions contribute to the success of the organisation as a whole.

To help coordination and maintain control within the firm managers, often introduce procedures such as budgeting, appraisal systems and management by objectives. Budgeting helps managers to plan and monitor what is being spent, appraisals provide a good opportunity to review what has been happening and set new targets for the future, while a system of management by objectives helps to ensure everyone is working towards the same goals. Without such systems running throughout the organisation, there may be no clear direction.

Good communication is of course also essential to effective growth. Employees, suppliers and investors must be kept informed so they are clear about what is happening at the moment within the firm and where the business wants to go next. Good communication is also needed to keep the organisation in close contact with its customers so it can meet their needs precisely.

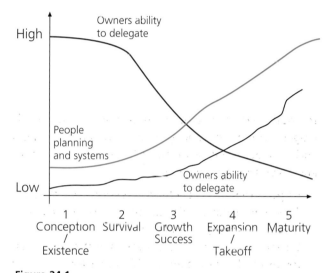

Figure 24.1

Source: Adapted from Churchill and Lewis 1983

The changes in the role of the founders of a business are highlighted above. As the business expands the owner's ability to actually do the job himself or herself becomes less significant. At the beginning they are very hands-on and have to actually provide the service, but over time others can do this for them. What they have to do is delegate and assume the role of a manager. To do this successfully they need good people around them, effective plans to show where the business is going and what everyone else has to do to contribute to this, and they need to ensure that systems are in place to control performance.

Growth therefore requires changes in the role of managers and changes in the style and structure of the business.

Internal and external growth

External growth occurs when one firm decides to expand by joining together with another. This may occur either by a takeover (also called an acquisition) or a merger. A takeover occurs when one firm gains control of another by acquiring a controlling interest in its shares. A merger occurs when one firm joins together with another one to form a new combined enterprise. Mergers and acquisitions are both forms of integration.

If one business wants to take over another it must buy up 51 per cent of the other firm's shares so that it has a majority vote. It may buy these shares either by using cash or by offering its own shares in return (this is known as a paper offer). The attacking company will make an offer to the shareholders of the victim company. The directors of the targeted company will decide whether or not they think the bid is fair and whether or not to recommend to their own shareholders that they should accept it; if they reject the offer the takeover becomes a 'hostile bid'.

If there are not enough shareholders willing to accept the offer, the attacking company may decide to increase the amount it offers for each share. There is, however, a strict timetable that the attacking company has to follow, so it cannot keep increasing its offer indefinitely.

In a merger the two (or more) firms agree to form a new enterprise; shares in each of the individual companies are exchanged for shares in the new business.

> **Key terms**
> **External growth** occurs when a business grows by merging with or taking over another business.

Types of integration

There are three types of integration:

1 horizontal
2 vertical
3 conglomerate.

Horizontal integration

Horizontal integration occurs when one firm joins with another at the same stage of the same production process. For example, when Ford took over Volvo this was an example of horizontal integration because they are both car manufacturers.

The possible reasons for this type of integration include:

- **greater market share** – by combining together the two firms will have a greater share of the market and, as a result, they are likely to have more power over other members of the supply chain, such as suppliers and distributors
- **economies of scale** – larger-scale production may bring a reduction in unit costs due to financial, production or purchasing economies
- **the opportunity to enter a different segment of the market** and thereby spread risks to some extent.

Vertical integration

Vertical integration occurs when one firm joins with another at a different stage of the same production process. Forward vertical integration occurs when one firm joins with another business at a later stage in the same production process. Backward vertical integration occurs when one firm joins with another business at an earlier stage in the same production process.

Firms may undertake vertical integration for various reasons:

- **In order to gain control over supplies**. This may be important for a firm to ensure it can maintain its suppliers (e.g. in times of shortage) or if it is essential to maintain the quality of its supplies.

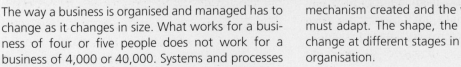

Key Issues

The way a business is organised and managed has to change as it changes in size. What works for a business of four or five people does not work for a business of 4,000 or 40,000. Systems and processes have to be reviewed, new structures and reporting mechanism created and the way the business is run must adapt. The shape, the rules and the style will change at different stages in the development of an organisation.

By gaining control of its inputs a firm may also be able to deny competitors the supplies they want.

- **In order to guarantee access to the market**. By buying up retailers, for example, manufacturers may ensure that their products actually get to the market and are displayed and promoted in the way they want.

A conglomerate merger

A conglomerate merger occurs when firms in different markets join together, for example, if a chocolate company joins with a paint company. Tomkins plc was one of the last big conglomerates in the UK and at one time sold guns, Mother's Pride bread and bicycles!

A firm may become a conglomerate in order to spread its risk. By operating in several markets or countries a firm is less vulnerable to changes in any one market. However, in some ways conglomerate mergers are much riskier than other forms of integration because managers may be entering markets in which they have relatively little experience.

Key terms

Horizontal integration is between organisations at the same stage of the same production process

Vertical integration is between organisations at different stages of the same production process.

Conglomerate integration is between organisations involved in different production processes.

Problems following a merger or takeover

Although, in theory, integration can offer many potential advantages such as economies of scale, many mergers and takeovers are relatively unsuccessful. One of the main problems following integration is coping with the different cultures of the organisations involved. Employees are likely to have different values regarding key areas such as customer service, quality, investment and training and this can cause conflict. Employees from one organisation may find that behaviour that was praised and rewarded in the past is now criticised. There will also be adjustment problems regarding pay and conditions, for example, employees in one of the organisations may have a significantly better remuneration scheme than in the other – either the firm increases the rewards for one (which is expensive) or tries to negotiate the rewards of the other downwards (which will be unpopular).

Many firms also find that they experience diseconomies of scale following integration. Despite improvements in information technology, communication can be a problem and there can be a lack of a common sense of purpose. The result is often demotivation and a lack of coordination.

Furthermore, many of the supposed benefits of integration do not appear – computer systems turn out to be incompatible, employees do not cooperate and share information and the business lacks focus or control. As a result, integrated companies can find that their costs increase and that the returns generated are lower than would have been expected if they had remained single. Studies often show that over 60 per cent of mergers and takeovers actually destroy shareholder value (i.e. the companies combined end up being worth less than they would if they had remained separate). It is surprising, therefore, how many large-scale deals continue to occur. Just think of AOL/Netscape, Exxon/Mobil, NationsBank/BankAmerica, Hewlett-Packard/Veifone/Compaq, Deutsche Bank/Bankers Trust and British Petroleum/Amoco.

In many cases the big deals are driven by a demand for greater scale. However, in reality diseconomies of scale seem to be the result, particularly when the merger or acquisition involves significant cultural, political, psychological and geographical differences.

Handy (1998, pp. 107–8) offers this perspective: 'Businesses can grow more profitable by becoming better, or leaner, or deeper, or more concentrated, without growing bigger. Bigness, in both business and life, can lead to a lack of focus, too much complexity and in the end, too wide a spread to control. We have to know when big is big enough.'

The cost of a firm being taken over

The amount paid by one firm for another will ultimately depend on its perceived value. This in turn depends on the assets of the target firm and how the attacker believes these can be utilised. A starting point in a bid may be the target company's balance sheet – this shows the 'book value' of a company. However, the book value will not necessarily reflect the actual value of the firm for several reasons:

- Some assets may not be valued, for example, the value of brands may not be included. In the case of many companies such as Microsoft, Sony, Apple or McDonald's the brand is clearly worth millions but is usually not listed in the accounts.

The balance sheet will also fail to value the quality of the employees – a very important asset in many organisations (think of the importance of the skills and ideas of employees for Manchester United, Oxford University and the advertising agency Saatchi and Saatchi).

- Some assets – such as property – may be valued at historical cost (i.e. the price paid for them) rather than their current value.
- The firm may have used window-dressing techniques (such as changing the depreciation policy) to flatter the accounts.
- These other factors may well be reflected in the current share price and therefore the market value of the business.

However, to make sure that the victim company's shareholders are willing to sell their shares the attacker is likely to have to pay a premium (i.e. to offer more than the existing share price). The amount of premium the bidder is willing to pay will depend on the extent to which it believes there will be gains such as economies of scale or synergy; the bigger the perceived gains the more it is likely to pay.

When deciding what a firm is worth there is inevitably a degree of risk. The risk involved will depend partly on whether it is a hostile or a welcome bid. If the bid is welcomed by the directors of the target company they will be willing to share information with the bidder. If the bid is hostile the attacking company will have no inside knowledge of the target firm and so may or may not be paying more than it should.

Going international

As well as growing within their domestic market, firms can also grow by expanding overseas. The benefits of this are that it provides new market opportunities. If, for example, the domestic market is saturated, selling overseas can provide new growth. Imagine you sell mobile phones; the UK market is fairly saturated so the majority of the sales which now occur are when people upgrade or replace a broken phone. In other countries with a lower standard of living the mobile phone market may still be in the growth phase of its life cycle.

The decision to sell overseas can be a difficult one to take. Along with all the usual problems of expansion a firm may face additional challenges, such as dealing with exchange rate fluctuations and coping with new legislation. A firm will also have to familiarise itself with market conditions and consumer behaviour, which can vary radically from one country to another.

Typically firms begin to sell abroad by exporting. They continue to produce in the UK but sell some of their products to overseas customers. If, however, demand from abroad continues to grow a firm may extend its operations by using an overseas agent. An agent will represent the business overseas and try to generate more sales on its behalf. An agent is likely to have more insight into the market than the UK firm and this should help to boost sales. Agents do not take ownership of the goods or services – they are paid on commission.

Instead of using agents, a firm may join up with a

Business in Focus

RBS and ABN Amro

According to the Barclays chief executive, Mr Varley, his rival, Sir Fred Goodwin of Royal Bank of Scotland, paid too high a price to take over ABN Amro. RBS beat Barclays in the bidding battle for the Dutch bank with an offer of £47 billion in the world's biggest ever bank takeover. The Barclays chief executive said: 'We weren't prepared to secure a win at any price. I think the RBS consortium has overpaid. We made a very clear commitment to our shareholders that we would not be irresponsible in this transaction and we have been faithful to that.'

RBS denied suggestions that its promised synergies of €1.8 billion were over-ambitious, claiming they were more conservative than those envisaged by Barclays.

Questions:

1 Discuss the factors that might have determined how much RBS paid for ABN Amro.
2 What do you think are the possible consequences of RBS paying too much for ABN?

local producer and either give or sell a licence to allow the products to be made there. The advantage of this approach is that the firm can benefit from local knowledge and skills as well as having lower distribution costs by producing in the region. In some cases, linking up with a local firm may be the only way to enter a market because the foreign government may insist that local businesses are involved.

Alternatively, a business may set up its own factory abroad and produce for itself. This is likely to involve high levels of investment and so will only be undertaken by firms if they are sure that demand will be sustained and profitable.

Financing growth

In order to grow, a firm will need to have the finance necessary to acquire resources such as new premises or equipment or to hire new staff. This finance can come from internal and external sources.

Internal sources of finance include:

- **retained profits**: the firm can invest its profits into stocks and new equipment
- **the sale of assets**: if firms have assets which are not being used (such as land) they may sell these to raise cash.

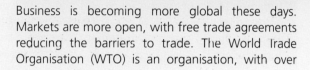

Key Issues

Business is becoming more global these days. Markets are more open, with free trade agreements reducing the barriers to trade. The World Trade Organisation (WTO) is an organisation, with over 150 member countries, which aims to reduce protectionist barriers. Other drivers of increased international trade are lower transportation costs and cheaper communication methods.

Business in Focus

Coca-Cola

In 2008 Coca-Cola announced it wanted to buy Huiyuan, China's largest fruit juice company, for $2.4 billion (£1.35 billion) in the biggest foreign takeover of a Chinese company. This was the second-largest acquisition in Coke's 122-year history.

The deal was intended to consolidate the soft drink maker's position in China where it already dominates the carbonated and diluted drinks markets.

Coke, which was an official sponsor of the Beijing Olympics, sells more than a billion bottles of Coke in China. According to its Chinese website, Coke has invested $1.25 billion since making its first entry in 1979. Analysts expect the Chinese fruit juice market to grow by more than 10 per cent in the next few years as the country's growing middle class become increasingly health-conscious.

'Though it's a relatively small market in the beverages space, it's a high-growth market because of the growing personal income in China and increased health awareness.'

Coca-Cola president and chief executive Muhtar Kent said: 'Huiyuan is a long-established and successful juice brand in China and is highly complementary to the Coca-Cola China business. This is further evidence of our deep commitment to China and to providing Chinese consumers with the beverage choices that meet their needs.'

State dominance of the corporate sector and strict red tape have made foreign moves into the country notoriously difficult.

Huiyuan, which has about a 46 per cent share of the pure-juice market exports drinks to about 30 countries, including Japan and the US.

Questions:

1 Analyse the possible reasons why Coca-Cola wanted to buy Huiyuan.
2 Discuss the factors likely to determine whether this takeover is successful.

External sources include:

- **overdrafts**: this is a short-term form of finance which can be called in at any time by the bank
- **mortgages**: this is finance acquired using property as collateral
- **loans**: this is long-term borrowing in which a firm agrees to pay back the borrowed money over an agreed period of time.

All of these forms of borrowing mean the firm is committed to interest repayments. This can cause problems if the firm's performance is poor since it may struggle to repay its interest.

Alternatively, a firm may raise money externally by issuing shares. This means that the control of the business is diluted among more owners.

Growth may therefore lead to changes in ownership and/or changes in the amount of debt the business has. This in turn can influence the decisions that are made and the impact of external change such as a change in interest rates.

Growth and cash flow

The expansion of a business may bring many benefits in the long term, but can also lead to cash-flow problems in the short term. As a firm expands it will be buying new fixed assets, purchasing stocks and investing in areas such as new product development. These all lead to cash outflows. Over time this investment should lead to more sales and cash inflows, but in the short term the business may have to plan carefully to avoid cash-flow problems. Its options may include:

- arranging a loan
- ensuring debtors pay on time
- delaying payment to suppliers as long as possible.

If a firm does grow too fast and fails to manage its cash flow effectively this is known as 'overtrading'. Overtrading occurs when a firm has too much money invested in building up stocks or has spent too much acquiring bigger premises and, as a result, has liquidity problems.

Imagine you have a successful idea for a cafe. The business does well so you decide to open two more. This requires investment and drains your cash flow, even though the first one is successful. The two new cafes eventually open and the first few months are promising. To exploit your idea as quickly as possible (and before others do), you decide to open another five cafes. Once again this leads to a drain on your cash. The business idea is a good one, but rapid growth can place an enormous strain on your cash-flow position – if you run out of cash you will experience overtrading.

Growth, therefore, will require careful planning to ensure that liquidity does not become a problem.

Retrenchment

Although businesses may want to grow there will be times when the managers decide to shrink the business. This may be because of a lack of demand and/or problems controlling a large-scale business. Retrenchment occurs when managers withdraw from some markets. This may involve the closure or sale of different divisions, or redundancies.

A company may pull out of a market because:

- the demand is no longer there
- it cannot manage operating on a larger scale (e.g. diseconomies of scale)
- it no longer has competitive advantage in that market (perhaps because of competitors)
- it wants to raise money by selling the business.

When scaling down the business managers should consider:

- How this is communicated to investors and the media. Is it planned and can the reason be explained so this is part of an overall strategy rather than seeming like a business in trouble?
- Consultation with employees to ensure they understand the reasons why the business is shrinking and how they will be affected. If redundancies are to be made can the business help employees find new jobs?

Key Issues

Retrenchment became a key issue in the UK in 2008 when the economy went into a recession. This led to a drop in profits for many companies and a delay in investment plans. Some business also started to close parts of their operations because they were not profitable enough. This was retrenchment caused by external factors.

The impact of new owners and leaders

As discussed, internal change may occur because of growth, which will alter the way the business is managed and organised. Another key driver of change is the impact of the owners and managers wanting to alter the way that the business is run.

New leaders in a business often want to make changes. This may be because they have a different vision of where the organisation is headed from the previous leaders, or because they have a different view of how to achieve particular goals. They may have different experiences, different values, different personal styles of leading and therefore they want to change the way things are done. In some cases managers might want to make change simply to show they have arrived and that they can and will make changes. Changes made soon after their arrival, for example, may include replacing some key personnel to mark a change of approach.

In fact, new managers are often brought in precisely to bring about change because of the failure of a previous strategy. For example, faced with falling sales or rising costs the owners may seek new leadership to bring about better solutions to the problems.

Differing expectations of employees

Change can also come from within the workforce. In the UK the nature of the workforce has changed in many ways in the last 20 years. For example:

- Employees are getting older due to demographic change.
- Employees are better educated than they were as more people have stayed on at school and gone to university.
- There are more families where both parents work.
- There is greater concern about a work–life balance.
- The workforce is more diverse in terms of gender and ethnic groups.

This will affect employees expectations, how they want to be treated, how they need to be motivated. For example, a better-educated workforce may want more involvement in decision-making and more opportunities to make decisions. This may require a change in management style and/or structure.

Poor business performance

According to Lewin, at any moment a business will be in a temporary equilibrium where the forces for change are exactly balanced by the forces resisting change. There may be pressures to change (either internal or external) but, at the same time, there are forces pushing against this.

For example, managers may not want to bring about change due to:

- the cost
- the likely opposition from some staff
- the extra work involved.

For change to occur there must be greater pressure for change or the resistance to change needs to decrease (e.g. it becomes cheaper to install new equipment; or employee relations improve). Greater pressure to bring about change is often caused by poor business performance because the owners want something done about it. Not surprisingly, a fall in sales and/or a decline in profits is likely to lead to pressure from investors for better performance. The existing managers are likely to feel pressurised to improve matters or they may fear they will lose their jobs. This may help managers to bring about changes they may have wanted to make anyway but now have the incentive and the justification. When asked why these changes are necessary they can point to a disappointing financial performance. The disappointing results can therefore be a factor for change and also help employees to understand why it is necessary, thereby reducing opposition to change.

Typical changes following poor business performance include:

- **Replacing some staff**. Specific employees may be held responsible for the firm's problems (see page 344 for the resignation of the chief executive of C&C following Magner's poor performance). There may also be redundancies in an attempt to cut costs.
- **Restructuring**. The managers may look at the structure of the business and decide that some parts are no longer necessary or are over staffed. They may also feel the structure hinders the efficiency and effectiveness of the business; perhaps a functional structure limits communication between functions and therefore a matrix approach may be better.
- **New processes and systems**. New ways of doing things, new ways of organising the work

and new technologies may all be introduced to reduce waste and improve quality.

Summary

Internal change may come from the growth of the organisation. This may be internal (through greater sales) or external (through mergers or takeovers). Expanding the size of a business brings many management challenges to maintain control and direction effectively. Changes are likely to the structure of the business and how it is managed.

Change may also be prompted by new managers in the business who may have their own ideas of how things should be done. New managers may be brought in because of poor business performance – given disappointing results managers are appointed to turn around the business by making changes.

Progress questions

1 Give two reasons why a business might want to grow. Explain these reasons. (6 marks)
2 What is meant by a takeover? (2 marks)

3 Explain two possible problems of a takeover. (6 marks)
4 Explain, with an example, what is meant by horizontal integration. (3 marks)
5 Explain, with an example, what is meant by vertical integration. (3 marks)
6 Why do new bosses often make changes? (5 marks)
7 Explain why poor business performance is often a trigger for change. (4 marks)
8 Explain two difficulties firms may face when entering overseas markets. (6 marks)
9 Explain how the role of the founders might change over time as the business grows. (6 marks)
10 Explain two factors that might affect how much a firm pays to takeover another. (6 marks)

Analysis and evaluation questions

1 Analyse the reasons why one bank may want to take over another bank. (8 marks)

Business in Focus

Magners

Figure 24.2

In 2008 C&C, the company that owns Magners cider, announced disappointing results. The profits of the company had been hit by poor weather, which reduced sales of cider, greater efforts by competitors owned by the huge Scottish and Newcastle and Bulmers, and the recession. Maurice Pratt, the chief executive of C&C, announced his resignation.

'I have to be accountable and take responsibility for business performance. The company has to take important strategic choices and I have therefore decided it is time to stand aside and allow a new CEO to bring fresh thinking and impetus to the business.'

Questions:

1 Analyse the factors that might have caused a fall in the sales of Magners.
2 Discuss the problems the new chief executive might face bringing about change.

2 Analyse the possible actions the managers of a major construction company might take after a significant fall in profits. (8 marks)

3 With reference to companies or industries you know, to what extent is a strategy of growth desirable? (15 marks)

One step further: Greiner's stages of growth

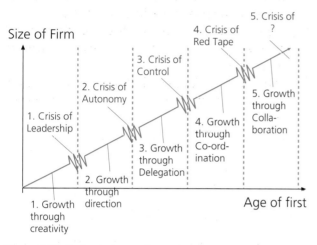

Figure 24.3 Greiner's stages of growth

According to Greiner (1972) the key stages of growth for a business are as follows.

1. Creativity

This is common with a start-up business when there are new ideas. Entrepreneurs may have created a new product or process and the business structure is fairly informal. Communication between employees is regular and frequent, typically employees work hard at this stage, often helping to do a range of jobs. They may not be paid particularly well but may be hoping to continue to be part of the business as it grows.

As the business grows there are more jobs to be done, there is greater complexity and there are more decisions to be made. The informal creative approach no longer works and there is a leadership crisis.

2. Direction

Typically a traditional functional structure is adopted at this stage, clarifying who does what and avoiding the overlap of jobs and decisions that was happening before as the business grew. Roles become more defined, budgets are set to determine how much can be spent, appraisals are introduced to review progress. Generally, systems are introduced to control the direction of the business.

However, if the business continues to grow with more products, more division and more regions then a centralised approach with one set of rules and systems may not be appropriate. In this situation there may be an autonomy crisis. The senior managers need to delegate.

3. Delegation

This occurs when a business decentralises and lets local regions or divisions make more decisions and react to local market conditions. Business units are likely to be run as profit centres, with reviews of progress and more independence.

The problem with this approach is that if the business continues to grow and be successful each section of the business may see itself as a separate unit and then there is a lack of control of what they are doing. This is a control crisis. To overcome this problem managers may enter phase four.

4. Coordination

This occurs when there is formal planning for the business as a whole. Key functions, such as human resources and purchasing, are centralised. The danger of this approach is that a large number of centralised forms and controls develop, causing a red tape crisis.

5. Collaboration

In this system teams work independently but collaborate. Cross-functional teams provide a common sense of purpose and work on projects the different units have in common. While this may work there is always the danger of another crisis occurring (shown by Figure 24.3) requiring some restructuring or some change of management style.

25 Planning for change

According to the management writer Peter Drucker, 'The greatest danger in times of turbulence is not the turbulence; it is to act with yesterday's logic.'

Managers should be looking ahead to anticipate change. Much better to be ready for what might happen than to have it happen to you. By anticipating change and planning ahead managers have more chance of being in control of their own destiny. The central plan of the business is known as the corporate plan.

In this chapter we examine:
- the purpose of corporate plans
- the internal and external influences on corporate plans
- the value of corporate plans.

Introduction

A corporate plan sets out what the business as a whole is trying to achieve and how it intends to achieve this. It will include the corporate objectives and the overall business strategy to be pursued. These overall targets and plans must them be turned into specific objectives and strategies for each of the functions.

A corporate plan may be derived from a process of comparing the internal **s**trengths and **w**eaknesses of the business with the future external **o**pportunities and **t**hreats. This process of strategic planning is known as SWOT analysis.

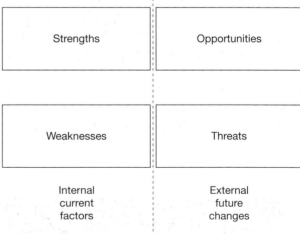

Figure 25.2 SWOT analysis

The plan may aim to build on the company's strengths such as its brand, its strong cashflow position, its broad portfolio or its expertise in order to exploit new opportunities.

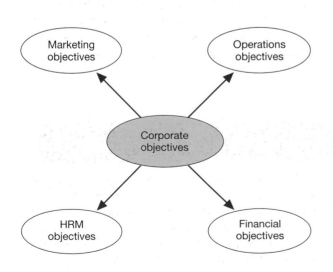

Figure 25.1 Corporate objectives leading to functional objectives

The value of corporate planning

The value of planning is that it makes sure that managers are looking ahead and thinking about what they want to achieve and how to achieve it, rather than just drifting along. Producing a corporate plan is also a useful exercise because it forces managers to consider the organisation's strengths and weaknesses in relation to its environment and to think about how all the different elements of the firm interrelate.

All other plans within a business can also be derived from the corporate plan. Each function can decide what it has to do to contribute to the overall direction and objectives of the business. Then, within each department, plans can be developed to contribute to the functional targets. Here is an example.

Corporate plan:
- Corporate target: grow the business by 15 per cent over three years.
- Corporate strategy: open new stores in the UK.

Operations plan:
- Open 5 stores this year, 10 stores the following year then 15 in year 3.

However, corporate planning can have drawbacks. There is a danger that a plan which sets out what a firm is going to do for, say, the next five years is soon out of date. If managers keep pursuing the original plan when all around them has changed there is a danger that they will actually be doing the wrong thing. It may be necessary, therefore, to ensure that the firm has a flexible approach to planning and keeps revisiting the original plan to ensure it remains viable and relevant.

Emergent plans

The end results of planning are often different from those initially intended. Businesses often end up with a different strategy from that intended as conditions change. Talk to your parents – did their careers end up the way they had initially planned, or did they take different turns along the way? The same is true for businesses – they often reassess their plans and alter objectives and strategies.

However, just because the environment changes and ultimately plans may change, this does not mean that planning is not worthwhile – on the contrary, it makes it all the more important. Without planning and review you will not know where you are headed and where you are at any moment. You may wander from the chosen track at any point and indeed may even change your destination, but without planning you do not know where you have come from, what resources you have, what your strengths are and what your options are. Imagine you set off travelling on a gap year without a map. By planning ahead you think about:

- where you might want to visit
- how long you have
- how much money you have
- how you prefer to travel.

You may end up staying somewhere a bit longer than you originally intended, or add a destination, or are delayed by some problems with the travel arrangements. However, because you have a plan you can estimate the knock-on effects, amend your arrangements without necessarily disrupting your overall plans and notify everyone of the consequences.

Key Issues

Planning is an essential part of management. You have to look ahead and see where you want the business to be in the future. Will it change what it does? Will it change where it operates? Will it change how it delivers its products? These are all key questions. You should be able to ask the boss of any organisation, 'where do you see the business in the next five years' time?' and get an answer. Of course circumstances, priorities and resources can change, but it is useful to have a sense of where you are heading, to know what might or might not be an opportunity or threat and to review where you are at any moment compared with where you want to be.

The corporate plan sets out what the business intends to do if it has anticipated the future environment correctly. For example, it may decide to focus on expansion overseas, cost reductions, investment in new products or diversification. However, managers may also want to plan for events that they hope will not happen but which might be very damaging if they do happen. For example, a school might plan for a fire – obviously we hope this will never happen but we need to have a plan in case it does, because it could be so damaging. Planning for the unexpected event is known as 'contingency planning' (see page 349).

Planning needs reviewing

Management is the 'process of getting things done through others' (Stewart). It involves:

- planning where the organisation is heading (this may be expressed in the mission statement and in its objectives)
- organising the resources needed to achieve its targets
- coordinating these resources to ensure everything is running on schedule
- controlling to review progress and, if necessary, change the plan (this may be achieved via systems such as budgets and appraisals).

Setting a plan is all very well. But effective management means you have to have the resources required to implement it. Do you have the people, the skills, the inclination, the finance, the capacity to fulfil the plan? Managers must organise these resources and ensure that the targets, the standards, the means by which they should be achieved and how they are to be achieved are all communicated effectively.

It is also important to assess the progress of the plan at any regular intervals. Where are we compared with where we expected to be? Reviews may occur informally or using formal mechanisms such as budgets and variance analysis and employee appraisals. By reviewing, changes can be made to get things back on track. You may plan to get the top grades in all your subjects; to help make sure you are on the way to achieving this it is helpful to have regular feedback (via mocks and reports) to let you know how it is going. If there are problems in one subject you can devote more energy to this or review your targets. If you never reviewed your progress

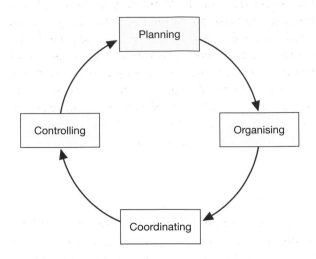

Figure 25.3 Management processes

you might get to the end of your two-year course before realising that your university and career plans were not going to be fulfilled.

Levels of planning

The problems of keeping to a given plan were highlighted by Carl von Clausewitz, a great Prussian military strategist, in his book, *On War,* in 1832. He argued that detailed planning necessarily failed due to chance events, problems in executing the plan and the actions of the opposition. Any grand strategy you have for a battle falls apart as soon as the opposition is met because they do not react the way you want and the battle conditions are never quite what you expect, and so you have to change the plan. What matters at times like these is leadership, good morale and the instinct of generals to react to the chaos of the battlefield. Clausewitz argued that it is vital to set broad objectives, but that you also need to be ready to seize opportunities as they evolve rather than stick rigidly to some plan drawn up away from the battlefield.

The same may be true of business; managers must rely at times on their feelings, on what needs to be done quickly, and must be prepared to jettison a plan that is no longer appropriate. However, it is still important to know the broad objectives and ways you want to compete because this will determine what you do overall. What Clausewitz's experience suggests is that some of the detail of any plan may be changed in the heat of battle as conditions turn out to be different from those you expected and because they change during the battle. So you need good generals (managers) who understand the overall strategy and objectives and know your resources so they can make the right decisions at any moment. This would suggest that getting the right staff and drawing the broad strokes of the plan are essential to success, but so is being prepared for details to change along the way.

Contingency planning

Businesses operate in uncertain and risky environments. Managers are always making decisions about the future and inevitably are not sure of exactly what the future will be like. This makes planning even more important; planning for a situation that is expected but also reviewing the plan regularly to assess where the business is compared with where it expected to be and to decide what to do next to get back on track if necessary. As mentioned above, one type of planning is known as contingency planning. This occurs when a firm prepares for unlikely events, such as:

- a fire
- the bankruptcy of a major customer
- the closure of an important supplier
- a major computer virus attacking the database
- an epidemic causing illness among staff.

Contingency plans might include:

- using two suppliers for the same part or component in case there are problems with one of them; this can safeguard supply
- paying a fee to be able to use computer facilities or office space elsewhere in case of flooding, earthquake or a terrorist attack *LOL!*
- training employees in several tasks so they can take over from others if there are major absences, illnesses or strikes
- ensuring new products are in development so that if there is a problems with existing products they can be replaced.

However, you cannot afford to have a contingency plan for every event (such as alien invasion or being hit by a meteorite). Managers must therefore decide exactly which events are worth preparing for and how many resources to put into contingency planning. Should the firm have back-up plans in case there are problems with suppliers? Should it have a plan for what to do if there is a safety problem with one of its products? What about planning for a situation where a competitor makes a takeover bid? Decisions must be based on the likely risk and damage of any event.

A contingency plan should provide a sense of direction and enable each element of the business to see how it should contribute. It should help managers set their priorities and allocate their resources.

Business in Focus

Extracts from Starbucks' Annual Report

Annual reports published by companies often include forward-looking statements. They use words such as 'believes', 'expects', 'anticipates', 'estimates', 'intends', and 'plans', highlighting how uncertain the future is.

In Starbucks' 2007 Annual Report it lists many possible future events that could make its projections inaccurate. These include exchange rate changes, epidemics (because people would not want to socialise at Starbucks anymore), changes in attitudes towards coffee if there were found to be

health issues, damage to the company's reputation, cost increases beyond the company's control, a downturn in the US economy, the loss of key personnel, and technology failure. No company can control the future but it can try to anticipate possible threats.

Question:

1 The risks and uncertainties above relate specifically to Starbucks. With reference to a business of your choice, analyse two significant risks it faces.

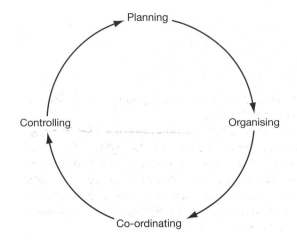

Figure 25.4

The greater the likelihood of an event and the greater the potential damage if it does occur, the more likely a firm is to plan for it. Food manufacturers, for example, are likely to plan for a situation where their products are contaminated and they have to recall them. An airline will plan for a crash. An oil transportation business will prepare for a spillage.

The need for contingency planning highlights the dynamic nature of business and the need to be prepared for the unexpected. Obviously a firm cannot prepare for every emergency but it is worth highlighting the biggest risks and preparing for these. Firms must continually examine their own operations and their environment to check that they are prepared for possible changes in the future; in this way managers will be proactive (anticipating and preparing for change) rather than reactive (having to react to crises as they develop).

Of course this does not mean that companies that have contingency plans are safe from disaster; unfortunately managers often do not or cannot foresee what events will occur. In 2008, for example, there was a major global financial crisis that few had predicted. This led to a problem gaining credit and lower customer spending which damaged many businesses, very few of whom would have had any form of plan for this scenario.

The impact of a crisis

When a disaster does occur, such as a fault in the product or a fire at the factory, this can cause panic. It is hoped that the firm will have a contingency plan which it can put into action, but even so this is likely to be a stressful time. It is easy to rush into a decision at times like these because of the pressure to do something and be seen to be doing something – this can lead to rushed and inappropriate decision-making. On the other hand, if you delay too long the crisis may get worse. As well as sorting out the crisis itself, the firm may have to handle the press as well. When managing a crisis it is important to:

- Identify the 'facts' as soon as possible. What is the scale of the problem? How many people are likely to be affected?
- Establish good communication systems. Managers must make sure that everyone is 'on line' and reacting in the same way. If, for example, different managers are giving the press different information following a scare about the safety of the

Business in Focus

Lehman Brothers

After the terrorist attacks on 11 September 2001 Lehman Brothers, an investment bank which had offices just across the road from the World Trade Center, was able to restart its business in New York almost immediately. This was thanks to careful advance planning which meant its computer systems allowed many of its staff to work from home, and others to set up in hotel rooms as a temporary measure. As a result, it came through the period after 11 September better than some of its competitors that suffered much less physical damage and disruption. (Despite such contingency planning Lehman Brothers later collapsed in the financial crisis of 2008, showing that no business is ever completely safe.)

Question:

1 To what extent is planning for terrorist attacks a good use of resources?

Business in Focus

Disaster planning

In 2008 over 5 million Southern Californians agreed to simultaneously drop to the floor on a given day and huddle face down under tables and desks for two minutes of imagined seismic turmoil in the biggest US earthquake drill ever.

The Great Southern California ShakeOut drill was organised by scientists and emergency officials as part of a campaign to prepare the region's 22 million inhabitants for a catastrophic earthquake that experts say is inevitable and long overdue.

The exercise is based on the premise of a magnitude 7.8 tremor striking the San Andreas Fault, similar in strength to a devastating earthquake that had hit China recently.

At precisely 10 a.m. on a given day people in classrooms, offices and homes throughout the region had to 'drop, cover and hold on' for two minutes, the duration of the hypothetical quake. They were guided by a public service message distributed to businesses and schools and played over the airwaves by radio and TV stations.

Question:

1   To what extent would disaster planning be useful for all businesses?

---

product, this will create the impression they are not in control and the public may lose faith.

* Have the authority and resources to make decisions quickly, rather than having to consult endless committees.

Business in Focus

Johnson & Johnson

Tylenol is a headache cure (like aspirin) produced by Johnson & Johnson. In 1982 it had 35 per cent of the US over-the-counter market and accounted for around 15 per cent of the company's profits. That year someone interfered with some of Johnson & Johson's Tylenol products and added cyanide. Seven people died as a result and there was widespread panic about how many products had been contaminated. The same situation occurred in 1986 but this time the company had learnt its lessons. It acted quickly, ordering that Tylenol should be recalled from every outlet, not just those in the state where it had been tampered with. Not only that, but the company decided the product would not be re-established on the shelves until something had been done to provide better product protection. As a result, Johnson & Johnson developed the tamperproof packaging that would make it much safer in future. The cost was extremely high. The share price fell, there was lost production and millions of packets of Tylenol were destroyed as a result of the recall.

However, the company won praise for its quick and appropriate action. Having sidestepped the position others have found themselves in – of having been slow to act in the face of consumer concern – they achieved the status of consumer champion. Within five months it had regained 70 per cent of its market share. By comparison, companies such as Cadbury and Perrier have been criticised for the way they handled crises when their products were contaminated. They were slow to react and accept there was a problem and lost customer goodwill which took longer to recover.

Johnson & Johnson reacted very quickly in 1986 because of its previous experience of how serious it could be and because everyone in the business knew that its mission statement (called Our Credo) stated that the business was there to serve the doctors, nurses, mothers and patients – so they had to take action and did not need to hesitate. This reaction is often quoted as evidence of how important the values of a company are and how they influence behaviour. A different business might have hesitated to act, might have tried to keep the incident quiet and might have tried to do as little as it could get away with.

Question:

1   To what extent would disaster planning be useful for all businesses?

Scenario planning

This is another technique to help managers plan ahead. In this approach managers try to imagine three or four possible scenarios that might develop in the future in their industry. Scenario planning does not assume the future will be like the past, but asks managers and experts to think of what the world might look like in the future. This could be very different from the past (as we have seen with the rapid collapse of financial markets in 2007 and 2008 across the world). This technique has been used widely by Shell where managers work with experts to create possible visions of what the world might look like in the future. For example, one scenario might include a stable political position in the Middle East, high levels of oil production and a low oil price. Another might focus on high levels of intervention by the government to reduce car usage, leading to high taxes and low levels of demand. Managers then work on how these scenarios might affect the business and the implications for their strategy. Schwartz describes scenarios as: 'Stories that can help us recognise and adapt to changing aspects of our present environment. They form a method for articulating the different pathways that might exist for you tomorrow, and finding your appropriate movements down each of those possible paths.'

Summary

Planning is an important part of the management process; it is then followed through by organising, coordinating, and controlling. The corporate plan is the overall plan of the business; this then influences the functional plans. The corporate plan should be linked to the external environment, the culture and the strengths and weaknesses of the business. Contingency planning is a particular form of planning which tries to prepare for dramatic and usually unwelcome change. Scenario planning may also be used to try and see what the future might hold and how the business should compete in different landscapes.

Progress questions

1 Explain what is meant by a corporate plan. (2 marks)

2 State three items likely to be in a corporate plan. (3 marks)

People in Business

Gary Hamel

Working with CK Prahalad, Gary Hamel developed the concept of core competencies in 1990. 'Core competencies are the collective learning in the organisation, especially how to co-ordinate diverse production skills and integrate multiple streams of technologies', i.e. they are the things that an organisation does extremely well and therefore its strategy should be based on this. If an organisation is not good at something it should consider outsourcing it to others that have competencies in these areas, i.e. business should concentrate on what they are good at. Hamel saw strategic planning not as a series of logical steps but as moments of dramatic change. He said that 'Strategic innovation will be the main source of competitive advantage in the future.' He believed great strategies come from challenging the status quo. He quoted Anita Roddick, the founder of Body Shop: 'I watch where the cosmetics industry is going and then walk in the opposite direction.'

'Management was designed to solve a very specific problem – how to do things with perfect replicability, at ever-increasing scale and steadily increasing efficiency. Now there's a new set of challenges on the horizon. How do you build organisations that are as nimble as change itself?'

In his book *The Future of Management* Hamel says: 'Management is out of date. Like the combustion engine, it's a technology that has largely stopped evolving, and that's not good ... My goal in writing this book was not to predict the future of management, but to help you invent it.' Businesses need to think about their purpose, seek out ideas from the fringes, and embrace the democratising power of the internet.

Books:

1 *Competing for the Future*, with Prahalad, CK, Harvard Business School Press, 1994

2 *Strategy as Revolution*, Harvard Business Review, July–August 1996

3 *Leading the Revolution*, Harvard Business School Press, 2000

4 *The Future of Management*, with Breen, B, Harvard Business School Press, 2007

Source: Adapted from Economist.com, 26 September 2008

3 Explain two factors likely to influence a corporate plan. (6 marks)

4 Explain the links between a corporate plan and the functional plans. (5 marks)

5 Explain two factors that might influence a corporate plan. (6 marks)

6 What is meant by a contingency plan? (2 marks)

7 What is meant by scenario planning? (2 marks)

8 Explain two reasons why a corporate plan might go wrong. (6 marks)

9 What is meant by an emergent plan? (3 marks)

10 Explain why a plan needs to be reviewed. (3 marks)

Analysis and evaluation questions

1 Analyse the likely key elements of a corporate plan for a business such as the BBC. (8 marks)

2 To what extent is contingency planning a worthwhile investment for an airline? (15 marks)

3 To what extent is corporate planning useful for an organisation such as General Electric? (15 marks)

Web link

For information on General Electric visit www.ge.com

Case study

Corporate objectives

In 2004 the directors of J Sainsbury outlined the plan to Make Sainsbury's Great Again ('MSGA').

Our vision is simple; we are here to serve customers well with a choice of great food at fair prices and, by so doing, to provide shareholders with strong, sustainable financial returns. This has driven everything we have done since we outlined our recovery plan in October 2004.

To enable us to measure our progress we set some key three-year targets:

- To grow sales by £2.5 billion, with grocery contributing sales of £1.4 billion, non-food products sales of £700 million and convenience stores sales of £400 million.
- To invest at least £400 million in improving product quality and our price position relative to competitors and to find annual buying synergies to be reinvested in the customer offer.
- To deliver operating cost efficiencies of at least £400 million.
- To generate neutral underlying cash flow in 2005/06 and positive cash flow thereafter.

These were demanding targets and the business has had to challenge itself in every area in response.

In 2007 the business reviewed in progress

Against these clearly defined key performance indicators we made good progress this year.

We grew sales by over £1 billion, taking our total sales growth over the past two years of the recovery plan to £1.8 billion and ahead of plan.

The £400 million of investment in the customer offer was completed by December 2006 and additional funds were invested in early 2007, improving product quality and giving us our most competitive price position for many years.

We increased our cost savings target to £440 million following our insourcing of IT in April 2006 and we are on track to deliver this.

We achieved an underlying cash flow positive position earlier than expected – in 2005/06 – so we targeted a cash neutral position in 2006/07 and have again exceeded that target despite increased capital expenditure.

These achievements give us a strong foundation on which to build.

We believe now is the right time to look to the next stage of our recovery and to expand the business to drive growth for the longer term. So we have set ourselves new three-year targets that build on the strong progress we've made so far and move us from recovery to growth.

(40 marks, 60 minutes)

Questions

1 Explain the features of an effective objective for Sainsbury's. (5 marks)
2 Analyse the difficulties Sainsbury's might have faced when trying to achieve the objectives it set for the first three years. (8 marks)
3 Discuss the targets Sainsbury's might set for the next three years. (12 marks)
4 To what extent do you think setting the targets above would have been useful to the business? (15 marks)

26 Key influences on the change process: leadership

How a business reacts to change and whether it leads change will depend in part on its leaders. Strong leaders may take a business in a new direction, may revitalise it and may bring about major change. In this chapter we examine:

- the meaning and significance of leadership
- the range of leadership styles
- the internal and external factors influencing leadership style
- the role of leadership in managing change
- the importance of leadership.

What is a leader?

Many business writers draw a distinction between a leader and a manager. A manager is someone who gets things done. They tend to focus on the present and the short term and are responsible for implementing the decisions of others. They manage but they also follow. Their role in many ways is to maintain things the way they are.

Leaders, by comparison, are people who are followed, who have a vision of the future and a clear sense of where they are taking the business. A leader decides what needs to be done and is prepared to shake things up to get them done. According to a significant writer in this area, John Adair, 'Leadership is the process of motivating others to act in particular ways.'

Leaders	Managers
Look to the future	Focus on the present
Are willing to break the mould, innovate	Maintain the status quo
Have vision	Are implementers

According to Drucker (1985) a leader has the ability to generate a commitment and is capable of 'lifting of

people's vision to a higher sight, the raising of their performance to a higher standard, the building of their personality beyond its normal limitations'.

A leader should understand where he or she wants to take the business. They should be able to provide a clear direction for the business and motivate and inspire others. A leader is often brought in to make changes. The leader will know what needs to be done and is responsible for making it happen. Leaders may or may not always be liked but should be pushing (or pulling) the business forward.

According to Kotter (1990), 'leadership and management are two distinctive and complementary systems of action. Each has its own function and characteristic activities. Both are necessary for success in an increasingly complex and volatile business environment.' Whereas management is about coping with complexity (i.e. making sense of a complex environment), leadership is about coping with change (i.e. coping with moving from one complex environment to another).

What makes a leader?

Given the importance of leadership in determining the direction (and therefore the success or failure) of a business it is not surprising that there have been many studies to try and identify what makes a leader. Some of these theories are examined below.

Trait theories

Early studies of leadership tried to identify qualities (or traits) that successful leaders possessed. They tried to identify exactly what it is that makes some one a leader (e.g. self-confidence, extroversion).

If we can identify a set of traits that all leaders have then we should be able to identify future leaders by looking at what they are like. However, despite numerous trait studies no common set of qualities has yet been identified. Some leaders seem to be loud, some seem quiet; some seem very confident, others less so. This difference in the qualities of leaders means that in practice trait theories have not been very useful. Nevertheless, according to Stodgill (1974) the most common traits that leaders seem to have include being:

- adaptable to situations
- ambitious and achievement oriented
- assertive
- decisive
- dependable
- dominant
- energetic
- persistent
- self-confident
- tolerant of stress
- willing to assume responsibility.

Unfortunately, this does not mean all leaders are like this!

Behavioural theories

These theories focus on how a leader behaves, trying to identify the right way of leading rather than what a leader is like as a person. Once again there have been many studies looking at styles of leadership. For example, researchers at Ohio State University used questionnaires to ask employees to describe the behaviour of their managers. They identified two dimensions: 'consideration' and 'initiating structure'.

- A **considerate style** focuses on the wellbeing of subordinates. Are they comfortable at work? Do they feel at ease? Do they feel well treated? This style listens to employees, encourages them and treats them with respect. This type of manager is approachable and rewards good performance.
- By comparison, an **initiating structure** focuses on defining and planning work. The leader concentrates on getting the work done. They allocate the tasks, inform subordinates of their task and monitor what is happening.

Another study by researchers at Michigan University called the relevant dimensions 'task orientation' and 'relationship orientation'. These different styles can be analysed using the Blake Mouton grid (1964). The vertical scale on this grid reflects a leader's concern for people. The horizontal scale reflects concern for the task.

Leadership styles can also be analysed in terms of the extent to which managers 'tell' or 'listen to' their employees.

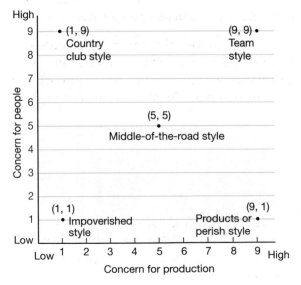

The Blake Moulton grid examines management styles in terms of their concern for production and their concern for people. You can plot a manager's style on the grid. Different styles of management include:

Country club leadership – this places a lot of focus on people and very little on the task itself. This type of leader is most concerned about the needs and feelings of members of the team. The work environment is likely to be relaxed and fun but the work may suffer due to lack of control and supervision.

Produce or perish leadership – this places a great deal of emphasis on the task and little on the people. It is likely to be very authoritarian. Employees are a means to an end; getting the job done is the key, regardless of the implications for the people.

Impoverished leadership – this has a low concern for the task and the people. The type of leader is ineffective. He or she does not focus on getting the job done or creating an environment where people want to work. The result is both work and people are neglected.

Middle-of-the-road leadership – this has some focus on the task and on people but not a great deal. It is a compromise between meeting peoples' needs and getting the job done but neither is fully met. The result is an average performance.

Team leadership – this approach has a high focus on the task and people. Employees are involved in the task and want to get it done. They are involved in the process and their needs are met by doing a good job.

Figure 26.1 The Blake Mouton grid

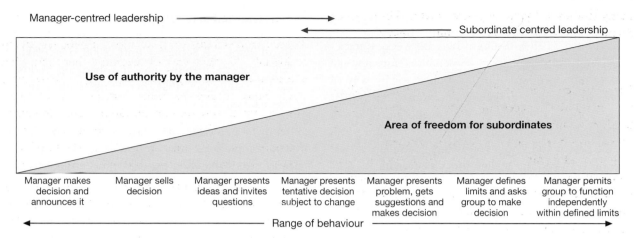

Figure 26.2 Tonnenbaum Schmidt Continuum (1973)

- An **autocratic (or authoritarian) leader** is one who tells employees what to do. This may make sense in some circumstances, for example if:
  - a decision needs to be made quickly
  - employees lack the skills and training to decide
  - the leader wants to keep control.
- However, it can:
  - demotivate staff who do not feel involved
  - mean that the leader does not benefit from the ideas and skills of subordinates.
- A **democratic approach** involves more consultation. The leader asks for the views of subordinates and discusses the options with them. This can be a slower decision-making process but may lead to better quality results because:
  - it utilises the talents of more people
  - ideas are discussed so better solutions may be found and flaws may be uncovered
  - employees feel more committed to the decision because they were part of it.

In fact there are a range of different styles of management which are shown on the Tannenbaum Schmidt continuum above.

The contingency approach to leadership

The contingency approach recognises that the 'right' leadership style depends on a variety of factors such as:

- The nature of the leader – Do they like to keep control? Do they like to know what is happening at all times? Has an autocratic approach worked for them in the past? If the answer is yes to all of these then an autocratic style is likely to be adopted.
- The nature of the subordinates – Do they have the skills and experience to make decisions for themselves? Do they expect and want to be involved?
- The nature of the task – Is the task simple (in which case employees may be able to decide for themselves)? Does a decision have to be made rapidly (in which case an authoritarian approach might be appropriate)? Would the decision benefit from debate and different perspectives?

This approach stresses that the style of leadership needs to be adapted at different times. This either means leaders themselves must adapt or that different leaders are appropriate in different circumstances.

Business in Focus

Barak Obama

In 2008 Barak Obama was elected President of the United States of America. He is the first black president of this country. He was elected on a message of change and inspired many people to become interested again in the political process and to go and vote. He is described by many as a transformational leader.

Question:

1 Can you think of any leader in the world of business, sport, politics, religion or any other field that you would regard as transformational? Justify your choice.

Transactional and transformational leaders

James Burn (1978) distinguished between transactional and transformational leadership. Transactional leaders influence subordinates' behaviour by way of a bargain. The leader enables followers to reach their goals if they contribute to the organisation's goals. You help the business to succeed and in return you get the salary and status you want. Essentially a deal is done between the leader and subordinate.

Transformational leaders, by comparison, get subordinates to change their goals, needs and aspirations. They change their subordinates. They raise subordinates views to a higher level. They demonstrate 'transcendent goals, demonstration of self-confidence and confidence in others, setting a personal example for followers showing high expectations of followers' performance and the ability to communicate one's faith in one's goals' (Fiedler and House, 1994).

Why do we follow leaders?

A leader is someone who is followed. Why do we follow others? Because they have power over us. According to French and Raven (1959) there are a number of different sources of power that a leader might have. These are:

- **Legitimate power** is the authority that flows from their position in the organisation; for example, they are the chief executive and are recognised as 'the boss' because of the job title they have.
- **Reward power** is power that comes from the leader's ability to give out benefits. For example, you may do as you are told because someone can decide whether you get a pay increase or a promotion.
- **Coercive power** occurs if someone has the power to force you to do something; perhaps they threaten you with redundancy? This is not a positive source of power – it may lead people to do as they are told but it does not mean they are willing followers.
- **Referent power** occurs when you follow someone because you respect them. You admire them and want to be like them. Philip Green, who owns Top Shop, Next, Burton, Wallis and Evans, is said to be a forceful and successful character who is very impressive for those who come into contact with him.
- **Expertise power** occurs when you follow someone because you respect their intelligence, their knowledge of an issue and their expertise. Sir Fred Goodwin, who was the chief executive of the Royal Bank of Scotland until 2008, was said to have superb insight into the banking industry (despite the fact that his bank ended up in financial difficulty).

Of course, a leader may have several sources of power. Employees may follow a chief executive because she is the chief executive, because she has a superb grasp of the direction the business should move in, because she has a brilliant personality, because she decides on your bonus and because she has the power to sack you – that would be one very powerful leader!

Why do leaders matter?

Leaders provide the vision that takes a business forward. They take the difficult decisions and bring about the difficult change. They can inspire or push through change. Leadership may not always be in the hands of one person – the leaders may be a team – but the direction needs to come from somewhere. Particularly in a crisis people look to a leader for guidance and to show them what to do; this is why, when an organisation is in trouble, a new leader is often brought in. Of course, leaders cannot by themselves save a business – they need the support and help of others, and great leadership may not in itself be enough if the external environment is too harsh or the weaknesses of the business too great. However, the ability of great leaders in sport, in business, in politics and in all aspects of life to achieve great things is inspiring. Just think of someone like Nelson Mandela who helped bring about the end of the division between blacks and whites in South Africa and made this a peaceful process through leading by example.

Summary

A leader drives a business forward. This may be important to push the business through a period of change or indeed bring about change in the industry. A manager is more of an implementer; someone who gets things done but does not necessarily inspire or have vision. Businesses need leaders and managers and these individuals are an important element of success. Managers are the ones who plan, organise, coordinate and control and, as such, they determine how the business performs.

Key Issues

All organisations need a direction. This may be expressed on paper in the form of a mission statement, but someone (or a group of people) need to lead the business forward. A key issue is where to find such people. Should they be recruited internally or externally? Can we train them to become leaders or are people born leaders? Should we always look for someone in our industry or would someone with a different set of experiences be better? How can we prepare someone for the role?

Business in Focus

Woolworths

In 2008 Trevor Bish-Jones was asked to step down as Chief Executive of Woolworths after more than six years as leader of the troubled variety retailer. He had found it difficult to turn around a business that had unfavourable leases and an outdated business model. He had some success in improving the wholesale side of the business, which distributed CDs and DVDs to other retailers. However, the Woolworths stores proved too difficult to sort out and Bish-Jones left with the shares at an all-time low. 'It has been agreed between the board and Trevor that this is an appropriate time to seek new leadership for the business,' said the chairman at the time. 'The search for his successor is underway. We will consider both external and internal candidates.' As well as trying to fix an ailing business, Mr Bish-Jones had to contend complaints from Baugur, the Icelandic investment group which owns a 10 per cent stake in the retailer, which last year said that the management 'have to get their act together'. The financial problems of Woolworth's were very severe and the business closed soon after Bish-Jones left. The biggest blame can possibly be put on the credit crisis – which stripped Woolworths' suppliers of their credit insurance and led to a dash for cash, causing problems with working capital plans and cash-flow projections on which the group's borrowing facilities relied.

Questions:

1 Should Bish-Jones be held responsible for the decline of Woolworth's?

Progress questions

1 What is a leader? (2 marks)

2 Distinguish between a leader and a manager. (4 marks)

3 What is meant by transformational leadership? (2 marks)

4 Outline three sources of power for a leader. (6 marks)

5 What is meant by trait theory? (2 marks)

6 Explain two factors that might influence the leadership style adopted. (6 marks)

7 Distinguish between autocratic and democratic leadership styles. (4 marks)

8 Distinguish between people-oriented and task-oriented leadership styles. (4 marks)

9 Outline the key features of the Blake Mouton grid. (5 marks)

10 Explain two ways in which a leader can affect the success of a business. (6 marks)

Analysis and evaluation questions

1 Analyse the difference between a leader and a manager. (8 marks)

2 With reference to organisations or industries that you know, discuss the ways in which a leader can affect the success of a business. (15 marks)

3 To what extent do you think a leader is born rather than made? (15 marks)

Case study

Sir Stuart Rose is the chief executive of Marks and Spencer plc and has helped turn the business around. He sees himself as independent minded and does not like some of the constraints he is supposed to adhere to as the chief executive of a public company. He was brought in as chief executive in 2004 from Top Shop to defend the business against Philip Green's takeover bid approach. He not only saved the company from takeover but also revived its fortunes, bringing in a new management team in a dramatic boardroom coup and pushing up profits. His dramatic strategy has involved buying the women's fashion brand Per Una from its creator George Davies and selling the firm's financial services division to focus on the chain's core business – women's fashion. Sir Stuart has used a number of high-profile advertising campaigns featuring celebrities, including 1960s model Twiggy and Hollywood actor Antonia Banderas, backed up by strong product offerings, which have helped to inject glamour back into the failing brand.

Perceived better value for money has also helped lure back disenchanted shoppers, which Sir Stuart has achieved through squeezing suppliers, while co-founder of Lastminute.com Martha Lane Fox was drafted in to improve the firm's internet offering. A strong commitment to ethical values and an environmentally friendly approach has also had a winning effect. Earlier in 2007 the chain announced a five-year plan to go carbon neutral, cutting energy consumption, stopping the use of landfill sites and stocking more products made from recycled materials. Under Sir Stuart M&S also launched a Fairtrade clothing range.

However, his decision to become executive chairman as well as chief executive was met with great criticism. By combining these roles he is, in effect, overseeing himself – this approach has been criticised by some for giving him too much power. Before the economic crisis hit in 2008 Stuart Rose looked likely to leave. He had turned the company around and was ready for another challenge. However, with a downturn in the economy and tough competition he was encouraged to stay even if it meant he became chairman and chief executive. Letting him go at this stage was not an option.

Sir Stuart believes the company is best led by one strong leader. Lord (Simon) Marks, the son of the founder, ruled as chairman for 48 years, as did all his successors until Sir Richard Greenbury agreed to become non-executive chairman in 1999, with Peter Salsbury as chief executive. That arrangement proved disastrous for the company. Some might ask, therefore, if M&S was highly successful for most of its 105-year history being run by an executive chairman, why not return to that arrangement?

Yet, far more important for M&S than a corporate governance controversy is the lack of succession. There was no one ready to take on Rose's role as chief executive.

- Sir Stuart started his career in retail in 1972 after joining M&S as a management trainee. He remained with the company for 17 years, holding a variety of roles in the textiles and food divisions, before being appointed commercial director heading M&S's European operations in Paris.
- He joined Burton Group in 1989, which included Debenhams department stores and the Top Shop and Dorothy Perkins fashion chains. The group later demerged into Arcadia and Debenhams. He joined the latter as a buying and merchandising director before going on to head Burton Menswear, Evans, Dorothy Perkins and Principles.
- In 1998 he was appointed chief executive of Argos – in the middle of its bid battle with retail giant GUS – and eventually secured a higher price for the catalogue chain.
- He went on to be the boss of troubled cash-and-carry business Booker; he arranged the merger with frozen food retailer Iceland, going on to become the enlarged group's chief executive.
- He became head of Arcadia, which he joined in

November 2000. He turned around this company, which had more than £250 million of debt, and then oversaw the sale in 2002 of Arcadia to BHS-owner Mr Green for £855 million, making £25 million out of the deal himself.

- He was knighted in 2007 for services to the retail industry and corporate social responsibility.

40 marks; 60 minutes

Questions

1 Explain the role of the chief executive of a business such as Marks and Spencer. (5 marks)

2 Analyse the reasons why some analysts do not like the idea of Sir Stuart Rose being the chief executive and chairman. (8 marks)

3 Discuss how you would recruit someone to replace Sir Stuart Rose. (12 marks)

4 With reference to the case above, to what extent do you think Sir Stuart Rose has contributed to the success of Marks and Spencer? (15 marks)

One step further: Mintzberg and management

In the 1970s Henry Mintzberg undertook a great deal of research into the nature of managerial work. From his studies he concluded that:

- Senior managers are very busy and have heavy workloads! There is little free time and trying to get away from work is difficult.
- The work is fragmented; you are moving from one task to another. You need to focus on what really matters and what really makes a difference (80 per cent of results usually come from 20 per cent of the effort, so try and work out what that 20 per cent is). Interruptions are common and there is little time to sit back and think.
- Managers focus on short-term immediate problems. They are often fire-fighting, dealing with the problem in front of them; this pushes them away from long-term planning and thinking.
- Verbal contact is preferred to written as with the latter lots of information is received but it takes longer to get a response.
- Managers seldom get out and about; walking around is useful because it makes you visible and makes you more aware of the issues within the business.
- Managers actually control little of what they do day to day – things happen *to* them!

It is all too easy to have a vision of calm logical planning by senior managers who are looking years ahead. In reality they are pushed and shoved by day-to-day emergencies.

27 Key influences on the change process: culture

Just as every person has their own personality, their own values and their own attitudes to things, so every business is different. There are, of course, obvious differences between, say, a car manufacturer and a software design business just in terms of the types of resource used, the working environment and the nature of the work. However, even if you visit two businesses in the same sector, such as two insurance firms, two clothes retailers or two banks, you will find enormous differences in the way they do things. This is because the culture of businesses varies.

In this chapter we examine:
• the meaning and significance of organisational culture
• types of organisational culture
• the reasons for and problems of changing organisational culture
• the importance of organisational culture.

What is culture?

The culture of a business can be described as the values, attitudes and beliefs of the people working for it. It describes 'the way we do things around here' (Ouchi 1981). Hoftstede (1991) describes it as 'the collective programming of the mind', which perhaps highlights how individuals' own values may change as they become accustomed to the established ways of doing things when they join a business.

In reality, there is no one culture in a business – different departments, different levels within the business, different groups of employees may all have their own way of doing things; nevertheless there may be some key areas where people generally agree and this can therefore help to define 'the overall culture' of a business.

> **Key terms**
> The **culture** of a business refers to the values, attitudes and beliefs of its employees; it refers to 'how we do things around here'.

Schein (2004) identified three levels of culture, as follows.

1. The artefacts

These represent the visible level of culture, e.g. what the buildings look like, what is displayed on the walls, what people wear, what stories are told. Within minutes of walking into any business we immediately get a sense of what it is like from the artefacts we see around us although we may not always understand the significance of them (do you have a school crest? Would an outsider understand what it represented without it being explained for them?).

2. The stated beliefs and values

This refers to the beliefs of employees about the work they are doing and the issues they face, for example:

• whether quality matters
• whether it is important to get it right first time
• whether teams are important
• whether people should be given room to try out their ideas.

Sometimes these values and beliefs will be written down; for example, they may be included in a mission statement.

3. Underlying assumptions

This refers to the assumptions that are deeply held by employees; these will determine the stated beliefs. For example:

- satisfied customers are essential for survival (that's why the customer comes first)
- people work better in teams (that's why we like teamwork)
- we employ capable people (that's why we can give them room to try things out).

Culture and mission statements

The mission statement of a business (if it has one) sets out what the main purpose of a business is, i.e. why it exists. This has to be influenced by the culture of the business. The mission is likely to be determined by the values of the organisation. An organisation that sets out to reward the owners clearly values investors more than other stakeholder groups. A business that values the environment is likely to include this in its mission statement. In fact, some companies do not have a mission statement, they simply have a statement of their values.

> **Key terms**
> The **mission statement** of a business sets out its purpose and values; the reason for its existence. It may also include the scope of its activities, e.g. in terms of products it wants to provide and the regions it aims to compete in.

How can cultures differ?

In the same way as people can differ and their attitudes can vary enormously, so the culture of businesses can be tremendously different. For example, organisations may be:

- entrepreneurial
- bureaucratic
- customer focused
- short run or long run.

Entrepreneurial

In these organisations (such as Google) you are highly valued if you try something, even if it does not necessarily work. The fact you had an idea and tried to make it work is regarded as worthwhile and commendable. This type of organisation may value people who 'think outside the box', try new approaches and show initiative.

Bureaucratic

This type of business may want people who stick to the rules and who do not make decisions for themselves. In some organisations you may not want people to start making up their own rules. At the Revenue and Customs you would want all the tax forms processed in the same way, for example. The risks of letting people use their initiative could be too high in some organisations or some part of organisations; for example, you may want nursing staff to concentrate on administering the treatment doctors have prescribed and not diagnosing people themselves or making decisions on the medication for themselves.

Customer focused

Some organisations clearly value their customers (most would, we hope, but in reality not all do!). This means getting it right for the customer, who is

Business in Focus

Premier Farnell plc

Premier Farnell plc is a leading UK business selling components to electronic engineers. Its values are: 'We are driven to deliver results by being:

- totally reliable (we deliver our promises)
- resourceful (we look for innovative ways to provide solutions)
- customer focused (we understand our customers and suppliers, anticipating their needs)
- with integrity (we are honest and trustworthy).'

Question:

1 How might these values affect the behaviour of employees in the business?

regarded as important – staff are expected to put themselves out to make sure the customers' expectations are met. Employees are not expected to find reasons why things cannot be done. While a customer-focused approach seems sensible and certainly advisable in competitive markets, some businesses have been much more inward looking and have focused on what they could do and what they wanted to do rather than what customers wanted. British Airways had a terrible reputation in the 1970s because it placed too much emphasis on flying planes and not enough on the customer experience. Money was being invested in engines, landing gear and pilots' uniforms but not into improving the in-flight entertainment or the cleanliness of the planes. A big push to refocus on customer needs led to a change in approach (which culminated in the rebranding of the business as the 'world's favourite airline'), training all staff to place the customer first. More recently, McDonald's has been accused of being too inward looking and not appreciating the change in the market demand towards wanting healthier food. Similarly the major American car manufacturers, such as General Motors and Ford, spent too long producing big, oil guzzling cars and did not appreciate that customers wanted more fuel efficient, smaller vehicles that were being provided by producers such as Toyota.

Conservative

In these businesses there is a tendency to avoid risks. Relatively safe decisions are taken and before any new ideas are accepted there is extensive, possibly overly extensive, research. At the other extreme are high-risk organisations where decisions are made without enough thought about the resources and the dangers involved. In 2008 the global banking system underwent major shocks due in part to high-risk lending – bank managers had taken undue risks in their attempts to increase their lending and this had damaged them in the long run when borrowers could not repay.

Short run, long run

Some businesses are very focused on the short term (perhaps because of pressure from investors for dividends); others look more towards the long term (e.g. they might plan 15 years ahead for the next revolution in the internet).

Business in Focus

Our Credo

The mission statement of Johnson & Johnson highlights the importance of the customer to the business. This set of beliefs has been proved on many occasions when employees have worked hard to make sure that customer service is outstanding and that customers are treated properly.

Our Credo

We believe our first responsibility is to the doctors, nurses and patients, to mothers and fathers and all others who use our products and services.
In meeting their needs everything we do must be of high quality.
We must constantly strive to reduce our costs in order to maintain reasonable prices.
Customers' orders must be serviced promptly and accurately.
Our suppliers and distributors must have an opportunity to make a fair profit.
We are responsible to our employees, the men and women who work with us throughout the world.
Everyone must be considered as an individual. We must respect their dignity and recognise their merit.
They must have a sense of security in their jobs.
Compensation must be fair and adequate, and working conditions clean, orderly and safe.
We must be mindful of ways to help our employees fulfill their family responsibilities.
Employees must feel free to make suggestions and complaints.
There must be equal opportunity for employment, development and advancement for those qualified.
We must provide competent management, and their actions must be just and ethical.
We are responsible to the communities in which we live and work and to the world community as well.
We must be good citizens – support good works and charities and bear our fair share of taxes.
We must encourage civic improvements and better health and education.

We must maintain in good order the property we are privileged to use, protecting the environment and natural resources.
Our final responsibility is to our stockholders.
Business must make a sound profit.
We must experiment with new ideas.
Research must be carried on, innovative programmes developed and mistakes paid for.
New equipment must be purchased, new facilities provided and new products launched.

Reserves must be created to provide for adverse times.
When we operate according to these principles, the stockholders should realise a fair return.

Question:

1 Discuss the impact Our Credo might have on the performance of Johnson & Johnson.

The culture of organisations was categorised by Deal and Kennedy in terms of the speed of reward and feedback and the risk involved. They identified four types of culture that relate directly to the nature of the businesses they are in.

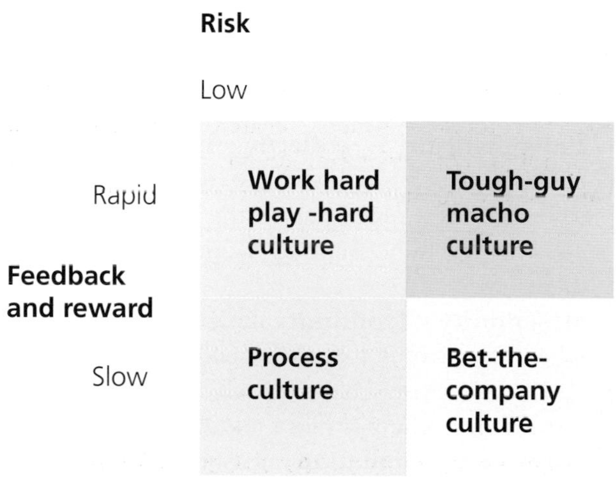

Risk

Low

Figure 27.1

- **Tough-guy macho culture** is an environment in which there is rapid feedback and rewards but also high risk, such as the operating theatres of hospitals, or the police.
- **Work-hard, play-hard culture** is a rapid feedback/reward and low-risk environment such as estate agents. There are lots of deals to be done but any one deal is unlikely to ruin the company if it goes wrong.
- **Process culture** is a slow feedback/reward and low-risk environment such as the civil service.
- **Bet-the-company culture** is a slow feedback/reward and high risk environment, such as pharmaceuticals; you plan ahead for years and then launch the product and hope it succeeds. Here, failure of the product could be distastrous for the whole business.

Types of culture

There are many ways of analysing the culture of a business although, given that every business will be unique, all these can do is describe in broad strokes some of the key features of an approach. One model is that of Charles Handy (1990) which outlines four types of culture. These are:

1 power culture
2 role culture
3 task culture
4 person culture.

Power culture

This type of culture is most common in relatively small, owner-run businesses. There is one dominant person (or a few key people) who makes all the major decisions and all employees refer to them if they want to know what to do. The 'boss' is in charge of all the operations of the business and its success depends very much on them. This can be very positive because it can lead to decisive leadership, quick decision-making and a consistent approach. However, if the business starts to grow the person or people at the centre may become overloaded and cannot cope with the number of decisions that need to be made. This can bring decision-making to a halt as employees wait to get a response. It also encourages employees to become reliant on the boss and not learn how to make decisions for themselves.

Role culture

This is very common in businesses as they grow and tend to adopt a more formal structure and culture. The importance of someone begins to be defined by their position in the hierarchy and their job title. This type of culture relies quite heavily on rules and procedures. To do well you need to follow the systems that are in place and do what is expected of you, rather than using your initiative to define your own job boundaries. Communication is via established channels of communication rather than being, say, through informal conversation. This leads to very predictable outcomes in terms of performance. Senior managers know what is going to happen because employees do what they have been told to do. This has the value of certainty. However, the danger is that the organisation is inflexible to change and is not prepared for unexpected challenges.

Task culture

This is relatively common in businesses such as design agencies or management consultancies, where the value of an individual to a project depends on their expertise rather than any formal title. In this approach teams are formed for particular projects and individuals brought into these as and when they can contribute. Your value depends on what you can add to the team rather than your age or how long you have been working there. This approach can bring together expert teams to help solve different problems; however, coordinating this approach can be difficult.

Person culture

This is not very common but occurs in an organisation or part of an organisation where there are groups of well-qualified individuals who respect each other's skills and knowledge. This may occur in a university or a doctors' practice, for example. Each individual is fairly self-reliant and can make decisions for themselves. They collaborate with each other and share their expertise and skills when needed but operate independently. This works well if the business can function with relatively independent units, but the danger is that the approach lacks consistency and may overlap (e.g. if university lecturers design their own courses independent of each other the student may find that elements of these courses overlap). Unfortunately, sometimes the individuals will resist if a more centralised approach is needed, because they are used to their independence.

National culture

In 1966 Geert Hofstede undertook what has become some of the most famous research on national cultural differences. Around 116,000 employees at all levels of the multinational, IBM, across 50 countries were involved. The result was a massive amount of data on employees within the same organisation but in different countries. This took Hofstede 15 years to analyse. He concluded that there were five major dimensions that can describe a national culture:

- **Power distance** is the extent to which there is a difference between who has the power within a business (e.g. a difference between the boss and the subordinate). A low power distance means that power is distributed fairly equally; a high power distance means there are big differences in power – for example, there are many levels of hierarchy in organisations.
- **Uncertainty avoidance** is the extent to which employees need to know exactly what they are supposed to do and how success is measured. A high uncertainty avoidance means employees want clear guidelines on what to do; a low uncertainty avoidance means employees are willing to be given general guidelines but do not need a high level of detail on what to do and when.
- **Individualism v collectivism** measures the extent to which employees feel they are supposed to be part of a team, part of the business 'family', or whether they want to work and look after themselves.
- **Masculinity v femininity** measures the extent to which employees feel they need to be dominant and assertive (masculine) or whether they feel that concern for others is more important (feminine).
- **Long-term orientation** measures the extent to which individuals plan ahead. Is the long term 5 years or 20 years?

There can be significant differences between societies in terms of how they score on these scales, and managers need to be aware of these differences when having meetings, making decisions and working with overseas partners. The differences that exist can be because of their history, society, traditions and politics. Look below at Hoftede's findings on the UK and China, for example.

The UK is strong on individualism – people recognise and reward individual performance rather than team players; the UK is low on long-term orientation, tending to be short-term planners. China, by comparison, tends to plan for the long term but place less emphasis on the individual. In China the hierarchy is accepted much more than in the UK. You can imagine how these differences could cause problems in business. Chinese managers might be interested in

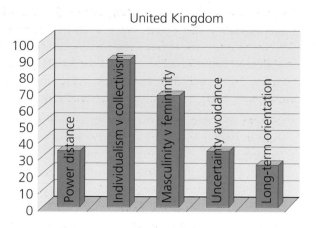

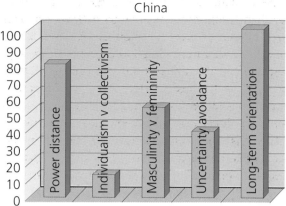

Figure 27.2

projects that generate a return in the long term; UK managers might not. In the UK junior managers might be asked for their opinion even if it contradicts the senior managers; in China they might not.

Of course, these findings do not represent every individual and every business in a given country (in fact, with globalisation and greater diversity among staff it becomes difficult to talk of a British or Chinese company), and these features will change over time. Nevertheless, they highlight that there can be significant differences in cultures between regions and this needs to be remembered when doing business with foreign partners. An understanding of Hofstede's cultural dimensions can help managers to understand the way business is done in different countries.

Business in Focus

WL GORE

Whenever business experts make lists of the best American companies to work for, or whenever consultants give speeches on the best-managed American companies, WL Gore is high on the list. It has a rate of employee turnover that is about a third the industry average. It has been profitable for 35 consecutive years and has growth rates and an innovative, high-profit product line that is the envy of the industry. Gore has managed to create a small-company ethos so infectious and sticky that it has survived their growth into a billion-dollar company with thousands of employees. And how did they do that? By (among other things) adhering to the Rule of 150.

Bill Gore, the founder of Gore Associates, a privately held, multimillion-dollar firm, understood from the start that smaller is often better and designed his organisation according to the Rule of 150 – each facility is limited to 150 associates. The size limitation enables this organisation to grow; yet it continues to behave like a small entrepreneurial start-up. This has not only proven to be a profitable strategy, but also it has created a culture of highly committed employees. Gladwell (2002, p. 182) comments:

'This organizational strategy is not unique to Gore and Associates. Semco, a Sao Paulo, Brazil-based manufacturer of industrial machinery, has a similar size strategy and, like Gore and Associates, Semco has experienced remarkable success. Semco has, in fact, grown 24 per cent annually for the past ten years – without an organizational chart or headquarters facility. Ricardo Semler, chairman of the board, reflecting on the decision to forego a traditional corporate structure, comments that traditional organizational hierarchies are "a source of control, discrimination, and power mongering" (Colvin, 2001, p. 60). The fact that Semco operates in a South American culture with patriarchal national values that are quite different from this company's participative organizational values, makes this a particularly noteworthy example of the paradoxical nature of successful organizations.'

Question:

1 Discuss the ways in which the decisions made regarding the structures of their business might affect or reflect the cultures of WL Gore and Semco.

Key Issues

The culture of a business, or the cultures within it, are not easy things to define or understand. They are also difficult to change. However, this does not make them less important. The culture influences the way everything is done and should not be under-estimated as a force that determines the success of failure of a business. Making a failing school successful for example, involves changing the culture so that staff, pupils and parents want it to win. It is not just a question of new rules or new funding.

How can we tell the culture of a business?

The answer is, you cannot! Not unless you actually spend time working there and realise what matters by working with other employees. And even then you may only be understanding the culture of a particular part of the business. The way the UK division works could be very different from the French division; the way the marketing department works could be very different from the operations department. So, you need to be careful when discussing the culture when you have only experienced a part of it. You must be careful not to base your decisions on a one-off visit. Imagine trying to explain the 'rules' of your family: what is and is not allowed, what do your parents value, what you would be praised for and what you would be criticised for, the 'family view' of sport, religion, charity, the death penalty, government intervention and education. Understanding the culture of a family would take a long time; understanding the culture of a business is just as difficult.

Whether or not you actually work in a business there are a few indicators that can help you understand its culture. According to Johnson and Scholes you will get some idea by looking at six interrelated elements:

1 **Stories:** What stories do employees tell about the business? What do these reveal about the attitudes of people within the business? Who are the heroes of the business and who are the villains? This will tell us something about who the managers value.
2 **The rituals:** All organisations have rituals. Think about your school. Does it have assembly every day? Does it have a sports day? Does it celebrate certain occasions? Is there a school song or uniform? These are all rituals and all businesses have them, each one revealing something about what is valued. At Honda the day may start with group meetings (highlighting the importance of the team compared with the individual); these meetings involve all employees, all of whom wear overalls (highlighting that everyone has a contribution to make and there is no 'us' and 'them'), and there may even be a company song (highlighting the loyalty to the company which is returned by company loyalty to the individual).
3 **The symbols**: What is on the wall of your school? Is it student artwork highlighting the importance of students and art to the life of the institution? Is there a list of sporting achievements or prefects or scholars? Who has the biggest office? What does the school look like? What investment has occurred in recent years? What do these developments tell us about priorities?
4 **Organisational structure:** How are things organised within the business? Who reports to whom? Is it a traditional hierarchy with small spans of control, suggesting long lines of authority and tight control over individuals? Or is it a flatter organisation in which spans are wider?
5 **Control systems:** How is control kept within the business? What is measured and monitored? This tells us what is regarded as important. Is the emphasis on reward for positive performance or punishment for poor performance?
6 **Power structures:** Who has the power to make decisions? Who really decides what happens?

Having analysed these six features of culture you should be able to summarise the key elements of an organisation's culture, which can be called its 'cultural paradigm'.

What determines the culture?

The culture of an organisation is originally derived from the attitudes and values of its founders. They often have a very strong influence on the business's values for many years, not least because of the people they employ, and then the people these

Figure 27.3 The cultural web

people employ, and so on. The culture comes from the views of those who are already there and this then influences who is selected to join the business. Once you have joined an organisation you are likely to adjust even more to become one of the 'insiders'. You will see what those at the top are doing and are likely to want to emulate them – leadership is therefore a key element of forming a culture. Those who do not 'fit in' may be ignored, punished or may be removed. Those who do fit in are likely to be rewarded, to get promotion and to receive praise. In this sense culture can be self-fulfilling.

But newcomers into the business will also be able to bring about change, as their own ideas will affect the thinking that goes on within the business. As society's values change, for example, this will influence what employees want and expect and influence the values within the business.

Employees will also be affected by investors who will demand certain forms of behaviour and by what is happening elsewhere. Seeing that a more cooperative approach with suppliers is benefiting competitors may change your own attitudes, and you may look for more ways of working with suppliers rather than always trying to beat them down on price. Realising that your customers really do value greater environmental awareness may make you reconsider your own attitudes on these issues.

The culture will also be shaped by the reward systems within the organisation. People tend to do more of the things they are praised for and rewarded for and less of the things they are criticised for. If a business seems to value someone who wins deals even if this is at the expense of other members of their team, then you will tend to want to go it alone and be highly competitive; sharing information and contacts with others in your team will not be on the agenda. If promotions go to those who 'don't rock the boat' you will tend to keep your head down and follow orders rather than question.

Business in Focus

Conservative Party logo

When David Cameron took over the leadership of the Conservative Party in 2005 he commissioned a new logo (shown on the next page). The result was a green drawing of a tree, which replaced the old torch emblem. The idea was to signify:

- Change: Cameron was showing he was the boss and things were going to change.
- Green: Cameron was keen to establish the green credentials of his party (e.g. environmentally friendly) and the green tree was to highlight this.

- Growth: symbolised by the tree.
- A link to the past: shown by the blue ground; blue was the colour traditionally associated with the Conservatives.

The logo was, therefore, a very significant development which made several important statements about Cameron's Conservative Party as opposed to his predecessor's. It cost £40,000 to design.

Figure 27.4 The logo introduced by David Cameron. One supporter said the logo looked like the work 'of a three-year-old'

Figure 27.5 Lady Thatcher introduced the previous torch logo in the 1980s

Why does culture matter?

The culture of a business or a part of a business matters because it determines how employees will behave in any given situation. This can work in an organisation's favour. Companies such as Google have a culture that recognises and rewards creative talent and technological skills. Bright computer programmers will go far in this organisation regardless of their age and, to some extent, regardless of their formal qualifications; if they can do the work and prove they can do it they will probably be promoted. This encourages ideas and new thinking which helps keep Google ahead of its rivals. A culture of accuracy and attention to detail, by comparison, may ensure your firm of accountants does not make any mistakes.

On the other hand, the culture of an organisation can limit a firm's success. In some retail organisations the customer seems an unwelcome visitor! Customers are not truly valued and employees do not make the effort to provide good customer service. This will lose business over time.

In other organisations, the unwillingness to take risks may mean market opportunities are missed. In Marks and Spencer ten years ago the culture was one of unquestioning agreement with the chief executive's decisions; this meant that when the wrong products were ordered and the wrong approach to displays was chosen no one dared to question. The culture did not encourage a questioning approach which meant that even though staff may have seen the iceberg ahead they did not shout out the dangers because they simply followed the course the captain set for them.

The importance of culture in terms of business success (or failure) should not be underestimated. Is the business full of ideas, encouraging initiative, stressing the value of working hard and working effectively? Are new projects met with open arms? Do individuals take care to get it right and show commitment to a project? All these issues depend on the culture of a business. It determines what people do, how they work together, how much effort they make, what they strive for and basically determines how the business 'ticks'. Whatever plans you bring in, whatever ideas you have, the culture of the business will influence whether they are implemented, how they are implemented and the level of commitment to them by employees.

Business in Focus

The Five Principles of Mars

QUALITY – The consumer is our boss, quality is our work and value for money is our goal.

Our company is dedicated to the highest quality in all the work we do. Quality is the uncompromising standard for our actions, and it flows from our passion and our pride in being part of the Mars community. Quality work, which results from our personal efforts, is the first ingredient of quality brands and the source of our reputation for high standards.

RESPONSIBILITY – As individuals, we demand total responsibility from ourselves; as associates, we support the responsibilities of others.

MUTUALITY – A mutual benefit is a shared benefit; a shared benefit will endure.

We believe that the standard by which our business relationships should be measured is the degree to which mutual benefits are created. These benefits can take many different forms, and need not be strictly financial in nature. Likewise, while we must try to achieve the most competitive terms, the actions of Mars should never be at the expense, economic or otherwise, of others with whom we work.

EFFICIENCY – We use resources to the full, waste nothing and do only what we can do best.

How is it possible to maintain our principles, offering superior value for money and sharing our success? Our strength lies in our efficiency, the ability to organize all our assets – physical, financial and human – for maximum productivity. In this way, our products and services are made and delivered with the highest quality, at the least possible cost, with the lowest consumption of resources; similarly, we seek to manage all our business operations with the most efficient processes for decision-making.

FREEDOM – We need freedom to shape our future; we need profit to remain free.

Mars is one of the world's largest privately owned corporations. This private ownership is a deliberate choice. Many other companies began as Mars did, but as they grew larger and required new sources of funds, they sold stocks or incurred restrictive debt to fuel their business. To extend their growth, they exchanged a portion of their freedom. We believe growth and prosperity can be achieved another way.

The Five Principles of Mars

www.mars.com

Question:

1 Discuss the ways in which the principles of Mars might affect the behaviour of employees and its business performance.

Business in Focus

Enron

Enron was one of the biggest corporate collapses ever. Once regarded as an amazing success story, it turned out that figures had been manipulated and there had been false reporting of profits (i.e. profits were being reported that did not exist). This happened on an extraordinary scale. This seemed to happen because there were no proper mechanisms in place to question employees' behaviour or check what they were doing. They were able to make up numbers without anyone asking where they came from. The culture of the business encouraged this behaviour. Each year in the company, poor performers were sacked and good performers were rewarded massively – the pressure was to deliver

1400 Smith Street

good figures whatever it took. The company recruited very able MBA graduates straight from university; these employees lacked experience and did not really know what was and what was not allowable behaviour. With unbelievable bonuses on offer all the incentives encouraged them to do what everyone else seemed to be doing and make up some profits. The example from the top seemed to further encourage this approach. The culture of Enron led to its collapse and the loss of thousands of jobs and millions of dollars for investors.

A special report commissioned to investigate the cause of the collapse found that the cause was 'A combination of self-enrichment by employees, inadequate control from the board and outside auditors, and an aggressive and overreaching corporate culture.'

How can you change culture?

With difficulty. To change the culture of an organisation you need to change what people value and what they believe is important. This can happen but often takes time. Imagine you were someone who does not like sport, who sees no point in taking part in it if you do not like it and who likes the freedom your sixth form gives you to choose whether to participate. If the school headmaster suddenly decides that your view on the importance of sports at school is wrong and that from now on it will be compulsory you would probably argue about this. It is possible that over time you could be convinced that compulsory sport at school would help your academic performance or help you feel better in yourself, but simply being told that this is true would not necessarily work. You would want to see some evidence or try it out for a while to see for yourself, or be talked through the arguments for and against until you were convinced and agreed with the case being made. Unfortunately, businesses do not always have time to go through this process with every member of staff. Sometimes culture needs to be changed faster than a process of education and discussion allows; sometimes leaders may think it is better to push on and let people see the benefits rather than spend the time trying to convince them in advance.

To achieve change quickly managers may:

- Offer incentives for those who agree to the changes and start adopting them (better reports for those who participate in sport); this is a 'carrot' approach.
- Punish those who do not adopt the changes (poor reports for those who do not participate in sport); this is the 'stick' approach.

Neither the carrot nor the stick approach will in itself change people's attitudes. They are simply changing behaviour. They do not change what you believe, simply what you do. This means people will not be very committed to the changes. However, in the long run if the changes are proved to be beneficial people may change their attitudes as well.

Other approaches include:

- educating people about the benefits of change
- reassuring people about the change, to reduce fears
- providing resources to enable people to prepare and train for change
- focusing on key people to get their support; once they are won over others will follow.

Summary

The culture of a business reflects 'the way things are done around here'. The culture within a business will influence the priorities set by individuals, the way they treat stakeholders, the way they plan and behave. The culture in some organisations clearly encourages and promotes innovation, it expects people to 'go the extra mile' and it puts customer service at the top of its agenda. In other organisations employees seem more interested in their own aims, and the culture permits complacency and waste. Changing culture can be a major managerial task to help improve performance. This can be a difficult task because it may involve trying to get employees to change long-standing attitudes and approaches.

Progress questions

1 What is meant by 'organisational culture'? (2 marks)

2 How can the culture of a business help its success? (5 marks)

3 Explain two influences on the culture of a business. (6 marks)

4 Why might it be wrong to try and describe 'the' culture of a business? (4 marks)

5 Outline four different types of culture according to Handy. (8 marks)

6 Explain one reason why the culture of an organisation matters. (3 marks)

7 Hofstede found five dimensions on which national cultures can differ. Outline these dimensions. (5 marks)

8 Why might changing the culture of an organisation be difficult? (5 marks)

9 Why is it difficult to identify an organisation's culture from the outside? (3 marks)

10 Outline the organisational culture of your school or college. (6 marks)

Analysis and evaluation questions

1 Analyse the ways in which the culture of a school might affect its success. (8 marks)

2 Discuss the problems new managers might have changing the culture of a highly successful premier football team. (15 marks)

3 Discuss how new managers might change the culture of a failing business. (15 marks)

Case study

Chrysler

The Daimler Chrysler merger in 1998 turned out to be a disaster because the companies operated in such different ways. A simple example illustrates the problems: in one meeting the German Daimler executive could not understand why a particular issue was being discussed when he felt that it had already been decided. He produced his minutes from the meeting which he had circulated. His American counterpart said he had received these but had assumed they were just some notes from the meeting and did not constitute a decision having been made. The Germans found the American style too informal; the Americans found the Germans too inflexible. One observer said, 'Germans analyse a problem in great detail, find a solution, discuss it with their partners and then make a decision. It is a very structured process ... Americans start with a discussion, and then come back to it with new aspects after talking with other people. Eventually – after a process which they call creative – they come to a conclusion.' In America it is common to pop into your boss's office and get an instant decision without having to explain it to everyone else. In Germany there tends to be more data analysis then formal recommendations and the involvement of all those affected.

These business differences mirror deeper differences in the societal values of the USA and Germany. According to Hofstede's study of global cultural differences, Germans are less individualistic than people in the USA. They also tend to feel more uncomfortable with uncertainty and ambiguity, and they have a longer-term time orientation. Germans are also found to be significantly more indirect in their communication styles and more respectful of title, age and background connections. These societal values are reflected in businesses from these countries. This is particularly apparent in preferred leadership styles. German managers frequently prefer a more autocratic style than their US counterparts and their employees expect to be treated accordingly. Research on obedience to authority indicates that a higher percentage of Germans are obedient to their managers than are US employees. For example, employees in a US organisation often feel comfortable challenging their managers, perhaps even giving them advice. German employees, on the other hand, expect their managers to give them specific instructions and they typically follow them unquestioningly.

There are differences in employment practices as well. For example, many Europeans view US hiring and firing practices as unnaturally brutal. In European companies, employees are protected by much stronger labour laws and union rules. Organisations in France and Germany are more concerned with protecting and nurturing the workforce than are US organisations. For example, in France and Germany, the average manager and worker get at least six weeks of paid vacation each year (most US employees get two weeks). French and German employees also enjoy a much wider range of benefits, such as paid maternity leave and layoff payments whose value increases as the number of years a person has worked for an organisation increases. Indeed, both France and Germany regard the US system of hiring and firing as harsh and exploitative.

The US-based Chrysler Corporation and German-based Daimler-Benz mirrored these cultural differences. Chrysler had a reputation for having a more freewheeling, open culture, in contrast with the more traditional, top-down management style practiced at Daimler. Daimler-Benz was synonymous with words like conservative, efficient and safe. Chrysler, on the other hand, was known as daring, diverse and creative. In fact, these cultural differences in many ways were the foundation for the mutual attraction between the two companies. However, like many marriages of opposites, the differences led to disaster. No one seemed to know how to discover common ground.

Source: 'The culture clash at DaimlerChrysler was worse than expected', by Dorothee Ostle, *Automotive news Europe,* 22 November 1999, Vol. 4, Issue 24

Questions

1 Explain the possible benefits of centralised decision-making at Daimler (5 marks)
2 Analyse the cultural differences at Chrysler and Daimler.
3 Discuss the factors that might have led to the merger of Chrysler and Daimler. (12 marks)
4 To what extent was the merger of Chrysler and Daimler bound to fail? (15 marks)

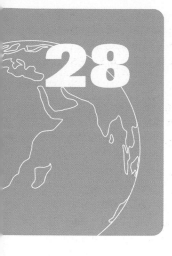

28 Making strategic decisions

In this chapter we examine:
- types of decisions
- the significance of information management
- different approaches to decision-making
- influences of decision-making.

Decisions

Management involves making many decisions. What to do, how to do it, who should do it and when all have to be decided. A decision involves a specific commitment to action (Boddy 2002). Making a decision will involve:

- knowing what you are trying to achieve
- considering the next-best alternative (i.e. the opportunity cost)
- committing resources to a course of action
- uncertainty about what will actually happen.

Types of decision

There are different types of decision that have to be made. Simon analysed types of decision in terms of programmed and non-programmed decisions.

Programmed decisions (Simon 1960) deal with problems that are familiar and where the information required to make them is easy to define and obtain. The situation is well structured and there are often established procedures, rules and policies. For example, reordering components is often a programmed decision. Employees know what has to be ordered, who to order from and how to order it. They simply decide issues such as when to order and how much to order.

By comparison, non-programmed decisions deal with situations that are unstructured and require a unique solution. These are unusual decisions that may be risky, such as a major investment.

> **Key terms**
> **Programmed decisions** are familiar and routine decisions.
> **Non-programmed decisions** are less structured and require unique solutions.

Decisions may also be categorised in terms of whether they are tactical or strategic. The strategy of a business is the long-term plan to achieve the business's objectives. For example, if a firm's target was to increase profits it might try and do this by reducing costs or by increasing revenue; these would be two strategies to achieve the same goal. Similarly, if a business was trying to boost overall sales the managers might take a strategic decision to do this by trying to sell more of its existing products or by increasing sales of new products; again these would be two different ways of achieving the same end goal.

Strategic decisions tend to be long term, involve a major commitment of resources and be difficult to reverse. For example, the decision to invest in new product development is likely to involve a high level of finance and take several years. Strategic decisions also tend to involve a high level of uncertainty. Over time market conditions often change significantly and so firms must change their strategies to cope with unfamiliar conditions.

The value of producing a clear strategy is that it sets out the firm's overall plan; this helps employees and departments develop their own plans to implement the strategy. If you know the firm wants to diversify, for example, you know that it is realistic to consider market opportunities in new segments of the market. If you know the strategy is to boost the firm's market presence in a particular region, you will know it is worth putting more resources into this area.

The decisions made about how to implement the strategy are called 'tactical decisions'.

Compared with strategic decisions, tactics tend to:

- be short term
- involve fewer resources
- be made more regularly and involve less uncertainty.

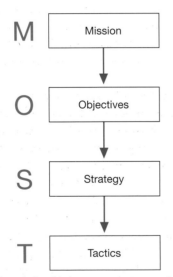

Figure 28.1 The relationship between strategy and tactics

Scientific decision-making

There are many different ways of making a decision: in some cases managers will research the decision thoroughly – they will gather data and analyse it before deciding what to do; in other cases they may rely on their own experience from the past or on their gut feeling. It depends on what the decision is, the risk involved and their own personality. If, for example, the decision concerns the purchase of new production equipment and involves hundreds and thousands of pounds, a manager will probably

research the decision very carefully; with an unfamiliar decision involving high levels of resources, managers would not want to risk getting it wrong. If, however, the decision simply involves ordering some more supplies of pens for the office, an employee might be more inclined to use his or her experience. The same is probably true of your own decision-taking – if you are spending a few hundred pounds on a new PC you will probably research the decision much more than if you feel thirsty and want to buy a soft drink, when you will rely on experience.

When you gather data and analyse it before making a decision, this is known as a scientific approach to decision-making. It is scientific because it is rational and logical and is based on data. Many of the mathematical topics you have studied are to help managers analyse the data as part of scientific decision-making. Break-even analysis, ratio analysis, investment appraisal and correlation analysis, for example, are all ways in which managers analyse the data to try and make the right decision.

Scientific decision-making should reduce the risk of error because decisions are based on information. On the other hand, the usefulness of this method will inevitably depend on the quality of the data. The better the information the more likely it is the right decision will be made; this is why market research is important and why managers need to ensure they have effective ways of gathering, analysing and circulating information within the organisation to ensure each manager has the information he or she needs at the right time.

> **Key terms**
> **Scientific decision-making** is based on data and uses a logical, rational approach to decision-making.

The scientific decision-making process involves:

- recognising that there is a problem or opportunity, i.e. recognising that a decision has to be made
- setting objectives for what you want to achieve
- setting decision criteria and deciding how important each one is
- developing and identifying alternatives
- comparing the alternatives
- choosing and implementing a course of action
- reviewing the effectiveness of the decision.

Decision-making is a dynamic process with continual review and assessment of what has been done and what needs to be done.

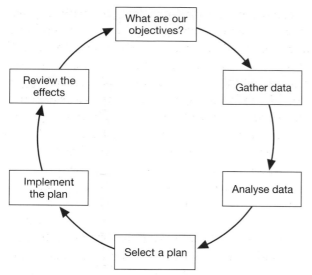

Figure 28.2 Decision-making is a dynamic process

A scientific approach to decision-making

A scientific approach to decision-making is rational and logical. Decisions are made based on information, not hunch. This approach is likely if there is high risk that managers are seeking to reduce.

When making a decision scientifically managers will want to understand the environment in which they operate. This means they need to consider the macro-environment and the microenvironment.

The macro-environment

This comprises factors that are not easily influenced by any one business. These are often analysed using the PESTEL framework: political, economic, social, technological, environmental and legal factors. Managers need to try to identify which factors in the macro-environment are most significant for the future. These will vary from business to business. In the cigarette industry the threat of even more legal restrictions on smoking must be a concern, as well as legal action by those whose health has been damaged by smoking. In the computer industry technological advancement is a concern if a business fails to keep up with the changes. In the healthcare market demographic changes may be a key factor. Managers must identify which factors are most significant for them.

The microenvironment

This relates to factors within a business environment which firms are more likely to be able to influence than those in the macro-environment. These include:

- competitors' actions
- suppliers
- buyers (customers).

The importance of market and competitor intelligence is clear in terms of strategic planning. You have to understand the markets and the business environment you are competing. This data may be gathered through many sources such as secondary research, your own databases or your sales force.

Once the external environment has been analysed, managers should be able to identify relevant opportunities and threats. An opportunity is a course of action that may provide benefits for a business. What is an opportunity for one business may not be an opportunity for another. Glaxo SmithKline may see an opportunity in a cure of the common cold; the managers of Cadbury may not see the same opportunity because they lack the skills and resources necessary to exploit this because their experience lies in other markets. A threat is a possible action that could cause harm to the business. A threat to one business may not be a threat to another. Changing legislation to insist cars are made more environmentally friendly may be a threat to car manufacturers because of the potential costs. It may be an opportunity to the developers of environmentally friendly engines.

To identify the relevant opportunities and threats we must therefore look at the specific circumstances of a particular business. This involves an examination of the firm's strengths and weaknesses. The strengths of the business may relate to any of the functions. For example, it could have a strong brand (marketing), good cash flow (financial), well-trained staff (human resources) or a good track record of research and development (operations). Equally, the weaknesses of a business could refer to any aspect of the business, such as falling sales (marketing), low profit margins (finance), high labour turnover (HRM) or a poor quality record (operations).

Decision trees

In order to make logical decisions, managers may use different approaches to help them organise their information and think through the various problems. These include decision-tree analysis. Decision-tree analysis tries to estimate the possible outcomes of different courses of action and work out the likelihood of these occurring. A decision tree is a mathematical model which can be used by managers

Business in Focus

SWOT analysis: Ryanair 2007

The process of considering the opportunities and threats created by the external environment relative to the strengths and weaknesses inside the business is known as SWOT analysis. This is a technique to help with strategic planning.

Shown below is a SWOT analysis for Ryanair in 2007. As conditions change so will the strengths and weaknesses of the business and the opportunities and threats it faces. This means SWOT analysis needs to be undertaken regularly.

Strengths of Ryanair:
Leading low-cost airline

The company operates short-haul, point-to-point routes between Ireland, the UK and Continental Europe. It operates 487 low-fare routes across Europe, carrying approximately 42.5 million passengers a year across 25 European countries. It has the best punctuality and highest frequency record, compared with its major competitors like Lufthansa, Air France, SAS, Aer Lingus, easyJet and British Airways.

A strong market position provides Ryanair with brand recognition which would help further expansion.

Strong revenue growth

Ryanair has been reporting strong revenue growth primarily attributable to an increase in passenger volumes. The company's strong consistent revenue growth provides its operations with financial stability and the ability to fund expansion strategies.

Business strategy

The company has a clear and focused strategy of being a low-cost airline. Its targets fare-conscious travellers and business travellers. It generally favours secondary airports as they are less congested and so it is more likely the planes can leave and land on time; it is also cheaper to operate from these airports. Faster turnaround times are a key element in Ryanair's efforts to maximise aircraft utilisation. In addition, Ryanair enters into agreements with third-party contractors to handle passenger and aircraft, ticketing and other services. The company fixes its contracts on competitive terms by negotiating multi-year contracts, at prices that are fixed or subject only to periodic increases linked to inflation.

Weaknesses of Ryanair:
Weakening employee relations

Ryanair has been involved in a number of union disputes.

Lack of scale

The company is small in size compared with its competitors. Many of its competitors, such as Air France, Lufthansa and British Airways are larger in size and enjoy a competitive advantage in accessing financial, technical and human resources.

Opportunities for Ryanair:
Launch of new routes

Last year, the company announced 153 new routes and extended its operations to three new countries, adding destinations in Marseille, Madrid and Bremen. It also started 16 new routes across Europe and its 19th base in Dusseldorf in February last year.

Fleet expansion

Ryanair entered into an agreement with Boeing in 2005 to purchase 70 new Boeing 737-800 series aircrafts over a five-year period from 2006 to 2011 and acquired additional option to purchase up to an additional 70 such aircraft. The new Boeing 737-800 is the most technologically advanced aeroplane in the single-aisle market. The new plane is outfitted with the latest entertainment system and safety systems (including autoland capability and traffic collision avoidance systems). The enlarged fleet would allow the company to support the existing capacity on existing routes and expand its network capacity to open new routes.

Global airline market

Demand for low-cost airlines is growing. Ticket price is the number one criterion for most passengers when selecting a flight, well ahead of the availability of a non-stop service.

Threats faced by Ryanair:
Increasing aviation fuel prices

Due to rising oil prices globally, the price of aviation fuel has gone up substantially in the past few years.

Threats to security

Security issues often pose a challenge to Ryanair. Security worries have led to passengers being body searched, and the banning of of certain liquids and gels in carry-on baggage.

The introduction of these measures led to passengers suffering severe delays while passing through these airport security checks. As a result, Ryanair cancelled 279 flights in the days immediately following the incident.

Source: Adapted from Mintel

to help them make the right decision. By combining possible outcomes with the probability of them happening, managers can compare the likely financial consequences of different decisions.

The value of the technique will, of course, depend on managers' ability to accurately estimate the options and their likelihood, but it does stress the key issues of risk and rewards. (For more on decision trees, see 'One step further' on page 389.)

Influences on corporate decision-making

The influences on the way that decision are made will include:

- **The success of a particular style of decision-making in the past.** A risk-taker who 'follows their instinct' and who has been successful so far may assume they have luck on their side and that they will continue to win (a dangerous assumption); they may be more likely to trust their instincts until it goes wrong, when it may be too late to change.
- **The nature of the industry and business.** In the film business great films sometimes break the mould and, on occasion, are successful despite initially poor feedback. Simply following research findings may lead to many films being similar and imitating the last blockbuster. Film makers may therefore decide to ignore or not even find out film goers' opinions and make the film they want to make. Having said this, film companies often show films to focus groups to get their feedback and amend the endings or the story line in response to this. The 'director's cut' is often the film the directors wished they had made but were not allowed to.
- **The risk involved.** If it is a high-risk decision, managers may want to reduce the risk or at least take steps to reduce the risk by gathering data on which they can base decisions. If it is a low-risk decision they may be more inclined to trust instinct. This links with the type of decision being made. With a small tactical decision you may rely on what you have always done; with a major strategic decision you may want to be more scientific because much may be unfamiliar.
- **The corporate values, mission and objectives.** Whether a particular decision is suitable will depend on whether it helps a business to do what it is there to do. A takeover may make sense if rapid growth is the objective. Giving suppliers longer to pay may make sense if you value suppliers. Trying to delay any redundancies may be essential if you are trying to treat your employees well. What is the 'right' decision for one business may be the wrong decision for another. Relocating to cut costs may be right for a profit-driven business and wrong for a business trying to look after existing staff.
- **The ethics of a decision.** This is linked with the point above in that the importance of ethics in decision-making may depend on the business. Some organisations want to try and do the right thing (Innocent Drinks founders say, 'we are not perfect but we are trying to make the world a bit better'); others may show less interest in social responsibility. What matters is what the owners and managers believe in and this will influence what they might or might not go ahead with. How important is the environment? What about suppliers? What about 'fair treatment' of customers (e.g. should we pass on a fall in our costs in the form of lower prices)? The 'supreme purpose' of John Lewis (which also owns Waitrose and Peter Jones) as stated in its constitution is 'the happiness of our Partners' (its employees); the managers here will take into account the partners' views when it comes to making decisions. More and more companies are taking their stakeholders into account when it comes to decision-making and showing an interest in Corporate Social Responsibility (CSR).

A CSR approach recognises the impact that a business can have on its staff, its suppliers, the community, the government, the environment and various other stakeholders; the impact on such groups is considered when setting objectives and making decisions. Several companies now produce CSR reports alongside their financial accounts to measure their progress in relation to the treatment of stakeholders. Greater commitment to reducing global warming, better treatment of staff or helping the community will affect the decisions managers take.

What also matters is the customers' and media's perception of a company's actions, i.e. do *they* think it is ethical? Ryanair may think it is fine to refuse a refund if you are late for a flight for reasons totally beyond your control but if there was enough media pressure it might change its approach. In some cases managers may consider the perception of their actions as much as what they actually believe, i.e. they may do something (give money to charity, sponsor an event or reduce emissions) because they want to be associated with this and think it will help their public image regardless of whether they believe in it.

- **Resources.** What you decide to do may depend on what is feasible, which in turn depends on your resources. When choosing a university you have to consider your likely results – there is no point applying to places that will not give you an offer. There may be many universities you would like to go to, but are they realistic options? Similarly there may be many decisions a manager wants to make, but how much money is available? How many staff? How much time? What is actually chosen will have to be the best of what is feasible.

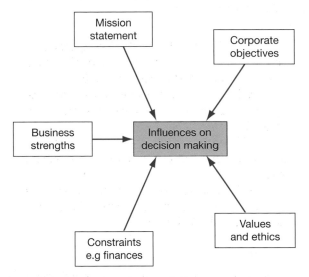

Figure 28.3 Influences on decision-making

Problems making decisions

Making decisions in business is not easy, not least because you will be dealing with many different stakeholders. A business is a political system (Pfeffer 1992) and made up of people with different opinions and sometimes very different views on what they want to achieve and how they think it should be achieved. Any major decision is likely to make some better off and others worse off; it is therefore likely to meet with opposition.

Every decision will involve different stakeholders and you will consider their objectives and their relative power. Do you want to listen to them? Do you need to listen to them? What will happen if you ignore them? This means you need to think about their relative power. A well-organised workforce that is unionised, for example, may be able to negotiate for more consultation and participation in decision-

People in Business

Warren Buffet

Warren Buffet is a well-known American investor. He is the largest shareholder and Chief Executive of Berkshire Hathaway and was ranked by Forbes business magazine as the richest man in the world in 2008 with an estimated worth of $62 billion. Despite huge wealth he does not display his wealth particularly and lives in the same house he bought in 1958 for $31,500. Buffet is a major philanthropist, using his money to help others. In 2006 he announced he was giving away his fortune to charity with 86 per cent of it going to the Bill and Melinda Gates Foundation. Bill Gates is the founder of Microsoft and he created this foundation with his wife to improve healthcare and reduce extreme poverty globally; Gates has donated millions of dollars to the foundation.

These highly successful businesspeople are now focusing on social causes; their decisions are no longer purely commercial – they are interested in what good they can do around the world.

Figure 28.4 Warren Buffet

making than individual employees could on their own. You may want to pay more attention to an investor who owns 65 per cent of the company com-

Business in Focus

CSR report

Along with many other companies Sony, the Japanese consumer electronics business, produces a Corporate Social Responsibility report each year. The 2007 report states:

'In light of increasing stakeholder interest and their importance in the context of Sony's business as a whole, four significant themes are specifically featured: climate change, supply chain management, innovation and China ... Sony has obtained third-party verification to ensure the reliability of environmental data reported and to facilitate the ongoing improvement of its environmental management ...'

In its climate change section it states:

'Climate change is one of the most critical global issues of the 21st century. Sony recognizes that addressing this issue is a task of paramount importance to ensure the sustainability of society as well as of Sony's business. It is expected that climate change will cause not only global environmental changes and large-scale natural disasters that have a significant impact on all life on this planet, but also the reinforcement of laws and regulations at various levels to mitigate climate change and a shift in consumer preferences to environmentally conscious products.

'These changes in the business environment will affect companies and their business activities. Sony's annual greenhouse gas emissions – the total of direct emissions from Sony sites and indirect emissions from product transportation and use by customers, all calculated in terms of CO_2 emissions – is estimated to be approximately 20.53 million tons.

'Sony is devoting extensive efforts to reducing greenhouse gas emissions in all of its business activities. It is not only making use of new technologies to reduce energy consumption by its products and direct CO_2 emissions from its sites, but also pursuing a number of other efforts, including forming partnerships with nongovernmental organizations (NGOs), actively promoting the introduction of renewable forms of energy and participating in emissions trading programs.'

It states:

1 The Sony Group will cut absolute greenhouse gas emissions, calculated in terms of CO_2, by 7 per cent from the 2000 level by 2010;

2 Sony will reduce CO_2 emissions from product use by lowering the annual energy consumption of major Sony products;

3 Sony will cooperate with the WWF to raise consumer awareness of global warming prevention; and

4 Sony will support the view that the average global temperature rise must remain below 2°C above pre-industrial times.

Questions:

1 Why do you think Sony is so concerned about climate change?

2 Why do you think Sony produces a Corporate Social Responsibility report?

3 Why do you think Sony has external verifiers?

---

pared with one who has 1 per cent. A key supplier of your major component will have more influence than the supplier of a component which can be bought in thousands of stores. So the more well organised, the more you need a particular stakeholder, the more you like or agree with them and their objectives, the more they are likely to influence your decision. This is why there is often an inner circle of senior managers who are powerful because they consult each other and look after each other; other employees sometimes feel they are not listened to.

The role of different stakeholders can be shown using a stakeholder map:

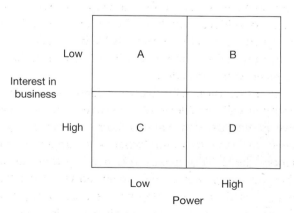

Figure 28.5 A stakeholder map

Groups in quadrant B are likely to influence decisions a lot. They are interested in what is going on in the business and are very powerful (e.g. a major investor); you will need to keep this group happy.

By comparison, stakeholders in quadrant C are not very interested and are not powerful (e.g. your milk delivery service or local newsagent); you do not need to worry much about this group.

Meeting the needs of different shareholders can, therefore, create difficulties for decision makers. Decision-making can also be difficult because of problems with the data. For example:

- The data you have gathered may be insufficient or inaccurate (it depends how you gathered it).
- The data may be incomplete; however much data you gather you often find you want more or you want it in a different format.
- The data may have been relevant when it was collected, but given the rate of change in some markets it can quickly become out of date; you may well produce a plan that is designed for a particular competitive landscape that has now changed.

Strategies must be continually reviewed, therefore, and managers must be prepared to adjust them (if they can) as times, resources and circumstances dictate. In many cases the changes that managers have had to make mean that the strategy that actually emerges may be very different from the one intended.

The limitations of scientific decision-making

Scientific decision-making is logical and rational. If the data is available is relevant and is not too expensive to gather, then it makes sense for it to feed into your decision-making. When big high-risk decisions are being made you often want to feel you have done all you can to make sure you get it right, and gathering and analysing data is part of this. However, data is not always reliable (political predictions of who will win an election are sometimes wrong, for example, despite fairly sophisticated ways of researching). Also there may not be the time or money for a scientific approach. In this case you may fall back on your intuition. In some instances you may think this is a better way of deciding anyway, for example, in the worlds of fashion, art and music it may be difficult to scientifically analyse what will work.

Even if there is enough data, at the end of the day you are likely to be influenced by your gut feeling (your intuition); you can research universities as much as you want but people often have a feeling about a course or place. A decision to do business with someone often depends on your feelings about them. So, however scientific your approach, intuition will often play a part in decision-making, whether we like it or not. We need to be aware of this (e.g. when interviewing people we sometimes let our feelings about whether we like them or not to override whether they would be good at the job), but also appreciate that not everything is quantifiable (e.g. whether two businesses could easily work well together, whether an advert which sets out to break the mould will immediately be appreciated by a focus group, whether a new logo works or not).

Business in Focus

The style of decision-making can vary considerably from organisation to organisation depending on the culture and management style. Some organisations are far more consensus based than others – they want the people involved to agree before going ahead. In other organisations the senior manager decides and will insist it goes ahead. This is often linked to the culture of different countries. In Japan, for example, the decision-making process is known as 'ringi'. Decisions go round and round for consultation. Everyone involved has a chance to input and their view is listened to, debated and taken into account; if someone raises an objection then the debate continues until a solution is found that is acceptable to all. This leads to a much slower decision-making process than in the US or the UK. However, everyone affected has seen how the decision has been made, they have all made a contribution and the chances are that it is a better decision than one person on their own would make. It may take longer but once made it probably works.

Corporate and functional strategies

The overall strategy of the business (e.g. to launch its products in new countries) is the corporate strategy. This will then have to be implemented by the different functions of the business; this requires functional strategies. For example, imagine that an airline decided to target the low-cost segment of the short-haul market – this is the corporate strategy. To achieve this each function must play its part. For example, the operations managers must work out how to keep costs down (e.g. by finding low cost airports to take off from and land at, keeping services offered to a minimum and speeding up turnaround time). Meanwhile the marketing function must promote this in a way that is cost effective (e.g. via the internet rather than mainstream advertising). The functional strategies, therefore, are developed to implement the corporate strategy.

group. The product is familiar but the way in which it is marketed may be new.

- Product development occurs when a business develops new products for its existing customer base. This involves risk because many new products are dropped before they are developed or fail when they are launched. Developing a new product can be very expensive and take time, only to flop when it hits the market (remember Wrigley's thin ice strips? Or Coca-Cola's vanilla Coke?).

- Diversification is the most difficult to manage because it involves new products and new markets. Therefore this strategy involves a high degree of risk in terms of making it successful. However, if it does work it means the business is operating in more than one market and so may be less vulnerable to change in any one of them.

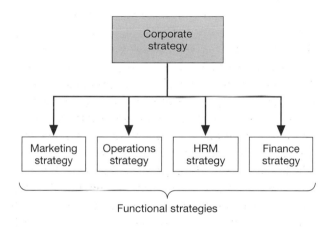

Figure 28.6

Figure 28.7 The Ansoff matrix

What types of strategy exist?

Strategies can be analysed in different ways. One way of categorising these is the Ansoff matrix, developed by Igor Ansoff in 1957. This examines strategies in terms of the products offered by a business and the markets in which it competes.

- Market penetration occurs when a business chooses to fight on its home ground. It is trying to sell more of its existing products. This may be achieved by more promotions, price cuts or greater efforts to get the product distributed. The aim is to gain more share of the existing market.
- Market development occurs when a business aims at a new segment; for example a business may try to sell in new countries or to a different target

The Ansoff Matrix highlights where firms are fighting i.e. in what products and in what markets. We are also interested in how they fight. This may be via differentiating their offerings or by offering a lower-cost strategy. These two alternatives were examined by Michael Porter in 1980. Porter argued that a business could achieve a competitive advantage by:

- Making its products so different from its competitors that it can charge a higher price for them. Better service, better reliability, better design, better response time, greater flexibility all provide possible ways of differentiating.
- Providing a similar service to competitors but at a lower cost; this requires a more efficient production system.

What businesses must not do is offer a similar range of products and services at a higher price than rivals. This would be to get 'caught in the middle'. It must focus on differentiation or low costs, according to Porter.

Why can strategies go wrong?

Strategies often do not turn out the way we want them to. This is because:

- It can be difficult to estimate what is going to happen in the future. In 2007, how many of us would have guessed that share prices worldwide were about to fall, that banks would be nationalised and governments would pour in billions of dollars to make funds available for lending? In such volatile circumstances as these it is no surprise that a firm's expansion plans may be put on hold or its decision to launch new products delayed.
- The implementation may prove far more difficult than you imagined; there may be technical problems, greater resistance to change than you imagined or costs may escalate.
- You may not have the resources to see the plan through.

Information management and decisions

Managers are in charge of various resources (such as people, money, machines and materials) and must decide how to use these most efficiently and most effectively. This involves hundreds of decisions every week. Every decision has an opportunity cost – this means managers must consider what they are sacrificing when they make a decision. They must also measure the success of any decision: Did it work? How effective was it? This highlights the importance of gaining feedback; whenever a particular course of action is taken data is needed to assess how well it is working so it can be corrected along the way and/or a different decision is taken next time. Imagine that you decide to write an essay using a different style. Does it work? Was it a good idea to change your style? You can only tell if you see what mark you get and read the comments on your work so you can assess the impact of your decision. Information, then, is at the heart of decision-making: you need information to decide what the present situation is, information to decide what your options are and information to assess whether a given decision worked or not.

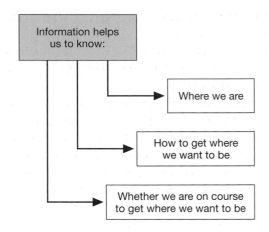

Figure 28.8 The importance of information

No manager will get everything right all of the time, but the good managers are the ones who get it right most of the time and who make sure the big decisions are correct. Getting it right matters because:

- You have limited resources and cannot afford to waste them.
- There is always an alternative; you do not want to choose the wrong course of action.
- There are competitors and if you get it wrong you are leaving it open to them to get it right.

To help get it right the management of information is important. Information can be used as a resource to help the business compete more effectively.

What is information?

Data consists of raw unanalysed facts, figures and events. Information comes from data that has been processed so that it has meaning for the person receiving it. £100,000, £200,000, £300,000 are just a series of numbers; if, however, you know that these numbers represent the turnover of a business they begin to have more meaning. If you know that this increase is following an increase of £15,000 on advertising then the figures begin to be very significant. As you know, in business studies we stress the importance of context. This means turning data into information – turning raw numbers into something meaningful by considering their context.

What is good quality information?

The quality of information depends on its

- reliability (accuracy): to be useful information must be accurate
- timeliness: information needs to be available at the right time to help make the decisions; it is no good if it arrives too late
- quantity: the amount of information must be appropriate – having too much information may mean that it cannot be digested and made sense of; most managers suffer from information overload and so do not process it all effectively
- relevance: good information is relevant to the user, i.e. it must not be too detailed nor too general but related directly to the needs of the user.

Information management (**IM**) involves the collection and management of information from one or more sources and the distribution of that information to different individuals. The management of information has, of course, been revolutionised by the growth in information technology. The amount of data that can now be transferred, the faster speed and lower costs of transferring and analysing data have significantly changed the way information is managed and the importance of information management.

According to the Carnegie Mellon School, information management (i.e. the organisation's ability to process information) is at the core of organisational and managerial competencies helping a business to compete successfully.

How can managing information help a business to compete?

Better management of information can help businesses to be more competitive in many areas. For example:

- It should provide better insight into the nature and behaviour of customers. Companies use loyalty cards, for example, as a way of tracking customer purchases and linking this to information held about the customers, such as their age, socio-economic group and home address. The effects of more promotional spending, price cuts or a changed store layout can all be measured directly.
- Stock management (information on the level of stocks held at any moment) can be useful to be able to tell customers quickly what is in stock, and good links with suppliers can help a just-in-time production approach to be developed. With good information passing between a business and its suppliers, the delivery of supplies can occur just when they are needed and they can be delivered in the order they will be used.

- Information is essential to know what resources are being used, how they are being used, what they cost and how effective they are. Systems such as budgeting and appraisal rely on information.

Information helps a business to:

- identify where it is at the moment (e.g. an internal and external analysis)
- evaluate different strategies to take
- review the results.

Information systems

Managers need to understand the importance of information and look at how they are managing it. Some organisations nowadays have knowledge managers which highlights how significant they think the management of information is to the business. Organisations gather lots of data all the time, such as who their customers are, what their sales are, what their costs are and what their competitors are doing. Just think of how much data there is in any organisation, often stored in different places and known by different people – often this information is not shared or analysed effectively.

Imagine if the information that exists in many different places about you at school or college could be made easily available in the right formats to those who need it: teachers, exam officers, parents, personal tutors, UCAS advisers. This would improve decision-making for the school and provide you with better advice and guidance.

Far too many organisations have very valuable information but keep it in all sorts of places where it cannot easily be found; some of it is on the marketing managers' shared drive, some on the operations director's memory stick, and some in the chief executive's brain. The information is stored in a way that does not make it very accessible.

An information system is a set of people, procedures and resources that collect and transform data into information and disseminates this information. Some of these systems are formal (e.g. computer systems); some are informal (e.g. gossip).

How do we manage information?

When developing a system to manage information we need to:

- **Decide what information we need.** There is sometimes a danger of collecting too much data and losing sight of the key issues, so it is important to be clear why you want something gathered.

- **Decide how to store the data.** In what format will it be stored? How and where will it be saved?
- **Decide who can access it and how.** For example, how do we keep managers up to date? How do we get information to them in a manner they can understand and that will inform their decisions?

Uses of information systems

There are many different types of information systems, such as:

- Enterprise resource planning systems which aim to coordinate activities and decisions across many functions by creating an integrated platform that integrates them into company-wide business processes. When an order is received, for example, this triggers decisions throughout the business in terms of ordering more materials.
- Customer relationship management (CRM) is intended to build and sustain long-term business with customers. It represents a move from mass markets and mass production to customisation and focused production. It helps to:
  - gather customer data quickly
  - identify valuable customers and less valuable ones
  - increase customer loyalty and retention
  - reduce the costs of meeting customers
  - make it easier to acquire similar customers.

Information systems can enable managers to:

- identify changes in conditions more quickly
- respond more quickly to change
- make better, more accurate decisions
- make fewer mistakes
- review their progress and identify what has and what has not worked in order to make better decisions next time.

Summary

Making decisions is an important part of management. Strategic decisions are non-programmed and long term. They often involve a high degree of risk. These are difficult decisions to make because they involve forecasting, dealing with unfamiliar scenarios in the future and a high degree of pressure because these decisions may be difficult to reverse. To help reduce the risk of such decisions managers are likely to take a scientific approach, which involves gathering and analysing data. They may also use techniques such as decision trees. Decision trees involve quantifying outcomes and risk to try and make the most rational decision on financial grounds. Of course there may be other motives driving the decision apart from the highest financial reward.

Progress questions

1. What is meant by scientific decision-making? (3 marks)
2. What is meant by a decision tree? (2 marks)
3. What is meant by probability? (2 marks)
4. What is meant by expected value? (2 marks)
5. Explain two benefits of using decision trees. (5 marks)
6. Explain one limitation of a scientific approach to decision-making. (3 marks)
7. Explain two reasons why strategies can go wrong. (6 marks)
8. Explain two reasons why information management can help a business compete. (6 marks)
9. What is meant by a management information system? (2 marks)
10. What is good quality information? (3 marks)

Analysis and evaluation questions

1 Analyse the benefits of a scientific approach to decision-making when undertaking a major strategic change. (8 marks)

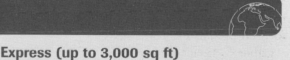

Web link

For more information on Nintendo visit www.nintendo.com

2 Discuss the possible reasons why managers of Nintendo might choose to change the strategy of a business. (15 marks)

3 With reference to organisations and industries you know, discuss how managing information can affect the success of a business. (15 marks)

Case study

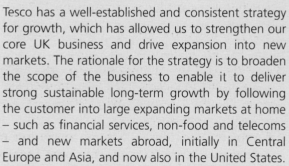

Tesco has a well-established and consistent strategy for growth, which has allowed us to strengthen our core UK business and drive expansion into new markets. The rationale for the strategy is to broaden the scope of the business to enable it to deliver strong sustainable long-term growth by following the customer into large expanding markets at home – such as financial services, non-food and telecoms – and new markets abroad, initially in Central Europe and Asia, and now also in the United States.

The strategy to diversify the business was laid down in 1997 and has been the foundation of Tesco's success in recent years. The new businesses which have been created and developed over the last decade as part of this strategy now have scale, they are competitive and profitable – in fact, the international business alone makes about the same profit as the entire Group did a decade ago.

Our core UK business is significant within the group, with over 280,000 employees and over 2,100 stores. Around 75 per cent of group sales and profits come from the UK business.

Store formats

We have four different store formats, each tailored to our customers' needs and one trial format called Homeplus:

Express (up to 3,000 sq ft)

Our Express stores offer customers great value, quality and fresh food close to where they live and work. They sell a range of up to 7,000 products including fresh produce, wines and spirits and in-store bakery.

Metro (approx. 7,000–15,000 sq ft)

Metro stores bring the convenience of Tesco to town and city centre locations. Metros cater for thousands of busy customers each week and offer a tailored range of mainly food products, including ready-meals and sandwiches.

Superstore (approx. 20,000–50,000 sq ft)

We have an ongoing programme of extending and refreshing our superstores to improve the overall experience for customers. In recent years we have introduced a number of new non-food ranges into superstores such as DVDs and books.

Extra (approx. 60,000 sq ft and above)

Extra stores offer the widest range of food and non-food lines, ranging from electrical equipment to homewares, clothing, health and beauty and seasonal items such as garden furniture.

Homeplus (approx. 35,000 sq ft to 50,000 sq ft)

Our Homeplus stores are dedicated to non-food, including clothing. These trial stores offer our widest range of non-food products in store, with more available through their Tesco Direct order and collection points. Our latest, largest stores have our Tesco Direct catalogue ranges on display, with most products available to take home today. Following the early promise of our first seven stores, we've committed to opening a further ten as part of the trial.

Broad appeal

We ensure we have a broad appeal by continually innovating and investing in new lines to increase choice for our customers. From Value to Finest and lifestyle ranges like Organic, Free From, Healthy Living and Wholefoods, our various own brands enable customers to buy products to complement their lifestyle. Our nutritional 'signpost labelling' aims to provide customers with the key information they need to help them choose a balanced diet.

Understanding our customers

Tesco Clubcard is a world-leading loyalty card scheme, with around 14 million active cardholders. Information provided by Clubcard enables us to better understand our customers and say thank you for shopping with us. There are over 8 million unique coupon variations with each Clubcard mailing, making sure that everyone receives the kind of offer that is appropriate for them.

Our international strategy

With more than ten years of experience overseas, Tesco has evolved a strategy based on six elements:

1 Be flexible – each market is unique and requires a different approach.

   In Japan, customers like to shop for small amounts of extremely fresh food, every day. Existing hypermarket formats do not meet the needs of local customers, so Tesco's entry into the Japanese market was through the acquisition of a discount supermarket operator.

2 Act local – local customers, local cultures, local supply chains and local regulations require a tailored offer delivered by local staff.

   In Thailand, customers are used to shopping at traditional wet markets, interacting with vendors and rummaging through piles of produce to choose what they want. Rather than adopting the Western approach of neatly packaged, convenient portions, our Rama IV store in Bangkok tries to meet local customers' expectations.

3 Maintain focus – we understand that customers want great service, great choice and great value. To become established as the leading local brand is a long-term effort and is not about planting flags in a map.

4 Use multi-formats – no single format can reach the whole of the market.

5 Develop capability – it's not about scale, it's about skill – so we make sure we have capability through people, processes and systems.

   We believe that investing in our people is the right way to live our values and brings sound business benefits, too. Developing individuals at every level means that we have home-grown managers who understand our culture and can effectively develop our business.

6 Build brands – brands enable the building of important lasting relationships with customers. In China, our first Tesco branded store called Tesco Legou opened in February 2007 and we have now completed re-branding of all stores.

All our customers are different, and their needs are continually changing. That's why we continue to offer more than one way to shop.

Non-food

Our strategy aims to be as strong in non-food as in food.

Our widest range of non-food can be seen in Extra stores and Homeplus, including electricals, home entertainment, clothing, health and beauty, stationery, cookshop and soft furnishings, and seasonal goods such as barbecues and garden furniture in the summer. Some of our stores also have opticians and over 240 have pharmacies.

In 2006 we launched Tesco Direct, a new online and catalogue non-food offer, with over 11,000 products available online. Next-day delivery is standard for small items with a unique two-hour delivery window. Customers also have a delivery to store option so they can pick up their order from their local store.

Tesco clothing brings fashion to a wide audience at fantastic prices. One in seven of our customers have bought from our clothing ranges. F&F is the label of fashion, style and great value, while our Cherokee brand offers essential trend-led kids clothing and adult casual wear. Visit tesco.com/clothing which enables customers to preview what's in store, find their nearest shop with clothing and sign up to the Fashionfile email.

Source: adapted from http://www.tesco.com

(40 marks, 60 minutes)

One step further: using decision trees

A decision tree is a mathematical model which can be used by managers to help them make the right decision. Imagine that a manager is trying to decide whether to cut the price of a product or increase the amount of money spent on advertising. These options can be illustrated as in Figure 28.09. The square shows that a decision has to be made, and the lines coming from it show the possible choices facing the firm.

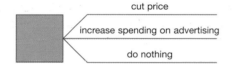

Figure 28.09

Whenever you choose a particular course of action such as advertising or cutting the price there will be a range of possible outcomes. For example, if the firm advertises its products there may be a big increase in sales or a small increase in sales. These possible outcomes are illustrated in Figure 28.10. The circles show that different outcomes are possible; these are then illustrated by the lines coming out of the circles.

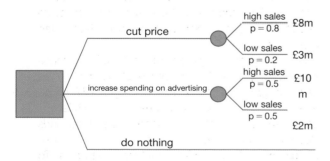

Figure 28.10

In Figure 28.10 we have also:

• estimated how likely it is that the predicted increase in sales will be 'high' or 'low' for each option. This is known as the probability of a particular outcome. The value of the probability can range from 0 to 1. The bigger the number the more likely it is that an event will happen. If the number is 1 this means that the event is certain to happen.

• added in the estimated benefits of each outcome. For example, if the firm advertises and there is a big increase in sales the benefit will be an increase in profits of £10m. A small increase would increase profits by £2m.

We can now work out 'the expected value' of each decision. This is basically a weighted average of the outcomes taking account of the probability of each one.

This can be calculated using the equation:

Expected Value = (probability1 × outcome1) + (probability2 × outcome2) + ...

[where 1 represents the first outcome and 2 represents the second outcome and so on].

That is, to calculate the expected value we multiply the probability of each outcome with the financial consequences of the outcome and add them all up. This shows how much the firm would earn on average if the decision was taken repeatedly.

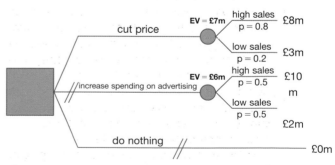

Figure 28.11

Expected value of advertising:

(0.5 × £10m) + (0.5 × £2m) = £5m + £1m = £6m

Expected Value of cutting price:

$$(0.8 \times £8m) + (0.2 \times £3m) = £6.4m + £0.6m = £7m$$

This has a higher expected value than advertising and so on this basis the manager would choose this option. The expected values are shown on the decision tree diagram above the outcome circles; the options which are not chosen are shown using a double-crossed line.

Using decision trees can be very useful for managers because it:

- makes them think about the different options they have and consider the possible consequences of each one
- forces them to quantify the impact of each decision

- helps them to logically compare the options open to them.

However, decision trees do have various limitations and drawbacks.

- Decision trees use estimates of the probability of different outcomes and the financial consequences of each outcome. The value of decision tree analysis depends heavily on how accurate these estimates are.
- Decision trees only include financial and quantifiable data; they do not include qualitative issues such as the workforce's reaction to different options or the impact on the firm's image.

29

Implementing and managing change

Given that change is going to occur, managers must consider the best way(s) of managing it.

In this chapter we examine:
• techniques to implement and manage change
• the factors that promote and or cause resistance to change.

Managing change

Lewin (1951) saw businesses as being in equilibrium at any moment between driving and restraining forces. At any moment, some forces are pushing for change and some are holding back change; a business is in temporary equilibrium. These are constantly interacting and pushing against each other. The task of change managers is to increase the driving forces or reduce the restraining forces. The equilibrium 'can be changed either by adding forces in the desired direction or by diminishing the opposing forces' (Lewin).

Imagine a situation in which managers want to introduce new technology. To bring about change managers must try to increase the pressure for it. For example, they might stress to employees:

• the dangers of holding on to old technology (e.g. loss of competitiveness and the possible loss of jobs)
• the benefits of new technology (in terms of boosting competitiveness)
• the threats from competitors who are already using this technology.

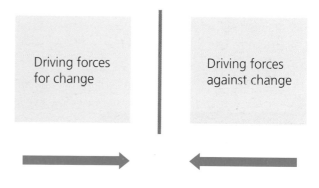

Figure 29.1 Managing change

Alternatively, managers might focus on reducing the resistance to change and perhaps:

• educate employees on the benefits of the change
• offer incentives to those willing to change
• threaten or intimidate those who resist
• guarantee jobs to reduce this insecurity
• offer training to those who need to re-skill.

This would reduce resistance to change and make it more likely to happen.

Why do people resist change?

Some people embrace change – they pioneer new ideas and new ways of doing things, But almost inevitably any innovation will meet resistance. Where there is a pioneer there is likely to be someone who does not want the change to happen.

According to Kotter and Schlesinger (1979) the main reasons why people resist change are:

- Self-interest – they do not want the effort of change or are better off as they are (e.g. their status or importance might be less after the change).
- Misunderstanding and lack of trust – they do not understand why change is necessary and/or are suspicious about why the change is happening.
- They prefer the status quo – they would rather keep things as they are because they feel comfortable with it.
- They do not think the new idea will work – they think there are flaws in this and therefore it would be wrong to pursue it.

Resistance to change may come in many forms, such as:

- a lack of effort to learn the necessary new skills or a general lack of cooperation
- a demand for more pay
- a refusal to use the new systems

Perceived Personal Risk from Change

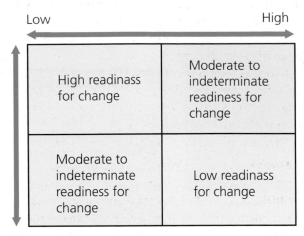

Figure 29.2 Employee readiness for change

- a demand for extended discussion to slow down the process of change.

Figure 29.2 highlights the different states that employees might be in when managers are introducing change. This model by Zeira and Avedisian highlights that the openness and readiness for change will depend on how dissatisfied employees are with the present situation and the extent to which they think they will suffer from change. The more dissatisfied they are and the less they think they will personally suffer as a result of it, the more open they will be to change.

Business in Focus

The England Football team

In 2008 Fabio Capello was appointed as the new manager of the England football team. The England team had been performing badly and had failed to qualify for Euro 2008. Change was badly needed. Capello came in and made a number of changes in the way the team was run. No player could guarantee his place any more, no matter how famous he was – all places were available to the best player at the time. To have a chance of a place all the players had to follow Capello's rules – they had to turn up to training, they had to train properly and they had to turn up for the pre-match preparations without their wives and girlfriends. From the very start Capello made it clear things were different. The result was a much improved team performance and

an approach that was competitive and where players wanted to impress. Capello made it clear he did not want to be friends with the players – they had to earn their places.

Capello was able to bring about such a change in the culture of the English camp because the poor performance up until then meant people were open to change and could see that the old ways of doing things did not work.

He showed leadership and made it clear that those who did not change would lose out.

Question:

1 Discuss the factors that are likely to influence the ability of a new manager to change the culture of a business.

Why else might change not happen?

Change may not happen because there is resistance to it. Also, it may be that the business lacks the resources to bring it about. We may know we need to update our database systems, improve our website or refurbish our stores but lack the resources to do so. Often the very time when change is needed (when a business is doing badly) is when a business is short of resources to bring it about.

The lack of resources may involve a lack of:

- **Money**, e.g. a business may not have the cash or access to credit to invest.
- **Skills**, e.g. a business may not have the talents, experience and abilities within its organisation to manage a change or bring about change effectively. This may be due to the recruitment policy, a lack of training and/or a new situation arising which requires new skills it does not have.
- **Time** – you should never underestimate time as a resource. There may be many changes managers want to bring about but they may be so busy fire-fighting (see Mintzberg's analysis of what managers do on page 361) that they cannot implement all the changes they would like to.

Another problem that can occur is that managers simply do not recognise that change is needed. They may be too inward looking and not appreciate that their market has changed. A manager like this is a reactive rather than a proactive manager.

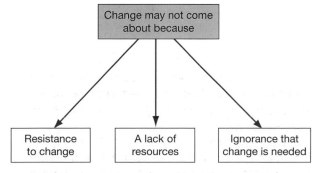

Figure 29.3 Unsuccessful change

What happens if you do not change?

The danger if you do not change is that you will be left behind: you are the only typewriter shop on the block (and not for much longer); you will have a lovely collection of cameras using photographic film but no customers. Change can, of course, go wrong but standing still is often dangerous.

Why can change go wrong?

Kotter (1990) studied over 100 companies going through change and identified the following most common errors that managers make:

1 Too much complacency – it is common to think problems can be dealt with later. Managers need to create a sense of urgency when introducing change.
2 Failing to build a substantial coalition – this means that forces opposing change often undermine the changes that managers are trying to bring in. Managers need to build a coalition to gain support and help push the change through.
3 Underestimating the need for a clear vision – without a clear vision of where you are headed you may end up with a series of initiatives that are rather disconnected.
4 A failure to communicate the vision – a vision needs to be shared.
5 Permitting roadblocks against the vision; allowing things to get in the way and delay change – managers need to empower people to clear obstacles.
6 Not planning or achieving short-term wins – it is important to sustain momentum. Managers need to secure short-term wins to show they can succeed.
7 Declaring victory too soon – managers need to keep moving.
8 Not anchoring changes in corporate culture – managers need to anchor change and make sure it is part of the culture (e.g. by rewarding those who have helped bring it about).

Kotter stressed the importance of using the sequence in the order shown above to bring about effective change.

Successful change

Change is most likely to be successful if:

- those affected by the change were involved in bringing it about (rather than having it imposed on them)

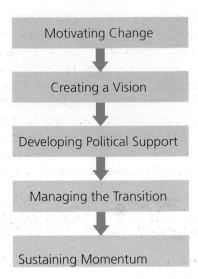

Figure 29.4 Successful change

- those involved in the change feel they have an opportunity to air their views
- the benefits of the change are made clear to those involved
- individuals feel able to cope with the change; they feel they have the resources and skills to deal with it
- the people involved agree with the reasons for the change.

SARAH

When a change is announced it often generates the following series of reactions from those involved:

1 Shock: people may be surprised that the change has to occur or has occurred.
2 Anger: people may be annoyed, perhaps because they did not know or expect it and/or because they may be worse off.
3 Rejection: people try to deny it is really going to happen; they think if they ignore it, it may go away.
4 Acceptance: eventually they accept that it is going to happen.
5 Help: at some point they decide to ask for help.

Project management

In many cases change may be ongoing; however, in some instances there may be a distinct project to manage (e.g. restructuring the business, undertaking a takeover or launching a new project). This requires particular skills to make sure that a project is completed on time, on budget and to the standards required. The process of ensuring these targets are met is known a project management.

What is a project?

A project occurs when an individual or team attempt to accomplish a specific objective by completing a set of interrelated tasks.

The features of project are that it has:

- an objective
- a series of interdependent tasks
- resources that will be used up
- a specific time frame by which it has to be completed
- a degree of uncertainty.

Examples of projects are:

- launching a new product
- moving offices.

Any project may face unforeseen circumstances such as delays from suppliers, difficulties completing some stages of the process on time and achieving quality targets on time. The challenge facing project managers is to prevent, anticipate and/or overcome such circumstances. This will involve planning to anticipate where possible and to set targets which will help define what is and is not possible. For example, you will need to estimate:

- the different stages of a project
- the order in which the stages must take place
- who is in charge of each stage
- the costs involved and the time allowed for each stage.

Project managing will involve a range of skills. These include the ability to:

- communicate to everyone what has to be done when and how
- organise and plan ahead
- set financial targets
- deal with and resolve conflict if necessary
- negotiate
- lead and inspire others to get the job done
- build a sense teamwork and common purpose.

Projects go through successive stages, and results depend on managing the project through these stages in an orderly way, i.e.:

1 define the objectives
2 allocate responsibilities (define who is in charge of what)

3 fix deadlines and milestones (what has to be completed by when)

4 set budgets (how much can be spent on any aspect or part of the project)

5 monitor and control (set targets and deadlines to review along the way; make sure action is taken if the project is not on target).

To bring about a successful completion of a project you may need internal support. This can be helped by finding people who will champion the cause (these are called **project champions**). They are the ambassadors telling others of the benefits of the project, enthusiastically pushing its benefits, and explaining its value. If you can identify such champions in advance (or appoint them as project leaders) this can help overcome resistance to the plan.

Project groups can also be helpful to identify possible problems. You may, for example, put together a multi-functional team with people from all the different areas of the business that might be affected by the project to get different perspectives on possible difficulties. This helps to flag issues before they occur and also helps to get people onside early because they have been involved in the planning. Without this people may feel that change is being forced on them and they may automatically resist because of this. Constructive criticism and debate is good in project teams because you are trying to flesh out problems, incorrect thinking and assumptions and flawed logic. This probably will not be highlighted if everyone agrees with everyone else out of politeness or if everyone has a similar background and training. In some organisations someone is specifically given the role of being 'devil's advocate' and trying to find flaws with the idea. However, disagreement and debate must be managed to ensure that progress is made and the whole project does not deteriorate into name-calling!

> **Key terms**
> A **project** is a 'unique set of coordinated activities, with definite starting and finishing points, undertaken by an individual or team to meet specific objectives within defined time, cost and performance parameters' (Office of Government Commerce).

Summary

Given that change is constantly occurring both within and outside the business, managers must learn how to cope with it and to manage it. This includes overcoming resistance to change. Resistance can occur for a number of reasons, not least because people think they will be worse off. To overcome resistance managers can use a number of techniques such as offering rewards for changed behaviour, training, education or even using punishments to force change through. Managers will also have projects to lead – to do this they need to plan carefully and be prepared to deal with delays and problems as they emerge, especially with major and new projects.

Progress questions

1 Outline Lewin's model of the forces of change. (5 marks)

2 What might increase the forces for change? (4 marks)

3 Explain two reasons, apart from employee resistance, why change may be difficult to bring about. (6 marks)

4 Explain two reasons why employees often resist change. (6 marks)

5 What is meant by project management? (3 marks)

6 Explain two features of effective project management. (6 marks)

7 Explain two reasons why change can go wrong. (6 marks)

8 Explain two ways of overcoming resistance to change. (6 marks)

9 Using an example, explain why one stakeholder group might welcome change while another might resist change. (6 marks)

10 Explain two factors that might help make employees open to change. (6 marks)

Analysis and evaluation questions

1 Analyse the reasons why employees might resist the introduction of new manufacturing technology. (15 marks)

2 With reference to examples you know, discuss the best way to overcome resistance to change. (15 marks)

3 To what extent is funding the key to effective project management? (15 marks)

Case study

Terminal 5

When Heathrow's $4.3 billion Terminal 5 finally opened there were terrible delays. Flights had to be cancelled and there was a backlog of over 15,000 bags which were stuck in transit.

Despite months of preparation at T5, its problems began almost immediately as staff arrived for their morning shifts. Many employees could not actually get to work on time because there was not sufficient space in the staff car parks.

Once inside the terminal building, workers also faced problems getting to the restricted 'airside' via security checkpoints. According to the GMB union, workers had not been familiarised with the new terminal and that many simply didn't know where to go.

The disastrous opening was a severe embarrassment for BA and BAA, the Spanish-owned company that operates Heathrow. Both had spent five years claiming that the new terminal would transform passengers' experience of Heathrow and work efficiently from Day 1. When it opened they blamed each other for the chaos inside Britain's biggest free-standing building.

BAA claimed that the baggage system was working properly but had become clogged with bags because BA had too few staff to unload them from conveyor belts. BA said that BAA had provided too few security staff to process its baggage handlers as they arrived for work. BAA had claimed that the baggage system was the most advanced in the world, with belts travelling at 23mph and capable of handling 12,000 bags an hour. The system had been operating in test mode with thousands of dummy bags for the past 18 months.

BA had been preparing for the switch to Terminal 5 for three years and claimed that it had trained thousands of staff on the new systems. But many were delayed after being unable to park their cars or to find their way to their work stations. Several lifts were also out of action and screens were wrongly showing that gates had closed when no one had yet boarded.

Simultaneously BA baggage teams struggled immediately with an automated system that, via handheld devices, told them which flight to unload and which flight to put bags onto. According to staff, the devices told handlers to sort bags for flights that were already cancelled. This meant they turned up to load flights that were not there while, in other parts of the sorting area, bags piled up unattended.

Without managers on the ground to allocate work, there appeared to be a communication breakdown between handlers and their supervisors in the BA control centre elsewhere in the terminal. By midday, 20 flights were cancelled as handlers frantically tried to reduce T5's inaugural baggage mountain.

(40 marks, 60 minutes)

Questions

1 Explain the possible costs of the problems experienced when Terminal 5 opened. (5 marks)
2 Analyse the reasons why people might have objected to Terminal 5. (8 marks)
3 Discuss the possible reasons why the opening of Terminal 5 may have gone wrong. (12 marks)
4 With reference to organisations or industries that you know, to what extent is effective project management a key element of the success of a business these days? (15 marks)

Tackling the Unit 4 Assessment

The main theme in Unit 4 is change. The topics covered consider the causes of change, the effects of change and the ways in which businesses react to change. The Unit also examines how businesses can manage the process of change- what determines how they respond to it and whether changes are damaging or not.

The first half of Unit 4 is concerned with the external environment, for example, political, economic, social and technological factors, changes in the competitive environment such as the entry of new firms, and changes in the power of buyers. Changes in the external environment create opportunities and threats for businesses.

The second half of Unit 4 considers topics such as how to manage change, the importance of culture, how businesses make decisions and the role of leaders in coping with changes in the environment.

The Unit 4 exam accounts for 50% of the A2 marks (that is, 25% of the whole A level).

Unit 4 is a synoptic examination. This means that whilst there is new material to study you can also build on the topics you have studied before in Business Studies.

The exam

The Unit 4 examination last 1½ hours. This should give you plenty of time to read the questions, choose which ones you want to answer and plan your responses. The exam consist of two essays and planning is an important aspect of a successful answer. An essay needs to be carefully thought through and well structured; you have time in this exam to think about your answer before writing so make sure you do this as it will improve your marks.

The first part of the exam is based on a case study that relates to a pre-released theme. A few months before the exam you will be told what this theme is. The theme is announced at the end of January and the same theme is used for that June's exam and the following January. You will also be given advice on what to study as part of the theme; this advice will set out exactly what areas need to be covered so keep referring back to this to make sure your studies are well focused.

The point of having a pre-released theme is that it gives you the opportunity to do some independent research; this should enable you to produce more analytical answers to the questions and you should be able to explore the issues in more depth. The theme will be fairly broad (such as "globalisation") and will often relate to many of the topics in Unit 4.

If globalisation was the theme, for example, this would involve ethical issues, strategic decisions, stakeholders, Corporate Social Responsibility, international business and corporate values and culture — all topics elsewhere in Unit 4. You are likely, therefore, to be referring back to the theme at many stages of your studies in Unit 4. Information on the theme will be readily available through research; type the word "globalisation" into Google, for example, and you will see what we mean — there will be thousands of results! You will certainly be studying the theme in your lessons but you will also have the opportunity to study more on your own based on the advice the exam board gives you. When researching independently you are trying to learn more about the theme and the key issues within it. You are trying to see how businesses are affected by this change and how the effects and their responses can differ. You are not trying to memorise a list of facts and figures but trying to understand the important issues and find useful data, evidence and examples to illustrate your arguments and thoughts.

In the exam itself you will be given a short case study (around one side of A4) and have the choice of one of two essays on the theme. The question will ask you about an issue relating to the case study but also give you the opportunity to bring in your own findings — better answers will to demonstrate evidence of research.

The second section of Unit 4 is also essay based. You choose one essay out of three. The essays will tend to have a given context (for example, they may relate to a particular industry or business) but again you are encouraged to bring in your own examples and evidence of what happens in different industries and to different businesses. Part of the aim of Unit 4 is to encourage you to study real business and to consider what determines how different businesses are affected by, or respond to, change and why this might be.

Skills assessment

	Unit 3	Unit 4
Content	20%	20%
Application	30%	20%
Analysis	25%	25%
Evaluation	25%	35%

You can see from the grid that Unit 4 places more emphasis on the higher level skills of analysis and evaluation relative to content and application. 35% of the marks are for evaluation. This means you need to think carefully about the judgements you make.

Judgements may refer to:

- the importance of one factor compared to another
- the extent to which a factor is likely to be significant
- the significance of the context, for example, the nature of the business or its particular circumstances.

Unit 4 will expect you to debate issues rather than to simply state or explain them. Knowing how the economy can affect a business is not enough, for example. In this exam you need to think about what determines how much it might affect a business, whether it is an opportunity or a threat, whether the effects are likely to be short or long term, and what determines the way a business might respond.

Writing an essay

As you will see from the section above, being able to write a good essay is extremely important in Unit 4. This means you need to work hard and practice your essay–writing technique. Here is some advice to help you improve the way you write essays:

a. Plan

A good essay has a shape to it. It sets out at the start the purpose of the essay and the key arguments and it has a clear conclusion at the end that follows on logically from the previous arguments. To have a structure like this you need to plan what you are going to argue before writing. Too many exam candidates start to write immediately and then gradually discover what they are arguing as they go along! You can see them changing their arguments as they jump from one point to another until they eventually decide what they are trying to say! This means the essay has no clear structure and the arguments are often less effective as a result.

b. Analyse

Remember that a good essay is not a series of points. You do not need to list lots of arguments — all this will do is to get you content marks. What we need at this level is debate and discussion. To do this you need to select a few key arguments and develop these in detail. An essay is marked out of 40 but this does not mean you need 40 different points! In your planning time you need to work out what your key arguments are and then focus on developing these into substantial arguments. Make sure you use your paragraphs properly. Each paragraph should be based on a particular argument. Don't have lots of different ideas in one paragraph. If you are about to launch into a new argument then start a new paragraph. This will also help you to appreciate whether you have enough detailed arguments or not. An essay made up of lots of small paragraphs is unlikely to do well because the analysis is likely to be undeveloped. Good analysis relates to good chains of arguments — it is not easy to do this in one or two lines.

c. Apply and evaluate

All essays will have a context. This may be a particular business or type of business or a particular situation. Keep this in mind at all times. If the question says the business is 'big', 'growing', 'traditional', 'bureaucratic' or 'heavily in debt' these are all important things to refer to. You can also refer to other businesses or industries you know about or what is happening in the real business world. By applying your answer you are making the response relevant and specific- this is essential for a good mark. Good application (where examples and insights into the firm or industry are used in the argument) is also a good starting point for evaluation. Evaluation involves judgement and where better place to start than judging what *this* business would do in *this* industry at *this* time in *this* situation? To answer the question properly and make effective judgements your arguments need to be in context, so application is vital for the top grades.

So, the key to an effective essay is:

- plan
- select a few key arguments
- apply and analyse
- evaluate your arguments
- conclude.

Useful sources of information

As you will have seen, studying what is actually happening in the business environment is particularly important for Unit 4. You need to know what is happening and how different organisations are affected by and react to change. You need insights into topics such as economic and social change, technological advances, leadership and contingency planning, by examining what businesses actually do. Reading a newspaper, downloading newsfeeds, tuning in to business programmes are all must-dos for this part of the course. That way you will have plenty of examples of business behaviour to compare and contrast in the exam. Someone who only knows theory but who cannot relate it to the theme or the given scenarios in the essays will be unlikely to score highly. You have to show your depth of understanding through your study of businesses.

There are many good sources of information but an obvious starting point is the BBC business website (www.bbc.co.uk/business). This is an excellent resource and one you should check regularly. In addition, you may find a national newspaper useful. Ones such as The Times, The Guardian and The Telegraph all have good business sections; alternatively buy one of the Sunday newspapers, which often have good features. These can all be found online (just type their names into Google). The Economist magazine is also useful (www.economist.com) and has some good surveys every few weeks. For general business information Wikipedia (www.wikipedia.co.uk) is generally very good but beware — anyone can contribute to this site so the information has not necessarily been checked; it may not be accurate! When studying business and doing your research do try to use more than one source so that you can gain from different perspectives and can also check the accuracy of some stories.

Success at this stage of the course involves studying what actually happens in business and thinking critically about change and business strategy. Keeping up to date with business events and developments, analysing what is happening in the business environment and thinking about the theory behind business decision-making should all make fascinating areas to study. Enjoy!

References

Pg 122 Bitner, J. and Booms, B.(1981), Marketing strategies and organizational structures for service firms" in Donnelly, J. and George, W. (1981) "Marketing of services", *American Marketing Association*, Chicago

Pg 122 McCarthy EJ (1960), *Basic Marketing: A Managerial Approach*, Irwin.

Pg 345 Greiner E.(1972), *Evolution and revolution as organizations grow*, Harvard Business Review July- August 1972

Pg 355 Kotter, J. (1990), *A force for change, how leadership differs from management*, Free Press, New York

Pg 355 Drucker, P. (1985), *The Effective Executive*, HarperBusiness

Pg 357 Tannenbaum, R. and Schmidt W.H (1957), *How to choose a leadership pattern*, Harvard Business Review

Pg 358 French, J. and Raven B. (1959), *Bases of Social Power, Studies in Social Power. Ed. Dorwin Cartwright*, University of Michigan, Ann Arbor

Pg 361 Mintzberg, H. (1973), *The nature of managerial work*, Harper Collins

Pg 362 Ouchi, W. (1981), *Theory Z: how American business can meet the Japanese challenge*, Avon books

Pg 362 Hofstede, G.(1991) *Cultures and organizations: software of the mind: intercultural cooperation and its importance for survival*, New York McGraw Hill

Pg 362 Schein, E. (1992) *Organizational Culture and leadership* San Francisco, Jossey Bass

Pg 365 Deal, T. E. and Kennedy, A. A. (1982) *Corporate Cultures: The Rites and Rituals of Corporate Life*, Harmondsworth, Penguin Books.

Pg 365 Handy, C. (1990) *Understanding organisations*, Penguin

Pg 366 Hofstede G (1991) *Cultures and organizations: software of the mind: intercultural cooperation and its importance for survival*, New York McGraw Hill

Pg 368 Johnson G and Scholes K (1997), *Exploring corporate strategy*, Prentice Hall

Pg 375 Boddy D (2002), *Management: an introduction*, Financial Times Prentice Hall

Pg 375 Simon, H.A. (1960). The new science of management decisions, New York, Harper and Row

Pg 380 Pfeffer, J. (1994), *Managing with power: politics and influence in organizations*, Harvard Business School Press.

Pg 383 Ansoff, I. (1957), Strategies for Diversification, *Harvard Business Review*, Vol. 35 Issue 5, Sep-Oct, pp.113-124

Pg 383 Porter, M. (1980) *Competitive Strategy: Techniques for Analysing Industries and Competitors*, Free Press

Pg 391 Lewin K. (1951), *Field Theory in Social Science*, Harper and Row, New York

Pg 392 Kotter JP, Schlesinger LA. (1979) *Choosing Strategies for Change*. Harvard Business Review.

Index